INVESTIGATING PRISTINE INNER EXPERIENCE

You live your entire waking life immersed in your inner experiences (thoughts, feelings, sensations, etc.) – private phenomena created by you, just for you, your own way. Despite their intimacy and ubiquity, you probably don't know the characteristics of your own inner phenomena; neither does psychology or consciousness science.

Investigating Pristine Inner Experience explores how to apprehend inner experience in high fidelity. This book will transform your view of your own inner experience, awaken you to experiential differences between people, and thereby reframe your thinking about psychology and consciousness science, which banned the study of inner experience for most of a century and yet continued to recognize its fundamental importance.

The author, a pioneer in using beepers to explore inner experience, draws on his thirty-five years of studies to provide fascinating and provocative views of everyday inner experience and experience in bulimia, adolescence, the elderly, schizophrenia, Tourette Syndrome, virtuosity, and so on.

Russell T. Hurlburt pioneered the investigation of inner experience, inventing (in 1973) the beepers that launched "thought sampling," the attempt to measure characteristics of inner experience. Despite the sophistication of his thought-sampling measurements, Hurlburt concluded (by about 1980) that science needed a better understanding of inner phenomena themselves. Therefore he developed "Descriptive Experience Sampling" (DES), the attempt to apprehend inner experience in high fidelity. That has led to four books: *Sampling Normal and Schizophrenic Inner Experience* (1990), *Sampling Inner Experience in Disturbed Affect* (1993), *Exploring Inner Experience* (with Chris Heavey, 2006), and *Describing Inner Experience: Proponent Meets Skeptic* (with Eric Schwitzgebel, 2007). A special issue of the *Journal of Consciousness Studies* (January 2011) was devoted to DES. Hurlburt is Professor of Psychology at the University of Nevada, Las Vegas, and is also the author of a highly regarded statistics textbook, *Comprehending Behavioral Statistics* (fourth edition 2006).

Investigating Pristine Inner Experience

MOMENTS OF TRUTH

Russell T. Hurlburt

University of Nevada, Las Vegas

CAMBRIDGE
UNIVERSITY PRESS

CAMBRIDGE UNIVERSITY PRESS
Cambridge, New York, Melbourne, Madrid, Cape Town,
Singapore, São Paulo, Delhi, Tokyo, Mexico City

Cambridge University Press
32 Avenue of the Americas, New York, NY 10013-2473, USA

www.cambridge.org
Information on this title: www.cambridge.org/9780521279123

First published 2011

Printed in the United States of America

A catalog record for this publication is available from the British Library.

Library of Congress Cataloging in Publication data
Hurlburt, Russell T.
    Investigating pristine inner experience : moments of truth / Russell T. Hurlburt.
        p.   cm.
    Includes bibliographical references and index.
    ISBN 978-1-107-00994-3 (hardback)
    1. Introspection.   2. Consciousness.   I. Title.
    BF316.H874   2011
    153–dc22   2011002454

ISBN 978-1-107-00994-3 Hardback
ISBN 978-0-521-27912-3 Paperback

To my wife

CONTENTS

FIGURES AND TABLES

FIGURES

TABLES

PREFACE

Here's a thought experiment: I have invented a machine I call the Expero. You strap yourself inside, like an astronaut into a rocket, except the Expero takes you to someone's *inner* space, not outer space. You get to choose a person, called the Objective – maybe a friend, or a lover, or a celebrity, or a perfect stranger. The Expero personnel painlessly, safely, and surreptitiously slip tiny electrodes into the Objective's brain and heart while the Objective continues going about her everyday business as if nothing had happened. When you, safely in the Expero, push a button, the electrodes transmit to you in high fidelity a moment of the Objective's thoughts, feelings, and sensations – you get to think, feel, and sense exactly what she happened to be experiencing at the instant you pushed the button. Push the button again and you get another helping of her inner experience. The thought experiment is: Would you queue up for a chance to ride the Expero?

This book is for those who answer yes. The Expero doesn't exist, sorry to say, but the idea that the Expero would lead to fascinating discoveries exists widely. People have been fascinated by inner experience ever since there were people: The earliest known writings (*Gilgamesh*, the *Iliad*) described the thoughts and feelings of the characters. Psychology was founded on the attempt to "introspect" the contents of consciousness, an attempt so problematic that the mere mention of "introspection" or "consciousness" became psychological heresy for most of the twentieth century.

In the early 1970s, I began to consider how to investigate inner experience in a scientifically adequate manner. In 1973 I invented a random beeper (Hurlburt, 1976) and, in 1974, began to use beepers in psychological research (Klinger and Csikszentmihalyi, working independently, launched similar studies using pagers within a few months). I called my method "random sampling of cognitions" (or "thought sampling" for short): Subjects carried beepers into their natural environments and, at the time of the random beeps, described their thinking by filling out a series of Likert scales, which I subjected to a variety of sophisticated analyses (correlational, factor analytic, etc.). The methods that are now called the Experience Sampling Method (ESM) and Ecological Momentary Assessment (EMA) are quite similar to thought sampling; such methods are now considered at the cutting edge of mainstream psychology.

By the early 1980s, as the result of ten years of research, I had concluded that (a) the understanding of inner experience was indeed central to psychology; (b) ecological validity such as provided by beepers in natural environments was necessary to the understanding of inner experience; (c) therefore thought sampling and similar methods were the best psychology had to offer for the exploration of experience; but (d) thought sampling and similar methods had not and probably could not productively investigate inner experience until an adequate exploration of the phenomena of experience had been accomplished.

So in the early 1980s I abandoned thought sampling and set about creating a new method aimed directly at exploring the phenomena of inner experience. That method has come to be called Descriptive Experience Sampling (DES), which uses beepers to trigger the careful description of phenomena. *Investigating Pristine Inner Experience* demonstrates that the apprehension of inner experience can be fascinating and that modern psychology has not adequately attended to the methodological requirements that the investigation of experience imposes. That is, *Investigating Pristine Inner Experience* shows why psychological and consciousness science must go through the same kind of transformation that I personally underwent in the early 1980s: Science must learn how better to explore psychological phenomena *and only then* to operationalize and measure psychological constructs. *Investigating Pristine Inner Experience* therefore suggests a far-reaching rejuvenation of psychological science. It contains, to be sure, a criticism of modern psychological method, but that criticism is always constructive. Alongside every criticism I show what I think is a better way, based on DES investigations I've been performing for thirty years.

I hope in *Investigating Pristine Inner Experience* to show you what it takes to apprehend inner experience in high fidelity. I hope to demonstrate that many people, probably most people, including many if not most consciousness scientists and very likely you, are mistaken about the nature of their own inner experience and that of others. I hope to reveal some genuinely fascinating and entirely surprising features of inner experience.

All of that may seem a lot to ask from the description of a few beeped moments. However, if you will meet me in Chapter 1 and let me walk with you through these experiences, I think you will come out at the other end with a changed perspective on moments of experience and on psychological and consciousness science.

ACKNOWLEDGMENTS

This book is built around the investigation of moments of pristine experience. Those experiences are always personal and private, often unforeseen in form or content, sometimes embarrassing or unflattering, occasionally unnerving or unsettling. To you who willingly shared in the struggle to be forthright about moments of your experience, I am deeply grateful; I have tried to honor your participation, to deserve your trust, to help us keep our footing in difficult terrain. I have learned from you and been deeply moved by you. To those whose names I have used, I thank you and trust that the reader will respect the courage you have shown by allowing others a glimpse into inherently private matters.

I am indebted to Chris Heavey, who has been a trusted colleague and collaborator as we have tried to sort through this subject matter; to Marta Meana, the foil for many discussions about issues at the core of this book and a thorough reviewer of an earlier draft; to Sarah A. Akhter, whose influence can be felt throughout the book; to Eric Schwitzgebel, who honed my thinking with his good-natured, precise, and persistent requests for refinement; to Susan Stuart, who helped me grapple with some core issues; and to the students at the University of Nevada, Las Vegas, who had the courage to venture into the unknown.

I am grateful to my coauthors Heavey, Akhter, Ricardo Cobo, Sharon Jones-Forrester, Michael J. Kane, and Arva Bensaheb for their substantial contributions to this work.

I thank Simina Calin, Emily Spangler, Josh Penney, Marcus Hinds, Amanda O'Connor, and the staff at Cambridge University Press for competently guiding this process from manuscript to reality, and Bindu Vinod and the staff at Newgen Publishing and Data Services for creating a handsome and carefully constructed volume.

1

Moments of Truth

[A warm mid-July evening, clear with high clouds. Sunset, bright oranges and golds. Jack and Jennifer stand on the beach, holding hands. Quiet and still.]

JENNIFER: "What are you thinking?"
JACK: "Right now?"
JENNIFER: "Yeah!"
JACK: "Just how spectacular the sunset is – and about sharing it with you."
JENNIFER: "Me too." [Leans closer to him.]

The omniscient being knows that at the moment Jennifer began to ask "What are you thinking?" Jack was seeing in his imagination Barry Bonds-at-bat in the All-Star Game he had been watching when Jennifer suggested walking to the beach to see the sunset. As he had clicked off the TV, Bonds was just coming to bat with a man on second. Now, as they stood on the beach, Jack was, in his imagination, seeing Bonds as if seen from the pitcher's mound, seeing Bonds tap the front of the plate with his bat, seeing his left elbow rock high in the air as he prepared for the pitch, hearing the crowd roar. The omniscient being knows that Jack's experience was, at that moment, totally absorbed in Bonds's at-bat, knows that Jennifer's question interrupted Jack's Bonds-at-bat experience and brought the sunset and Jennifer into the foreground of Jack's experience.

The omniscient being also knows that at the moment Jennifer began to ask "What are you thinking?" Jennifer was feeling a dryness in her throat and a caving-in sensation in her chest – a worry/guilt/tension about whether someone had told Jack that she had flirted with the sales rep that afternoon. The omniscient being knows that when Jennifer asked "What are you thinking?" her real question was whether Jack knew about her flirting.

Jack did not tell Jennifer about his real chain of inner experiences. Jennifer did not tell Jack about her real chain of inner experiences.

PRISTINE INNER EXPERIENCE

This little melodrama illustrates that quite a lot happens in Jack's experience in the second it takes Jennifer to ask, "What are you thinking?" Jack's experience changes from innerly seeing Bonds-at-bat to something about the sunset and Jennifer. Let's call Jack's Bonds-at-bat experience his *pristine inner experience*. By *inner experience* I mean directly apprehended ongoing experience, that which directly presents itself "before the footlights of consciousness" (as William James would say) at some particular moment. A thought, a feeling, a tickle, a seeing, a hearing, and so on count as experience by this definition. Seeing a baseball player in your imagination is an experience; seeing the orange-and-gold of a real sunset is an experience. Elsewhere (Hurlburt, 2009; Hurlburt & Schwitzgebel, 2007) I have explained why I refer to this as *inner* experience when it includes things like seeings, hearings, smellings of the outside world, but let's not get distracted by terminology yet. Here suffice it to say that inner experience means directly experienced, apprehended directly before the footlights of consciousness. Sometimes, when there is little room for ambiguity, I will refer to inner experience as simply "experience."

By *pristine* I mean naturally occurring in natural, everyday environments, *not* altered, colored, or shaped by the specific intention to apprehend it (Hurlburt & Akhter, 2006). I use *pristine* in the same sense as we would say a forest is pristine – before the loggers clear-cut, before the Park Service installs the walkways and the signage, before the visitors leave their plastic bags and bottles. Pristine does not necessarily mean "clean" or "tranquil"; much of a pristine forest is mucky, bloody, brutal, and so on. Jack's pristine inner experience at the moment Jennifer's question begins is his innerly seeing Bonds-at-bat. Jennifer's pristine inner experience at that moment is her throat-dryness and chest-pressure, and her worry about whether Jack knows about her flirting.

Jack's reply to Jennifer ("Just how spectacular the sunset is – and about sharing it with you.") is *not* a description of his pristine inner experience; let's say it is about his *reported «experience»*. Let's examine Jack's pristine experience first; then we'll return to his reported «experience». For now we need only observe that in the second it takes Jennifer to ask her question, Jack's pristine inner experience disappears, chased away by Jennifer's question and his response to it, and is replaced by his reported «experience».

Bonds-at-bat was, at the moment Jennifer began her question, arguably the most interesting thing in the universe for Jack. At that moment, Jack's pristine experience could have been focused on the orange-and-gold of the sunset (but it wasn't); he could have been focused on the warmth of Jennifer's hand in his (but he wasn't); he could have been remembering Obama's speech at the 2004 convention (but he wasn't); he could have been focusing on the story he had heard about Jennifer with the sales rep (but he wasn't). Out of the millions of things that Jack could have been experiencing at that moment, Jack created a seeing of Bonds-at-bat.

We mustn't make too much of one moment of Jack's pristine experience. His at-that-moment creation of Bonds-at-bat does not necessarily imply that he prefers baseball to Jennifer. Jack created, say, 200 moments of pristine experience between the clicking off of the TV and the setting of the sun; maybe (as known to the omniscient being) this was the only moment that happened to involve the All-Star Game, and Jack's other 199 moments had been occupied by enjoying the sunset and being with Jennifer. Or maybe he's been thinking about the All-Star Game in nearly every moment, the imaginary seeing of the game alternating with resentment over the interruption. Or maybe this thinking about the All-Star Game was (finally!) a relief that replaced his insecurity over Jennifer's flirtation. The omniscient being knows about the stream of Jack's pristine experiences; we can't know from this one snippet.

But we mustn't make too little of it, either. Jack's pristine experiences are his creations, one momentary experience after the next, created by Jack himself, created for Jack alone, created just how Jack created it at that moment, not tied to or constrained by reality or by anyone else. Seeing Bonds-at-bat is a moment of truth about Jack's by-Jack/for-Jack/how-Jack pristine experience. It embodies Jack's interest at that moment, displays that interest in precisely the way Jack knows how to – and does – display it. This Bonds-at-bat is created by Jack for Jack, just how Jack creates it and understands it. There is no producer, screenwriter, or director standing between Jack and his experience, interpreting Bonds-at-bat for Jack – Jack is his own producer/screenwriter/director of his experience. There is no viewer or critic other than Jack himself – no fellow viewers with whom to compare notes. Even granting that Jack was to think about the All-Star Game, there was no necessity for him to *see* Bonds or to see anything – he could have been *talking* to himself about the All-Star Game (but he wasn't – he was *seeing* it). Even granting that he was seeing Bonds, there was no necessity for Jack to be seeing him from the pitcher's mound, or that the seeing was in motion – it could have been more like a snapshot (but it wasn't); it could have been a silent seeing without crowd noise (but it wasn't); it could have been in black-and-white (but it wasn't). *Everything about this momentary pristine experience is Jack*: created by Jack, created for Jack, created just how Jack creates it, created free of any real-world constraints (although perhaps reflecting some aspects of the real world).

Jack lives his life occupied by a series of these moments of personal truth, pristine experiences well and truly created by, of, and for Jack. These moments of truth are Jack's property, his own private way of apprehending the world of reality and imagination. There is no one telling Jack that it would be better if he saw Bonds-at-bat from the batter's perspective, no one saying "Rewind that – I want to see it again," no one else clicking Jack's experience to a different channel. Jack sees Bonds-at-bat *exactly* Jack's way until Jack's interest takes him elsewhere.

«EXPERIENCE» IS NOT EXPERIENCE

When Jennifer asks "What are you thinking?" Jack could have described his pristine experience, could have said, "I was imaginarily seeing Barry Bonds at the plate in the All-Star Game, as if I were seeing him from the pitcher's mound." But he didn't. Instead he «described» his «experience» of the spectacular sunset. It may seem that describing Bonds-at-bat and «describing» the spectacular sunset are two very similar occurrences, but nothing could be further from the truth. Jack's seeing Bonds-at-bat is a moment of pristine experience – something that Jack directly apprehended, something that presented itself directly to Jack, something that appeared directly before the footlights of Jack's consciousness – and therefore it makes perfect sense to say that Jack could *describe* his Bonds-at-bat *experience*. However, the spectacular sunset was *not* a moment of pristine experience, was not directly before the footlights of Jack's consciousness, was not directly experienced by Jack in the moment about which Jennifer inquired (he was absorbed in Bonds-at-bat, not the sunset). Therefore, *it is not possible* for Jack to describe his pristine experience of the spectacular sunset – there *was no pristine experience* of the spectacular sunset to be described. Therefore, I have put «describing» and «experience» in angle braces to indicate that "Just how spectacular the sunset is – and about sharing it with you" *appears* to be a description of experience but is in fact not a description and not of experience.

> **Q:** That's not fair. By the time Jennifer gets to the *end* of her question, Jack had a direct experience of the sunset – Jack stopped experiencing Bonds-at-bat and started experiencing the sunset. So both are experiences; the only difference is that one is a second or so after the other.
> **A:** It is indeed *possible* that Jennifer's question caused Jack immediately to experience the sunset. If so, seeing the sunset is not his *pristine* experience – it is his experience *after* Jennifer asks him to inspect his experience. And it is not the experience about which Jennifer presumably inquired – "What are you thinking?" is not a question about what his experience *will* be as he tries to respond to her question. Furthermore, it is possible that Jack's experience did *not* shift immediately to the sunset but rather involved a series of experience-lets that may be characterized by *Oh! I can't tell her I'm thinking about the game! I'm still mad to have been forced to leave the game. What does she want me to say?!? Ah yeah! She said let's go see the sunset. Of course! The sunset!* In that case, the sunset itself might never have been directly experienced.
>
> It is also possible that Jack's experience *ceases to exist* for the second or so that is required to say "Just how spectacular the sunset is – and about sharing it with you." Jennifer's question might have triggered a mélange of processes, like those characterized above but also about how much he trusts Jennifer to recognize that this moment may or may not be typical of his other moments, by how he wants to present himself to her, about how Jennifer's friends might react if she were to tell them he was thinking about baseball, about what

Jennifer's mother might think, about what Jack's friends would say, and so on. However, none of those processes are necessarily *experienced* in that second where Jack is required to say *something* in response to Jill's query. There may well be no direct experience at all in that interval (hold your fire on this point until after Chapter 9).

Thus it is likely that Jack's [I'm thinking about] "just how spectacular the sunset is" is an impure mixture of his real experiences and fabrications, aimed at some impure take on what Jennifer really wants to hear and what he supposes she wants to hear. There is no easy and probably no possible way of sorting through the strands that twist and melt together to contribute to what Jack says.

APPREHENDING PRISTINE EXPERIENCE

Jack's pristine experience is Jack for Jack by Jack how Jack. It is pure Jack, an elixir, eau de Jack. Jack's innerly seeing Bonds-at-bat is one drop of pure Jack. Jack's reported «experience» is a mess, an inextricable combination of Jack and not Jack, of Jennifer and the Jennifer of Jack's imagination, of Jennifer's friends and mother (both of reality and of Jack's imagination), of Jack's experience and supposition.

Pristine experience exists only one drop at a time – one momentary experience after another – but there are lots of drops – twenty or thirty a minute, maybe. If the omniscient being revealed a dozen randomly selected drops of Jack's pristine experience between the clicking off of the TV and the setting of the sun, a dozen pure Jack-for-by-how-Jack moments, then we'd have some insight into whether the All-Star Game dominated his experience, whether he was angry, hurt, or neither about Jennifer's flirting. If the omniscient being revealed enough randomly selected moments of truth over a long enough period, we could know with some assurance whether imaginarily re-created seeings dominate Jack's experience; we could know quite a lot about Jack.

With this little melodrama, and with this entire book, I'm trying to deepen our appreciation of Jack by/for/how Jack, of what pristine inner experience is and is not. Here's what the melodrama suggests (it doesn't prove or demonstrate anything – that is the task of the remainder of the book):

- Precisely defining the moment is of fundamental importance. In a second or so, Jack's pristine Bonds-at-bat experience is replaced by an inextricable mess.
- Carefully defining experience is of fundamental importance. Jack's pristine Bonds-at-bat experience is fundamentally different from Jack's spectacular-sunset «experience».
- There is some important technique involved in the apprehending of experience. Jennifer's asking Jack about his experience was not good enough to reveal his pristine experience.

I also observe that Jack's pristine experiences are Jack's alivenesses, Jack's scintillations, Jack's idiosyncratic Jack-y-nesses, Jack before he puts on the mask and filters that hide/distort some, much, most, or all of his pristine experience from external view. At that moment, pure Jack was *interested* in Bonds-at-bat. Of the millions of things he could have been interested in at that moment, he created Bonds-at-bat.

Pristine experience is fundamentally interesting because we know what we're talking about. Jack's Bonds-at-bat is pure Jack. Otherwise, we don't know what we're talking about. When Jack says "Just how spectacular the sunset is," we don't know whether we're talking about Jack, or Jennifer, or Jennifer's friends or mother, or some mush of all of them together.

All we need is an omniscient being to reveal Jack's pristine experience, but as it happens, no omniscient being is forthcoming. Jack for Jack by Jack how Jack remains Jack's private, confidential preserve; if we're interested in it, we'll have to ask Jack to tell us about it.

> **Q:** Isn't "asking him about it" just what Jennifer did? Yet you criticized that thoroughly.
> **A:** No it isn't. Jennifer did *not* ask Jack about his pristine experience. Instead, she expressed, in a disguised manner, her worry about being caught flirting. She used words that *sounded like* an inquiry about Jack's pristine experience, but were not *in fact* an inquiry about his pristine experience.
>
> Jack and Jennifer engaged (knowingly or otherwise) in a collusion about inner experience: Jennifer used words that seemed to be asking about Jack's inner experience (but weren't really) in the expectation that Jack would respond in a way that seemed to be answering about his inner experience (but wasn't really), so that both could avoid revealing their actual pristine experience.

This book is about the possibility of structuring situations in which Jack (and others) can tell us in pretty darn high fidelity about his pristine experience. This telling will doubtless fall short by the omniscient being's standards, but I'm pretty sure we can learn how to talk about *mostly* Jack for, by, and how Jack. We'll have to develop some skills in doing so, learn to avoid the misrepresentations and disguised interests à la Jennifer, figure out how to develop Jack into being a good describer of his pristine experience, to earn his trust, to teach him what pristine experience is and is not, to separate out pristine experience from other candidates for conversation. And we will have to discover whether such a structuring is worth the effort.

I'm convinced that it is possible to get pretty darn faithful descriptions of pristine experience. I assure you that encountering Jack for/by/how Jack is a fascinating endeavor, fascinating for Jack himself and fascinating for the explorer. I hope to demonstrate that fascination in this book. I hope to demonstrate that describing Jack for/by/how Jack is necessary for a science that concerns itself with persons and/or with experience.

Q: Are you claiming that Jack's pristine experience reveals the *essence* of Jack?

A: No. There may well be important aspects of Jack that do not figure directly in his pristine experience. Pristine experience is a fascinating view of the true Jack, not necessarily a complete view of the essence of Jack.

Catch-484

In a *Catch-22*, you have to do X before you can do Y, but it is impossible to do Y before you have done X. Webster's example is that you can't publish a book before you have an agent, but it is impossible to get an agent before you have published a book. *Moments of Truth* reflects a second-order Catch-22 (perhaps we should call it a Catch-22² or a Catch-484): It is impossible to understand moments before you have understood truth and experience; it is impossible to understand truth before you have understood moments and experience; and it is impossible to understand experience before you have understood moments and truth.

Q: It is impossible, ultimately, to access these moments from the outside. Right? Isn't all this an approximation at best?

A: Yes, but this book will show how we might increase the fidelity of our approximations.

The way out of a Catch-484 (this applies also to a Catch-22) is to start anywhere, but start small. Start with a little bit of X so that then you can understand a little bit of Y, so that then you can understand a little bit of Z, so that then you can understand a bit more of X and then a bit more of Y, and so on. It is a screwy (meant literally) approach; each turn of the screw takes you a little deeper, a little more securely, into exactly the same X, Y, Z, X, Y, Z, X, Y, Z place that you started from. There is no progress, except in depth. This approach requires patience because of the appearance of lack of progress and repetitive redundancy. However, that appearance is deceptive: There is indeed progress, but it is downward, into security.

I adopt this approach in this book and beg for patience from the reader. Our Jack/Jennifer melodrama serves as the first turn of the screw. That melodrama was a fiction, meant to soften us up, to whet our appetites for a sustained interest in the facts of inner experience and its exploration. It introduced us to X (the importance of precisely defining moments), to Y (what is and is not experience), and to Z (that some methodological sophistication will be required). Those early turns of any screw are very insecure – it's easy to aim a dismissive argument at the Jack-and-Jennifer melodrama and knock the screw clean out. The deeper into the book you go, however, the harder it will be to dismiss.

Now we leave melodrama behind and aim at the reality of inner experience and its exploration. Here is a second turn of the screw, the whole book in about ten words:

> Experience inheres in moments; experience can and should be faithfully apprehended.

That experience inheres in moments is obviously not an original idea. For example, "A lived experience which is not a singular moment in the life of a given person is not a lived experience" (Vermersch, 1997, p. 8). Our aim here is simply to take that common observation seriously.

Moments, experience, and faithful apprehension are the *X*, *Y*, and *Z* of our Catch-484. We will have to elaborate moments before we can grasp experience and before we can faithfully apprehend moments; but we will have to elaborate experience before we can grasp moments and before we can faithfully apprehend experience; but we will have to discern what is meant by faithful apprehension before we can grasp moments and before we can grasp experience. I don't expect you to accept any of this now, at this early stage.

Here is a third turn of the screw, the whole book in about 50 words:

> By "inner experience" I mean thoughts, feelings, sensations – anything that "appears before the footlights of consciousness" at some moment. Inner experience is important, and almost everyone is interested in it. Inner experience can be apprehended with high fidelity, and we should do so.

All this might appear obvious, just a restatement of the Jack/Jennifer melodrama. Good! But I will say this in a preliminary way: The science of psychology in general and consciousness science in particular does not have an adequate appreciation of the importance of moments; it does not have an adequate appreciation of experience; and it does not have an adequate appreciation of faithful apprehension. Those are doubtless fighting words for some readers, but I urge us to postpone the fight until we are more secure about all three concepts. Here, I'm merely sketching the concepts; I'm not trying to support or defend them yet.

Here is the whole book in about 100 words:

> By "inner experience" I mean thoughts, feelings, sensations – anything that "appears before the footlights of consciousness." Inner experience is important, and whereas almost everyone is interested in it, few concern themselves adequately with the necessaries of its apprehension: that inner experience inheres only in moments and that accounts of experience must relentlessly separate truth from fiction. Thus, a high-fidelity apprehension of experience must concern itself with moments of truth. Moments of truth are bits of the human condition, objective enough to merit personal and scientific consideration.

Q: This last sentence is a powerful statement that is alone worthy of detailed analysis. How can we define "objective" in this context?

A: You highlight an inherent frustration of the Catch-484 and the turn-of-the-screw method of its exposition. I do indeed intend to focus on "objective enough," but we will need some substantial groundwork. I hope you will accept that I owe you that and will repay that debt in Chapter 17.

This book explores an obvious truth: Experience inheres in moments. Nothing could be simpler. Unfortunately, this simple truth is almost always overlooked, blurred, ignored, denied, repudiated in all manner of ways. An obvious truth that is almost always denied deserves exploration.

Thus this book is about experience, about moments, and about apprehending moments of experience; those are the *X*, *Y*, and *Z* of the Catch-484. My intention is gradually to explore those three concepts until their interrelationships are irretrievably, unalterably secure.

MOMENTS

By *moment* I mean a specific point in time, the present time, the experientially naturally occurring shortest unit of time.

Now! The camera flashes, capturing the scene shown in Figure 1.1. What moment is caught there?

- Is the moment *the baseball game*? No. A game is not the experientially naturally shortest unit of time. There are lots of experientially shorter units than a game: an inning, an out, an at-bat, a pitch, a release. A game is the setting for many moments.
- Is the moment *the pitcher sets, checks the runner at first, and delivers the pitch*? No. That's still too long – that's at least three experientially naturally occurring moments (the set, the check, and the pitch).
- Is the moment *the pitch*? Well, yes, that seems like a moment.
- Is the moment *the pitcher's arm moves forward from 57° to 58°*? No, that's too short. That's a true *physical* characterization of the pitcher at the instant of the flash, but I don't have the *experience* of the pitcher's arm moving forward from 57° to 58°. I experience the man as *pitching*; I don't experience him as *flinging his arm forward from 57° to 58°* Furthermore, if you allow *flinging his arm forward from 57° to 58°* as the moment, then *moment* can be indefinitely subdivided: *flinging his arm forward from 57.23° to 57.24°* is also a moment, and so on. There's nothing experientially natural about that.

Q: I think you are vague or ambiguous in your use of the word "experience" here.

A: I agree. This vagueness is part of the Catch-484: We have to understand moments before we can understand experience, but we can't understand

FIGURE 1.1. What moment is caught here?
Photo is by Photographer's Mate 2nd Class Damon J. Moritz. From http://en.wikipedia.org/wiki/
File:Baseball_pitch_release.jpg

experience until we have understood moments. This is where I need
your patience as we successively approximate everything at each turn
of the screw. Here all that is required is a rough approximation of what
is experience: We can easily accept that the three hours of a baseball
game involves many experiences: of the pitches, of the catches, of the
peanut vendor, of the spilled beer, of the woman in the next row, of the
recollection of.... With that rough approximation of what is experience,
we can easily accept that *the game* is too long, too complex, too
sequentially diverse to be a moment. *From 57° to 58°* is too elemental
to be a moment; *the pitch* seems to be about right as the shortest
experientially natural unit of time. You may quibble, but the size of
the quibble will be pretty small, I think.

This simple example illustrates:

- That moments are defined by the stream of experience, not by the stream of physical time. It is a true statement of physics to say that the camera's flash occurred at 5:27:31.07 P.M. Eastern Daylight Time, but that's not a true statement of the experience of a "moment." A hundredth of a second later (5:27:31.08) is a separably different instant of physical time but the same moment (still part of *the pitch*).
- That the physical duration of a moment is brief but indefinitely so; it is not possible to say, for example, that moments last .573 seconds. A moment lasts until a new naturally occurring moment begins (the *set* lasts until the *check* begins; the *check* lasts until the *pitch* begins).
- That moments depend on private experience. If there are 30,000 fans in the stadium at the physical instant of the flash, there may be 30,000 different moments at 5:27:31.07 P.M. Eastern Daylight Time. For maybe 25,000 fans, experience dictates that the moment encompasses the pitch; for 1,000 other fans, experience dictates that the moment encompasses wondering where the beer man is; for 500, experience dictates that the moment encompasses the wish that my boyfriend didn't like baseball; for 1, experience dictates that the moment involves a sudden insight into Gödel's last theorem, and so on. Some of those moments of experience are longer than others, if measured in physical time; the duration in physical time is not crucial to the definition of a moment.
- We have to be very specific about identifying the precise Now! if we are to examine moments carefully. The moment that is occurring at 5:27:31.07 may involve excitement and tension (*the pitch* with bases loaded, tie score), whereas the moment that is occurring a half second later at 5:27:31.57 may involve disappointment and anger (*Ball four!*).

There is, at least sometimes, maybe always, some fuzziness inherent in the apprehension of moments: Did or did not *the pitch* include the last-minute adjustment of the fingers on the baseball? That is, it may be impossible to ascertain precisely when, in physical time or in the stream of experience, a moment begins and ends. Usually, I have found, that fuzziness is relatively small.

We, each of us separately, live in a series of moments, a stream of Now!s. Now! I watch the batter foul off the pitch. Now! I feel the crunch and taste the saltiness of the peanut. Now! I see the pitcher shake off the sign. Now! I smell the perfume of the woman next to me. Now! I see the pitcher shake off the sign again. Now! I feel impatient. Now! I see the pitcher set. Now! I feel a wave of tension in my shoulders. Now! I see the pitcher check the runner at first. Now! I watch the pitch, simultaneously keeping my eye on the runner. Now! I see the catcher reach too high. Now! I feel my body curl in disappointment and anger at ball four. And so on.

Thus, moments are not intervals in physical time; they are defined by experience. We cannot have a genuine understanding of moments without already having a genuine understanding of experience. And we cannot have a genuine understanding of anything without being concerned about truth.

> **Q:** Your baseball example makes it seem that moments are cleanly separate things, like pearls on a string. It seems to me that experienced moments overlap: The saltiness of the peanut continues as you watch the pitcher shake off the sign, for example.
>
> **A:** I agree that that is possible, and perhaps I should have written: "Now! I feel the crunch and taste the saltiness of the peanut. Now! I see the pitcher shake off the sign while simultaneously continuing to taste the saltiness." Yet it is also possible that saltiness passes through the footlights of my consciousness, then disappears as I zoom in on the pitcher, and then experientially returns. Any careful examination of moments will have to try to make such distinctions as carefully as possible. Sometimes it will be obviously simultaneous: The saltiness continues while the main focus shifts to the pitcher. Sometimes it will be obviously sequential: The saltiness disappears as the new focus takes over. Sometimes it will be fuzzily difficult to determine.

INNER EXPERIENCE

By "inner experience" I mean thoughts, feelings, sensations, anything that "appears before the footlights of consciousness." Some would call it "experience," "lived experience," or "phenomenal consciousness." I don't think there is a best term (Hurlburt & Schwitzgebel, 2007, esp. Box 2.1), so I don't care much about what we call it as long as we understand that by "inner experience" (or whatever) I mean what presents itself to you directly, in your conscious awareness at some particular given moment.

As I write this, I happen to be sitting in an airport, waiting for a delayed flight, trying to make the most of the four hours I will be here. I'll use this opportunity to provide an example of real (not melodramatic Jack and Jennifer) moments of (pristine inner) experience. I resolve to notice what passes through my inner experience for the next few minutes and take notes about it. Then I'll double back and make those notes coherent enough for you to understand. Here's the result, which I will refer to as the "airport stream of consciousness":

RUSS'S AIRPORT STREAM OF CONSCIOUSNESS

I see a man in a gray shirt walk by; I notice his slight limp and I recall seeing him pass by an hour ago. I wonder if he works here. I imagine a conversation with my colleague George, who was to pick me up at the airport – I see a clear image of George's face with its look of empathic distress as I describe the weather in Dallas that delayed my flight. I hear the morning TV show on the TV monitor and am irritated by the too-enthusiastic voices of Regis and his guest and by the unnatural laughter; I wonder whether the laughter is electronically enhanced or just the result of "Laugh" signs on the TV studio stage; I wonder whether anyone is really watching that airport TV; I wonder whether I could figure out how to turn it down. I see a woman on her cell phone; I'm attracted to her pretty blond hair as it falls across the phone but then am repelled by her whiny voice, which is too loud, like many people when they talk on cell phones. I take a deeper-than-usual breath/sigh that has a catch to it, which doubtless reflects the pressure of being made late by the delay. My knee twinges under the inactivity caused by the computer on my lap. I wonder if I have to explain to the reader why I've been delayed. I see a black man walk right to left. I hesitate: Do I mention in my account that he's a *black* man, or should I just say a man walks right to left? This hesitation is a tightness in my chest that seems to refer to the political-correctness of either mentioning or not mentioning blackness. The woman next to me gets up, takes off her coat, and walks away; she's very heavy, and I'm somewhat fascinated by the fleshy rolling of her hips and cheeks as she walks away. I debate the words: "very heavy" seems too general; "obese" seems too formal but more accurate. I debate how to write "hips and cheeks"; "ass" is too low-brow, "butt cheeks" seems not kind. I get no resolution; I have a sense, like a slight relief in my shoulders, that the reader will know what I mean and leave it at that.

That's a minute or so of some molecules of my inner experience as collected by a casual method of observation we might call "armchair introspection": I set myself the task of observing what was in my experience and then did so. About this airport example we can notice that:

1. Experience inheres in moments. My pristine experience while waiting at the airport at one moment is quite different from my pristine experience while waiting at the same airport the next moment. Experience inheres in moments. Strictly speaking, I don't have an airport-waiting experience; I have a seeing-a-limping-man experience; then I have a wondering-if-he-is-an-employee experience; then I have an imaginary-conversation-with-George experience; and so on.

2. Moments are short. In this minute or so of experience, I have had at least seventeen experiences, maybe more depending on how you break it down: limp, recall seeing him before, wondering about employee, imaged conversation with colleague, irritated by Regis's voice, unnatural laughter, anyone really watching? turn it down? pretty hair, whiny voice, sigh, knee twinge, explain delay? PC black debate, fleshy hips, P.C. "heavy"

debate, reader will know. That's a new experience every few seconds, and that rate might be slowed down (or perhaps speeded up?) by my note taking.

3. Experience is fleeting. In the procession of moments, I am interested, aggravated, attracted, repelled, neutral, and so on; in the procession of moments I think, feel, experience pain, and so on. One experience comes, another comes and the first goes, and so on. These are abrupt transitions: from attraction almost immediately to repulsion; neutrality to pain and back to neutrality in a few seconds; from idle observation quickly to PC debate, and so on.

4. Experience is private. I create this experience in a way that is hidden from your view. The neurons that are involved in my experience are firing inside my skull and body, entirely disconnected from your neurons and everyone else's. Even if you had been watching me intently during that minute, you'd know very little about my experiences, very little about my lived reactions to the gray-shirt man, the blond woman, the fat woman, the black man. You'd see me typing on my computer, glancing up impassively when someone walks by, resuming typing. That's all; you'd have little idea of the micro-significances, the experiential realities of these moments.

5. I create these experiences – they are not forced on me by the external or internal environments. At every instant during my airport minute, there was a welter of stimuli occurring all around and inside me – visual, auditory, olfactory, kinesthetic, proprioceptive, and so on – a disorganized riot of energy fluctuations available to be transduced by my sensory apparatus. My experience sometimes incorporated some of those stimuli (e.g., the gray shirt, the laughter sound), never incorporated all of those stimuli (that would have been chaotically overwhelming), sometimes incorporated none of those stimuli (during the moment I was engrossed in the image of the distant colleague I excluded all the present stimuli). Thus, my stream of experiences says a lot about me; that out of the literally millions of possibilities presenting themselves to my sensorium during that airport minute, I created those particular 17 experiences and annihilated the remaining 999,983 possibilities. My pristine experience may have something to do with the immediate environment, but it is by no means entirely driven by the environment; George is a thousand miles away and draws my attention anyway. My pristine experience is my personal, idiosyncratic creation, manufactured by me out of (perhaps) my immediate environment, my interests, my skills, my history, my blind spots, my desires.

6. Experience is personal. Had you been, at that minute, sitting next to me typing on your laptop, bathed in the same (or at least highly similar) riot of energy fluctuations, you might not have noticed the TV and the blond woman at all; and had you noticed, your experience might not have been

annoyance by the laughter or attraction and then repulsion by the blond woman. At the same instant that I'm annoyed by the Regis laughter, your inner experience might have been about the terrorists in Afghanistan, or about the plans for the Christmas party you're going to have, or …. Your inner experience is your personal, idiosyncratic creation, the result of your constellation of skills/desires/interests as well as (perhaps) your immediate environment.

TRUTH

Experience inheres in moments. If you want to apprehend my experience, really know about my experience as I experience it, you have to specify precisely which moment you are enquiring about. You can ask, "How was waiting in the airport?" and I will likely say "Fine" or "Boring" or "I was productive" or "I felt bad because I inconvenienced George." However, none of those actually describes experience as I actually experienced it; all of them actually *hide* the experience as I actually experienced it, hide the attractions, annoyances, PC debates, and so on.

Thus, if you begin with an interest in experience, you are immediately confronted with an interest in personal truths, the Z aspect of our Catch-484, to which we now turn.

By truth I mean the genuine article, the real deal about a person, a faithful apprehension of the phenomenon of interest and a straightforward communication about it. This personal truth is not necessarily easy to apprehend:

1. The privacy that we just discussed is partially innate (my neurons are in a different bag from your neurons), but beyond that, maintaining that privacy is a learned and highly practiced skill. The impassivity that you observed when I looked up and saw the gray-shirt man, the blond woman, the fat woman, and the black man is largely an acquired expertise. My reactions to those men and women were undetectable to you at least in part because I have practiced suppressing the expression of my inner experiences, probably the result of a lifetime of sometimes painful consequences of freely expressing attraction/repulsion/interest/criticism of people or events in my environment: parents or teachers saying "Don't you be angry at me!"; girls spurning my attraction to them; and so on.

   My experience has gone underground, and I'm by no means unusual in this regard: Nearly everyone hides most of their inner experience from view (recall Jack and Jennifer). Some would argue that the ability to hide inner experience has been evolutionarily selected: It can be dangerous indeed, for example, openly to express anger, jealousy, envy, sexual feelings, or guilt (to the king, for example; Kagan, 2007).

Perhaps it is merely the expression of my experience that has gone underground: Perhaps I acutely experience my anger but have learned (or over-learned) to hide the main features of its expression. My research shows that some people acutely experience emotion but suppress its expression, whereas others do not experience emotion at all (hold your fire on this score until we get to Chapter 13).

Thus, an interest in personal truth leads us back to a careful concern with experience (and therefore also to a careful concern with moments). And if not the experiencing itself, at least the communication about my inner experience may put me diametrically at odds with my own skills that are likely part of my genetic equipment and that I have practiced or over-practiced throughout my life.

2. Experience is evanescent. Despite the vividness-at-the-moment of my apprehensions of the gray-shirt man, Regis's audience, the blond woman, the fat woman, and the black man, within a minute or two I doubtless would have entirely forgotten that I saw/heard them at all, entirely forgotten that I had engaged in an inner political-correctness debate and a slight crisis of kindness. Like a dream that can be vividly recalled on waking but that soon disappears completely, those experiences would have vanished had I not been actively engaged in the task of recording them. That has methodological implications: If I want to apprehend my personal truths, and therefore, necessarily, my moments of experience, I'll have to do that in a way that does not overlook the evanescence of experience. Probably that will require minimizing retrospection, but there may be other ways as well.

Some people maintain that they recall everything that passes through their experience, and that is perhaps possible for some people. But do the math: If you roughly assume that experiences last a few seconds, that's roughly 20 experiences per minute × 60 minutes × 16 hours = 19,000 experiences per day. (Maybe it's really 9,000 or 29,000. I don't really know the number; but it's a lot!) I doubt that most people can remember the details of all those experiences.

3. Because experience goes all over the place, it is sometimes at odds with my overt intentions, and therefore may not get observed, much less reported. For example, I was typing notes on my computer throughout my airport minute, and yet the note taking itself does not figure at all in my account. Why not? Probably because I had ruled the note taking to be irrelevant at the time – I was interested in conveying what a minute of sitting-in-the-airport was like, *not* what a minute of sitting-in-the airport-trying-unobtrusively-to-record-my-sitting-in-the-airport was like. So I systematically overlooked a large part – quite possibly the largest part – of my experience, the experience of note taking: that I hit Caps Lock by mistake and felt my usual angry-at-Microsoft surge that there is no software switch

to disable that key; that I was deciding whether to spell "gray" or "grey"; that I misspelled "twinge" and had to go back and fix it; and so on. That is, due to some *a priori* understanding of my task, I had somehow agreed with myself to overlook important, real aspects of my experience, even though I was ostensibly trying to give a complete account of my experience.

That is therefore another methodological implication: However I go about apprehending my real pristine experience, I'll have to suspend my sense of task, my presuppositions about what is "supposed" to be in experience.

4. Once the personal truth/moment of experience has been apprehended (assuming for now that that is possible), it has to be straightforwardly communicated if it is to be useful to someone else or to science.

How should we approach the genuine article, the real deal about a person's experience, a faithful apprehension of the phenomenon of interest and a straightforward communication about it? We can learn much from Harry Frankfurt's delightful little book *On Bullshit*, the main theme of which is conveyed in an anecdote Frankfurt relates about the philosopher Wittgenstein and his friend Fania Pascal. Wittgenstein visited Pascal shortly after she had her tonsils out, and Pascal said, "I feel like a dog that has been run over." Wittgenstein disgustedly replied, "You don't know what a dog that has been run over feels like" (Frankfurt, 2005 p. 24). Frankfurt examines what disgusts Wittgenstein about Pascal's report. It is not that she is lying, as she would have been if she had actually felt good when she said such a thing. Frankfurt's Wittgenstein finds Pascal's statement objectionable because

> it purports to convey something more than simply that she feels bad. Her characterization of her feeling is too specific; it is excessively particular. Hers is not just any bad feeling but, according to her account, the distinctive kind of bad feeling that a dog has when it is run over. To the Wittgenstein in Pascal's story, judging from his response, this is just bullshit ... because he perceives what Pascal says as being ... unconnected to a concern with the truth....

> The point that troubles Wittgenstein is manifestly not that Pascal has made a mistake in her description of how she feels. Nor is it even that she has made a careless mistake. Her laxity, or her lack of care, is not a matter of having permitted an error to slip into her speech on account of some inadvertent or momentarily negligent lapse in the attention she was devoting to getting things right. The point is rather that, so far as Wittgenstein can see, Pascal offers a description of a certain state of affairs without genuinely submitting to the constraints which the endeavor to provide an accurate representation of reality imposes. Her fault is not that she fails to get things right, but that she is not even trying. (Frankfurt, 2005, pp. 29–32)

Frankfurt holds that liars and bullshitters have something in common: They mislead us about their intentions. However, his analysis shows that the directions of their misleading are very different. Liars lead us away from a correct apprehension of reality, whereas bullshitters lead us away from recognizing that they have no real concern for whether reality is or is not correctly apprehended. The liar knows the truth and deceives us about it; thus the liar is in fact acutely connected (albeit falsely) to the truth. By contrast, the bullshitter essentially ignores the truth; Pascal's feel-like-a-dog-run-over comment is made without adequate care about whether or not that comment is true – her utterance is a tool in her interaction with Wittgenstein, not to be evaluated on its truth value any more than a screwdriver would be evaluated on its truth value.

Because liars are connected to the truth whereas bullshitters are disconnected, Frankfurt concludes that "bullshit is a greater enemy of the truth than lies are" (Frankfurt, 2005, p. 61). I accept Frankfurt's analysis; I think that avoiding bullshit is a high ideal (arguably the highest ideal, but that is not my point). The term "bullshit" has a, well, stinky connotation, and I wish there were a better term. For those who don't like the term, every place you read "bullshit" you may substitute Frankfurt's definition of it: "a description of a certain state of affairs without genuinely submitting to the constraints which the endeavor to provide an accurate representation of reality imposes."

I also wish to emphasize that to bullshit does *not* imply mean-spiritedness or the intention to misrepresent. Wittgenstein's Pascal was not mean-spirited when she said she felt like a dog run over; doubtless she was warmly disposed toward Wittgenstein and was trying to demonstrate it. Pascal was not intending to misrepresent her condition to Wittgenstein. Pascal doubtless had no negative motive whatsoever; she simply was not adequately connected to the truth.

To bullshit is an inter-personal act: I'm deceiving you about my disconnection from the truth. (Perhaps it is possible to bullshit oneself, but I think that is more confusing oneself rather than deceiving oneself, and therefore it is not actually bullshit.) To avoid bullshit is also an inter-personal act: I will try to avoid bullshitting you. That leads, I think, empirically if not necessarily, to the encounter with personal truths, which, as we have seen leads to experience, which leads to moments.

> **Q:** Wittgenstein sounds like a pain-in-the-neck kind of friend! But my main concern is the role of metaphor or art or other representations of human experience that avail themselves of imagination. If I told you that I felt like a plant that hasn't been watered, I think you would have some sense of what I am trying to communicate.
> **A:** I accept that I would know *something*, but how much I would know is open to question, as is how much of what I *think* I know about your experience is actually my misguided projection. That's why science can't rest on metaphor or art, has to avoid bullshit.

MOMENTS OF TRUTH

Thus, a genuine interest in moments energizes an interest in experience and energizes a genuine submission to the constraints that the endeavor to apprehend moments of experience imposes. A genuine interest in experience energizes an interest in moments and a genuine submission to the constraints that the endeavor to apprehend moments of experience imposes. A genuine submission to the constraints that the endeavor to apprehend moments of experience imposes energizes an interest in experience and moments. And so on. It is a reflexive system: Everything potentiates everything else.

However, the opposite is also true: It is *not* possible to be genuinely interested in experience without being genuinely interested in moments and/or without a genuine submission to the attendant constraints. It is not possible genuinely to submit to the attendant constraints without being genuinely interested in moments of experience. It is not possible to be genuinely interested in moments without truly encountering experience. It is not possible to be genuinely interested in experience without genuinely submitting to the constraints that the endeavor to provide an accurate representation of experience imposes. You can't turn any one aspect of the screw farther than you turn the other two aspects of it.

> **Q:** Is Jack's "Just how spectacular the sunset is – and about sharing it with you" bullshit?
> **A:** Yes. He wasn't lying to her – he did in fact find the sunset spectacular. He wasn't mean-spirited – he was trying to do what he thought Jennifer wanted him to do. But Jill had asked what he was thinking and his answer was not connected to the truth about that.
>
> **Q:** Then isn't your airport stream of consciousness bullshit, too?
> **A:** Yes. It was not "a description of a certain state of affairs that genuinely submits to the constraints which the endeavor to provide an accurate representation of reality imposes." I wasn't lying – I sincerely tried to give an account of a few minutes of my experience at the airport. I wasn't mean-spirited. But there are many reasons that the airport stream of consciousness account fails genuinely to submit to the constraints that an attempt to describe pristine experience imposes: There was no provision for the possibility that my notes could not "keep up" with my experience (that I can think faster than I can type); there was no provision for the possibility that I would filter my account because I knew that I was preparing this account for your perusal; there was no provision for the possibility that I would have a blind spot (or hypersensitivity) to some aspect of my experience; there was no provision for the possibility that I would have to learn how to engage in this task; there was (as we mentioned earlier) no provision for including the experience of the note taking; there was no provision for the inclusion of

adequate detail (my airport account has 17 moments: there are 384 words in the whole account, roughly 22 words per experience); and so on.

Q: You're too hard on yourself. Your airport account isn't bullshit, it's just an approximation. Everything is an approximation.
A: By that logic, you could say that Pascal's "I feel like a dog that has been run over" isn't bullshit – it's just an approximation: *Of course* she doesn't feel *exactly* like a dog that was run over, but Wittgenstein should get the idea. That is exactly Frankfurt's point. The expected acceptance of the presentation hides the fact that the presentation itself is estranged from the truth in important ways. It is a form of collusion: I'll say, imply, or otherwise represent that my airport stream of consciousness is a faithful account of my experience at the airport if you promise not to notice the shortcomings of that representation. We are both estranged from genuinely considering whether I faithfully apprehended my experience in the airport.

Q: Still, your airport account was very vivid and "real" to me. I can relate to having such experiences; it was very momentarily (literally) concrete, unlike Pascal's (in which she describes her whole experience in terms of a clever metaphor).
A: You are saying that my airport account has high "truthiness," higher truthiness than Pascal's metaphor, and I agree. I wrote it to have high truthiness. Comedian Stephen Colbert coined the term "truthiness" to mean "the quality of preferring concepts or facts one wishes to be true, rather than concepts or facts known to be true" (it was Merriam-Webster's number-one word of the year in 2006; Merriam-Webster, 2009). The point of Colbert's wit is to demonstrate that truthiness is not good enough, and I agree with that, too. Frankfurt's bullshit and Colbert's truthiness come from the same motive.

We are observing, by our melodramatic and armchair introspection examples, that we need to be very specific in targeting moments; that we need to be very careful in understanding what *is* experience and what only *seems* to be experience; that we need genuinely to submit to the constraints that the attempt to apprehend moments of experience imposes. Our melodramatic and armchair introspection examples have fallen short on all three counts.

Let's have a look at another example. Here is a portion of an interview that "Nancy Nichols" and I conducted with "Stephanie Peterson." Nancy is a graduate student; I'm supervising her training in the interview techniques we're using at the University of Nevada, Las Vegas. Stephanie is an advanced undergraduate who had expressed interest in our work. We had given Stephanie a beeper and asked her to report the experience that was ongoing at the moment just before the beep began (we'll talk more about our method of using beepers in Chapter 3 and beyond). This example is the fourth sample from Stephanie's fifth sampling day, six samples per day, each day followed by a sixty to ninety minute interview designed to train her to be a good observer as well as help her to describe what she has observed. The transcript is almost entirely verbatim, although I have removed some sections that involved training for Nancy and a few false starts that seemed distracting to the transcript.

INTERVIEWING STEPHANIE

NANCY NICHOLS: Can you tell me your experience at the moment of beep four?

STEPHANIE PETERSON: Yeah. At the moment of beep four I was talking in class [a senior seminar] and I was feeling a little bit pressured because, um, Dr. Rodriguez had asked me directly a question about whether I liked or disliked Las Vegas, so I was [hesitates] talking but I was more aware of [hesitates] I guess, I mean I was formulating what I was gonna say. But I was also feeling a little bit of pressure 'cause he kind of put me on the spot. I didn't want to offend anybody.

NN: So, right at the very moment of the beep, what was in your awareness?

SP: Feeling a little bit pressured and also kind of like coming up with what I was going to say, or coming up with ... I mean I was talking at the moment of the beep, so, um, I mean, I was formulating what I was going to say and saying it. But I was much more aware of feeling pressured, like put on the spot.

NN: Can you tell me what that experience was like, or how you experienced feeling pressured?

SP: [pauses, sighs] I don't really know how to describe it other than just feeling pressured. I mean I felt like I needed to say something PC ["politically correct"], like I needed to say the right thing. That there wasn't ... I mean I wasn't thinking I need to say the right thing, but there was that awareness that, like there was a right answer and a wrong answer, even though it wasn't that kind of question. So, I don't know, kind of just pressure and maybe like a little bit of conflict between what I wanted to say, or like what I would have honestly said and what I did say. So I was like spinning it, I guess [laughs]. I was like self-editing in my head before I said it. So at the moment of the beep I was thinking, I mean, I was doing that editing what I would have ... what I was saying, but I was feeling kind of like startled and put on the spot by the question.

NN: The conflict and the editing and the feeling pressured, are those the same thing, or are they two [she means three, and Stephanie understands that] different experiences?

SP: Um, the conflict and the editing are part of whatever process is going on when I'm thinking about what I'm going to say. But those are [sighs] secondary to the feeling of, like, feeling pressure to say the right thing.

NN: OK. So, Stephanie, I'm trying to figure out, do you mean being pressured in a cognitive sense? Do you mean it in a physical/emotional sense? Neither ...?

SP: Um, I would say that it's more cognitive than physical. I'm not aware of any physical anything [pause] at the moment of the beep.

NN: Is their any emotional part of being pressured?

SP: [tentatively, questioningly] Yeah [strained laugh] probably.

RUSS HURLBURT: So you listed sort of a lot of things going on about that pressure: There was the conflict of what you wanted to say and didn't say, something about being honest, something about spinning it ...

SP: Um hm.

RTH: ... Is all that stuff somehow present to you right at the moment?

SP: Uh, [sighs] it's like implied, I guess, at the moment. Because I'm talking, but as I'm talking I'm thinking, well, I can't really say that, I don't want to, you know, piss such and such off, and I don't want to do this, and I don't want to do that, and so I'm editing, and I'm ... I wouldn't say that I'm actively aware of that, but I'm talking and I know that I'm like holding certain things, certain opinions or whatever, back.

RTH: And do you know what those opinions are? Like do you have specific opinions that you then clamp off? Or do you clamp them off before they even come to you? become conscious, so to speak?

SP: Well, some of, I think, some of them, when he *first* asked me the question, some of them I was like, [in an ironic tone] OK! I'm not going to say that!

RTH: Some specific things ...

SP: Some specific things. But ...

RTH: ... that were in your awareness right then?

SP: Um hm.

RTH: OK.

SP: But, I mean, I would venture a guess, although I wouldn't say it was in my awareness, but I would say there were definitely other things that probably didn't even get to the surface before I just was like, Nnaahh! [a negative grunt] I'm not gonna say that!

On the basis of this interview, I think we can write with substantial confidence this description of Stephanie's moment:

STEPHANIE'S MOMENT

At the moment identified by this beep, Stephanie had been asked by her professor how she liked Las Vegas. Her experience was largely occupied by a felt pressure to say something politically correct about it, and she was in the process of reviewing and rejecting things she could say. This reviewing/rejecting was actively in her experience – she understood herself to be examining and rejecting alternatives – but the alternatives themselves were *not* in her experience – she had a hint or an intimation or an implication of what she might say and then rejected it. The pressure itself was a cognitive experience – she did not feel pressure in her body, nor was this pressure an emotional experience. Although this pressure was clearly understood to be cognitive, her experience of the decision/rejection process did not involve words, images, or any other symbols. At the same time that she was feeling this pressure, Stephanie was talking, but not paying attention to what she was saying – the spoken words were mostly rolling out as if automated.

> **Q:** You say Stephanie's pressure was not an emotional experience. I would argue that there *was* an affective element to her experience of being pressured, and that she even said as much in response to Nancy.
>
> **A:** Perhaps so. But your question exposes again the inherent frustration of the Catch-484 nature of this subject matter and the turn-of-the-screw method of its exposition. In Chapter 8 we will discuss why Stephanie's word "probably" and her strained laugh undermine my confidence in that portion of her interview, and in Chapter 13 we will discuss the experience of emotion. At this early stage in the exposition, I can only beg that you forgive such incompletenesses.

That is an example of what I take to be a moment of truth, a bit of Stephanie's actual pristine experience faithfully described. It illustrates some of the constraints, paraphrasing Frankfurt, that the endeavor to apprehend experience in high fidelity imposes:

- *Constraint: It is risky to infer inner experience from external behavior.* There is a huge difference between inner experience and outer behavior. Stephanie is asked whether she likes Las Vegas and she says, aloud, that she does. However, at the same time, her main experience is of pressure and the filtering out of her honest opinions.

> **Q:** If you looked at Stephanie very closely you could see signs that she was not merely candidly answering the question.
>
> **A:** Perhaps. But (a) see the next observation, and (b) such signs are always to some degree ambiguous – the apparent lack of candor might mean that she doesn't like Las Vegas, or that she just had a fight with her boyfriend and doesn't want to say anything about anything, or that she has stomach cramps, or any of a variety of other experiential realities.

- *Constraint: People hide their experience.* Stephanie has substantial skill at *not* saying what is going on in her experience. Stephanie is far more skillful at hiding her experience than she is at simply straightforwardly describing it: We worked for fifteen minutes to get a moderately faithful account of her experience; by contrast, in the classroom she successfully deflected questions about her experience on the fly in a matter of seconds. Her hiding of her experience is almost entirely automated. She doesn't have to articulate an impression fully before recognizing that that should be suppressed. That is evidence of a highly skilled behavior, skilled in the same way that we don't need to fully articulate that the road turns left before engaging in left-turn behavior.

- *Constraint: Experience changes dramatically and quickly.* Had the beep occurred five seconds earlier, there would have been no experienced pressure – the professor's question would not have occurred. Had the beep occurred five seconds later, the experienced pressure would likely have been replaced by something else – a consideration of the advantages and disadvantages of quasi-experiments, interest in the next student's hairstyle, or whatever might occupy Stephanie's experience at the next moment.

- *Constraint: Experience is evanescent.* Stephanie's micro-experiential pressure, had we not subjected it to the scrutiny we undertook, would likely be completely forgotten within a few minutes; feeling pressured was just one experience among the hundreds that occurred during the class.

- *Constraint: Casual characterizations of experience are often not accurate.* If there had been no beep, and someone asked her, when the class ended, about the class, she very likely would give a characterization entirely unrelated to the pressure of the moment: She's really looking forward to the class, she might say; or she really likes the professor; or she wishes the class were not so early in the day.

- *Constraint: Experience is apprehendable.* Regardless of whether her experience is quickly forgotten, her experience is available to her and important to her at that moment: Stephanie *did* feel pressured, and she adjusted her speech accordingly.

- *Constraint: Experience reveals something about a person.* Not everyone would react to the same kind of circumstance in the same way: Alice would react with anger; Betsy would just say what she thinks, consequence be damned; Connie would never even have noticed; Diane would feel pressured but that experience would be bodily, in her heart, not cognitive; Evelyn would be attracted to Dr. Rodriguez's wavy black hair; and so on. Stephanie reacts the way Stephanie reacts, not the way Alice, Betsy, Connie, Diane, or Evelyn would react. This experience does reveal a bit of the truth about Stephanie.

- *Constraint: Experience is not essence.* That this reveals a bit of truth about Stephanie does not necessarily mean that it reveals the True (with a capital *T*) Stephanie or the essence of Stephanie or even an important characteristic of Stephanie. It is entirely possible that that was the only time in Stephanie's life that she felt that kind of pressure – it may have been a mere chance occurrence.

- *Constraint: Apprehending and describing experience requires skill.* Stephanie could describe some aspects of her experience easily – she said in the interview's opening sentence that she felt pressure. However, that ease comes at least in part from the fact that this was her fifth day of wearing the beeper, so she has had quite a bit of practice at understanding what is meant by experience and how to observe and describe it. Had this beep occurred on her first sampling day, her opening line in the interview would likely have been something like, "We were in class introducing ourselves," or "I was telling Dr. Rodriguez that I liked Las Vegas," or "Dr. Rodriguez is funny." You might retort that that isn't about experience at all, and that is exactly the point: People do not, typically, have a clear understanding of what experience is or how to observe it or describe it.

- *Constraint: Experience is detailed.* It required 165 words to describe this single moment, and from some points of view this description is still incomplete. Contrast that with the airport armchair introspection, which required only 384 words for about 17 moments, or about 23 words per experience. About eight times as many words were required for the careful description of a moment of Stephanie's experience as for an armchair report.

That's a lot to infer from one inconsequential moment of truth. Much depends on whether this interview can be said to have provided a faithful account of Stephanie's experience. As we have seen, an account of experience requires at least three aspects: focus on a concretely specified moment, focus on experience, and genuinely submitting to the constraints that the apprehension of experience imposes. We were, I think, largely successful in identifying a precise moment, using the beep to focus on a moment with a precision probably measured in some fraction of seconds in real time. We were, I think, largely successful in distinguishing, again and again, between what was and what was not actually experienced: Pressure? Yes. Emotion? Probably not. Bodily? Yes. Meta-awareness? No. And so on. We used, I think, a method that genuinely submits to the constraints that the endeavor to provide an accurate representation of reality imposes.

As a result, I think this is a pretty low-bullshit account of Stephanie's classroom moment. The account may be false: Stephanie may be lying, the interviewers may not be adequately skillful, and so on. However, it is not bullshit as Frankfurt used the term. It seems to me that our description of Stephanie's classroom experience *does* genuinely submit to the constraints that the endeavor to provide an accurate representation of reality imposes. We tried hard to get things right, used a method that took the science of experiential report seriously.

> **Q:** It's not quite fair to compare your interview to a fiction and to your own admittedly flawed armchair introspection, and then to conclude that your interview is a good one. I could advance several criticisms of your interview.
> **A:** I ask again for your patience. This is still an early turn of the screw, and I haven't tried to convince you of any of this at this point. So far, I've tried only to *begin* the conversation about the importance of moments, about what

are and are not bits of pristine experience, about the possibility of faithfully apprehending moments of truth and giving low-bullshit reports about them. We will examine all these concepts in much more detail.

Q: OK. Let's accept, at least tentatively, that you have provided a low-bullshit account of one inconsequential moment of Stephanie's experience. Yet that moment is, as you say, *inconsequential*. You spend, by your own account and your Stephanie example, an inordinate amount of time and energy trying to get straight about something that doesn't matter!

A: I agree that we spent *a lot* of time and energy apprehending Stephanie's experience in as high fidelity as we could, but I don't think that is *inordinate*. Chapter 2 illustrates why apprehending moments of truth may be of fundamental importance to a science of persons, and if it takes a long time to get each moment apprehended, then that's the price of admission.

EPILOGUE

Your pristine experience is your unscripted, unedited, naturally occurring moments of you, by you, for you, just how you experience them. However, as we have seen, pristine experience is usually hidden from the view of others and from your own retrospection, buried by scads of practice, social pressures, personal insecurities, and perhaps even by genetic endowment. Instead of describing experience, we «describe» «experience» – we use explicitly or implicitly created and rehearsed scripts that mask or otherwise distort pristine experience. Jack doesn't tell Jennifer about his pristine experience; Stephanie doesn't tell her professor/classmates about her pristine experience. And that's too bad: Jack's and Stephanie's pristine experiences are much more fascinating, genuine, illuminating than the mush they actually say.

We miss a lot when we fail to attend to pristine experience, and we miss it so thoroughly we are not likely to notice its absence. We will reconsider this omission throughout the book. The omission is personal, one person at a time, but it is also scientific, one scientist at a time. Pristine experience is *not* a topic well known to science. And that's too bad, because in a human science, pristine experience may be where the gold is.

Perhaps by coincidence, I watched, while taking a break from writing this chapter, well-known comedian Conan O'Brien being interviewed on *Inside the Actor's Studio*. He said:

> I don't pretend that I've learned the true craft of improv, but what I did learn is that people respond to something that happened in the moment much more than they will respond to the most brilliant thing that was thought of ahead of time and prepared. There's something in us – and they'll find it some day, it's like a tiny piece of zinc in our cerebral cortex. They're going to find out what it is. But when we see something that

unfolds naturally and is real, people love it. The biggest laughs I've ever had in my life are something going off the rails, something going wrong, something happening that wasn't supposed to happen. Improv teaches you not to fear those moments. That's where the gold is. (Conan O'Brien, *Inside the Actor's Studio*, January 26, 2009)

Q: I get it that pristine experience might be interesting and fascinating. I get the analogy between pristine experience and the real events that O'Brien is talking about when scripts go wrong. But your claim that such things are *necessary to science* seems a long stretch from their being interesting to you or to O'Brien's late-night audience.

A: I agree that I haven't demonstrated that. I encourage you to read Chapter 2 and see if it answers your question.

2

Fragmented Experience in Bulimia Nervosa

WITH SHARON JONES-FORRESTER

Chapter 1 made the case, preliminarily, that it was possible to describe moments of truth, bits of pristine experience. We discussed what we called a Catch-484: You can't really understand moments without first understanding experience and genuinely submitting to the constraints that the apprehension of experience imposes; you can't genuinely submit to the constraints without first understanding moments and experience; and you can't really understand experience without first understanding moments and genuinely submitting to the constraints.

We said that the way out of a Catch-484 is to start anywhere: Start, say, with a little discussion of moments, so that then we can have a little discussion of experience, so that then we can have a little discussion of the constraints, so that then we can have a deeper discussion of moments, so that we can have a deeper discussion of experience, and so on. It is a screwy (meant literally) approach; each turn of the screw takes us a little deeper, a little more securely, into exactly the same moments ↔ experience ↔ genuinely-submitting-to-the-constraints place that we started from.

The present chapter will focus primarily on experience. However, moments, experience, and the constraints co-determine each other, so every discussion of experience is also a discussion of moments and the constraints – we can never talk about one while completely ignoring the other two. The illustration at the top of this chapter is intended to convey this: Chapter 2 will focus primarily on experience but will always keep moments and the constraints in mind.

APPREHENDING EXPERIENCE

If we tentatively accept that moments of truth are apprehendable, we are still left with the question of whether such moments of truth have any value. Perhaps moments of truth are inconsequentialities, mere faithfully apprehended minutiae, too small to be useful in any way. Or perhaps they are of interest to the person whose moments they are but useless to others. Or perhaps these moments are of interest to the person and to the person's acquaintances but useless to science.

This is another Catch-22: There's no sense bothering to apprehend moments of truth unless you can be assured that it's worth the trouble, but it's impossible to discover whether it's worth the trouble until you have apprehended them. This Catch-22 is therefore overlaid on the Catch-22^2 of Chapter 1, making it a Catch-22^3, or Catch-10648. As before, the way out of these catches is to turn the screw gradually: We went some ways into the possibility of apprehending moments of truth in Chapter 1; now we'll go a bit into the value of doing this; and in subsequent chapters we will return to both.

Over the course of my studies of inner experience, I have observed that usually, if I stay with a person's microscopic moments of truth long enough, I discover there are strong regularities/patterns/salient characteristics in the person's experience, and that pausing to observe those regularities can offer deep, sometimes startlingly new and seemingly useful insights into a person. If I observe a group of individuals who share a common characteristic, I discover that there are strong regularities/patterns/salient characteristics *across* people. I don't expect you to believe that without evidence; this chapter provides the beginning of that evidence, provides an example of the potential within-person and across-person insights achievable by examining moments of truth.

Stephanie Doucette, Sharon Jones-Forrester, and I have explored the pristine inner experience of twenty-four women with bulimia nervosa using a method that carefully examined moments of experience and that genuinely submitted, I think, to the constraints that the attempt to apprehend experience imposes. Let's have a look at a few moments of truth of one of those women, whom we will call "Jessica" (Jones-Forrester, 2009). The question we mean to discuss is whether we learn something worthwhile about bulimia by apprehending Jessica's pristine experience or that of other individuals with a similar affliction.

JESSICA'S EXPERIENCE

Jessica was a twenty-two-year-old university student with a long history of binge eating, purging, laxative misuse, and excessive concern about her weight, shape, and appearance. Traditionally evaluated, she was at the eighty-ninth percentile on the bulimia sub-scale of the Eating Disorder Inventory-3 (Garner, 2004), the state-of-the-art eating-disorder measure, indicating that she reported bulimic behaviors that were severe even when compared to those in treatment for bulimia nervosa. She volunteered for the bulimia study after hearing it described in one of her university classes. We gave her the same kind of beeper and the same instructions we gave Stephanie in Chapter 1 (for more details, see Chapter 3 and beyond); Jessica wore the beeper on five sampling days. As is usual, we interviewed her about her experiences on either the day she wore the beeper or the next day. A total of seventeen samples were discussed extensively.

Here are a few examples of Jessica's experience, as discovered through beeps and interviews at least as thorough as the one we conducted with Stephanie in Chapter 1.

Sample 2.4 [second sampling day, fourth sample]. Jessica was in class and was directly experiencing about ten simultaneous, chaotic unworded thought/feelings. These experiences were in her head, were all jumbled together so that none was clearly differentiable or separable. Jessica knew them to be related to the day's activities: her paper is due, about the final exam, wanting her teacher to shut up, wanting the class to be over, realizing that she was going to be late to her sampling appointment, wanting to leave the class. These experiences were neither thoughts nor feelings, or perhaps were both thoughts and feelings, or were somewhere between thoughts and feelings, and were apprehended as simultaneous experiences; that is, it was *not* one thought with ten aspects or ten thoughts quickly in a row. All of these thought/feelings were apprehended to be in her head except the wanting to leave the class, which involved an undifferentiated bodily urge to get up and go as well as a cognitive wanting to leave.

Simultaneously, Jessica was feeling a complex nervousness/worry/anxiety that was also undifferentiated but contained all three aspects (nervousness, worry, and anxiety); this feeling included a bodily sensation of her stomach's turning upside down. She also was seeing her teacher in the front of the room.

Q: Stomachs don't turn upside down, so we have no idea what it would feel like if they did. Isn't this another example of what Pascal did when she said she felt like a dog run over? Yet you don't seem to have a problem with it here.
A: I accept that all description contains some ambiguity, but the degree thereof can differ dramatically. I think the stomach-flipping description unpacks quite unambiguously into: "Jessica felt a sensation in the midsection of her body, in the region she takes to be occupied by her stomach, that was a twisting or flip-flopping sensation." There is little question about *what* is experienced (a bodily sensation); there is little question about *where* that sensation is (*here* in my midsection); there is little question about *how* that sensation feels (flip-flopping).

By contrast, Pascal's <<description>> provides no details whatsoever about *any* such major aspects of experience: Is Pascal talking about *physical pain* or the *psychological pain* of abandonment (left by the side of the road)? Is she talking about the risk of being run over *again*? We don't know. These are not details; they are entirely separate ontological realms that have not been specified.

There are ambiguities of our description of Jennifer: one or many flips? Left to right or front to back? And so on. But those are indeed details that, if they were judged to be important, could be elaborated. (In Chapter 10 we will return to a discussion of how to perform this elaboration.)

Sample 3.2. Jessica was watching the TV show *Scrubs*, a scene in which a skinny blond female doctor walked into a room and all of the male doctors froze and stared at her. As she watched, Jessica was innerly speaking words in two distinctly separate parts of her head. In the front of her head, she was innerly saying, in her own normal speaking voice, the words "blond," "skinny," "guys," and "stare." These words were clearly apprehended as if spoken aloud except there was no external sound. At the same time, in the back part of her head, she was also saying, in another inner voice, "Why is it that movies and TV shows always have," "girls for," "to," and "at." These words were also apprehended as being said in her own inner voice, but this voice was quieter. At the moment of the beep, these two voice streams were not temporally coordinated or synchronized; that is, both the front/louder and the back/softer voices were simultaneously speaking jumbles of words like pieces of a puzzle. If one were to combine the puzzle pieces from both streams and arrange them in order, one would get, "Why is it that movies and TV shows always have blond skinny girls for guys to stare at?" but at the moment of the beep Jessica did *not* experience that coherent sentence – that meaning was fragmented across the two simultaneous voice jumbles.

Simultaneously, Jessica was recalling perhaps eight or ten separate scenes from movies or TV shows in which skinny blond girls were featured, a jumble of incompletely articulated thoughts that somehow existed in a pile or heap outside and behind her head. There were no words, visual images, or other symbols in these recallings.

Q: What the heck do you mean by two separate voices? By distinctly separate parts of her head? How can Jessica make such distinctions? Sounds like bullshit to me. Also, what do you mean "in a lower voice" when no one is actually hearing anything?
A: In this chapter I am asking you to bungee jump with me into some pretty complex experiences, and I recognize that the leap might have been less frightening if I had placed this chapter at the end of the book. But if I don't give you, early on, a glimpse of some pretty remarkable experiences, you will have little reason to do the work necessary to *get* to the end of the book. That is, of course, one of the Catch-22s of this book. I assure you that Jessica's sample 3.2 is as straightforward a description of Jessica's experience as we can manage, and that we will discuss reasons to believe that description throughout the book.

For now I'm asking you to accept *the possibility* that, at the moment of the beep, Jessica experienced herself as speaking in two separate but simultaneous voices, each with different vocal characteristics and locations, and each conveying only part of a meaning. If that sounds highly implausible to you, then I note that one of the constraints that the exploration of experience imposes is that you not judge others by yourself. We will, as the screw turns, repeatedly discuss those constraints; don't judge others by yourself will be a consideration of Chapter 9.

Sample 5.2. Jessica was looking at her digital camera display, seeing a photo of her and her boyfriend taken on a recent trip to Chicago. While seeing this photo, she was also innerly seeing at least five separate, simultaneous, overlapping visual scenes of places she had visited in Chicago. These inner seeings were fuzzy or indistinct, and were apprehended as if looking at snapshots – the scenes had edges, for example.

Simultaneously, she was innerly seeing herself and her boyfriend standing close together at the kitchen sink. In this seeing, which was somewhat clearer than the Chicago scenes, Jessica was on the left, the boyfriend on the right, and both were seen from the back. This was a re-creation of an event that had actually taken place, but viewed from behind her, an obviously impossible perspective for her to have taken in reality.

Simultaneous she was feeling happy, apprehended as a volleyball-sized sensation deep in her stomach but also all over her stomach.

Certainly there is a pattern in these samples: All include a strikingly fragmented multiplicity of experience that is impossible to overlook. Such multiplicity was evident in twelve of her seventeen samples (70 percent). The multiplicity cut across aspects of her experience: multiple thought/feelings in sample 2.4, multiple inner speakings and non-symbolic recallings in sample 3.2, and multiple inner seeings in sample 5.2.

The question we are asking in this chapter is whether it is worth the trouble to try to get to moments of truth, and a first step in answering that question is to try to discover whether we learn something about Jessica by examining her experience. It seems that we *have* learned something about Jessica: that she has fragmentedly multiple inner experiences. That is a salient characteristic of Jessica as a particular individual; that is, fragmented multiplicity is an idiographic (Hurlburt & Heavey, 2006) characteristic of Jessica. Regardless of the characteristics of other individuals, whether others do or do not have this characteristic, Jessica has frequent fragmentedly multiple inner experiences.

Q: I don't think anyone has experience – Jessica's "descriptions of experience" are merely fabrications designed to please the interviewer or to serve some other unstated goal. Experience doesn't exist for anyone, including Jessica.

A: Such thoroughgoing skepticism is impossible to refute, I think. Yet it is also hard to maintain in the face of so many compelling reports – of images, dreams, inner speech – from so many people. I personally am entirely agnostic on this point: I don't at the outset presume that people have experiences or that they don't. I try to structure occasions where they can describe experiences if they exist, and, equally, where they can report that no experiences exist. You can judge for yourself whether that is adequate.

I will not try to talk you out of your skepticism, but I urge you to try to bracket it – cultivate your own personal agnosticism about it – so that you can see for yourself whether that is a productive point of view. Keep in mind that we are still very early in our discussion of the apprehension of experience.

IS JESSICA UNUSUAL?

A second step in determining whether it is worth the trouble to try to get to moments of truth is to try to discover whether Jessica's experience is similar to or different from that of other individuals. Let's recall our glimpse of Stephanie's experience from Chapter 1: Stephanie had basically one thing ongoing: a felt pressure to say something politically correct about Las Vegas, a process of reviewing and rejecting things she could say about it. Stephanie's experience in that sample was *far less* complex than Jessica's experience. Stephanie's Las Vegas sample was rather typical of her other samples – none was remotely as complex as any of Jessica's examples here. So it seems, preliminarily, that there are substantial differences between people in their inner experiences.

Chris Heavey and I (Heavey & Hurlburt, 2008) used this sampling procedure with a stratified random sample of thirty college students in the same large urban university that both Jessica and Stephanie attended. We found the median frequency of multiple experience to be zero, with the highest frequency of multiple experience 30 percent. Jessica's 70 percent is therefore very extreme by these standards; Stephanie's 0 percent was typical.

Q: I don't think Jessica's *experience* is that different from Stephanie's experience. It's just that Jessica has a strange, idiosyncratic way of *describing* her experience. For whatever reason, she gives reports that sound like fragmentedly multiple experience, but that doesn't mean that her experience is really fragmentedly multiple.
A: That is a reasonable concern at this point. I think her reports reflect her experience, but I don't wish merely to assert this as an established fact. For now, I ask only that you accept the *possibility* that they are faithful accounts of her experience. It will require several more turns of the screw for you to decide that for yourself, one way or the other.

JESSICA'S PARADOX

Jessica's fragmented multiplicity is striking. It jumps out at you, inescapably, unavoidably. The rough implications are astounding: Assume, as we did in Chapter 1, that experiences last a few seconds, resulting in roughly 20 experiences per minute × 60 minutes × 16 hours = 19,000 experiences per day. If roughly 70 percent of those experiences are fragmentedly multiple, that's 13,000 multiple experiences per day. To be conservative, cut that estimate in half: Jessica has perhaps 6,000 fragmentedly multiple experiences per day, or 2,000,000 per year.

And yet *Jessica herself, prior to sampling, didn't know that her own experience had this fragmentedly multiple characteristic, didn't know that her experience differed from others in this way.* This we will call Jessica's paradox: that her experience, on millions of concretely existing occasions, is fragmentedly multiple, and yet she does not know that her experience is frequently fragmentedly multiple.

Here are six potential explanations of Jessica's paradox. First, *no comparison*: Fragmented multiplicity emerges starkly as a salient phenomenon for *us* because *we* have something to compare it to (you have your own experience and Stephanie's; I have my own, Stephanie's, and the hundreds of other people's with whom I've sampled). *Jessica has nothing to compare her experience to.* Everywhere she looks, experience is always the same (always hers).

Second, *no interest*: Jessica has never really been interested in her experience per se. People are generally more interested in the *about what* of their experience than the *how* of their experience. Were it not for the beep and her participation in our study, at the time of her sample 2.4, Jessica would have been interested in her upcoming exam, in wanting her teacher to shut up; she would have no natural interest in the fact that these interests presented themselves simultaneously as part of a complex experience.

Third, *presumed similarity*: In the (unlikely) event that she would focus on the fragmentedly multiple way her experience presented itself, she would naturally assume that everyone (obviously!) has fragmentedly multiple experience. She's not unusual in this regard: Most people (including most consciousness scientists) assume that everyone's experience is just like their own.

Fourth, *no attention*: Jessica has never really paid attention to moments, never really paid attention to experience, never really paid attention to the careful apprehension of moments of experience. Chapter 1 showed that all three are necessities for the faithful apprehension of experience.

Fifth, *multiplicity hides multiplicity*: Those first four explanations pertain to all kinds of characteristics of inner experience. The fifth and sixth are focused particularly on Jessica's particular kind of inner experience: The existence of multiplicity of experience makes it harder to notice multiplicity of experience.

If you have one single, stable point of view (as did Stephanie in Chapter 1), then it is easy to notice the characteristics of experience – that would be simplicity aimed at simplicity, relatively easy to accomplish. However, if you characteristically have lots of things going on, then it may be more difficult to notice that lots is going on – that would be complexity aimed at complexity, a difficult feat.

Sixth, *focus destroys multiplicity*: Even if Jessica were to wonder whether she had multiple experience, the specific, premeditated, and therefore focused intention to examine her experience may cause that multiplicity to disappear for the duration of the self-examination (the risk of armchair introspection; see Hurlburt & Schwitzgebel, 2011b).

However, I say again, I am not trying to convince you; for now all I wish is that we make this remarkable observation: In response to beeps, Jessica provided, over and over, compelling accounts of fragmentedly multiple experience that differed, apparently, from her own understanding of her own experience.

By the way, once Jessica saw for herself fragmentedly multiple experiences at moment after moment of her own experience, it became easy for her to observe that multiplicity frequently as it naturally happened in herself and to recognize how that multiplicity seems to have impacted her life.

FRAGMENTED MULTIPLICITY OF EXPERIENCE IN BULIMIA

Stephanie Doucette and I (Doucette, 1992; Hurlburt, 1993b; Doucette and Hurlburt, 1993a, 1993b) and Sharon Jones-Forrester and I (Jones-Forrester, 2006, 2009) have used this same beep-interview procedure to examine the moments of inner experience of twenty-four women with bulimia. *Everyone of these women had frequent fragmented multiplicity of experience.* The largest and most recent of these studies is Jones-Forrester's dissertation (Jones-Forrester, 2009), in which we sampled the inner experience of thirteen bulimic women. The frequency of multiply fragmented inner experience ranged from 44 percent to 92 percent. Recall that Heavey and Hurlburt's (2008) normative sample (a stratified random sample of fifteen men and fifteen women from the same basic general population) found the median frequency of multiple experience to be 0 percent and the *highest* frequency to be 30 percent. The lowest multiplicity frequency in our bulimic sample is half-again as high as the *highest* frequency in the normative sample. That's a huge difference.

This difference in the frequency of multiplicity cannot be explained away by differing definitions of "multiple" between investigators in the two studies: I myself was intimately involved in the samplings in both studies. I attest that the bulimic women have *far* more multiplicity of experience than do non-bulimic subject individuals.

Compared to our sample of bulimic women, Jessica is not at all unusual. Her 70 percent is right in the middle of the 44 percent to 92 percent range. We selected Jessica to be the example in this chapter because the features of her fragmented multiplicity are pretty typical of the bulimic women that we have studied.

None of these women, prior to sampling, knew that her own experience was fragmentedly multiple; none knew that her own experience was similar to other bulimic women but different from non-bulimic women in this way. That is to say, Jessica's paradox applies to every woman in our sample. One cannot, therefore, dismiss our characterization of Jessica's experience as being merely the result of Jessica's strange, idiosyncratic way of describing her experience.

> **Q:** OK. So it's not Jessica who has a strange way of talking. It's *you* who has a strange way of listening. You are the common denominator in all these observations; you have some delusional fantasy that leads you to project multiplicity into bulimic women's experience. You saw multiplicity in 1980s in your case study (Hurlburt, 1993b), and then again in1992 in your study with Doucette, and ever since you have been infecting your own observations.
>
> **A:** That is a criticism that I take very seriously. I think it's incorrect, but I accept that all delusional people think their critics are incorrect. I would be delighted if some investigators unrelated to me would carefully explore the inner experience of bulimic women and either corroborate or disconfirm our observations.
>
> I have, over the course of my career, gone to great lengths to examine whether I do in fact have such delusions, whether I am effective in bracketing presuppositions (I generally call the delusions that you refer to "presuppositions"; Hurlburt & Heavey, 2006; Hurlburt & Schwitzgebel, 2011c). In the most prominent example, I invited noted introspection skeptic Eric Schwitzgebel to conduct jointly with me six hours of interviews with a subject we called Melanie; we've published transcripts of those interviews and Eric's critique of them (Hurlburt & Schwitzgebel, 2007); we've made audio files of those interviews available on the Web (http://mitpress.mit.edu/inner_experience) for those who wished to hear the original interviews. Eric grants, after careful examination, that I am "a careful and even-handed interviewer" (Hurlburt & Schwitzgebel, 2007, p. 221). A reviewer of that book says that "Hurlburt shows an almost flawless use of a Rogerian-Husserlian interpersonal phenomenological dialogue" (Faw, 2008, p. 121).
>
> I am not asserting that I am an excellent interviewer – perhaps I have fooled Schwitzgebel, Faw, and others, including myself. However, it does seem to me that it shouldn't *glibly* be presumed that my presuppositions are the culprit here. Replication by others is required.

By the way, like Jessica, once these women saw, for themselves and in themselves, fragmentedly multiple experiences at moment after moment, it became easy for them to observe that multiplicity in themselves and to recognize how that multiplicity seems to have impacted their lives.

It is a stark conclusion: *The existence of fragmented multiplicity of experience in bulimia is ubiquitous but essentially entirely unknown, even among people who experience it at most of their waking moments.*

"TAILS"

In 1984 I sampled the experience of "Ashley," a bulimic operating-room nurse; I reported this case in Hurlburt (1993b), in which I described a phenomenon that Ashley, and subsequently I, called "tails." Since that time, we've observed the tails phenomenon in at least a half dozen of our bulimic women, but never in the hundreds of non-bulimic subjects with whom I have sampled.

Ashley said her experience was like an aquarium with lots of fish in it, her metaphor for describing multiplicity of awareness. Metaphors are dangerous – their brilliance may lull you into falsely believing that you understand what is meant (recall Pascal's run-over dog). Genuinely submitting to the constraints that the endeavor to provide a faithful description of experience imposes requires careful questioning to delimit the metaphoricity of a description. Such questioning revealed that Ashley meant to convey that her several or many simultaneous experiences were not coordinated – each fish appeared when it wanted to appear, stayed as long as it wanted, traveled at its own speed, and disappeared when it wanted to disappear, apparently independent of the other fish in the aquarium. In that regard, Ashley is very similar to Jessica and the other bulimic women we have studied.

Ashley extended her metaphor, saying that some of the fish in her aquarium were "under the rocks," mostly disappeared but with their tails sticking out. By this, Ashley meant that when she stopped thinking about *X* to think about *Y*, she didn't *completely* stop thinking about *X*; *X* simply "parked under a rock" while she thought about *Y*. The "tail" of *X* continued to be a directly experienced reminder that *X* was there, waiting to be thought. Then, if she was attracted to think about *Z*, she parked *Y* and now had *three* things simultaneously in awareness: *Z*, the tail of *Y*, and the tail of *X*. And it didn't stop at three; she frequently reported having about five fish and ten or more tails all simultaneously in awareness.

When most people turn their attention from *X* to *Y*, *X* vanishes completely from their direct experience. *X* may continue to be important, and perhaps to be processed, but that takes place *outside* of direct experience while attending to *Y*. Ashley's description was different; she continued to experience a bit of *X*, an explicit-in-awareness I-should-get-back-to-thinking-about-*X*. In 1984 I found that hard to believe, figured she was just using florid language to describe the everyday fact that sometimes she returns to thoughts. However, six years later, Stephanie Doucette and I sampled with a few more bulimic women (Doucette, 1992; Doucette & Hurlburt, 1993a, b). One of these women said that she had, in her awareness, "strings," by which she meant that there were thoughts that had stalled and were waiting to be restarted; being stalled didn't mean the thoughts were entirely out of her awareness; instead, there was a hint or a sign, directly in her awareness, that the thought was there, waiting. Another of these women said she had "threads." Tails, strings, threads: different metaphors, apparently the same phenomenon.

Now for the interesting part: Sometimes there were more tails than at other times, or more strings than at other times, or more threads. As the threads began to build up, her awareness became "webby," and that webbiness was nauseating; same for the tails and the strings.

And now for the even more interesting part: When the number-of-tails nausea became strong enough, Ashley induced vomiting. When the vomiting was done, the tails were gone, for a while. Why should emptying the stomach have anything to do with emptying the mind? I have no idea.

> **Q:** Your descriptions make many uses of the word "simultaneous." Everyone knows that the mind can think about only one thing at a time. I think it likely that Ashley's and Jessica's mental events happened very quickly, right after the other – *badabadabing*; Ashley and Jessica mistakenly apprehend that as simultaneous.
>
> **A:** First, "the mind can think about only one thing at a time" is the presupposition of a particular form of mental realism. By its proponents, it is accepted as "obvious," but it is not at all obvious to me. There are individual neurons, and collections of neurons, firing simultaneously all over the brain, so the notion of parallel processing is by no means absurd.
>
> Second, I make no claim about whether the mind actually does only one thing at a time (or whether the mind exists, for that matter). This book is not about the *mind* and what happens in it; it is about *experience* and what presents itself. What presents itself, for some non-bulimic subjects and all bulimic subjects some of the time, is simultaneity. Perhaps the underlying neurological or cognitive mental processes are actually sequential, but they happen so fast that they appear simultaneous. I know nothing about that. This book is about what presents itself in experience, which is, in these samples, simultaneity.
>
> Third, and related to the second point, I think you underestimate the importance of the iterative process (see Chapter 10). These women are not merely asked once, "Was your experience multiply simultaneous?" They are not asked whether there is multiple simultaneity at all. Instead, the conversation goes something like this: Investigator: "What was in your experience at the moment of the beep?" Subject: "I was thinking *X*, and at the same time I was thinking *Y*, and at the same time I was thinking *Z*. I had three simultaneous thoughts." Investigator (whose skill is to remain neutral): "Really simultaneous? Maybe it's *badabadabing*, mental events happening very quickly, right after the other." Subject: "Maybe so, I don't know." Investigator: "I don't know, either. Let's suppose that either simultaneity or quick sequentiality is possible – the question is what it's like for you. It's too late to figure that out

for this beep (we can't go back and experience this again), but not to worry – if this simultaneity or rapid sequentiality is a frequent phenomenon, we'll see it on later beeps, and maybe we can figure it out then."

After several days of practice, subjects are, I think, just as good at differentiating simultaneity from *badabadabing* sequentiality in inner experience as they are in reality, which is to say, pretty good but not perfect. The bulimic subjects say, convincingly, that the experience is of simultaneity.

IS APPREHENDING EXPERIENCE IMPORTANT?

This book is not about bulimia per se. We are using our investigations of bulimia as a case study to discover whether investigating moments of experience might be fruitful for science.

The Hay in Every Haystack

Fragmented multiplicity is not a needle in some haystack; it is the *hay* in the haystack. In fact, it is the hay in *every one* of our bulimic haystacks. Our investigations of bulimic women find fragmented multiplicity to be an enormously salient characteristic of their inner experience. *All* our bulimic women experience fragmented multiplicity frequently – the *lowest* frequency was 44 percent (recall the *highest* frequency in Heavey and Hurlburt's (2008) non-bulimic sample was 30 percent).

But the Hay Has Been Overlooked

Most modern theories of bulimia nervosa believe that inner experience is an important, probably causative feature in bulimia nervosa. Typical and influential in this regard is Fairburn's cognitive behavioral model of bulimia nervosa (Fairburn, Cooper, & Shafran, 2003), which suggests that a cognitive over-emphasis on the importance of weight, shape, and eating leads to dietary restriction, compensatory behaviors, and preoccupation with weight, shape, and eating. This dietary restriction and cognitive preoccupation then trigger binge-eating behavior, which then triggers purging behavior. Intense self-criticism and negative self-evaluation appear to play an additional active role in maintaining these cyclic bulimic behaviors.

Despite the perceived importance of inner experience, the science of bulimia nervosa is essentially unaware of the existence of fragmented multiplicity of experience in bulimia. There is no scientific recognition that bulimic women may have very high frequencies of fragmented multiplicity by comparison to non-bulimic women; no scientific exploration of whether the degree of fragmentation is related to purging.

Our own work agrees with the bulimia literature that preoccupation with weight, shape, eating, self-criticism, and negative self-evaluation are indeed important. For example, Jessica's sample 3.2 (skinny blond girl on *Scrubs*) was about the thin ideal. However, the most striking feature of our observations of bulimic women is their complex multiplicity.

The Hay Might Be Important

Assuming that our observations of the connection between multiplicity of experience and bulimia are correct, the source of that connection remains to be explored. We don't know whether bulimia causes multiplicity, multiplicity causes bulimia, or some unknown third factor causes both. That will require substantial additional study, probably including prospective studies of the inner experience of women at risk for bulimia but not yet bulimic.

However, there is reason to suspect that working through those connections might be of vital importance for the science of bulimia and the women it affects. First, the standard therapies for bulimia aim primarily at altering cognitions about weight and shape, thus interfering in the Fairburn sequence described earlier, but bulimia therapies are not highly effective. Our research suggests that it might be prudent to explore therapies that aim at the focusing of inner experience (the reducing of multiplicity), rather than (or along with) altering the contents of experience (reducing preoccupation with weight and shape). As far as we know, that is an unknown therapeutic strategy for bulimia. Just how such a therapy might be implemented has never been investigated, but we note that most of the women who have participated in our studies have claimed some therapeutic benefit from participation. Our studies have never attempted to be doing therapy – we have done nothing except relentlessly inquire about experience at the moment of the beep. Nonetheless, many of our subjects report that their bulimic symptoms have improved over the course of their participation. Perhaps our systematic requirement to pay attention to the details, to slow down and tell us about one (of the multiple) aspect of experience at a time, serves as some sort of calisthenic for focusing experience. Note that we are not making that as a claim, only suggesting it as a possibility. Others may have different or better suggestions for a therapeutic intervention.

A Wild Speculation

Bulimia science rests on the assumption that preoccupation with weight and shape leads to bulimia. Our observations can be interpreted to reverse that logic: that bulimia *leads to* preoccupation with weight and shape. We do not claim that that is true; the mere existence of such a counter-intuitive explanation of bulimia shows the potential fertility of the faithful apprehension of inner experience for science. So here is how this counter-intuitive claim goes:

Suppose that fragmented experience leads to nausea, and that the more fragmented the experience, the stronger the nausea. (Why might that be? Fragmented experience requires having several simultaneous points of view: here looking that way; there looking this way; hither understanding this way; yon understanding that way. Maybe such multiple points of view confuses the circuitry connected to the inner ear; a confused inner ear leads to nausea. [I remind the reader that the heading of this section is "wild speculation."]) Now suppose that teenaged Bonnie learns that inducing vomiting eases her nausea, leaves her in a peaceful state that she doesn't comprehend but sure feels good. She doesn't need to understand the connection between multiplicity and the inner ear or between the inner ear and nausea or between a peaceful feeling and lack of fragmentation; all she needs to have discovered (perhaps by accidental observation, as in illness) is that vomiting leads to an inner peace that lasts for a while. So Bonnie starts to induce vomiting, begins acquiring the skills of inducing vomiting – how to do it, when to do it, how to hide it, who to tell and not tell about it, how to lie about it, and so on. That is, she learns the bulimic behaviors. Note that becoming bulimic is about cultivating a peaceful feeling, *not at all* about the socio-cultural thin ideal.

Now suppose Bonnie's friend Nora, who is not bulimic, discovers that Bonnie is self-inducing vomiting and tries to figure out why. Like most people, Nora *presumes* that everyone else's inner experience is just like her own – that is, Nora presumes that Bonnie is pretty much just like Nora herself except that Bonnie self-induces vomiting. Nora tries to imagine why she herself would self-induce vomiting and finds that the only imaginable reason is weight control – the socio-cultural thin ideal and its concomitant weight-control behaviors are pretty important issues for Nora, and self-induced vomiting seems like a solution. Therefore, Nora *presumes* that the self-induced vomiting *must be* a weight-control behavior *for Bonnie*. Nora notices, furthermore, that she herself does not self-induce vomiting; therefore the socio-cultural thin ideal must be a *stronger* issue for Bonnie than it is for Nora herself.

Because of Jessica's paradox, *Bonnie, too, presumes that everyone else's experience is just like her own*. Bonnie observes that she herself induces vomiting and Nora doesn't; therefore Bonnie, too, thinks her connection to the socio-cultural thin ideal *must be* stronger than is Nora's – Bonnie accepts that she must be preoccupied with the socio-cultural thin ideal whereas Nora must just be influenced by it.

Note that Bonnie's interest in and her connection to the socio-cultural thin ideal is *independent of* her bulimia – she's no more impacted by the magazines, billboards, TV shows, and so on than is Nora. However, her presumption about the *strength* of her connection to the socio-cultural thin ideal – that hers is a preoccupation rather than merely a strong influence – is the *result* of her bulimia, not its cause. More precisely, Bonnie's preoccupation about the socio-cultural thin ideal is the result of her bulimia *and* the fact that both she and Nora systematically fail to notice the huge differences between their experience.

The stakes are high: If our speculation is in the ballpark of correct, it is a tragedy. Nora's theory imposes a substantial untruth on Bonnie, forces her to look in the wrong direction for self-understanding.

How to See

As we have said, it is not our aim to provide a theory of bulimia, but rather to provide a way of investigating that may provide constructive alternatives to or extensions of present theories. That bulimia causes preoccupation is a wild speculation, and I have no attachment to that theory, make no claim that it is true. I'm quite confident in the robustness of the fragmentedly multiple observations – I have made the same observations over a span of twenty-five years. However, how to explain those observations is another matter.

The failure of observers early in the history of a science to theorize correctly about their observations should not be held against them. Van Leeuwenhoek, looking through the home-built microscopes he was perfecting, saw "many very little living animalcules, very prettily a-moving" (Van Leeuwenhoek, Letter to the Royal Society, September 17, 1683). He was quite mistaken about the nature of these animalcules (for example, he thought sperm cells were complete animals whereas egg cells were just "nourishment for the sperm animal"), but that theoretical misstep in no way diminishes his contributions to the development of microscopy on which modern biology rests. Van Leeuwenhoek's contribution was to the science of how to see, not to the science of what was seen.

> **Q:** I don't believe you when you say you have no attachment to your theory. Everyone is attached to their theories! I think you should just be honest.
> **A:** What you, with evident passion, see as obvious, I see as a profound dilemma. I do *not* in fact have a theory about bulimia. It seems to me that you are falling into the same trap that both Bonnie and Nora fell into.
> I would urge you, as my mother urged me countless times, not to judge others by yourself. Psychologists are selected, bred, trained, and rewarded to value theory (as your question suggests) with insufficient recognition of the blinders that theory imposes. Just because *you* may (over)value theory does not imply that *everyone*, including me, (over)values theory.
> Having a theory about bulimia would seriously harm my ability to apprehend faithfully the phenomena in the vicinity of bulimia, would cause me too look too hard in some directions and not hard enough in others. Over-valuing theory is, I think, a primary culprit leading five thousand

studies of bulimia to miss the fragmentedly multiple hay in the haystack. So it may well be that the explorer of phenomena should be firewalled away from the theorizer (Hurlburt & Akhter, 2008). I have spent the better part of a lifetime working at bracketing the influence of theory (cf. Hurlburt & Schwitzgebel, 2011c). I accept that I am well short of perfection in this regard, but I do think it reasonable to suppose that I have improved my abilities.

I'm not opposed to theory. I am opposed to *premature* theory, theory that is advanced before the relevant phenomena have been thoroughly explored. Further, I'm opposed to theory that seeps into or otherwise clouds careful observation of phenomena. We will return to this topic in Chapter 21.

Q: Might I register a stylistic complaint? This book includes many forward references, which frustrates me. Here, for example, you refer to Chapter 21, so I have to leave one finger holding my place here while paging forward to find Chapter 21. That's happened a half dozen times already. Couldn't you have eliminated forward references?
A: I agree that forward references are generally annoying. However, here they derive from the "screwy" organization of this book, which is essentially one big forward reference. I have inserted some explicit forward references to make it *possible* for you to look ahead if you so desire. I assure you that it is *unnecessary* to follow any forward reference; the text will read coherently without them.

IMPLICATIONS FOR GENUINELY SUBMITTING TO THE CONSTRAINTS

Let's accept (which I think is fair, now that we have conducted three studies of the phenomena of bulimia spanning twenty years) that fragmented multiplicity is a strongly salient characteristic of women with bulimia. Let's accept that bulimia science has not noticed fragmented multiplicity. What can we glean about the constraints imposed by the attempt to apprehend pristine experience faithfully?

Constraint: There is no safety in numbers. Our consideration of bulimia demonstrates that an entire science, literature, and lore can be oblivious to important aspects, perhaps the most important aspects, of experience. Therefore one of the constraints that the faithful apprehension of experience imposes is that the fact that everyone is saying the same thing does not automatically engender confidence. It is possible, as perhaps here, that everyone employs the same or similar flawed methods (universal Jessica's paradox), leading to the same or similar incomplete or otherwise flawed descriptions. This constraint applies to all science of phenomena; there is nothing unique about bulimia that makes its experience particularly invisible to science, literature, or lore (we discussed the particular difficulty of multiplicity viewing multiplicity difficulty earlier, but I think that is a small effect by comparison to others).

Constraint: You can't find out about a phenomenon unless you talk about the phenomenon. The Eating Disorder Examination (EDE-12; Fairburn & Cooper, 1993) is a widely used structured interview for the scientific exploration of bulimia. Perhaps we would understand why bulimia science's five thousand articles overlook fragmented multiplicity if we understood why the structured clinical interview tools of that science overlook fragmented multiplicity. Here, then, is a typical question from the EDE-12:

> Over the past 4 weeks have you spent much time thinking about your shape or weight? Has thinking about your shape or weight interfered with your ability to concentrate? How about concentrating on things that you are interested in, for example, reading, watching television, or following a conversation? Concentration is regarded as impaired if there have been *intrusive thoughts about your shape or weight that have interfered with activities.* (Fairburn & Cooper, 1993, p. 350)

This question does not ask about fragmented multiplicity, and neither do any of the other questions of the EDE-12. If you don't ask about fragmented multiplicity, you can't find out about fragmented multiplicity. That may seem so obvious as not to require comment, but it is of such fundamental importance that it is frequently ignored. This will lead us to the necessity of "open-beginninged" questions in Chapter 10.

Constraint: Bracket the influence of theory. The EDE-12 asks questions that are suggested by current theory; anything off the current theoretical radar is ignored. The attempt to apprehend pristine experiences as they actually exist requires that you be indifferent to theory, or at least behave indifferently to the implications of theory – that is, you should suspend or "bracket" your current theories. Phenomena that are relevant to current theory should be asked about but not exaggerated; phenomena that are not deemed relevant by current theory should be asked about but not minimized. Even-handedness about one's own theoretical persuasions is no mean feat, but it is possible to cultivate (Hurlburt & Schwitzgebel, 2011c).

Constraint: Ask about moments. The EDE-12 question, "Over the past 4 weeks have you spent much time thinking about your shape or weight?" does not ask *at all* about *any* specific moment. It asks about undefined times over four weeks.

Constraint: Manage retrospection. There is lots of psychological evidence (eyewitness testimony, for example) that shows the inadequacy of memory. People's "recollections" are shaped at least as much by recency, salience, plausibility, and other heuristics than by direct recall of events. Remember that there are roughly 19,000 experiences per day; that's roughly 500,000 experiences over four weeks. It is highly doubtful that those will be even-handedly remembered. Any attempt at apprehending experience must somehow manage the difficulties of retrospection.

Constraint: Clarify what is meant by "experience." When the EDE-12 asks, "Over the past 4 weeks have you spent much time thinking about your shape or weight?" what is meant by "thinking"? You might believe that it is obvious what "thinking" means, but a careful observation of experience reveals the opposite:

> In fact, there is substantial variability from person to person in what is intended by the phrase "*I was thinking....*" For example, when Alice says "*I was thinking...*" she means that she was saying something to herself, in her own naturally inflected inner voice. When Betty says "*I was thinking...*" she means that she was seeing a visual image of something. When Carol says "*I was thinking...*" she means that she was feeling a sensation in her heart or stomach, and that she had no awareness of cognition whatsoever. (Hurlburt & Heavey, 2001, p. 402; cf. Hurlburt & Heavey, 2006, p. 36)

The foregoing refers to differences in the direct experience of what is called "thinking." However, "thinking" also refers to underlying cognitive processes that are not directly present to experience.

As it happens, our research with bulimics shows that many (most, in our sample) are quite strikingly confused about what is and is not thinking. Most non-bulimic people experience a clear distinction between thinking and feeling, but our bulimic subjects often have a very difficult or impossible time in this regard.

Constraint: Remove ambiguities. What, for example, does "much time" mean in "Over the past 4 weeks have you spent much time thinking about your shape or weight?" Does "much time" mean the same thing to Anne as to Betty? Does the administrator of the EDE-12 know what it means to either of them? I fear not.

Thus the EDE-12 question asks whether you have spent "much time" thinking about shape or weight, as if you were (a) capable of knowing what is meant by "thinking"; (b) capable of noticing what you're thinking about in all moments; (c) capable of remembering those thinkings across four weeks; (d) capable of "averaging" across all those moments; and (e) sharing a common understanding of what "much time" means. I think there is ample reason to believe that *none* of those considerations is true; at the very least, there is little reason to believe that we know the extent to which those considerations are true. Therefore, the EDE-12 question and its answers should not be taken as attempts to describe experience in high fidelity. If Anne says, "Over the past 4 weeks I have spent much time thinking about my shape or weight," she "offers a description of a certain state of affairs without genuinely submitting to the constraints which the endeavor ... imposes" (Frankfurt, 2005, p. 32).

Constraint: Be skeptical about reports of experience. We have indicated many reasons for skepticism about people's reports of experience. The same applies for our own reports. We say that fragmented multiplicity is frequent. Is that so? Maybe the questioner is right: It is my delusion and I have infected my students and our subjects. I can assure you that I have tried not to do so, and that assurance is offered in good faith, offered by a careful practitioner who has subjected his technique to extraordinary scrutiny by many. But you should be skeptical anyway. To be skeptical is not blindly to disbelieve. True skepticism is to keep your eyes wide open; to desire corroborating or disconfirming evidence *and to be equally happy with either outcome*. There is no substitute for corroboration, either by others using adequate interview methods or by objective performance measures that validate our observations. Unfortunately, most people, when they say "I am skeptical of your observations," really mean something closer to "I am closed-mindedly positive that you are full of baloney."

Constraint: Particulars can lead to generalities, but generalities cannot lead to particulars. Recall that Jessica's paradox referred to the fact that Jessica might be able faithfully to describe the details of a specific concrete experience while not having a clue about the main features of her experience in general, and it turned out that Jessica's paradox applied to all the women in these studies. There is nothing unique about bulimia that leads to Jessica's paradox; it may well apply to you as well – the chances are good that you are ignorant about some important feature of your experience, but that you could describe your individual experiences faithfully, one at a time, if you used a proper method.

It is possible to derive a generality from a stream of particulars; it is not possible to derive a particular from the general, no matter how often the general is restated. In our investigations of bulimia it was a very straightforward thing for us to begin with a stream of moments of experience, each faithfully described, and notice the frequency of fragmented multiplicity. That allowed us to draw a generalization about experience: Fragmented multiplicity occurs often in bulimic women and rarely elsewhere. Subsequent research may discover some limitations of that generalization, perhaps even discovering that that generalization, although true for the twenty-four subjects whose experience we have explored, is not true for any other bulimic women. However, no matter how often scientists have asked bulimic women about the features of their experience, they have never provided a generality that noticed the fragmented multiplicity that populated most of their moments. A science of experience must begin with particular moments and build upward toward generalities.

Constraint: The exploration of experience probably has to be a first-person-plural endeavor. Reports of inner experience are often called "first-person" reports, a phrase usually meant to imply "first person singular": one person observing his or her own experience. Jessica's paradox implies that the exploration of inner experience is best undertaken as a first-person-*plural* endeavor. Jessica's first person *singular* reports do not reveal important features of her experience, because she is blind to her own blindnesses, forgives her own exaggerations, takes as fact her own delusions, sees the wisdom only in her own conclusions, and so on. There is an intimate choreography between observer and observed when both are the same person. But when *two* (or three, as in the case of most of our bulimia observations) people are involved in the fist-person-*plural* observing of one of their experiences, that oh-so-intimate dancing-with-myself rhythm gets interrupted. It is easy for *me* to notice Jessica's fragmentedly multiple experience because I myself don't have fragmentedly multiple experiences; and even if I did, I don't have them in exactly the same way at exactly the same time as does Jessica. *We* (first person plural) can do what *Jessica herself* (first person singular) cannot. This is not an idiosyncrasy of Jessica; *everyone* (short of nirvana) is blind to their own blindnesses, forgives their own exaggerations, takes as fact their own delusions, elevates the wisdom of their own conclusions, and so on.

> **Q:** You're pretty hard on the EDE-12. The EDE-12 does a good job of discriminating bulimics from non-bulimics.
>
> **A:** Yes, it does. I am not at all critical of the EDE-12, which is indeed a highly useful tool in the diagnosis of bulimia and for validating some hypotheses about bulimics. The point is that whereas the EDE-12 is a useful *validational* tool, it is *not* useful for exploring pristine experience. That is not a criticism of the EDE-12 any more than it would be a criticism of a hammer to observe that it is not good at tightening nuts and bolts. The mistake (which I think is frequent) is to believe that the EDE-12 provides a forum for subjects to reveal in high fidelity their inner experiences.

DISCUSSION

This chapter has focused on the fragmented multiplicity that is characteristic of our bulimic subjects. Chapter 16 describes sensory awareness, another frequent characteristic of the experience of our bulimic subjects.

This book is attempting to turn the screw into the notion that these three aspects co-determine each other: moments ↔ experience ↔ genuine-submission-to-the-constraints-that-the-exploration-of-experience-imposes. By co-determine, I mean that it is impossible to be good at apprehending moments but bad at apprehending experience and/or bad at genuinely submitting to the constraints, and all possible combinations of vice-versa. Either an investigation is good at all three, or bad at all three.

We have tried to show that investigating moments of experience using a method that genuinely submits to the constraints might produce observations of substantial importance: The complex multiplicity of experience is, we think, an enormously salient feature of experience in women with bulimia (for other characteristics of experience in bulimia, see Jones-Forrester, 2009). If our observations are correct (and we've replicated them three times), and if experience matters, this discovery might be of substantial consequence for some, maybe many, bulimic women.

We have also tried to show that the bulimia literature falls short of exploring experience on all three counts: It does not consider moments, it does not consider experience, and it does not genuinely submit to the constraints that that interest imposes. As a result, bulimia science has overlooked a large part of the hay in the haystack.

We used bulimia science as an example *not* because bulimia science is particularly inexpert in the exploration of inner experience. In fact, we think that bulimia science is typical: Modern science does not explore moments of experience; does not genuinely submit to the constraints that such exploration imposes. I have not proven that to you yet; I'm turning the screw into it.

If experience is important in bulimia, and if there are huge but unknown aspects of that experience, the same seems likely to be true of schizophrenia, and/or of old age, and/or of work performance, and/or of reading, and/or of guitar playing – of some if not in most everyday human activities. If experience is important, then moments and genuinely submitting to the constraints must be important.

In our moments ↔ experience ↔ genuinely-submitting-to-the-constraints revolution, we haven't yet discussed in much detail what is entailed by genuinely submitting to the constraints. We've seen ten constraints suggested by the discussion in this chapter; we turn now to the method that is my best shot at genuinely submitting to the constraints.

3

Apprehending
Pristine Experience

Chapter 1 concluded that a genuine look at inner experience must apprehend moments of truth, and that it must do so by genuinely submitting to the constraints that the exploration of inner experience imposes. It made the moments ↔ experience ↔ genuinely-submitting-to-the-constraints co-determination case: You can't encounter moments without encountering experience and vice versa; and you can't encounter moments or experience without genuinely submitting to the constraints that that endeavor imposes. Chapter 2 focused primarily on the experience portion of that co-determination, using the example of the experience of bulimic women to demonstrate that apprehending pristine experience might well be worth the effort required, might well be a matter of substantial consequence in some cases.

Now we turn the screw into moments of truth by focusing primarily on the genuinely-submitting-to-the-constraints aspect, but because of the co-determination, that will also require deepening our appreciation of moments and experience. Descriptive Experience Sampling (DES) is the concrete instantiation of my best efforts toward genuinely submitting to the constraints imposed by the exploration of pristine experience. My colleagues and I have subjected DES to some substantial scrutiny (Hurlburt & Heavey, 2002, 2006; Hurlburt & Schwitzgebel, 2007). In a fundamental way, the moments ↔ experience ↔ genuinely-submitting-to-the-constraints analysis and DES are two sides of the same coin, two complementary perspectives on the apprehension of pristine experience. Moments ↔ experience ↔ genuinely-submitting-to-the-constraints is the analytic side; DES is the action side of the same coin. Across my career, as I developed my understanding of moments ↔ experience ↔ genuinely-submitting-to-the constraints, I evolved DES; and as I evolved DES and applied it with a variety of people, I deepened my understanding of moments ↔ experience ↔ genuinely-submitting-to-the-constraints.

This chapter describes the methodological aspects of DES, describes what I take to be one way of genuinely submitting to the constraints that the exploration of experience imposes. In Chapter 1 I described the "whole book" in ten, then in fifty, and then again in one hundred words. Here I describe the "whole book," at least from the methodological side of the coin, in one chapter. All those whole-book accounts, including the present chapter, are incomplete; they are turns of the screw, ever deeper into the exploration of experience, with details to be discussed later.

DESCRIPTIVE EXPERIENCE SAMPLING[1]

Descriptive Experience Sampling (DES; Hurlburt, 1990, 1993a, 1997; Hurlburt & Heavey, 2006) is a method for apprehending and describing inner experience that follows the guidelines discussed by Hurlburt and Heavey (2001, 2004) and Hurlburt, Heavey, and Seibert (2006). Briefly, DES subjects wear random beepers in their natural environments. The random beep cues the subject immediately to pay attention to the inner experience that was ongoing at "the moment of the beep" – the last undisturbed moment before the beep interrupted their natural environment.

Thus DES aims at apprehending natural occurrences – experienced phenomena in their pristine state, unspoiled by the act of observation or reflection. As we have seen, pristine experiences can be simple or complex, clean or messy; "pristine" refers to experiences in their natural state, not disturbed by the act of observation, unplanned, unpremeditated, unmapped, un-"figured-out" already, uninterpreted, un-heuristicized real experience.

Constraint: Aim at pristine experience. DES aims at apprehending pristine experience, actual phenomena that are actually being experienced by actual people at actual moments during actual natural activities, free of any artificial interference by the investigator.

Constraint: Concede imperfection. Of course, DES falls short of that aim because no technology for capturing/transporting/importing experience directly from one person to another exists. DES makes no pretense about the fact that it falls short; all methods in science fall short of their ideal. The object is not perfection, but to create a method that aims to glimpse actual experience and falls short in manageable ways. DES attempts to accomplish that in the ways described as follows.

Pristine experiences are fundamental data of consciousness studies in particular and of psychology in general – pristine experience is the way real

[1]   This section and the final section of this chapter are revised with permission from part of Hurlburt, R. T., & Akhter, S. A. (2006). The Descriptive Experience Sampling method. *Phenomenology and the Cognitive Sciences, 5*, 271–301.

people experience real things in their real lives. I as a person am who I am in large part because of the things I experience and the way I experience them; I differ from you not merely because you and I have different histories and different physicalities, but because you and I have different experiences and different ways of experiencing them (a central theme of most humanists, e.g., Rogers, 1959; Kelly, 1955). In any given moment of any real person's existence, there is a welter of potential experience, some external (arising from a myriad of surrounding objects, people, and features of the environment such as temperature, wind, brightness, sounds, tastes, smells, etc.), some interoceptive, proprioceptive, or kinesthetic (pressures, pains, hunger pangs, limb/joint positions, tickles, itches, etc.), some innerly created (thoughts, images, feelings, etc.). At every moment, a person selects/creates some very small number (often just one) of those potential experiences to form that moment's actual pristine experience. Different people do that in different ways: One person may consistently create visual images that are quite unrelated to the immediate environment; another, in exactly the same environment, may consistently attend to emotional experience; whereas a third, also in the same environment, consistently pays attention to the sensory features of that external environment. Those three people may differ from each other in other important ways – or maybe not. Science needs to figure that out; to do so depends on methods that apprehend adequately pristine experience with an adequate degree of fidelity.

DES is an attempt at such a method.

Brief Description of the DES Method

Hurlburt (1990, 1993a), Hurlburt and Heavey (2006), and Hurlburt and Schwitzgebel (2007) have discussed at some length the rationale behind DES, how to perform the DES method, and its results. As we have seen, DES subjects wear random beepers in their natural environments. The random beep, which is delivered through an earphone, cues the subject to pay attention to the inner experience that was ongoing at the moment of the beep and immediately to jot down in a notebook (or otherwise record) the features of that ongoing experience. Within twenty-four hours after collecting a number (typically six) of such samples, the subject meets with the DES investigator for an "expositional interview" designed to help the subject provide faithful descriptions of the sampled experiences. After the expositional interview, the investigator prepares a written description of the ongoing inner experience at each sampled moment. The sample/interview/describe procedure is repeated over a series of (typically four to eight) sampling days until a sufficient number (typically twenty-five to fifty) of momentary experiences have been collected. The investigator then surveys all that subject's moments of experience and extracts their salient characteristics.

Constraint: The exploration of pristine experience is fundamentally idiographic. Pristine experience is never a shared phenomenon – it is always *my* experience, presented by me, for me, to me. Of course, many people may have similar experiences; but each pristine experience itself always uniquely belongs to one person. Therefore DES produces a characterization of one particular person's experiences. From the idiographic perspective, it is irrelevant whether that person's experiences are similar to or different from some or most other people's experiences.

Some DES studies investigate a collection of subjects who have some feature (for example, psychiatric diagnosis, as of bulimia nervosa in Chapter 2) in common. In those studies, the investigator produces an idiographic characterization of each subject as previously described and also examines the entire collection of subjects' experiences to discover whatever salient characteristics might emerge across the collection. This allows the investigator to produce an across-subject or "nomothetic" characterization of the collection's in-common salient inner experiences.

Thus a DES investigation uses its idiographic procedure in one of two basic ways: as a purely idiographic procedure to encounter/describe the experienced phenomena of one individual; and as a series of idiographic procedures as steps in the direction of a nomothetic goal.

The salient features that emerge from DES studies (both idiographic and nomothetic) are often features of the *form* or pattern of *how* experience occurs within individuals. For example, frequent salient form characteristics are inner speech, inner seeing (aka visual images), unsymbolized thinking (unworded, unimaged thinking; see Chapter 15), sensory awareness (see Chapter 16), or feelings (see Chapter 13). *Content* features, a pattern of the *about what* of experience, can also emerge as salient characteristics; in practice, content features have been less common.

DES is a simple procedure: A subject wears a beeper and notes the inner experience that was ongoing at the moment of the beep; an investigator interviews the subject about each of those experiences and characterizes their patterns. However, behind this simplicity are considerations of substantial subtlety, to which we now turn.

Inner Experience

DES seeks to describe as faithfully as possible pristine experience, by which we mean anything that is going on in awareness at the particular moment defined by the beep, whatever is "before the footlights of consciousness" at that moment. That experience can be of interior events (thoughts, feelings, tickles) or external events (seeings, hearings, smellings). DES rules out anything that is outside of ongoing awareness. Thus DES rules out "unconscious" processes of any kind. DES rules out physiological events (neuron firings, peristalsis, homeostatic adjustments, and the like) unless they are specifically part of awareness. DES rules out explanations and interpretations unless they are specifically part of awareness. DES rules out events that have occurred before or after the moment of the beep unless they are somehow present in awareness at the moment of the beep.

Constraint: Rule out everything that is not directly experienced. It seems simple; explore what you are interested in (pristine experience) and avoid all else. We shall see in subsequent chapters that that simplicity is by no means trivial or easy.

For example, a DES subject we will call "Juanita" is reading *Messenger,* a novel by Lois Lowry, when the DES beep sounds. At the moment of the beep, Juanita is seeing an imaginary scene that she has created in harmony with her reading: She sees the book's main character Kira seated on a log facing Matty, who is to the left. The seeing is quite visually detailed: Kira is wearing a blue dress that reveals her deformed leg; Matty's arms are seen to be swollen from the injuries he has received; the trees of the forest are seen in the background behind the clearing; and so on. At the same time, Juanita is aware of an itch in her nose, near the openings of both nostrils. We question Juanita thoroughly and conclude that the inner seeing of Kira and Matty and the itch in her nose are experienced to be simultaneous, and that no other phenomena are being experienced in her awareness at the moment of the beep.

Constraint: Distinguish pristine experience from the welter of potential experiences. We consider Juanita's seeing of the imaginary scene and the nose itch to comprise Juanita's pristine experience at the moment of this beep. We do *not* consider the act of reading to be in her pristine experience. Doubtless her eyes are moving across the page; doubtless some kind of representation of the printed page occurs on her retina and at other places in her visual system; doubtless she is in fact processing the meaning of the words according to some cognitive principles; doubtless the kinesthetic, proprioceptive, and tactile sensors are firing where her body contacts the chair in which she's sitting; doubtless she could, if she chose, make some portions of those processes and many others part of her awareness. Yet at the moment of the beep, those processes were not part of her awareness, as best that we could ascertain under our careful questioning. Therefore those processes *do not* count as parts of Juanita's inner experience at the moment of the beep.

It can be argued, on a rich view of consciousness, that Juanita's consciousness at the moment of the beep in fact included, simultaneously, the seeing of the printed page, the bodily sensations, and all the rest of the welter of inner and external phenomena. DES takes no position on that issue. DES seeks to discover the main characteristics of whatever phenomena is/are immediately present in experience. It tries to do that as completely as possible, but makes no claims whatsoever about the exhaustiveness of that effort. We inquired as carefully as we could about whether the printed page was in Juanita's awareness at the moment of the beep, and she consistently claimed that it was not. That is, we would have included exterior visual perception as "inner experience" if it had been part of Juanita's ongoing phenomenal awareness, but it was not.

Constraint: Concede incompleteness. DES does not contend that it makes an exhaustive survey of pristine experience; we believe that an exhaustive survey is beyond the possibility of any introspective technique. DES examines the salient phenomena of experience; it does that as completely and thoroughly as possible but accepts that there may well be faint or subtle aspects of experience that are not described. As an empirical fact, most DES subjects, once they have some practice, believe that there is little ambiguity about what is and what is not experienced at the moment of the beep. For example, for Juanita there was a huge experiential difference between the inner seeing of Kira and Matty and the exterior seeing of the book page. The first was a clearly, unambiguously manifest phenomenon directly experienced at the moment of the beep; the second was not part of experience at all. (See Hurlburt & Schwitzgebel, 2011a.)

The Targeted Experience (AKA the Data)

DES uses the beep to aim at randomly selected, specific, manifest, ongoing, natural, contemporaneous, personal experiences. We will discuss each of those modifiers in turn.

Randomly selected. DES chooses to discuss random moments for two related reasons: first, for the same reasons that pollsters take random samples of voters, so that the experiences that are discussed are representative of the person's actual experiences.

Second, discussing randomly selected experiences is one important way that DES brackets presuppositions. The random beep says, in effect, "Let's discuss this particular experience, not because Juanita or the investigator thinks, in some presuppositional way, that this experience is important, significant, or interesting, but merely because it was selected by a neutral, dispassionate, external, random trigger." If Juanita strays from the moment of the random beep to other experiences, she would necessarily be describing experiences that *she* selected on the basis of some presuppositional self-theory or other personal characteristic.

Constraint: Develop mechanisms to help bracket presuppositions. People are blind to their own presuppositions, cannot be trusted to be even-handed about their presuppositions. DES accepts this human frailty and believes that some methodological procedure is necessary to help counter it. One such procedure is to require that the moments to be examined be selected at random. Selecting on the basis of one's personal proclivities can be powerfully biasing.

To illustrate, imagine a couple that has communication/anger-management issues. The truth, as an omniscient observer would know, is that the man is a jerk and is frequently mean to his wife; the wife is long suffering and usually patiently endures it; occasionally she can't take it any more and says something nasty. However, we non-omniscient mortals don't know these true dynamics, so we must collect some data. Data-gathering strategy A: Beep the man at random and ask him to report what's going on. The data will show that the man is frequently a jerk. Data-gathering strategy B: Have the man self-monitor his anger; every time the anger gets strong, he is to report what's going on. The data will show that the woman frequently says nasty things. Strategy B distorts reality because the man collects data based on a personal characteristic of his – when he gets angry. He doesn't get angry while he's being a jerk; he gets angry only when she finally reacts. (We return to the discussion of bracketing presuppositions later; see also Hurlburt & Schwitzgebel, 2011c.)

Specificity of time. DES uses the beeper to identify with substantial precision the specific moment to be examined: We are interested in the phenomena that was ongoing at the "last undisturbed moment before the onset of the beep" (an instant that DES usually calls the "moment of the beep") and no other. DES does not care about phenomena that occurred a second, a minute, an hour, or a day before or after the moment of the beep.

The substantial precision of temporal selection is not perfect: It does take some time for subjects (even skilled subjects) to process the physical sound waves that impinge on their eardrums and recognize the presence of the beep. Between people there is some variability in the time it takes to accomplish that recognition. Within a single person, there may be some variability from one occasion to another in the time to recognize the beep (Hurlburt, 1990), and it is possible that this variability may systematically depend on the specific characteristics of the ongoing experience, and therefore may introduce some systematic bias into the data. How much bias is yet to be investigated; our sense is that it is generally not significant.

Thus, for example, in Juanita's example described earlier, we were interested in just one moment in time, the one that, it turned out, happened to involve imagining Kira and Matty and the nose itch. We did not ask questions such as, "For how long had your nose been itching?" because that would have inquired about events before the moment of the beep; and we ignored Juanita's comments such as, "I reached for my pen and wrote it down" because that describes events after the moment of the beep.

Specificity of experience. DES focuses on the specific beeped experiences, not on generalities about or responses to those experiences. Subjects often avoid the specific by making statements about themselves that sound like generalities; for example, Juanita said, "I *usually* create images as I read." DES refers to such statements as "faux generalities" because although they appear to be statements about general characteristics, an actual generality is the result of an inductive process. For example, "I have systematically observed myself reading, and the majority of those observations include visual images" is an actual (inductive) generality. However, the statements that most people make about themselves are faux, rather than actual, generalities, and are based on heuristics such as recency or salience rather than on inductive process. Many faux generalities are entirely or to some degree false: People are not necessarily accurate observers or reporters of their general characteristics. Some faux generalities are quite accurate, but people are not generally good at judging whether or not their faux generalities are accurate. Therefore, DES brackets faux generalities, for example, by saying to Juanita, "You may well create images as you read, but let's suspend judgment about that. If it's true, we'll probably discover that in subsequent samples." (We discuss bracketing presuppositions further later.)

The avoidance of faux generalities follows from the *Rule out everything that is not directly experienced* constraint described earlier. DES supports the induction of actual generalities based on specific experiences: Over the course of many samples, the DES investigator may discover that Juanita frequently creates images as she reads, and if so, may well state that as an actual generalization. However, DES does not encourage faux generalities; for example, it avoids asking whether a particular feature of experience is frequent or infrequent, typical or atypical.

Manifest. The data of DES are experiences that are immediately recognized, manifest phenomena – experiences that take place in immediate awareness, experiences that are directly before the footlights of consciousness. DES does not consider processes, constructs, or structures that are presumed (whether correctly or incorrectly) to lie behind those manifest phenomena. DES does not explore constructs such as meanings, significances, explanations, or general characterizations unless those constructs are specifically present as some aspect of the phenomena present at the moment of the beep. It does not consider anything that is unconscious or so faint as to be subliminal (or very nearly so; this is the mistake that Titchener and the Würzburgers made with respect to "imageless thought" a century ago; Monson & Hurlburt, 1993; Hurlburt & Schwitzgebel, 2007, 2011a). DES focuses simply on describing what are obviously apparent phenomena that manifestly appear in awareness at the moment of the beep.

Ongoing. DES targets specific, concrete slices of experiences that are ongoing at the moment of the beep. DES seeks to use the beep to "catch experiences in flight," as it were, much like a photographer's flashbulb catches an event in the midst of its occurrence. DES is not interested in experiences that are after or in reaction to the beep (e.g., "The beep made me think of"); DES is not interested in experiences that are presumed to have caused the present experience. The DES interest is *only* in the actual phenomena that are actually already ongoing at the exact moment of the beep, because the ongoing event is the only one truly randomly selected by the beep.

Natural. DES seeks to investigate naturally occurring ("pristine") experiences, not experimentally contrived or otherwise manipulated or forced experiences. Therefore DES asks people to wear their beepers in their natural environments and report their experiences at random times in those environments. DES does not typically set out to examine theoretically important experiences or specific topics of interest, although, with appropriate safeguards, it can be used in that role.

An a priori focus on some particular experience (rather than simply on randomly selected natural experiences) may infect the entire process, making it likely that subjects will create or exaggerate some aspects of experience and overlook or minimize others.

Contemporaneous. DES seeks to investigate contemporary experiences with as little retrospection as possible, following the *Manage retrospection* constraint described in Chapter 2. There is abundant evidence from orthodox psychology (Hurlburt, Heavey, & Seibert, 2006) as well as sampling studies (e.g., Hurlburt & Melancon, 1987a) that show the distortions of memory that occur when reporting an experience much after it occurs, so the less memory is involved in the process, the better.

DES typically asks subjects to jot down notes about their experience immediately after (within a few seconds of) the beep, to capture experience while traces of it are still available in short-term memory. DES interviews subjects about those experiences within twenty-four hours, which is a compromise balancing the desire to disturb the natural experience as little as possible with the desire to discuss experience as soon as possible. We have informally explored variations on this jot-notes-immediately/interview-within-twenty-hours theme: We have interviewed subjects immediately after the beep (minimizing retrospection but at the expense of intrusiveness); we have asked subjects to dictate extensive descriptions into a portable tape recorder instead of jotting down notes; we have interviewed subjects after more than twenty-four hours; and so on. Our sense is that the jot-notes-immediately/interview-within-twenty-four-hours procedure is generally a good one, although for some purposes we prefer other variants.

Personal. Phenomena present themselves to individual persons, that is, to real flesh and blood individuals undergoing real events, not to people in general. Furthermore, phenomena are actual experienced events, not abstractions such as cognitive processes (e.g., learning or memory). Therefore, because DES seeks to apprehend phenomena, it is fundamentally a personal encounter, the investigator along with the subject seeking to apprehend the subject's personal phenomena. Sometimes (usually, in fact) those personal phenomena are mundane and everyday; nonetheless they are fundamentally personal events. This is part of the DES submission to the constraint described earlier: *The exploration of pristine experience is fundamentally idiographic.*

The Beep

Constraint: Relentlessly pursue concrete moments. Experience inheres only in moments, and being absolutely clear about this temporal specificity is a cornerstone of DES. Specifying the time allows subject and investigator mutually to consider a clearly defined slice of experience, which grounds the conversation and enables a real discussion of the phenomenal details of experience.

As we have seen, DES aims at randomly selected, specific, manifest, ongoing, natural, contemporaneous, and personal experiences. It is the beep that makes that aim possible; Hurlburt and Heavey (2004) gave five desirable characteristics of the DES beep (or other signal): It should be unambiguous, easily detectable, private, portable, and have a rapid onset.

Many who have not participated in DES believe that it is difficult if not impossible to apprehend experience clearly; this mistaken belief usually arises from a failed simulation of the introspective task. They imagine asking themselves, "What's my inner experience like right now?" and then "discover" that nothing seems to be in experience because the "What's my inner experience like right now?" question is itself in their awareness but is ruled out as irrelevant. When they rule out the very thing that is most saliently occurring, it seems to them (incorrectly) that nothing is ongoing. (It is not adequate to attempt to improve on that simulation by using, for example, their cell phone ring to simulate the DES beeper. When the cell phone rings, the person has to think something like, "I'm not supposed to *answer* the phone – I'm supposed to *pay attention* to my inner experience!" But now *that* thought is in fact central to awareness but is again ruled out.)

Those failed simulations should *not* be understood as evidence that paying attention to inner experience is impossible. Instead, it is evidence that some care must be taken in creating the occasion on which to observe experience. The effect of using an appropriate beeper is striking. Typical DES subjects prior to sampling believe that they will not be able to perform the task at all. After sampling those same people believe that the task was relatively easy.

The Expositional Interview

DES subjects receive beeps in their natural environments and immediately jot down notes about the experiences that were ongoing at the moment of the beep. After capturing a half dozen experiences in this way, they meet with the DES investigator for an "expositional interview" about the characteristics of those half dozen sampled experiences. The expositional interview is described in detail by Hurlburt and Heavey (2006); we highlight some of its main characteristics here.

High fidelity observation and faithful description. The intent of DES, and therefore the intent of the expositional interviews, is to help subjects gain a high fidelity view of their own randomly selected, specific, manifest, ongoing, natural, contemporaneous, personal experiences and then to provide faithful descriptions of those experiences (Hurlburt, 2011). The aim of the expositional interview is simple: to help the subject stay focused on the experience that was ongoing at the moment of the beep and no other; to help the subject describe the features of that particular ongoing experience and not experience in general; and to help the subject describe the ongoing phenomena as they actually present themselves, not according to some a priori understanding or expectation. In a very real sense, the interviewer asks repeatedly one and only one question during the entire interview: *What was ongoing in your experience at the moment of the beep?* Hurlburt and Heavey (2006) called that the one legitimate question about pristine experience.

However, for a variety of reasons (among them avoidance of pain and/or boredom, desire to impress, self-theories, self-aggrandizement, greed, delusion, fear of exposure, of rejection, of consequences etc.), people (both investigators and subjects) at first find that question difficult; they flee from actual phenomena and distort or mask them in a variety of ways. The expositional interview is a performance art designed to support, inform, constrain, restrain, instruct, and guide both the subject and the investigator so that together they may apprehend in high fidelity and faithfully report the subject's beeped ongoing phenomena.

Co-researchers. DES views investigator and subject as co-investigators. The subject has something DES needs – access to inner experience; the investigator also has something DES needs – skill and expertise in exploring that inner experience. Together, as indispensable partners, subject and investigator might apprehend experience in high fidelity, something that neither can likely do alone. DES takes that co-researcher relationship seriously. For example, DES encourages subjects to help shape the investigation by suggesting particular lines of questioning, particular situations to investigate, and so on. Therefore, as we saw in Chapter 2, we consider DES to be a first-person-*plural* method: We (Juanita and investigator together) examined Juanita's inner experience and evaluated her/our characterizations thereof.

Iterative. Most subjects are not very skilled observers or reporters on their first sampling day or days. Despite the investigator's best efforts at describing the apprehension-of-phenomena task prior to participation, subjects are usually surprised and unprepared for the level of specificity and detail required by the expositional interview, saying things like, "I didn't realize you would ask that! Had I known, I would have paid closer attention at the beep."

Constraint: Develop the subject's abilities. There is no reason to presume that subjects will be skilled at paying attention to their experiences, and if they do pay attention to their experiences, there is no reason to presume that they will be skilled at describing them. Both are abilities that have to be iteratively developed, requiring instruction, practice, and support.

Constraint: Develop the interviewer's abilities. There is also no reason to presume that interviewers will be skilled at helping subjects pay attention to and describe their experiences. Interviewing is a high art, acquired as the result of talent, work, and practice. Many of those skills are applicable across subjects; some apply to particular subjects but not to others.

No amount of interviewer skill can make up for a subject's lack of observational skill at the time the phenomenon occurred; if the subject did not observe the phenomenon in high fidelity, a probing interview is much more likely to produce confabulation than faithful description. As a result, DES usually discards the reports of experience on the first sampling day, and considers the first expositional interview to be primarily training for the second sampling day rather than a data-gathering procedure. As a result of the first-expositional-interview training, the subject's second-day observational skill is typically substantially improved, so the second day's expositional interview can be partly data collection and partly training for the third sampling day. The third day's observational skills are typically again improved, allowing the third expositional interview, typically, to be mostly data collection along with some additional refinement of observational skill.

This iterative training procedure is integral to DES. The faithful apprehension of pristine experience requires that the subject acquire improved observational skills, and that takes time: observation, feedback, new observations, more feedback, and so on.

For example, the subject "Ahmed" said during an expositional interview, "I was saying to myself, 'my girlfriend should buy some bananas.'" The interviewer, noting that people don't generally say to themselves, "*My girlfriend should*" – they say the much more natural, "*Janet should*" – recognized that Ahmed was probably not quoting himself accurately and therefore asked Ahmed, "Exactly what were you saying?" Ahmed replied, "My girlfriend was on the way to the store and I thought maybe I should call her cell phone and tell her to buy bananas." The interviewer, now noting that Ahmed wasn't responding to the "Exactly what were you saying?" question, asked, "Yes, but exactly what words, if any, were you saying?" Ahmed replied, "I'd like to have bananas for a sundae that evening and Janet could bring them." That again was not responsive to the "Exactly what were you saying?" question, so the interviewer continued to press Ahmed for the details of his experience. Ahmed said he was talking to himself, but he was unable to say exactly what the words were; that inability was frustrating to Ahmed.

DES interviewers see this particular kind of interchange with its attendant frustration frequently, and it often means that at the moment of the beep the subject was experiencing thinking that was occurring without words, images, or any other symbols (a phenomenon DES calls unsymbolized thinking; see Chapter 15). Ahmed (incorrectly) assumed that *all* thinking is in words (an incorrect presupposition held by many philosophers and psychologists as well), so if he's thinking, he must be talking to himself. When he couldn't remember the words that he must have been saying, he became frustrated.

The interviewer reassured Ahmed by saying, "Sometimes words are present during thinking, sometimes not; either way is OK. We don't have to worry too much about this particular sample – if this phenomenon is important, we'll see it on subsequent sampling days and we can figure it out then." That aimed to relax Ahmed's defenses and to help him truly describe his subsequent experience.

The point here is that Ahmed's statement, "I was saying to myself that my girlfriend should buy some bananas," was probably not true. That doesn't invalidate the method; it does mean that the interviewer has to be careful to help Ahmed *become*, on subsequent sampling days, a better observer/reporter, to help undermine Ahmed's commitment to presuppositions, to help Ahmed become more adept at paying attention to the actual phenomena present to him. That requires the iterative, day-to-day skill building and new observations that are essential to DES. We will return to the discussion of the iterative nature of DES in Chapter 10.

Successive approximation to faithful reporting. The iterative process we have just described refers to an improvement in apprehensional and reporting skill that gradually accrues over several days of sampling and expositional interviews. Now we note that the description of a phenomenon typically alters within each interview; the interview about any beeped experience can be considered a series of successive approximations leading to a more faithful reporting of the phenomenon. Much of what a subject jots down in the notebook or says early during the expositional interview is incomplete, misleading, partially incorrect, or completely false. This is particularly so on the first sampling day or two, but it at least potentially characterizes every interview about every experience on every sampling day. People take things for granted that aren't true; experiences are often quite difficult to put into words; subjects may not be linguistically skilled; they try too hard to please the investigator; and so on. The interviewer's iterative task is to help subjects improve, revise, or outright reject and replace what they say early in an interview in favor of a more faithful alternative.

DES investigators are supportively candid with their subjects about the importance of limiting themselves to the high fidelity truth. The investigator emphasizes that not knowing at all is better than knowing a half-truth; that we'd much prefer an honest "I don't know" to an answer driven by social desirability. As in the previous section, the interviewer can reassure the subject that if a phenomenon is important, we will encounter it on subsequent sampling days and perhaps will be better able to describe the phenomenon then. DES interviewers reassure subjects that we expect them to say things that aren't true or at least are not confidently true – they are learning a new skill and shouldn't expect to be good at it on their first attempts. Until subjects become confident that they are not going to be punished (shamed, embarrassed, made to feel inadequate, etc.), they cannot legitimately be expected to admit ignorance and/or mistakes of observation in trying to discover what is true for themselves, let alone to tell it to the investigator.

This alteration of reports as the interview progresses does provide the risk that the interviewer will coerce the subject into giving skewed or biased reports. I believe that is an unavoidable part of the DES process and that the risk can be limited by the asking of non-leading questions and bracketing of presuppositions (see the following sections). The alternative, I think, is worse; for example, if we required subjects to be very careful when they jot in their notebooks to write only things that are perfectly true, we would put a substantial chill on notebook jottings. Instead, we want subjects to jot something that is an approximation or clue to the truth, something that can serve as a starting point and be elaborated, refined, and corrected through the interview process.

Non-leading. Part of the expositional interviewer's skill is to ask non-leading questions and give level-playing-field alternatives. For example, when the interviewer reassured Ahmed that sometimes words are there, sometimes not, and that either way is OK, the object was to raise the question about Ahmed's possible presupposition that all thinking is in words while at the same time accepting that Ahmed's thinking may well have been in words. That is, the interviewer's skill requires leaving equal room for any characteristic of a phenomenon until the characteristics are confidently observed and described. Skilled DES interviewers undermine everything including the importance of the distinction they are currently making: Thinking could be in words, could be not in words, or it could be that knowing whether words are there is not important. The object is to provide a level playing field on which any phenomenon can emerge precisely as it occurs. Hurlburt and Heavey (2006) and Hurlburt and Schwitzgebel (2007, 2011c) discussed in depth the skills required for this non-leading, level-playing-field questioning and their importance.

Bracketing presuppositions. A central and pervasive component of the DES method is the bracketing of presuppositions of both the investigator and the subject. To bracket presuppositions (following the lead of Husserl, 1913/1982) is to suspend or put out of play a priori views of the way phenomena or processes occur. To apprehend phenomena as close as possible to the way they actually present themselves, it is necessary to hold your own ideas, expectations, characteristics, beliefs, and predispositions in abeyance.

However, most people have strong a priori presuppositions about the nature of inner experience (recall Ahmed's presupposition about the necessity of words in thinking), and these presuppositions interfere with the subjects' ability to apprehend their phenomena and the investigators' ability to hear the descriptions in high fidelity and to help the subject describe carefully.

Presuppositions can interfere with the apprehension of pristine phenomena in two ways. First, they can create the appearance of experience when it actually didn't exist. For example, Ahmed presuppositionally believed that he always talked to himself when thinking. Therefore when the beep caught him thinking, he incorrectly "observed" himself as talking to himself. Second, presuppositions filter experience, causing experience to be selectively overlooked or minimized.

Presuppositions are difficult to bracket in large part for two reasons: They are "pre" – they operate prior to all cognition and analysis – which means that they are so taken for granted that it doesn't seem that the world could be any other way; and they are insidious, sneaky, and attractively seductive – they aim directly at each individual's particular vulnerabilities and weaknesses. Your presuppositions are based on *your* history, *your* experiences, *your* environment, *your* reality, *your* desires, and you are likely to be exquisitely skilled at hiding their operation from yourself. As a result, DES believes that it is necessary to work relentlessly, effortfully, repeatedly, and fastidiously at the task of bracketing presuppositions.

Presuppositions operate for both investigator and subject. The investigators' task is not only to bracket their own presuppositions but also to help subjects bracket theirs. Phenomenologists have written volumes on bracketing presuppositions, and Hurlburt and Heavey (2006) devoted a chapter to how to attempt to accomplish it in DES.

As previously mentioned, randomness is a powerful, consistent guide to the bracketing of presuppositions. DES discusses an experience not because our presuppositions say that a particular kind of experience is important, but because a dispassionate random beep selected it. DES subjects (and investigators, too) are constantly tempted to leave the experience at the moment of the beep and discuss events surrounding that moment, because those surrounding events may be more interesting, less boring, less embarrassing, more macho, more theoretically important, more scientifically understood, and so forth. All those temptations reflect presuppositions; every departure from the discussion of the moment of the beep is a sign that a presupposition is at work. If you let it, the randomness of the beep will break you, one presupposition at a time.

We will return to the discussion of the bracketing of presuppositions throughout this book, especially in Chapter 12; see also Hurlburt and Schwitzgebel (2007, 2011c).

Attending to non-content cues. In determining whether the subject's statements are true or false, on target or misleading, complete or unfinished, the expositional interviewer pays attention to a wide variety of verbal and non-verbal cues, many of them similar to the cues used by other skilled interviewers (Petitmengin, 2006; Hurlburt & Heavey, 2006). One that is particularly important for DES is noting the subject's use of what Hurlburt and Heavey (2006) called "subjunctifiers."

The object of DES is to describe a specific, manifest occurrence. People who are in fact describing such occurrences generally speak in simple declarative sentences: "I saw an image of Kira sitting on a log"; "I was saying to myself in my own inner voice, 'I should make a ham sandwich'"; "I felt a squeeze in my heart." People who are not describing a specific, manifest phenomenon often signal that non-specificity by using a subjunctive, rather than a declarative sentence: "It was *as if* I were seeing an image." Subjects use many words to signal this shift to the subjunctive: "It was like"; "Maybe I was"; "Well, I don't know, but"; "Probably I was." We call all such phrases "subjunctifiers."

It is striking how consistently people, even linguistically unsophisticated people, switch back and forth between declarative and subjunctified sentences as they switch from describing actual experiences to speaking in general terms. Like all other human behaviors, this consistency is not perfect; it is a clue (and a pretty good one at that) that needs to be examined and confirmed or disconfirmed. We will return to the discussion of subjunctification in Chapters 5 and 8.

Bottom-up Theorizing

As we have seen, DES fundamentally creates an idiographic portrait, the result of making actual (rather than faux) generalizations about the experiences within a single person. Thus all DES generalizations begin at the bottom – faithful descriptions of single experiences – and work up to descriptions of an individual person's salient experience.

We have also seen that DES can be used to draw actual (rather than faux) nomothetic generalizations across several idiographic portraits of individuals who share a common characteristic. Thus the DES nomothetic generalizations also begin at the bottom: Faithful apprehensions of single experiences lead to careful descriptions of persons that lead to true nomothetic generalizations. All DES theorizing is thus a bottom-up process; it avoids beginning with a theory or hypothesis (that would be reifying a presupposition) and instead arrives at a theory as the result of a series of specific observations.

By contrast, psychological science almost always works from the top down. Based on prior theory or casual observations, the typical psychological study advances a hypothesis and then conducts an experiment to test it. I'm in favor of experimentation – in fact, I've written textbooks in the area (Hurlburt, 2006). However, I think that experimentation is likely to be most valuable following careful examination of the relevant phenomena. In my view, adequately careful observations are rarely made, and that undermines psychological science. This section is an elaboration of the constraint stated in Chapter 2: *Particulars can lead to generalities, but generalities cannot lead to particulars.*

MOMENTS

This section elaborates two constraints stated previously: *Relentlessly pursue concrete moments*; and *Rule out everything that is not directly experienced.*

DES, as we have seen, aims at "the moment of the beep," the last undisturbed moment just before the beep is heard. That may seem like a simple, unambiguous instruction, but the fact is that very few subjects grasp the moment-of-the-beep concept on their first sampling attempt. DES subjects seem actively repelled by the moment of the beep; it requires considerable interviewing patience, skill, and tenacity to help, encourage, and instruct a subject to become and stay focused on the moment of the beep. We'll give an example of that in Chapter 5 and in later chapters.

If the instruction "What is in your experience at the moment of the beep?" does not produce descriptions of events at the moment of the beep, what, then, does it produce? In broad strokes, five kinds of things:

First, people give universalist statements. We ask, "What was in your experience at the moment of the beep?" and they say, for example, "I *always* am talking to myself"; or "*Whenever* I _____ I feel _____"; or "I'm *usually* thinking about politics nowadays." *Always, whenever,* and *usually* signal that those statements are *not* (or at least not necessarily) statements about any specific moment in time. Some people do, of course, always talk to themselves, but that is the exception.

Second, subjects describe intervals of time that are far too long to count as moments. They say, for example, "I was in class watching a documentary about Reconstruction. It was interesting." Watching a documentary involves not one but hundreds of moments, hundreds of experiences. We need to encourage the subject to zero in on the particular moment that was ongoing when caught by the beep.

Third, people describe moments that are *after* the moment of the beep. They say, for example, "The beep startled me, and I jumped." The startle is *in response to* the beep, whereas the moment of the beep is the last undisturbed moment *before* hearing the beep.

Fourth, people describe times that are before the moment of the beep. They say, for example, "Ever since I put the beeper on I was waiting for the beep to happen." That is not a moment (it is a long interval of time), and it is not at the moment of the beep (and it probably also is not a description of experience).

Fifth, people give responses that have no temporal significance whatsoever. They say, for example, "I think this is a very interesting experiment."

A large part of the DES interview skill is to train subjects to get to the moment of the beep. It's not nearly as easy as it sounds; in fact, students learning DES have a great deal of difficulty mastering this.

> **Q:** What difference does it make whether we get the moment right at the moment of the beep or a bit before or after? A moment is a moment.
>
> **A:** First, it has been my experience that the only moment that can actually be firmly grasped is the moment of the beep. Any other moment, even if it is actually a moment, is slippery, because it is not clearly defined. So in a very real sense, the only moment capable of being adequately described is the moment of the beep.
>
> Second, even if you could grasp and describe some moment other than the moment of the beep, then you could not claim that that moment was randomly selected. Now you are describing some moment that you, for whatever reason, prefer to discuss over the randomly selected moment of the beep. Random selection is, as we saw earlier, a strong aid in the effort to bracket presuppositions.
>
> So the moment of the beep is, because of its ordinariness, a very special thing.

When we said at the beginning of this section that "DES subjects seem actively repelled by the moment of the beep," we did not mean to imply that DES subjects were somehow different from other people. In fact, our DES subjects at least sometimes have been randomly selected from large populations (Hurlburt & Heavey, 2002; Heavey & Hurlburt, 2008), so it seems safe to say that many people would be actively repelled by the moment of the beep.

Furthermore, we think that it is not only the moment of the beep that repels people, but moments, period. Thus the sentence could equally well be written as "People seem actively repelled by moments." In this book, I do not presume to know *why* that is so, but I'm pretty sure *that* it is so. Being unambiguously specific does not come naturally to many, if not most, people.

(I should add that most of our studies have been undertaken in the United States, and a few in the EU; none has been undertaken in non-industrialized countries. I don't know whether the repelled-by-moments conclusion would apply across cultures.)

Most people do not know that they are repelled by being unambiguously specific, apparently because one doesn't know much about what one actively avoids.

Recognizing that people are repelled by moments, and fashioning a method that takes that seriously, is part of genuinely submitting to the constraints that the exploration of inner experience imposes. DES responds to those pressures in a variety of ways. It uses a signal that is clearly apprehendable, has a rapid rise time, and is unambiguous. As we saw earlier, some have tried to use vibrating signals such as those used by pagers; they take too long to be apprehended (Is that the vibration? Yes! But by now the experience is gone). Some have used cell phones as beepers, but that is not ambiguous (Ah! There's the phone. But I'm not supposed to answer it – I'm supposed to pay attention to my experience. But by now the experience is gone). We don't wish to claim that the beep is the only way; we do wish to note that there are some constraints here about what is and what is not a good signal.

Training people not to be repelled by moments requires a series of successive approximations; that's why DES requires the iterative training sketched previously and discussed in detail in Chapter 10. We generally discard the data from the first sampling day. The first expositional interview provides training for the second day but, for most subjects, produces little of descriptive value.

Recall that we said in Chapter 1 that moments and experience co-determine each other. Therefore it would be just as appropriate to say that people are repelled by *experience* as that people are repelled by *moments*.

Let's make this as clear as possible. Before a subject wears the beeper for the first time, we give extensive instructions, usually for about forty-five minutes. Much of that is aimed precisely at what is the moment of the beep. For example, we typically show the illustration displayed in Figure 3.1, explaining that it is meant to depict a movie with frames a fraction of a second apart. It shows a car driving past a sign; the beep comes at the third frame, and the time that we are interested in is the frame *just before* that.

We also use a flash photograph metaphor: You're walking down the street and someone takes a flash picture of you. You turn toward the camera. The moment of the beep is what the flash catches – your undisturbed walking. Your turn toward the camera comes *after* the beep.

Those illustrations seem clear and unambiguous, and the subjects invariably say they understand, but the empirical fact is that *most people do not get it!* No matter how we say it, until subjects have undergone the first (or perhaps more) expositional interview, they do not grasp the concept of the moment of the beep. Instructions are not adequate to teach people to describe moments. It requires iterative training.

There is a very important corollary to this set of observations: Descriptions of inner experience that are collected after one set of instructions are not to be trusted. That includes, sad to tell, most of the descriptions of inner experience collected by psychological science. DES believes that genuinely submitting to the constraints that the exploration of inner experience imposes generally

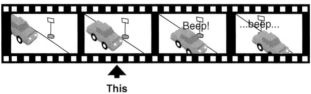

This
is the "moment of the beep"

FIGURE 3.1. What we mean by "the moment of the beep."

requires discarding as worthless the data that is generated by subjects after one set of instructions.

> **Q:** You stress the importance of the precise moment, but you are ambiguous in your terminology. Sometimes you use "at the moment of the beep," sometimes "the last undisturbed moment before the beep," sometimes "the moment caught in flight by the beep," and so on. I think that inconsistency confuses your subjects and maybe you yourself.
>
> **A:** There is no single best way of describing the moment we're interested in. "*Just before* the beep" is temporally ambiguous, perhaps measured in seconds, perhaps in millennia (the Paleozoic Age comes *just before* the Cenozoic Age). "The last undisturbed moment before" implies that we are not interested in the "in-flight" experience, because the in-flight experience will certainly be interrupted by the beep. "At the moment of the beep" implies that the experience should take place *during* the beep. "One millisecond before the beep" implies a temporal precision that is unobtainable. And so on.
>
> The way I have discovered to overcome the idiosyncratic limitation of each phrase is to use all the phrases intermittently, in the expectation that the idiosyncrasies will cancel each other out. *This* is what I mean by "just before the beep"; *this* is what I mean by "the last undisturbed moment before the beep"; *this* is what I mean by "at the moment of the beep"; eventually the subject will come to understand what I mean by *this*.

EXPERIENCE

This section elaborates two constraints stated previously: *Aim at pristine experience*; and *Rule out everything that is not directly experienced*.

Moments and experience co-determine each other. We observed earlier that if people seem actively repelled by moments, then people must also seem actively repelled by experience, and that is indeed the case. DES subjects, early on, before the iterative training has taken hold, avoid describing experience.

"Experience," as we use the term, refers to directly observed apprehensions, events that take place before the footlights of consciousness. Most subjects, early in sampling, instead of describing the experience that was ongoing at the moment of the beep:

- give faux generalizations, for example, "I *always* feel angry when he is in the room."
- give self-characterizations, for example, "I like to read." Such a self-characterization may well be true, probably is true, in a manner of speaking, more often than not. But it is not a description of experience.
- opine about causation, for example, "I was tired *because* I was up studying last night." The tiredness might be a statement about experience, but the causative link between last night's studying and today's tiredness is (at best) inferred, not directly experienced.
- describe what we call facts of the universe, for example, "I was sitting with my legs crossed." It is possible that the legs-crossedness was actually being experienced at the moment of the beep, but more often that is not the case; this has to be discovered by careful interviewing.
- describe behavior, for example, "I was playing chess." In actuality, people rarely experience *playing chess*; instead, they experience wondering whether they should sacrifice the rook for the knight.
- describe a presupposition about experience. Recall Ahmed's presupposition that he was "saying" something.
- describe presumed or theoretical aspects of themselves, that their ego was involved, or that their self was under attack, and so on.
- describe the environment, say, the room was noisy or the doctor was running late.

I don't mean to imply that these are the only things that people talk about when asked what they were experiencing, only that they are common things, and that they are not being directly experienced. Furthermore, there are doubtless other ways of categorizing these distractions from experience (for example, describing the environment might reasonably be lumped in with the "facts of the universe"). However, to quibble about that is to miss the main points: that there are *many* ways that people have of avoiding describing experience, and that iterative training is required to help the subject reduce that avoidance.

GENUINELY SUBMITTING TO THE CONSTRAINTS

Constraint: The exploration of pristine experience is a personal endeavor. It is not to be expected that you and I will discover exactly the same things when exploring someone's pristine experience.

People avoid moments. People avoid experience. Subjects have to be trained genuinely to submit to the constraints that the apprehension of experience imposes.

Relentlessly keeping the subject aimed at the experience at the moment of the beep can at least to some degree overcome those avoidances. That requires skill, patience, repetition, and on-the-job training. As I have said, I don't think it can be done in one shot; some kind of iterative training is required (see Chapter 10).

DES *investigators* are also tempted to avoid moments and experience. The same forces that drive subjects away from moments and experience also drive investigators away from moments and experience, which makes conducting DES interviews a high-skill endeavor, requiring a substantial amount of training, itself iterative.

The challenges don't end once one acquires some DES skills. The beep's instruction is simple – let's communicate honestly, straightforwardly, truthfully about whatever makes its way into the subject's experience. Yet as in all human endeavors that involve truth, there are a myriad of distractions (comfort, promotion, tenure, merit, grant money, attraction, peer acceptance, jealousy, competing responsibilities of all kinds, etc.), always personally created and always seemingly innocuous. It requires substantial courage to set all that aside and go about the slow, repetitive, demanding, painful, seemingly boring business of bracketing presuppositions.

Apprehending pristine experience must therefore be recognized as being a highly challenging endeavor with a strong tendency to avoid it at every level. Challenging does not mean impossible; I believe that DES can be performed adequately or well, probably not by everyone but by more than a few. The situation is quite similar to that of good meditation: It requires work, patience, and perseverance over the long haul.

There is a range of depths possible in the application of DES. At the shallower end of this range, the DES beep can be simply a signal for the gathering of data about the characteristics of experience (for example, investigating how frequently inner speech occurs in some population). At the deeper end of this range, the beep can be a relentless and unflinchingly impartial guide or taskmaster to those who would give themselves over to communicating fearlessly about all aspects of experience; the beep, if you let it, can break you of the sloppy habits of fleeing from uncomfortable or conflictual experience.

In that regard, DES is like an elevator into the crypts of inner experience. You can choose to get off at a variety of depths; the deeper you choose to go, the more committed you have to be to overcoming presuppositions, not just bracketing them. To examine pristine experiences deeply and thoroughly, you have to make yourself vulnerable to the truth, which means letting go of the very ground you (presuppositionally) stand on, so that you can encounter experience directly – including encountering things you don't want to see about yourself and others. The deeper you want to go into personal truths, the more courage is required and the more you must open yourself: You must be willing to get bruised; be willing to become transparent; be willing to see your own unbridled greed as well as the neurotic fallout that seems inevitably to follow the exposure of greed; be willing to be deconstructed (a process, which, if you want to avoid complete disorganization, requires varying periods of digestion, integration, maturation) with no guarantees about what gets reconstructed in its place and no guarantees about how long and deep the process has to go.

The same phenomena exist outside every door of this elevator: Sooner or later, among the ham sandwiches, gas stations, and television shows you must encounter sexual desire, anger, love, hate, jealousy, temptation, disappointment, guilt, competition, frustration, lust, insecurity, fear, death, despair, longing, responsibility, failure, prejudice, heartache, and so on. All these experiences, from the banal to the difficult, can be examined at a variety of depths. At the shallower doors, those phenomena can perhaps be glossed over; at the deeper doors, they have to be confronted and personally examined when they occur. The deeper the elevator descends, the more direct the impact, sometimes with foundation-shattering ramifications for the investigator when his or her defenseless sensitivities somehow line up with the subject's experience.

Here again, there are parallels to meditation. There is a range of ways meditation can be used, from a simple relaxation exercise to a tool to burn out impurities until perfection is attained. We have no wish to overdraw this comparison; the Eastern traditions have spent centuries exploring methods that train practitioners to pay attention to experience at a far deeper level than DES has attained. The DES beeper can be seen as a way of jump-starting that kind of meditation practice, using the portable beep in place of the monastery gong that calls monks to pay attention now.

Thus DES has the virtue that within it there is the possibility of substantial depth, regardless of whether that depth is plumbed by any particular applier at any particular time. DES observes the phenomena of experience, and those phenomena can be observed at a variety of levels.

4

Everyday Experience

We have been discussing the co-determination of pristine experience ↔ moments ↔ genuinely submitting to the constraints that the exploration of experience imposes. Chapter 2's discussion of bulimia showed that submitting to those constraints may be worth the required effort and may provide outside-the-box perspectives on vitally important matters.

All that presumes that pristine experience exists. However, there are many who believe that inner experience *doesn't* exist, or if it does exist it can't be apprehended or described in any scientifically useful way. There is good reason to be wary of introspective methods; the introspections on which nascent psychology was founded were a spectacular failure, leading to nearly a century in which introspection was effectively banned from orthodox psychology (the term "introspection" rarely appears in modern textbooks on psychological method except in the history-of-psychology chapter where it is criticized). As I have explained elsewhere (Monson & Hurlburt, 1993; Hurlburt & Schwitzgebel, 2007), I think the early introspections were interpreted incorrectly, so psychology's banning of introspective techniques was an over-generalization and an over-reaction. However, that history does suggest that skepticism about introspective techniques is justified, as long as by "skepticism" one means "suspending judgment" rather than being "unwilling to admit or accept what is offered as true."

Chapter 3 sketched DES, a method (or approach, or instrument) for the exploration of pristine experience. The practitioner of DES, I claimed, can genuinely submit to the constraints that the endeavor to apprehend experience imposes. In the present chapter, I present two DES interviews so that the reader can begin to get a feel for what a DES expositional interview looks like, feels like.

These two interviews were conducted jointly by me and graduate students who were learning the DES method. The subjects were undergraduate students who participated in exchange for meeting a research requirement in their introductory psychology courses. I chose these two examples (a) because the experience being described is relatively uncomplicated (pristine experience exists along a range of complexity, with Chapter 2's bulimic women at the complex end of that range); (b) because they came from the subject's third or fourth sampling day (so the subject had acquired some skill in observing and describing experience; see Chapter 10); and (c) because they are more or less typical (every pristine experience is personally unique, but these are *not* unusual in any particular sense). Thus these interviews serve as a rather "easy" introduction to DES: These examples do not struggle against complexities (that is, are not like the bulimic subjects of Chapter 2), and do not present the struggles frequent on the first day or two of sampling. "Easy" does not mean "unusual" – in fact, these interviews are not at all unusual.

The interviews are complete and unedited. They will serve as a yardstick against which to compare more complicated, problematic interviews that we will discuss later in this book. I'll call the first subject "Luke Jones," or "LJ" for short. The interviewers are graduate student I will call "Amanda Clark" (AC) and me (RTH).

LUKE JONES SAMPLE 3.5

RTH: [upon finishing the conversation about the fourth sample on the third sampling day] Beep number 5?
AC: Yes. So tell me about your experience.
LJ: Yes. I pictured the equation *g* equals *v* squared over *R* ...
AC: Could you say that one more time?
LJ: [laughs] I pictured the equation *g* equals *v* squared over *R* in my head, and that was like a, kinda like a, like how I actually had just written it down. So it was in pencil, written with a mechanical pencil on a white note card. Um, but it was not ... But what I pictured in my head was not what it was written on, so it was more so "floating" [said quizzically] in my head, but like at the, probably, closer to the forefront of my head. But probably between my frontal and parietal lobes, I would say [chuckles]. [pause] Let's see. Was the print large? [This is a reference to a conversation about a previous beep, and is largely irrelevant to the present beep.] [pause] It's hard to determine like relative size when, like ... um ... [pause]

One of arguments against the existence or scientific adequacy of pristine experience is that subjects confuse – don't adequately distinguish between – their experience and real events in the world. In the present case, that argument would imply that Luke does not have any inner experience of an equation; instead he *remembers* seeing a real handwritten equation and then, swiftly, *mistakenly believes* that he innerly sees it. That explanation does not square with the facts of Luke's report. Luke is effectively making exactly that distinction: He is carefully and confidently distinguishing between seeing real pencil marks on a real note card and imaginarily seeing an *impossible-in-reality* equation floating in space, innerly seeing pencil marks on nothingness.

> RTH: Did it look like the original?
>
> LJ: [nods affirmatively] Yeah, it was like a copy of it.
>
> RTH: And are you seeing the original of it at the same time, the original?
>
> LJ: Um … [pause] No, I wasn't. Um, no, I was, sorry, looking at it, I was looking at my notes. Wait, yeah … [pause] And … [pause] any other questions?
>
> AC: You said it looked like how you had written it. So was it, was it written like in handwriting, versus being …
>
> LJ: Printed?
>
> AC: … like in typed letters?
>
> LJ: Yeah.
>
> AC: You said it was v squared over R?
>
> LJ: Yeah, g equals v squared over R. [He gives a slight emphasis on the "g equals" portion of this statement, as if correcting Amanda's omission.]
>
> AC: So you said that you had written on a note card but it seemed like it was floating in your head? [Amanda says this quizzically; LJ nods affirmatively.] Were you seeing the note card? Or were you just seeing the equation g …
>
> LJ: Just the equation. Just the handwritten part.
>
> AC: Um. Was it v squared *over* R or was it more like a slash R?
>
> LJ: [confidently interrupts] Slash.
>
> [pause]
>
> AC: I don't know if I have any questions further.
>
> RTH: Does it look like you're looking forwards at it, downwards at it, backwards at it, or doesn't that make any sense?
>
> LJ: Um, you mean in my mind's eye?
>
> RTH: Yeah.
>
> LJ: Like if we were right in front of me, like here … OK, it's probably easier to visually describe it. Let's say my brain is like right here [uses his hands to map out a three foot deep region of space in front of him meant to represent his brain].
>
> RTH: OK.
>
> LJ: The back of my head right here [indicates the region closest to him]; the front over there [indicates three feet in front of him]. So I'm looking as if I'm viewing it from the back, and it's right here [gestures perhaps two or two and a half feet in front of him].
>
> RTH: So sort of closer to the front of your head than the back of your head …
>
> LJ: Yeah, like between my frontal and parietal …

This is Luke's second reference to the imagined equation's being between the frontal and parietal lobes of his brain. There are lots of potential explanations why Luke might say that – an attempt to impress me with his knowledge of brain physiology, a theory about where images are located in the brain, and so on. None of that is of interest to me, because my goal is descriptive, not explanatory. So instead of trying to *interpret* this, I accept it as being descriptive of experienced location. That is, I understand him to be saying that the imagined equation seems to be in his head maybe two thirds or three quarters of the way toward the front. Whether or not that corresponds to the actual location of the division between his frontal and parietal lobe is inconsequential to me.

> RTH: … and viewed from the back looking forward.
> LJ: Yeah. Yeah. Yeah, like you're sitting in a drive-in movie theater and you're looking forward.
> RTH: And does it seem like a long way away like in a drive-in movie theater or does it …
> LJ: No [confidently]. It seems pretty close.

One of arguments against the existence or scientific adequacy of pristine experience is that subjects are taken in by their own metaphors (e.g., Schwitzgebel, in Hurlburt & Schwitzgebel, 2007, p. 99). In the present case, that argument would imply that once Luke invokes the drive-in theater metaphor, then he will likely confuse the characteristics of the drive-in with the characteristics of his experience. That explanation does not square with the facts of Luke's report. Luke invokes the drive-in metaphor, but backs away from its viewed-from-a-distance ramification. Luke seems quite capable of limiting the range of the metaphor only to those aspects that effectively illustrate his experience.

> RTH: OK.
> AC: And it's facing you, as in like you would read it? g equals v squared …
> LJ: Right.
> AC: … not like reversed?
> LJ: Right … [pause] And the awareness of looking at my notes versus what I'm seeing in my head are very equal, equal shared, equal percentage of whatever I was focused on. Like the focus was pretty much split between the two.
> AC: So you're also looking at something?
> LJ: Right. I am looking at notes. I don't remember if they had the equation on it or not – but it most likely did. Um, but I did say, like there was a shared percentage of focus or whatever …
> AC: Um hm.
> LJ: … there's a slightly more focus on the equation in my head.

One of the arguments against the existence or scientific adequacy of pristine experience is that subjects merely try to maintain verbal consistency – "That's my story and I'm stickin' to it." In the present case, that argument would imply that once Luke says that the amount of attention he was paying to seeing in reality and in imagination are equal, that saying would reify the experience. That does not square with the facts: Luke is now doubling back, trying to correct or at least amend his earlier statement.

AC: Um … [pause] So in your experience was this mental equation that you're seeing [LJ nods affirmatively], and then also looking at your notes [LJ nods affirmatively]. Were there any specific parts of looking at your notes that were in your experience?

[pause]

LJ: Um, I may not have been focused on the whole page, but I'm not sure. Sorry.

One of arguments against the existence or scientific adequacy of pristine experience is that subjects make things up merely to try to please the investigator. Here, by contrast, Luke explicitly indicates that, in his view, he is *not* pleasing the investigator, but regardless he is not going to say anything more.

By the way, "I'm not sure" is a delightful answer, as far as I'm concerned; it indicates, as Luke is indicating here, that the subject takes the task seriously and is willing to accept ambiguity or uncertainty where it arises.

AC: It's OK. Was it like a notebook that you're looking at? Was it a textbook?

LJ: A notebook.

AC: And were, like … was it your notes that was in the notebook?

LJ: Um hm.

AC: OK. I don't know if there are any other questions.

RTH: I think I'm set.

It seems to me that the most reasonable, defensible understanding of this interview is that Luke was, at the time of the beep (or very close thereto) innerly seeing an equation, $g = v^2/R$, that this imagined equation seemed to be handwritten in pencil, that there was no seen background, and that this imagined equation seemed to exist in the interior of his head slightly in front of the middle. And at the same time, part of his attention, though somewhat less, was aimed at the real notes that were in front of him.

This apprehension of Luke's experience is not intended to be nor understood to be entirely complete: There may have been several or many other aspects of experience (the sounds around him, the pressure on his buttocks, the proprioception of his joints, and so on) that occupied some small part of his direct experience. Yet these aspects, if they existed at all, were of much smaller magnitude than the innerly seen equation and the exteriorly seen notes (Hurlburt & Schwitzgebel, 2011a).

This apprehension of Luke's experience is not intended to be nor understood to be absolutely accurate.[1] It did not describe the spacings between the

---

[1] In previous writings (e.g., Hurlburt & Schwitzgebel, 2007) I have stated that the object of DES was *accurate* description. I have now tempered that view: inner experience is (sometimes) too complex and/or multilayered for accuracy to be attainable, so it makes more sense to say that the object of DES is *high fidelity* apprehension. High fidelity is attainable; accuracy is not.

characters in the equation, the variations of the width of the pencil line, and so on. Our goal in this exercise is a *faithful apprehension*, not an entirely complete or absolutely accurate apprehension. It seems a high fidelity account to say that Luke was innerly seeing an equation; it would seem to be mistaken to write that Luke was innerly seeing a Cadillac Escalade parked next to a Hummer H3; mistaken to write that Luke was *saying* "*g* equals *v* squared over *R*" at the moment of the beep; mistaken to write that Luke's attention was primarily focused on the feeling of the desk top against his elbows as he leaned on it.

We call Luke's innerly seen equation and exteriorly seen notes his "pristine experience", his "pristine inner experience," his "inner experience," or, when unambiguous, his "experience." There is no best term (Hurlburt & Schwitzgebel, 2007). "Inner" seems to favor the image over reality, but as this interview shows we do not intend that favoritism. "Pristine" seems to imply purity or simplicity, but we do not intend that. "Experience" unmodified seems to include the sounds around him, the pressure on his buttocks, the proprioception of his joints, and so on, and we definitely do *not* want to imply that unless those are directly experienced. I urge you not to get hung up on the terminology; there's little doubt that, in this instance, whether we call it pristine, inner, or unmodified, the innerly seen equation and exteriorly seen notes count and the surrounding sounds, the buttock pressure, the joint proprioception do not.

There are other defensible understandings of this interview, for example, that at the moment of the beep Luke had no experience whatsoever. Instead, the beep caused him swiftly to manufacture an "experience" that was understood (incorrectly) to have been ongoing. Although perfectly defensible, it seems to me that there is no evidence whatsoever in favor of this understanding.

PATRICIA SMITH SAMPLE 4.3

I'll call our second subject "Patricia Smith," or "PS" for short. The interviewers are graduate student we will call "Debra King" (DK) and me (RTH).

DK: [upon finishing the conversation about the second sample on the fourth sampling day] OK. Go to beep 3.
PS: I was warming up some food in the microwave, and I was staring at the numbers when … the countdown thing, and I was counting in my head when I looked at the numbers.
DK: OK, so when the beep hit you're warming up the food in the microwave and you're staring at the timer …
PS: Yes.
DK: … and you're counting …
PS: Well, it would be like, I got to "8," and it was like "9 … 8"; you see it [points to her eyes] and then you say it [gestures away from her face] also.

DK: And did you say you were counting out loud?

PS: [shakes head negatively] In my head.

One of the arguments against the existence or scientific adequacy of pristine experience is that subjects are easily led by the investigator. That does not square with the facts here: Debra suggests that Patricia was counting aloud, but Patricia easily denies that.

DK: OK. So at the moment of the beep, what's in your awareness?

PS: The number on the timer screen and the counting in my head.

DK: OK. So let's start with the number on the timer screen. How is that in your awareness?

PS: Like seeing the number physically, kind of, if that ... I'm not sure if that makes sense.

DK: Do you remember what number it was?

PS: 8.

DK: 8? So you're seeing the number 8. Was there anything in particular you're paying attention to or ...

PS: No. Just ... it was 8 and then the beep went off. So I was looking at the numbers. Not the color or anything, just the number, kind of.

DK: Just kind of taking in the number 8?

PS: Um hm. I wasn't like really focused on any physical thing to it.

DK: OK. And the counting in head. How was that in your awareness?

PS: Saying it. Usually, like ... [now becomes substantially more definite] In my head I'd be like, "9 ... 8," but it'd be ... it wasn't like low tone or anything, it's just in my same, normal voice. ["Low tone" is a reference to a previous sample where she had been saying something very softly in her inner voice.]

DK: So at the moment of the beep you were saying ...

PS: "8."

DK: "8." And that's not ... So that was in your own normal voice, you said?

PS: Yes.

DK: And that was more like you were saying it? [This is a reference to a previous sample where Patricia had been more focused on the *hearing* of her own inner voice rather than on the *speaking* of it.]

PS: Yes.

DK: Is there anything more that you can say about that?

PS: No. [laughs/sighs nervously] Just it was in my voice and counting, usually, and I could ... Like saying it but you could still hear it. More the saying it than the hearing it.

DK: And this one was more saying than hearing.

PS: Um hm. [pause]

DK: Is there anything else going on?

PS: [shakes head negatively] No.

RTH: So I have one question about it. So this was in normal volume by comparison to the first one, which was said normally but the volume was then cranked down on it [in your experience] ...

PS: [has been nodding affirmatively throughout the question] Yes.

RTH: … Is that right? So this [the current beeped experience] is said normally but *not* cranked … the volume was not turned down. Is that right?

PS: [continues to nod affirmatively] Yes.

RTH: OK. And as far as you know, are you in sync with the numbers? So when the microwave says "9" you're saying "9" and then when it turns to 8 you say "8," …

PS: Yes, um hm.

RTH: … so you're like an attachment of the microwave?

PS: [laughs] Yes. It wasn't like 9 and then I'd say "9," it was both at same time, like [gestures with her hand, as if pointing to the microwave, at the same time she says] "9 … 8."

RTH: [in unison with Patricia] "9 … 8." [pause] I'm happy.

It seems to me that the most reasonable, defensible understanding of this interview is that Patricia was, at the time of the beep (or very close thereto) innerly saying "9 … 8" in sync with the exteriorly seen microwave timer. This saying was apprehended to be in her own normal speaking voice.

As with Luke, this apprehension of Patricia's experience is not intended to be nor understood to be entirely complete or absolutely accurate. Our goal is a *faithful apprehension*, not an absolutely complete or accurate apprehension. It seems a high fidelity account to say that Patricia was innerly saying "9 … 8"; it would seem to be mistaken to say that she was innerly saying "I like Cadillac Escalades more than Hummer H3s"; mistaken to say that her attention was primarily focused on the aroma of the spaghetti she was heating.

DISCUSSION

One aim of this chapter is to give you a sense of what goes on in DES interviews. These are more or less typical.

Another aim of this chapter is to refine our understanding of pristine inner experience. I see little reason to doubt that Luke was innerly seeing the equation $g = v^2/R$, that this seen equation was created by Luke for Luke and how Luke created it: seen in handwritten pencil, seen with no background, experienced slightly forward of the middle of his head. It would be hugely weird to write that at the moment of her beep *Patricia* was innerly seeing the equation $g = v^2/R$; that would be something like by Luke *for Patricia* how Luke. That's just not how pristine experience works.

To hold that Luke at his moment was seeing $g = v^2/R$, and that Patricia at her moment was innerly saying "9 … 8" seems pretty uncontroversial. There are cavils: Luke and Patricia were lying; Luke and Patricia had no experience at the moment of the beep but swiftly made it up in response to the beep; and so on. However, such thoroughgoing skepticism hardly seems productive.

In fact, it is the other side of the coin that may engender the more opposition: Luke's and Patricia's pristine experience is so obviously acceptable that it cannot possibly be of interest to science. Who cares whether Luke was seeing an equation with no background? Who cares whether Patricia was innerly saying numbers in sync with her microwave? Those are nano-details, doubtless true, but so tiny, so situation specific, so fleeting, as to be entirely inconsequentially trivial in the scheme of things.

And maybe they are. But remember Chapter 2. The fragmented multiplicity that occurred in one of Jessica's samples was itself a nano-detail; it didn't become interesting until we discovered that Jessica had a lot of such nano-details, as did many, maybe most, other bulimic women. Until one examines the nano-details, as they actually occur, using a method that has a chance to reveal the nano-details, we cannot know whether they are vitally important or trivial.

5

Moments Are Essential

This book attempts to tighten our grasp of moments of truth, which, as we have seen, requires deepening our understanding of all three aspects: moments ↔ experience ↔ genuinely submitting to the constraints. Chapter 2 focused on the experience aspect, using bulimia to illustrate the potential profit of investigating experience. Chapter 3 focused on the genuinely-submitting-to-the-constraints aspect, laying out a method (Descriptive Experience Sampling, or DES) that tries to take that genuine submission seriously. Chapter 4 returned to the experience aspect, providing some straightforward experiences to illustrate DES and to provide some perspective against which to compare the fragmented experience of the bulimic women.

Now we deepen our focus on the moments aspect by presenting a transcript of a DES expositional interview that I conducted with a twenty-five-year-old college student we will call "Kathy Talbert" ("KT" in the transcript); this is her first beep from her third sampling day. The question, as always, that DES seeks to answer is, *What was in your experience at the moment of the beep?* During the first two expositional interviews, I had pressed without success to get to her experience at the moment of the beeps. Now, in the third hour of interviewing, I continue that relentless (but supportive) pressure toward the moment with, at first, equally little success. However, six minutes into this third interview we finally arrive at the moment of a beep. There is, I think, a huge difference between talking about experience at the moment of the beep and talking about anything else. I'd like you to experience that difference for yourself, so I present this interview essentially unedited from the beginning.

We pick up the transcript after two minutes and seventeen seconds of pre-liminaries – setting up the video camera, small talk, and so on. Kathy knows full well (the result of two prior hours of intensive interview) what my question is (*What was in your experience at the moment of the beep?*). As we shall see, she doesn't yet know how to answer it. I put superscripts on each conversational turn so we can refer back.

KT[1]: When the first beep went off I was looking in the mirror putting some
lip gloss on 'cause I was wondering which was … looks best with my skin
colors, or something like that. And I was just like, when I was looking in the
mirror, I was wondering, How is it that …how does makeup make someone
look better? 'Cause I was like … I was like … I don't know, I was like looking
at my own face in the mirror and I was like, What is it that's so special about
it that makeup makes someone look better? I was probably just like messing
around in my mind, and like, like, like I was thinking, like this feeling …
I was probably just like curious, curiously like messing with my makeup
and just trying … just like trying a different style or something. And I was
probably more like trying … transitioning faces, like [inaudible] lips, like …
what's … I was more like trying to change my makeup, to make my makeup
work, or something. That's more what I was doing.

Constraint: Subjects say things that are not true. In Kathy's opening remark,
she advances five "descriptions" of her experience:

- Wondering which looks best
- Wondering how makeup makes someone look better
- Wondering what's so special about makeup
- Curiously messing with makeup
- Trying to make her makeup work

You may wish to add or subtract something from that list – that is, you may
slice up the pie of Kathy's opening remarks somewhat differently. Yet no matter
how you slice it, this is evidence that Kathy is not unambiguously describing a
moment of her experience. Beyond that ambiguity of content, there are many
linguistic signs that Kathy's talk in KT[1] should not be accepted as a simple
description of her momentary experience. We called these signs "subjunctifiers" in Chapter 3, and will return to their discussion in Chapter 8; for now
we merely wish to notice that Kathy gives lots of signals that she herself does
not believe what she is saying. For example, when Kathy says "or something
like that" at the end of her first sentence, that phrase implies that what she has
just said is not right, or not accurate, or is in some way contrary to her experience. "I don't know," "I was probably," "or something," and the frequent use of
the word "like" have (or may have) the same subjunctifying significance. For
example, when Kathy said "I was *like* looking at my own face in the mirror,"
like in that sentence means (or at least may mean) that she was not *really* looking at her face, but was only doing something *more or less similar* to looking at
her face. Therefore *like* counts (at least potentially) as a subjunctifier.

By my count (I'll list them in Chapter 8) there are twenty-one subjunctifiers in KT[1], which is a lot in a 175-word utterance. You may disagree with some
subjunctifiers on my list, or perhaps will spot some that I missed. The exact
count is not important; any way you slice it, there are a lot: Kathy is telling us,

in her linguistic/behavioral side-channels, that she is not, or at least may not be, describing her experience at the moment of the beep.

> **Q:** You're making far too much of locutions like *like*. *Like* is just a speech ornament that people use out of linguistic habit. It means nothing.
> **A:** First, as the result of my experience with DES, I'm confident that *like* is often a subjunctifier. But the conclusions in this chapter and book do not in any way hinge on that.
> Second, I think *like* is *not* merely an ornament, even for Valley girls. I suspect that the reason that that "ornament" caught on is that there is some truth to it. When the Valley girl says "I was *like*, 'Oh my god!'" she means, "I was surprised, and *could have (but probably didn't)* indicate that by saying 'Oh my god!'" That is, *like* intentionally indicates a lack of precision or approximateness of description.
> Third, whether *like* is a subjunctifier or an ornament is an empirical issue. We will see later that six minutes into this interview subjunctifications of other kinds decrease dramatically. If *like* is a subjunctifier, then its frequency should also decrease; if *like* is an ornament, its frequency should stay the same.
> Fourth, we're still early in the screw-turning process. I aim here only to sensitize you to the *possibility* that subjunctification (however you define it) might serve as an important clue to whether Kathy is actually describing the moment of the beep. For now, I ask only that you keep an open mind about subjunctification.

That Kathy says lots of things that are not true does *not* make DES a flawed procedure or Kathy a bad subject. It demonstrates that if we are, paraphrasing Frankfurt, genuinely to submit to the constraints that the attempt to provide a faithful account of experience imposes, we have to take seriously (a) that Kathy is currently unable to provide the account we desire; (b) that down deep in her grammar-producing soul she recognizes her inability; and (c) that she lets us in on her inability in the (probably) only way she knows how, by sub-junctifying her talk. Because moments ↔ experience, if I am to help her get, precisely and straightforwardly, to her experience, I will have to help her get, precisely and straightforwardly, to the moment of the beep.

> RTH²: OK. And so, the … there's a lot of things that might be candidates for being inner experience at that particular moment, and I'd like to know exactly what's going on. So here's what I think may be possibilities, and I might be off the track here, too. But one is that you've got a thought process going on, about, sort of, makeup in general: How is it that makeup makes people look different. That's one possibility.
> Another possibility is that you're just looking at your makeup, and so right at the moment of the beep (snaps fingers) you're just seeing the way the makeup looks on your face…

Note that I subjunctify my own response ("might be," "may be," "might be off the track," etc.; for that matter, the advancing of the list of possibilities is itself one big subjunctifier). My object here is to leave room for her to clear things up – to deny or accept all, part, or none of what she has already said.

> KT[3]: Um hm.
>
> RTH[4]: … in the mirror. And another possibility is that you're actively engaged in making this face, that face, whatever, watching the face more than you are watching the makeup. Or maybe all three of those, or maybe none of them. But I'm interested in what the details are right at that (snaps fingers) *Flash!* moment.

Constraint: Subjects are co-researchers. Note that I am discussing my thought process about Kathy's experience directly with Kathy; I'm not hiding from her my inability to understand her talk. I want to apprehend in as high fidelity as possible her private experience; I think if I manipulate her in any way, that manipulation will likely backfire in the end. So I am candid with her, as I would like her to be candid with me.

Constraint: Clarify rather than interpret. Note that I do *not* try to figure out what Kathy means; I do *not* try to infer which of Kathy's five statements about her experience is correct or the most believable. Instead, I lay out in plain view that I don't understand and ask for Kathy's help. DES is *never* about inference; it is about observation. If something is worth interpreting, it is even more worth getting in a position to observe directly.

> **Q:** You ask too much of Kathy. If she knew which of those was the right one, she would have told you right away. So you will never get in a position to observe directly what you need to observe.
>
> **A:** You are absolutely correct. Kathy was not a good observer at the time of the beep, and therefore she is not to be trusted, no matter how skilled my questioning, in her descriptions of this beep. However, and this is a very important "however," Kathy can learn to be a good observer and describer for *tomorrow's* sampling. That is why the following constraint is so important.

Constraint: The exploration of pristine experience has to be iterative. As we sketched in Chapter 3 and will elaborate in Chapter 10, an essential feature of DES is that it is iterative – that each sampling interview involves training the subject to be a better observer on subsequent sampling occasions. Kathy does not yet understand what is a moment of experience. The rest of this interview will aim, relentlessly, at clarifying the moment of experience as best we can (recall from Chapter 3: *Constraint: Relentlessly pursue concrete moments*). However, we have to accept that at the moment of this beep, Kathy did *not* have an adequate grasp of the concept of the moment of experience, and therefore Kathy's description attempts are problematic. Our task today (and yesterday and the day before – it is not always an easy concept for subjects to grasp) is to clarify the moment of experience; if we are successful, tomorrow Kathy will be in a better position to apprehend and then to describe.

> KT[5]: Right at the beep I was like looking at myself in the mirror and more like I was just ... I was like looking at myself in the mirror, putting some lip gloss on, some different shade or something, and then I'm ... I was just like looking at myself in the mirror and like wondering, Would that color look better than the other color? Y'know like ...

Kathy uses the right words ("right at the beep"), but then she advances a sixth potential description of experience:

- Wondering whether that color would look better than the other color

But this is also heavily subjunctified ("more like," "or something," etc.). So I don't think her use of "right at the beep" is to be accepted at face value – she doesn't yet have a solid grasp of the precision necessary to apprehend the moment.

> RTH[6]: And does that mean that you're looking at your lips right at that moment ...?
> KT[7]: I was looking in the mirror.
> RTH[8]: ... or at your whole face?
> KT[9]: My face, 'cause I was looking at the color, whether it looked good on my skin tone or not. And I was ...
> RTH[10]: OK. And so, so the hard distinctions (and they are hard distinctions – they are hard for everybody, not just for you – this is ... these are genuinely hard questions for everybody, or almost everybody) ... So are you more just paying attention to the color? [Kathy nods affirmatively] Or are you thinking? Is this more like a thought process? Or more like a perceptual process?

Constraint: Maintain a level playing field. Just as we press relentlessly (but gently) toward the moment, we have to press relentlessly (but gently) toward experience until Kathy gains the skills necessary to describe it faithfully. But that pressure can't be in one direction or another; that is, I try to keep the playing field level. Here, I indicate that I would be equally accepting of Kathy's experience being primarily either a thought process or a perceptual process (and by implication any other kind of experience).

> KT[11]: Prob– ... I would probably think it was more of a perceptual ... Not, not really a thought process. It was more like a perceptual, like, That color lip gloss looked good for my skin tone – why did I even buy it? And so I was like, I don't know why. I was, it was in the evening and I was messing with like ...
> RTH[12]: OK.

KT¹³: … like different lipsticks and stuff, and I was … so I was like percept–
    … perceiving it in different ways, like, the shade, the skin tone.
RTH¹⁴: So the main aspect of your experience, the main content/thrust,
    whatever you want to call it, is the color of the lip gloss …
KT¹⁵: Um hm.
RTH¹⁶: … and the color of your face? Or just the color of the lip gloss?

Constraint: Clarify the details. The art of high fidelity communication
requires attending to the details. DES pushes for details not because the details
themselves are particularly important, but because of the belief that, at least
for most people, experience is specifically detailed, at least to some degree,
and if subjects cannot give details, they probably have not apprehended their
experience.

Experience is usually concretely specific; if we are to submit to the constraints that exploring experience imposes, we have to be concretely specific,
at least until we determine that some particular experience is *not* concretely
specific.

Occasionally, clarifying a detail results in a substantially new and deeper
way of apprehending the phenomenon.

KT¹⁷: Probably more … I was looking at the color of the lip gloss, how it
    looked with the skin tones. I was … I got a little tan, a little bit. So I was
    probably just looking at the color, and how it looks good with my skin. Or
    something. More like that.
RTH¹⁸: OK. And, and so you were noticing the color …
KT¹⁹: Um hm.
RTH²⁰: … and it did look good to you?
KT²¹: Yes.
RTH²²: OK. And is this a new color? Not the color that you usually wear?

This question was intended to clarify what Kathy meant by the KT¹¹ question "Why did I even buy it?" However, it turns out to be a bad question as
evidenced by the fact that it leads Kathy away from the moment of the beep in
the first two sentences of KT²³:

KT²³: No, I usually buy different colors. But usually I use natural colors, so
    I was like … it was … What was going on is I keep getting it on my teeth,
    and I was like messing with it trying not to get it on my teeth, like, lipstick
    and lip gloss, I'm trying not to get it on my teeth, so it looked like, trying
    to fix it so it looks like … so it won't get on my white teeth, and so I was
    more … I was probably focusing more on the lip gloss than I was worried
    about not getting it on my teeth at the same time.

At the beginning of KT²³, Kathy is clearly not describing experience, not
describing the moment of the beep – she is describing what she *usually* does.
Even if her description of what she usually does is correct (and there is reason

to be skeptical of such faux generalities), it is *not* a description of what she actually did on this particular occasion.

Furthermore, Kathy advances a new potential description of inner experience:

* Trying not to get makeup on teeth

However, at the end of KT[23] she backs away from the on-the-teeth worry and gives a description that does sound like experience, that she was focusing on the lip gloss. However, that too is subjunctified ("probably").

> RTH[24]: So at the same time there's a worry about not getting it on your teeth …
> KT[25]: Yes. Because I was … I have a habit of getting it on my teeth.
> RTH[26]: OK. And so there's sort of two things going on? There's the noticing the color and liking …
> KT[27]: Um hm.
> RTH[28]: … something about liking that, that this is a good … a good match with your skin?
> KT[29]: Um hm. Yes.
> RTH[30]: And also a trying not to get it on my teeth, is that right?
> KT[31]: Um hm. Or I try not to put too much on to make it… so it won't go, it won't rub on my teeth. And the other thing is like… 'cause when I do it, it sometimes gets, like, sometimes the skin on it, well, the color would get on, grab on my teeth, and…

Kathy's sentence structure indicates that she is not talking about experience at the moment of the beep. Experience is concretely specific, but she is talking in generalities. "I try not to put much on" is a generality, has the implication of "always," as in "I [always] try not to put much on." If she were describing a specific moment, she would likely say, "I *was trying* not to put much on."

The rest of K[31] is similarly not about a specific moment, but about always, sometimes, or never:

> 'cause [always] when I do it…
> sometimes it gets…
> [whenever] I smile, it gets…

> RTH[32]: Right.
> KT[33]: … and when I smile it's like, Oh my god! And then I kept rubbing it off my teeth, and so it was more … It was more a perceptual thing, but really I was just worried about not getting it on my teeth, 'cause I have a habit.
> RTH[34]: OK. So, right at the very moment of this beep (snaps fingers), are there two things going on with you? One is noticing the color and the other is trying not to get too much of it on?

Note that I don't confront her – that is, I *don't* say something like, "Those are generalities and so couldn't be about experience." Instead, I simply relent-lessly push her toward describing her experience at the moment of the beep.

> KT[35]: At the beep it was more about the color of the lip gloss. It was not … It was more about the color of the lip gloss, not more … It was more about the color of the lip gloss and the skin, rather than the teeth. I wasn't looking at the teeth, but at the moment of the beep it was more the color …
>
> RTH[36]: So the teeth comes after the beep or before the beep …
>
> KT[37]: … and that … Before. Way before.

Beginning at KT[35], that is, six minutes into the interview, Kathy's talk undergoes a dramatic shift. At the same time she begins to identify with con-fidence the moment of the beep (distinguishing clearly between what comes before the beep and what comes at it), she ceases to subjunctify her talk. In fact, as we will see, there is very little subjunctification for the remainder of this interview. She now uses relatively simple declarative sentences: She says quite straightforwardly (without subjunctification), it was the lip gloss, not the teeth. She is no longer equivocating, but instead is speaking quite clearly and definitively.

Experience is concretely specific; Kathy is now speaking concretely specif-ically. I take that as evidence that she is now beginning to describe the actual experience that was ongoing at the moment of the beep. This evidence is not conclusive, of course – there might be many other reasons for the change in language use.

The remainder of the interview is self-explanatory; I present it with-out comment. Note that she continues to talk about the moment with little equivocation.

> RTH[38]: OK. So right (snaps fingers) at the very moment of the beep, if we could just … if we could just take a s–… a flash picture of your experience right then, you were, I'm gathering, looking at the color of your lip gloss …
>
> KT[39]: Yeah. I am … I was putting it on, and then … because at the moment of the beep it was more I was putting it on and looking at myself in the mirror and looking at the color on it, compared to the skin tone …
>
> RTH[40]: OK.
>
> KT[41]: … but the … Yeah.
>
> RTH[42]: OK. So, so what we're finding here is that … What we're doing in these conversations is that we're really narrowing down the time frame, down to just right at the very moment of the beep …
>
> KT[43]: Um hm.
>
> RTH[44]: … and what we're discovering is that the sort of the wondering about how lip gloss works, how makeup works, that might have been a *long* time ago …
>
> KT[45]: Um hm.

RTH[46]: ... and the how ... I gotta keep it off my teeth, that was a *little* bit of ago, but both of those are *ago* ...

KT[47]: Yes.

RTH[48]: ... both of those are in the past.

KT[49]: (emphatically) Yes.

RTH[50]: What I'm gathering right at the moment of the beep is just noticing the color, sort of being absorbed by the color ...

KT[51]: (emphatically) Yes.

RTH[52]: ... and your attention is just going toward the color...

KT[53]: Yes. At the moment of the beep it was more about the color of the lip gloss.

RTH[54]: OK. And is it *more* about the color, right at ... So right at this very moment (snaps fingers), is it mostly about the color of the lip gloss? Or is it about the color of the lip gloss *and* your skin?

KT[55]: It was more about the lip gloss.

RTH[56]: So you're zeroed in. Right at (snaps fingers) that particular moment ...

KT[57]: Yes.

RTH[58]: ... you're zeroed in on the color of the lip gloss.

KT[59]: Yes. 'Cause it was on my lips and I was looking at it. That's, that's ... At the moment of the beep that's what I was doing.

RTH[60]: OK. And you're ... Are you in the act of putting it on at that ...?

KT[61]: Ye– ... No ... I had it on. I had it on before the beep, but then I was looking in the mirror with ... at my lip ... But at the beep I was looking at the color on my lips, not ...

RTH[62]: OK.

KT[63]: At the moment of the beep that's what happened.

RTH[64]: So right at the moment of the beep basically all that's in your awareness is the color of the lip gloss ...

KT[65]: (emphatically) Yes.

RTH[66]: ... is that right?

KT[67]: (emphatically) Correct.

RTH[68]: OK. And all those other things are somewhat before ...

KT[69]: Everything else was right before ... Everything was *way* before the beep (everything I said before was right before the beep). But then at the moment of the beep I was noticing the color of the lip gloss on my lips, and I was focused on the color at the moment of the beep.

RTH[70]: OK. And is there anything else in your experience right at the moment of this beep?

KT[71]: No, no, I was just looking at (inaudible) the color.

Kathy has, since KT[35], dramatically reduced her frequency of subjunctification. I invite you to check this for yourself by comparing Kathy's talk at KT[69] or KT[71] (or any of her talk after KT[35]) with her talk at KT[1]. At KT[1], Kathy's deep structure, the part of her that creates the grammar, that apprehends the connection (or lack thereof) between what she is about to say and the reality that she is trying to describe, was shouting at us (and at herself): *This stuff that I'm about to say is contrary to fact! Or at least only tenuously related to the facts! Or I don't know whether it is related to the facts! I don't know! I'm trying to answer your questions, but it's not right!* Now, at KT^{69} or KT^{71} (or any time after KT^{35}) Kathy's deep, grammar-creating structure is telling us that she is now connected to her experience.

The subjunctifications at KT^1 are *not* the result of Kathy's logical analysis of what she has just said – they are pre-logical qualifications of what she *is about to say*. They diminish the truth value of her *upcoming* utterance. That is, they are evidence that Kathy is *in touch with the truth*, is trying to utter the truth, is recognizing that she is unable to utter the truth but feels compelled to utter something anyway. Kathy is, down to her grammatical core, *connected* to the truth – she just doesn't know how to get to it cleanly, to put it into words properly, to communicate effectively about it. This makes Kathy distinctly different from Frankfurt's Pascal, whose "fault is not that she fails to get things right, but that she is not even trying" (Frankfurt, 2005, p. 32). Thus in Frankfurt's terms, Pascal was bullshitting Wittgenstein; Kathy was not bullshitting me in KT^1. Kathy was trying to describe her experience; she was simply incapable of it.

However, something dramatic happened at K^{35}, something that had a deep impact on her, transforming not merely the content of her talk but her way of talking – its very grammar – something that altered her pre-logical apprehension of what she was about to say.

This is what I think happened. Kathy grasped at KT^{35}, for the first time, the concept of the *moment*, and that new grasp unlocked, for the first time, her ability to describe experience. Or, equivalently, Kathy grasped the concept of experience, and that unlocked her ability to describe a moment. It is simple: Experience exists only in moments, but Kathy, like most people – including most psychologists and philosophers – had not grasped that simple truth adequately. So in KT^1, instead of describing experience (which was impossible for her because she had not differentiated the importance of the moment), she was describing some generalities about herself, or some theories about herself, or some glosses of herself, or some self-presentations, or some partial truths about her general condition – I don't really know what she was doing *and neither did she*, except that she knew, down deep in her grammatical soul, that what she was about to say wasn't true, wasn't right, didn't fit. She didn't, at KT^1, know what to do about that, didn't have the skill to make her upcoming utterance conform to her apprehension of her experience; so she signaled, in an inchoate but loud and clear way, that what she was saying was not to be understood as being true.

Then, for six minutes (on top of the two previous hours) I struggled in the best way I knew how to help her grasp that I wanted us to be talking about a *moment of her experience*, a brief, specific, concrete, not necessarily particularly important occurrence of her experience. I conveyed to her that I was relentlessly interested in what happened in her experience at the moment of the beep, no interpretation, no self-presentation, no gloss – just the momentary experience. She finally grasped that at KT^{35}, with dramatic effect on her prelogical, grammatical soul: After KT^{35}, what she was about to say seemed right, seemed to conform to her experience as she apprehended it, as evidenced by the fact that her need to subjunctify fell away.

> **Q:** I don't buy this moment stuff. I think you badgered her, and badgered her some more, and at KT^{35} she finally gave in. You exhausted her. *That's* what changed her way of talking.
> **A:** You might be right. I don't think there is any analytic way of rebutting your contention except to say that this is your first look at subjunctification; we will discuss it in more detail in Chapter 8. Also, I would note that if you asked Kathy and the other subjects who have participated, they would tell you they didn't feel badgered. I urge you to keep both your point of view and mine in mind as you read the remainder of the book. Perhaps you will feel your faith in noticing subjunctification grow.
>
> Let me remind you that your previous objection was that I made too much of the word *like*; I called *like* a subjunctifier when you held it to be merely an ornament. I asked you to keep an open mind, that perhaps there would be evidence. Now we have some evidence. Before K^{35}, Kathy utters a total of 641 words and uses the word *like* 40 times – every sixteenth word is *like*. Beginning at K^{35}, Kathy utters 288 words and *not a single time* uses the word *like*! I take that as evidence that *like* is *not* a meaningless ornament for Kathy, that *like* is connected to her subjunctifying process.
>
> I don't mean to imply that *like* is a subjunctifier for all people all the time. I can say with confidence that *like* is a subjunctifier for many DES subjects, and the evidence makes it likely that it is so for Kathy.

> **Q:** But even if I accept that something changed at KT^{35}, I still don't think it is because she "got to the moment." You asked her question after question; you polluted the well; she could not reasonably be expected to get to her pristine experience after such an onslaught.
> **A:** I agree. The longer an interview drags on, the more "pollution" is created (or at least likely created) by the interviewer. So I think it is entirely reasonable to be skeptical of Kathy's account here. But that doesn't damn the method: *tomorrow* Kathy will be more skilled at identifying the moment, more skilled at apprehending her experience; *tomorrow's* interview about that experience will be more efficient, shorter, less polluting. That's an application of the constraint (discussed earlier) that an exploration of experience must be iterative (see Chapter 10).

Thus, in my view, it took six minutes into the third interview (several hours of interviewing in total) before Kathy grasped the concept of the moment;

when she got to the moment of the beep (as I see it), she maintained that her experience at the moment of the beep was of seeing the color of the lip gloss – only that, nothing else. Note that seeing the color of the lip gloss was *not* among the previous (prior to KT[35]) attempts at characterizing her experience, which, as you may recall, were:

- Wondering which looks best
- Wondering how makeup makes someone look better
- Wondering what's so special about makeup
- Curiously messing with makeup
- Trying to make her makeup work
- Wondering whether that color would look better than the other color

What should we make of that?

There are at least two possibilities. First, she was in fact, at the moment of the beep, zeroed in on the color of the lip gloss with nothing else in experience. If that is true, then that is a classic example of what DES calls sensory awareness. As we will see in Chapter 16, it is often, perhaps usually, the case that when DES subjects experience frequent sensory awareness, it takes several sampling days for that phenomenon to emerge, apparently because those subjects (a) don't know that they experience that phenomenon and/or (b) pre-suppositionally believe that such a phenomenon is not part of experience.

The other possibility is that Kathy was not, when the beep sounded, zeroed in on the color of the lip gloss with nothing else in experience – that is, her final report is mistaken, perhaps because I had badgered her. I think that is unlikely, because even if I had badgered her, why would she have chosen a strange thing like sensory awareness as a story to cling to? Any one of her previous alternatives would have been an easier, less controversial characterization of her experience.

However, I fully accept that I don't know whether Kathy was or was not zeroed in on the color of the lip gloss when the beep sounded, and in an important way, I don't really care. I accept that, when this beep sounded, Kathy was *not* a good observer of her experience – she didn't really become adequately sensitive to the definition of the moment *until KT[35] in this interview*, and that took place some number of hours after the actual experience. If you don't know what a moment is, you cannot adequately apprehend experience. So this interview should be thought of primarily as training to help Kathy become a better observer on subsequent sampling days, *not* as a data-gathering exercise. Tomorrow (or whenever Kathy wears the DES beeper next), she will likely be substantially more knowledgeable about the importance of attending precisely to the moment and substantially more skilled at doing so. This is an example of what we call the iterative training nature of DES, to which we will return in Chapter 10.

Constraint: Getting to the experience at the moment can be quite difficult.
Either way, most, if not all, of what Kathy said about her experience prior to
KT[35] was not true. (Maybe what she said about her experience after KT[35] was
also not true, but that's a different matter.) Kathy is more or less typical of other
subjects in the time it takes to get to the moment of the beep – we haven't collected systematic data on this, but my impression is that only a few subjects
get adequately to the moment on the first sampling day; the majority get to the
moment on the second sampling day, some, like Kathy, get there on the third
sampling day, and a few never get there.

I have been training people to conduct DES interviews for quite some
time, and I can say with assurance that one of the major difficulties that novice DES investigators face is accepting the rigors of getting to the moment of
the beep. I tell them repeatedly, "You *have* to develop a shared understanding
with your subject of precisely what the moment of the beep is; there is no
sense going forward to inquire about the details of experience until you have
precisely identified the momentary experience to be apprehended." However,
novice investigators, as well as subjects, have great difficulty with that.

To recapitulate: If you're genuinely interested in experience, then you
(paraphrasing Frankfurt) genuinely have to submit to the constraints that the
endeavor to provide descriptions of experience impose; one important constraint is that it takes time (often a *lot* of time) and iterative effort to train the
subject to recognize a moment, and until you have recognized the moment,
there is no point in inquiring about experience.

> **Q:** It can't be! The moment is just not that hard a concept! Why could
> people possibly have difficulty reporting on a moment?
> **A:** *Everyone* thinks they know what a moment is! (Well, almost everyone.)
> All my subjects think they know what a moment is. All my interview trainees
> think they know what a moment is. Almost everyone, including most likely
> you, is mistaken in the belief that they grasp the moment. I don't now wish
> to speculate about *why* grasping the moment is so difficult, but I do wish to
> convey, as clearly as possible, *that* it is difficult.
>
> The important corollary is that any study that presumes to inquire about
> moments without adequately (read, *iteratively*) training the concept is
> problematic.

6

Experience in
Tourette's Syndrome

WITH MICHAEL J. KANE

Mike Kane is a cognitive psychologist who studies the dynamic interaction between attention and memory. Mike has Tourette's Syndrome (TS), a disorder characterized by multiple motor tics and at least one vocal tic. His first professional paper, while still a graduate student in psychology, was an introspective case study of his own experience of TS tics. Whereas the tics that characterize TS have typically been thought to be involuntary, Kane's observations and the work of others have suggested that TS tics tend to be compulsory, perhaps emitted in response to a subjective tactile/kinesthetic/sensory experience. Kane observed in himself, as have others, that tics are preceded by premonitory sensations:

> These sensations are not mere precursors to tics; they precipitate tics. ...
> I experience the TS state as one of keen bodily awareness, or a continual consciousness of muscle, joint, and skin sensations. For example when sitting in a chair, I do not lose awareness of the tactile sensation of the seat against my body, nor can I ignore the deeper somatic sensations of what my back and legs feel like.

> The TS state is omnipresent with few exceptions (e.g., during intense concentration or attentional focus, such as in lecturing), but it is not constant in bodily location or intensity. ...

> If a tic is temporarily stopped, its respective bodily location becomes less ignorable. If all tics are suppressed, virtually all of my joints and muscles begin to demand my attention. The TS state heightens to a stiffening feeling, such that my skin feels like a hardened casing and my joints feel as though they are becoming rigid. The intensity rises until it becomes so unpleasant and distracting that tics must be executed (with a compulsion that rivals the scratching of a severe itch). (Kane, 1994, p. 806)

If this description is accurate, it suggests that premonitory urges – sensory experiences – could be at the root of a disorder that, although not common, causes a good bit of suffering.

Kane's account is an attempt to describe his pristine experience – it says, for example, that the bodily/tactile sensations are omnipresent (or nearly so) but that they wax and wane and change bodily location. However, that account was written without the benefit of a systematic exploratory tool such as DES, so it might be biased or distorted by any of the heuristics known to affect memory for complex events.

Furthermore, it had occurred to Mike that his (and other TS patients') experience of this bodily/tactile awareness may be, in large part, much like everyone else's, but that TS patients, for some reason, simply find this awareness aversive. There's no way to answer this given the kinds of data currently available. There is no perfect way of ever answering that question, but DES may provide an across-person perspective that might be illuminating.

Because Mike knew of my interest in sensory awareness, he e-mailed me his TS paper. In response, I asked Mike whether he still experienced the same kind of TS phenomena, and if so, whether he would be interested in exploring his experience with DES. Mike said yes, he did, and that he was interested. However, he had reservations. Here's the e-mail exchange:

> MIKE: I've got strong beliefs about my experiences that, in some ways, I'm also motivated to hold on to, so I'm concerned about my biases corrupting my data. I don't fear that I'll be dishonest, but rather that the confirmation bias will be a big challenge for me to overcome. I may be motivated (consciously or unconsciously) to "look for" or pay particular attention to, any possible sensory-awareness-type experience I have at the moment of the beep. In your terms, I'm not sure how well I'd be able to bracket my own assumptions about my own experience.
>
> RTH: The fact that you recognize the importance thereof is a good first step, perhaps an adequate first step, which, combined with the randomness of the method and my ability to help you along, might be enough to be successful. The only way to tell would be to try it, with no convictions about whether we would be adequate at it. I have a pretty good "nose" for such things, developed over 30 years of trying, so I suspect I'd be able to tell. But one never knows for sure, either looking forward or at the conclusion.

We agreed that I would mail Mike a beeper; Mike would use it in the standard DES way, and I would interview him about his sampled experiences by telephone (and tape record the process). I requested that Mike wear the beeper in typical everyday activities, and Mike did so for three sampling days, each followed by a DES expositional interview with me within twenty-four hours of Mike's collecting the samples. As requested, Mike brought six beeped experiences to each interview. Two of those were unusable, one because it came within a few seconds of the previous beep and one because Mike was not sure he had heard the onset of the beep.

Mike thus produced sixteen usable samples over three sampling days. Here's what we found.

SENSORY AWARENESS

By far the most salient characteristic of Mike's experience was sensory awareness, occurring twenty-eight times in sixteen samples (many samples included more than one sensory awareness). As we will discuss in detail in Chapter 16, sensory awareness, as DES defines it, involves being immersed in the experience of a particular sensory aspect of the external or internal environment without particular regard for the instrumental aim or perceptual-objectness. For example, if I'm reaching for the door handle to open the door, that is *not* sensory awareness – I'm perceiving the handle for its instrumental use. By contrast, if I'm noting the particular shiny goldness of the handle, the way the light happens to glisten off the upper right part of it, then that *is* sensory awareness – I'm interested in the shiny goldness for its own sake, not as a means to get the door open.

Many people, probably most, experience sensory awareness only very rarely, but Mike's experience was dominated by it – only one of his sampled moments had no sensory awareness; the rest had at least one and as many as three separate sensory awarenesses. Here are some examples:

> Sample 2.2. Mike is in the act of pouring honey mustard onto his son Ryan's plate. He's watching the flow/shape of the mustard stream – seeing the thick liquid hit the plate, watching the shape of the honey-mustard dollop as it spreads onto the plate. He's also saying aloud, "What d'ya say?!" and he's hearing his voice say that, hearing the sing-song, leading-question-to-a-juvenile characteristic of his voice. This is a hearing experience – he does not experience himself as saying these words (although obviously he is). The experience is entirely of hearing the sounds of the words.

Sample 2.2 involves two separate sensory awarenesses – a seeing of the shape of the honey-mustard dollop and a hearing of the characteristics of his voice. As Chapter 16 will discuss in much more detail, sensory awareness as DES defines it is a particular attention to a sensory aspect. For example, was Mike just watching the honey mustard to determine when he had put enough on Ryan's plate, that would *not* be sensory awareness by the DES definition – the sensations originating in the honey mustard would merely be building blocks heading toward a perception. Instead, Mike is particularly interested in, drawn to, absorbed in the sensory aspect of the honey mustard – focused on the shape of the flow.

> Sample 3.1. Mike is on the way home, walking from his office to the bus stop. There are two or maybe three simultaneous strands of experience ongoing at the moment of the beep:

1. He is visually focused on the pink of a crepe myrtle bloom against the slate-gray of the building behind it. The pink was "popping" at him. The sensation was pink-against-gray, not merely strong pink.

2. He's innerly hearing the chorus from Paul Simon's "Mother and Child Reunion." As best he can tell, it is an accurate re-hearing, just like hearing it on the CD, probably including the accompaniment, but he's focused on the singing, not the accompaniment. However, it's not like an *a cappella* version; it sounds just like the original.

3. (He's not at all sure about this aspect.) It is possible, maybe even probable, that he was innerly talking to himself, or maybe hearing himself talk. The topic, if there was one, was how to explain the beeper earpiece to his neighbor Wesley who sometimes picks him up at the bus stop and gives him a ride home. Mike had the sense that he was just missing catching fragments of a conversation he might have with Wesley, but he "couldn't catch" the words at all.

The pink-against-gray (strand 1) is a sensory awareness, an absorption in the visual aspect of the scene. DES calls the "Mother and Child Reunion" experience (strand 2) an inner hearing. We will discuss inner hearing later. We will also discuss the possibility of an ongoing thought (strand 3).

Of the twenty-eight sensory awarenesses, sixteen were visual (the shape of the honey-mustard dollop and the pink-against-grayness of the crepe myrtle are good examples), and four were auditory (the hearing of the sing-song qualities of his voice as he said "What d'ya say?!" is a good example). That is, twenty of the twenty-eight sensory awarenesses were not of his own body.

Prior to sampling, Mike had no understanding at all of himself as being visually/auditorially focused on the sensory aspects of the external world. This focus on the sensory rather than on the meaning was striking. For example, at one sample he is focused on the redness of the "marks" on the whiteboard. The "marks" are words, but Mike's interest is so focused on the redness that the "wordness" doesn't even register.

BODILY SENSORY AWARENESS

Eight of Mike's sensory awarenesses were bodily. For example:

Sample 3.4. Mike is at home holding his daughter Emily. There are three or possibly four simultaneous strands of experience:

1. He is seeing her face and hair in profile – she's looking to the right. He's focused in on the visual aspects of her face and hair.

2. He is feeling a burp in his throat and chest – the air moving through. (He presumes the air escapes through his nose, but he's not aware of that.)

3. He is feeling tension – a pulling feeling – in the left side of his neck. He's craning his neck, but he's not so much aware of the craning as of the pulling feeling.

4. He has a sense that there is a thought about something, but he has no idea about what.

Strand 1 is a visual sensory awareness as discussed previously. Strands 2 and 3 are two separate bodily sensory awarenesses. Strand 4, like strand 3 in sample 3.1, involves the experience of "just missing" some aspect of experience; we'll discuss that later.

Of the eight bodily sensory awarenesses, three were questionable in the sense that Mike was not really sure whether they were or were not ongoing at the moment of the beep.

This result is far different from Mike's expectations. Recall that Mike's published self-characterization was that he had an omnipresent bodily awareness of muscle, joint, and skin sensations (Kane, 1994, p. 806), a self-understanding that Mike continued to hold at the outset of his sampling participation. Yet that is not at all what the sampling showed. There were indeed some samples (3.4 is an example) where he had the bodily awareness he described in 1994, but they were by no means omnipresent and in fact were of far less salience than other kinds of sensory awareness (e.g., visual, auditory).

THINKING

Prior to sampling, Mike understood himself to be nearly constantly engaged in some kind of thinking. As it happened, there were only two of sixteen samples that unquestionably involved the experience of thinking.

Sample 2.4. Mike is walking toward the laptop, which is in the dining room. There are three strands of his experience:

1. As he approaches the laptop he sees the silhouette of his head and shoulders against the white stripes of the Venetian blinds, all reflected in the screen of the laptop. He is interested in the shape/color/form of the silhouette, more or less as he would be interested in a painting. That is, he doesn't see the laptop; he doesn't see *himself* reflected in the laptop; he sees a "really cool" visually interesting display. (This is an example of a visual sensory awareness.)

2. He is thinking something like "Wow! If the beep goes off now it would be a really cool one!" But there are no words. He's confident he is thinking this. It is not merely that he takes the scene to be cool; more than that, he recognizes himself to be specifically, cognitively regarding the coolness and the potential for reporting it at a beep.

3. He's clearing his throat, feeling it in his throat (not hearing it, for example). (This is an example of a bodily sensory awareness.)

Sample 2.5. Mike is sitting at the computer reading an e-mail from the editor of a paper that Mike had reviewed. There are three strands of experience ongoing:

1. [most dominant] He's innerly hearing the words that he is reading. This is clearly a hearing phenomenon – he doesn't feel himself producing the words. He innerly *hears* them, as if they had been tape recorded and are now being played back. (We will discuss inner hearing later.)
2. [maybe equally dominant to 1] He's thinking a thought that if in words would be something like "Oh! They just gave their identity away!" But this thought is not in words.
3. [and least dominant] He's noticing the shape/visual aspect of the words on the computer screen. He is noticing their shape, and not immediately apprehending their meaning. (This is a visual sensory awareness as described previously.)

The two thought strands in these samples (sample 2.4, strand 2, "Wow! If the beep goes off now it would be a really cool one!" and sample 2.5, strand 2, "Oh! They just gave their identity away!") are probably examples of unsymbolized thinking as will be described in Chapter 15. In unsymbolized thinking, the subject is sure a thought is ongoing, sure about the *about-what* of that thinking, and sure that there are no words, images, or other experienced symbols. That seems to characterize both these two thought strands. As we will see in Chapter 15, it often takes more than two samples for us to become confident that a sample includes unsymbolized thinking.

Mike's sampled experiences are strikingly at odds with his prior-to-sampling self-understanding. There is not much thinking in his experience, despite the fact that prior to sampling he understood himself to be thinking almost all the time.

There were six occasions (as in samples 3.1 and 3.4) where Mike had the impression that there was a thought ongoing but he couldn't grasp it. In all those cases, he had no idea about the content of the thought – there was just some nagging sense that there was something more to his experience, something that seemed to be or must have been a thought.

The fact that Mike did not have much thinking *experience* does not in the slightest imply that there is not much thinking *process* ongoing. Our DES investigation of Mike (and all other DES investigations) are only of experience, *not* of underlying thought processes. We can say with some confidence that Mike experienced very little thinking; we cannot say anything whatsoever about Mike's ongoing thought processes.

THE HAPPENING OF SPEAKING/INNER HEARING

On two occasions (of sixteen), Mike was hearing his own voice. We've encountered one of them already. In sample 2.2, Mike was saying aloud to his son, "What d'ya say?!" and hearing his own voice say that, hearing the sing-song, leading-question-to-a-juvenile characteristic of his voice. Here is the other example:

> Sample 3.5. Mike is holding daughter Emily, and there are two strands of his experience:

> 1. He's looking down on her face, focused on the broadness of her nose. He's mostly seeing her nose, but also her eyelids (she's looking down) and maybe a little of her hair. He's not thinking about the broadness of her nose, just noticing it. Her nose is more like her brother's than his own or his wife's, but he's not thinking that – he's just noticing its shape. (This is an example of visual sensory awareness described earlier.)
> 2. He's hearing himself say aloud, "My nose!" They're playing; Emily has grabbed his nose and said "I've got your nose!" and he's responding playfully. He hears his voice say "My nose!" The phenomenon is much more the hearing of it than the saying of it.

In both those examples, Mike's experience of his voice is as being the *recipient*, not the creator, of it. That is, Mike's experience of his own words is very similar to the experience of hearing someone else's words – as if they were created outside of his control and come to him.

This is, in my experience, a fairly rare phenomenon, which I have called the "happening of speaking" (Hurlburt, 1993a). Most people with whom we have sampled experience themselves as being the driver or creator of their own speech. (That does *not* imply that they have some prior experience of the words that they will say before they say them; it does imply that they directly grasp themselves as the doers of the words being said.) This is a very distinct phenomenon for most people, as illustrated by this experiment: Imagine yourself speaking into a tape recorder; now imagine yourself hearing the recording of what you just spoke. For most people, the speaking and the hearing are dramatically different experiences. Mike's experience at these samples is more like hearing than of speaking.

The same phenomenon applied to his imaginary voice. For example, at sample 2.5, Mike is reading an e-mail and innerly hearing the words that he is reading. This is clearly a hearing phenomenon – he doesn't feel himself producing the words. For most people, inner speaking has the same sense of driving/producing that external speech has.

Combining inner and outer, there were seven examples of this sense of hearing rather than speaking. Prior to sampling, Mike had no explicit view of this one way or the other, but he found it surprising when we discovered it during sampling.

NOT DOING

Mike's samples contain very few experiences in which Mike experiences himself as the doer, the driver, the author of his experience – he is nearly always the receiver of his experience. The happening of speaking that we just discussed is one example of this. Instead of experiencing himself as speaking (an active, doing experience), Mike experiences himself as hearing himself speak (a receptive, non-doing experience). Here are additional examples:

> Sample 1.6. Mike is feeling his teeth being pressed against by his tongue (he is *not* experiencing himself as pressing his tongue against his teeth, even though he is of course doing that).

> Sample 2.2. He is seeing the honey-mustard dollop spread (he is *not* experiencing himself as pouring the honey mustard, even though he is of course doing that).

> Sample 3.4. He is feeling the stretching of his neck (he is *not* experiencing himself as craning his neck, even though that is what is causing the stretching).

He has only one sample in which he experiences himself as being the doer of some aspect of his experience: In sample 2.4, described earlier, Mike is thinking something that if expressed in words (which it was not) would be "Wow! If the beep goes off now it would be a really cool one!" That thought seems to come *from him*, not *to him*; he experiences himself as being the creator of that thought.

There are two additional samples in which he had an experience about which he was not confident, not sure. In samples 3.2 and 3.3, Mike *may* have been seeing a visual image, and if so, these images would have been experienced as being of his own creation.

The scientific literature does not include any exploration (or notice) of this doing/non-doing phenomenon (see Hurlburt & Raymond, 2011). It is my is my impression that doing is by far the more common among the hundreds of people with whom I have sampled. However, whether that is cultural artifact (most of my subjects have been American or European) is unknown.

DISCUSSION

After the last day of sampling, Mike and I had a conversation about the characteristics of Mike's samples of experience, more or less as is written previously. Mike expressed his opinion that I had characterized with high fidelity what he had said about his experiences. Further, Mike believed that what he had said about his experiences was a high fidelity apprehension of the experiences themselves.

There were three aspects of his sampling experiences that were especially surprising to Mike. First, he was surprised at the high frequency of visual and auditory sensory awarenesses. He apparently had never thought about such experiences at all, apparently for the same reason that one never thinks about oxygen – it is so ubiquitous that it is entirely taken for granted. He was amazed when I told him that some people (most, in fact) do not have frequent sensory awareness. Recall our discussion of Jessica's paradox in Chapter 2.

There is a powerful lesson to be learned here about psychology. When I describe sensory awareness to psychologists, most are surprised by the possibility that it exists in high frequency for some people. By distinct contrast, Mike (a highly competent, highly knowledgeable, and highly regarded psychologist) was surprised by the possibility that sensory awareness *does not exist at all* for some people. That some psychologists could think that the base rate of sensory awareness is close to 0 percent whereas others could think that it is close to 100 percent shows how little psychology knows about inner experience.

Second, Mike was surprised by his low frequency of bodily sensory awareness. His belief prior to sampling was that he had bodily sensory awarenesses nearly *all* the time; in fact, he had such experiences about one-third of the time (six of sixteen). Much of his understanding of TS hinges on his understanding of bodily sensory awareness, so his misapprehension of the frequency of his own bodily experiences may indicate that he misunderstands its significance for TS. On the other hand, Mike's six-of-sixteen frequency of bodily sensory awareness is quite high compared to those without TS with whom I have sampled, so bodily sensory awareness may indeed be important to TS. Further still, I have sampled with a few without TS who have as high or higher frequency of bodily sensory awareness as does Mike.

Third, Mike was surprised at how little cognition appeared in his experience; in particular, he was surprised how little inner speech occurred. He had understood himself to be more or less constantly engaged in some explicit, usually innerly spoken, kind of thought process, when almost none appeared in his samples.

There may be a powerful lesson to be learned here about TS, mostly that there's lots of interesting work yet to be done. Are Mike's patterns of experience typical of all, many, some, or no other TS patients? We don't know. And if they are, we don't know whether the experience pattern causes TS, TS causes the experience pattern, or whether both are caused by some third thing (gene sequence, for example). And if we knew that, we don't know whether the experience pattern could be altered, and if it were, whether that would alter the tic frequency, and if it did, whether that would be a good thing.

Mike found the sampling task somewhat difficult (Kane, 2011), was particularly worried that the beep disturbed his experience and therefore that his reports did not faithfully apprehend pristine experience. What should we make of that? Here are three possibilities: (a) Maybe the failure of Mike's sampling to confirm his presuppositions about his experience leads to skepticism about the DES method; (b) maybe consciousness scientists, including Mike, are particularly careful observers who recognize difficulties that non-scientists overlook – some other consciousness scientists who undergo DES have had similar reactions to Mike's (see Chapter 12); (c) maybe TS patients, including Mike, have difficulty apprehending their experience. That such disparate interpretations all seem reasonable indicates that consciousness science is in its infancy.

Mike Kane comments: So, I'm left to wonder: Have I apprehended these sampled moments accurately? If so, then one way I may come to understand myself is that I do have these "thoughty" and "speechy" moments, but they don't happen all that often and they tend to revolve around work; so when I'm not actively thinking about weighty work stuff, I tend not to have them. Another possibility is that I have these thoughts more frequently than we picked up in our sampling, but that the beep/DES procedure got in the way of my apprehending them on the wing. Although I'm entertaining the latter possibility, I'm leaning toward the former – that I sometimes have these thoughty/speechy experiences but much less frequently than I'd previously believed. Of course, it would probably take more sampling to get to the bottom of things.

Constraint: It's risky to pre-define the phenomena that will emerge from an investigation. Prior to sampling, Mike characterized himself as a "thoughty" person, and it might have been tempting to launch an investigation of the characteristics of his thinking. Such an investigation would likely create faux descriptions of thinking and would likely overlook the dominant characteristics of Mike's actual experience (sensory awareness).

7

The Moment (*Not*):
Happy and Sad

This chapter examines the co-determination of moments ↔ experience ↔ genuinely submitting to the constraints from the perspective of highlighting what is *not* a moment. Most of psychological science does not appreciate the inherent difficulty of recognizing the moment and therefore (as implied by the co-determination) does not appreciate the difficulty of recognizing experience.

CAN PEOPLE FEEL HAPPY AND SAD AT THE SAME TIME?

We begin by examining a study by Larsen, McGraw, and Cacioppo (2001) called "Can people feel happy and sad at the same time?" I choose this example because it is a well-done study by orthodox psychology standards, and because it deals with moments *more carefully* than do most orthodox psychology studies. However, I will show that despite this care, Larsen, McGraw, & Cacioppo (2001) do not define moments carefully enough to be considered to be genuinely submitting to the constraints that the study of moments of pristine experience requires.

My critique is aimed at orthodox psychology in general, *not* at Larsen and his colleagues (2001) in particular. My logic is: The Larsen et al. paper is an exemplar of very good orthodox psychology; that paper does not define moments carefully enough; therefore orthodox psychology's treatment of moments is not adequate for the genuine exploration of pristine experience.

Our concern is the way moments are used by Larsen, McGraw, and Cacioppo (2001). They wished to know whether people could experience happiness and sadness at the same time, and they investigated that by trying to identify a place or situation in which happiness and sadness might be expected to co-occur. They settled on the lobby of a movie theater where the film *Life is Beautiful* is playing. That 1997 film is set in a World War II concentration camp where Guido, a Jewish-Italian father, and his five-year-old son Joshua are interned. Guido uses his fertile imagination in often comic attempts to keep Joshua alive and blissfully ignorant of the true nature of the camp. For example, Guido tells Joshua that they are playing a game: The first player to one thousand points wins a tank. Joshua can win points by not complaining to the guards about hunger and so on. The film ends with Guido's engineering a way to save Joshua's life but is himself shot dead by a Nazi guard.

Larsen and colleagues reasoned that viewers of such a film might feel both happiness (at the son's survival and the father's resourcefulness) and sadness (at the father's death) at the same time. Here's their method:

> Participants completed a 10-item emotion survey ... as they entered a Columbus, Ohio, theater to see *Life Is Beautiful* or as they left the theater. Oral and written instructions asked participants to indicate how they felt "right now, at this very moment." Participants were then presented with 10 questions intended to measure their current emotional state. Items consisted of five pairs of emotion terms ...: *calm – tense, relaxed – stressed, happy – sad, pleased – displeased,* and *excited – depressed.* In this and all studies, the questions were of the form, "Do you feel happy? _ Yes_ No. If you checked yes, how happy are you?" The scale ranged from 1 to 5. The numbers 1, 3, and 5 were labeled *slightly, moderately,* and *extremely.* (Larsen, McGraw, & Cacioppo, 2001, p. 689)

This instruction to subjects "to indicate how they felt 'right now, at this very moment'" would seem to be entirely consonant with our understanding of the importance of moments. However, our discussion of Kathy in Chapter 5 showed that there is reason to believe that it took several hours of intense interviewing to help Kathy grasp the concept of a moment of experience. If that is true, Larsen and colleagues' one-occasion instruction to subjects to report about "this very moment" cannot be expected adequately to induce subjects to report how they felt at that very moment.

In fact, I think it likely that many if not most of Larsen and colleagues' subjects specifically *excluded* consideration of the actually present moment when responding to the questionnaire. If we really had access to a subject's inner experience, I think it would be something like this: Ah, this pretty girl is giving me this clipboard – I wonder what she wants – I feel a bit turned on by her – But I see my girlfriend looking at me – I sense her disapproval – Oh, this girl's asking how I feel right now, at this very moment – Obviously she's not asking about how I *really* feel right actually now because that would be about being attracted to her and my girlfriend's jealousy – That can't be it! – Ah! She must be asking about *the movie*! – Of course! – Well, I felt happy that Joshua survived the concentration camp, but I felt sad about Guido – I'll check *Yes* to "happy" and *Yes* to "sad" – *that's* what they must mean by "how do I feel right now, at this very moment."

Thus I think a reasonable understanding of this study is that the context of the instruction (people with clipboards in a movie theater lobby) overrules the instruction (how do you feel "right now, at this very moment"). Thus the study can be understood to be *ruling out the very thing that the study seeks to explore*: how people felt at this very moment.

Larsen and colleagues' conclusion reflects the indeterminacy of their moments: "[This] study ... demonstrates that people can feel happy and sad at the same time during a powerful and emotionally complex film" (Larsen et al., 2001, p. 690). If "this very moment" refers to the instant the subject is responding to the questionnaire, then their study is *not* about what happens *during* the film – that was minutes or hours ago – so their conclusion is unwarranted. If "this very moment" refers to what happened *during the film*, then despite the "this very" modification, the moment's duration is of the order of hours.

This highlights the co-determination of moments ↔ experience ↔ genuinely submitting to the constraints. Had they been less ambiguous about what they meant by "this very moment," they would have had to submit to the constraints that specifying the moment imposes, and vice versa.

If moments are ambiguous, then moments ↔ experience implies that what Larsen and colleagues and their subjects meant by "feeling" must be ambiguous. "Feeling" is often used in the emotion literature to refer to the *experience* of emotion. It is widely accepted that feeling is only one aspect of emotion; that it is possible to be in an emotional state without experiencing that emotion. (DES agrees with that, and uses the word "feeling" to refer to emotion *experience*.) For example, it is possible at some particular moment to *be* sad but not to *feel* sad (perhaps because you are distracted by some extraneous event).

But sometimes "feeling" is broadly used to refer to the emotion state itself. Those two uses of "feeling" are very different – one refers to an experience and the other to a state.

However, I think that it is not possible to keep those two meanings distinct unless the moment is adequately specified. Because Larsen and colleagues' subjects were ambiguous about the moment, they must have been ambiguous about whether "how they felt 'right now, at this very moment'" referred to some presumed emotion *state* or to a directly apprehended emotion *experience*.

As a result, during the movie, one subject might now experience sadness, now experience happiness (while the sad *state* continues outside of experience), now experience sadness (while the happy *state* continues outside of experience), now experience happiness (while the sad *state* continues outside of experience), and because of the indeterminacy of the "moment" characterize his experience as "happy and sad at the same time." Another subject, during the movie, might now experience sadness, now experience happiness, and now experience happiness and sadness at the same time, and because of the indeterminacy of the "moment" characterize her experience as "happy and sad at the same time." I don't think the Larsen' et al. method can distinguish between those two importantly different kinds of experience.

Therefore I don't think the Larsen et al. study can distinguish among (a) happy and sad states existing at the same time, (b) happy and sad experiences existing at the same time, (c) happy and sad states occurring in close proximity but not at the same time, (d) happy and sad experiences occurring in close proximity but not at the same time, or (e) some combination of those.

In fact, I believe that it is possible actually to experience happiness and sadness at the same time – the bulimic women that we described in Chapter 2 occasionally do that – so I'm not at all opposed to Larsen and colleagues' view. However, I don't think their study demonstrated what they said they demonstrated, primarily because they didn't develop with sufficient care their subjects' (and perhaps their own) sense of the moment (or of experience).

I do think that it would be possible to conduct a variant of Larsen and colleague's study that could investigate whether the *feelings* (that is, the emotion experience) of happiness and sadness can occur simultaneously: Train a group of subjects in the standard DES procedure in their daily lives; that likely would take three to five sampling days with an hour expositional interview for each sampling day, iteratively building their skills until they become adequately skilled at apprehending experience at the moment of the beep. Then arrange that they see *Life Is Beautiful*; and arrange that some beeps occur at specified times during that film. Ask about those beeps the standard DES question: *What was ongoing in your experience at the moment of the beep?* Do *not* ask them particularly about their *emotion*; if they happened to be experiencing emotion at the moment of the beep, then they will naturally describe it as part of the discussion of the beeped moments of experience. In that way you could *discover* whether feelings are experienced in such situations, and you could *discover* whether those feelings include seemingly conflicting simultaneous feelings. Such a study is obviously substantially more difficult to conduct: You have to invest substantial time in the training of individuals so that they will be ready to observe what you want to observe. "Substantially more difficult" does not mean "impossible"; it's just a matter of resource allocation. It seems to me that is what is required if one is genuinely to submit to the constraints that the exploration of experience imposes.

I repeat that my critique is not aimed specifically at the Larsen et al. study. That study is *more* careful about moments than are nearly all orthodox psychological studies, but not careful enough to apprehend experience, so I conclude that orthodox psychology does not genuinely submit to the constraints that identifying the moment requires and therefore cannot apprehend pristine experience in high fidelity.

STERN'S PRESENT MOMENT

Daniel Stern's *The Present Moment in Psychotherapy and Everyday Life* (2004) is evidently driven by much the same interests as drive the book that you are holding. Here is the opening paragraph:

> The idea of a present moment is put forward to deal with the problem of "now." It is remarkable how little we know about experience that is happening right now. This relative ignorance is especially strange in light of the following:
>
> First, we are subjectively alive and conscious only *now*. *Now* is when we directly live our lives. Everything else is once or twice removed. The only time of raw subjective reality, of phenomenal experience, is the present moment. (Stern, 2004, p. 3)

That could equally well serve as the opening paragraph of *Apprehending Pristine Inner Experience*. Further, *The Present Moment* recognizes, as does the present book, that the examination of the present moment must aim directly at the phenomena that are apprehended:

> The conception of the present moment relies heavily on a phenomenologic perspective. Phenomenology is the study of things as they appear to consciousness, as they seem when they are in mind. This includes: perceptions, sensations, feelings, memories, dreams, phantasies, expectations, ideas – whatever occupies the mental stage. Phenomenology is not concerned with how these things were formed by or popped into the mind. It also avoids any attempt to explore the external reality that may correspond to what is in mind. It concerns only the appearance of things as they present or show themselves to our experience. It is about the mental landscape we see and are in at any given moment. (Stern, 2004, p. 8)

Further, *The Present Moment* recognizes, as does this book, that there are methodological challenges in reaching the *now*:

> There is, however, a large question. The present moment, while lived, can not be seized by language which (re?)constitutes it after the act. How different is the linguistic version from the originally lived one? At this point, even the neurosciences can make only limited suggestions. In spite of this, the book is largely about the unreachable present moment. Such a lived experience must exist. It is the experiential referent that language builds upon. It is the ungraspable happening of our reality. So it must be explored, as best we can, to better think about it and devise therapeutic approaches. (Stern, 2004, pp. 8–9)

I agree with nearly everything Stern has written so far. However, he then advances a method, the "micro-analytic interview" (originally called the "breakfast interview") to explore present moments, and it is here that Stern and

I part company, because the micro-analytic interview method, in my view, is far too retrospective and far too open to the imposition of plausible speculations to produce observations that are robust enough to ground a science of experience. (They may well be adequate to facilitate other endeavors – psychotherapy, for example; I take no position on that.)

Stern describes the micro-analytic interview as follows:

> I ask individuals, "What did you experience this morning at breakfast?" (I ask several hours after breakfast is over.) They usually answer, "Well, nothing, really." I pursue it until they recall something. I am looking for any happening that has a clear beginning and end (good boundaries). This is an example of what they might recall: "Well, I remember picking up the teapot to pour my tea. Actually, I don't remember picking it up, but I must have done that. Anyway, while I was pouring, I had a memory of something that happened last night. Just then, the telephone rang and I became conscious of pouring the tea because I wondered if, I should finishing [sic] pouring to the top of the cup or put the teapot down and get the phone. I put the pot down, got up, and answered the phone." (All this took about five seconds.)
>
> I then conduct an interview about what was experienced in that five seconds. ... I ask what they did, thought, felt, saw, heard, what position their body was in, when it shifted, whether they positioned themselves as an actor or an observer to the action, or somewhere in between. I ask them to make a movie of their experience as if we could make a montage of what was on their mental stage. They are the director and I am the cameraman. They have to tell me what to do with the camera. Is this shot a closeup or a distance shot? How am I to cut from one scene to the next? Where is the camera and its angle relative to the action? In other words, I ask about anything I can think of to capture their subjective experience most fully. (Stern, 2004, pp. 9–10)

I don't think people can be relied on to recall accurately such details of an event (a) that took place hours ago; (b) that they had no special skill or training to observe; and (c) about which they were not prepared to observe or even particularly interested in when it occurred. Therefore, I think the result of a breakfast interview will be some combination of experiences that actually happened at breakfast, some omissions of experiences that actually happened at that time, and some insertions of "experiences" that didn't actually happen at all, strung together under the influence of self-presentation pressures in an impure amalgam of speculations about what might plausibly have happened at breakfast.

Stern himself understands this; I insert superscripts so that we can discuss this sentence by sentence:

> It must be noted that the present moments ... are not *original* present moments[1]. Rather, they are the told recollections of moments that were,

earlier in the morning, actually lived present moments[2]. Obviously,
we cannot get a verbal account of experience as it is happening without interrupting the experience[3]. The goal is to draw a picture of what a
present moment is probably like[4]. (Stern, 2004, p. 11)

1. I agree. It seems that Stern's "*original* present moments" are what we are
   calling pristine experiences.
2. I think this sentence assumes what is very much at issue. I don't think
   Stern's present moments can be assumed to be "told recollections of
   moments that were ... actually lived." They are, I think, told *stories* about
   something that may or may not have been an actual lived moment. I accept
   that the stories are *intended* to be accounts of an actual lived moment, but
   it is one thing to intend to recall and quite another actually to recall. In
   some situations those things are pretty similar; in others, very different.

   Q: Surely, the intended recall has some connection to what actually
   happened. People don't just confabulate.
   A: I agree that the intended recall *may* have some relation to what happened.
   But maybe not. The lesson we learned from the bulimic women in Chapter 2
   and from Mike Kane in Chapter 6 is that people's reports of experience can be
   quite discrepant from actual experience. Furthermore, even if there probably is
   some (perhaps vague) relation to what really happened, that is hardly satisfying
   from a scientific point of view. We can and should do better than that. See
   Hurlburt and Akhter (2006) for a similar but more detailed discussion.
       Furthermore, the eyewitness testimony literature and the false memory
   literature demonstrate the unreliability of recollections (Schwitzgebel, in
   Hurlburt & Schwitzgebel, 2007, chapter 10).

3. I agree. That's why I think it is necessary, if one is genuinely to submit to
   the constraints that the exploration of experience imposes, to interrupt
   the experience.
4. If Stern were to replace the word "probably" with "plausibly," and so state
   that "the goal is to draw a picture of what a present moment is *plausibly* like," then I would agree with this statement. However, this is a very
   important difference, to which we now turn.

PLAUSIBILITY

"Probably" implies a direct connection to the truth; by distinct contrast,
"plausibly" has no direct connection to the truth. When you say, "This is probably how the victim's blood got on the floor of the defendant's automobile," you
are stating your belief that your account is likely true, but you are acknowledging
that there is some doubt. However, when you say, "The defendant gave a *plausible* account of how the victim's blood came to be on the floor of his automobile,"

you are specifically *avoiding assessing the truthfulness* of the story – you are underscoring that the defendant's account is merely a story. It may of course be true, but you are specifically denying having any knowledge about its truth.

Constraint: The plausible is the enemy of the truth. When you say an event is probable, you define the possible outcomes (either it happened or it didn't happen) and throw your support behind one of those outcomes (it happened). When you say an event is plausible, you explicitly *decline* to define the possible outcomes (you imply that there are a whole range of possibilities) and you *decline* to support any of them – you merely observe that the story you have presented aligns with the facts in some way.

I think Stern's breakfast table accounts are plausible stories: They may of course be true, but we should specifically deny any knowledge about whether they are true. They are *not* probably true. As our bulimia and Kane examples demonstrate, they are also probably *not true* in important ways. Stern, by contrast, apparently believes his breakfast table observations are probably true (in sentence 4 and throughout his book). That is a hugely important distinction in my view, roughly the same as between Colbert's truthiness and truth (recall Chapter 1). Stern's breakfast table observations have a certain truthiness to them, but that does *not* make them probably true.

Recall from Chapter 1 that because liars are connected to the truth whereas bullshitters are disconnected, Frankfurt concludes that "bullshit is a greater enemy of the truth than lies are" (Frankfurt, 2005, p 61). The same can be said about plausibility, for exactly the same reason plus this important additional one: Plausibility is currently acceptable in the science of experience (as the two examples in this chapter show), and therefore plausibility *impedes* attempts to apprehend experience in high fidelity. Plausible accounts seem good enough and therefore sap the intention to advance. Science is justly built on probabilities, not plausibilities, and a science that fails to recognize that cannot in the long run be productive.

I fully accept that Stern's main interest was in psychotherapy. In psychotherapy, blurring the distinction between the probable and the plausible may be unimportant or even desirable. I take no position on that. Stern's breakfast interview seems to be an effective way to bring a plausible account into the here and now of the psychotherapy session. That is a substantial accomplishment, because plausible accounts are typically there and then, and Stern is correct in pointing out that psychotherapy is often at its best when it is brought into the here and now. So I am supportive of the overall thrust of his book. However, if our interests are in attaining not merely plausible but actually faithful accounts of actual in-the-natural-environment experiences, then we should be clear that Stern's micro-analytic "breakfast" interview falls short. The distance between a retrospectively constructed narrative and the actual lived breakfast experience is potentially great.

A PLAUSIBILITY NATURAL EXPERIMENT

Here is a natural experiment that illustrates why distinguishing between plausibility and probability is crucial. It's a single example, to be sure, but it presented itself unbidden while I was writing this chapter. It is quite unusual in its specifics and therefore can be instructive.

Yesterday, May 24, presented me with a little serendipitous opportunity to "relive" experience, more or less the way Stern desires in his breakfast table interviews. Sarah Akhter, a graduate student, asked me to join her in watching a video of one sample from a DES interview that she and I had jointly conducted three weeks earlier, on May 1; that interview was the fifth with an adolescent boy we will call "TJ." Here's a description of the beeped experience in question:

> Sample 5.3. TJ is sitting on his bed with the bottom half of his legs hanging over the wooden footboard. At the moment of the beep he feels a painful burning sensation in the back of his knees, where the footboard is pressing into him. At the same moment, TJ is thinking that he should probably move his legs. The thought is not in words, it is just an idea that has not yet translated into a decision to act. Though the thought is in reference to the burning sensation in the back of his legs, it is somehow disconnected from the sensation, as if the sensation and the thought are abstracted from one another. When they finally do come together, a bit after the beep, TJ takes action and moves his legs off of the footboard.

Sarah wanted to discuss this sample with me because her notes from the interview indicated that I had set aside my usually relentless moment-of-the-beep focus to inquire about what happened *after* the beep; she wanted to know what had led me to depart from my usual procedure. Sarah said it would be useful to know what had been passing through my experience as I had conducted this interview, so that she could come to an understanding about when and why to make exceptions to the moment-of-the-beep focus.

That seemed an eminently reasonable request from a gifted student, and I was strongly motivated to be candid in providing my best recollections of my experience. So as we watched the video, I paused it every few seconds and tried to articulate exactly what had been going on with me at each turn in the interview. I said that I had been imagining what it had been like for me, as a child, to sit on my own bed with my legs hanging over the footboard. I said I currently had my own childhood bed in my garage and could imagine it clearly, and I could feel the rounded top of the footboard pressing against the soft flesh in the back of my knees as my legs draped over it. I said that on May 1 I had been wondering whether TJ's experience was like mine – that I recognized that it might have been the same or might have been different, and was therefore inquiring about it. Furthermore, I said that as I asked the questions about what happened after the beep, I knew I was departing from the DES strategy; that I knew that the answers TJ would give would be more speculative and therefore more deserving of skepticism, but that I was willing to enter into that discussion because it might shed light on TJ's process that would prove useful in some later beep discussion.

This was a nearly ideal situation for reliving an event. Sarah was an excellent student and I was highly motivated to be forthcoming with her. We had a high-quality video of exactly the moment in question. We could watch it, pause it, try to get the relived experience right.

It turned out, as we discovered a few minutes later as we continued to watch the video, that Sarah had had the same curiosity on May 1 during the interview as she had had in reading her notes about it yesterday (May 24), and that she had interrupted the May 1 interview to ask me about the same thought process that we had just discussed. We had both entirely forgotten our May 1 conversation that had occurred during the interview, but that conversation had been captured on the video! That presented a unique opportunity. We now had two descriptions of the same experience, both the result of the same student asking the same question about my same experience: one from May 25 as we watched the video of the interview, one from May 1 during the original interview.

Here's what I had said on May 1 as captured on the video: I had recalled that one of TJ's beeps from an earlier sampling day had involved an event where his mother was talking to him. TJ's experience was that he was only half listening to her, that he hadn't yet "latched onto" the meaning of his mother's words. He had also used the phrase "latched onto" in the description of the knee-burning thought. Given that he used the same phrase in somewhat different situations, I wondered whether "latched onto" had some particular experiential significance for him – whether the use of the same phrase conveyed that the two processes were in some way experientially similar. I therefore relaxed the DES moment-of-the-beep focus and inquired about what happened next; perhaps that would give me a clue about how he understood his experience and therefore what "latched onto" meant to him. I recognized, I said in the May 1 conversation, that my question was non-standard and his answer should be treated with more skepticism.

Thus it turned out that my May 24 "relived" account of my May 1 thought process was almost entirely different from my May 1 account of the same thought process. My May 1 account centered on TJ's twice-used phrase, "latched onto"; by contrast, my May 24 account centered on my own feeling of my own knees on my own childhood bed's footboard. The two accounts were similar only in that both recognized the non-standardness of the interview and the recognition that I would treat TJ's answer with substantial skepticism.

My May 24th relived account was *plausible*: it was coherent, believable, and fit all the facts of the video that we were watching. Yet it was wrong in important ways. (Or at least one of the two accounts was wrong. I don't know for sure which, but it would seem reasonable to give more credence to an account given on May 1, a few minutes after the event and taken in the identical situation and state of the original experience, rather than to an account given May 24, twenty-three days after the event.) It would have been a mistake for me to have told Sarah, on May 24, that my account was *probably* correct – it was only plausibly correct. My May 24 account is *still* plausible, even now when we are confident that it is wrong.

The problem with plausible accounts is that they line up oh-so-intimately with our presuppositions about what must have been experienced. Plausible accounts are created exactly out of our presuppositions. To create and/or accept a plausible account is the antithesis of the bracketing of presuppositions. We will return to the bracketing of presuppositions throughout this book.

DISCUSSION

It is substantially distressing for me to criticize the studies by Larsen and colleagues (2001) and Stern (2004). These studies take experience seriously, placing them among the few that do so, and I obviously think that taking experience seriously is of fundamental importance to understanding the human condition. These studies also recognize the importance of moments, making them the exceptional among the exceptional.

However, I have felt compelled to criticize them anyway because both, as it seems to me, blur the critically important distinction between the plausible and the probable. It is indeed *plausible* that Larsen and colleagues' subjects simultaneously experienced happiness and sadness, but I fear we know little about whether that probably, plausibly, or actually occurred in the theater.

The plausible is a threat because it is so seductive: It sounds so right, feels so right, that it dulls our sensibilities about whether it *is* right. That's why Frankfurt's Wittgenstein was critical of Pascal – not because she was mistaken about her experience, but because she was fundamentally alienated from the attempt to describe that experience *and she didn't recognize her alienation*. I must criticize Larsen and colleagues and Stern not because they are mistaken in their results (I think, as do Larsen et al., that it *is* possible for at least some people to feel happy and sad at the same time), but because they do not, in my view, genuinely submit to the constraints that the attempt to apprehend experience imposes. Stern seems to acknowledge that ("Obviously, we cannot get a verbal account of experience as it is happening without interrupting the experience") but then proceeds anyway. Science is not likely to advance in that manner.

Plausible accounts of experience abound. We must learn to recognize them for what they are; and the science of experience, if it is to advance, must learn to mistrust them.

Notice, by the way, that in this chapter we started out talking about Larsen and colleagues' (and Stern's) failure to be specific about moments; that led us to the conclusion that they could not apprehend experience in high fidelity and also to a consideration about whether they genuinely submitted to the constraints – about the distinction between plausibility and probability. That's what co-determination means: There is no consideration of moments without also consideration of experience and consideration of genuinely submitting to the constraints. In the next chapter, we will start with a focus on genuinely submitting to the constraints, but we will also necessarily deal with moments and experience.

Moment Experience Constraints

8

Subjunctification

Our aim in the present chapter is to deepen our understanding of the constraints that the exploration of experience imposes by highlighting one important methodological thread: subjunctification.

> **Q:** Subjunctification again? Haven't we talked about that enough?
> **A:** I agree that it may seem redundant. However, I think it necessary to turn the screw gradually into such concepts, to build progressively the skills of recognizing and appreciating subjunctification. Skill acquisition does not happen in one shot; the appreciation for subjunctification is the result of repeated contact in a variety of situations. Since we last focused on subjunctification, we have deepened our appreciation of moments and experience; now we're ready for a deeper grasp of subjunctification.
>
> To appreciate experience, you have to appreciate the genuine submission to the constraints that the apprehension of experience imposes. Appreciating subjunctification is an important constraint.

As you will recall, DES asks only one thing of its subjects: to give a straightforward description of experience that was ongoing at the moment of some beep. We call a subjunctifier anything that gives a sign that a subject's utterance is not to be confidently understood as a straightforward description of momentary experience. Subjunctifiers include

- Verb forms in the subjunctive mood (e.g., "I would think," "If I were"). The subjunctive mood grammatically signals that what follows is contrary to fact. "I would think that I was hearing the TV" means "I have no directly recalled experience of hearing the TV."
- Generalities (e.g., "Whenever I X, I experience Y"). As we have seen, experience inheres in the moment; experience is never general. "Whenever I read, I talk to myself" means, or at least might mean, "I have no direct recollection of talking to myself, but I must have been talking to myself." Such "generalities" are often false (DES calls them "faux generalities").

- Theoretical inferences (e.g., "All thinking involves," "I must have been"). "All thinking involves words, and I was thinking, therefore I must have been using words" means "I have no direct recollection of using words."
- Undermining expressions (e.g., "Well," "or something," "like," "I don't know," "maybe," "it could be," "probably," "I think I," "I'm not sure, but," or "I guess"). Those expressions are generally meant literally to undermine confidence in descriptions. "It might be" also means that "it might not be."
- Plausibility indicators (e.g., "Of course"). Plausibility is an enemy of description because it gives the impression that something has already been described or does not need to be described.
- Causal inferences (e.g., "because"). Causation is never, or at least hardly ever, directly observed. Causation is inferred (rightly or wrongly), perhaps from what is observed. The "because" portion of "I was seeing an image because images help me remember" leads *away* from the description of the image to a speculation about the cause of the image.
- Intentional expressions (e.g., "I was trying to," "I was about to"). "I was trying to see an image" means, or at least may mean, "I was not seeing an image."
- Distancing or depersonalization expressions (e.g., "you're feeling," "it is seen"). A straightforward description is always in the first person singular: "I was feeling" or "I saw it." Using the second or the third person may imply that experience is not being described: "When it rains *you* feel depressed" does *not* necessarily mean that *I* felt depressed at some particular moment.
- Metaphors (e.g., "Her voice was a beacon of hope"). There are lots of aspects of "beacons" that might be being invoked, so invoking a metaphor hides, or at best makes ambiguous, a description.
- Procedural discussion (e.g., "Am I supposed to ...?"). A comment or question about the procedure indicates that the subject is not (yet) doing the procedure, that is, is not describing his experience.
- Behavioral indicators (e.g., false starts, groans, shrugs, deer-in-the-headlight stares, quizzical tones, or long pauses). Most often, when subjects apprehend their experience clearly, they simply say something like, "I was seeing Kira and Matty sitting on a log" without hesitation or distress. Any behavioral sign of hesitation or distress is therefore evidence that experience is not being straightforwardly described.

Subjunctifications are *signs* that expressions are not to be taken at face value. That is, subjunctification is evidence, not conclusion. There are lots of reasons that a person might use a theoretical inference, might insert an undermining expression, might show distress, or use some other subjunctifier even while faithfully describing experience. Perhaps the describing causes some embarrassment and the subjunctification has a temporizing function, merely allowing the subject to "catch his breath" before launching into the embarrassing detail. Perhaps the subject clearly apprehends experience but is finding it hard to put into words, so the subjunctification refers to the difficulty of description, not the difficulty of apprehension. Perhaps the subject uses subjunctifying words merely as ornaments.

There is nothing essentially new in the concept of subjunctification. Psychotherapists interviewing clients about sensitive issues recognize the hemming and hawing that precedes the client's revealing a sensitive issue; detectives recognize when a witness is not telling the truth; and so on. However, for reasons we will discuss, subjunctification is particularly noticeable when people try to describe moments of pristine experience.

RECOGNIZING SUBJUNCTIFICATION: KATHY

In Chapter 5 we mentioned that there were many subjunctifications in the first half of Kathy's interview, twenty-one in her first statement alone. Here is that first paragraph with the subjunctifications set in bold face with superscripts:

> KT[1]: When the first beep went off I was looking in the mirror putting some lip gloss on **'cause I was**[1] wondering which was ... looks best with my skin colors, **or something like that**[2]. And **I was just like**[3], when I was looking in the mirror, I was wondering, How is it that ... how does makeup make someone look better? **'Cause I was like**[4] ... **I was like**[5] ... **I don't know**[6], **I was like**[7] looking at my own face in the mirror and **I was like**[8], What is it that's so special about it that makeup makes someone look better? **I was probably just like**[9] messing around in my mind, and **like, like, like**[10] I was thinking, **like**[11] this feeling ... **I was probably just like**[12] curious, curiously **like**[13] messing with my makeup and just trying ... **just like**[14] trying a different style **or something**[15]. And **I was probably more like**[16] trying ... transitioning faces, **like**[17] [inaudible] lips, **like**[18] ... what's ... I **was more like**[19] trying to change my makeup, to make my makeup work, **or something**[20]. That's **more**[21] what I was doing.

All are undermining expressions except 1, which is a causal inference, and 4, which is both a causal inference and an undermining expression. You could quibble about my count; perhaps you would count numbers 9, 12, and 16 as two underminers each (separating the "probably" from the "like"), and the three "likes" in 10 separately, giving you twenty-six subjunctifiers instead of twenty-one. And I haven't counted the pauses and changes of direction (indicated by the ellipses; there are nine of them, bringing the total to thirty-five. No matter how you count, twenty-one, twenty-six, or thirty-five subjunctifiers in 175 words is a lot, one subjunctifier every 8 (or 5!) words.

RECOGNIZING SUBJUNCTIFICATION: DUNCAN SMITH

Here is the opening statement by "Duncan" about the third beep from his first sampling day. Our task, as before, is to recognize the subjunctifiers, which I again set in bold face with superscripts:

> DS: **The third one?**[1] **Let me see what I was**[2] ... Contentment ... I felt contentment, and I was starting to feel a little tired. And while I was doing it I was forming an APA citation for my project. And I felt contentment **probably**[3] **because**[4] I had just learned how to do an APA formation ... citation. **But, yeah, those two were the things that stuck out, definitely.**[5]

1 and 2: "The third one?" and "Let me see what I was" are both procedural comments. I view them as subjunctifiers because they are not simple, straightforward descriptions of his experience at the moment of the beep. The skilled subject, when prompted to describe a beeped experience, simply launches into the description or gives a bit of background so the description is intelligible. Duncan, by contrast, talks about the procedure instead of talking about his experience.

> **Q:** I think this is nit-picking. It is entirely natural for Duncan, a subject on his first sampling day, to inquire about the procedure.
> **A:** I entirely agree. However, our task at this part of the chapter is not to debate the *why* of what Duncan says, but only to notice those occasions in which he is signaling (or may be signaling) that for whatever reason he is not (yet) heading directly toward the description of beeped experience.

3: "Probably" is an undermining expression: Duncan is not aiming directly at some experience.

4: "Because" signals that Duncan is inferring causation, not describing a phenomenon. Duncan was *not* experiencing the learning of APA formation; he was *not* directly *experiencing* the causation between that learning and the contentment he felt. Therefore his talk about causation is not talk about experience.

5. "Those ... things ... stuck out, definitely" is a procedural comment that indicates that he is *not* sure that he knows what he is to describe. If he really were confident, it wouldn't occur to him to prop up his confidence.

A minute later Duncan says what is transcribed at DS[10]. I provide this as an exercise for the reader: Identify the subjunctifiers in DS[10] and determine what kind of subjunctifier each is (that is, choose from among: verb in subjunctive mood, generality, theoretical inference, underminer, plausibility indicator, causality indicator, intentional expression, distancing or depersonalization, metaphor, procedural discussion, or behavioral indicator).

> DS[10]: Well, I felt content because I had just learned how to do an APA formation, and I guess typing makes me feel content and I guess I attach

contentment with level, too. Maybe … I don't think "accomplished" would have been a better word, because I didn't feel very accomplished, I felt very, very just satisfied because I had just learned how to do an APA formation, and I was doing it correctly, in the middle of it while I was … right before the beep went off.… [pause] And there was an underlying feeling of me feeling moderately tired.

By my count there are fourteen subjunctifiers in this paragraph. I list them in Table 8.1 overleaf. Reasonable people can disagree about some of those subjunctifiers – maybe your list included eleven or seventeen. The point is not to be exact about what is or is not a subjunctifier – no matter how one counts, Duncan's talk is heavily subjunctified, about one subjunctifier every nine words.

Q: I still think you're nit-picking. Everyone uses words that could be called subjunctifiers. If Duncan uses more than someone else, it's just his verbal style. **A:** As you may recall, you raised a similar objection in Chapter 5, saying that Kathy's use of *like* was just a meaningless ornament. I noticed that that was an empirical issue; we then noted that Kathy used *like* once every sixteen words in the first half of her interview, but *never* in the second half of the interview. I don't think subjunctifiers are merely style.

The instruction "Report your experience at the moment of the beep" seems so simple that many researchers seem to assume that merely giving the instruction is adequate training. It is not simple, and it requires consistent iterative training, and that training requires the investigator to be sensitive to clues that the subject is or is not describing experience. Recognizing subjunctification is an important cue because the "density of subjunctification" provides real-time evidence. Here's a good rule: The lower the density of subjunctification, the better the description. That rule is like a compass that generally points north. A compass doesn't *always* point north (because it is not level, because there is ferrite in the vicinity, etc.), but it's usually a pretty darn good indicator.

WHY DO PEOPLE SUBJUNCTIFY?

We have noted that subjunctification, whether revealed by the grammatical subjunctive mood, behavioral waverings, or any of the other methods, signals that what follows is contrary to fact. It may seem obvious, but that implies that the person who subjunctifies *must know, in his or her grammar-producing core, at some (perhaps inchoate) level*, that what he or she is about to say, or is in the act of saying, is not true, is misleading, is contrary to fact in some way.

Subjunctification was an issue in the Kathy and Duncan interviews because we had made, repeatedly, skillfully, relentlessly, across several hours of prior interviewing, a clear distinction between what was actually experienced at the moment of the beep and all else. At the outset of their interviews, Kathy and Duncan subjunctify because they grasp, in an as yet inchoate way, that they are not doing what we are asking. They understand, inchoately, that we are asking purely about directly observed, concrete experience but that they are telling us about some impure admixture of not only directly observed experience but also of self-theory, social desirability, self-presentation, projections about what we think is important, psychological knowledge, expectations, background, context, self-protection, habit, sexual interest, and so on. They know, as yet inchoately, that there is a difference between direct apprehension of experience and all the rest, but they do not have the skill of self-observation. Out of this inchoate recognition of the failure to distinguish between the directly observed and all else comes subjunctification. That is, subjunctification is the body/mind/soul's inchoate way of conveying: *I know (in a deep and perhaps still inchoate way) that you want me to describe directly apprehended experience-at-the-moment-of-the-beep; I know (in a deep and perhaps still inchoate way) that there is a huge distinction between experience-at-the moment-of-the-beep and all else; I know (in a deep and perhaps still inchoate way) that I'm not cleaving to experience, not carefully distinguishing between experience and all else; but I don't know how to cleave to experience, don't know for sure what it means to describe experience. So I pepper my utterances with "sort of," "as if," "maybe," or "like"; with behavioral hemmings, hawings, and false starts; and so on as a signal from my grammatical soul that I am not doing what I know I should be doing.* That is, subjunctification reflects the recognition of the fundamental importance of the distinction between the apprehended and the not apprehended in the absence of the skill (or inclination) necessary to be faithful to that distinction.

Subjunctification becomes particularly salient to the extent that *all* these conditions are met: (a) The person understands that there is a clearly defined target (experience at the moment of the beep and nothing else); (b) there are pretty darn right (on-target) and pretty darn wrong (off-target) descriptions about the target experience (either Kathy was wondering which makeup looks better or she wasn't); (c) the person is at least somewhat motivated to hit the target; and (d) the person recognizes (at least inchoately) that she is not hitting the target. If all conditions are met, the person is likely to subjunctify. If any one of those conditions is not met, then there is little or no motivation for the person to subjunctify. All four aspects were present in Kathy at the outset of her interview, so she began the interview with heavy subjunctification; the same was true for Duncan. Halfway through each subject's interview, the knowledge and skill required in (d) dawned on her (Ah! You mean *experience* only and *at the moment of the beep* only!), so she became able to align her utterances with her understanding of the task.

TABLE 8.1. *Subjunctifiers in the DS[10] paragraph*

Count	Subjunctifier	Kind
1	Well	Undermining expression
2	Because	Causal inference
3	I guess	Undermining expression
4	typing makes me feel	Causal inference
5	I guess	Undermining expression
6	I attach	Causal inference
7	maybe	Undermining expression
8	…	Behavioral indicator (false start)
9	I don't think	Undermining expression
10	would	Verb in subjunctive mood
11	because	Causal inference
12	because	Causal inference
13	…	Behavioral indicator (false start)
14	[pause]	Behavioral indicator (pause)

As a result, the motivation to subjunctify disappeared and subjunctification fell away almost completely.

SUBJUNCTIFICATION IS NOT AS IMPORTANT ELSEWHERE

Subjunctification is much more important in DES investigations of experience than in other studies of experience, because DES draws a bright-line distinction between what is directly experienced at a moment and all else. Maintaining this bright-line distinction is rare in studies of experience. In Chapter 7, for example, we saw that Stern (2004) did *not* clearly maintain a bright-line distinction between experience and all else when he inquired about "the present moment" during the breakfast-table interviews. His subjects reported some messy combination of actual experience at the breakfast table and plausible speculation about experience at the breakfast table. If there was no bright-line distinction between actual and plausible experience, then there was no clearly defined target, and therefore there was no motivation for subjects to subjunctify.

Also in Chapter 7 we saw that Larsen and colleagues did *not* clearly maintain the distinction between experience at the moment and all else when they asked their subjects leaving the movie what they were feeling "right now, at this very moment." Larsen and colleagues' subjects may have been talking about feelings at that very moment, states at that very moment, feelings during the movie, states during the movie, the plot of the movie, some messy combination of all or part of those, or about something else. If there was no bright-line distinction between experience and state, and/or no bright-line distinction between now and during the movie, then there was no clearly defined target, and therefore there was no motivation for subjects to subjunctify. Moreover, because their subjects used rating scales (simply checking *slightly*, *moderately*, or *extremely* when asked, "How happy are you?"), there was no *possibility* of subjunctification.

Subjunctification is a highly informative clue to the fidelity of descriptions of experience only when all four of the conditions described previously are met. Most studies do not meet them, so subjunctification is not important. As a result, subjunctification is not a frequent topic in the modern science of experience.

> **Q:** I find your description of subjunctification pretty unbelievable. For Duncan to go from one subjunctifier every nine words to one every fifty-five (or never, depending on how you count) seems like a too-good-to-be-true effect, more dramatic than most anything else in the psychological realm.
> **A:** To be sure, I chose cases (here and in Chapter 5) that made clear the notion of the density of subjunctification. And I don't wish to imply that all subjects go suddenly from a high rate of subjunctification to a low or zero rate when they get to the moment of the beep. Yet many (perhaps most) do, and I'm quite sure the change in the density of subjunctification is often very large, including larger than that discussed here.

APPRECIATING SUBJUNCTIFICATION

DES is a simple task. There is really only one thing to do: to describe the experience that was ongoing at the moment of the beep. When you know what your momentary experience was, or at least what the main characteristics of that experience was, that is indeed a very simple task, and you just provide a description straightaway. However, if you were not attentive to your experience at the moment of the beep, or if you have presuppositions that work against your direct reporting, then the simple task becomes dramatically complex: You have to *guess* what you were experiencing, or you have to *fight* your tendency to theorize, or you have to *try to reconstruct*, or invoke something other than simple direct description. If you know what the task is (which you probably do because it's pretty simple) but you recognize that you're not doing it, then you subjunctify, one way or the other.

When you're driving and you know where you are going and how to get there, you confidently, unhesitatingly make the corners and skillfully make the adjustments that the traffic and the conditions require. However, when you're not sure where you're going, you slow down, you hesitate at intersections, you consult the map, you ask questions, all of which give away the fact that you don't know where you're going. Subjunctification is like that. There's nothing at all magic about it; it's the result of a simple task that either can be done easily or cannot.

Constraint: Appreciate subjunctification. Genuinely attending to subjunctification, and to increases and decreases in its density, is one of the constraints that the exploration of inner experience imposes, for two reasons. First, if the subject's talk is subjunctified, it should not be taken at face value. Such talk is not a straightforward description of experience at the moment of the beep.

Second, attending to the shifts in the density of subjunctification can provide instantaneous and high-quality feedback about the interviewer's technique. If the interviewer asks a question and the density of subjunctification goes up, it was probably a bad question, probably a question that led the subject *away* from experience-at-the-moment-of-the-beep. If the interviewer asks a question and the density of subjunctification goes or stays down, then it was probably a good question. Looked at in this light, acquiring the DES interviewing skill is straightforward: Ask whatever questions lead your subject to less and less subjunctification.

That is, of course, a bit of an oversimplification. Sometimes subjunctification is a good thing. Subjects sometimes subjunctify when they have a clear apprehension of their experience but are struggling to put it into words. Subjunctification in those cases is not a sign of a bad question, but of a good (albeit difficult) question. So as a first approximation to skillful DES technique, trying to reduce subjunctification is a good thing. An even better thing is to recognize when subjunctification indicates estrangement from experience and when it indicates a faithful apprehension of experience but difficulty in describing.

It requires substantial skill to conduct an interview that stays directly in touch with experience at the moment of the beep. Genuinely submitting to the constraints that the endeavor to explore inner experience imposes requires developing that skill. Attending to the shifting density of subjunctification will contribute to that development.

9

Before and After Experience?
Adolescence and Old Age

Recall that in Chapter 2 we explored the pristine experiences of bulimic women; we discovered fragmented multiplicity, multiplicity that increases with the urge to vomit and decreases after vomiting. Those results were unpredicted and provocative, which we took as evidence that carefully examining moments of truth might unlock experience in ways that reveal characteristics of people that are obvious and immediately at hand (the hay in the haystack) but systematically overlooked by almost everyone.

Now, we again focus on the pristine experience portion of the moments ↔ experience ↔ genuinely-submitting-to-the-constraints co-determination by exploring the experience of adolescents and older adults. We will see that we get some perspectives on the development of experience that, as in bulimia, have rarely if ever been noticed.

Our aim here, as in Chapter 2, is to demonstrate the productivity of carefully focusing on experience. I will make a few provocative speculations about the development of experience. I do not intend this chapter to be anything remotely resembling a treatise on developmental psychology. Our samples of younger and older individuals are not as large and not as well replicated as the bulimia studies of Chapter 2. However, we have seen enough to make some provocative suggestions, enough to demonstrate the essentiality of carefully observing experience.

SPECULATION 1: FEELING IS AN ACQUIRED SKILL

We use the term "feelings" in the same way most psychologists (Kagan, 2007) do: to refer to emotion *experience*. Emotion itself covers a broad waterfront

Portions of this chapter are revised with permission from Akhter, S. A. (2007). *Exploring adolescent inner experience.* Unpublished Master's Thesis, University of Nevada, Las Vegas, and from Seibert, T. M. (2009). *The inner experience of older individuals.* Unpublished dissertation, University of Nevada, Las Vegas.

in the modern literature, including behavior, brain state, context, appraisal, bodily expression, function, situation, experience, and so on. Feeling (= emotion *experience*) is only one (albeit an important) aspect of emotion.

Feelings can be an aspect of pristine experience: If I am angry, and that anger is directly present to me, then DES would call the anger a feeling and include it in the exploration of pristine experience. The physiological (adrenal secretions, etc.), behavioral, contextual, and any other aspects of my anger do *not* count as feelings unless they are directly part of my pristine experience. It is possible, for example, to *be* angry but not to *feel* angry – perhaps my attention is drawn completely to the task at hand, distracting me from the angry process that continues in my body (Heavey, Hurlburt, & Lefforge, in preparation).

Sarah Akhter and I set out to observe a few pre-adolescents' pristine experience, whatever that happened to be – that is, we did *not* set out specifically to observe feelings. Along the path of that investigation, we made some chance observations of feelings (or lack thereof), which led us to some provocative speculations. I start by describing some features of the inner experience of two young adolescents that Akhter and I investigated.

Eleven-Year-Old AV

"AV" was an eleven-year-old female who collected a total of twenty-five samples on five separate sampling days. One of AV's classmate friends had died unexpectedly the week before and AV was visibly upset about it: She appeared sad and downcast; in casual conversation she had often reported feeling sad about this; the sadness figured somehow in five of her twenty-five samples.

Remarkably, however, *none* of AV's samples directly manifested sadness or any other feeling experiences. However, *emotion* broadly defined did play a very important indirect role in eight (including the five sadness samples just referred to) of AV's twenty-five samples (32 percent). Here are three examples:

> Sample 2.1. AV was watching a TV show in which her favorite contestant was about to lose a competition. At the moment of the beep AV was innerly saying to herself in a sad tone, "Melrose is going to lose." AV was confident that her inner voice *sounded* sad; at the same time she was confident that she was *not* actually *feeling* sad at that moment.

> Sample 2.4. AV had been watching TV, an episode in which one of AV's favorite TV show characters died. AV had turned off the TV, gone into her room, turned off the lights, and lain down on her bed. She stared at the ceiling while repeating aloud to herself, "I'm sad, I'm sad, I'm sad, I'm sad ..." At the moment of the beep, AV was saying the final "I'm sad" in the chain. Remarkably, even though AV was in the act of saying she is sad, and even though her voice sounded sad (by her own report), she was *not* actually feeling sad at that moment.

Sample 4.4. AV was at the doctors' having her blood drawn for the first time ever. Her eyes were squeezed shut as the needle was just beginning to pierce the skin in the inside crease of her right arm. At the moment of the beep AV was commanding herself in a rapid, high-pitched, dramatically anxious squeaky little inner voice, "I'm not going to cry!" She felt the uncomfortable sensation of the needle entering her skin. At the moment of this sample, AV clearly was undergoing an anxiety/panic/worry/fear process; that anxiety/panic/worry/fear was clearly expressed in her squeaky little inner voice; and yet she did *not* directly experience any of the anxiety/panic/worry/fear.

These samples make it clear that we must separate the *feeling* of emotion from the *state* of emotion – that it is possible to have an emotion state in one's body and yet to have no emotion experience at the same time. There is nothing new about that observation: The emotion literature clearly distinguishes between emotion as an experience and emotion as a state, and we all can recall episodes where we were in a sad state (for example, at the funeral for a family member) but that occasionally (as when someone presents a funny reminiscence) we briefly "escape" that sad state, we "forget for the moment that we are sad," we get carried along by the current situation into neutrality or even joy, only to return to the experience of sadness a bit later.

There are two things about AV's samples that are different from such escape occasions. First, there is absolutely *no escape* in AV's samples. In all three of the cited examples (and others as well), AV is *directly engaged in the emotional situation* and yet she feels no emotion. In Sample 2.4 AV is so engaged that she is saying "I'm sad, I'm sad, I'm sad," and yet she does not feel sadness. Second, AV does not experience emotion in *any* of her samples, despite the fact that emotional processes are salient in many (32 percent) of them.

> **Q:** Maybe AV is just reluctant to talk about her feelings. She feels them, alright, but she doesn't want to tell you about them. Or maybe she just doesn't have the vocabulary to talk about feelings.
> **A:** I don't think that accords with the facts. In casual conversation she spoke openly and descriptively about her sadness over her friend's death. Furthermore, at the examples I have cited, she freely described aspects (tone of voice, TV content) of emotions. Why would she be not free to describe feelings? I think AV knew what it meant to be sad, was not reluctant to describe sadness, and had the vocabulary and lexical skills necessary to describe moments of sad experience. She simply did not have any such moments.

Thirteen-Year-Old RD

"RD" was a 13 year-old male who sampled over six days and participated in an expositional interview after each sampling day, thirty-four samples in all. In twenty-three of these (68 percent), RD was speaking to himself in his own inner voice (the phenomenon DES calls inner speech). In eight of these twenty-three inner-speaking samples (35 percent), RD recognized his inner voice as showing emotion such as anger, excitement, sadness, or happiness. Strikingly, in all but one of these samples, *he did not experience any feeling*, even though his inner voice had an emotional sound, tone, and speed. Here are two examples:

> Sample 3.1. RD was saying to himself in his head, in an angry voice, "Why did he kick me in my sore knee?" All of his awareness was focused on this thought. RD's inner speech was angry and rapid yet he was not feeling angry. Immediately after the beep, RD recognized that his voice was angry, and he acknowledged that his angry tone of voice reflected that somehow he was angry. However, at the moment of the beep RD was not *experiencing* being angry: not experiencing tenseness in his body or any other aspect of experience that might be indicative of anger.

> Sample 5.2. RD's mom was showing him some DVDs she brought home. At the moment of the beep he was exclaiming to himself in his head, "Oh! Crap! You got *Rocky*?!" His voice contained a mix of delighted surprise and excitement, which accurately reflected his state, but he did not *experience* any delight, surprise, excitement, or any other feeling directly in the moment.

Though RD frequently (in eight of his thirty-four total samples) *expressed* emotions (in his inner-speaking tone, as we have just seen), he *experienced* emotion as a distinct inner experience only twice in thirty-four samples (6 percent). Here are those two examples of experienced feeling:

> Sample 5.1. RD was saying to himself in inner speech, "Aw, man ... Dude, that really sucks," and was feeling sorry for his friend, J, who had just fallen and appeared to be hurt. The tone of his voice was sympathetic; it had a feeling-bad-for-J sound to it. Most of his awareness (about 70 percent, he said) was of this inner speaking itself, but the rest (about 30 percent) was of actually feeling sorry for J, which he felt on the inside surface of his chest and in his head, but not in any other part of his body. He had difficulty describing it other than to say that the sorry feeling seemed natural to RD, his natural response to seeing someone get hurt, and it was similar to a sad feeling but not exactly the same.

> Sample 6.6. RD was watching football on TV; the Eagles (RD's favorite team) had just lost. At the moment of the beep RD was exclaiming aloud with frustration, "How could they lose?!" RD felt a tiny bit of disappointment, and although he could not describe how the disappointed feeling manifested itself to him, he seemed confident that he experienced the disappointment as separate and distinct from his speech.

Thus in seven of the nine samples where RD was *expressing* emotion in his inner or outer voice, RD did not *experience* any emotion. The two remaining samples indicate that RD was capable of describing emotion experience, and therefore lend credibility to the observations about moments that had *no* felt emotion.

Of course, we or RD may have been mistaken, but it is striking that RD *recognized* his own emotion *not* by *feeling* it but by *observing* the characteristics of his inner or outer tone of voice, much like he would recognize the emotion in another person.

Inchoate Emotional Experience

Thus AV and RD have in common frequent emotional expressions that were not accompanied by simultaneous feelings. There are doubtless many ways to interpret such observations, but we will advance one speculation that we think is worthy of consideration and that is in accord with our observations of AV, RD, and a few other pre-adolescents. Our main goal in this book is to discuss the exploration of experience; we hope to contribute to the study of experience in a how-to-fish rather than in a here's-a-fish manner. We advance this speculation because it may demonstrate the fertility of the careful observation of experience.

Let's consider AV's "I'm sad, I'm sad, I'm sad" experience (AV's sample 2.4). Why would AV lie in the dark saying aloud to herself, "I'm sad, I'm sad, I'm sad"? Before we speculate on an answer, let's recall two things about AV: She manifested substantial sadness noticeable by any external observer during the period that we sampled with her, but she had no direct experience of sadness in *any* of her samples.

Sarah Akhter and I speculate that AV is telling herself repeatedly "I'm sad" because *she hasn't yet acquired the skillful ability to feel sadness immediately and coordinatedly*; she *is* sad, and she *knows herself to be* sad, but she does *not feel* sad. AV says, "I'm sad, I'm sad, I'm sad" *not* because she feels sad but because she does *not feel* sad. She says, "I'm sad, I'm sad, I'm sad" as a way of building/ practicing the organized experience of feelings (which currently exists only in a nascent or inchoate way) in the same way that a new driver learning to drive a stick shift says about the clutch, "let it out slowly, let it out slowly, let it out slowly" – as a way of focusing attention on an as yet nonexistent skill. Sooner or later, AV will learn to *feel* sad, but at this point in her development she does not skillfully, automatically know how to do that.

On this view, AV is saying, "I'm sad, I'm sad, I'm sad" as if she were saying, in effect, "My eyes feel moist, and I can touch them and notice that they are in fact moist. When my mother's eyes are moist she says she feels sad, especially when she watches a TV show where someone dies. So I'm pretty sure I'm sad. I'm apparently supposed to feel something in situations like this; I wonder what that would be like? I guess I have to learn to do that the same as I learned to ride a bicycle. I'll pay attention to myself. I'll try to practice feeling sad. My eyes feel moist – that's got to be part of this sad-feeling. My shoulder itches.

Is that part of this thing they call sad? I don't think so – yesterday when I was teary my shoulder didn't itch. My chest feels empty. Is that part of this thing they call sad? Maybe – I've heard my mother talk about heartache, whatever that is. There's a lot else happening in my body, some parts of which are no doubt sadness – I wonder which parts? I should pay attention to my bodily sensations as a way of learning something about the experience of sadness." Of course, AV probably does not engage in such a specific inner dialog – she just repetitively "plays" with aspects of what she will eventually immediately *feel*.

On this view, feelings are coordinated skills. AV will learn the skill of recognizing sadness and other feelings in herself in roughly the same manner as a toddler learns fine motor skills: build blocks, stack blocks, knock over blocks, throw blocks, over and over until the fine motor skills are secure. In some number of years, AV will likely immediately, directly feel sadness, and then she will forget what it was like to be unable to do so, just as she has forgotten what it was like not to be able to stack blocks.

Both RD and AD frequently expressed emotion, recognized emotions in others, recognized the emotionality of their own verbal expressions, but did not feel emotion. Our speculative explanation is that the first-person skill of feeling emotion in oneself (*I* feel sad) is *more difficult* than, and therefore is acquired developmentally later than, the third-person skill of recognizing emotion in others (*he* feels sad). That speculation is the reverse of the common view that the development of the understanding of the feelings of others comes *after* the development of one's own feelings (e.g., Saarni, Campos, Camras, & Witherington, 2006), and also quite different from the common view that feelings are pretty well in place by the third year (e.g., Lewis, 2008).

Here is the speculative logic of this understanding of the development of feeling: (a) Emotional behavior is innate: Infants cry when hungry or in pain. On the assumption that infants do not have organized inner experience (that is, do not have thoughts, feelings, images, etc., that would be recognizable to an adult), this suggests that one does not need to have a clear inner experience of emotion to engage in a behavior that can be called emotion. (b) The third-person skill of observing/recognizing/interpreting emotion expression in others is taught directly by the verbal community early in development. When Mom smiles and says softly and warmly, "I love you," the child learns to match her smiling face, warm body language, and soft sounds with the word "love" as a characteristic of Mom. On other occasions, when Mom's eyebrows furrow, her arms cross, and she uses a loud and harsh voice while she snaps, "I'm angry at you," the child learns to match this rigid posture and harsh sound with the word "angry" as a characteristic of Mom. Thus acquiring the third-person skill of recognizing emotion in others is relatively easy: Mom tells the child directly what the emotions are ("I love," "I'm angry") and all the child has to learn is which behavioral and vocal sounds are related.

(c) The first-person skill of recognizing emotion in oneself has to be learned on one's own with little or no help from the verbal community. The pattern-recognition skill is actually quite complicated, involving the recognition that this feature (my heart is racing) goes along with that feature (my eyes are moist), and goes along with that other feature (my muscles are tense), and goes along with yet that other feature (my visual perception has narrowed), but does *not* go along with this feature (my skin is sensitive) or that feature (I hear music), and so on. These are disparate micro-processes, represented quite separately in different regions of the body and the brain and at different temporal rates (I hear my voice get louder within milliseconds of its occurrence, but the nervous rush sensation comes some seconds after the adrenal glands secrete). All that pattern recognition has to be done without an instruction manual, and with little, if any at all, direct training by adults. Sometimes, of course, parents or other adults correctly acknowledge the child's emotional state ("You must be sad."), but parents and others often supply *mis*information ("You're not angry!")

Thus the developmental acquisition of the first-person skill of feeling has to be made despite indifference to, suppressions of, or interference with the nascent skill of feeling recognition. The child has to learn (without much guidance) to discern the differences between sadness and other feelings. For example, we have a beep that seems to catch AV in just that activity:

> Sample 4.5. AV's younger brother had messed up a computer game being played by her older brother, Marcus. As the beep sounded, AV is asking, "Marcus, are you sad?"

This sample might be taken as suggesting that AV is in the process of developing her abilities to recognize feelings in others, is figuring out what is meant in the linguistic community by the audible grunt "sad." The grunt "sad" does not arrive for the child with a dictionary definition – that definition has to be inferred over many occasional interactions with many members of the linguistic community. This sample further illustrates the developmental difficulty of acquiring the emotion-recognition/language-honing skills (see the discussion of B. F. Skinner and discriminating the language of private events in Chapter 11). It is likely that Marcus is *not* sad, but rather is angry or frustrated at his younger brother. AV herself, however, is likely in a sad state, the result of her friend's death. Her developmental task is to extricate Marcus's state from her own, and at the same time to differentiate the language used to communicate about those states, and *also at the same time* to discern the similarities and differences between how sadness and anger/frustration *feel* all over her body and mind. Recognizing the states in others, differentiating the vocabulary, and figuring out how to feel are three very different skills that have to be acquired at the same time in a noisy, inconsistent, and idiosyncratic environment.

The notion that the third-person recognition of emotion is easier than the first-person recognition gets some support from the scientific emotion literature:

> So, although people can automatically and effortlessly perceive instances of *anger, sadness, fear,* and so on, in others (especially when they are asked to assign facial muscle configurations to emotion categories), individuals do not consistently characterize their own experiences in such terms. The fact that people differ in emotional granularity suggests that not everyone knows the difference between a sad feeling, an angry feeling, a guilty feeling, and so on. (Barrett, 2006, p. 38)

Barrett's aim was not to characterize development or even to describe emotional experience, but her observations are in accord with the speculation being presented here.

If this is indeed how feelings develop, or at least one way that they can develop, it seems reasonable to speculate that children/adolescents learn the first-person recognition of their own emotional states (that is, learn the skill of feeling) by observing their own behavior (tone of voice, behavioral expression) in the *same third-person way* as they would observe the behavior of others. Thus RD observes the angry tone of his inner voice saying, "Why did he kick me in my sore knee?" and *infers* his own anger in the same third-person way as he observes his mother's tone of voice and infers that she is angry.

This speculation views feelings as skills that have to be acquired through a combination of maturation and practice. All skills are fragile early in their acquisition – watch kids learning to add and subtract fractions in fifth grade and you'll probably see that they forget how to multiply two-digit numbers – a skill they had easily mastered in the fourth grade. That evidences the fragility of a nascent skill – when doing one thing, the concentration is robbed from the ability to do another, even when (or especially when) they are related. It follows that when a pre-adolescent is (innerly or outerly) speaking, he *can't* simultaneously feel. Inner speaking is a skill that has to be acquired as well; it is possible that he can speak, or he can feel, but he can't do both in his nascent state. From an adult-centric point of view that may be hard to imagine, just as it is hard to remember that at one time it took all your attention to operate the clutch.

RD had two samples that included feelings. That in no way implies that he *always has* feelings. Just because he *can* perform a skill doesn't mean that he *always does* or that he *easily can* perform the skill, especially when the skills are nascent. In fact, it lends credibility to the claim that RD does *not* always have feelings: He *can* describe feelings (as the two examples demonstrate) but he doesn't always.

If our speculation (that feeling is a skill that develops quite late) is true (or even, as is more likely, if it is half true, or if it is true for some kids but not for others, etc.), the ramifications could be substantial. When you observe Johnny to be obviously angry, but he (angrily) says, "I'm not angry!" he may not be as defiantly stubborn as you think him to be. "I'm not angry!" may well be a perfectly true description of his feelings (or lack thereof), despite his angry tone. He may be merely not yet able to feel anger, or not able to feel it securely enough to recognize it under the current conditions. That may seem impossible from your adult-centric point of view; that's why it is necessary to bracket presuppositions in the exploration of another's pristine experience (and why that bracketing is so difficult).

This book, and this chapter, is not about the development of experience; it is about the faithful apprehension of moments of experience. I happily accept that I know little about the development of experience, that the conjecture that feeling comes developmentally later than the expression and the recognition of emotion is highly speculative and based on only a few observations (that is, is much more speculative than the bulimia observations of Chapter 2, which have been replicated in three separate studies). Our aim in this book and this chapter is to demonstrate the potential fertility of apprehending pristine experience using a method that genuinely submits to the constraints imposed by the intent to apprehend faithfully. This speculation requires substantial replication and scientific evaluation.

Constraint: Bracket presuppositions. Whether our speculation is or is not true is beside the main point: If you would apprehend pristine experience with high fidelity, you must bracket presuppositions on all fronts. To make the observations that underlie the present speculation, you must be able to observe a girl lying in the dark on her bed, crying, and saying, "I'm sad, I'm sad, I'm sad," *and still be open to the possibility that she does not experience sadness.* That requires the willingness to listen with a high degree of attentiveness to the details of what she says without jumping to conclusions about anything that might seem obvious. That requires a high degree of skill and practice, but that is a constraint imposed by the subject matter.

The bracketing-presuppositions constraint is a stern taskmaster. *Everything* that seems obvious must be bracketed (Hurlburt & Schwitzgebel, 2011c). We will return to discuss the bracketing of presuppositions frequently in the remainder of this book. From the perspective of someone who is highly skilled at bracketing presuppositions, the bracketing task is very easy: just relentlessly pay attention to experience regardless of all else; just help the subject describe the phenomena without straying from it. However, from the perspective of someone who is not highly skilled at bracketing presuppositions, it seems impossible or nearly so. How would it occur to you not to assume that someone feels sad if she is crying on her bed, saying, "I'm sad"? It is easy once one clearly makes the distinction between experience and all else. "I'm sad" is *not* a description of experience (or at least *may not be* a description of experience); it is a characterization of some state of the universe. Once you realize that, then if your aim is to apprehend experience, you realize that you have to ask carefully about experience regardless of how obvious it may seem that you already understand it.

There is no reason to believe, a priori, that adolescent or childhood feeling is merely a simplified version of adult feeling. Maybe it is, but that would have to be established by direct observations more thorough than those we have conducted. Modern psychology has not conducted those investigations in a way that genuinely submits to the constraints that the exploration of inner experience imposes, so I think it makes sense to hold that the jury is still out.

Constraint: Clearly differentiate between state, knowledge of that state, and experience. Let's use AV's "I'm sad, I'm sad, I'm sad" example. "Sad" has three quite different meanings in this sample: (a) AV *is* sad. "Sad" refers to AV's emotional state as a fact of the universe. Any halfway observant person seeing AV would recognize her as being sad from her tears, her quavering voice, and so forth. (b) AV *knows herself to be* sad refers to AV's self-characterization or self-knowledge. That self-knowledge may have been honed in the third-person world: She has observed others' tears and had conversations with them and others about them, thus differentiating her use of the word "sad," among other things. However, knowing something about oneself does not necessarily imply experiencing that at any particular moment. I know about myself that I am six feet one inch tall, but I rarely *experience* my "six-feet-one-ness." (c) AV does *not feel* sad – she does not have a direct, first-person apprehension of her feeling. Even though she *is* sad, and even though she *knows herself to be* sad, she does not feel sad. Most modern scientific discussions of emotion acknowledge a distinction between the emotion state (a) and emotion experience (c), but (b) and (c) are not usually adequately differentiated. For example:

> Emotional experiences require an organism to possess some fundamental cognitive abilities including the ability to perceive and discriminate, recall, associate, and compare. Emotional experiences also require a particular cognitive ability – that is, the development of a concept of self. Emotional experiences take the linguistic form "I am frightened" or "I am happy." In all cases the subject and the object are the same: that is, oneself. Until an organism is capable of objective self-awareness, the ability to experience may be lacking. (Lewis, 2008, pp. 312–313)

Lewis's "I am frightened" does not, strictly speaking, have the linguistic form of a statement about experience; an unambiguous statement about experience would be: "I feel fright." The failure to make such a distinction unambiguously clear perhaps reflects Lewis's *assumption* that if I am frightened, I also feel fright. That assumption may well be true some of the time, for some people and for some emotional experiences, but it is not always true, as our AV and RD examples show.

Of course, the development of feelings may proceed along different pathways from the one suggested here. However, our findings confidently suggest that the nature of emotion experience in pre-adolescents *may be* much different from emotion experience in adults; specifically, pre-adolescents may be in the process of developing the capacity to experience emotions directly whereas adults have already mastered that capacity.

Constraint: Don't judge others by yourself. This is a corollary of *Bracket presuppositions*, but because it is of such strong influence in consciousness science, it deserves separate notice. It is, I think, *not* true that because I experience feelings much of the time, therefore AV and RD must experience feelings much of the time. Unfortunately, I think, the failure to take the *Don't-judge-others-by-yourself* constraint seriously undercuts much, if not most, consciousness science, much of which rests on armchair observation. I have argued against the adequacy of armchair introspection (Hurlburt & Schwitzgebel (2007, 2011b). Even if the introspector could overcome the difficulty of observing a pristine phenomenon under inherently un-pristine circumstances (introspecting at precisely those times when you have specifically set yourself the task of introspecting), there remains the difficulty that what is introspected may not be typical of every other, or even many other, people.

SPECULATION 2: INNER SEEING IS AN ACQUIRED AND LOST SKILL

Hurlburt and Heavey (2006) presented this example:

> On October 16, 1987, when the beeper sounded at 18 seconds after 2:47 in the afternoon, 9-year-old Jimmy was in his bedroom playing with his cars. The DES interview revealed that instead of paying attention to the cars that were arrayed on the floor in front of him, he was at that moment seeing in his imagination an image of a big hole he had been digging for the last several days in his backyard. The hole in his image was about a foot deep, and his red tricycle was seen to the left of the hole, with its front wheel partly down into the excavation. The imaged scene was viewed as if from a perspective standing on his back porch.
>
> "Was this hole in your imaginary picture just like the real hole in your backyard?"
>
> "Yes," he said, "except that the real hole has more toys in it. If you had beeped me in a couple minutes, I would have had time to finish the picture."
>
> If Jimmy was right (and we think he was) when he said that he had put only his tricycle in the imaged hole because he hadn't yet had time to elaborate the entire image, and that if we had beeped him a bit later, there would have been more toys in the imaged hole, it suggests that seeing an image may be a skill that is acquired gradually. As children just begin

to acquire this skill, it may take many minutes to construct an image, to "draw in the details," so to speak. (Hurlburt & Heavey, 2006, p. viii)

The parallel between the acquisition of the skill of inner seeing and the skill of feeling is striking. Here is the logic of this speculative understanding of the development of inner seeing: (a) Visual responding to external stimuli is innate. For example, newborns discriminate brightness (Lamb, Bornstein, & Teti, 2002). However, newborn seeing is not the same as performed by an adult; for example, the fovea does not form until after birth (Banks & Shannon, 1993). (b) The skill of external seeing is given substantial exercise and training in the real world by the (to some extent) consistently patterned visual stimuli of real objects and the guidance by the verbal community ("Get the red ball!" "Put the triangle in the hole!"). But (c) the skill of *inner* seeing is probably more complex than the skill of external seeing for at least three reasons: First, one has to learn to "turn off" the experience of external seeing to be able to experience inner seeing (that is, the child first cannot see objects; then has to learn to *see* objects; and then, later, to learn to *decline to see* those same objects even though the eyes are open and aimed at the object); second, there is no external stimulation that drives the seeing (the "image" has to be created in the absence of reality); and third, there is no instruction manual, no help from others.

Most adults, including most psychologists and philosophers, assume that children's images are just like their own (a failure to submit to the *Don't-judge-others-by-yourself* constraint); that is, they presume that children's images, like their own, seem to happen in an instant and appear fully formed. There is little basic developmental science of the image that answer questions such as, "Is inner seeing a skill that has to be acquired gradually?" (The previous example suggests yes.) "And if so, at what age?" (I don't know.) "Does everyone see images?" (Heavey & Hurlburt, 2008, suggest no.) "Are the first images in color or black-and-white?" (We will suggest black-and-white.) "Is early inner seeing schematic or simplified?" (I don't know.) There is little or no scientific effort aimed at these basic science questions.

To summarize: There is reason to believe (but little or no scientific study) that the ability to innerly see (to form an image, as it is usually stated) is a skill that is acquired gradually across childhood, a skill that is acquired with substantial proficiency by some and very little or no proficiency by others. Todd Seibert (Seibert, 2009) and I have observed that this skill may *decline* in older adults.

Eighty-One-Year-Old Clara

Clara was an eighty-one-year-old woman with no apparent cognitive impairment. On the Mini-Mental State Exam (MMSE; Folstein, Folstein, & McHugh,

1975), a widely used screening device for Alzheimer's disease and other dementias, she received a perfect score of thirty, suggesting no dementia. She had a Master's degree in a health-related field and was very adept at DES – she was apparently able to narrow her focus to the moment of the beep and describe her experience reliably.

About one quarter of Clara's samples (nine of thirty-five) included inner seeing. On eight of these nine occasions, Clara's inner seeing was in black-and-white; on the ninth occasion, it was in brown-and-white. Here are examples, adapted from Seibert (2009):

> Sample 3.5. Clara was sitting in her front yard watching traffic and recalling an experience she had had the previous week. She had been at the Department of Motor Vehicles, and because she had a walker, she had been instructed to go to the beginning of a very long line of people. At the moment of the beep, she was innerly seeing a long line of people. This line was on her right and the people were facing largely away from her at a diagonal, left to right. There was no background. This seeing was clear and detailed but in black-and-white.

> Sample 5.2. Clara was sitting outside knitting. She was innerly speaking in her own voice, "Flowers, leaves, and green grass in March." The beep came on the word "grass." She was also innerly seeing a small group of flowers planted in a dirt bed. The flowers were small and similar to pansies and viewed from a perspective as if she were just a few feet from them. This inner seeing was in black-and-white.

> Sample 5.6. Clara was outside knitting. The previous day she had received a reproduction of photographs of her brothers, four pictures on an eight-by-ten inch sheet. At the moment of the beep, Clara was innerly seeing this sheet, apparently much as it exists in reality. This seeing was very clear: She saw the details in each of the four pictures (who was in each picture, the positions of those people, and some of the surrounding details). These pictures were seen in sepia tones as were the actual reproductions. Also at the moment of the beep, she was also innerly speaking in her own voice something like, "The pictures of my brothers were reproduced and came out better than the originals." Clara was not sure if this was the exact sentence she was innerly speaking, but she was certain that the beep came on the word "reproduced."

All nine of Clara's inner seeings were experienced to be monochromatic (shades of gray in eight and shades of sepia in one). There is little possibility that this is the result of failure to communicate adequately about her experience for four reasons: First, the interviewers (Todd Seibert and I) were highly skilled and queried her in detail about this aspect of her seeings. Second, she was herself very surprised by her first sample that contained a black-and-white image; she didn't really believe her own observation. She became highly motivated to ascertain whether her initial observation was correct; pretty clearly she would have been satisfied if not delighted to find that the first observation was an anomaly. This is an example of the importance of iteration in the apprehension of pristine experience; see Chapter 10. Third, she was very clear and articulate about her communication of her experience and in general, so that deficits in communication ability is not a likely explanation. Fourth, she was also very detailed and careful about what was and what was not in her experience, so it is unlikely that it is merely "sloppy reporting."

Constraint: Do not trust self-characterizations of experience. The most likely scenario here is that Clara had frequent inner seeing (roughly a quarter of her waking moments) and yet did not know, prior to sampling, that these were all or predominantly monochromatic. This is, I believe, another example of what we called in Chapter 2 Jessica's paradox. People are often mistaken, sometimes dramatically mistaken, about the characteristics of their own experience, often mistakenly believing what we have called faux generalizations about their experience.

Some people, of course, are quite accurate in their self-characterizations. However, I have observed that many people who are quite confident about their inner characteristics are also quite mistaken about them.

If we accept (which I do) that Clara's imagery was monochromatic, how should we understand that? There are at least three possibilities: (a) Her usual imagery is *not* monochromatic – for whatever reason we saw an unusual sample of her experience. This seems pretty unlikely because the samples were random across five sampling days spread over a month. (b) She has, throughout her life, *always* had monochromatic imagery. This also seems pretty unlikely – monochromatic imagery is very rare in our DES samples with younger adults (but see Schwitzgebel, 2002). Furthermore, her ability to see color in the external world seemed quite normal. And (c) Clara, when younger, had frequent color imagery, but that as she aged she stopped producing colored imagery. This seems a reasonable understanding, and is elaborated in the following section.

Color in Imagery

What follows is speculation that clearly needs to be validated in a variety of ways.

There have been very few if any investigations of color in adult mental imagery, perhaps because of the failure to take seriously the *Don't-judge-others-by-yourself* constraint. However, other aspects of mental imagery in older individuals have been experimentally investigated. For example, older individuals consistently perform more slowly in mental rotation tasks relative to their younger counterparts (Dror & Kosslyn, 1994); it appears to take longer for elderly individuals to form, maintain, and manipulate mental images (Dror & Kosslyn, 1994; Palladino & De Beni, 2003). Palladino and

De Beni (2003) had participants generate a mental image for each word on a forty-word list. Older individuals produced fewer overall details than did younger individuals when the time to produce the image was kept relatively short (twenty seconds). Furthermore, various studies on imagery suggest that more detailed images take longer to construct (see Kosslyn, Pinker, Smith, & Schwartz, 1981), and the vividness of an image is inversely related to the time one is allowed to form that image (Campos, Perez-Fabello, & Gomez-Juncal, 2006). Those experimental results suggest that the quality and detail of images (e.g., vividness) may not be present instantly but rather take time to develop, and that more detailed images take a higher level of mental processing. All that is consonant with the view that "mental computational power," however that is defined, declines in older individuals. That is certainly true at the extremes (as in dementia), and seems to me to be quite likely to be true in normal aging after, say, thirty years old.

It is reasonable to presume that it requires much more mental computation to create a colorful image than to create a monochrome image. For example, a full-color computer image requires perhaps eight times the computer memory of a gray-scale image. A computer program that has to coordinate color information is substantially slower and requires substantially greater resources than a program that coordinates only gray-scale information. It seems likely that a "mental program" that coordinates (or creates!) color information would also be slower and require greater resources.

Thus it seems to me to be quite natural to suppose that as people's mental computational power decreases, they have to simplify their computational tasks. One (apparently) obvious way to simplify is to eliminate the color from imagery, as Clara's examples show, but there is little or no discussion of that in the scientific literature.

> **Q:** Wow! That seems really ridiculous to me! Aren't you committing the fallacy of treating the brain like a computer? I don't think we know much about which parts of the brain are involved in imagination or visual experience, or how much processing power it takes to do something in black-and-white versus color. It sounds really implausible that one takes less energy than the other. It seems like changing the way you do visual processing after all those years would take more energy than leaving it the same.
>
> **A:** Let me ask you this: Do you think it's possible that people lose the ability to see imagery at all? That when they were young, they could see imagery, but when they're old they can't?
>
> **Q:** I don't know, but that seems totally possible.
>
> **A:** And if that happens, do you think that imagery just suddenly switches off? One day they wake up and no more imaging? Or do they lose it gradually?

Q: Hm! It doesn't sound ridiculous that they would lose it gradually.
A: And if they lose it gradually, what does that mean?

Q: Yeah. I suppose one way that could happen is that they could lose color, or lose definition, or something like that.
A: Right. So I don't see it at all as ridiculous. I see it as quite plausible, but clearly much more work needs to be done.

If this speculation is true, why don't Clara and older people in general notice a loss of color in their imagery? That is, why do people fall victims to Jessica's paradox? My guess is that there are at least five reasons: First, the loss of color happens gradually across many years, so the person habituates to it. Second, a black-and-white image contains a *lot* of information, probably all that is needed in most situations, so there is no need to notice the black-and-whiteness. Third, people don't really pay attention to the characteristics of the display itself – they are really interested in what is displayed. For example, if you watch a black-and-white television long enough to habituate to it, and the screen happens to show a Fourth-of-July parade, you wouldn't notice that the American flag is really black and white – you'd naturally understand yourself as *seeing* a red, white, and blue flag. Fourth, in inner seeing, you *know* what you are representing (after all, you are representing it), so the color is, in a way, an extraneous detail.

Fifth, the lack of color in Clara's sampled imagery does *not* necessarily imply that Clara lacks the *ability* to see color in her imagery; it merely implies that Clara doesn't *usually* see color in her imagery. This is a big distinction. Clara may well be *able* to create colorful imagery, and may well do so, either on some experimenter's demand or when she naturally desires to see an innerly detailed representation. What is at issue here is whether she typically *does* create color-ful imagery as she goes about her everyday activities. *Constraint: That one* can *experience X does not necessarily imply that one frequently* does *experience X.*

This fifth possibility is important because it has methodological implications. It seems likely (or at least possible) that if Clara armchair introspected her imagery, that is, if she premeditatedly instructed herself to see an image so she could report its details (or was so instructed by some consciousness scientist), she would produce color imagery, but that might be very atypical of what she *usually does* in her pristine (unpremeditated) experience. At sample 3.5, for example, she was more or less *idly* recalling the line at the DMV. It is not necessarily the case that an inner seeing whose idle intent is to reflect the actual DMV line would have the same characteristics as an inner seeing whose premeditated intent is to examine the details of inner seeing. Perhaps some people's idle and premeditated inner seeings have the same characteristics; perhaps that is true for all people. But it cannot be uncritically assumed. See Hurlburt and Schwitzgebel, (2011b).

Inner Seeing as a Skill

I think it is reasonable to presume that inner seeing is a skill that has to be acquired, much like playing tennis is a skill that has to be acquired. It requires maturation; some people doubtless have more of the necessary genetic/neu-rological/muscular/biochemical ingredients than do others; some have more opportunity than do others; some engage in more practice as children than do others; and as a result some are more skilled inner seers (or tennis players) than are others. Inner seeing is not present at birth; it is acquired somewhere along the developmental arc, probably substantially later than is frequently assumed. With normal or abnormal aging, the skill gradually deteriorates, and as a result the inner seeing (or tennis playing) competence diminishes and the quality and the detail of the inner seeing declines. Eventually inner seeing (and tennis) may be abandoned as the abilities continue to decline.

I think you will find very little of that account in a standard textbook on development.

> **Q:** All that is pretty wild speculation.
> **A:** Maybe, but I think it is more important to observe that such speculation is *possible*, not that it is *wild*. There is *no science of the characteristics of imagery* that constrains such speculation. How is it possible that such a gigantic lacuna exists in 2011? There is a science of the *function* of imagery (e.g., mental rotation), but all that science presumes that science already knows the characteristics of the imagery itself. I think that presumption is likely entirely false, the result of the failure to bracket presuppositions about phenomena. I think if careful studies of the phenomena of imagery were conducted, there would be plenty of new speculations that could be tested.
>
> And there is a retrospective science of imagery in children. As should be obvious to the reader, I am highly skeptical regarding retrospection in general, and doubly skeptical about adults' retrospections of childhood memories. As a result, I didn't include such reports in the foregoing exposition, but they do accord with the speculation. For example, investigations into the presence of color in early childhood memories have found a range of approximately 10 to 40 percent of memories in which colors are directly mentioned (for a review, see Clark, 2004). In one study that asked participants directly if color was a part of their childhood memories, only 34 percent of the memories contained color (Howes, Siegel, & Brown, 1993). Clark (2004) estimates that if you ask children to report their memories, and do not directly ask about color, approximately one out of six reports contain color.

SPECULATION 3: INNER EXPERIENCE IS A SET OF SKILLS

Let's accept for the sake of argument the premise of the previous sections: (a) that feeling is a skill that has to be acquired, and that there is developmentally a time (perhaps at or before pre-adolescence) when there are no feelings (that is, when there is no emotion experience), even though there are emotion processes and emotion expression; and (b) that inner seeing is a skill that has to be acquired, and that there is developmentally a time (perhaps at or before pre-adolescence) when there is no inner seeing, even though external seeing is quite skilled.

If feeling and inner seeing are skills that have to be acquired, then it is likely that inner speaking is a skill that has to be acquired, that unsymbolized thinking (see Chapter 15) is a skill that has to be acquired, and that sensory awareness (see Chapter 16) is a skill that has to be acquired, and so on for *every* feature of experience.

If all those are skills that have to be acquired, then it follows that there is a time when *none* of those skills has been acquired; that is, it follows that there is a time when there is no inner experience at all.

Perhaps that doesn't surprise you – a newborn certainly doesn't have inner experience of any kind that would be recognizable to an adult – no inner speech, inner seeing, and so forth. But I have much older children in mind.

Twelve-Year-Old BC

Sarah Akhter and I sampled with twelve-year-old "BC" on five occasions, collecting a total of twenty-two samples. Of those samples, we came to believe that only *one* included pristine experience as we generally understand it; perhaps two more included pristine experience if we loosen our procedure. In the rest of her samples, BC apparently had no pristine experience at all. In most (twelve samples), BC was just doing things (listening, talking, watching, cleaning, etc.) without any inner experience that we could discover.

Concluding that there is no inner experience is rather like proving the null hypothesis: Maybe we didn't discover inner experience because we employed a bad procedure; maybe we were not adequately skilled; maybe BC didn't understand what we were asking about. So that you may judge for yourself, here are some details.

Sampling with BC was remarkably different from our experiences with other subjects in our study of adolescents (and from adults, too). She had prolonged difficulty mastering the sampling task. Whereas most of our subjects become increasingly interested in the task and its results, BC became less and less interested over time. On the first sampling day, BC appeared to struggle with the sampling task as most subjects do: She was visibly surprised by the detailed interview questions, she could not locate the exact moment of the beep, she could not identify her inner experience, and she resorted to describing outer events instead. That is typical of first sampling days, so we reassured her as we always do with the expectation that the following day might be somewhat easier.

By the end of day two, BC decidedly was not reporting her inner experience as most subjects do. Instead, she communicated to us with increasing frequency and confidence that she was just doing things, without any corresponding inner experience. For example:

> Sample 2.5. BC was scrubbing the counter closest to the stove. At the moment of the beep there was nothing in her awareness. She had finished doing the dishes – specifically, finished washing the last knife – and had begun to wipe down the counters. It was a fact of her universe at the moment of the beep that she was scrubbing the counter hard, but she was not aware of that, or of anything else at that moment. In this sample BC was confident in describing the details of her activity; she reported the sequence of events and what she was doing at the moment of the beep without hesitation (scrubbing the counter closest to the stove). Yet there was nothing in her inner experience at the moment.

There was, however, some inkling of inner experience on day two when BC was able to describe two instances in which she may have been experiencing perceptual awareness:

> Sample 2.1. BC was looking at the leaves on a tree in her front yard, though she was not focused, drawn in, or "into" the leaves in any sensorial way – she just happened to have her eyes pointed at the leaves at that moment. We are not confident about the accuracy of this description. For example, we couldn't (or at least didn't) distinguish unequivocally between "looking at the leaves" as meaning that she was interested in the leaf-ness of her perception or as meaning that she was merely seeing the top half of the tree (the part where the leaves were as opposed to the trunk), or whether her eyes were merely aimed in that direction and she was experiencing nothing.

> Sample 2.3. BC was perceptually aware of pain in her front tooth, but she was not aware of the pain in any deeper way than knowing it was there at the moment. We could not unequivocally discern whether the toothache was just a fact of the universe or was actually present in her experience in some way.

Those are the two samples that we said earlier *might* include inner experience.

It was possible that BC's difficulty in describing experience was the result of memory difficulty, so for the remaining sampling days we eliminated memory as much as practicable. On days three, four, and five, we sat in the car on the street in front of BC's house while she wore the beeper inside. When each beep sounded, she came to the car and we conducted the interview immediately. However, even with the change in format, we still could not discover inner experience ongoing at the beep, and BC continued to become increasingly desultory during the conversations. For example:

> Sample 3.2. BC's mother had sent her next door to borrow a cup of sugar. At the moment of the beep, BC was walking home, just passing her mailbox. That she was walking past the mailbox was a fact of the universe; there was no experience – no seeing of the mailbox, no thinking about the sugar that she was carrying, no thinking about what she might say to her mother in a few seconds, no nothing.

We watched this sample occur, watched BC turn off the beeper and come directly to us. There was no violation of procedure; we had as good an opportunity to observe experience as is possible to have, but the interview produced no inner experience. The interviews themselves seemed to be frustrating to BC, as if we were persistently asking her about something that she knew nothing about.

BC's increasingly confident reports of "nothing" in her inner experience led us to wonder whether (a) she didn't understand what we were asking of her; (b) she had inner experience but was incapable, for whatever reason(s), of capturing and reporting it; or (c) she simply did not have inner experience at those sampled moments. A clue to this question arrived at the end of the third sampling day:

> Sample 3.4. BC was watching the actress Halle Berry on TV. At the moment of the beep, BC was paying attention to the way Berry was speaking, to Berry's accent, which BC recognized as unusual. BC was confident that her attention was focused on the sound of Berry's speaking, not on Berry's white dress or the Oscar statuettes that were also on the screen at the same time.

BC was uncharacteristically enthusiastic during the interview about this beep. She was animated and energetic, and easily and precisely defended the fact that she was listening to Halle Berry's accent at the moment of the beep, not looking at Berry's dress or the Oscar statuette or anything else. This was a markedly different interview from any other we had encountered over three full days of sampling with BC.

It was possible that as a result of the Halle Berry sample, BC would be more able to describe her experiences. However, that was not the case. Subsequent samples produced no clear experience. For example:

> Sample 5.2. BC was hitting her friend in the face with her right hand. She had no experience.

We asked BC whether she was feeling something that caused her to hit her friend, but BC said there was no such experience.

In the spirit of discovery, near the end of the fifth (and last) sampling day we relaxed the DES procedure and reminded BC of her inner experience of attending to Halle Berry's accent a few days back. Did she have any inner experience similar to that in any of her more recent samples? BC enthusiastically recalled her experience at the Halle Berry beep, but maintained that none of her samples since included inner experience.

Did BC really have, most of the time, no inner experience? Clearly we do not have enough information to answer that question unequivocally. But there is evidence in favor: BC apparently had inner experience at least once (the Halle Berry sample), so it can't be argued that BC simply didn't know what inner experience was. Furthermore, BC apparently could generalize the concept of inner experience. For example, on her first sampling day BC reported seeing an image of herself and her brother playing one-on-one on a basketball court. In the image, BC had the basketball and was standing in front of her brother, who was gesturing in frustration because BC had won. Though she knew it was a basketball court, she did not see the basketball hoops or any other distinctive features of the court in her image. The image was still (i.e., not moving) and was in black-and-white. This image was reported with more or less the same amount of detail that other DES subjects report images. However, careful questioning revealed that BC's basketball image came perhaps five seconds *after* the onset of the beep; therefore, it does not count as an experience at the moment of the beep. However, the recounting of this image does provide evidence that BC knew what "having an image" was, and that she was capable of describing an image if it occurred. That lends credence to the speculation that she just didn't have any such images at the moments of the beeps.

Constraint (from earlier): Don't judge others by yourself. This is a corollary of *Bracket presuppositions*, but because it is of such strong influence in consciousness science, it deserves separate notice. It is, I think, *not* true that because I have inner experience most of the time, therefore BC must have inner experience most of the time.

The Flavell Work

In Hurlburt and Schwitzgebel (2007, chapter 11) I reconsidered the enormous work by the Flavells. In a typical experiment, the Flavells seat a child on a carpet and say:

> I'm going to ask you a question, but I don't want you to say the answer out loud. Keep the answer a secret, OK? Most people in the world have toothbrushes in their houses. They put their toothbrushes in a special room. Now don't say anything out loud. Keep it a secret. Which room in your house has your toothbrush in it? (Flavell, Green, & Flavell, 1995, p. 57)

The Flavells then move the child to a table and ask the child if she had been thinking while seated on the carpet, and if so, about what. The Flavells apparently believe that everyone, while seated on the carpet, is thinking about the bathroom, and that indeed is what most older children and adults report. However, most five-year-olds deny that they were thinking while seated on the carpet. If they say they were thinking, they typically say they were thinking about something other than the bathroom. As a result, Flavell and his colleagues conclude that five-year-olds lack the ability to observe the thinking that was taking place:

> Children lack the disposition and the ability to introspect. Lacking introspective skills, they would be unlikely spontaneously to notice and reflect on their own mental experiences and, consequently, unlikely to attribute such experiences to others. (Flavell et al., 1995, p. 52)

The Flavells go to great lengths to set up a variety of situations where five-year-olds can report their thinking, and always reach the same conclusion: Five-year-olds lack introspective skills.

I think the Flavell studies are at least as straightforwardly interpreted as showing that five-year-olds *are usually not thinking*, if by thinking we mean engaged in some cognitive act that appears before the footlights of consciousness. However, the Flavells do not reach such a conclusion:

> We can imagine a number of possible reasons why … 5-year-olds tend to perform poorly on introspection tasks. (1) The 5-year-olds had no thoughts of any kind … and therefore had nothing to report. *This explanation seems implausible on its face. It is tantamount to saying that, unlike older people, young children do not have a continuous or near-continuous stream of consciousness when in a conscious state.* There is also empirical evidence against it…. Flavell et al. (1995) found in several studies that 5-year-olds would often deny having had thoughts even when it was not just likely, *but virtually certain*, that they had just had some (e.g., about which room they keep their toothbrush in). (Flavell, Green, & Flavell, 2000, p. 108, emphasis added)

When the Flavells write, "This explanation seems implausible on its face," I think they fall victim to the judge-others-by-yourself mistake: They reject out of hand the *possibility* that children do not have a continuous or near-continuous stream of consciousness. They run experiment after experiment where their five-year-old subjects say they have no experience, but the Flavells remain "virtually certain" that their five-year-old subjects had experience but can't report it. I fear that this virtual certainty comes from presupposition (that everyone is like me, and I have a continuous stream of consciousness), not observation.

My point is not to prove that BC and the Flavell subjects in fact have no inner experience. I think that is likely, but by no means certain. My point is that *to have the possibility of discovering whether* BC and the Flavell subjects have no inner experience, scientists would have to *admit that as a possibility*, and that would require submitting to the *Don't-judge-others-by-yourself* constraint. Unfortunately, I think that is rare in consciousness science.

Seventy-Year-Old Fay

Fay was a seventy-year-old woman with a Bachelor's degree in political science who volunteered for sampling after reading a story in a local newspaper about a study Todd Seibert and I were conducting. She received a perfect MMSE score of thirty, suggesting no dementia.

Although Fay was clearly quite intelligent (evidenced by her eloquence and substantial vocabulary), she had substantial difficulty describing her inner experience. She was very easily led by the interviewers and often changed and contradicted her reports. For example, at every beep on days three and four, Fay described long conversations that were either innerly or outwardly spoken. However, she could not describe at all which portion of the conversation was ongoing at the moment of each beep despite our considerable pressure to do so. Likewise, even though we told Fay repeatedly that we were interested only in her inner experience rather than background information or facts of the external situation, Fay would nearly always describe background information or facts of the external situation as if they were events that were in her experience.

As a result of these difficulties, on day five, we altered the standard DES procedure, much as Akhter and I had done with BC, to reduce as much as possible the interference that memory disturbances may have played. Seibert and I sat in a back bedroom of Fay's house while she wore the beeper and went about her activities in the rest of the house. When the beep sounded, she came to us immediately and we conducted the expositional interview on the spot. Here is a sample from day five:

> Sample 5.3. Fay was playing Scrabble on her computer and at the moment of the beep was apparently somehow thinking about the word "slotter." The gist was that she was wondering whether or not "slotter" was a word; that she could play it and find out if the computer would reject it; that she could remember that the word had been played in some past Scrabble game where there had been a protest, but she couldn't remember the outcome of the protest. But Fay's descriptions of this thought process were inconsistent, so it is impossible to know exactly what was in her awareness at the moment of the beep. We were unsuccessful in determining whether these wonderings/rememberings were all parts of the same thought process that were all present at the moment of the beep; or if they had been explicit but separate thoughts experienced in the vicinity of the beep but not simultaneous; or whether they were simply ways of describing her activity, none of which was actually present in her experience at the moment of the beep.

We pressed Fay on those issues. For example, we repeatedly asked if there were words in her experience at the moment of the beep, but she responded by describing external reality (e.g., she described the words on the Scrabble board, restated that she didn't know if "slotter" was a word) instead of answering directly about her experience. Fay did not, even when interviewed immediately after the beep, distinguish adequately between what was in experience at the moment of the beep and what were the characteristics of the situation surrounding her at the moment of the beep.

There are many possible explanations for Fay's difficulties: (a) that she has no inner experience at all; (b) that she has inner experience but it is so undifferentiated as to be impossible to report; (c) that she has clear inner experience but cannot introspect; (d) that she does not have the cognitive ability to focus on the moment of the beep; (e) that she has inadequate memory for the sampling task details; (f) that she has rigid presuppositions about inner experience that don't match what she actually experiences and so can't apprehend her experience; and doubtless others.

The most likely option seems to us to be (a), that she has no inner experience at all. Clearly this cannot be inferred from the one sample we have presented, but it is made more plausible by the fact that Seibert and I have sampled with a half dozen individuals who have MMSE scores between eighteen and twenty-nine, *and, like Fay, none of them was able to perform the DES task adequately* (Seibert, 2009).

> "Henry" (seventy-two-year-old male, MMSE score of twenty-nine) Sample 3.3. Henry was at home eating lunch with his wife, and they were discussing going out later that evening with friends. Initially, Henry reported that he was asking his wife aloud, "What clothing are you going to wear?" and that the beep had come between "you" and "going." As the interview about this sample progressed, however, he reported that he had specific clothing in mind that he was going to wear and that at the moment of the beep he was asking for approval from his wife about what *he* was going to wear that night. It was difficult to discern whether this was a change in his report about his experience (from being about his wife's clothing to being about his own clothing) or whether the question about his wife's clothing was actually a part of his consideration of what he should wear. We tried to differentiate those aspects without success. (Adapted from Seibert, 2009)

Q: So are you saying that having inner experience is a developmental skill we acquire as children and lose in our old age? Like we learn to experience and then we forget to experience?
A: Yes, that is exactly what I am speculating. I accept that we don't have enough observations to be positive, but that speculation is in accord with my sense gleaned from my thirty years of sampling.

Q: But how can that be? What does it mean to have no inner experience unless you are in a coma or dead? Isn't inner experience synonymous with consciousness or being?

A: This is a crucially important question, which I'll answer on five levels.

1. First, that it is impossible to have, generally, no inner experience represents a *very* powerful presupposition, but a presupposition nonetheless. Maybe it is true (I don't think so), but whether it is true or not, if you wish to apprehend experience with fidelity you have to genuinely bracket that presupposition. That is the *only* way you can possibly *arrive at the conclusion* that inner experience always exists. Otherwise you are just accepting your presupposition that inner experience always exists.

2. Having no inner experience is not merely a characteristic of infancy or old age. Chris Heavey and I (Hurlburt & Heavey, 2006, chapter 2) described "Amy," a university student who, we argued, did not have inner experience. Amy was a pathological liar – she lied about everything, all the time. She lied about inconsequential details such as what she had for lunch today or whom she had seen at the library. She often didn't know that what she had said was untrue until corrected by her friends. Her lying didn't seem motivated by trying to hide something or for personal gain – she just lied as if she couldn't help it. When her friends wondered if she was bisexual, she thought they might be right – not that they *were* right, but that if they thought she was bisexual, it was perhaps so. Heavey and I concluded, as the result of long sampling, that the lying and the lack of identity were likely the result of Amy's having no inner experience – she said things about lunch that weren't true because she hadn't really experienced the lunch in the first place. She wondered about her bisexuality because she had no direct sexual feelings one way or the other, nothing "inside" to "consult" regarding her sexual interest. Actually, she had no feelings at all, about anything.

   Amy is not unique. I have encountered other adults who did not, as it seemed to me, have any inner experience, but I have not published those cases. Some of these individuals were successful pillars of the community, and none at the outset recognized that her lack of experience was in any way different from the norm.

3. Here is a "subtraction" way of approach that may make the concept of no inner experience seem less impossible. Let's begin with our finding (Heavey & Hurlburt, 2008) that there are five main forms of inner experience: inner speech, inner seeing (aka having images), unsymbolized thinking, sensory awareness, and feelings. There may be other less-frequent forms, and others may have somewhat different definitions of our forms – neither affects the present discussion.

Now ask yourself: Does it seem possible for a person to have only four of those – say, to have all the kinds of experience *except* inner speech? Most people would say yes – not everyone has to talk to himself. So we conclude that inner speech is not an essential feature of experience.

Then might a person have only *three* of those – say, all *except* inner speech and inner seeing? Yes. And we can do the same for all the other forms of experience, one at a time subtracting a form of inner experience, and eventually conclude that *no* form of experience is essential.

Then we can ask, If no form of experience is essential, is it possible to have *none* of those forms of experience? Answering yes still requires a conceptual leap here, but perhaps not as long as before.

4. Here is a "boundary condition" approach that may help. Most people would accept that inner speaking is a characteristic of at least some adults' inner experience. Most people would also accept that people are *not* born innerly speaking. That implies that somewhere between birth and adulthood a person acquires the skill of innerly speaking, and before that time did not experience inner speech. The same logic can be applied to all other forms of experience. Therefore there may have been no inner experience early in development. (By the way, contrary to some opinion, our observations show (as did Vygotsky's) that inner speech is a skill that is acquired substantially *after* the external speaking skill: First the child has to learn to speak externally; *then* she has to learn how both to speak and simultaneously to suppress the vocalization of that speaking. Speaking and suppressing is a substantially *more* complicated coordination than speaking itself.)

5. Whether or not you find the subtraction logic or the boundary condition logic compelling, the only way to discover the characteristics of experience is to inspect experience very carefully with adequate bracketing of presuppositions. I'm pretty sure you will, occasionally, find people with no experience, not only children and the elderly but also adults.

DISCUSSION

I know of no human ability that appears suddenly and completely formed; all human abilities commence in fits and starts – here today, gone tomorrow, here again the next day and the next, gone the following, finally here to stay. The early forms of all human abilities are crude approximations of the final forms, usually including steps in the *opposite* direction from the final forms – skins that must be shed completely before the current skin fits. That seems to apply to experience as well as to other abilities.

This book is about how to explore experience, not particularly about developmental psychology (or bulimia or any other specific topic). Our discussions of nascent feelings and nascent and declining images illustrate some features of what is required genuinely to submit to the constraints that the exploration of inner experience imposes.

Constraint: Accept that orthodox psychological instruments never discover phenomena. We could have given AV or RD every test or questionnaire known to psychological science, and subjected them to every structured interview yet devised, and we never would have discovered the characteristics of nascent feelings. Psychological instruments are always backward looking, seeking to validate what has already been discovered. Psychological instruments are not designed for the discovery of phenomena. (We will return to this discussion in Chapter 21.) One could interpret this constraint as a corollary to Chapter 2's constraint: *You can't find out about a phenomenon unless you talk about the phenomenon.*

Constraint (from Chapter 2): *The exploration of experience probably has to be a first-person-plural endeavor.* Neither AV nor RD could have *possibly* described their nascent emotional experience by themselves. It is not merely that it would have been *difficult* for them; it would have been *impossible*, for two reasons: First, whenever they would purposefully examine their emotions, they would experience them (something like an external beep is required to overcome that); and second, the recognition that nascent emotional experience might be interesting requires knowing how other people experience emotions, and they are not in a position to know that.

Constraint: Lightly hold observations. We need to be very alert and at the same time lightly hold everything we find (including everything said in this chapter) until we have observed long enough to be confident about the phenomena (cf. Hurlburt & Schwitzgebel, 2011b).

We will return to a discussion of RD and some additional speculations about development in Chapter 20.

10

Moment Experience
Constraints

Iteration Is Essential

If a man will begin with certainties, he shall end in doubts, but if he will be content to begin with doubts, he shall end in certainties.
– Francis Bacon

In Chapter 5, we noticed this constraint: *The exploration of pristine experience has to be iterative.* As we turn the screw ever more securely into the notion of faithfully apprehending experience, it's time to return to that constraint, which I think is of fundamental but largely overlooked importance to consciousness science. We could not have discovered the fragmented multiplicity of bulimia (Chapter 2) without an iterative method; we could not have made the slow-forming images or black-and-white images speculations (Chapter 9) without an iterative method. This chapter explains why.

I use *iterative* in the same way a mathematician uses it: a series of successive approximations leading to a satisfactorily close approximate solution. Suppose a mathematician uses an iterative method to determine the value of x when $f(x) = F$. She guesses an initial value x_1 and determines $f(x_1)$. If $f(x_1)$ is satisfactorily close to F, then she's done: x_1 is the desired solution. Otherwise, she uses this new information ($f(x_1)$) to make a second (better) guess x_2 and then determines $f(x_2)$. If $f(x_2)$ is satisfactorily close to F, then she's done: x_2 is the desired solution. Otherwise she uses this new information ($f(x_2)$) to make a third (even better) guess x_3. If all goes well, x_{n+1} is a better guess than was x_n (that is, $f(x_{n+1})$ is closer to F than was $f(x_n)$), and eventually $f(x_m)$ will be close enough to F to consider x_m a satisfactory solution.

Iteration is therefore not merely repetition; it requires refinement – making a better and better guess – at each step. Iteration does not produce an exact result; it produces a satisfactory approximation. Iteration is a common process

---

Much of this chapter is revised with permission from Hurlburt, R. T. (2009). Iteratively apprehending pristine experience. *Journal of Consciousness Studies, 16* (10–12), 156–188.

in everyday life: The successive drafts of an academic paper can be considered iterative steps – each one an improvement on the previous one.

This chapter shows why an iterative process can lead to a more faithful apprehension of pristine experience. We begin by discussing the apprehension of pristine experience in a single interview and then across a series of iterative interviews. Then we examine a concrete example of the first interview in an iterative series. We use a DES interview as an example, but the argument applies to any interview.

A SINGLE INTERVIEW

Suppose that at time t the subject undergoes a pristine experience, and at some later time a highly skilled interviewer attempts to apprehend that experience. The model shown in Figure 10.1 illustrates that the interviewer's initial apprehension of the subject's experience will arise partially from the pristine experience as conveyed by the subject (e.g., "At time t I felt ..."), but also from four other sources: (a) the subject's presuppositions (e.g., "I *always* feel," "*Everyone* always feels," "I presume you want to know how I felt"); (b) the interviewer's own presuppositions (about the content that the subject begins to describe, about the subject, about the mask that the interviewer wants to display to the subject, about the interview process, etc.); (c) miscommunication (lack of vocabulary, failure of the interviewer to understand the subject's terminology, lack of understanding of the task, distraction, etc.); and (d) reconstructions that the subject has used to recall or otherwise re-invoke the pristine experience between time t and the interview. The first three of those (subject's and interviewer's presuppositions and miscommunication) are non-experiential impediments to the faithful apprehension of the pristine experience; the fourth (reconstruction) is an experience (or a series of experiences) that occurs at a time removed from the original pristine experience.

There may well be other ways to slice this apprehensional pie. I use the pie-chart format only for its heuristic value; I don't presume to know the actual sizes of the slices in this pie; it is primarily the *change* in size of the slices within and across interviews that I wish to discuss. Figure 10.1 illustrates a highly skilled interviewer: The interviewer's presuppositions are shown to have a relatively small effect on apprehension.

Now suppose that over the course of the interview the interviewer attempts to refine his or her apprehension of the pristine experience. Clarifications will be requested (e.g., "What did you mean when you said you felt..."), attempts to bracket presuppositions will be made ("Yes, I understand that you may *usually* feel ..., but at time t did you ...?"), and so on. In responding to these requests, the subject will likely attempt, repeatedly, to reconstruct the original experience, either spontaneously or by

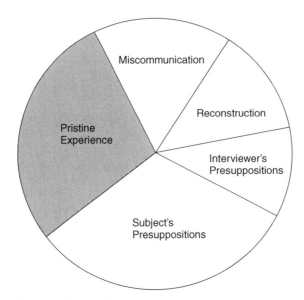

FIGURE 10.1. Contributions to the interviewer's apprehension of the subject's experience at the beginning of the interview.

explicit instruction (e.g., Petitmengin, 2006). Let's suppose that this interview is skillful, careful, and extensive, lasting, say, fifteen minutes or an hour. Figure 10.2 illustrates the possible contributors to the interviewer's apprehension at the *end* of the interview.

If the interviewer is skilled, the influence of the non-experiential impediments can be reduced: Some presuppositions of both subject and interviewer can be exposed and bracketed (Hurlburt & Heavey, 2006), and terminology can be refined and aligned. Figure 10.2 shows, therefore, that the relative contribution of those three aspects to the interviewer's apprehensions has been reduced compared to the beginning of the interview (Figure 10.1).

On the other hand, the interviewer's probing questions strongly encourage (explicitly or implicitly) the subject to try to reconstruct the pristine experience during the interview; the reconstruction slice is therefore substantially *larger* in Figure 10.2. The longer and the more intensive the interview, the more reconstructions.

The proportion that the original pristine experience contributes to the interviewer's apprehension is therefore likely to be *less* at the end of the interview than at the beginning, because of the difficulty extricating the pristine experience from the reconstructions thereof. It is possible that the contribution of pristine experience will increase, but only if the reduction of presuppositions outweighs the effect of reconstruction.

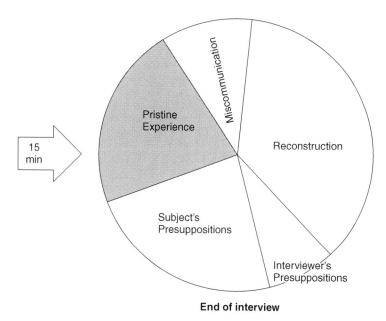

End of interview

FIGURE 10.2. Contributions to the interviewer's apprehension at the end of the interview.

ITERATIVE INTERVIEWS

The preceding section concluded that the direct contribution of pristine experience to an interviewer's apprehension is likely to *decrease* across one interview as the reconstructed experiences increase. I now argue that an iterative series of interviews can increase the direct contribution of pristine experience and decrease (but not eliminate completely) the reliance on reconstruction.

There are four main aspects of an iterative method, all of which can contribute to the faithful apprehension of experience: (a) the refreshment by new experience; (b) the improvement of the apprehensions; (c) the multiple perspectives on experience; and (perhaps most importantly) (d) the "open-beginningedness" of the process. I will discuss these as separate aspects, but they are, in practice, synergistically interrelated.

Refreshment by New Experience

Suppose that the interview illustrated in Figures 10.1 and 10.2 is the first in an iterative series of interviews. The second interview is illustrated in Figure 10.3. At some time after the first interview, the same subject undergoes a new pristine experience and is interviewed about it by the same interviewer. This is a fresh start. The pristine experience to be discussed in this second interview is

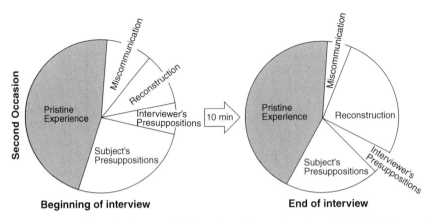

FIGURE 10.3. Contributions to the interviewer's apprehension at the beginning and end of the second interview.

not merely one more reconstructed experience overlaid onto the same original pristine experience – the new occurrence of a new pristine experience has the potential to refresh the entire process from the beginning.

The sources of the interviewer's apprehension of the subject's experience at the beginning of the second interview are illustrated in the left side of Figure 10.3. Whatever progress was made during the first interview in reducing the non-experiential impediments (bracketing the influences of the subject's and interviewer's presuppositions, clarifying communication) is likely to be at least to some degree maintained. Thus these three slices are shown to be roughly the same at the beginning of the second interview as they were at the *end* of the first interview (Figure 10.2). The necessity for reconstruction between the new pristine experience and the second interview should be no greater than between the first pristine experience and the *beginning* of the first interview (the reconstruction slice in the left side of Figure 10.3 is about the same as in Figure 10.1). The result is that the relative contribution of the new pristine experience at the beginning of the second interview is *greater* than it was at the beginning of the original interview.

The right-hand side of Figure 10.3 illustrates the end of the second interview. The second interview is likely to be more efficient and probably shorter (let's say ten minutes instead of fifteen minutes) because some progress was made in bracketing presuppositions and in communication – no need to do that again. Reconstruction still occurs during the second interview, but because the interview is shorter, it is likely that there will be less reconstruction required here than in the first interview. The second interview may make further progress on bracketing presuppositions and clarifying communication.

The net result is that the direct contribution of pristine experience can be expected to *decline* across the second interview (as it did in the first) but *remain greater* than at any point in the first interview.

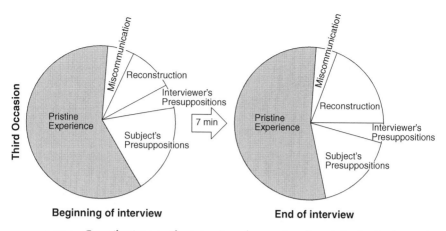

FIGURE 10.4. Contributions to the interviewer's apprehension at the beginning and end of the third interview.

Nth occasion. Now let's suppose that at some time after the second interview, the subject undergoes a new (third) pristine experience and undertakes to describe it in a third interview (Figure 10.4), and then another new (fourth) experience and fourth interview, and so on. At the beginning of the nth interview, the relative contribution of pristine experience is the whole pie minus the non-experiential impediments (presuppositions and miscommunication) minus the reconstructed experience. The sizes of the non-experiential impediment slices at the beginning of the nth interview are likely to be roughly the same as those at the *end* of the $(n-1)^{st}$ interview, because the progress participants made in the $(n-1)^{st}$ interview is likely to be maintained. However, the size of the reconstruction slice is similar to that at the *beginning* of the $(n-1)^{st}$ interview, because each interview starts fresh with a new pristine experience. (Actually, the size of reconstruction slice may lessen across occasions; see the subsection *Lessening reconstructions.*)

To the extent that genuine progress is made in the bracketing of the subject's and/or the interviewer's presuppositions and/or the clarifying of communication, the relative contribution of the pristine experience at step n will be greater than at step $(n-1)$. This improvement is made possible by the refreshment of each interview by an always new pristine experience, the starting over and over again with new pristine experience at each step.

To summarize, the direct contribution of pristine experience is likely to *decrease within each interview*, because the influence of reconstructions during the interview is likely to outpace the bracketing of presuppositions, even if genuine progress is made in bracketing presuppositions and clarifying communication. However, if genuine progress is made in bracketing presuppositions and clarifying communication, the direct contribution of pristine experience is likely to *increase across interviews*, because of the refreshment by the new pristine experience at each step.

I make no claim that the non-experiential impediments can be eliminated completely – presuppositions are stubborn. I therefore do not claim that pristine experience can be apprehended with absolute accuracy. I do claim that genuine skill at bracketing presuppositions can lead, across interviews, to an increasingly faithful apprehension of pristine experience.

Improvement of the Apprehensions

We have seen that each step in the iterative process can be refreshed by new pristine experience and therefore the relative contribution of pristine experience can increase across interviews. Now we notice that, beyond this increase in contribution, each iterative step can improve the quality of the apprehensions of the pristine experience themselves. That is, not only can the pristine experience slice of the pie increase in size, the slice itself can become of higher quality, for six main reasons: (a) Practice may refine the observational skill; (b) practice may improve interview skill; (c) iteration allows the synergy of refining observation and improving interviews; (d) iteration may make the observer more prepared to observe; (e) iteration may lessen the need for reconstructions; and (f) iteration may improve the fidelity of reconstructions.

Practice in observing. Any subject's first observation of a pristine experience is likely to be of low quality: The subject doesn't skillfully know what experience is and what it is not, doesn't skillfully know the difference between observation and theorizing, doesn't have an appreciation or skills for holding presuppositions at bay, and so on. The first interview, skillfully conducted, may incrementally improve some or all of those skills, allowing the subject to become more skillful at the time of the second observation. This incremental refinement of observational skill may occur at each occasion.

Practice in being interviewed. Because the subject has little practice in carefully describing inner experience, the first interview is itself likely to be quite rudimentary, making only relatively crude distinctions about what was and was not apprehended as well as only crude characterizations of the pristine experience. At each subsequent occasion, those distinctions and characterizations can become incrementally refined.

Synergy of observation and interview. Not only may practice improve observation skills and interview skills, the improvement in those skills interact synergistically. If the nth interview provides an incremental improvement in the skill of bracketing presuppositions about experience, that bracketing skill may carry over to the $(n + 1)^{st}$ *observation* of pristine experience. Presuppositions blind, amplify, or otherwise distort, and to the extent that subjects learn to bracket them in the first interview, the second observation may be less distorted. However, the $(n + 1)^{st}$ observation serves as the starting point for the $(n + 1)^{st}$ interview; the improved quality of that observation can lead to an improved ability of the *interview* to focus more directly on the characteristics of the subject's own particular experiences and more able to bracket the subject's own particular presuppositions. That can make the $(n + 1)^{st}$ interview more effective than was the nth interview, not merely because of the practice effect but because of the improved observational input. This improvement in the $(n + 1)^{st}$ interview can lead to an improved quality of the $(n + 2)^{nd}$ observation, which can lead to a better $(n + 2)^{nd}$ interview, which can lead to an improved quality of the $(n + 3)^{rd}$ observation, and so on.

Readiness to observe. Pristine experience always comes "out of the blue," is unanticipated, more or less surprising. The practice gained in early observations and early interviews may help the observer become more prepared, more poised, more ready to observe a subsequent pristine experience when it occurs. As a result, the subject may well be quicker and more effective at apprehending the subsequent pristine experiences. This increased readiness to observe is separable from the skill of observation in the same way that a news photographer's learning to carry a camera that is prepared (What lens is likely to be useful here?) is separable from the skill of composing the photograph. The skilled photographer's readiness makes her more likely to be able to deploy her composition skill when the emergent situation occurs.

Lessening reconstructions. The subject acquires, over the course of the iterative interviews, an understanding of the kinds of questions the interviewer might ask, the kinds of features experience might have, and so on. As a result, the subject becomes more and more able, *at the time of the occurrence of each successive pristine experience*, to make contemporaneous observations that will later require less and less reconstruction. Thus the reconstruction slice of the pie may decrease across interviews.

Improvement of reconstructions. The sixth aspect of the subjects' successive skill acquisition is that subjects may iteratively learn the skill of conforming their reconstructions more and more closely to their pristine experiences. Reconstructing experience is a skill like any other skill, and the practice of that skill can lead to improvement (e.g., learning how to take better contemporaneous notes about the experience, and how to refer to those notes effectively when reconstructing). If the reconstructions are more faithful, then apprehensions (which rest on both the original pristine experience and reconstructed experience) may mirror pristine experience with higher fidelity.

But not necessarily. The foregoing has assumed a skilled interviewer; in particular, it has assumed that the interviewer is effective at bracketing his own presuppositions as well as helping the subject bracket hers. Without such skill, iteration can lead to the *amplification* of presuppositions: The subject or the interviewer may start to develop a theory about the subject's experience based on early observations, and that theory then can inform and distort future reports. If presuppositions increase, fidelity of apprehension of pristine experience decreases.

Multiple Perspectives on Experience

Pristine experience at any moment is determined by the characteristics of the subject, the features of the environment, and many other factors. Suppose a subject describes her pristine experience on a series of occasions. On the first occasion her pristine experience is $X + A$; at the second occasion her pristine experience is $X + B$; at the third occasion her pristine experience is $X + C$; and so on. X could be said to be a salient feature of the subject's experience. For example, on the first occasion, Sally is simultaneously smelling pizza and recalling a scene from *Schindler's List*; on the second occasion she is smelling the sea breeze and worrying about the stock market; on the third occasion she is smelling the dog's fur and contemplating a move in chess.

There are two ways that an iterative method aids in the faithful apprehension of X. First, at the outset, neither the interviewer nor the subject needs to know that X even *exists*, much less that it is a salient feature of experience, and even less what the essential features of X are (Sally needn't know, prior to the interviews, that she frequently pays attention to smells in the environment). If X is a salient feature of the subject's experience, it will *emerge* from a series of careful examinations of pristine experience. On the first occasion, the recollection of *Schindler's List* was no more and no less an important feature of Sally's pristine experience than was the smelling of pizza. However, *across occasions*, X (the smelling) occurs again and again, and will therefore be naturally recognized as salient, whereas the non-recurring features (*Schindler's List*, stock market, chess) will therefore naturally be recognized as incidental and not salient. Thus the multiply refreshed instances of pristine experience allow the more central features to emerge, unbidden, as salient.

Second, each fresh encounter with pristine experience is a view from a somewhat different direction, highlighting experience from a new perspective on each occasion. The first occasion highlights smelling from the concrete perspective of *pizza*; the second highlights smelling from the concretely different perspective of *the sea breeze*; the third highlights smelling from the yet again concretely different perspective of *fur*. The features of the experience of smelling can be discovered by triangulating from the several vantage points.

Thus iteration allows both for the emergence of salient phenomena and for the elaboration of phenomena once they emerge. Both those characteristics taken together can, across occasions, allow a greater clarity of apprehension of the central features of pristine experience.

Open-beginninged Probes

Presuppositions about experience are a primary, if not *the* primary, impediment to faithful apprehension of experience (Hurlburt & Schwitzgebel, 2011c).

Presuppositions can be held by the subject or by the interviewer (or worse, both), and they blind or otherwise distort the apprehension of experience.

One of the most insidious but frequent presuppositions is the presumption that people have the kind of experience that the interviewer seeks. Interviewers interested in images, for example, frequently ask subjects to form an image and then to answer questions about it, without leaving adequate space for the possibility that the subject never actually formed an image. That procedure can have very negative consequences for an investigation: The results are an inextricable aggregate of responses by those subjects who have images and those who don't have images but answer the questions anyway.

Constraint: Use open-beginninged probes. There is an alternative: Use only open-beginninged probes (Hurlburt & Heavey, 2006, chapter 8; Hurlburt & Schwitzgebel, 2007) about experience.

Open-*ended* probes are "designed to permit spontaneous and unguided responses" (Merriam-Webster), but it is only the *end* of the response that is "spontaneous and unguided" – the beginning is entirely specified by the probe. "Tell me about your image" is an open-*ended* probe, but it nearly always produces talk that *begins*, "My image was," even in subjects who do not create images in such situations. Such talk may be a plausible characterization of "my imagery" that has nothing at all to do with my experience.

An open-*beginninged* probe is one that leaves *both* the beginning and the end of the response spontaneous and unguided. There is, as far as I know, only one open-beginninged question about experience: "What, if anything, was in your experience at the moment?" Hurlburt and Heavey (2006) called this the "one legitimate question" about experience. However, calling this the one legitimate question is not to say that this precise wording is the best or only instantiation. On the contrary, it is desirable to be deliberately inconsistent (Heavey, Hurlburt, & Lefforge, 2010; cf. Hurlburt & Schwitzgebel, 2007, p. 15) in the framing of this and other questions and let the iterative process do the work of sharpening the meaning. Deliberate inconsistency means using a variety of versions of this question (e.g., "What is your experience at the moment?" "Right then, what were you aware of?" "What if anything presented itself before the footlights of consciousness right then?"), each with its own advantages and disadvantages. If those questions aim (each imperfectly) at pristine experience, and pristine experience is a robust phenomenon, then pristine experience will (iteratively) emerge, free from the specific influence of any specific version of the question. If there is not a robust phenomenon, no amount of care in crafting the question will help.

A genuinely open-beginninged probe adumbrates the general arena (experience or lack thereof) but provides no specification of alternatives and no pretraining, because either may limit the potential beginning of a subject's reports. The genuinely open-beginninged probe simultaneously conveys (explicitly or implicitly) all the following: I don't know what the features of your experience are; I don't want to speculate about some potential aspect of your experience because then you may "go looking for" that aspect; I'm interested in whatever presents itself directly to you, whatever is before the footlights of your consciousness; maybe there is nothing in your experience; maybe your experience is different from anything I have previously encountered; I don't know what is in your experience so I can't tell you what to look for; if thinking is in your experience, I'd like us to talk about thinking; but if you're not experiencing thinking, then I don't want to talk about thinking; if you're feeling something I'd like us to talk about that, but if not, not; same for seeings, tickles, hunger pangs, hearings; I'd like us to talk about whatever you *actually* experience out of the welter of possibilities that you *might* experience; I emphasize that I don't know what you experience; maybe you will be able to perform this task, maybe you won't – either way is fine with me because I'll probably learn something either way; if you can report your experience, fine, but if you can't, fine as well; maybe you'll find it easy, maybe you'll find it difficult at first and then it will become easy, maybe you will find it always difficult, maybe you will find it impossible – any of that is OK with me; I'm sincerely interested in your experience, whatever that is, including nothing; I'm interested in our talking honestly about your experience, including that this task is difficult or impossible if that's the way it is; some people can do it easily, some find it difficult or impossible, and either is OK with me; perhaps together we will be able to apprehend faithfully your experience, and if so, that would be good; but if not, that would be good, too; I want you to observe your experience; I don't want you to guess about it or theorize about it; I want you to describe exactly what you directly observe; I don't want you to explain it or speculate about it.

Obviously an interviewer can't say all that at once – it would overwhelm – but an interviewer can consistently convey that stance with every utterance, and eventually, across occasions, *iteratively*, the subject will get the message: *The interviewer really does want to hear about the details of my experience, whatever those details happen to be (or not, if I have no experience).* However, that can happen only if the investigation is genuinely open-beginninged. Sooner or later, any un-genuineness will bleed through.

Open-beginning probes are designed to be nebulous and ambiguous, designed to create a level playing field when approached from any direction, thus allowing subjects to penetrate their own experience on their own terms. Any other approach favors one thing over other things and therefore distorts the process. In some ways an open-beginninged probe is similar to applying gesso to a canvas prior to painting. The gesso has no relationship at all to what you will paint; you don't plan, at the end of the painting, to see the gesso; applying the gesso is a temporal distraction, seems to waste time you'd rather spend painting. But the gesso, once applied, allows your artistry to flourish: The oil doesn't bleed into the canvas, the colors stay purer, the imperfections of the cloth disappear, and so on.

Even if the interviewer's probes are genuinely open-beginninged, the subject will likely not initially *believe them* to be open-beginninged. The investigation operates in a context of psychological and philosophical studies, almost all of which are manipulative and goal-verification oriented, if not downright deceptive. There is little historical context for the genuine appreciation or apprehension of pristine experience. It is naïve to expect that a one-shot open-beginninged conveyance, no matter how sincere or eloquent, can overcome that context. A series of open-beginninged probes delivered in an arena where the subject can test the intention and veracity of the interviewer *for himself or herself* may be able to overcome the context, but that can happen only iteratively across occasions.

Constraint: Pre-training about what might be observed is inimical. Asking open-beginninged questions is an inefficient approach – as inefficient as possible, one might say. However, if the aim is a faithful apprehension of experience, there is, as far as I have been able to see, no alternative, because pre-training about potential observations is *inimical* to the faithful apprehension of pristine experience. Because pre-training takes place before concrete observations have been made, pre-training must be about abstract concepts: Pre-training defines a concept, teaches how to recognize that concept, teaches what to do about that concept. But *experiences are not concepts.* If the object is to apprehend pristine experience, then non-experiential aspects are to be avoided. It is often useful, after the fact, to determine whether some particular pristine experience can be considered an instance of a concept, but the order must be to apprehend pristine experience first and to make abstract determination second. Otherwise the concept pollutes the experience.

For example, Chapter 16 describes the concept of sensory awareness, saying that it is a frequently occurring characteristic of inner experience that is usually overlooked by subjects and interviewers. But Hurlburt, Heavey, and Bensaheb (Chapter 16's authors) *should not* (and in fact did not) pre-train subjects about the potential existence and characteristics of sensory awareness; subjects' descriptions of sensory awareness emerged unbidden.

Suppose you pre-train subjects on the characteristics of sensory awareness (or some other aspect of experience) and then ask them to apprehend their pristine experience. To the extent that subjects paid attention to and were impacted by the pre-training, the pre-training will have three undesirable effects: (a) distraction, (b) selective sensitization, and (c) leading. (a) Distraction: When they should be engaged in the direct observation-of-pristine-experience task, they will instead (at least in part) be engaged in a conceptual task: They will be rehearsing the definition of sensory awareness, recalling what was said in the pre-training about sensory awareness, and so on. That conceptual focus distracts from, if not obliterates entirely, the direct observation of pristine experience. (b) Selective sensitization: Subjects will approach the apprehending-pristine-experience task sensitized to the possibility of sensory awareness, and therefore selectively *de*sensitized to other potential aspects of experience. The attempt at apprehending pristine experience is no longer a level playing field but is tilted in the direction of sensory awareness and away from other potential aspects. (c) Leading. Any report that the subject provides that sounds like sensory awareness is now quite possibly the result of having been led to sensory awareness by the (explicit or implied) pre-training suggestion of the interviewer.

Suppose a subject says: "I was driving. I know this sounds weird, but I wasn't paying any attention at all to my driving. My entire focus was on the particular yellow color of the yellow line; it was like I was drawn to the color of it. I guess my driving was happening on auto-pilot." If this was given as a "free-range" report, that is, by a subject who has *not* been pre-trained about sensory awareness, and particularly because it was advanced with some misgivings ("sounds weird"), this apprehension of pristine experience is quite believable. However, if the subject had been pre-trained in sensory awareness, instructed that sometimes people are "immersed in the experience of a particular sensory aspect of his or her external or internal environment without particular regard for the instrumental aim or perceptual objectness" (Chapter 16), then the same report may well be merely a reflection of the training. As a result, pre-training should *increase* the skepticism about the possibility of apprehending pristine experience. This pre-training dilemma presents itself not only for sensory awareness, but for *all* features of experience. Every pre-training reifies some presupposition about what will or won't be found in experience. It is impossible to provide pre-training that keeps a level playing field for reports of all sorts of inner experience.

An open-beginninged probe avoids that dilemma. If sensory awareness is indeed a characteristic of a subject's inner experience, it will emerge from a series of pristine experiences faithfully apprehended even if (or especially if) no pre-training has been given (it will become the X of the preceding "Multiple Perspectives on Experience" section). The price for reducing the dilemma is the inefficiency and discomfort – open-beginningedness often is initially uncomfortable for both subject and interviewer because it involves genuinely acknowledging ignorance.

Fortunately, in our DES studies, we have found that the open-beginninged approach is not as inefficient as it might appear. Most people apparently can, within two or three interviews, become adequately skillful in apprehending their experience. In fact, what appears to be an inefficient procedure may be not only the most direct path, but perhaps the only path to faithful apprehension.

Open-beginningedness is inextricably related to an iterative process. It's likely to be a waste to ask an open-beginninged question in a single interview: It requires one occasion to clarify what the beginning might be, and then another occasion to reap the benefits of that clarification. Moreover, it's likely to be a waste to conduct an iterative process that is not open-beginninged; the improvements brought about by iteration will then be built on a substantially impure foundation.

Synergistically Interrelated

For analytical purposes, I have separated out refreshment by new experience, improvement of the apprehensions, triangulation of the observations, and the open-beginninged process, but these are all synergistically interrelated. Refreshment by new experience results in improvement of the apprehensions; but improvement of the apprehensions also increases the refreshingness of new experience. Refreshment by the new experience is what makes an open-beginninged process possible, but the open-beginning process improves the observations, which increases the refreshingness of the new experience. And so on. All these features work in concert to potentiate each other and may lead to the high fidelity apprehension of pristine experience.

A FIRST INTERVIEW

First interviews occupy a unique position in an iterative (and therefore open-beginninged) investigation: They have to start nowhere, say nothing, and head some unknown place – head with as little interference as possible in the direction of some yet to be discovered experience. I now comment on a word-for-word transcript of the beginning of a typical first DES interview.

This interview was conducted by Nellie Mihelic (a graduate student training in the DES method, called NM in the transcript) and me (RTH) with "Joshua Thomas" (JT), a subject who was recruited as a practice participant for Nellie's DES training. Prior to the interview, we knew nothing about Joshua other than that he was a student in an introductory psychology class who volunteered for this study as a course requirement. Joshua's first beep occurred on September 21 at 2:14:38 P.M. The expositional interview was the following morning; we join the interview thirty seconds into the recording, during which time the camcorder was set up and adjusted, small talk exchanged, and so on. I superscript each conversational turn for ease of reference.

NELLIE MIHELIC:[1] Joshua, when did you collect your beeps?
JOSHUA THOMAS:[2] Yesterday between about 2:30 and 5:30 or 6:00.
NM:[3] And did you collect all six?

JT:[4] Yes. Except for the last one. I kind of rushed it. I pretended there was a
   beep. I just want to be honest.
NM:[5] [inaudible] OK. And the other, the first five, they were all beeps?
JT:[6] Um hm.
NM:[7] OK.
JT:[8] I don't know if that ruins anything for you guys, but . . .
RUSS HURLBURT:[9] Well, let's see when we get there.
JT:[10] Alright. [laughs]

Constraint: Subjects (initially) do not follow instructions. One basic reason
that iterative training is necessary is that subjects often don't follow the instructions given on a single occasion. In JT's instruction session, which had lasted
about forty-five minutes, we had emphasized, re-emphasized, given verbal
descriptions, used visual aids, and employed metaphors all aimed at raising JT's
appreciation for the importance of attending to the exact moment the beeper
sounds. Despite that effort, he still thought it was OK not to use a beeper.

This kind of imperviousness to instruction is not peculiar to JT; most
subjects have preconceived notions about what is important to a study and
what is not, and pre-training has difficulty penetrating those preconceptions.
It is not the result of naiveté. To the contrary, very sophisticated DES subjects
(consciousness scientists, for example; see Chapter 12) often fail to follow
important basic instructions. If you want someone to follow your instructions, you have to instruct him, then ascertain what he actually does, and then
instruct him again, and so on. That is, instruction itself must be iterative.

Note that at RTH[9], I *don't* say it's OK to pretend a beep (which it is not;
Hurlburt & Heavey, 2006), but I also don't say that it is not OK. JT has just demonstrated (by allowing himself to pretend the beep in the first place) that he is
currently incapable of understanding why such a pretending is not OK. I'm confident that this understanding will naturally arise in him later in the interview
when he discovers the difference in his ability to describe a beeped experience
and a non-beeped experience. Thus the iterative nature of DES allows his failure
to follow instructions to be a valuable training experience *for the next occasion.*

That JT volunteered the fact of his pretending augurs well for the future: It
demonstrates that he is motivated (even though he is currently failing) to
apprehend his experience faithfully.

NM:[11] Well, why don't you tell us what was in your experience at beep 1.
JT:[12] Beep 1. . . .[pause] Ah, well, I guess I could tell you what was happening
   right before. I was actually learning how to drive stick shift and I had the
   earpiece in my ear and then I just got out of the car 'cause the cops pulled
   up, and like "What are you doin'?" And my friend said, "Well, I'm teaching
   him how to drive stick." So I got out of the car and I was thinking, "It
   still hasn't beeped yet" and it beeped. And I was also thinking that, um, I
   wanted to drive on the street to get some gas for my friend's car.

Constraint: Subjects (initially) don't know what a moment is. We had, in his pre-training instructions, tried to convey to JT the "flashbulb" brevity of a moment, but JT, like most subjects, didn't grasp that and refers instead to a whole series of moments: the cops pulling up; the cops asking "What are you doin'?"; the friend's reply; JT's thinking about the beeper; JT's thinking he wants to drive on the street; JT's thinking about getting gas. JT's pristine experience is doubtless quite different from one of those moments to the next. We have found it impossible to convey, before sampling has been attempted, the brevity of a moment as we intend it; an iterative procedure is necessary to refine the subject's initial (mis)understanding of the moment.

> NM:[13] OK. So, I know you gave me some background there, so if you can help me clarify. Right when the beep went off, what was in your experience?
>
> JT:[14] Um. What do you mean, in my experience? [sounds puzzled] What was I thinking?

Constraint: Subjects (initially) don't know what experience is. JT's puzzlement is a typical and necessary first step of an open-beginninged iterative procedure. We had said in the initial instructions that experience was anything that is occurring directly before the footlights of his consciousness at the moment of the beep, but that instruction is apparently (and not surprisingly) difficult for him. Evident here is JT's presupposition that *thinking* is the primary feature of experience or the primary goal of the study; sooner or later we will iteratively have to disabuse him of that notion.

> NM:[15] Whatever was in your awareness or in your experience right at the moment of the beep. That could be …
>
> JT:[16] Well, I was standing like right at the hood of my friend's car, and, and then I was just thinking, it still hasn't beeped yet. And I actually said that out loud, too, to my friend, 'cause I had told him about the experiment. And it beeped.
>
> NM:[17] OK. Um, so the beep came right after you had said, "It still hasn't beeped yet"?
>
> JT:[18] [laughs] Yeah, like, pretty much. [laughs]

Constraint: Subjects (initially) don't know how to describe experience. The JT[18] "Yeah" seems to be an agreement with Nellie's NM[17] characterization of his experience. But JT[18], like most of JT's responses so far, is highly subjunctified (see Chapters 5, 8). The subjunctifiers ("like, pretty much") indicate Nellie's NM[17] summary is probably *not* what actually was ongoing in JT's experience at the moment of the beep, or is at best a loose approximation thereof.

JT's willingness to go along with loose approximations is quite typical of most subjects on their first attempt at describing experience. It requires an iterative procedure to refine JT's understanding that a faithful description requires reporting the specific details, not an approximation.

NM:[19] [laughs] And did you, um, you said that you said that out loud, but then, before, you also said you were thinking it? Was it both? One or the other?

JT:[20] It was both, pretty much. Is that normal? I don't know. [laughs nervously]

Constraint: Subjects (initially) may be reluctant to describe experience. JT, like nearly all others, has never had the opportunity or occasion to expose his moments of private experience. This makes it likely that he will be reluctant to reveal his private experience on the first day. When he discovers that the interviewers are sensitive and skillful, he will likely drop that reluctance, but that will require more than one occasion.

RTH:[21] Yes. That's normal.

JT:[22] I'm the kind of person that says what they think, usually, so ...

Constraint: Subjects (initially) don't distinguish between apprehension and theorizing. As evidenced by "I'm the kind of person" and "usually," JT[22] is a statement about a theoretical presupposition about himself, *not* a statement about a direct apprehension of his experience. Our aim is to get a faithful apprehension of JT's experience, so eventually, iteratively, we will have to convey to him that we are *not* interested in his self-theorizings. We had told him that in the pre-training, but that instruction (as expected) was not effective.

RTH:[23] I would like to clear up the "pretty much" part, because I'm not exactly sure what you mean by that. So, first off, let me get the sequence right. So you had been driving, you stopped driving – did the cops pull you over while you were driving? Or were you ...

JT:[24] Well, we were driving in the Thomas & Mack [a basketball arena] parking lot, it was like a whole empty parking lot, and I had just parked the car and the cop came over. And my window was rolled down, and my friend was in the passenger seat of his car ...

RTH:[25] But that was all before the beep, and then you ...

JT:[26] Um hm. It was all leading up to the beep.

RTH:[27] OK. And then you got out of the car and moved to the front of the car
...

JT:[28] Yeah.

RTH:[29] ... next to the hood of the car, and then you say out loud [questioningly], "It still hasn't beeped yet"? You say that to your friend? Or is that, or was that before ...

JT:[30] I said that like, I said that out loud, because that was what I was thinking.

RTH:[31] OK. And when you said "because that was what I was thinking," are you separately thinking, "I'm thinking this hasn't beeped yet," and *then* I say, "This hasn't beeped yet!" er, [uncertainly] "Still hasn't beeped yet"?

JT:[32] Yeah.

RTH:[33] And where does the beep come exactly in that sequence, as best you can say?

JT:[34] Like right after I said "yet" it beeped.

RTH:[35] OK. So the sequence is something like, *thinking* this thing hasn't beeped yet, and then *saying*, "It still hasn't beeped yet," beep! Is that right?

JT:[36] Yeah. Exactly.

RTH:[37] OK. Cool.

Constraint: Subjects (initially) don't know what the moment of the beep is. In the pre-training instruction, we had given JT considerable training about the importance of the moment of the beep. We had stressed that experience was fleeting and momentary, and apprehending experience would therefore require being very careful to note exactly where the beep occurs. However, it is clear that that training did not "take"; we are about three minutes into this interview, pressing to ascertain with some precision where the moment of the beep had occurred in the stream of JT's experience. RTH[35] summarizes, and JT[36] assents, but I'm quite skeptical of the veracity of this summary. JT wasn't prepared, *at the time of the first beep*, to note with precision where in his stream of experiences the beep occurred.

JT is entirely typical in this regard. Regardless of how often we say in the necessarily abstract pre-training instruction, "We want to know the exact microsecond of the beep," only the very rare subject actually understands this.

Now, however, as a result of the concrete conversation RTH[23-37], JT *does* probably have a clearer idea of what is meant by "the moment of the beep" and its importance. He will be far better at observing the precise moment of the beep when he wears the beeper next time. That, however, is the result of the concretely literal iterative training, not the pre-training abstract instruction.

Note carefully that even though the conversation RTH[23-37] appears to be my attempt to determine when the beep occurred in the stream of experience that was ongoing at 2:14:38 P.M. September 21, that is really not my aim. Instead, I am attempting here to improve, iteratively, his ability to apprehend the moment of the beep *on future occasions*. He was not a skilled observer at 2:14:38 P.M. September 21, and I completely accept that, and so am highly skeptical of his accounts of that experience. It's *tomorrow's* experience that I am primarily interested in here, not *yesterday's*.

[Here I omit 30 seconds of training conversation between Nellie and me that would distract us from our present purpose.]

RTH:[38] So, so far I've understood you to be saying, I first of all *thought* this thing hasn't beeped yet, and then I *said* it. Now is that really the case? That … Some people would say that what really happened was that it was both at the same time, and some people say, well I just said it so I *must* have been thinking it, so I want to be as explicit about that as we can be.

JT:[39] Well, OK. In that case it could have been I said it and it must have been what I was thinking.

RTH:[40] OK. So there's no really separate thought, then?

JT:[41] I don't think so.

RTH:[42] ... as far as you know at the moment?

JT:[43] As far as I know.

Constraint: Subjects (initially) don't bracket presuppositions. All iterative interviews are a balance of backward looking (ascertaining what was in pristine experience on some past occasion) and forward looking (skill building for future occasions). In first interviews, this balance is predominately forward-looking iterative improvement; in later interviews, the balance shifts toward the backward-looking data gathering.

Here, my aim is to level the playing field about what I take to be JT's presupposition about a sequence in inner experience: First think, then say. I don't *disbelieve* his report about this sequence; I am *skeptical* about it, and those are two very different things. I would be delighted to discover that his sequence actually is first think, then say. But I would be equally delighted to disabuse him of this presupposition if presupposition it is. So my aim here is forward looking: I raise the question about his presupposition so that the *next* occasion's interview may shed light on it.

> **Q:** It seems to me that you are leading JT in the direction of your presuppositional theory about thinking/saying and away from his presupposition.
>
> **A:** I disagree. First, I don't have a theory of thinking/saying – I don't care whether or not there is an experienced thought before an utterance. Second, it is JT's own comments, not my presuppositions, that lead me to this speculation about his presupposition. His utterance at JT[22] ("I'm the kind of person that says what they think, usually") is a general statement about something he presumes about himself, not a description of a particular experience; thus this statement was *his* announcement of the potential existence of *his* presupposition. It is my (iterative) obligation to try to level the playing field for JT with respect to his own presuppositions. That is not a presupposition on my part; that is proficiency at hearing JT's actual talk and expertise at helping him improve his faithful observation skills.

Such skill building *must be* iterative, and could not possibly have been performed before JT's participation in this interview for five reasons: (a) Prior to this interview, we had no way of knowing that JT had (perhaps) this thinking-and-saying presupposition. (b) Even if we had clairvoyantly known about his thinking-and-saying presupposition, a pre-training conversation about it would necessarily have been abstract. Now, by contrast, JT has a specific, real-in-his-own-life example of what is meant by a distinction between thinking-and-saying and just saying. (c) He is innately, personally involved in the process: The question stems from his own concrete behavior and his own inability to answer my questions. (d) I have demonstrated that I am interested in JT's getting it right about his own experience, that I am willing to work hard at it, and that I have some skill in training him to report his experience with fidelity. He can't just blow it off as mere boilerplate about the quality of science – this is about one real individual really wanting to know the details of what is going on within another real individual, with as much fidelity as possible and with no expectations of form or content. Finally, (e) presuppositions are mini-delusions, and attempting to argue someone out of his delusions is generally futile (Hurlburt & Schwitzgebel, 2011c).

[Here I omit 30 seconds of training conversation between Nellie and me that would distract us from our present purpose.]

RTH:[44] So you're standing at the hood of the car, the cops are around …

JT:[45] The cops had left.

RTH:[46] The cops had left. And so you're saying to your friend, "It hasn't beeped yet." Are those the exact words?

JT:[47] Yes.

RTH:[48] "It still hasn't beeped yet." And is anything else in your awareness other than the saying of those words?

JT:[49] Well. I know you showed me that whole slide [Figure 3.1 in Chapter 3] on, like, whenever the different situations leading up to the beep, but right before I was thinking it still hasn't beeped yet, I don't know if that's pertinent, but I was thinking that I could drive on the street to get my friend some gas.

RTH:[50] OK. But that was before the beep? That was like …

JT:[51] That was before…. It still hasn't beeped yet.

RTH:[52] And is that still present to you or has that come and gone? So the sequence is, the cops come, the cops go, I want to drive on the street, now I say to my friend it still hasn't beeped yet, and then it beeps, like separate links in a chain of sausages, one thing and then another thing and then another thing? Or do these things overlap?

JT:[53] I'm pretty sure it's still in the back of my mind, the driving on the street, and then I was just thinking it still hasn't beeped yet and I say it out loud, and then it beeps. But, I don't know, like the beep kind of like interrupted my thought process, y'know.

RTH:[54] Right.

JT:[55] It's really hard to narrow it down. It really throws you off.

RTH:[56] OK. I agree with all that. But this is only the first beep, and you're probably going to get somewhat better at that, or maybe you won't. But most people do get a little better at it as they get accustomed to what the beep …

Q: I think you pressure JT here in ways that might lead to construction in the future. If JT hears that most people get better, he may not want to appear to be one of the few that don't.

A: I agree that that is a risk. But I'd say three things: First, I think it is a small pressure. I explicitly acknowledge that he might not get better. (I discussed such pressure at length in Hurlburt & Schwitzgebel, 2007, pp. 285–289.) Second, in fact, I am not pressuring him. It may not be clear in this passage, but I think my entire interview demeanor conveys that high fidelity is of more value to me than an interesting story. I have told him or will tell him repeatedly on other occasions that I'll be happy to learn about why the DES process doesn't work for him, if that indeed turns out to be the case. Third, there are two competing pressures that need to be balanced. I agree that I don't want to lead the witness. But I also recognize that DES first interviews are frustrating, and it is simply unkind to let that frustration sit without support.

JT:[57]   Conditioning!
RTH:[58] I would think of it as sort of a practice, that after a while you figure out, Well, *that* is what the beep is! and it doesn't startle you as much. That's probably conditioning, if you like.

Constraint: Subjects (initially) don't observe skillfully. The heavy subjunctification ("I'm pretty sure" and "I don't know" at JT[53]; "It's really hard to narrow it down. It really throws you off" at JT[55]) indicates that JT thinks he is not adept at apprehending his experience, and I agree with him. Most people are not very good at apprehending their experience on their first sampling occasion. So subjects need support, and I try to provide it. Note, however, that even while supporting, I allow the subject ("or maybe you won't" at RTH[56]) the opportunity to advance an alternative that differs from my expectation and permission not to be a "good subject." Both are parts of the open-beginningedness of the process.

RTH:[59] So now I'm a little bit confused. A bit ago I thought there was no thought that was before the speaking. But now it seems like maybe there is a thought that it still hasn't beeped yet, that's before the speaking.
JT:[60]   Well, there must have been. Maybe it was a thought at the same time as I was saying it, you know. Maybe I was thinking that it still hasn't beeped and then I say that out loud, "It still hasn't beeped yet" (snaps fingers simulating beep).
RTH:[61] OK. And that's fine with me. I'm not trying to talk you into or out of what's in your experience.
JT:[62]   Right.
RTH:[63] What I'm trying to do is to say that we are interested in that fine of a distinction. If you're saying, "It still hasn't beeped yet," and as part of your experience you're also thinking that separately from the saying of it, we would like to know about that. But we don't want to just *presume* that that's the way it is, because we're trying to find out the way it *really* is. So we're ... and so we're happy with your saying, if it's true, "I was just saying out loud, 'It still hasn't beeped yet.' And that expressed myself. But I didn't really have a

thought first." That's possible. And it's also possible, "Well I thought to myself, Hm, this still hasn't beeped yet, and then said, 'It still hasn't beeped yet.'" And it's also possible that, "While I'm saying 'it still hasn't beeped yet,' I also am separately thinking, in my experience, that it still hasn't beeped yet. All those things are possible. And we're trying to figure out, what's that like for you?

Constraint: Make distinctions when and where distinctions are important. The repetition and the fine distinctions at RTH[59–63] are possible *only* because JT now has a personal stake in the discussion. This discussion is squarely on his turf, and he knows it. It fascinates him because it is *his*. It would have been impossible to have a discussion this precise before JT had himself struggled to try to make the distinction.

I'm not attempting to argue JT out of his mini-delusion; I'm trying, *with him*, to understand exactly what he meant about a particular pristine experience. JT himself indicated that there is a fissure in his presuppositional structure: He himself is not certain that there was a thought before a speaking (as evidenced by the subjunctifiers). We express a sincere interest in what he is saying, including a sincere appreciation for his qualifying expressions. We are trying to understand what he is telling us. As a result, we never attack, so he doesn't have to defend.

However, I re-emphasize the main point of iteration: This conversation is primarily aimed at skill building for *tomorrow's* sampling, *not* at trying to figure out *yesterday's* experience. Yesterday he didn't have adequate observational skill to support the kinds of distinctions we are raising.

RTH:[64] And I think we told you when we talked to you last week that we didn't expect you to know what this was going to be like until we've done it. And this is an example of that. You had no way of knowing that we were going to be interested in that fine a detail of what your experience is like. And nobody does. There's no way that you can know that until after we've had this kind of conversation. So basically, the first sampling day or two is our trying to convey to you, we really want to know about the microscopic details of what's in your experience, as best you can report it. It could be that you can say, "You guys are asking me questions that are way too difficult for me to answer! My experience isn't like that! I can't make that distinction." That would be fine, too. But we want to get sort of right up to that point, where we can take you as far as you are willing to go, or can go, or your experiences can take us, about what your experience is like.

JT:[65] Alright. I'll try my best.

RTH:[66] That's what we're here for.

Constraint: Recognize that iterative training is inherently frustrating. We don't tell subjects what they should be looking for, but then we ask detailed questions about what they have experienced. It's like walking into an exam on a surprise topic. It is frustrating but unavoidable because the alternative would be worse: We *do* tell subjects what they should be looking for and then feign discovery when they report it.

So we get to the end of the first interview *without collecting any reports that are believable*. It appears that all we have done is to point out to JT his inadequacy, that we have done nothing of positive value. But that's not true. He *was* an inadequate observer of his experience, and we have demonstrated our willingness to speak the truth about his inadequacy. We have demonstrated that we are skillful at understanding what he is saying and what he is not saying, and skillful at knowing the difference between apprehension and speculation, between truth and plausibility. We have demonstrated that we are supportive of him and non-judgmental. We have demonstrated that we are sincerely interested in obtaining faithful reports about experience. All that is really quite a lot. Even though it does not get us believable reports today, it sets the stage for obtaining believable reports *tomorrow*.

The fact is that JT (like most first-time subjects) was *not* ready to apprehend – he didn't have the skill, wasn't prepared, didn't accept that we really were interested in what was really in his pristine experience, didn't know what experience was, didn't really trust us to take him seriously, didn't understand how brief a moment is and how much pristine experience may change from one moment to the next, didn't really know the difference between apprehending and theorizing/speculating, didn't really adequately distinguish between what was truly apprehended and what was plausibly present. So yesterday his original pristine experience came and went, was apprehended in a low fidelity way, mixed with presupposition and self-presentation. *No amount of interviewing, no matter how skilled, could have reversed that*. Next time, however, he can, perhaps, do better. And the time after that, better still.

DISCUSSION

This chapter has drawn three main conclusions: (a) In any interview, an interviewer's apprehension of a subject's pristine experience arises from conflated contributions of pristine experience and reconstructed experience diminished by non-experiential impediments (subject's and interviewer's presuppositions, miscommunication); (b) regardless of skill, within-occasion interviewing is likely to *decrease* the direct contribution of pristine experience (because of the increase in the contribution of reconstructed experience); and (c) skillful across-occasion "iterative" interviewing may, incrementally on successive occasions, *increase* the direct contribution of pristine experience (and decrease the contribution of reconstruction).

An apprehension that arises from a conflation of pristine and reconstructed experience may well be quite similar to an apprehension that might arise from pristine experience alone. A reconstructed experience is, after all, itself an experience; the subject may well have intended the reconstructed experience to mirror the pristine experience; and the reconstructed experience was created by the same bag of bones and neurons that created the pristine experience. To the extent that the reconstructed experience is similar to the pristine experience, the interviewer's apprehension of (pristine and reconstructed) experience at the end of an interview can more faithfully mirror the subject's pristine experience than was possible at the beginning of the interview (the combined contribution of the pristine and the reconstructed experiences in Figure 10.2 is larger than in Figure 10.1). However, Hurlburt and Akhter (2006) argued that it is unwise to assume similarity between reconstructed and pristine experience – after all, the situations are much different (interview versus the original), subjects may not have been skilled observers at the time of the pristine experience and so may not know what they are trying to reconstruct, and the reconstructions may reflect presuppositions as much or more than the pristine experience. At present, the science of experience has no effective way of determining in what kinds of situations and for what kinds of experiences the reliance on reconstructed experience is useful.

I have argued that these features of iterative interviews may lead to higher fidelity apprehensions: (a) refreshment by pristine experience; (b) commitment to bracketing presuppositions; (c) practice in observing; (d) practice in being interviewed; (e) readiness to observe pristine experience; (f) reducing the need for reconstructions; (g) improving the fidelity of reconstructions; (h) multiple perspectives on experience; and (i) open beginning. A science of experience should examine which of these features is important in what situations. For example, clinical interviews could be said to be iterative: The therapist gets to know the client better on each occasion. However, clinical interviews have no procedure designed to assist in the bracketing of presuppositions by either therapist or client. Armchair observation can be said to be iterative – always trying to improve the observation of experience – but armchair observation is not about pristine experience: Armchair observation occurs only after a self-initiated intention to observe (Hurlburt & Schwitzgebel, 2007, 2011b). The Experience Sampling Method (ESM; e.g., Csikszentmihalyi & Larson, 1987) uses beepers to trigger subjects to fill out questionnaires about the experience that was occurring when beeped. Those repetitions could be called iterative, but the use of a pre-constructed Experience Sampling Form at each beep eliminates the possibility of bracketing presuppositions from one observation to the next, and ESM typically trains subjects in the use of the form on only one occasion. DES incorporates all the iterative features described in this chapter, but perhaps that slows the method down too much to be useful in science. At present, the science of experience does not know which features of iteration are useful under which circumstances.

I have observed that iteration does not always or automatically increase the contribution of pristine experience; that the beneficial effect of iteration depends on interviewer skill, particularly the skill of bracketing presuppositions. At present, the science of experience does not expend much effort training its practitioners in the bracketing of presuppositions.

I have argued that iteration can increase fidelity, not that it leads to complete accuracy. At present, the science of experience has not worked out a method to measure the fidelity of an observation.

At present, most empirical studies in the science of experience rely on one-occasion, non-iterative observations. The analysis in this chapter suggests that such reliance is problematic.

Consciousness science can be said to be caught in the crossfire between those who think experience is easy to apprehend (and therefore attempt to do so without much concern for methodological niceties) and those who think experience is impossible to apprehend (and therefore eschew the attempt altogether; Hurlburt & Heavey, 2004). Iterating the observing of experience/interview sequence may improve the apprehension of experience and thus reduce the crossfire.

Iteration is an essential feature of DES, an essentiality imposed on it by the genuine attempt to apprehend pristine experience in high fidelity. We will therefore return to iteration frequently in this book, particularly in the discussion of Figure 12.1 in Chapter 12.

> **Q:** You have in this book discussed a *lot* of constraints – fifty-nine so far, by my count. Which of those are important at which times, if I am genuinely to submit to them?
>
> **A:** All are important at all times. I expect that is not the answer you wanted to hear, but it's similar to classical violin playing: There are constraints about the bow: right number of horsehairs, right tension, right balance, right amount of rosin, and so on; there are constraints about the bowing: held at the right place, right amount of tension in the fingers, right angle (actually three angles) to the string, right amount of weight on the strings, and so forth; there are constraints about the violin: right construction, right strings, right intonation, and so on; there are constraints about the left hand … well, you get my drift. The virtuoso must genuinely submit to all those constraints simultaneously if the sound production is to be beautiful.
>
> The good news is that as violin performance skills become perfected, those constraints become automated, and the virtuoso has only to concentrate on making beautiful music. When the beauty is corrupted in a particular way, the artist knows that his right hand is rotating the bow at the wrong angle and automatically corrects it; when the beauty is corrupted in a different but still particular way, the artist knows that his left hand is slightly too far up the neck and automatically corrects it; and so on. The artist continues at all times genuinely to submit to those constraints, but automatically. Once that

automaticity is achieved (10,000 hours later), submitting to the constraints is easy – just try to make beautiful sounds.

The same is true for exploring inner experience. The constraints can become automated, so all the "artist of inner experience" has to do is to pay attention to moments of experience, and when the purity of description is corrupted in a particular way, the artist knows that the subject needs help sticking to the moment; when the purity of description is corrupted in a different but still particular way, the artist knows that the subject needs help differentiating experience from all else; and so on. The artist continues at all times genuinely to submit to those constraints, but automatically. Once that automaticity is achieved, submitting to the constraints is easy – just help the subject describe moments of experience.

Q: Yes, but how do you acquire fifty-nine skills all at the same time? That's impossible.
A: No, it's not impossible, it's just difficult. You screw into all of them, each revolution more securely than the last. The violinist does the same thing. He concentrates for a while on right hand technique, until that is better than left hand technique. Then he concentrates on left hand technique, not entirely ignoring right hand technique, but with the bulk of the focus on the left hand, until the left hand is more skillful than the right. Then he goes back to the right hand. All the while, he's listening to the beauty of the production, seeing what goes with what, what gives this color or that, and so on.

It's the same with exploring pristine experience. Cycle through all the constraints, focusing particularly on one but not to the exclusion of the others, all the while paying attention to moments of experience, seeing what leads toward, what leads away from moments of experience. It is by no means impossible. It is by no means easy.

Q: The least you could do is to provide some helpful organization for the constraints.
A: This book is about the necessity of genuinely submitting to the constraints, not about the constraints themselves. I do not pretend to be presenting a complete set of constraints, nor a set of constraints reduced to their minimum number. The constraints imposed may well depend on the particular situation and the persons involved, so an efficient set of constraints may well be impossible.

My aim is to demonstrate that if you are to apprehend experience with fidelity, you need to ascertain what constraints are imposed and then genuinely submit to them. I expect that many if not all of the constraints I am discussing here may also apply in your situation; that is, I expect that my discussion of constraints may be helpful to you. I do not wish, however, to be understood as providing a complete catalog of constraints.

11

Epistemological Q/A

The questions in this book are based on real questions from reviews, e-mail exchanges, and question-and-answer sessions following presentations. I have edited the questions for readability, coherence, and context while trying to keep their flavor.

BRACKETING PRESUPPOSITIONS[1]

Q: You have referred throughout this book to the "bracketing of presuppositions." Can you elaborate on what a presupposition is?
A: Chris Heavey and I described presuppositions this way:

> A presupposition is a preconception, something that is taken for granted. It is a notion about the world that is so fundamental that it exists prior to critical examination. It is something accepted without controversy as being true, something that shapes perception, behavior, and affect without the fact of that shaping being noticed or recognized. It is an unquestioned manner of relating to the world that chooses what is seen and what is not seen, what is experienced and how it is experienced, so invisibly that what is seen and experienced seems to be the world itself, not aspects of the world selected, shaped, and distorted by the presuppositional process. (Hurlburt & Heavey, 2006, p. 151)

Presuppositions cause you to turn away from evidence that might change your mind, cause you to assume that your currently used methods and procedures are adequate (if not downright virtuous). Presuppositions arise from (and at the same time create) a personally advantageous and self-sustaining mix of prideful, professional, social, economic, and other influences.

---

[1] Parts of this section are adapted with permission from Hurlburt, R. T., & Schwitzgebel, E. (2011c). Presuppositions and background assumptions. *Journal of Consciousness Studies.*

Q: You said in Chapter 9 that bracketing presuppositions is a stern taskmaster, that *"everything* that seems obvious must be bracketed." I think that evokes the ill-conceived scientific ideals of Bacon (1620/2000) and Descartes (1641/1984) – in particular the ideal of conducting inquiry completely free of background assumptions. The incoherence of that ideal was, I think, amply demonstrated by twentieth-century philosophy of science (especially Popper 1935/1959 and Kuhn 1962/1970) and twentieth-century cognitive psychology. Without background assumptions, and the categories and schemata that depend on and embody them, one is as cognitively naked as the empiricists' baby, all sensory input only a buzz of confusion. Presuppositions are both *necessary* and *good* because presuppositions are built into the very having of concepts, into every action, and into every perceptual, theoretical, memorial, and introspective judgment. When I walk into a building, I presuppose that the floor will support me. When I sit on a bus, I presuppose that the person next to me won't punch me in the nose for no reason. Walking past an orchard, the splashes of red I see among the trees I assume more likely to be apples than coffee mugs. Do you really want me to bracket *everything*?

A: I want you to bracket every presupposition that arises (I elaborate this view in Hurlburt & Schwitzgebel, 2011c). You say you presuppose that the floor will support you, and so do I. But we presuppose that exactly because the system has created a particular class of individuals ("building inspectors") whose job is precisely *not* to presuppose that. Building inspectors are trained to set aside appearances of solidity and structural adequacy and examine the solidity and structure for themselves. I want the building inspector to try to bracket all presuppositions related to construction adequacy, to try not to be taken in by the surface appearance, or by the adequacy of the drawings, or by the reputation of the builder, or by anything that you or I would take for granted when we step out of the elevator. I want the building inspector to look for herself: to take her own core samples, X-rays, ultrasounds, whatever it takes to establish for herself that the construction is adequate.

Q: But it seems impractical, maybe even impossible, for the building inspector to bracket all presuppositions relevant to construction adequacy (e.g., about steel's retaining its strength over time, about the floor's being solid at point D given that it is solid at A, B, and C, etc.). Maybe you mean she can bracket one or a few presuppositions at a time, and the rest she can try to hold lightly, in the sense that she would be willing to change her mind if contrary evidence presented itself.

A: No, that's not what I mean, on two counts. First, I think it is *harder* to bracket one or a few presuppositions than to bracket many. That's like bringing an elephant into the room and then trying to imagine what it would be like without one.

Second, "holding presuppositions lightly" is a far too passive stance. I think you need to be actively, relentlessly on the lookout for such presuppositions, sniffing them out. In Hurlburt and Schwitzgebel (2011c) I listed a series of researchers who would probably insist that *of course* they were attuned to signs of trouble in their theories, and *of course* if they spotted such signs they would change their minds. *Yet they don't spot such signs of trouble*, because it is the nature of presuppositions to blind one to such trouble spots.

A presupposition is a skill (or set of skills), a dextrous coordination of learned tasks. That skill is perhaps counter-productive or self-defeating, but it is a skill nonetheless. A presupposition is a skillfully built, elaborated, and maintained coordinated, self-amplifying system of beliefs, fears, professional advantages, anxieties, economic incentives, narcissisms, and the like, each aspect supporting and defending itself and the other aspects. Part of that skill is to spot potential disconfirming evidence and, to turn away, defocus, and aim attention elsewhere – whatever it takes to defuse the potential disconfirmation. An obvious example is the conservative who turns away from MSNBC and turns toward Fox News, whereas a liberal would do the opposite. But presuppositions are high skills, practiced across a lifetime, so this turning away is usually not obvious. The skill is to turn away, defocus, aim attention elsewhere – to do whatever it takes to undermine disconfirmation *when there is only a trivial hint of it*, at its first whiff, when it is a mere speck on the horizon. At the same time, one learns, with the same level of at-the-first-whiff subtlety, to spot potential confirmations when they appear and to turn toward them. Because the first whiffs, in either direction, are probably not explicitly recognized (and if they are recognized, they are dismissed as trivial), the *world itself* seems full of confirmations and devoid of disconfirmations, and there is no appreciation for the highly refined (albeit self-defeating) skill that warps the view of the world.

The bracketing of presuppositions is also a skill, a personal set of coordinations that must be relentlessly sensitive and powerful enough to be able to counter the deeply rooted and taken-for-granted presupposition skill. It is an ongoing battle, pitching one set of coordinations against another set within the same individual. I'm pretty sure it is possible for the bracketing skill to make progress against the presupposition skill; I don't know whether the bracketing skill can win once and for all (perhaps that is what is called nirvana, about which I have no personal knowledge).

"Hold presuppositions lightly" simply does not connote an activity that is energetic enough, relentless enough to penetrate the presuppositional self-containment; it does not acknowledge the difficulties presented or the courage required; it contains the implication: *Of course! I'm already doing that.* It implies that skill and practice is not required; it does not undermine the overconfidence that people have in their own positions. Most scientists, it seems to me, believe that they hold their presuppositions lightly, so if I were to exhort my colleagues to hold presuppositions lightly, as you suggest, I think I would be de facto saying to them: *Stay the course! No big deal here! Everything will be cool, just as now!*

But I don't want to communicate that. I want to say: *It's not good enough, and it is a huge deal! We have to do better! Consciousness science is full of unwarranted presuppositions, and we have persistently, continually, aggressively, fearlessly to fight to get them under control.*

I elaborate all these views in Hurlburt and Schwitzgebel (2011c).

Q: I'm still struggling to understand what you mean by bracketing of presuppositions, and would like to know what you think of this: Samuel Taylor Coleridge, the novelist and poet best known for *The Rime of the Ancient Mariner* and *Kubla Khan*, talked about "suspension of disbelief" as a process that a good novelist evokes from readers. It basically consists of instilling a narrative with enough realistic or human elements for the reader to accept all sorts of fantastical elements in a story. The reader suspends his disbelief to be able to follow and become engaged in a fantastical story. So, I can enjoy the movie *Spiderman* because I have suspended my disbelief for a couple of hours and am choosing to believe that there is this guy who can propel himself across New York skyscrapers through the webs that flow from his fingers.

It seems to me that you are asking your reader to do the opposite: Suspend *belief*. Put your beliefs aside, some of which may indeed be fantastical, so that you can follow and become engaged in the only real story. So Coleridge had the suspension of disbelief and you have the suspension of belief. Is that what you mean?

A: Exactly! Coleridge adds enough truthiness to make a story compelling. I want to subtract enough truthiness to make an account faithful.

REPORTABILITY

Q: Russ, you tell interesting stories about what you call experience, but in doing so you naïvely ignore a central concern of consciousness studies: whether reportability and experience go together. Ned Block gives this example: You are reading at the kitchen table when you notice the compressor on the fridge switch off. It seems to you that you have been aware of the compressor's hum all along. But if asked about your experience prior to its turning off, you would not have reported the hum (while you were reading you weren't attending to it). Block says that you were experiencing the hum all along (see Block's **2007** *Behavioral and Brain Sciences* paper for the most extensive discussion of this issue). Block concludes that what we report is distinct from what we experience: Though we *may* experience everything we report, we fail to report, or to be able to report, everything we experience. We only can report what we attend to. Now, if Block is right this is very bad news for your work.

Of course, Block might be wrong, but the rival view that Block's opponents promote is no better for your project. On the rival view, what happens when the compressor switches off is that your attention is drawn to an alteration in the environment. That your attention is drawn to it implies that the information that was until then not experienced was, rather, being registered sub-personally, and is now made available for experience. That is, because the alteration in the environment might be important, the information is made available as if it were the content of experience all along. However, this is a reconstruction, caused by mechanisms that promote representations to phenomenal consciousness. On this view, attending to information alters the experience. If this view is correct, then there is no reason at all to think that what your subjects report as their experience really was their experience. Rather, the beep sets in motion sub-personal processes that select from among the representations that were available those that will be made available to phenomenal consciousness.

For your project to succeed, you need a third view to be correct, on which experience and reportability always (or pretty much nearly always) go together. Both Block's view and that of his rivals may be wrong, but it demonstrates that there are deep problems with thinking that experience and reportability go together in normal life. You have not shown why this third view is more plausible than both the more popular views. Therefore, what you give us is just what the introspectionists gave us: a fascinating set of descriptions of experience but little reason to take the descriptions seriously.

A: Let's accept your characterization of Block (Block might have some quibbles, but they need not concern us here) and his rivals. I do not accept your conclusion, though, that I "need experience and reportability always (or pretty much nearly always) [to] go together." For my project to succeed, I need only that experience and reportability *sometimes* (not necessarily even often) go together, and to have a principled way of knowing with some probability (not necessarily perfect) when those goings-together might be expected to occur. The distinction between "always (or pretty much nearly always)" and "sometimes" is substantial.

Both sides of the Block debate agree that experience and reportability *sometimes* go together. Block's fridge scenario, for example, depends on your noticing that the fridge switches off; both sides accept that experience and reportability go together *then*. The link between experience and reportability is called into question only about the *ongoing* compressor hum.

About the off-click itself, there is no nicety of wording or definitional detail required: "Did you hear the click?" "Did you experience the click?" "Did you attend to the click?" will all elicit a confident and relatively uncontroversial "Yes." By contrast, as the rival opinions you cite demonstrate, whether the ongoing hum is experienced is a difficult if not impossible question to answer, dependent on the exact wording of queries and the details of definitions of terms like "experience" and "attention." "Did you hear the hum?" "Did you experience the hum?" "Did you attend to the hum?" will properly elicit unconfident (probably highly subjunctified) and perhaps disparate responses, such as, "Well, I don't know. Maybe, it depends, y'know, on what you mean by 'hear' (or by 'experience' or by 'attend to')." Such responses will be considered controversial not only by the interviewer but by the subject herself.

I and DES take this difficulty entirely seriously by attempting to develop the skill of being interested in the kinds of experiences where experience and report are likely to be linked and by *declining* to be interested in the kinds of experiences where experience and report are *not* likely to be linked (see Hurlburt & Schwitzgebel, 2011a).

At least as importantly, I would like us to be crystal clear that the fridge scenario is *not* about experience as I define it in this book. Pristine inner experience, the topic of this book, inheres in moments, and there is *no moment specified in the fridge scenario*. When you cite the fridge scenario, you *presume* that your listener can *imagine* a concrete moment, but that is likely not true.

Q: OK, then I'll say, "Let's presume that the fridge clicks off at 11:47:06 A.M.; the moment I'm interested in is the second before, namely 11:47:05." *That's* a concrete moment.

A: No it is not – it is a figment of your imagination and is therefore neither concrete nor a moment. Moments of experience, the topic of this book, are real experiences at real times, not imagined experiences at presumed or imaginary times. It would of course be possible to arrange a beep to occur at some real particular 11:47:05 and for the fridge to click off a second later. Under those circumstances, there *would be* a concrete moment to consider.

Q: I don't see the difference. When you say you could arrange a beep, you're making up a hypothetical moment just like I did.

A: Not at all. When I say we *could* arrange a beep and then explore experience, I am saying that *we haven't* arranged a beep, and therefore we have *no* concrete moment to consider, and therefore we have *nothing* to say about experience, whether it includes the fridge hum or it doesn't. Your question, by contrast, presumes that you *can* and *do* imagine the fridge situation, and that that imagining allows you to say *something* about experience, to have an opinion about whether experience includes the hum. Me: *Potentially accomplishable in some future (not yet existing) reality.* You: *Already accomplished in imagination.* Those are not in the slightest the same.

If we *did* arrange a situation where we could apprehend experience at a series of moments, and that situation included a humming fridge, then we might be able to ascertain, at each particular moment, whether the hum was or was not experienced, but so far, we *haven't* done that. If we went to the trouble of arranging such a situation, and one of those moments happened to be 11:47:05, then the result would probably be either that the hum was directly experienced at 11:47:05 or that there was little or no experience of the hum at 11:47:05. But until we run the experiment, we don't know which.

LITTLE OR NO, RICH OR THIN EXPERIENCE

Q: You say that there might be "little or no" experience of the hum. There's a huge distinction between *a little* experience of the hum and *no* experience of the hum. You can't just lump them together like that.

A: Eric Schwitzgebel and I have written at length about little or no experience (Hurlburt & Schwitzgebel, 2011a). I will summarize here, but this is an important topic and I refer you to the original. For all people at all moments, there is a welter of events/processes/occurrences that are candidates for experience. Some of those events are external: breezes, pressures, fridge hums, seen objects, and so on. Some of those events are internal: kinaesthetic, proprioceptive, imaginary, and so on. There are, depending on how you count, hundreds or thousands or millions of events/processes/occurrences in the welter. DES shows that out of that welter of potentialities, most people at most particular moments bring one experience or a very few experiences directly before the footlights of consciousness and pretty much annihilate, for that moment, the welter of other potential experiences.

For example, in Chapter 6, Mike at sample 3.1 was walking to the bus stop on his way home. Presumably there was a welter of events/processes/occurrences ongoing in and around Mike at that moment, some external (the sound of the traffic, the smell of the asphalt, the breeze against his right wrist, etc.) and some internal (the feel of his foot against his shoe and his shirt against his neck, the flex of the left leg, the hunger contraction, the recollection of the unhappy conversation he had had earlier that afternoon, etc.). Of that hundreds- or thousands-strong welter, at the moment of beep 3.1 there were two that were, from Mike's point of view, uncontroversially directly experienced: the pink-against-gray "sensory pop" of the crepe myrtle bloom against the gray wall and the inner hearing of Paul Simon's "Mother and Child Reunion." There was one that was controversially directly experienced: whether he was imaginarily telling his neighbor about the earpiece. He had *little or no* experience of the rest of the thousands of events/processes/occurrences in the welter – little or no experience of the rub of his collar against his neck, little or no experience of the flex of his left knee as he walked, little or no experience of the earlier unhappy conversation, and so on.

From an experiential point of view, it is impossible (or at least practically impossible) to distinguish between "a little experience" and "no experience" about the collar, the knee, and so on. Depending on the details of the definition of "experience" and how assertively one probes, I think one could conclude that Mike had *a little* experience of his collar or that Mike had *no* experience of his collar. I have been able to find no experiential way out of this inability to determine whether the collar is (a little) or is not experienced at that moment – that is, I don't think Mike can reliably contribute to disentangling those options – so DES concludes that Mike had "little or no experience" about the collar, the knee, the conversation, and the hundreds or thousands of other events in the welter, and declines to proceed further.

Q: That's a cop out. Distinguishing between *a little* and *no* is crucially important.
A: There is a clear dividing line between *a little* and *no* for some things – money, for example: If I have one cent, I have a little money, but if I lose that

cent, I have no money. Other things, however, have no such clear borderline – there is no clear-cut distinction between mountain and no mountain; instead, the term "mountain" loses its range of convenience in some indeterminate place (Hurlburt & Schwitzgebel, 2011a). Experience is more like mountains than money, so I think it is not possible to distinguish unambiguously between little and no experience. That is not a cop out; it is submitting to the constraints that the exploration of experience imposes.

I think consciousness science focuses on such difficult or impossible distinctions and then over-generalizes that difficulty. I think it is possible to say with some confidence that Mike was experiencing, before the footlights of consciousness, the pink-against-gray sensory pop and the inner hearing of the of the Paul Simon song; and that there is a huge experiential difference between those two experiences and the rest of the welter, of which he has little or no experience. There are, occasionally, some experiential controversies (for example, whether Mike was also imaginarily talking to his neighbor). As discussed in Chapter 6, there are lots of reasons that such controversies may arise, including that Mike may have had the false belief that he frequently talked to himself and therefore scoured the moment for something that *might* have resembled talking to himself.) But that is the exception that proves the rule: There is a big experiential gap between a few directly experienced experiences and the welter of little-or-no-experience experiences. I think it is of value, at this point in the history of science of experience, to explore the big distinctions (that's what led to the bulimia discoveries of Chapter 2). When we have accomplished that, then it might be possible constructively to explore little distinctions.

Q: Maybe the entire welter of experience was equally directly present to Mike at that sample, but by the time he has jotted down notes about the pink-and-gray and Paul Simon, he has forgotten about the neck-against-collar and flex-of-the-knee, and so on.

A: That possibility (among others) is precisely why the exploration of experience has to be iterative (see Chapter 10). The interviewer should (and did) say something like, "Y'know, Mike, you say that you experienced only two things (or maybe three), but maybe there were lots of other events/processes/occurrences that were equally directly present in your experience, but by the time you jotted down notes about the pink-and-gray and Paul Simon, you have forgotten about those other things. *So on your next sampling day,* please be aware of that possibility *before you jot anything,* survey your experience as completely as possible and jot down one word about each experience before you go back to fill in any details."

I accept that such iterative training does not *solve* the issue, but I think it does limit its scope substantially. Most subjects, including sophisticated subjects like Mike, seem to find the possibility of quickly evanescent experience interesting and take the search for it seriously, and at the end of a series of iterative attempts convincingly say something like, "I looked hard for more experiences, but there weren't any."

Q: Suppose I accept that. But if we limit ourselves to directly-experienced-at-particular-times studies as you suggest, we limit ourselves to discussing only those obvious things that we all know about: *Of course* people occasionally hear refrigerators switch off, *of course* people occasionally notice the pink of crepe myrtle blooms. Your science would be epistemically adequate but trivial.

A: I think you are mistaken that such a science would be trivial – it is the point of this book to demonstrate that (think bulimia). And I think you are mistaken in your estimation that science already knows about such things. Let's use your reference to Block (2007) as an example.

Block, as you recognize, is a highly regarded consciousness scientist who uses an analytic strategy that is common among consciousness scientists; understanding his strategy will provide some insight into whether the DES strategy is trivial and whether consciousness science is as knowledgeable as you seem to think.

Block (2007) wondered whether there was consciousness within each of the perceptual modules described by Fodor (1983). Those modules are, for example, small bits of the visual system; for instance, one module reacts to sharp changes in luminosity. There are, presumably, hundreds or thousands or millions of such modules (Fodor, 1983, p. 47). I call Block's question about whether some one particular perceptual module has consciousness a *micro* question, whereby "micro" I am merely referring to the size of the bit of consciousness involved (loosely speaking one one-hundredth or one one-millionth of a person's total consciousness).

Block attempts to answer this micro question by considering, for the most part, a host of what I will call *special* situations, where by "special" I mean only that they are unusual by comparison to everyday situations. Here are some of his examples: binocular rivalry, where, for example, a face-stimulus is presented to one eye while at the same time a house-stimulus is presented to the other eye (the subject's experience alternates between face and house); various kinds of particular brain injury such as *visuo-spatial extinction syndrome*, where if a fork is shown to the left, the patient can identify it, and if a knife is shown to the right, the patient can identify it, but if the fork-on-the-left and knife-on-the-right are shown simultaneously, the patient sees the fork but not the knife; change blindness, where a photograph is presented to a subject, followed by a pause, followed by another photograph that is similar but different in some large but not primary detail (the subject typically says the photos are identical); and so on. Those are all *special* by my definition: Rarely does anyone, in her everyday activity, simultaneously see a face with her left eye and a house with her right eye.

Block's strategy relies heavily on considering a series of special situations and how they might apply to a micro question. However, Block's primary interest is neither in the special situations nor the micro questions; those are special/micro means to a macro end: the understanding of consciousness itself. Block strategy is common in consciousness science.

Block does *not* spend much time or energy directly investigating the macro issue – experience itself. Introspection has indeed a problematic history, so it is entirely reasonable, in my view, for a consciousness scientist to rule out of consideration *all* reference to introspected conscious experience. Block, however, does not rule out all such consideration. Instead, he seems to assume that he knows quite a bit about everyday (macro) conscious experience, as indicated by statements such as "Of course some states that have phenomenology, for example, emotions and thoughts, are not experienced as spatially located" (Block, 2007, p. 482).

However, whereas my research shows, as Block says, that emotions and thoughts are *often* (probably even usually) not experienced as spatially located, I'm quite sure that there are many instances in everyday situations where everyday people *do* experience emotions and thoughts as spatially located. For example, when some people say they had a thought "in the back of my mind," they intend that to be an *entirely literal description of the experienced spatial location of their thought*: They describe a thought that is phenomenally located in the rear of the cranium (Hurlburt & Schwitzgebel, 2007, p. 160). (Other people, perhaps most people, perhaps including Block, intend "in the back of my mind" as a metaphor. However, I speculate that the persistence of the metaphor derives from the fact that it is not metaphorical for some people.) Similar things can be said for emotion.

Thus it seems to me that Block is substantially mistaken in at least this aspect of his view of the macro characteristics of the phenomena of consciousness, and that's a pretty big thing for a consciousness scientist to be mistaken about, in my view. It is the "of course" in his statement that draws my particular attention: It carries the implication that Block is *entirely confident* about his (I think) mistaken view of the macro characteristics of the phenomena of consciousness, that there is *no question* about the macro characteristics of phenomenal experience, that *everyone knows* how thoughts and feelings are experienced, that there is *no need to explore* the macro characteristics. You, dear questioner, seem to share that (over)confidence, which is a characteristic of, I think, the presuppositions about experience that I have discussed in Hurlburt and Schwitzgebel (2007, 2011c), Hurlburt and Heavey (2006), and here.

Thus it seems to me that Block is interested in macro phenomena of consciousness and bases his understanding of that on (a) at least partially mistaken but taken-for-granted views of macro phenomena and (b) careful consideration of micro phenomena and the evidence that can be gathered thereabout from special situations.

I wish to be clear that I am in no way singling out Block in this regard – I think many if not most consciousness scientists hold similar views about the macro phenomena of experience with equally unjustified overconfidence. As evidence of that, Block (2007) was a target article in one of the top journals in consciousness studies; there were thirty-two commentaries to that article, and unless I missed it, *none* pointed out his overconfident mischaracterization of the spatial phenomena of thought.

I also wish to be clear that I have no objection to the strategy of examining special situations and micro phenomena as a means of understanding consciousness. My objection is to the *over-reliance* on that strategy and the corresponding *under-appreciation* for the careful direct observation of experience. Just as a cabinetmaker would not use fine sandpaper until she was finished with coarse sandpaper, I think it is likely to be unproductive to over-consider micro issues until we have the macro issues well understood. Is fine sandpaper important? Yes. Could the cabinetmaker do the whole job with only fine sandpaper? Maybe, but it would take a very long time and wear out lots of sandpaper (and probably lots of cabinetmakers).

Q: It is possible that it is *you*, not Block, who is mistaken about the spatial location of thinking. I'm deeply skeptical about your project. You believe that your subjects learn to describe their pristine experiences as a result of your questioning and training. It seems to me more likely that your subjects learn what kinds of responses to your questions will satisfy you, and then give them.

A: I happily accept that I may be mistaken; one of the purposes of this book is to encourage others to engage in similar or better apprehensions of experience. Let's note that the claim under consideration – that thoughts are or are not experienced as spatially located – is decidable *only* by some form of introspection (broadly defined). This is a question about experience, and there is no experimental, analytic, or neurophysiological evidence that can be brought to bear here. Therefore, it seems that the choice is either to dismiss the whole introspective enterprise (which neither I nor, apparently, Block is willing to do) or to develop methods that try to do the introspective enterprise well.

The subjects-pleasing-the-investigator issue is important. I've discussed related issues in Hurlburt and Schwitzgebel (2007, e.g., pp. 285–289), and take great pains to limit their force. For example, I typically sample with *two* interviewers, on the probability that what is pleasing to one may not be pleasing to the other. In particular, I co-interviewed with Eric Schwitzgebel, a noted skeptic about introspection; pleasing Eric would seem to be just about the opposite from pleasing me. What's a poor investigator-pleasing subject to do in such a situation? Such steps of course provide no guarantees, but they do make it less likely that subjects will be captured in the way that worries you.

Furthermore, if you are worried about subjects pleasing the investigator, it seems you should apply that worry also to Block and inquire what introspective-type investigations Block has consulted to provide evidence for his claim. I don't know Block, but it wouldn't surprise me if much of his (over)confidence about the thoughts-have-no-spatial-location issue come from his own observations of his own thoughts. If so, it seems you should be an order of magnitude *more* worried that Block's subject (himself) tries to please Block than that *my* subjects (who don't really have much investment in me) try to please *me*.

I criticized such armchair introspection in Hurlburt and Schwitzgebel (2007); I thought (and think) that armchair introspection is a substantial impediment to the progress of consciousness science. I amplified that view in

Hurlburt and Schwitzgebel (2011b). Even if an armchair introspector is right about his own experience (a dubious assertion), whether one's own inner characteristics are shared by everyone else is still an open question.

I wish to be clear that I have no particular knowledge of how Block arrived at his (I think) incorrect view of the lack of localization of thoughts – perhaps armchair introspection played only a minor role for him, and if I have overemphasized his reliance on armchair introspection, I apologize. The point is not particularly about Block; it is about the many consciousness scientists who hold overconfident but (I think) incorrect views about the macro characteristics of pristine experience that they have not investigated adequately.

Q: Even if I grant all that, again borrowing from Block, how do you distinguish what is dispositionally available to report – the contents of access consciousness – from what is phenomenally present? *Availability to report at the moment of the beep is not phenomenal consciousness at the moment of the beep*, at least according to many thinkers; further and worse, *there may be no way to distinguish empirically between what is actually present at the moment of the beep and what can be retrieved from non (phenomenally) conscious systems for report*, because what is retrieved for report will be a representation with a phenomenal feel and which will be backdated to the moment of the beep.

A: I fully accept the possibility that the act of responding to the beep may diminish, warp, or completely wipe out the pristine experience that was actually ongoing at the moment of the beep and replace it with some new phenomenon that *seems like* it had been ongoing; I accept that there may be no empirical way to rule out that possibility. However, as I said in Hurlburt and Schwitzgebel (2007) and amplified in Hurlburt and Schwitzgebel (2011b), that is at least as serious a problem for *all* introspection as it is for DES: The armchair decision, *Ah! I think I will introspect now about what was ongoing in me!* seems at least as likely (probably more likely) to produce a backdated phenomenon as is an exteriorly generated, unambiguous signal such as the DES beep. Therefore, as I have said, I think it is a perfectly legitimate principled position to rule out *all* introspective reports including DES. I do *not* think it is fair to single out DES in this regard.

There's lots of pretty compelling evidence that people can report quite a bit of detail about what is present in experience. The now-classic Sperling (1960) studies and the extensions that build on it indicate that experience (or some detailed representation of it) persists for perhaps a second or more. For example, consider the experiment schematized in Figure 11.1. Landman, Spekreijse, and Lamme (2003) briefly displayed Stimulus 1, eight rectangles arranged in a circle more or less like the face of a clock, as sketched in the left side of Figure 11.1.

Stimulus 1 lasts .5 seconds, and is followed by a blank interval, whose duration was varied by the experimenters from .4 to 1.5 seconds. For the moment, ignore the "cue." Then Stimulus 2 is briefly (.5 seconds) presented; Stimulus 2 is either identical to Stimulus 1 or identical except that one rectangle's orientation has been rotated ninety degrees; Figure 11.1 shows that the rectangle at middle-

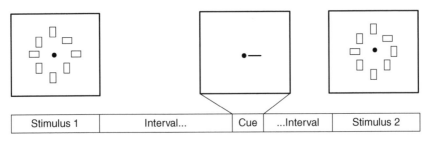

FIGURE 11.1. A study that combines change blindness with Sperling. Revised[2] from Landman, Spekreijse, & Lamme (2003).

right has been rotated. Then the subject is to indicate whether Stimulus 2 is identical to Stimulus 1 (here the answer is no).

So far, this is an example of a change-blindness study, and subjects do little better than chance in determining whether the two stimuli are identical.

Of particular interest to us here, Landman and his colleagues also sometimes inserted a "cue" somewhere in the interval. The cue was a line segment that started near the fixation point and extended in the direction of the one rectangle that may or may not change. In Figure 11.1, for example, the cue's line segment points to the right, indicating that if a rectangle is to change, it will be the one at the right. It turns out that the cue is indeed effective in helping subjects determine whether Stimulus 2 is the same or different from Stimulus 1.

Landman and his colleagues found that the cue would be effective even if the interval between the offset of Stimulus 1 and the onset of the cue was as long as 1.5 seconds. Because the cue does not appear until after Stimulus 1 disappears, the fact that such a cue is efficacious in reducing change blindness implies that the subject must continue to maintain some kind of *large-capacity representation* of Stimulus 1 for a second or so after the actual Stimulus 1 disappears.

This is only one study, but even Block agrees that, in general, William James was right when he held:

If we open our eyes instantaneously upon a scene, and then shroud them in complete darkness, it will be as if we saw the scene in ghostly light through the dark screen. We can read off details in it which were unnoticed whilst the eyes were open. (James, 1890, p. 645)

The Landman study shows that this interval of 1.5 seconds may be far longer, at least under some conditions, than the .3 seconds interval in which James believed. That there is an interval of a second or so during which a departed

---

[2] Their actual presentation had a background that is much more organic in appearance, like a burlap fabric with a pronounced diagonal grain. Furthermore, the rectangles do not have straight borders as I have drawn them, but rather are rectangular patches where the grain runs at right angles to the background, so the rectangularity is indicated by the contrast in the diagonality. However, this is not integral to our discussion.

visual scene can be accessed is important to DES in the sense that when the beep occurs, a large-capacity representation of pristine experience can be expected to persist for at least a while.

Furthermore, Landman and his colleagues also reported that the effective length of the interval between Stimulus 1 and cue *increased with practice* with the task: For naïve subjects, that interval was 1.2 seconds, rather than 1.5 seconds. This is a "special" task as I have defined it; most subjects have very little experience with displays of rectangles, one of which may rotate. If subjects can substantially improve their ability to maintain such special visual presentations over the course of a few hundred trials over a few hours, it seems reasonable that people's pristine experience may be apprehended for substantially longer than 1.5 seconds, the result of millions of trials over the few *hundred thousand hours* in which an adult has practice creating pristine experience (cf. Hurlburt & Schwitzgebel, 2011b). (I note that the DES skill depends both on the ability to create and store pristine experience for a few seconds, and also on the ability to encode and recall it. Most people have far less practice in the second ability, which is why (a) they are frequently mistaken about the characteristics of their experience and (b) why DES training over the course of several hours can be effective.)

Q: Even if we accept that a large-capacity representation persists for a second or so after the beep, the details of DES subjects' reports are still far too richly populated, exceeding the capacity of working memory by orders of magnitude, even when working memory is probed just a few seconds after the encoding, never mind twenty-four hours later. This richness contradicts the findings of the enormous literature on the sparseness of actual perception. For example, in Chapter 3, Juanita said that, while reading the novel *Messenger*, she saw Kira seated on a log facing Matty. There are too many details: Kira, Matty, the log, Matty to the left, Kira wearing a blue dress, Kira's deformed leg; Matty's swollen arms, trees in the background; and so on. And at the same time Juanita feels an itch in her nose. Such detail far exceeds the verified richness of perception.

A: I think your question reflects a confusion between pristine experience and perception. I accept that recalling that much detail may be impossible for any given perception. However, pristine experience is *not* perception, either external or internal; pristine experience does *not* follow the laws of perception, as your question seems to presuppose. Juanita is *not* observing an externally created scene of Kira and Matty sitting on a log; she is probably *not* even observing an *internally* created scene of Kira and Matty sitting on a log. Instead, Juanita's *seeing Kira and Matty sitting on a log* is the unitary event to be described. The inner seeing and the innerly seen thing are likely best considered two aspects of *the same* process, *unlike* observation of any kind.

Observation requires some kind of *transfer* or *transduction* from the thing observed to the observer. Furthermore, a thing observed contains all sorts of details that are irrelevant to the observer; observation requires sorting out which aspect to attend to and which to ignore. By distinct contrast, I think pristine experience requires *no* such transfer/transduction and contains *nothing* that is irrelevant. Whatever Juanita innerly sees is exactly what Juanita is disposed to see. If she is disposed, for whatever reason, to see the log with two people seated thereon, then she sees the log. If she is disposed, for whatever reason, to see two seated people who are seated on an unseen log, then she sees the people and does not see the log. If she is disposed, for whatever reason, to create a visually detailed seeing, then her seeing will be visually detailed, but if she is disposed to see just one isolated thing, then she will see one isolated thing. Juanita may well not know why one experience is detailed and another is of an isolated thing, but the detail or lack thereof is an integral, organic part of her inner seeing, *not* a characteristic of the thing seen.

The previous paragraph is about *processes* – how pristine experience works. I wish to emphasize that DES per se doesn't speculate, know, or much care how these processes work – its aim is to describe experience so that others may so speculate. I mention processes here in an attempt to disabuse you of the presupposition that pristine experience follows the same rules as external observation. Maybe there is some sense in which pristine experience *does* follow the rules of external observation, and I would be happy to have that explored. But until such exploration has been accomplished, I strongly recommend bracketing such presuppositions.

Q: Even if I accept that, I think we ought to suspect that Juanita is over-reporting the richness of her experience. Even if she sees it at the moment of the beep, it is extremely unlikely that she could recall such detail long enough to jot it down, as the DES procedure requires. Therefore, it seems likely that she confabulates some of the detail.

A: Here again, I think you confuse external observation and pristine experience. I don't think that the laws for the memory of pristine experience correspond to the laws for the memory of external events (or at least that that correspondence has not been demonstrated). That you can remember only about 7 ± 2 chunks of an external scene, as Miller (1956) suggested, does not necessarily imply that you can remember only about 7 ± 2 chunks of a pristine experience. The external scene was created by an entity other than you, according to procedures that are foreign to you, whereas *every bit* of the pristine experience was created by and for you yourself in just exactly the way you were disposed to experience it. Maybe at some point in the future that correspondence will be demonstrated, but so far as I know, it has not been explored yet.

That said, I grant that memory for inner experience is limited, and that it is likely that Juanita has confabulated some of the details of her report, and I discussed this issue at length in Hurlburt and Schwitzgebel (2007, e.g., pp. 96–97, 102, 119–120, 153–154, 254–255). It is important to bear in mind the *size* of the confabulation. Perhaps at the moment of the beep Juanita did not actually see the log on which they were sitting; to say that she saw it was a confabulated detail. However, it seems to me that even if the log was confabulated, that confabulation may be in the service of a larger truth. Juanita understood herself as experiencing a detailed seeing, and it is possible to get some detail wrong in the service of conveying the detailed seeing. For example, it would have been grossly *un*faithful to her experience for her to have said, "I saw Kira and Matty sitting, but I specifically *didn't* see the log on which they were sitting, even though I know they were sitting on a log." Such a description *would call attention to the log*, would elevate the importance of the log, when Juanita's pristine experience was apparently to *diminish* the importance of the log.

Even more importantly, if confabulation is occurring, it is likely to be about *a detail* of an experience. Juanita is *not* likely to say, at the moment of this beep, I was saying to myself, in my own voice, "I want a hamburger." Juanita's experience was of a seeing, *not* of a saying, and it was about Kira and Matty, not about lunch. Juanita is *not* likely to be mistaken about either of those.

Q: I think it likely that Juanita has confabulated some of the major aspects, not merely details, of her report. The eyewitness testimony literature robustly documents such gross confabulation. The DES procedure, with its incessant probing, invites confabulation.

A: I accept that eyewitness reports are often grossly untrustworthy, a literature Schwitzgebel summarized in Hurlburt and Schwitzgebel (2007, pp. 234–244). However, the argument I have just been making, that pristine experience is not observation, applies here as well: Eyewitness testimony is about events that are outside the observer, where the important details have to be culled from the extraneous. By contrast, in pristine experience there are *no* extraneous details. Furthermore, I discussed at length in Hurlburt and Schwitzgebel (2007, particularly pp. 281–289) how DES reports are distinctly different from eyewitness reports, including: Eyewitnesses are reporting events on one occasion whereas DES subjects are describing events on multiple occasions; eyewitnesses are not prepared to observe, whereas DES subjects have been trained to observe; eyewitnesses observe unusual events, whereas DES subjects apprehend common-to-them events; eyewitnesses do not receive any training at all prior to the observation, whereas DES subjects get high-quality iterative training; in particular eyewitnesses are not pre-trained in the valuing of bracketing presuppositions, whereas DES subjects are helped to discover the importance of bracketing; and so on.

Q: Dennett and others have shown that we cannot rely on subjects' fine-grained judgments of the timing of mental states, that there may be brain systems that reshuffle the timing of states so that the timing a subject reports reflects the rearranged time of experience, not the actual time of experience. I don't think that DES solves that problem.

A: I agree that there may be brain or other systems that can and do reshuffle the timing of states. I wrote about one such case, the DES investigation of a schizophrenic individual, in Hurlburt (1990, chapter 13). The subject, "Bob," reported an experience that had six quickly occurring phases. I speculated that the experienced phases (4), (5), and (6) reflected processes whose beginnings were actually sequenced (6), (5), (4). Furthermore, I noted that two additional of my four schizophrenic subjects

> show a disjunction between the perceptual beginnings of a thought process and its appearance in awareness.... All interfere with the ability to report accurately when a particular event occurred. All posit a process that is extended in time much longer than most normal thought processes. (Hurlburt, 1990, p. 242)

Therefore I agree that it would be a mistake to presume that people's reports of judgments of timing are always correct. I have tried to say repeatedly and explicitly in this book that science *should* avoid (and DES tries hard to avoid) inferring, explicitly or implicitly, *any* characteristics (including timing) about unobserved processes.

However, if your implication is that science should eschew careful introspection of phenomena because of the possibility of time-shuffling experience, I think you hamstring science in an undesirable way. I think it is, and should be to science, hugely interesting that Bob might shuffle his experience. In most everyday situations, the brain and other systems do a pretty good job of keeping timings straight: Most people most of the time feel the pool cue slide across the finger, *then* hear the soft thud of felt against phenolic, *then* see the white ball roll, *then* hear the loud click of white ball against red and *simultaneously* see the balls collide, *then* see the red ball roll, *then* hear the kiss of the red ball against the bumper, and so on, all in the temporal order that the physics of billiards would predict. If some people get such details out of order, then science should be hugely interested in what kinds of people, what circumstances, and what kinds of details. For example, if Bob, who happens to be schizophrenic, gets such details out of order, then that might provide some insight into Bob's delusional claim that he knows the outcome of events before the events occur – such a claim might genuinely reflect an experiential reality for Bob. For example, I pointed out to Bob the possibility that he had shuffled his experiential timings and explained the physics behind my reasoning. But he argued vehemently against the shuffling possibility – he had, after all, *just seen the events with his own eyes.*

However, to be interested in which people, which circumstances, and which details of experience are shuffled away from the underlying process order *requires a careful paying of attention to pristine experience*: You can't notice that the details of experience are shuffled without noticing the details of the experience. In this example, as I discuss in more detail in Chapter 13, I think it plausible that many schizophrenic individuals *do* get the timings of experience wrong. That observation could be useful in a variety of ways that are hard to predict: For example, perhaps a psychiatrist could titrate the dosage of a particular drug by gradually increasing dose until experience becomes unshuffled; or choose drug A over drug B because evaluations have shown that drug A is more effective when experience is unshuffled than is drug B; or perhaps it could contribute to the early detection of schizophrenia – experience shuffling may precede the appearance of frank clinical symptoms.

Therefore it seems to me that a scientist can fall into one of two traps: (a) A scientist could mistakenly suppose that a subject's reports about experiences temporally reflect underlying processes. That is the trap you seem to be worried about, but the second trap is equally important: (b) that a scientist would eschew the investigation of pristine experience because of the risk of falling into trap (a). Science's task, as it seems to me, is to learn to value the apprehension of pristine experience without falling into *either* presuppositional trap, and toward that end I think scientists should always bracket all presuppositions that arise about the relationship between experience and underlying processes.

IMPOSSIBILITY

Q: I don't think it is possible to investigate inner experience. Nisbett and Wilson, in their influential **1977** review, examined a whole series of studies and concluded:

> The accuracy of subjective reports is so poor as to suggest than any introspective access that may exist is not sufficient to produce generally correct or reliable reports. (Nisbett & Wilson, 1977, p. 233)

What makes you think DES is exempt from Nisbett and Wilson's scathing critique?
A: Because Nisbett and Wilson themselves exempt it:

> We also wish to acknowledge that the studies do not suffice to show that people *could never* be accurate about the processes involved. To do so would require ecologically meaningless but theoretically interesting procedures such as interrupting a process at the very moment it was occurring, alerting subjects to pay careful attention to their cognitive processes, coaching them in introspective procedures, and so on. (Nisbett & Wilson, 1977, p.246, italics in original)

Nisbett and Wilson's "ecologically meaningless but theoretically interesting procedure" is a perfect description of DES. Nisbett and Wilson were correct to note that people are *often* (maybe even usually) substantially mistaken about their inner experience, but they themselves accept the possibility that DES-type investigations might be successful. (The whole point of this book is to show that they were mistaken in their "ecologically meaningless" label.)

Q: B. F. Skinner, arguably the most influential psychologist of the twentieth century, thought that private events did not exist, or if they existed, they were unimportant. That's what led him to his behaviorist views. Just because behaviorism has fallen largely out of favor, you can't sidestep his critique.
A[3]**:** I consider Skinner to be one of the four or five people most influential on my thinking, and DES is designed to be *exactly in accord with*, not to sidestep,

---

[3] This answer is adapted from Hurlburt & Heavey, 2001, with permission.

Skinner's views. So we should take some time to understand Skinner and to see how DES is in accord with him.

First, you are mistaken when you assert that Skinner thought that private events don't exist; in fact, he quite explicitly denied that position:

> The statement that behaviorists deny the existence of feelings, sensations, ideas, and other features of mental life needs a good deal of clarification. Methodological [non-Skinnerian] behaviorism and some versions of logical positivism ruled private events out of bounds because there could be no public agreement about their validity. Introspection could not be accepted as a scientific practice, and the psychology of people like Wilhelm Wundt and Edward B. Titchener was attacked accordingly. Radical [Skinnerian] behaviorism, however, takes a different line. It does not deny the possibility of self-observation or self-knowledge or its possible usefulness (Skinner, 1974, p. 16).

In fact, Skinner believed that private events have the same essential nature as public events:

> We need not suppose that events which take place within an organism's skin have special properties.... A private event may be distinguished by its limited accessibility but not, so far as we know, by any special structure or nature. We have no reason to suppose that the stimulating effect of an inflamed tooth is essentially different from that of, say, a hot stove. (Skinner, 1953, pp. 257–258)

However, Skinner did identify three main limitations on the scientific use of private events: (a) that verbal behavior about private events may be impoverished because it is difficult for the verbal community to shape a person's speech about inner experience; (b) that it is impossible for a person to have access to his or her thinking in its entirety; and (c) that it is a mistake to give causal significance to mentalistic events. All three criticisms are entirely justified, but the first is most important for our purposes.

According to Skinner, a main difference between private events (like toothaches or thoughts) and public events (like hot stoves) is that the community of speakers has more control over the speech about public events:

> The verbal response "red" is established as a discriminative operant by a community which reinforces the response when it is made in the presence of red stimuli and not otherwise. This can easily be done if the community and the individual both have access to red stimuli. It cannot be done if either the individual or the community is color-blind. The latter case resembles that in which a verbal response is based upon a private event, where, by definition, common access by both parties is impossible. How does the community present or withhold reinforcement appropriately in order to bring such a response as "My tooth aches" under the control of appropriate stimulation? (Skinner, 1953, pp. 258–259, italics in original)

If a community wishes to develop a differentiated usage of the talk "I see red," it can give a series of trials in which it presents external objects that are variously rose, auburn, russet, rusty, carnation, strawberry, cerise, and carmine, appropriately reinforcing or punishing talk about each specific variation of red. Thus the community can shape "I see red" with great precision and thus can reliably differentiate such statements as "I see auburn" from "I see cerise." However, if the community wishes to develop a differentiated usage of the talk "I am depressed," it cannot present a series of internal states that are variously melancholic, downcast, downhearted, droopy, low, blue, bummed out, and down. It therefore cannot directly reinforce or punish talk about such states. It is forced to rely on public accompaniments of private events, such as withdrawal, failure to eat, or crying, to shape statements about the private events themselves. Even though such public accompaniments may in fact be correlated with depression, those correlations are far from perfect. Therefore talk about the experience of depression receives only impoverished differential reinforcement and is not likely to have the same precision as talk about external events.

We saw in Chapter 2 an example of Skinner's claim that private events receive impoverished differential reinforcement. There we noted that subjects early in their DES participation refer to their own inner experience as "thinking," and various subjects use that term to connote a wide variety of experiences, ranging from inner speech, to inner seeing, to feeling some bodily sensation, to feeling an emotion. That is, "thinking" when applied to one's own experience *does not necessarily connote a cognitive event at all*. My explanation is exactly in accord with Skinner's: that when applied to one's own experience, the term "thinking" is typically not differentiated much beyond the fact that it refers to a private event – it connotes whatever is a frequent inner experience, and that may differ dramatically from one person to the next. Over the iterative course of the DES training, subjects can learn to differentiate the talk about such experiences, including how to use the term "thinking."

Constraint: Limit ourselves to talk that has been adequately differentiated. Said another way, Skinner was right! If talk cannot be adequately differentiated, don't engage in it! Once subjects are trained in DES, they can report, for example, whether or not at any particular moment they were engaging in inner speech, precisely what words were being spoken at that moment, and the perceptual characteristics of that speech. Because inner speech has some of the same characteristics as external speech, you can differentiate communication about inner speech with quite a bit of precision, including those aspects where it is different from inner speech.

However, it is far more difficult, if not impossible, to differentiate adequately such talk as "I am sad all the time." That is an item from the most widely used depression inventory, and I think we don't know what endorsement of that item means. What does "sad" mean? What does "all the time" mean? Those are not trivial questions (remember that even "thinking" has widely disparate meanings). Sampling studies frequently show that individuals who endorse

"I am sad all the time" are actually sad at fewer than half their sampled moments. It is thus simply wrong to accept the endorsement of "I am sad all the time" as a description of inner experience. If we want to know whether someone is sad all the time, there is no substitute for collecting a large number of random samples and inquiring whether sadness is present at each sample.

Q: Even if I accept that you can differentiate your talk about inner experience, Skinner held that mentalisms should be banished from science. DES is one mentalism after another.

A: Skinner was right about that, too: The core of his critique of psychology was his anti-mentalistic polemic. However, you're mistaken about DES, which is *not at all* mentalistic. I designed DES, with Skinner in mind, explicitly to *eliminate* all talk of mentalisms.

A mentalism is an unobserved but assumed-to-exist inner psychological event that is said to explain behavior. For example, in "John eats because he is hungry," hunger is a mentalism: It is presumed that John has some inner psychological state (hunger) that causes him to eat. Skinner objected to science's crediting such mentalisms for two main reasons. First, hunger is not a directly observable or measurable state. Many scientists have tried, not very successfully, to measure hunger: In rats, for example, scientists have measured how long the rat has been food deprived; measured what percentage the rat is of his free-feeding weight; measured how much electrical shock the rat will endure to engage in feeding; measured how much a rat's food can be laced with quinine before the rat declines to eat; and so on. It turns out that those measurements of hunger don't correlate very highly, leading Skinner to conclude that hunger as a unitary construct probably doesn't exist, and I agree.

Second, according to Skinner, allowing science to posit the existence of mentalisms such as hunger discourages scientists from searching for really existing, really important causes or features of behavior:

> When what a person does is attributed to what is going on inside him, investigation is brought to an end. Why explain the explanation? For twenty-five hundred years people have been preoccupied with feelings and mental life, but only recently has any interest been shown in a more precise analysis of the role of the environment. Ignorance of that role led in the first place to mental fictions, and it has been perpetuated by the explanatory practices to which they gave rise. (Skinner, 1974, pp. 17–18)

> The exploration of the emotional and motivational life of the mind has been described as one of the greatest achievements in the history of human thought, but it is possible that it has been one of the great disasters.... The objection to the inner workings of the mind is not that they are not open to inspection but that they have stood in the way of the inspection of more important things. (Skinner, 1974, p. 165)

> We must remember that mentalistic explanations explain nothing. (Skinner, 1974, p. 224)

Skinner was right about that, too, and has never been refuted, as far as I can see. He has been widely ignored, including by most of modern cognitive psychology (Skinner, 1977), but that is entirely his second point.

Now that we have seen what Skinner meant by mentalisms, we can determine whether the features of experience, as described by DES, are mentalisms, and I think the answer is no. Inner speech, for example, is a directly observable event. Granted, that observation can be made by only one person; that is, the event is private. I (along with Skinner) accept that the privacy of observation makes for some methodological difficulties in the observation of inner speech, but that difficulty is not because the observation is mentalistic; it is because it is private. By contrast, there is no possible direct observation of hunger; that's one thing that makes it mentalistic.

The second defining feature of mentalisms is that they are used to explain behavior: John eats *because* he is hungry. DES explicitly rules out such explanation.

Constraint: Eliminate mentalisms. DES does not discuss mentalisms, does not discuss associations, ideas, concepts, identity, will, causation, preference, intention, knowledge, propositions, representation, encoding, storage, retrieval, or cognitive rules (those are all examples from Skinner's 1977 paper, "Why I am not a cognitive psychologist.") As Skinner observed, such concepts are not directly observable by anyone; talk about them cannot be differentially reinforced. DES limits itself to directly (albeit privately) observable phenomena that can be differentiated. For example, inner speaking is not a mentalism but is a directly (privately) observable phenomenon, and the talk about its characteristics can be differentiated by the verbal community: Are there words? If so, exactly which words? Is there a voice? If so, what are its characteristics? (Soprano or bass? Vocal characteristics like your own or someone else's voice? inflected? And so on.) There is nothing mentalistic about inner speech or any other phenomena investigated by DES. (We will return to this discussion in Chapter 17.)

CRITICISM

Q: You have throughout this book given a particularly uncharitable reading of the positions you have used as foils, for example, of Larsen, McGraw and Cacioppo (2001) in Chapter 7. It is obvious that these authors were not aiming at capturing what you call experience, so their failure to use a methodology appropriate for capturing experience hardly counts as a criticism.

A: It is not my intention to be critical of Larsen, McGraw and Cacioppo – in fact I said their study was excellent by psychological standards – or the others whom I have cited in this book. My intention is to hold up a mirror to *consciousness science* and to point out that consciousness science is not attending to what I take to be important phenomena (pristine experience). I did try clearly to state my contention that Larsen, McGraw and Cacioppo were examining neither moments nor pristine experience.

Q: The claims you make in this book are far too strong and are based on far too few observations of far too few subjects for science to take seriously.

A: I acutely feel the sting of the "based on far too few observations" criticism, and sincerely wish I could provide more observations of more subjects. It is up to the readers, not me, to judge whether I have provided enough examples to make the case that the study of inner experience is important.

As for my claims being too strong, I accept the probability that I have in some places, perhaps in this book, overstated my position. I have tried to state my positions as speculations, not claims; as positions in need of validation.

I have, really, made only one cluster of claims in this book: that it seems reasonable for science to investigate pristine experience, and that to do so requires careful attention to moments and methods. Even that is a pretty weak claim. I am not claiming that such investigations *will* successfully advance science, only that such investigations *might* successfully advance science and therefore deserve consideration.

In my view, the role of apprehensions of pristine experience and the salient characteristics thereof is the *beginning* of a claim process, a scouting report that should be confirmed by other scouts (who have different sensitivities and presuppositions) and subjected to validation by objective performance measures. Then there would be enough evidence to warrant a claim. We are far short of that in all the aspects that I have discussed in this book.

I suspect that some of my speculations will not be borne out or will be transformed substantially by the validation process. That does not dismay me – that is the natural life of observation and validation. As I said in Chapter 2, many of the conclusions van Leeuwenhoek reached as he developed his microscopes – the existence of "animalcules," for example – turn out to be mistaken, but that does not in the slightest lessen the value of the microscopes and the importance of examining small details.

12

A Consciousness Scientist
as DES Subject

A few years ago, a world-class consciousness scientist engaged me in an e-mail and telephone conversation about the exploration of inner experience. He knew of my DES work, found it interesting but problematic, and wanted to know more about it. We eventually agreed that he should wear the DES beeper and I would interview him by telephone – then he would know about the process first hand.

For a variety of reasons, some of which may be obvious and some others might become clear, I prefer not to identify this person. Serious students of consciousness would recognize his name and his work. In the transcript I will call him "CS," for "Consciousness Scientist," and I note that I had not previously met him and never published with him. This chapter is *not* about CS; it is an example of how a serious student of consciousness went about undertaking the task of encountering DES. In many ways, CS is similar to many students of consciousness as they approach the possibility of exploring inner experience. In other ways, he is unique, with his own personality and his own proclivities and experiences.

Constraint: Consciousness science proficiency does not facilitate and might actively interfere with the ability to observe pristine experience. Over the years, many consciousness scientists have expressed interest in DES. I have offered many of those the opportunity to wear the beeper and have me interview them about their experiences; most have declined out of what seemed to me (rightly or wrongly) to be defensiveness (Eric Schwitzgebel and Mike Kane are notable exceptions; see Hurlburt & Schwitzgebel, 2007, and Chapter 6.) CS is to be commended for his open-minded willingness to participate and, moreover, strongly applauded for allowing me to publish the upcoming transcript of our interviews, which are highly personal. The transcript will expose some of the difficulties many scientists will have when observing experience, but as with any real example, it exposes *his* particular difficulties and makes *him* the target of my commentary. It takes courage to allow that kind of exposition.

The transcript itself is word for word except that I have altered it where necessary to mask particulars that might reveal CS's identity. If I have not been successful in this masking, and you discover his identity through some clue that I have overlooked, I think you owe it to CS to keep this discovery to yourself.

I conducted five expositional interviews with CS, all by telephone with CS in his home state and me in Nevada. Each of these interviews was roughly an hour; as a way of condensation, I will present (and comment on) the first part of the interview from each of the first three sampling days.

THE FIRST SAMPLING INTERVIEW

This interview began before the tape was started because I always re-establish permission to record. During that interval, CS mentioned that he had worn the beeper on two days, getting four beeps on the first day and five on the second. Then we start the tape, which is transcribed here.

> RTH:[1] I'm starting a tape now. And … We … I don't have any plans for the tape, except that it's frequently the case, in the business that I do, that there are times when I get to the end I say, "Damn! I wish I'd taped that!"
> CS:[2] Yep.
> RTH:[3] OK. So you were saying.
> CS:[4a] Well, I've got some general issues to discuss with you before we talk about specific beeps …

The DES task is simple: to discuss as faithfully as possible specific, concrete moments of experience as they occur at the precise times selected by random beeps. Most DES subjects, as CS here, initially prefer to talk about the general before we talk about the specific, which is exactly backward from the DES approach (recall the constraint from Chapter 2: *Particulars can lead to generalities, but generalities cannot lead to particulars.*

> CS:[4b] I think, y'know, I'm a sort of master of mindfulness and consciousness, and it's very hard to do this beeping because I use every second of my time for various tasks …

Constraint: Avoid ungrounded, premature, or otherwise faux generalities. CS states what appears to be a generality about his experience (beeping is hard because …); DES calls this a faux generality because it is probably not really the result of an inductive procedure, as actual generalities must be. Faux generalities are always problematic for DES – they distract from careful observation. One of the things that makes DES difficult for many consciousness scientists is that their professional identity stems from their ability to advance hypotheses. However, hypotheses are usually faux generalities, so consciousness scientists, if they are to apprehend pristine experience, have to learn how to suspend one of their primary and highly valued skills.

CS's faux generality about why beeping is hard seems based on his assumption that he knows how to respond to a beep. I doubt that that is true; most subjects require some training in the skills necessary to apprehend experience, and I expect that that will be the case for CS as well. So I recognize that I will have to help him work through his probably incorrect presuppositions about DES.

> CS:[4c] Like on Friday, three of the beeps occurred when I was reading. And when you're reading, it doesn't seem like anything else is going on, if you read with a kind of concentration that I do. Your mind is filled up with the content of the material that you're reading. And I was unaware, at three of the four beeps that occurred that day, of anything else besides what I'm reading. Now I'm editing my own material, so I say, Well, in order to free things up a bit here, I'd better stop editing. But that's not … that's not naturalistic. I mean, what I wanted to do with that time was *edit*. And I got three beeps while I was editing, and I mean, as far as I know, all that I could recall was what I just read.

His second faux (or at best premature) generality is a characterization of the experience of reading. This generalization is premature because we have not examined a single beep. Note that his generalization is a universal, as evidenced by "when *you*'re reading." This kind of statement assumes that others' experience is just like his (we'll return to the *Don't-judge-others-by-yourself* constraint of Chapter 9). CS does limit himself slightly to the semi-universal by saying "if you read with a kind of concentration that I do," but that still assumes that others who are concentrating have the same kind of experience he does.

His general characterization of the experience of reading may, of course, be correct (I doubt it), but even so, such a generalization is precisely what is at issue, so we shouldn't assume it at the outset.

Because many psychologists and philosophers encountering DES for the first time make similar faux generalities, let me state this as baldly as possible: CS, on the basis of a few untrained, probably not very skillful, observations of one subject (himself), has with apparent confidence stated a universal conclusion about experience. Besides being probably incorrect, such a generalization undermines his ability to observe experience faithfully. So I will have to discourage such generalizations while at the same time encouraging him to observe moments.

> RTH:[5] And …
> CS:[6] So I put that down.
> RTH:[7] Well, it seems to me that if that's what's going on, then that's what's going on. And I don't see that that necessarily makes the task hard; what …
> CS:[8] No it doesn't, but … it doesn't make the task hard, but it's sort of a trivial result. I mean, it doesn't tell you about, well, what you might call a freer range of consciousness. I mean, the consciousness is locked in by the task, and so, the fact that I'm, y'know, aware of reading, and I mean

very aware, because I'm paying very close attention – I'm editing my own papers. What was the fourth one that day? I'll tell you in just a minute. It was better, for me it was more interesting. But then I began, y'know ... What I'm trying to tell you, I think, is that your [sighs in distress] or my expectancy set is such that I think I am not doing a good job, or this isn't very interesting, or something.

Many (probably most) subjects initially think they are not doing a good job of DES, and that their experiences are not very interesting. So far, CS's reports are indeed *not* very interesting to me because we are discussing probably untrue faux generalities – we haven't begun the probably true, moment-by-moment exploration of his experiences that is the source of genuine interest. My task will be to help him ride out the uninteresting non-experiences until we get to the very interesting actual experiences, which may not happen until the second or third sampling day.

RTH:[9]   Well ...

CS:[10]   I just want you to know that. The second day I was sleepy, and I knew if I went to sleep I wouldn't ... Oh! I did go to sleep on the first day! I went to sleep and then I couldn't remember a thing! And the beeper ... Of course, that's not uncommon.

RTH:[11]   Right.

CS:[12]   But the second day I was aware that ... I was in the car driving back to the city from my friend's house, and I was aware of the problem of, y'know, what was going to be going on in my mind at the time of the beeps.
And I was actually *programming*, and that's not good at all! But it's very interesting, I mean what happened was very interesting, and I'll tell you about it, because you can decide to go into sort of fantasy mode. I've been ... I was working over this problem in my mind which is kind of a moral problem, a dilemma in my life ... And I do a lot of that, too, I mean that's very interesting. That's more interesting than editing the material. But I was doing it in part to have material to ... so I wouldn't go to sleep, you know...

As CS reports here, many subjects on their first day try to manipulate ("program") what they do while wearing the beeper to get what they think will be "interesting" beeps. Such programming is undesirable, but I don't feel the need to respond to it because of the iterative nature of DES: Most subjects naturally abandon that kind manipulation as they discover (a) that I really am genuinely interested in unprogrammed experience (many people, as apparently CS did, mistakenly assume that I will find their everyday experiences boring); (b) that *they, too,* are genuinely interested in their own unprogrammed experience; and (c) their attempts to program were largely unsuccessful anyway. That is, subjects don't need to be *told* that manipulations dilute interest – they will naturally notice that for themselves when they see the alternatives.

RTH:[13] Right.

CS:[14] ... and have nothing to report. I'm just telling you that there's a lot of self-consciousness that enters in here, at least in me.

RTH:[15] OK.

CS:[16] I don't think I'll ever get over that. I mean, I'm probably too experienced to be one of your subjects or something.

CS[14] and CS[16] continue to be context or faux generalization, not description of experience at the moment of the beep.

> RTH:[17] Well, why don't we start with the first beep on the second day. And let's go through the beeps, and we'll discover as we go whether they're interesting or whether they're not, or whether they're focused or whether they're not. I would say at the outset that most of the subjects in our research – I wouldn't say all of them but many of them – say on the first day of sampling, "Well, I'm not a very good subject, and it wasn't very interesting, and sorry about that."

I have let CS approach the interview his way, which was (not too surprisingly) far too overly faux-generalized for my taste. So I indicate that I have heard him, and I try to be supportive, and I start the task of corralling him into discussing the specific moments of the beep.

Note that CS didn't follow the DES procedure that I had laid out for him and for all other subjects – he sampled on two occasions instead of one. He doesn't seem to see an important difference between sampling immediately before and several days before the interview. As a result, I do *not* expect, no matter what I ask, to obtain faithful reports about experience on this day. Today's interview will be *entirely* iterative training (see Chapter 10) to improve tomorrow's sampling.

I elected to begin with the second sampling day only because it's the most recent – the beeps are "fresher." (It is not that I expected the content of the second day to be more interesting.) I nearly always start with the first beep for bracketing-of-presuppositions reasons – otherwise CS gets to select the beep on the basis of some a priori interest. I'd much rather let the beeper's random process select our topic of discussion.

> CS:[18] Well, I'm going to try some more. Don't worry about that. But I'm telling you that I was already aware on day 2 that I was ... Plus I think the beeps are predictable. I get ... I think I got four of them in each three-hour period, except that one of the periods was a little longer and I got five beeps or something like that. And they don't occur in proximity to each other. That's another issue, because after thirty minutes have gone by, you begin to think, Well, a beep is going to come pretty soon. I mean, you can't avoid that! I mean, your mind is just ... That's part of your task is to have the beeper on. My friend thought I was listening to music, by the way. [laughs]

Seeing a predictable pattern in randomness is an example of premature generalization in its rawest form. Many subjects believe there are patterns in the beep sequences, but none actually exists: CS's beeper was programmed to create its own random intervals uniformly distributed between about half a minute and sixty minutes.

Note that I don't try to talk him out of this, either; I have faith in the power of the specifics of our upcoming interviews to disabuse him of such notions naturally (another example of the importance of iteration).

RTH:[19] Yeah. That's a real common response.

CS:[20] But anyway, let me get my notes. Just a minute.

[a minute of silence]

CS:[21] OK. They're sitting right here on my desk. I was looking in the wrong place.

RTH:[22] I hate it when that happens.

CS:[23] OK. Day two?

RTH:[24] Day two.

[We skip here discussion of the first beep because CS was not sure that he heard the onset of the beep.]

Let's review: The DES aim is to describe concrete, specific experience that occurs at carefully defined moments. So far, CS has neither described concrete, specific experience nor described anything that occurs at carefully defined moments. Instead, he has made a series of gross faux generalizations about himself and/or about universal human characteristics:

- It's hard to beep because I use every second of my time
- There is no experience when reading
- I get a trivial result from DES
- I'm not good at beeping
- I programmed my experience
- It was interesting
- I work out moral dilemmas a lot
- DES gets a lot of self-consciousness
- I'll never get over my self-consciousness in DES
- The beeps are predictable
- Predictability is a problem for DES

I make no claim that that list is the best way of characterizing CS's generalities, but to quibble about that misses the point that *none* of his talk so far is about the concrete, specific experiences that occur at carefully defined moments.

I emphasize that CS is somewhat typical of most DES subjects in this regard. Despite the initial instructions that I am basically interested only in beeped, concrete, specific experiences, very few subjects appreciate that on the first sampling day.

This list illustrates the "might actively interfere with" portion of the constraint from earlier: *Consciousness science proficiency does not facilitate and might actively interfere with the ability to observe pristine experience.* By their training and reward structure, consciousness scientists probably have *more* faux generalizations at their disposal than do non-scientists.

> RTH:[25] Beep number 2.
>
> CS:[26] OK. I'm seated in the car about to go back to the city having an imaginary dialog with my co-worker, who has, I think, plagiarized an article of mine, publishing it without my permission. And I'm wondering how to deal with this problem. I'm wondering what my strategy should be, how I should get information before confronting him. Because I might have forgotten, you know, having given him permission to do this. And I don't want to have ... I don't want either to blow my cover or falsely accuse him. So I'm thinking about what my strategy should be. And I'm talking, I'm telling him (Oh yeah) ... I'm telling him about my resentment in a list of particulars about his behavior. So in other words, this is occurring in a context of a variety of behaviors which I think are usurping, and I was very surprised, very upset by this. I picked up his article a couple days ago at a conference, and I didn't even *know* he was working on it. And there's my article with somebody else's name on it. It's very upsetting.

Constraint: The narrative is a distraction from apprehending experience. CS[26] is the beginning of an interesting story, told by an interesting guy, in an interesting way. But most of CS[26] is *not* his experience at the moment of the beep – it's background, context, strategy, gloss of one kind or another. There are lots of questions that I could ask, and *would* ask in an everyday let's-trade-narratives conversation (What do you mean, "*my* article"? Was it your idea or did you actually write it? How much of it? Word for word? etc.). Any such interest in the narrative would take us *away* from CS's experience that was directly ongoing at the moment of the beep.

The constraint about narratives is a corollary of the constraint from Chapter 3: *Rule out everything that is not directly experienced.* CS[26] is an impure mixture of narrative and experience, and we will have to develop our (my and CS's) skill of sticking to experience and ruling out everything that is not experience. I'm confident that in the long run that focus will reveal something far deeper than the narrative – what CS *actually* experienced while confronting plagiarism is, to my mind, far richer than the largely pre-packaged story that he might tell about plagiarism – but CS does not (yet) have that confidence. So I will have to establish with CS that I (unlike perhaps anyone else with whom he has conversed) am *not* particularly interested in the narrative – I want to focus directly on his experience.

Even when we set aside narrative, it is hard to tell what of CS[26] actually is direct experience. "Having an imaginary dialog" might be a description of experience, but he also says he is "wondering how to deal with this problem." Dialog and wondering may be, experientially, two quite different things: A description of a dialog would be something like, "I'm saying in an angry tone, 'You have no right!'" A description of wondering would be something like, "I was musing to myself, considering different options." So it is possible that both of these are descriptions of the beeped experience; it is possible that one is (but we don't know which one), or maybe neither are. Until we build CS's skill of apprehending experience at the moment of the beep, we will not be able to sort this kind of thing out.

Despite the substantial imperfection in CS's getting faithfully to his experience here in beep 2, I note that he has made a *giant* leap from the realm of making gross generalizations (before getting his sampling notes) into the realm of trying to describe his actual experience. Prior to getting his notes, our difficulty was that he was inclined to talk entirely in generalizations. Now we have arrived in the neighborhood of a specific (something having to do with plagiarism), but he hasn't (yet) said what his actual experience was at the moment of the beep – that is, he hasn't grasped the DES directive to capture and describe his actual phenomenological experience (very few subjects grasp this on the first day). However, he has made a big step forward, which apparently has been aided by the beeper and the notes that he has taken. It is, I think, more than coincidence that the shift in emphasis takes place when he retrieves his actual notes, as if the absence of notes about beeped experiences encourages gross generalizations, and the presence of the notes ties him at least loosely to the concretely specific.

Constraint: The exploration of pristine experience has personal and interpersonal risks. This passage illustrates the moral dilemmas/bracketing of presuppositions that the faithful apprehension of experience frequently provides *to the investigator*: He plagiarized your work? How could he?! Who is the bastard!? Wait! Maybe I know him! What am I to do if in this interview I find out who it is? I don't want to know. Yes I do! Is it good for CS to tell me this? How much about this do I have to know? Is it going to put me in the middle of something that I can't handle? Can I ask about CS's experience without knowing the details of the plagiarism? Probably not. I need the details. I *want* to know the details! No I don't – it's none of my business!

The task of bracketing presuppositions is to be equanimous in the face of such personal involvements/entanglements/attractions/repulsions. However, that is not easy, and the decisions to be made happen fast. This sample happens to concern plagiarism, but there are lots of human conditions that present similar dilemmas: sexual interest, interpersonal gossip of all kinds, and so on. Random samples always run the risk of presenting such features without warning.

RTH:[27] I can ...

CS:[28] I'm wondering what to do about that.

RTH:[29] OK. And I can certainly sympathize with the upsettingness of the situation. But right at the moment of the beep, right at that ...

CS:[30] Yeah.

RTH:[31] ... millisecond before the beep begins, you're having a dialog with him in your imagination? Is that correct?

CS:[32] Yes. It was inner speech, what you'd call inner speech.

RTH:[33] OK. And are you speaking, or is he speaking?

CS:[34] I'm speaking.

RTH:[35] And what exactly are you saying? Right then, at that moment.

CS:[36] I'm saying, uh, oh gosh, I ... I'm saying ... y'know ... I didn't write it down. I mean, I'm saying that, uh, there are a number of things that have been bothering me. This one has really pushed me over the edge. And it's been ... it's gone on for five years, this guy and I have worked together, and this ... You know, this is a common scenario, this kind of thing is all too common.

Constraint: If the details don't cohere, be skeptical of the experience. CS[32] ("It was inner speech") *sounds* like a description of beeped experience, but if a person is innerly speaking at the moment of the beep, he should be able to quote the words he is speaking and the characteristics of the inner voice. CS cannot do that. Why not? I don't know. Maybe he *was* innerly speaking at the moment of the beep, but he *just didn't* write it down and so forgot it. But maybe there was *no* inner speech in the first place, so he *couldn't* write it down. The constraint from Chapter 5, *Clarify the details*, is important not because the details themselves are important, but because the details can reveal the referent (or lack thereof) in the subject's report.

By the way, screwing down further into the topic of Chapters 5 and 8, we might note the heavy subjunctification in CS[36]. Nearly every word, every behavioral indicator, indicates that CS is *not* telling me about experience at the moment of the beep, retreating instead into context.

RTH:[37] Right.

CS:[38] And, uh, my wife has been very upset about it. More upset than I am. Trying to sensitize me to this. But I'm trying to tell him, y'know, by leaving me off as author [chuckles] it looks like he's done the work, and he didn't write *anything* – he wrote, like, two paragraphs. It's all *my* stuff. And I had given it to ... I'm not responding to your question now, I'm wandering around. But I'm trying to figure out how to speak to him and what to tell him about this.

RTH:[39a] OK. And I think we have sort of the general context understood. What I would like to get is as close as we can, given that this is actually our first conversation about beeps, I'd like to get us as close as we can to the actual moment of the beep.

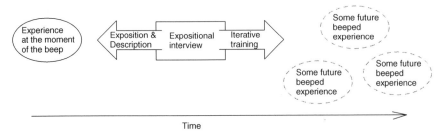

FIGURE 12.1. The interview as simultaneous forward looking and backward looking.

This illustrates a nice moment in the DES "dance": the joint acceptance (CS[38] "I'm not responding to your question" and RTH[39a] "I'd like to get us as close as we can") that we have understood part of what we're interested in, but we haven't yet gotten to the heart of it.

When, in RTH[39a], I say "I'd like to get us as close as we can to the actual moment of the beep," I don't expect him to be able to do that successfully – this is the first sampling day and he has shown by his lack of adherence to the procedure (e.g., two sampling days, not one) and the generalities of the conversation so far that he probably did not pay adequate attention to his experience at the moment of the beep. He is very typical of DES subjects in this regard – that's why the iterative procedure is necessary.

Constraint: Balance (forward looking) iterative training with (backward looking) data collection. "I'd like to get us as close as we can to the actual moment of the beep" may *appear* to be a look *back* at the beeped moment, but my *actual* aim here is to look iteratively *forward* to the next sampling days. In asking any question, the DES interviewer is simultaneously looking both backward and forward: looking backward, trying to help the subject expose/describe what was ongoing at the moment of the (past) beep; and looking forward, trying to help the subject become a more skillful observer of future experiences. These two tasks are fundamentally different, even though the questions posed are almost identical. Figure 12.1 shows a schematic.

The interviewer is nearly always asking a series of questions aimed at some past event: at the moment of the beep. To the extent that the interviewer judges the subject's skills to be adequate, those questions serve, as depicted in the left half of the schematic, a backward looking aim: The interviewer is trying to help the subject recall the past moment and describe it faithfully.

However, to the extent that the interviewer judges the subject's skills to be not (yet) adequate for faithful apprehension and description, those same questions serve, as depicted in the right half of the schematic, a forward looking aim: The interviewer is engaged in iterative training, trying to help the subject build the requisite skills so that future events can be apprehended more faithfully.

Despite their fundamental differences, the two tasks are usually worded in (almost) exactly the same way: some variant of *What was in your experience at the moment of the beep?* The careful reader will have noted that in RTH[39a], by my own subjunctifications I have grammatically signaled that I am not really asking about the past: "would like," "as close as we can," "I'd like to get us as close as we can," "*If* you're talking," and "can you say?"

In the typical series of DES interviews, as here, the first few interviews are aimed primarily at the future: We ask about past beeps as a way of iteratively building skills. Typically by somewhere between the second and fourth interview, the balance shifts so that later interviews are aimed primarily at the past.

> RTH:[39b] If you're talking, can you say as precisely as you can what you were saying to yourself right then?
>
> CS:[40] Yeah, I mean, I've already done that. I'm telling him that this is just one of a number of problems, but it's one that has to be settled, because he should have included me as an author or obtained a written statement from me giving him permission to leave my name off.

Despite his claim that "I've already done that," CS has *not* reported precisely what he was saying at the moment of the beep – CS[36–38] was a general gloss of what he was thinking about, not a description of what he was actually saying or of any other aspect of his experience. I will have to help CS master the distinction between experience and context/generalization.

> RTH:[41] OK. And … That's a fairly long sentence, or a fairly long thought. Do you think all that is in your …
>
> CS:[42] No. Probably not.
>
> RTH:[43] OK.
>
> CS:[44] I mean I think what is in my mind at the time of the beep is that I'm having this imaginary dialog with him. That is clear. There's no question about that. What I actually said, what he said, I'm not sure.

There is indeed some question about whether there was actually a dialog at the moment of the beep. He may indeed have been having the dialog he describes, but as we saw previously, until a subject can say exactly what words were being said, there is reason to be skeptical that words were being said. Inner speech has specific vocal characteristics and specific words, and unless the subject can report them with convincing confidence, then it is possible – perhaps likely – that the report reflects the common *presupposition* that thinking is in words rather than a direct apprehension of words. There is no way to sort that out about this beeped experience. Therefore although it *sounds like* I am interested in *yesterday's* beep, the aim of my questions here is iteratively *future* oriented: to raise CS's sensitivity to the issue, so that should such thinking occur on some subsequent sampling day, he will be prepared to capture its characteristics (words or not).

The upcoming portion of the interview marks the beginning what might be called the sweet spot of the day one interview. The object of the whole interview up until now could be said to have been to get to this very spot – the point at which CS is tenderized and open enough to hear/take in/comprehend/assimilate/ingest the next level of the iterative instruction. As we've seen, I have tried to steer the interview to a description of concrete, specific experiences that were occurring at precisely defined moments in time. As we've observed, I have not been very successful at doing that – CS has strayed from experience into generality and context; strayed from the moment of the beep into broadly defined or undefined sweeps of time. As we've seen, I have pointed all that out to CS repeatedly in a very personal, very directive, and yet supportive manner. In essence, we (CS and I) have demonstrated that his method of observing and reporting experience has been substantially inadequate.

That series of supportive confrontations has, I think, left him potentially receptive to the next level of instruction. So now is the time to consolidate that instruction, which I do in the next five conversational turns.

> RTH:[45] OK. And the conversation that we are having – that the two of us are having right now – is a very typical first-sampling-day conversation in the sense that you're responding in a … about what is going on at the moment of the beep in broader strokes than I'm actually interested in.
>
> CS:[46] Yep.
>
> RTH:[47] I would like us to zero in on exactly what was going on right at the moment of the beep; catch you in exactly what those words were …
>
> CS:[48] Yep.
>
> RTH:[49] … and almost nobody does that on the first sampling day. That is a characteristic of this method. And I've tried over the years to figure out how speed this process up, and haven't been able to figure out how to do it, so maybe it's … maybe this is just the way it is. But our interest is in exactly what you were saying if that's possible to apprehend.

Constraint: Iteration has to be specifically confrontational. At RTH[47–49] and their precursors, I am saying, directly to CS, in effect, "You report here a general thought without the actual words. *That is not adequate for DES purposes!* I want you to try to do better the next time you sample!" I am not trying to create a general skill; I am trying to build CS's skills in precisely the specific area where he needs it. Confrontation, in its etymological essence, is a face-to-face encounter. I am looking him directly in the eye and saying we haven't yet done what we need to do. Confrontation does not at all have to be negatively valenced – in fact, it can be quite supportive.

> CS:[50] Yep. And if it isn't?
>
> RTH:[52] And if it isn't, then it's not, and we'll get as close to it as we can. And maybe we'll figure out why.

CS has asked an attuned question, giving me the chance to reassure him that I will maintain a level playing field, that I do not intend to squeeze him.

CS:[53] OK.

RTH:[54] So I'm not ... We do have to, sometimes, as probably in this case, find out something about the background of the situation, but that's sort of the context in which the actual ... what I would call the actual experience takes place...

CS:[55] Yep.

RTH:[56] ... which is what you were actually saying. And so, I ... we would be asking questions like, "Well, what ... Do you know exactly what the words were?" And then you'd be saying, well, "Yes I do," or "No I don't," or "Yes, I wrote them down and here they are," or whatever. And then we would be asking, "Well, what is the characteristics of your voice, if this is a speaking thing?" or "What does your voice sound like?" "Do you sound happy? Sad? Fast? Slow? High? Low?" Whatever. Um ...

CS:[57] I understand. I understand perfectly clearly.

RTH:[58] OK. And it is just a characteristic of the method that we are more interested in, I guess, the molecules of the phenomenon ...

CS:[59] I understand that ...

RTH:[60] OK.

CS:[61] ... Yeah, I do. I have a question about whether you're really gonna get it, you know, because you're demanding the details that aren't there, I think.

RTH:[62] Well, in the first one I would say there were no details there ...

CS:[63] OK. We'll just see what happens.

RTH:[64] In the second one, in the second beep it sounds like there might very well have been details there ...

CS:[65] Yep.

RTH:[66] ... and I don't want to presume that there are details there. I think it's quite possible that you said ... Well, at the beginning of this beep, you said, for example, I was having an inner dialog with myself ...

CS:[67] Um hm.

RTH:[68] ... and that may mean that at the moment of the beep you were saying, quote, whatever it was that you were saying. Or it may mean that you were just thinking about this in general, and there would not be any words present. Either one of those things is totally OK with me.

Constraint: The apprehension of another's pristine experience is a skilled performance art. This exchange from CS[61] to RTH[68] illustrates what I think is my quite skillful helping of CS to bracket his presuppositions. CS[61] stated the presupposition ("you're demanding the details that aren't there"); that may or may not turn out to be true, and I want us to bracket any presupposition that leads one way or the other. I level the playing field by giving both an example that agrees with his presupposition (at RTH[62]) and an example that disagrees with it (at RTH[64]); and then I give an explicit leveling-the-playing-field comment (at RTH[66–68]). That series specifically calls his presupposition into question on his own terms. I do not impose my authority; I do not invoke my experience; I do not squeeze him one way or the other. And yet I think I successfully transmitted to him the very personal desirability *for himself* of being equally open to his presupposed result or to a contrary result. To be able to transmit that consistently and adroitly is quite high art.

Note that I never asked CS about the plagiarism, which illustrates the fundamental difference between a narrative and experience. CS could have provided countless details about the plagiarism narrative, related the significance of the plagiarism, the impact of it on his personal and professional life, the importance of plagiarism to research, and so on. But he could not provide a single reliable detail of his experience. The narrative and the experience are ontologically different entities. My failure to ask questions is doubtless somewhat disappointing or frustrating to CS: I didn't seem interested in what he expected me to be interested in. The art of the interview is to transmit that there is something that is even more interesting than that, if we can just pay attention to it.

THE SECOND SAMPLING INTERVIEW

CS opened the second interview by saying that he had not brought his sampling notes – he had left them in his other briefcase – but he assured me he could recall his experiences. Now there are lots of ways to interpret this, but I will decline such speculations. However, I would like the reader to understand four aspects.

First, it is probably *not* true that he can adequately recall his experiences (remember, after CS[26], that his ability to report his experience in the first sampling interview improved only *after* he retrieved his sampling notebook), and even if he *can* recall his experiences, neither he nor I have the right to *assume* that he can. Retrospection is not to be trusted, even (or perhaps especially!) by consciousness professionals.

Second, almost everyone *believes* they can adequately recall their experiences. This is perhaps because of faulty reality testing: If I want to know whether I recalled something adequately, I consult my *recollection* and see whether what I recalled matches my recollection. It always does!

Third, it may indicate that CS believes he knows what is necessary about the DES procedure, knows what about DES can be ignored, and so on. He is probably mistaken about that. CS is by no means alone in this regard – many of my subjects initially think they know more about how to study experience than I do.

Fourth, the constraint (from Chapter 10): *Subjects (initially) do not follow instructions.* There are all manner of ways that subjects manage to torpedo the mechanics of the DES process in their first few sampling days: They don't use the beeper at all (they "mentally simulate the beep"); they don't wear the earphone, using the beeper's on-board speaker despite specific instructions to use the earphone; they leave the beeper in the next room; they sample several days before the scheduled interview instead of the day of or the day before; they don't take notes; they get fifteen beeps instead of the six we asked for; they get one beep instead of six; they wear the beeper while asleep despite instructions to the contrary; and so on.

Genuinely submitting to this constraint requires accepting that the subject's not following instructions is simply part of the cost of doing business. It used to frustrate me – How could you not follow these simple instructions! – but hundreds of exemplars later I came to recognize that the mechanics of the method need to be iteratively trained as much as does the understanding of the moment of the beep and what is experience. *Nothing* is skillful on the first sampling day or two. Subjects eventually master the mechanics of the procedure in the same way and at the same time as they master the moment and master experience: through a series of successive approximations. This is part of the evidence for the co-determination of moments ↔ experience ↔ genuinely submitting to the constraints.

As with all iterative training, I don't criticize CS for not following the procedure. I have confidence that he will come to recognize *for himself* that he *needs* to follow the procedure if he *himself* wants to be able to answer the kinds of questions I will ask.

Given the absence of the sampling notes, I allowed CS to choose a beep to describe. I would have preferred to follow unwaveringly the order dictated by the random beeper, because randomness is an effective aid in bracketing presuppositions, but in the absence of the notes, that seemed impossible. We join the interview at the eleventh conversational turn, as he begins to describe the first sample of his choosing. We'll call this CS[211] to indicate the second sampling interview, eleventh conversational turn. At the time of the beep he was relaxing on the commuter train.

> cs:[211] I was thinking about, uh ... I'm a regular volunteer, sort of a coordinator, in a program at a school in my neighborhood. Um, and I was thinking about my telephone conversation with the teacher that I had yesterday. And we were talking about the general status of the program. And she was telling me that one of the teachers who had been in the first ... this thing has been going on ... this is the third year of it ... she was telling me that one of the teachers had quit after one year because she wanted to have a baby, and her name was ... what's her name? I can't think of it. But I was talking to her about helping us out. Now we're talking about the beeper, OK?

All this is background, which is not an unusual part of the early DES exposition of a beep.

RTH:[212] OK.

CS:[213] The beeper goes off and I'm saying, "Stufer! Stufer! You were really super!" But I said "stufer"! Have you heard things like this? I mean, this is a neologism! I thought I was saying "super." Only on the third repetition of "stufer" did I say "super."

CS now appears to be giving a description of experience at the moment of the beep – an inner speaking that contains a neologism. His ability to describe his experience seems far better than any of his descriptions during the first interview, so I will try to stay out of his way to let him elaborate.

RTH:[214] Hah!

CS:[215] And what I was trying to do was to compliment her, but... Not to flatter her, because she *was* very good, but to let her know that I had noticed how effective she was in getting these kids ready for their trip. And, uh, she has this kind of spirit that comes out of her, that people just gravitate to. So that was sort of surprising to me. I mean, I've never had a ... I've never been aware that I was, you know, when I was having fantasies, or what I call behavior rehearsals like this one, which was obviously one of that kind, that I said "stufer"! There's no question that I said "stufer."

However, he returns to giving background, not experience (except the last sentence, which seems to indicate that he knows our target is concrete experience). This peek at experience and then retreat to background is very typical of DES subjects, especially early in sampling. The DES interviewer's task is iteratively to help the subject learn the difference between direct apprehension of experience and background, and to value direct apprehension.

RTH:[216] So you're sort of half asleep on the train, or resting on the train ...

CS:[217] Well, I'm thinking! I'm thinking. I'm thinking about ... I'm probably half asleep.

RTH:[218] Right.

CS:[219] But I'm thinking about this program and how I can get things better organized, and I'm thinking that I'm going to call her up. This is not ... I don't think this is ... That's not sleep related. What may be sleep related is the actual locution.

RTH:[220] Right.

CS:[221] You know, this "stufer" business is just amazing to me, amusing, very amusing.

RTH:[222] So you're saying to yourself, if I'm understanding you correctly, "Stufer! Stufer! Stufer!"

CS:[223] It's as if I were talking to her.

RTH:[224] As if you are talking out loud.

CS:[225] Yeah.

RTH:[226] And does your voice sound natural to you, as if ...

CS:[227] No. No it doesn't. It's not … It's not … I don't overhear the conversation. It's almost as if after the beeper goes off, if I'm even faintly attentive (as I was in this case), then the last words of whatever the internal dialog was, whether they're mine or somebody else's, are actually re– … sound like they are replayed to me. I can *hear* them. I could hear "stufer." Now again I'm not sure whether I heard that before the beep or after the beep, but it was right around there, somewhere. And, you know, I certainly heard "stufer" said in my dialog with her. No question about it.

CS[217-227] is a still a mixture of apprehension and context, but more apprehension than was present in the first interview. Progress!

CS[227] illustrates the confusions that must be sorted through, if we are to apprehend experience. There are at least three separate themes twisted together in this paragraph: The pristine experience (at the moment of the beep), the "replay" (after the beep), and the speculations (at the time of the interview).

Constraint: Cleave to pristine experience. In Chapter 3 we noticed the constraint *Aim at pristine experience.* Now, with several turns of the screw under our belts, we notice that "aim at" is merely a preliminary step to "cleave to." "Cleave to" has a loyalty or unwaveringness denotation that is, I believe, imposed by the intention genuinely to apprehend experience. It is *not* sufficient merely to aim at pristine experience, because merely to *aim* implies the satisfactoriness of *Oops, I missed! Oh well!* By contrast, to *cleave to* implies the *successful* aiming at pristine experience, the successful eradication of interest in anything but pristine experience. A two-year-old can *aim at*; it requires mature high commitment to *cleave to*.

There are lots of things that can interfere with the apprehension of pristine experience; if one is genuinely to apprehend pristine experience one must apprehend it and only it. Here, there are two competitors: the "replay" experience and theoretical speculation.

Pristine experience takes place at the moment of the beep – that is, a split second *before* the beep disturbs it. The DES object is to apprehend pristine experience. Pristine experience has to do, here, with "Stufer, stufer, super." The report that CS is saying "stufer, stufer" is evidence that CS is in some way tapping pristine experience – that seems the most reasonable explanation of such a neologism, particularly given CS's evident surprise at its existence. It seems likely that *something* about "stufer" was experienced in the vicinity of the beep.

The "replay" seems to come a second or so after the beep. CS reports that he was saying "Stufer, stufer, super" at the moment of the beep (the pristine experience), and then *again* hearing those same words a second or so later. We have to try to discriminate carefully in such cases. Were there indeed two experiences in close proximity (a second or so apart) and they are in close similarity ("Stufer, stufer, super" both times)? If so, they are, in the eyes of DES, fundamentally different: One is pristine experience, our primary interest, the kind of thing CS engages in "free range" (or at least minimally interfered with). The other, the replay experience, is entirely a product of the DES beeper or CS's reaction to it. Or maybe the replay isn't really an experience, but instead is the result of CS's presupposition about how recall works.

CS[227] also includes some general/theoretical/universal speculations about the apprehension-of-experience process: "It's almost as if after the beeper goes off, if I'm even faintly attentive (as I was in this case), then the last words of whatever the internal dialog was, whether they're mine or somebody else's, are actually re– ... sound like they are replayed to me" is a (faux) *universal* statement about how he responds to beeps. He is not describing how he responded to *this particular* beep; he is describing how he *always* responds to beeps. Many DES subjects engage in some sorts of universal speculations; students of consciousness, in my experience, do so often and with energy. Part of cleaving to pristine experience is to eradicate as completely as possible this kind of speculation; that is often difficult and requires iterative effort.

So without being critical of CS as an individual, it is necessary to be blunt about the process. First, it is noteworthy that he would engage in such speculation with so little evidence – he's not very good at the DES procedure, and this is his first beep of this kind. Second, it turns out that *his own other samples* do not actually accord with the theoretical universal he has advanced here – that is, he doesn't always have the replay he describes here. He has apparently overly faux-generalized from one (probably not very skillful) "observation."

Regardless of whether this generalization is true, the generalizing *interferes* with the apprehension of pristine experience. At the very best, it distracts; it focuses on something other than pristine experience. But more realistically, it *competes with* or *confuses* the apprehension of pristine experience. To the extent that CS believes his universals, he will twist his observations to match, and that is problematic even if the generalization is true.

I'm quite sure we will not be able to disentangle CS's pristine experience/ replayed experience/universalization about this particular beep. Therefore, the aim of the rest of this interview will be entirely iteratively forward looking. I will ask questions about this particular beep to help us to discern, as best we can, exactly what was experienced and when, *not* because I expect to be able to discover his (past) pristine experience, but because I want to build the (future) skill of cleaving to pristine experience, which will require distinguishing between pristine experience and all else.

There is no guarantee that it will *ever* be possible for CS to separate his pristine experience from all else. I have no preconception that CS can get to pristine experience – maybe he can, maybe he can't. Most subjects find that they can apprehend their experience at the moment of the beep, but that in no way implies that CS can do so.

It is clear that we are not yet following an adequate procedure, even down to the basics of having the notebook at hand during the interview. Subjects have the right to discover whether the procedural details I ask for are really important. Just because I *say* that X is important does not really mean that I *believe* that it is important, and much less does it mean that I will behaviorally value its importance and interpersonally require its adherence. Part of the iterative sequence is to build the subject's understanding of what is procedurally important and the extent to which I am committed to it.

The interview about this beep will go on for another fifteen *minutes*, during which there is probably only about fifteen *seconds* of talk about experience at the moment of the beep. That is not at all unusual early in DES, but we clearly have our work cut out for us in future interviews. Our task will be iteratively to raise the amount of time and attention we aim at the experience at the moment of subsequent beeps.

This sampling day illustrates the basic tension that fuels the DES iterative process. In the beginning of DES sampling, subjects do the best they can to understand the DES procedure and to follow instructions. They fall short, however, because the DES procedure and instructions, despite their seeming simplicity, are very demanding: They request subjects to perform a task that is beyond their current skill repertoire. Because subjects don't know what they don't know, they interpret the DES procedures and aims according to their own (mis)understandings, but in so doing they fall short of the actual DES aims. Subjects typically recognize that they have fallen short; that is typically somewhat frustrating, which can provide the energy for improvement.

> **Q:** I understand that you don't like "why" questions, but why is it so difficult for him to get to the moment of the beep? Couldn't you speculate just a little?
> **A:** Most subjects have some trouble getting to the moment of the beep. It has never been my aim to analyze *why* that is; it has seemed enough for me to notice *that* it is difficult. But here's my speculation: The *experience at the* moment is where the truth about yourself inheres. It is at particular moments that you are angry, or are fascinated, or are jealous, or covet, or like someone, or are afraid of someone, or are sexually interested, or are thinking about someone other than who you are with, or have to pee, or are repulsed, or however the world and its inhabitants presents itself/themselves to you. You are not angry, or fascinated, or whatever *in general*; you are angry or fascinated or whatever at specific, concrete times in specific, concrete ways about specific, concrete people or events. Those experiences can be dangerous: to be angry at someone who has power over you; to like someone who doesn't like you; to be sexually interested in someone who is involved with/married to someone else; and so on. So it can be smart to hide your experience, even from yourself.
>
> So pristine experience, and/or the process of noticing it, can become, over the long haul, defocused, undermined, diluted, confused. One effective way

to make experience go unfocused is to make the moment disappear: no moment, no experience. And therefore, no moment, no danger. Different people have different things that are saliently dangerous; and the same person has different things that are saliently dangerous at different ages and situations. But developing the skill of defocusing the moment (I do think it is a skill or a collection of skills) will serve to defuse all sorts of dangers at all ages.

    Once that skill begins to be developed, which may occur at age one or ten or one hundred, the ingrained habitualness of not encountering momentary experience is likely to persist long after the original danger has passed, because the habitualness is self-perpetuating: It hides/masks/defocuses the very thing (direct experience) that is at the center of itself. As a result, you don't know what you're missing or even *that* you're missing it, and therefore you have little impetus for changing it.

    I don't know whether any of this is true for most people; and if it is, I don't presume to know whether it is true for CS. For the present purposes, it doesn't matter. It is a direct observation (without speculating *why*) that CS's analyses, generalities, and presuppositions are extremely layered and difficult for him to set aside. I don't wish to opine about whether that is a good thing or a bad thing for CS in general: It may well make him a good scientist, for example. Or not – it requires omniscience to know the answer to those questions. For now it is enough simply to observe that CS has difficulty getting to the moment of the beep, and because one has to get to the moment of the beep before (or at the same time) one gets to the *experience* at the moment of the beep, he therefore has difficulty describing his beeped experience.

THE THIRD SAMPLING INTERVIEW

CS:[301] I just got back[1] from a meeting in New York last night, and I'm writing in my journal. And I have the beeper in my ear and I'm just writing[2] a specific detail about a guy I met at the meeting, and the beeper goes off. I know[3] exactly what I was writing because it's already written. And I'm trying to figure out[4] whether I actually heard the voice or not. You know, when the beeper goes off – we talked about this last time – when the beeper goes off it's as if you then replay what you've been thinking or, in this case, writing, and it's almost as if you hear the voice.[5] But when the beeper goes off, you're just writing, it's completely silent.[6]

    And I'm just fascinated by this detail.[7] It's the only beep that I have to report today, because it's the first beep that I've gotten today. I mean, I started at about ten.

RTH:[302] OK.

CS:[303] I don't know what you think about that[8], if you want … If that's…
Is that inner speech or something else?[9] I feel like when I write it's totally silent.[10]

As we have seen throughout this book, DES tries to be as precise as possible about pinpointing the moment of the beep. As do many subjects, CS starts out quite *un*focused about timing. Referring to the superscripts in CS[301-303]:

1. "I just got back" is well before the beep.
2. "I have the beeper in my ear and I'm just writing" is in the vicinity of, but not necessarily specifically at, the beep.
3. "I know" is temporally ambiguous: It could refer to the moment of the beep, the time of apprehending the beeped experience (a few seconds after the moment of the beep), or the time of the present interview.
4. "I'm trying to figure out" is equally ambiguous.
5. "You know, when the beeper goes off … you hear the voice" is a universal – it refers to no specific time at all.
6. "But when the beeper goes off … it's completely silent" is also ambiguous – it might be a description of the phenomenon at the moment of this particular beep, but the "you're" and "it's" can be taken to imply an impersonal generality, a universal theory of beep-responding.
7. "Fascinated by this detail" ambiguously refers to the time between beeping and the interview or during the interview, and the remainder is context.
8. "I don't know what you think about that" apparently refers to the time of the interview.
9. "Is that inner speech or something else?" is about a universal.
10. "I feel like when I write it's totally silent" is a universal.
    For whatever reason, CS has not zeroed in on the experience at the moment of the beep, so I will have to help him to do so.

    RTH:[304] Well, I'm not sure that I understand the phenomenon, so let me ask a little bit more about it. Are you free to tell us what the detail was, what you were writing?

It is my intention here to bring him to the concrete, to the actual at-the-moment-of-the-beep experience, and to do that I want him to tell me exactly about that experience. I'm actually not primarily interested in what he was writing – I'm interested in his experience. Because experience inheres only in concretely explicit events, I'm trying to get us to talk about some concretely explicit detail of this moment.

Sometimes subjects are ambiguous about the moment because the moment contains something private, embarrassing, or otherwise personal. So I asked permission to proceed.

[CS gives background for eighty seconds. He tells me that this colleague, whom he previously had not known well, had invited CS to a high-level meeting in San Francisco, which is to take place in a building that CS knew

well. He proceeded to tell me about the building that sits picturesquely on
a hill overlooking the San Francisco Bay]

RTH:[305] [interrupts] Well, that [the building] sounds pretty cool, but I'd
rather get to talking about that after we get to your experience.

I'm interested in CS's experience. The background that CS reports,
although perhaps an interesting part of CS's narrative, is not his experience. I
try to convey that to CS directly, to let him know that I heard him, but I want
us to cleave to his experience.

CS:[306] OK. I'm setting this up.

RTH:[307] Right.

CS:[308] I'm writing him a note, you see, in my journal, saying how excited I am
by this prospect [of the invitation to the San Francisco meeting]. But then
when the beeper goes off, I know that I was writing before the beep, or at
the beep ...

RTH:[309] You were in the act of writing.

CS:[310] I'm in the act of writing and the language is sort of coming out of my
brain. But I don't think it's spoken.

I think he is now trying to tell me about his experience at the moment
of the beep, and I try to support that but stay out of his way. However, "the
language is sort of coming out of my brain" is probably not a description
of a phenomenon for two reasons. First, "language" is an abstract concept;
English is a language; one *never* (or at most extremely rarely except perhaps
among multilinguals) directly experiences English. One experiences concrete
words or the meaning that those concrete words convey or the sound of those
concrete words. One does not experience the entirety of the word-producing/
receiving art that is language.

Second, "coming out of my brain" is entirely ambiguous: It may be an
explanatory concept (my brain cells are firing) or it may be a description of a
phenomenon (I experience the words moving, coming out of my head).

"I don't think it's spoken" is also ambiguously descriptive or theoretical.

Thus CS probably mixes a bit of description of a phenomenon with a lot of
theorizing or interpreting. The DES task is, iteratively, to reverse that balance.

RTH:[311] OK.

CS:[312] I don't hear anything. But when the beep goes off, I hear the voice
saying, you know, "Thank you for your invitation ..." I mean, everything
gets replayed. It's like déjà vu or something.

We discussed during the second sampling day (cf., CS[227]) the importance
of distinguishing between the pristine experience at the moment of the beep
and the replay, but despite that training he does not keep them adequately

separate here. This illustrates that iteration is a process of successive approximation – this may be better than day two, but it is not yet good enough. We will have to provide additional training (see CS[325]).

> RTH:[313] OK. So let's ... What exactly were you writing at the moment of the beep? When the beep caught you....

Q: Why are you asking about his writing? That's not experience!
A: You're right, I would much rather ask only about experience, but until we get to the moment of the beep, that is not possible. This question is a compromise in the service of the iterative training. I focus on the concreteness of the writing in the attempt to help bring him back to the moment of the beep, to make clear the distinction between the moment of the beep and everything else (after the beep, context, generality, etc.).

> CS:[314] I could go get it [the journal in which he had written]. I was writing, "It's auspicious that my trip to New York would lead me to San Francisco." And I write, "might lead me to."

I'm wary of the accuracy of his report: His first self-quote was "*would* lead me to" but the second was "*might* lead me to." Recall the constraint from Chapter 5: *Clarify the details.*

I don't really care whether the written word was "would" or "might," but I do care about getting it right, whatever *it* was. Being careless about such things leads to being careless about the faithful apprehension of experience.

> RTH:[315] And so you're in the process of writing "might lead me to" at the moment of the beep?
> CS:[316] I had already assembled that sentence, in my head I think. I mean, it's so hard to know, because language just seems to assemble itself.

This is not a description of experience: "assembling" is a presumed-to-exist cognitive process, not an experience. This is a theoretical characterization of language.

This giving of theoretical explanations rather than phenomenological descriptions is, I think, characteristic of many consciousness scientists' responses to DES beeps, but I bracketed that hunch during the interview. That is, I did *not* entertain a line of reasoning that went: CS is a scientist; scientists give theoretical explanations; therefore CS is likely to give theoretical explanations. Instead, I simply noted that *for whatever reason* CS was not simply describing experience, and therefore I had to help him describe experience.

> RTH:[317] Right. So ...
> CS:[318] So I had just written, "might lead to ..."
> RTH:[319] "Might lead to."
> CS:[320] Yeah.
> RTH:[321] OK.

Note that at CS[314] he had said he had written "might lead *me* to." This discrepancy, small though it may seem, continues to indicate that CS has *not* paid adequate attention to his experience at the moment of the beep. DES subjects, once they master the task, become quite exactly consistent about verbal details, not merely approximately consistent as here.

> CS:[322] And then the beep goes off. And then I hear this voice repeating the previous sentence, as I'm trying to recall – I'm trying to recall it, you see?
> RTH:[323] Right.
> CS:[324] So I can give a report.
> RTH:[325] So let's keep very separate the moment of the beep, which is like that microsecond right *before* the beep, in which you're writing "might lead to," and the time of the *report* of the beep, which happens after the beep begins …

Iterative training requires repetition. We had made the same distinction (differentiate carefully the moment of the beep from all else) on CS's second sampling day (see CS[227]) and at other times that I did not transcribe. If a subject has an entanglement, as here, it generally takes several or many passes to unravel it. It's quite *un*likely that we will be able to disentangle those time frames for this beep; our interview here is still primarily future-oriented training, aimed at CS's next sampling day.

> CS:[326] Oh, long after, yeah.
> RTH:[327] Right. Let's focus first on the, on the moment of the beep, the undisturbed (as best we can get to it) …
> CS:[328] Right.
> RTH:[329] … time just before the beep occurs. So you're writing, and is there anything in your experience while you're writing?
> CS:[330] [tentatively] Not … not that I know of. You know, I'm in my dining room, so presumably I'm monitoring all of that stuff, but it's not part of my perceptual consciousness.

CS is distinguishing between what he directly apprehends and what he presumes. Good! I will have to help him be more attentive to this distinction …

> RTH:[331] And how about the guy, is he somehow present to you, the guy that you're writing to?

… and I do that by following his lead of talking about the dining room. I'm affording him the opportunity to differentiate direct apprehension on a different topic, and that seems to help his confidence.

> CS:[332] [with apparent confidence] Well, previously I see him. But …
> RTH:[333] OK. But not at the moment of the beep?

CS:[334] Not at the moment, not as I'm writing. I see him as I'm getting ready to write, because I'm recalling this whole interaction.

I'm happy that CS is discriminating between at-the-moment and any other time.

RTH:[335] OK. And how about the San Francisco building. Do you see that at the moment of the beep?
CS:[336] [with apparent conviction] No, not at all.

I'm impressed with his straightforwardness in this latest section of the interview (beginning at about CS[326]). No longer is he evading the experience at the moment of the beep in favor of some other time; no longer does there seem to be an impure amalgam of generality/speculation and experience.

RTH:[337] So at the moment of the beep you ...
CS:[338] It's completely dominated ... my consciousness is completely dominated by this linguistic act or writing act. It seems to me!
RTH:[339] OK. So it seems like now you've said it sort of in two different ways. One way that you said a few minutes ago was it was like your consciousness was turned off while you were writing ...

That actually is a misstatement of what CS has said. I didn't intend to misstate; I just got it slightly wrong.

CS:[340] Well, that *is* my consciousness.
RTH:[341] Right.
CS:[342] It is ... there is no other [sighs/laughs resignedly] ...you know, there is no other aspect of my conscious experience which is verbalized. I mean, there is no internal propositional thought about the dining room. Obviously I'm in the dining room, but that doesn't get it. That doesn't have any place in the foreground of my consciousness ...
RTH:[343] Right. And that's quite usual. That's the way it almost always is.
CS:[344] Yeah ...
RTH:[345] What I guess I'm trying to get at is the details of the phenomenon that *are* in your consciousness, in your awareness, in your experience ...
CS:[346] [inaudible] "that New York leads to" – that's what comes, that's what's in my mind. It's the assembly of that sentence.
RTH:[347] "New York leads to" or "might lead to"?

I press for the careful report of the details because experience actually resides in those concrete details. The distinction between "New York leads to" and "New York might lead to" may seem trivial, as if it were merely a matter of linguistic expression style (and that may be true in some cases, but we never know which ones). The fact is, however, that experience is (usually) specific, so to allow ourselves to speak non-specifically about any of its specific detail is to lose the fidelity of the account.

My questions here are about what he was writing at the moment of the beep, even though my main interest is in what he was experiencing *while* he was writing. These questions are part of the iterative successive approximation procedure: I am first trying to get us to focus on the *moment* of the beep; then I will encourage us to be as specifically detailed about what was *happening* (he was writing) at the moment of the beep; then, if successful, I will inquire about the details of his *experience* at the moment of the beep. I'd prefer to leave out the second step, but CS and I are not ready for that yet.

Also noteworthy is CS's presumption that he doesn't really need to have the notebook. That's part of the basics of the DES procedure; CS has not yet accepted that he might need to perform the whole procedure as I've specified it if he is to apprehend his experience faithfully. We have discussed this earlier; see the discussion before the beginning of the second sampling day. I re-emphasize that CS is not unusual in this regard; many subjects are quite cavalier, at first, about the details of the procedure.

> CS:[348] [exasperated] Well, I mean I could go … the thing [the journal] is sitting on the table in the next room.
> RTH:[349] It might be a good idea to get it.
> CS:[350] [still exasperated] Just a minute.
> [1:20 of silence]
> CS:[351] [consults his journal] It says, uh, let's see, the blurb was actually written … this is the whole thing. I'm commenting on the page in the meeting manual that describes my lecture. This was actually not … this stuff about me here was written for a different grant application. [reads] "Auspicious that New York might lead to San Francisco" beep. So "San Francisco" was before the beep.

Most of this is background or context. It is noteworthy that he notices that San Francisco was before the beep – that he had misstated this fact earlier in our discussion. That demonstrates that he is trying to get his descriptions right, which is a good sign for the future faithful apprehension of experience. It also demonstrates on his own turf (no abstract conversation about memory here) why he should *not* rely on his memory for the details of experience.

> RTH:[352] So "New York might lead to San Francisco," and then the beep comes right after that.
> CS:[353] Yeah. The beep comes right after "San Francisco."

From my point of view we have, nine minutes into the third sampling interview, finally nailed down the moment of a beep. That is frequently how long it takes to get the kind of precision that I think is necessary.

Now that we have determined the moment of the beep as well as we are going to be able to do so, I will turn my attention to the experience that was ongoing at the moment of the beep.

RTH:[354] OK. And so now the question that I would like be as careful about as we can get is, so you're in the act of writing "New York might lead to San Francisco," and is there anything in your awareness *at all* other than, well, just that those words are coming out the end of your pen?

CS:[355] Doesn't seem to be. Yeah, that's it. Of course, I mean, you know, I'm aware that I'm sitting in the room, but I'm not, I'm not focused on that *at all*.

RTH:[356] Right. And so the ...

CS:[357] I'm aware of the whole orientational context of the situation. But what is really occupying my mind to the *oblivion* even of my surround is this, you know, how to say what I want to say to this guy.

RTH:[358] And it sounds to me – and I'm just trying to interpret what you're saying, so if I'm mistaken about this let me know – but it sounds like almost everything including what you're going to say is in the oblivion of your consciousness, so to speak. It's not ... My understanding of what you're saying is it's not like you are, in your direct phenomenal consciousness, aware of what you're going to say before you're saying it.

CS:[359] Totally not. I'm aware of the task. I mean, the task is to write this guy and acknowledge our meeting and convey enough enthusiasm to keep him interested, let's put it that way.

RTH:[360] Right.

CS:[361] I mean, those things are clear. Those are motives, and I mean ...

RTH:[362] But those motives, I'm understanding, are not in your direct experience right at the very moment of the beep?

CS:[363] No, no. At the time that I'm writing, I'm just writing. I've already prepared the text in a way, if you want to be ... this is interpretation, but I've thought a little bit about him and what he said to me ...

RTH:[364] Right.

CS:[365] ... and what I should say to him at this point – it's carefully measured. But then it's *completely* unselfconscious ...

RTH:[366] Right, OK ...

CS:[367] The writing is virtually automatic. But then the beep comes on and it makes you think or you feel like you're assembling that ... It's a funny ... it's a mirroring or an echoing effect.

[End of discussion of this beep]

To my ear, beginning at about CS[353], CS's statements are quite different from those that have come before. Now he is much better at distinguishing between the moment of the beep and what comes after and before it; between the experience at the moment of the beep and theory. This change, as it seems to me, began nine minutes into the third interview, at the time (CS[353]) when we finally got some clarity on the moment of the beep. Until the moment of the beep is made precise (as precise as can be done), there is room for equivocation, interpretation, abstraction, unclarity. Once we have established the moment of the beep, however, then the clouds lift and the distinctions between what was precisely then and not then, and between what was actually in experience and what was not, is made possible.

Q: It took you two entire interviews and nine minutes into the third interview finally to get to the moment of the beep. Two hours and nine minutes seems excruciatingly long. Is that typical?

A: There are big individual differences in this regard. A few people (but not many) grasp the concept from the initial instructions and are pretty secure about the moment of the beep during their first sampling. Quite a few (probably the majority) grasp the concept during the first interview, and therefore are pretty secure about it during their second sampling day. Some take longer. But the moral is clear to me: *It takes as long as it takes.* Until the subject is indeed secure about the moment of the beep, all reports about experience are suspect.

There is also a moral for those interested in acquiring the DES skills. I'm pretty good at these interviews, and it took me two hours and nine minutes to get, for the first time, to the vicinity of the moment of the beep. Maybe someone else might accomplish that twice as fast as I can; either way, substantial patience is required.

There is also a moral for those interested in pristine experience in general: Reports about pristine experience that come from a first (or only) interview (which means almost all reports used in psychological research) are not to be trusted.

DISCUSSION

I again thank CS for allowing these interviews to be transcribed and published.

I hope the reader has not come away with the impression that CS is a particularly intransigent subject – nothing could be further from the truth. As DES subjects go, he is not that unusual. As consciousness scientist DES subjects go, he is way out front: Most consciousness scientists have avoided *altogether* the prospect of wearing the DES beeper. I decline to speculate too strongly about their motivation, but it seems reasonable that if they did participate, DES would be at least as difficult for them as for CS.

Being a DES subject may be more difficult for consciousness scientists than for non-professionals. Here are two competing explanations. First, perhaps consciousness scientists are more careful observers than are non-professionals. They make important distinctions that others are not competent to make. That is, non-professionals oversimplify, with the result that for them the DES task is overly simple.

On the other hand, perhaps consciousness scientists are more thoroughly attached to their theoretical positions, and therefore have a harder time bracketing them than do non-professionals. As a result, direct observation is overly difficult for consciousness scientists.

I don't know which, if either, of these is correct. Maybe some of both. But if I had to bet real money, I'd bet on the second option; CS is an example. The distinctions that CS had difficulty with – between experience at the moment of the beep and experience a few seconds thereafter, between experience and theory – are not any more or less complex than the distinctions faced by non-professional subjects. But overcoming them was more difficult for CS because of, as it seems to me, the strength of his commitment to theories about the way consciousness works.

Again, I emphasize that my data are limited and my sample non-random. I do think I've seen enough to counsel against any smugness on the part of consciousness scientists.

We are turning the screw into the notion of the co-determination of moments ↔ experience ↔ genuinely submitting to the constraints. We've focused primarily in this chapter on the difficulty that consciousness scientists might have in genuinely submitting to the constraints, but we could as well have focused on the difficulty of getting to the moment or the difficulty of cleaving to experience. We noticed, for example, that at CS[353] a transformation seemed to take place in all three simultaneously. Co-determination implies that a focus on one aspect entails a focus on all.

13

Pristine Experience (*Not*):
Emotion and Schizophrenia

In this chapter, we put pristine experience into bolder relief by considering what is *not* pristine experience. We first examine a paper titled "The Subjective Experience of Emotion in Schizophrenia" (Kring & Germans, 2004) and conclude that, despite its title, this paper does not investigate the pristine experience of emotion in schizophrenia. We then discuss some DES findings about the experience of emotion in schizophrenia. Then we repeat that process for emotion in general, examining a paper titled "The Experience of Emotion" (Barrett, Mesquita, Ochsner, & Gross, 2007).

KRING: "THE SUBJECTIVE EXPERIENCE OF EMOTION IN SCHIZOPHRENIA"

Ann Kring is a noted schizophrenia and emotion researcher, and "The Subjective Experience of Emotion in Schizophrenia" (Kring & Germans, 2004) is a highly competent example of how the discipline of psychology attempts to tackle inner experience. We will critically examine that paper. First, we will ask whether Kring and Germans mean by "subjective experience" in the title of their paper the same thing that we mean by pristine inner experience; we'll answer yes. Then we'll examine Kring and Germans's methods and conclude that despite the article's title, they actually examine neither moments nor experience, that their method does not genuinely submit to the constraints that the examination of experience requires, and therefore that the paper is not genuinely about pristine experience.

I emphasize that I choose the Kring and Germans article for us to examine for four reasons: First, understanding schizophrenia is a vitally important task; I commend researchers who undertake studies of schizophrenia. Second, Kring and Germans (2004) (and many of Kring's other papers) aim frankly at experience; Kring recognizes, more acutely than many psychologists, the desirability of confronting experience. Third, Kring and Germans (2004) is of high quality – it is a sophisticated orthodox-psychology study of experience.

Any criticism that I level against Kring and Germans is a criticism of the science of psychology, not of any weakness in their particular application of that science. Fourth, I have myself made a few observations of the experience of emotion in schizophrenia (Hurlburt, 1990).

Subjective Experience Equals Pristine Experience

Our first task is to determine whether Kring and Germans mean by "subjective experience" the same thing that we mean by "pristine experience" – that is, something occurring before the footlights of consciousness at a particular moment. Here is the opening of Kring and Germans (2004):

> The notion that schizophrenia patients' subjective experience of emotion might not match their facial expressions is not new. Indeed, early theorists, including Sullivan and Bleuler, among others, commented on an apparent discrepancy between what schizophrenia patients reported feeling and what they outwardly expressed to others. Moreover, family members have noted that their ill relatives often report experiencing strong emotions. For example, Bouricius (1989) presented samples of her son's diary writings, which articulated the experience of clear and complex emotions. Nonetheless, psychological research into the emotional features of schizophrenia has lagged behind the astute observations of the early theorists and family members.
>
> In this chapter, we will concentrate on one aspect of the subjective experience of schizophrenia, namely the subjective experience of emotion. (Kring & Germans, 2004, p. 329)

The main thrust of the Kring and Germans article is thus the discrepancy between the overt expression and the subjective experience of emotion. I conclude that Kring and Germans use the term *subjective experience* to refer to phenomena directly apprehended before the footlights of consciousness, which we call *pristine inner experience*.

It is the thesis of this book that if one wishes to examine pristine experience, one must examine explicitly defined moments of experience and must do so in ways that genuinely submit to the constraints that that endeavor imposes. Let's examine the extent to which Kring and Germans do that.

The Studies Cited: Not Pristine Experience

Broadly speaking, Kring and Germans cite three kinds of evidence about the subjective experience in schizophrenia: the Bouricius diary, orthodox psychological investigations that use emotion rating scales, and experience sampling method (ESM) studies. I examine each from the perspective of whether they apprehend moments of experience.

Diary

Jean Bouricius is the mother of a thirty-two-year-old son who had been diagnosed with schizophrenia. Bouricius (1989) quotes many entries from her son's diary and infers that he experiences emotion, even though his expression of that emotion is blunted. For example, Bouricius writes:

> As evidence that my son does experience strong emotions that are appropriate to his circumstances … I offer some samples of his writing. … He wrote
>> I am a lonely nothing, a being, but pass me by. Forever pass me by. Strangers, I don't see you. My afflictions fill the place that was meant for sharing love. I am crying in despair.
> Although he speaks of inability to share love, this passage surely cannot be construed to mean that he feels no emotion. (Bouricius, 1989, p. 202)

In my view, that diary entry, like all the diary entries that Bouricius cites, cannot be unambiguously construed either as being a statement that he feels emotion or that he feels no emotion. Here are three reasonable construals of the diarist's words: (a) that he experiences love and is sad that he can't share it (apparently Bouricius's view); (b) that he doesn't experience love and therefore experiences despair; and (c) that he experiences neither love nor despair (that is, the diary entry is a general statement or universal assertion about the diarist's *being*). On this third understanding, "I am crying in despair" means that the diarist knows of the human potential for emotional experience but himself feels none, and therefore recognizes his loss.

I fully accept that I don't know how the diarist's statement should be construed, but neither, I think, does Bouricius, Kring, or Germans. Is the diarist attempting to describe the experience of emotion? Maybe so, maybe not. The co-determination of moments ↔ experience ↔ genuinely submitting to the constraints that we have been discussing implies that ambiguity about moments must imply ambiguity about experience must imply failure to employ a method that genuinely submits to the constraints that the endeavor to provide a faithful representation of pristine experience imposes.

> **Q:** It seems that the natural understanding of "I am crying in despair" is that the diarist experiences love and is sad that he can't share it. The mother's intuition is right! You should just accept that and move on.
> **A:** That is *one* understanding, and it *may be* what the diarist meant. However, to accept that understanding because it seems natural or intuitive is *antithetical* to the constraints imposed by the genuine investigation of experience. Implied in your "natural accepting" is the presupposition that the schizophrenic diarist's lack of love is just like your own non-schizophrenic lack of love, and that his sadness/despair reaction to lack of love is just like your own reaction would be. The schizophrenic's emotion experience *might*

be the same as yours, but it might be different. To act on your presupposition ("to accept that and move on") *guarantees* that you can *never* discover a difference if there be one, and that, at this stage of the knowledge of experience, is problematic. Recall the constraint from Chapter 9: *Don't judge others by yourself.*

Note carefully that the antidote to presupposing emotional similarity is *not* presupposing emotional *dis*similarity, it is the *bracketing* of the presupposition of similarity, the maintenance of a level playing field toward all experiential possibilities, the ability to explore even handedly possibilities that seem natural and possibilities that seem strange. We have seen three different takes on what the diarist means; doubtless there are other interpretations. *We don't know what the diarist meant*, and it's a mistake to presume that we do. (By the way, "it seems natural" usually means that a presupposition is in the vicinity.)

Q: We can't bracket everything!

A: No we can't. But we can try to bracket everything *that arises* (Hurlburt & Schwitzgebel, 2011c). Here, for example, the diarist writes "My afflictions fill the place that was meant for sharing love." Most nonschizophrenics would not write that, so that should alert you, I think, to rev up your bracketing of presuppositions engine and open yourself to the possibility that his experience is importantly different from yours. I discuss in detail a similar example in Chapter 19.

Q: It seems you are criticizing the diarist for something he doesn't deserve. He did *not* set out, as far as we can glean, directly to describe moments of experience, and did *not* seek to use a method that sought to minimize the experiential ambiguity of his writings. So you shouldn't criticize him for failing to do so.

A: You're right that the diarist is under no obligation to describe pristine experience, so I am not criticizing the diarist. I criticize those who would (without warrant, as it seems to me) accept the diary as a description of pristine experience.

Emotion Rating Scales

Most of the investigations Kring and Germans cite use emotion rating scales such as the Positive and Negative Affect Schedule (PANAS; Watson, Clark, & Tellegen, 1988) or the Chapman Scales (Chapman, Chapman, & Raulin, 1976) to examine the "subjective experience" of emotion. (Kring and Germans also explore physiological reactions [e.g., EEG, EMG], behavioral observations, and facial expression observations; those are important ways of investigating emotion and schizophrenia, but Kring and Germans do not hold them to be revealing a person's *experience* of emotion, so we will not examine them here.)

The PANAS presents twenty adjectives that are designed to represent two concepts (ten adjectives each): positive affect (PA: adjectives such as "enthusiastic," "interested," "determined") and negative affect (NA: adjectives such as "scared," "afraid," "upset"). The subject is to rate each of these twenty adjectives on five-point Likert-type scales ranging from *very slightly or not at all* to *extremely*. Subjects are instructed to rate the PANAS adjectives in a variety of time frames, ranging from "right now (that is, at the present moment)" to "during the past week" to "in general, that is, on the average."

Let's consider a representative PANAS study, Kring and Neale (1996). Kring and Neale showed schizophrenic patients and non-patients three kinds of film clips: (a) clips designed to elicit positive emotion (happiness; e.g., slapstick comedy); (b) clips designed to elicit negative emotions (sad, fear; e.g., a dying parent, a man being swarmed with cockroaches); and (c) clips judged to be emotionally neutral (nature scenes). The clips were about five to six minutes in length. Emotion expression was measured by videotaping subjects while they watched each clip; facial expressions were videotaped and subsequently rated by the experimenters. Emotion experience was assessed by asking the subject to fill out the PANAS following each clip, using the at-the-moment instruction: "To what extent [do] you feel this way right now, that is, at the present moment?" (Kring & Neale, 1996, p. 251).

For us, the question is whether, for example, a subject's set of PANAS ratings should be considered an apprehension of her pristine experience; I think the answer is no. First, Kring and Neale do not adequately specify the moment under consideration. Kring and Neale's instruction is "to what extent [do] you feel this way right now, that is, at the present moment?" which is highly similar to the instruction in the happy/sad study we discussed in Chapter 7: "indicate how [you] felt 'right now, at this very moment.'" It seems likely that Kring and Neale's subjects understand the rating task in much the same way as did the subjects in the happy/sad study: The investigator is probably not really asking about how I feel *right now* – she must be asking about the movie clip. That clip was of five to six minutes' duration, and if moments of experience have durations on the order of a few *seconds*, each subject had on the order of hundreds of moments of experience during that movie clip. I think neither Kring, Neale, nor their subjects know with precision what moment the subject is actually rating. Perhaps Kring and Neale assume that emotion experience that started in a film clip five minutes ago will continue unaltered through the rating process, but that (a) assumes what is at issue (that we know the characteristics of emotion experience in schizophrenics); (b) is unlikely given the fleetingness of experience as discussed in previous chapters; and (c) is perhaps even more unlikely in a population noted for erratic, labile responding.

Second, Kring and Neale do not adequately specify for their subjects what they mean by "feel." As we have seen throughout this book, it requires training and practice to separate what is directly experienced from what is presupposed to be ongoing, and Kring and Neale provide no such practice. Their subjects' ratings are most likely some unspecified (probably unspecifiable) combination of a general aspect of the clip, a general characterization of mood, some expectation about what the experimenter wants to be rated, the subjects' self-view/ presuppositions about the nature of their emotions, and pristine experience.

Third, Kring and Neale have no way of knowing whether their rating scales are used in the same way by all subjects. I see no reason to presume that a schizophrenic subject's rating "enthusiastic" a 3 means the same thing as does a control subject's rating "enthusiastic" a 3. That assumption may be true, but it may also be the case that a person who would write "My afflictions fill the place that was meant for sharing love" might have a different way of rating "enthusiastic" than would a person who could never write such a thing.

Thus I conclude that the Kring and Neale (1996) study does not adequately specify the moment, does not adequately inquire about experience, and does not use a method that genuinely submits to the constraints that an exploration of experience requires. Therefore I think it should not be understood to be an exploration of pristine experience.

However, it seems to me that Kring and Neale write about their study as if it *were* a study of pristine experience. Here is their statement of their main results:

> Schizophrenic patients in the present study reported *experiencing as much emotion* during positive and negative films than [sic] controls, and in some cases, they reported *experiencing more* than controls. ... That is, although schizophrenic patients differed from controls in the amount of outwardly expressed emotions, they did not differ in the amount of reported *experienced emotion*. Additionally, these effects were consistent across both positive and negative films. Stated differently, schizophrenic patients reported *feeling positive emotion* during a positive film and negative emotion during the negative films, despite showing relatively little facial expression in response to these films. (Kring & Neale, 1996, p. 254, emphasis added)

Q: You should have italicized *reported* in each one of those instances. That is an important qualifier.
A: I don't think adding *reported* changes anything substantial. This paragraph implies that Kring and Neale put their subjects in a position to report *emotion experience*, and I don't think that's true. They put their subjects in a position to report *some unspecified combination of a general aspect of the clip, a general characterization of mood, some expectation about what the experimenter wants to be rated, and pristine experience*. It's not the *report* that is a problem, it is the *about what* and the *how* of the report.

It is not my intention to criticize the Kring and Neale (1996) study per se; I wish to hold a mirror up to the way psychology investigates experience, and the Kring and Neale study is merely a means to that end. I selected the Kring

TABLE 13.1. *Mean PANAS scores by film and group*
(excerpted from Table 3 of Kring & Neale, 1996, p. 254)

Film	PANAS Scale			
	PA		NA	
	Schizophrenia	Control	Schizophrenia	Control
Negative	25.27	24.48	19.70	18.08
Positive	28.34	27.15	17.21	11.25
Neutral	26.70	21.20	16.83	10.70

and Neale study because it is a high-quality study by orthodox psychological science standards. Understanding how that study deals with experience will help us understand how psychology deals with experience. So if it is not pristine experience that Kring and Neale are investigating, what is it?

I understand the main results passage just quoted as being a summary of the results shown in Table 13.1. When Kring and Neale write, "Schizophrenic patients in the present study reported *experiencing as much emotion* during positive and negative films than [sic] controls, and in some cases, they reported *experiencing more* than controls," I take them to be comparing their schizophrenic patients' mean PA and NA scores to those of the control subjects; that is, 25.27 is as large as or larger than 24.48, 28.34 is as large as or larger than 27.15, and so on, six comparisons in all. If that interpretation is correct, then, strictly speaking, Kring and Neale's "reported experiencing as much emotion" means "rated the PA and the NA adjectives as high as."

To make the jump from "rating adjectives as high as" to "reported experiencing as much emotion as" requires, as we have noted, the mostly unexamined but large assumption that the rating scales are used the same way by both schizophrenic patients and controls. I think it is possible to re-analyze Kring and Neale's results without making that assumption by assuming that patients and controls have similarly neutral reactions to film clips that are designed to be neutral. On that assumption, the ratings that patients and non-patients give of the neutral scenes can serve as a zero point on the scale, and the data analysis would proceed by subtracting the neutral rating from other ratings. Then, for example, if schizophrenic patients rate "enthusiastic" differently from control subjects, that difference would be assumed to apply equally in all conditions, and subtracting the neutral condition should remove the difference. Such a re-analysis is shown in Table 13.2. For example, the schizophrenic patients' mean rating of PA for the negative clip is $25.27 - 26.70 = 1.43$, lower than their mean PA rating of the neutral film.

The pattern of Table 13.2 is very different from that of Table 13.1. Table 13.2 shows that schizophrenia patients, as a group, have *smaller* differential

TABLE 13.2. *Differential PANAS scores by film and group*

Film	PANAS Scale			
	PA		NA	
	Schizophrenia	Control	Schizophrenia	Control
Negative	-1.43	3.28	2.87	7.38
Positive	1.64	5.95	.38	.55
Neutral	0	0	0	0

reactions to emotional scenes than do control subjects, as a group. The main disparity between Tables 13.2 and 13.1 arises from the schizophrenics' ratings of the neutral films (bottom row of Table 13.1): While watching neutral films, schizophrenics rate both their positive and their negative emotionality higher than do control subjects. It is not possible to tease apart whether this is due to stronger experienced emotionality or differences in use of the rating scales.

There are thus at least two importantly different ways to analyze these data, with different results. I don't wish to claim that the second analysis is better than the first – both make assumptions that can be criticized. The point that I wish to emphasize here is we are forced to consider such ways of analyzing the data because the original data – the adjective ratings – are problematic if they are held to be measures of experience. There is no statistical procedure that can overcome those problems.

> **Q:** Even folks who use the PANAS in emotion research admit at least privately that it is a pretty impoverished approach to measuring emotion experience.
> **A:** Then perhaps making its weaknesses more public will encourage the development of better methods.

> **Q:** The validity of a scale does not depend on the content of the items – if the scale distinguishes consistently between groups, that is all that is required for validity.
> **A:** That is true. But Kring and Neale's use of the PANAS goes beyond mere validity. They write, for example, "schizophrenic patients reported feeling positive emotion during a positive film and negative emotion during the negative films," which is a statement about experience, not merely about valid differences between groups.

In addition to the PANAS studies just discussed, Kring and Germans (2004) review schizophrenia emotion studies that use the Chapman Scales (Chapman, Chapman, & Raulin, 1976). All of the criticisms we aimed at the PANAS apply here; furthermore, it will be instructive to recall the origins of the Chapman

Scales. The Chapmans and their colleague gave the following instruction to "our item writers for their guidance" (Chapman et al., 1976, p. 375):

> The anhedonia which we wish to measure is a life-long characterological defect in the ability to experience pleasure. We are not interested in a more transient loss of the experience of pleasure. Pleasure is characterized by a strong positive affect, by a keen anticipation of the experience that evokes it, by a satisfying recollection of the experience, and by a willingness to expend effort to achieve the experience. Behaviors which evoke pleasure tend to be repeated.
>
> Pleasures may be grouped into three categories:
>
> 1. Physical pleasures, that is, pleasures of eating, touching, feeling, sex, temperature, movement, smell, and sound.
> 2. Interpersonal pleasure, for example, nonphysical pleasures of being with people, talking, exchanging expressions of feelings, doing things with them, competing, loving, and interacting in multiple other ways.
> 3. Other pleasures which are neither physical nor interpersonal. Examples are intellectual pleasure and the pleasure of achievement.
>   Item writers were asked to construct items for physical pleasure and for interpersonal or social pleasure but (in the interest of time) to omit the third category of "other pleasures." Items were categorized as physical or social by their dominant theme. (Chapman et al., 1976, pp. 375–376)

The item writer's task was, apparently, to look at those instructions and write a series of items that try to instantiate those instructions.

The item writer's task was *not*, by distinct contrast, to observe as carefully as possible the features of anhedonic schizophrenic subjects' experience and then write items that instantiated that experience. Chapman and colleagues' item writers were apparently not directly informed by *any* careful observation of *any* actual phenomenon, particularly not by any careful observation of actual schizophrenic phenomena.

The items thus generated were then subjected to a standard item analysis, excluding items that correlated minimally with the other items, that correlated with a desirability scale, or that favored one gender over the other.

Here are a few typical items on the Chapman Scales Physical Anhedonia Scale (PAS): "The beauty of sunsets is greatly overrated"; "I have seldom cared to sing in the shower"; "I have always had a number of favorite foods"; "Sex is OK, but not as much fun as most people claim it is"; and "I have always loved having my back massaged" (Chapman et al., 1976, p. 376). The analysis in this book shows that such statements should *not* be considered descriptions of experience. "The beauty of sunsets is greatly overrated" is *not* about any particular moment – it asks about sunsets in general – and the same is true of the other items. Furthermore, the "beauty of sunsets" item does *not* ask about the subject's experience at all – it asks for the subject's opinion of *other people's characterizations* of sunsets – whether others overrate them. The same can be said of the "Sex is OK" item.

None of the Chapman Scale items submits to the constraints that the endeavor to apprehend pristine experience imposes – they were not the result of a careful encounter with the phenomenon of interest, they do not aim at particular moments, they are not all aimed at experience.

I accept that the Chapman Scales may have validational utility in some situations, so I am not criticizing the Chapman Scales per se. My aim is to demonstrate why I think it is unlikely that Chapman Scale scores can be useful discovering something about pristine experience.

The Experience Sampling Method (ESM)

The studies we have just been discussing rely on questionnaires to some degree retrospectively applied. Kring and Germans (2004) also cite studies that use the experience sampling method (ESM), which seeks to minimize retrospectiveness. For example, Myin-Germeys, Delespaul, and deVries (2000) gave programmable wristwatches to patients with schizophrenia and to non-patients. The wristwatches were programmed to beep at ten unpredictable times on each of six consecutive days. Immediately following each beep, subjects were to rate ten adjectives on Likert-type scales. The "positive mood" scale consisted of ratings of the adjectives happy, cheerful, relaxed, and pleased; the negative mood scale consisted of ratings of angry/irritated, lonely, anxious, insecure, down, and guilty. Myin-Germeys and colleagues used these ratings in a variety of ways. For example, *Emotional intensity* was defined for each subject by computing the positive scale scores and the negative scale scores for each moment and averaging these scale scores across all moments. ESM can therefore be thought of as the ultimate attempt repeatedly to administer something like the PANAS in its "present moment" format and in natural environments (ESM typically uses somewhat different adjectives and fewer of them, but those are not essential differences).

ESM seeks to be an improvement over methods that use the PANAS and the Chapman Scales in two ways. First, ESM more carefully defines the moment under consideration. Whereas Kring and Neale's subjects were aimed at a five to six minute window, Myin-Germeys and colleagues' ESM subjects were aimed at the time the wristwatch beeped. That is an improvement; however, as we discussed in Chapter 5, we have found that beeper subjects require substantial iterative training if they are to focus on the actual moment of the beep. Merely telling subjects to rate "the present moment" or "the moment of the beep" is not adequate; careful interviewing shows that subjects so instructed very often rate events that are minutes or hours away from the actual beep. Furthermore, the repeated-day format of ESM should not be considered iterative in the sense of our Chapter 10; there is no training between sampling days in ESM, no successive approximation to any desired result. In ESM there is repetition, not iteration.

Second, the Myin-Germeys et al. ESM procedure seeks to be ecologically valid: It conducts research in the natural environments of the subjects, unlike the artificial laboratory environment of the film Kring and Neale created. I believe that ESM succeeds admirably in this regard.

I therefore accept that the Myin-Germeys and colleauges procedure is in important ways an improvement over Kring and Neale (1996) and can be quite useful in validating aspects of schizophrenic daily life. However, I emphasize that ESM as used by Myin-Germeys et al. (2000) cannot be thought of as providing a high fidelity glimpse into pristine experience – it does not solve the same rating-scale dilemma we discussed earlier in the context of Kring and Neale (there is no reason to believe that one subject's use of a 3 rating is the same as that of another subject's 3). Furthermore, as we discussed previously with respect to the Chapman Scales, the items on the ESM questionnaire were not constructed by a careful investigation of the phenomena of schizophrenia.

Overall

This has been a long section, so I review: We considered Kring and Germans (2004) paper "The Subjective Experience of Emotion in Schizophrenia." We saw at the outset that Kring and Germans seem to use "subjective experience" to mean what we call pristine experience: They were indeed interested in emotional experience as it appears before the footlights of consciousness and whether what is experienced is different from what is expressed. Yet when we considered the kinds of studies that Kring and Germans (2004) reviewed (diary, rating scales, ESM), we determined that none of them should be considered as apprehending pristine experience.

My aim is not to criticize Kring and Germans – they are doing exactly what the science of psychology says they should be doing. And my aim is not to criticize diaries, the PANAS, the Chapman scales, or ESM – they all have their legitimate roles. My critique is aimed at the confusion that I think presides over modern psychology about what is and is not pristine experience and what does and does not constitute the investigation of experience. The accepted psychological methods are not adequate to explore pristine experience.

Pristine Experience in Schizophrenia

If the studies of the kind that Kring and Germans have reviewed should not be considered investigations of pristine experience in schizophrenia, is it *possible* to investigate pristine experience in schizophrenia while genuinely submitting to the constraints that such investigations impose? There has been (that I know of) one study of experience in schizophrenia that attempts to do so: *Sampling Normal and Schizophrenic Inner Experience* (Hurlburt, 1990). That book used an early version of DES; relevant to the present chapter, feelings were a salient aspect of at least two of the four schizophrenic patients ("Bob" and "Sally"). Here's what I said about Bob's emotion experience:

> Five of Bob's samples … included some clear emotional experience which was a central feature of the sample. Most of Bob's samples involved some feeling aspect, but in these five the Feeling was a salient part. In general, Bob could give a clear description of the subjective aspect of the Feeling, saying he felt low and desperate, or slightly self-critical, for example. … However, unlike most of our subjects, Bob experienced his Feelings to reside in precise, clearly demarcated, vivid bodily locations, and these locations could be described in detail.
>
> For example (Sample #10), Bob was sitting in the information center of the hospital. Someone had just asked where the academic center was, and Bob had mentioned a similar center in another city to him. At the moment of the beep, he felt unsure of himself, felt perhaps that what he had said was not quite right. The Feeling was slightly self-critical and was not an extremely strong emotion. The experience had both a bodily and cognitive component. The bodily Feeling was in his chest, in a well-defined teardrop-shaped area extending from the center of his chest, where it was relatively narrow (perhaps 3 inches wide), down to his waist where it was approximately as wide as his body. The region where this Feeling was located existed in depth, also: at the top of his teardrop-shaped region this Feeling of unsureness extended from the surface of his skin to perhaps an inch into the interior of his body, and it gradually increased in depth as it descended, so that at the waist area it extended from the surface to perhaps four inches into his belly. …
>
> Bob's experiences of Feelings had thus three major features: First, they were very vividly experienced. Second, they were clearly and unambiguously apprehended; that is, Bob had no difficulty in recognizing the subjective significance of a particular emotional experience. … The third characteristic of Bob's Feelings was that they were clearly localized in particular parts of his body. There was nothing vague or general in these descriptions; instead they were highly specific. This exactness of bodily description was different from that of most of our earlier [non-schizophrenic] subjects, whose reports of bodily Feelings have tended to be rather indistinct. (Hurlburt, 1990, pp. 228–230)

"Sally" was another schizophrenic patient. Here is an example of her emotion experience:

> Sample #5 took place while Sally was in conversation with her mother about Dollie and Dollie's husband, who were in the process of getting a divorce. At the moment of the beep, Sally herself was talking aloud to

her mother, and at the same time the gods were talking to each other in a conversation that Sally could overhear [for Sally, the gods existed as shadowy visual presences in a rectangular area of her experience that she called the "alternate reality"], and that their general tone of voice was cynical at the moment. She could not remember the exact words of the voices, but the general sense of their conversation was that they were critical of people of the world in general. This critical conversation seemed to trigger in Sally a clear, strong Feeling of anger or aggression, like "of taking a machine gun and shooting everybody down that I see," which had both a bodily and an Image aspect. The bodily aspect was characterized by tension in her hands and stomach. The Image aspect of this aggressive Feeling involved seeing an inner moving picture of approximately ten people riddled with machine-gun bullets, covered with blood and falling down and screaming. The Image was like a moving picture, in color, of the people in various stages of falling while being gunned down. The color was accurate, with red blood, etc., except that the people's skin was very, very pale, almost white. (Hurlburt, 1990, pp. 248–249)

First, I note that these descriptions are of particular moments: The beep occurred at particular points in time (when Bob was talking about an academic center; when Sally was talking to her mother). Second, these are meant to be straightforward, non-metaphorical, differentiated descriptions of something directly experienced at the moment of that beep: Bob means his teardrop-shaped region to be a physically dimensioned reality where his experience of emotion resided; Sally means that she both directly felt angry and directly saw her image of shooting. Third, these descriptions were created with a genuine concern for the constraints that the endeavor imposes: We bracketed presuppositions (by choosing the moment at random, for example); we selected a specific concretely targeted experience (identified by the beep); we minimized retrospection; we used talk that could be differentiated by the verbal community ("3 inches wide," "as wide as his body," etc.)

The question to be faced here is the extent to which observations such as Bob's teardrop-shaped unsureness and Sally's imaged anger can be scientifically useful. Here is what I concluded about emotion experience in schizophrenia in 1990 (italics in the original):

Schizophrenics, when not decompensating, may have extremely clear emotional experiences; inner emotional experience is not blunted. It is frequently said that schizophrenics have "blunted" affect, that most of the time their emotional experiences are shallow or nonexistent until sudden emotional outbursts occur. Our samples force us to make the distinction more clearly between the inner experience and the outward expression of emotion. Our schizophrenic subjects simply did *not* have blunted inner emotional experience. On the contrary, their emotional experiences were quite clear to them; they were easily capable of describing nuances and discriminations of their inner emotional experiences; and the range of such emotions was quite varied.

At the same time, however, some of our subjects outwardly appeared to have the characteristic affective blunting; this was perhaps most evident in Sally. Since the inner emotional experience was clear at the same time that the outer expression of emotion was blunted, our interpretation is that what is identified as blunting of affect is at least sometimes the result of *hiding* clear inner emotional experience from expression in the external world, not the result of flattened inner emotional experience. For example, when Sally experienced the aggressive image of gunning down people all around her, that feeling of aggression was clearly available to her; but an external observer of Sally at that moment would have seen her as emotionally flat and detached.

In fact, inner emotional experience in our schizophrenics sometimes seemed *hyper*-clear. Our schizophrenic subjects were *more* adept than our normal subjects in describing the exact physical location of their emotional experience. ... Thus we are led to speculate that *the externally observed blunting of affect in schizophrenics is the result of hiding extra-clear inner emotional experience rather than deficient emotional experiencing.* (Hurlburt, 1990, pp. 254–255).

We shouldn't make too much of my 1990 observations: They were based on a very small sample and performed by an early version of the DES method. Yet we shouldn't make too little of them, either: Bob and I (Sally, too) were at least *trying* to describe his experience faithfully, a trying that genuinely considered the constraints that such an endeavor imposes: minimizing retrospection, clearly specifying the moment, bracketing presuppositions, and so on. Bob and I cleaved to his experience with as much care and concern as we could muster.

> **Q:** Bob and your observations about his emotion experience (his teardrop-shaped self-criticalness, for example) are highly problematic: I'm forced to take Bob's and your word for it; Bob might be unusual; your samples are small; you might have a hidden (perhaps even to you) penchant for teardrop-shaped regions or whatever; and so on.
> **A:** I agree that that is possible. However, I note that my investigations described the discrepancy between the experience and the expression of emotion in 1990, *before* that discrepancy was *begun* to be explored by modern orthodox psychology (hyper-clear feelings are still not explored), so it is not likely that I had presupposition-driven leanings toward those views.

A Few More Observations of Schizophrenia

I am not an expert on schizophrenia. I have not conducted anywhere near the number of careful observations of schizophrenic experience that I have argued ought to be conducted. However, Hurlburt (1990) made some observations, and it seems worthwhile to give a few examples. I am not in a position to know which of these would be replicated by other observers (or by me with other subjects), but they may give the flavor of the range of phenomena that might turn out to be characteristic of schizophrenia or in some way interesting to schizophrenia research.

- Hyper-clear bodily emotion. Example discussed previously.
- Imagery used to represent emotion. Example discussed previously.
- Bent or tilted visual phenomena. Example: Innerly seeing the table top, except that the iced tea glass, which is in actuality sitting on the table, is seen floating at an angle above the table.
- Inaccurate color in imagery. Example: When you are talking to me, instead of paying attention to me, you are innerly seeing me. But in your inner seeing, I'm wearing a red shirt instead of the blue shirt I'm actually wearing.
- Images have concrete characteristics. Example: Imagery in non-schizophrenic subjects is typically clear in the center and then fades to indistinct nothingness at the edges. Imagery in schizophrenic subjects has its own reality: An image might be seen to curl up, to float away, or to rip in half. Or you're seeing an image of my face except that the image has an abrupt edge that happens to pass down my face between my nose and my left eye. Or the image of me has black stuff splattered on it – it's not *me* that has the black stuff on it – it's the *image* of me, as if someone dipped a toothbrush in black ink and flicked it on a photograph of me.
- "Visual hallucinations" are not always visual phenomena. Example: "At the moment of the beep I see the virgin Mary on a path in front of me" would likely be interpreted as a statement of a visual hallucination. However, when I asked this subject for the details of this seeing (Was Mary facing toward you or to the side? Do you see her body or just her face? What was she wearing? Was this seeing in black-and-white or in color?) she was unable to provide any of those details, despite practice. I concluded (Hurlburt, 1990) that she was not having a visual experience at the moment of the beep. I don't know how many reports of visual hallucinations actually refer to visual phenomena and how many do not, but a science that doesn't carefully make such distinctions cannot know, either.
- Spiraling of experience. Example: You see a beam of light that seems to spiral or corkscrew away from you; or you hear a buzzing sound that seems to travel from left to right in a spiral path.

Let me state as clearly as possible that *I don't know* whether these are typical of schizophrenic experience; whether they are typical of medicated but not unmedicated schizophrenics (or vice versa); whether these are typical of some types of schizophrenia but not others; whether they are typical with medication

A but not with medication B; and so on. I believe that careful observations might lead to answers to these questions.

> **Q:** Your conclusions here are wildly speculative, based on far too few observations of schizophrenics by far too few observers, and not validated by any of the conventional methods of psychology.
> **A:** You are making exactly my point. Psychological science *could* structure itself so that more observers, perhaps more skillful than I at submitting to the constraints that such an endeavor imposes, actually observe the actual experience of many schizophrenics. Then those observations could be validated by conventional methods and by other methods yet to be elaborated. Science could do so if it had the will: One could perform a lot of DES investigations for the price of a single fMRI magnet.

> **Q:** You say that schizophrenics might use the 3 on a rating scale differently from non-schizophrenics. Doesn't that same argument apply to everything your schizophrenic DES subject says to you about his experience?
> **A:** Yes and no. For example, when Bob said he felt unsure and self-critical in a teardrop-shaped reason, there is, as you say, absolutely no guarantee that what Bob means by "unsure" is the same thing that you or I would mean by "unsure." Yet some aspects of his talk *can* be disambiguated in a way that the rating scale 3 cannot. For example, Bob said he experienced emotion in a teardrop-shaped region. I could (and did) inquire about what he means by "teardrop," in the same way that one could ask for any clarification in any conversation. I don't have a transcript, but that conversation was doubtless something like this: "When you say 'teardrop-shaped region,' do you mean that metaphorically or descriptively?" "Descriptively." "You mean you actually feel your feelings in a teardrop-shaped region?" "Yes." "By 'teardrop-shaped region' do you mean wide at one end and narrow at the other, or something else? Either way is OK with me." "I definitely felt it right here. It was about this wide here (indicates three inches at the top) and it got wider as it went down to here (indicates the whole width of his body at his waist)."
>   Now it is of course possible that his entire lexicon is in some ways different from mine, or that he is lying, or that he is making something up on the spot and saying it was at the moment of the beep. We can and do inquire about those possibilities. However, Bob's saying, for example, "the top of the region is 3 inches wide" is fundamentally different from ticking off a 3 on the enthusiasm rating scale. "Three inches wide" has a definite, unambiguous, universally accepted referent: It's wider than a Coke can, narrower than a softball, *this* wide (thumb to forefinger), half the length of a dollar bill. The 3 on the enthusiasm scale has no such objective referent. Even if there were a possible referent, there is typically no effort made to teach the subject what it is.

> **Q:** I still don't think you can blindly trust what Bob says, even if you are a highly skilled interviewer.

A: I agree. We *need* studies that validate observations. Careful exploration does not guarantee accuracy, much less utility, so we need to validate every important observation we make, multiple times and in multiple ways, as is well known in science.

Validation Following Observation

In this chapter I have tried to emphasize that *validation studies should follow careful observation*. For example, Kring and Germans (2004) followed observations by Sullivan and Bleuler. However, Sullivan and Bleuler's observations were casual by their own accounts and were made more than a half century ago. It is, or at least should be, remarkable that Kring and Germans could find, in the intervening half century, observations of experience in schizophrenia no better than those of Bouricius's diary. Science does *not* value observation of phenomena (see Chapter 21).

Let's consider how Chapman-like scales might look if the items on those scales had been constructed on the basis of careful observations of schizophrenics, rather than on the imagination of item writers who are ignorant about schizophrenic experience. Instead of items such as, "The beauty of sunsets is greatly overrated" and "I have seldom cared to sing in the shower," which have nothing in particular to do with experience in schizophrenia, items might be something like: "I experience my emotions in clearly defined regions of my body" or "I frequently have violent visual images." The new Chapman-type process would start with a large number of such observation-based items, provided by a relatively large number of observers (canceling out my own observational idiosyncrasies) and a relatively large number of schizophrenic subjects (canceling out the idiosyncrasies of Bob and Sally and the few other schizophrenics with whom I have sampled). Those diverse observation-based items would then be subjected to the same kind of standard item-analysis procedure as used by the Chapmans, winnowing out those that are too narrowly focused or otherwise problematic. The result of that procedure would be a validity-based scale that began with actual observations of the phenomena of interest: observe first, validate later. Would such a procedure be scientifically useful? Probably, but I don't really know – it has never been tried.

If science aimed its substantial collective talents in that direction, it may well be able to evolve other methods that incorporate faithful observation, with hard to predict but potentially fascinating results. If we wish to advance the understanding of experience in schizophrenia, we have to observe the experience in schizophrenia as carefully as we can for as long as we need to from as many different perspectives as is required, and *then* formulate a theory and validate it. I think there is reason to believe that the result of such an effort might be of substantial importance.

Here's how one such a study might proceed. Identify a group of individuals at risk for schizophrenia (risk defined by family history, genetic marker, or whatever) but not currently schizophrenic. Use a method such as DES and characterize the inner experience of each of the individuals in that group. Then wait a decade or so and determine which individuals become schizophrenic. Then go back to the original observations to determine the actual characteristics of experience that discriminated between those who did and who did not become schizophrenic. If nothing else, such a prospective study might be able to provide clues about the actual characteristics of experience that might be useful in early detection of schizophrenia, which would be a valuable contribution – perhaps scales could be constructed based on such clues.

However, there is potential beyond early detection. Most people who are at risk for schizophrenia do not become schizophrenic. Why not? No one really knows, but it is at least plausible to suspect that some people fall into patterns of inner experience that lead to schizophrenia, whereas others fall into patterns that do not lead to schizophrenia. If that is so, it is also plausible that *those patterns are skills that can be learned or unlearned if identified early enough*. This is an old idea (Harry Stack Sullivan wrote in 1927: "The psychiatrist sees too many end states and deals professionally with too few of the pre-psychotic . . . . I feel certain that many incipient cases [of schizophrenia] might be arrested before the efficient contact with reality is completely suspended" Sullivan, 1927/1994, p. 135). That view is widely accepted within modern psychiatry ("Identifying this prodromal phase...is the essence of indicated prevention, providing the possibilities . . . of preventing, delaying or ameliorating the onset of diagnosable psychotic disorder"; Yung et al., 2007, p. 636).

Without wishing to make too much of Bob's teardrop-shaped emotion, let's pretend that we have conducted the prospective study just described, and we have discovered that clearly demarcated regions of the experience of emotion differentiates those who become schizophrenic from those who do not. (I accept that this is a largely unwarranted speculation, but it will serve to make the point.) Perhaps the young person at risk for schizophrenia could be taught to notice that emotion affects the body not only *there* but also in other bodily regions, thus reducing the clear demarcation of experience. Would that be enough to alter the course of incipient schizophrenia? I don't know, but neither does science. I return to the discussion of early detection of risk for schizophrenia near the end of Chapter 19.

BARRETT: "THE EXPERIENCE OF EMOTION"

We turn out attention now from emotion in schizophrenia to emotion more generally. Lisa Feldman Barrett is a highly respected researcher in the science of emotion, the author of many papers on emotion, including one titled

"The Experience of Emotion" (Barrett, Mesquita, Ochsner, & Gross, 2007). We will examine that paper in the same way as we did Kring and Germans (2004). First, we will ask whether Barrett and her colleagues mean by "experience" in the title of their paper the same thing that we mean by pristine inner experience; we'll answer yes. Then we'll examine Barrett's method of attempting to examine experience and conclude that she actually examines neither moments nor experience, and that her method does not genuinely submit to the constraints that the examination of experience requires, and therefore that the paper is not genuinely about pristine experience.

What do Barrett and her colleagues mean by *experience*? Here is their opening paragraph:

> As psychology transformed from the science of the mind ... into the science of behavior ... an important topic slipped from scientific view: the subjective experience of emotion. Recently, scientific discourse on this topic has reemerged ... but the prevailing wisdom remains that "emotion researchers need to figure out how to escape from the shackles of subjectivity if emotion research is to thrive" (LeDoux, 2000, p. 156). Our current, impoverished understanding of emotion experience is due not only to American psychology's behaviorist legacy, but also to a view of the mind that eschews phenomenology and characterizes mental states as nothing but their causes. Consequently, knowing the causes of emotion is presumed sufficient to answer the question of what the experience is. While expedient, this scientific approach leaves out an important aspect of reality: *people feel something when they experience emotion*. Describing how emotion experiences are caused does not substitute for *a description of what is felt*, and in fact, *an adequate description of what people feel is required* so that scientists know what to explain in the first place. (Barrett et al., 2007, p. 374, emphasis added)

It seems that by "experience" Barrett and her colleagues mean "what people feel," and that this feeling is directly apprehended. Thus I conclude that Barrett means by "experience" the same thing that we call "pristine experience."

However, despite the fact that this paper is called "The Experience of Emotion," and despite the fact that Barrett and her colleagues open the paper calling for a description of what is felt, I would like us keenly to understand that Barrett and her colleagues do *not ever* in this paper directly examine what people feel, do not ever apprehend pristine emotion experience. As we have seen, apprehending experience, including emotion experience, requires carefully defining moments, carefully defining experience, and genuinely submitting to the constraints that the exploration of inner experience imposes; Barrett's research, in my view, does none of those things adequately.

Not Pristine Emotion Experience

Barrett is among the most sophisticated users of rating scales, presenting them both in their classical paper-and-pencil form and using experience sampling methods – she deserves substantial credit for furthering the cause of PalmPilot-based sampling in natural environments. She uses highly complex analyses to arrive at provocative conclusions about emotion that may be substantially useful as long as we acknowledge that these studies do not investigate what emotion feels like.

Many of Barrett's studies of emotion are based on the PANAS, which we have seen earlier does not apprehend the phenomena of emotion experience. So let's examine one of Barrett's most sophisticated non-PANAS studies, Study 2 of Barrett (2004):

> Participants were assigned a palm-top computer ... and received instructions regarding the experience-sampling portion of the study. The palm-tops [presented] affect terms ... in a random order at each trial. Participants made their ratings on a 7-point Likert scale (o = *not at all*, 3 = *a moderate amount*, 6 = *a great deal*) measured by pressing numbers on the keyboard of the palm-top computer. Participants were told that they would be beeped randomly 10 times per day for a 28-day period and asked about their momentary affective experience using 29 emotion-related terms (potentially resulting in 280 affect measurement trials per participant, each of which contained ratings for 29 terms). Participants were told to respond as quickly as possible without compromising their accuracy. (Barrett, 2004, p. 274)

This study would seem to be quite precise in the way in which the moment is defined – delivered by a beep from a palm top computer. However, our own results, as we saw in Chapter 5 (and mentioned in the ESM section of the present chapter), suggest that this seeming precision is not to be trusted; we find that we must work iteratively with our subjects for days before we are confident that they understand what is meant by the moment of the beep.

Yet even if we accept that Barrett's pre-training is capable of conveying to subjects exactly what is meant by the moment of the beep (a dubious assumption), I think Barrett's subjects cannot be assumed to be describing experience. They are asked to rate twenty-nine adjectives such as "enthusiastic," "peppy," "happy," "satisfied," "relaxed," "sluggish," "sad," "nervous," and" aroused" on seven-point Likert-type scales. We saw when discussing Kring and Germans (2004) that there is no reason to believe that two subjects mean the same thing when both rate "enthusiastic" a 3. One subject might actually directly feel mild enthusiasm, and so rate "enthusiastic" a 3; another might not be feeling enthusiasm at all but because the *situation* is interesting she rates "enthusiastic" a 3. Phenomenologically those are two very different experiences, but they are represented by exactly the same 3. I conclude, therefore, that Barrett (2004) does not actually examine emotion experience; the adjective ratings are an ungrounded mix of observation of emotion experience, inference about emotion state, judgment about the situation, and so on.

Disentangling feeling from state and situation is important to a science of emotion experience. Recall AV's "I'm sad, I'm sad" experience from Chapter 9: AV was *not* experiencing sadness at the moment of that beep, as best as extremely careful interviewing could determine, but there can be little doubt that without extremely careful iterative training she would have rated "sad" a 6 had that adjective been presented on the palm-top computer.

Barrett (2004) is thus about some mixture of experience, state, situation, and perhaps other factors; and Barrett (2004) is typical of the papers Barrett and colleagues (2007) review. Therefore I conclude that Barrett and colleagues' article entitled "The Experience of Emotion" is *not* about the experience of emotion. I conclude that their stated aim of obtaining "an adequate description of what people feel" is not fulfilled; although they say "it is necessary to ask people what they experience," they fail to do so.

As with Kring and Germans (2004), I emphasize that my critique is not aimed at Barrett and colleagues (2007) – their paper constitutes exemplary psychological method. My critique is aimed at the psychology community that does not discriminate adequately between experience and all else.

Pristine Experience of Emotion

If we accept, as Barrett and her colleagues apparently do, that an important aim of the science of emotion is to investigate the experience of emotion, but we conclude that psychological science has not actually done that, then we are left to ask: How *would* one investigate emotion experience? And what would one discover if one *did* carefully investigate emotion experience?

The argument of this book is that any study of experience, including any study of emotion experience, must carefully identify moments, carefully apprehend experience, and genuinely submit to the constraints that such an investigation imposes. I don't think the science is mature enough to know yet exactly what constraints are necessary in what situations. At the state of my understanding, that requires something like the DES iterative procedure, but there may be other ways. Simply saying, "tell me about your experience at the moment" or "rate your experience on this scale" is not good enough (or at least would have to be shown to be good enough).

Once moments are clearly demarcated, whatever experience happens to be ongoing at those moments must be investigated, whether or not that experience happens to include emotion. Some of those experiences will include emotion – probably roughly one quarter of them, if the subjects are more or less randomly chosen and our DES experience is representative (Heavey & Hurlburt, 2008). Then those experiences can be examined for salient features; some of those salient features will be of emotion.

The typical DES studies do investigate emotion experience when it occurs, and Hurlburt (in Hurlburt & Schwitzgebel, 2007) summarized some of those results; I will slightly amplify a few here:

1. Feelings exist.

Nearly all subjects make a clear, unshakeable distinction between thinking and feeling. They may use different words, but the distinction seems obvious to them. When pressed for the source of this obviousness, they are typically frustrated and say something like, "Well, this is thinking and that is feeling!" as if that were an irreducible fact of experience. (Hurlburt, in Hurlburt & Schwitzgebel, 2007, p. 187)

That there is a clear distinction between thinking and feeling might seem obvious, but notice that that distinction may be entirely missed by subjects in Barrett's procedure. When subjects are required to use Likert scales to rate "enthusiastic," "peppy," "happy," "sluggish," "sad," and "nervous," they may use those adjectives indiscriminately for thought and feeling experiences. The bright-line distinction between the experience of thinking and feeling emerges *only* when moments of experience are adequately apprehended.

2. There are large individual differences in the frequency of the experience of emotion. Some people directly experience emotion in all or nearly all of their randomly selected moments. Other people directly experience emotion in *none* or very few of their randomly selected moments. Still others (the majority?) directly experience emotion in some (one quarter, one half) of their moments.

When we say that some people experience emotion never or rarely, we say nothing whatsoever about their underlying emotion *states*. Perhaps there is an ongoing emotion state in everyone all the time, but only sometimes is there a direct experience of that emotion state. We have sampled with some adults who clearly have ongoing emotional states but no experience of emotion. For example, Chris Heavey, Noelle Lefforge, and I report this sample from "Barry":

Example 28: Barry screeched his chair back, jerked to his feet while nearly screaming "You #!%@ don't know what the #$@% you're talking about!", yanked open the door and slammed it behind him. The beep occurred between the scream and the slam. Barry experienced himself as simply yelling at his idiot colleagues and *not* experiencing anger or any other feeling. (Heavey, Hurlburt, & Lefforge, in preparation)

Barry has a strong emotion *state*; Barry does not *experience* emotion. If the *experience* of emotion is indeed scientifically important, then that science has to be based on the fact that emotion process and emotion experience are not always parallel. This may seem patently obvious, were it not that noted emotion researchers opine to the contrary, for example, "waking consciousness is experienced as a continuous *stream of affect* such that people are always experiencing some type of mood" (Watson, 2000, p. 13, italics in original). Watson's research, like some of Kring's and Barrett's, is based largely on the PANAS, which, as we have seen, does not adequately distinguish between actual emotion experiences and presumed emotion states.

> 3. There are robust individual differences in how emotion is experienced.
>
> Some people experience emotion as being primarily in their bodies; others experience emotion as being primarily in their heads. Here again, these descriptions are made with confidence. Furthermore, subjects who report that emotions are in their heads are not at all confused about the distinction between thinking and feeling. "They're both in my head, but one's thinking and the other is feeling!" (Hurlburt, in Hurlburt & Schwitzgebel, 2007, p. 187)

This difference is striking. When Mary says, "I feel a pain in my heart," she is describing a directly apprehended, sharply stabbing pain in the middle of her chest, just as experientially real as if a knife plunged into her chest. But when Sally says, "I feel a pain in my heart," she is saying that she has a deep understanding of the difficulty of the situation, that she recognizes the seriousness of the problem. Mary's heart pain is directly experienced; Sally's "heart pain" is metaphorically intended. Experientially, this is a huge difference, and I think our research has shown this difference to be robust. Mary and Sally's PANAS or palm-top ratings would be identical.

The fact that I say that these differences are robust doesn't make it so. Others who apply the DES procedure find the same differences (which is why I think the finding is robust), but at this point in the history of the universe, all appliers of DES are working more or less with me. Certainly, we need independent investigators to corroborate or disconfirm this finding. Furthermore, we need to triangulate such findings by objective performance measures. For example, Barrett and colleagues (2004) used the ability to detect one's own heartbeat (Whitehead & Drescher, 1980) as a measure of interoceptive (bodily) sensitivity. It seems reasonable to suppose that people who experience emotions as bodily sensations (as identified by DES) would be more likely to be able to detect their own heartbeat than would people who experience emotions in their heads. However, such experiments have not been performed, and it is also reasonable to expect the opposite: It is possible that people's bodily experience of emotions *interferes with* their ability to detect merely bodily events such as heartbeat. I don't know, but neither does emotion science.

4. Reports of emotion experience that are taken as metaphorical may be straightforwardly descriptive.

> The literature has overlooked the experience of color along with emotion. I am quite confident on the basis of my own work and that of my colleagues that *some* people literally experience color along with emotion. My subjects have (I think credibly) reported "seeing red" when angry, "being blue" when depressed, and "seeing rose-colored hues" when optimistic; furthermore, my careful questioning leads me to conclude that these phrases were meant to be straightforward descriptions of robust visual phenomena (they can specify the precise color of blue, for example), not mere metaphors. (Hurlburt, in Hurlburt & Schwitzgebel, 2007 p. 72)

In my casual conversations with psychologists, "seeing red" and "being blue" are understood as being *of course* merely metaphors; psychologists invariably steer the conversation toward wondering what accident of history or literature led to this metaphor. When I observe that some people *actually* see red when angry, *actually* see blue when depressed, psychologists typically are surprised or, more often, disbelieving.

I'm quite confident that some people do in fact see particular colors when experiencing emotion, and while this is not exactly common, it is more common than most psychologists expect. Or maybe it's not. My ignorance here is exactly the point. I'm pretty sure some people see colors as part of their emotion experience; I don't know how frequent such seeing of colors is; I don't know whether there is any scientific significance in the seeing of such colors – that is, I don't know whether there are correlates (personality, situation, gender, neuropsychology, endocrinology, language skill, etc.) of seeing such colors. But neither does emotion science.

The point here is that these are the kinds of things that, our investigations have shown, populate the experience of emotion; Heavey, Hurlburt, & Lefforge (in preparation) elaborate these and discuss other features. If a science of emotion is to take emotion *experience* seriously, these are the kinds of phenomena that have to be investigated. But they are not investigated by modern psychology.

EPILOGUE

I wish to observe that the commentary I have aimed at the work of Kring and Barrett could just as well be aimed at my own early thought-sampling work.

For example, the subjects in Barrett's (2004) experience sampling study took palm-top computers into their natural environments; when the computers beeped, they responded with Likert scales to twenty-nine emotion adjectives presented in random order by the palm-top computer. Barrett computed P-correlation matrices within each subject's data, and used a sophisticated analysis of these matrices to show that the subjects' ratings were not purely language-based.

For comparison, the subjects in my own (1980; see also Hurlburt & Melancon, 1987b) thought- and mood-sampling study took beepers into their natural environments; when the beepers beeped, they responded with Likert scales to twenty-nine emotion adjectives presented in always the same order on paper pads. I computed P-correlation matrices within each subject's data (the first large-scale P-technique analysis, I believe), and used a sophisticated (at the time) analysis of these matrices to show that the subjects' ratings had common factors from one subject to the next. Barrett's work is incrementally more sophisticated than my efforts a generation earlier, but it should be clear that, research-wise, Barrett and my own early studies are soul mates; every critique I have aimed at Barrett applies equally well to my own work.

However, in the middle of many sleepless nights in the early 1980s I came to believe that my data, although mountainous, were not a firm enough foundation for analysis, no matter how sophisticated. There was no reason to believe that the subjects really knew what they were rating; there was no reason to believe that one subject's Likert-scale 3 meant the same thing as another subject's Likert scale 3. My 1980/1987 study gathered 125,000 data points; I could not vouch for a single one. In the language of this book (which, of course, was less than inchoate in the 1980s), I had collected a mountain of data without ever genuinely submitting to the constraints that the exploration of experience imposes.

Furthermore, considered when I should have been sleeping, that mountain of data did not reveal anything about the phenomena that I thought were interesting – did not reveal anything about the experience of a single one of my subjects. I had concluded that many (but not all) individuals' P-technique factor structures were more or less similar to some others' P-technique factor structures and to the R-technique factor structure produced by groups of individuals. But what did that say about Jane Smith's experience at any particular moment? Nothing. What did it say about Jane Smith's way of experiencing *that would be specifically applicable or useful to Jane Smith or that would differentiate Jane from John Doe*? Midnightly considered, nothing.

In fact, I was not exploring Jane Smith's experience. I was using techniques on the cutting edge of sophistication of that generation's psychology. Yet I was not exploring Jane's experience. I was exploring ratings that were correlates of Jane's experience.

I have great respect for Kring's and Barrett's work. However, they study experience in only an incrementally more sophisticated way than I did in 1980, which is to say, midnightly considered, that they don't really study experience any more than I did.

This chapter is not really about Kring's or Barrett's studies – I use them only as exemplary instances of orthodox psychology. I wish to comment on what I take to be the blinkered state of orthodox psychology, which could produce review articles called "The Subjective Experience of Emotion in Schizophrenia" and "The Experience of Emotion," written by the discipline's most competent researchers, published in the top journals, but which do not really examine experience in an adequately careful way. Kring and Barrett are at the forefront of their discipline, not only because they are sophisticated researchers but because they recognize that the phenomena of experience are important – recall Barrett's "an adequate description of what people feel is required so that scientists know what to explain in the first place" (Barrett et al., 2007, p. 374). I could not say it better. However, psychology has been wearing blinders against experience for so long that it has forgotten that it is wearing blinders.

> **Q:** I just don't believe it is possible to have a strong emotional state and not feel it. *Of course* Barry felt anger when he screeched his chair back, when he slammed the door! He simply didn't want to tell you about his feelings, for whatever reason.
> **A:** That is, of course, possible, but let me try to weaken the presupposition that leads to your "*of course!*" I have tried to show, in Chapter 9 and this chapter, that feeling is a skilled activity, and that feelings are complex skilled coordinations of disparate physiological and psychological sub-processes: heart palpitations, muscle contractions, sweat, facial musculature, and so on. Please permit me to tell a fairly long story about skill; bear with me – I'll eventually show how the story relates to your question.
>
> In 1975, I performed a simple study that, other than in my dissertation (Hurlburt, 1976), I have never reported. It was a behavioral study, designed to explore of the acquisition of a simple behavior under conditions of intermittent reinforcement in the subjects' natural environment.
>
> I outfitted three graduate students (one of whom was me) with a beeper (an early version of the ones used in this book) and two small counters (one marked YES and the other marked NO). The beeper emitted signals at random intervals whose mean length was five minutes. Each subject was to try at all times to keep his left thumb and forefinger in contact – like making the "OK" sign – throughout his everyday activities. The question was whether random self-monitoring would reinforce the acquisition of this simple habit.
>
> At each beep, the subject was to self-monitor his OK sign; if his thumb and forefinger were in contact, he was to press the YES button; if not, he was to press the NO button. Clicking YES was presumed to be reinforcing; if that was true, behavior theory predicted that the frequency of the OK behavior should increase.

All three subjects quickly learned to maintain the OK behavior close to 100 percent of the time. All three subjects reported similar subjective experiences. Subjects were extremely aware of the procedure during the first two or three days, reporting that maintaining the OK position was effortful at that time. By about the fifth day, however, the effort involved had declined and the OK position began to "feel normal." By the tenth day, the whole process was habitual and without effort. The OK position had become a most natural one, and monitoring only minimally interfered with everyday activities. All that was a mildly interesting confirmation of behavioral principles: We set out to use self-monitoring to increase the frequency of the OK behavior, and we did so.

What was striking, and relevant to our current question, was *how* the OK behavior was acquired. All subjects found that the muscles being trained during the experiment were *not* merely the muscles directly controlling the thumb and forefinger. The *whole body* – head to toe – adjusted itself in relatively unpredictable ways to assume postures that conveniently maintained the thumb and forefinger OK position. One subject while driving an automobile learned to grip the steering wheel between the third and fourth finger so that the steering wheel automatically supported the thumb's pressing into the forefinger; learned to stand with his arms folded and the left-hand OK nestled in the crook of the right elbow, which pressed the OK together; learned to walk keeping his hands in his pockets because the pocket constriction helped keep the thumb and forefinger in contact.

Thus subjects did *not* merely learn a new way of keeping their thumbs and fingers together – they learned a new way of driving, a new way of standing, a new way of walking, and so on. This simple experiment makes it easy to see that the patterns of coordinations that we develop may be only remotely related to their initial contingencies. (By the way, the subjects in this study felt that the breaking of the habit was more difficult than had been the formation of the habit in the first place.)

That's the story. Now back to Barry's feelings-at-the-moment. Let's imagine that Barry as an adolescent has parents who punish him for any expression of anger. To avoid punishment, Barry learns to suppress anger expression. In so doing, he becomes acutely aware of the *very earliest beginnings* of an angry emotion state, learns to notice, say, a tiny change in skin tightness on the back of his neck, so as to be able effectively to launch behavior that hides his anger. If my OK study is a model (which I think it is), over the course of many potential punishment trials, Barry learns to notice back-of-neck skin tightness and immediately to adjust his whole body to *turn away* from emotion expression – maybe he will dig his fingernails into his palms so he can concentrate on that pain, or to study intently the patterns of dust on the floor, or to squeeze his abdominal muscles – whatever it takes to distract him from the experience of emotion. After a while, that avoidance process becomes second nature, so that when an anger process ever-so-slightly begins, Barry immediately, automatically launches his *avoidance of experience* fingernail-digging, dust-examining, abdominal-squeezing – anything that disrupts the

feeling of anger. As a result, Barry learns to *not experience* anger, even when
it physiologically courses through his body. That skill was highly adaptive in
his adolescence but is perhaps quite counter-productive as an adult: The anger
physiology continues to build in Barry's body but he doesn't *experience* it;
eventually it becomes so strong that he blows up, which takes him by surprise.

So I don't think that you should hold that *of course* Barry feels his anger.

(By the way, in Chapter 11 I noted that the operation of presuppositions was
an at-the-first-whiff skill. The process described here is an example: Barry
learns to avoid evidence contrary to his I'm-not-angry presupposition by
turning away from that evidence at its first whiff.)

Q: If Barry does not experience anger, how can something like DES ever
be useful to Barry? If he doesn't have any experience, it won't be discovered
by DES.
A: That may be true, but it largely remains to be seen. It is possible that if
beeps were to come early in an anger process that Barry *does* have *very small*
experiences of anger, perhaps before the fingernail/dust/abdominal pattern
has been invoked. It is quite possible that learning to pay attention to those
minor angers would be constructive for him. But that is speculation. It is also
possible that his anger-avoidance skill acquisition has been so complete that
there is *no vestige* of anger in his experience, in which case you're right – DES
would never discover it. There is lots of room for investigations of such topics.

14

Multiple Autonomous Experience
in a Virtuoso Musician

WITH RICARDO COBO

Have you ever sat in a concert and wondered what was going on with the performer, what it was like to be a virtuoso performer? In this chapter we'll ask a virtuoso to take a DES beeper on stage during a performance and give us a glimpse.

Colombia-born classical guitar virtuoso Ricardo Cobo gave his professional debut with the Orquesta Filarmonica de Bogota at age sixteen for a nationwide telecast audience of over nine million. He later won the prestigious Guitar Foundation of America International Guitar Competition and has gone on to a successful recording and performing career.

Cobo is one of the foremost students of master guitar teacher Aaron Shearer. Shearer was the author of one of the most successful guitar methods of all time, and was creator and a tireless promoter of a method of visualization he called "aim directed movement" or ADM, which Anderson (1980) described as follows:

> Visualization requires that before a note (or note group) is played, the guitarist can see, in his mind's eye, which string and fret the note(s) will be played on, and which fingers of the left and right hands will play the note(s). Once the guitarist has cultivated the ability to perceive these images on the guitar, then he is at least on his way to practicing accurately. (Anderson, 1980, p. 10)

Cobo emphasizes ADM visualization in his own playing, in his master classes, and in his own teaching: He exhorts his students to form a mental image of the guitar fingerboard, to see in this image exactly where you want your fingers to go, and then to move them there. Cobo says he always has such an image present when he plays. He says all great musicians on all instruments describe the same phenomenon – the virtuoso's secret to security in performance is *first* to see clearly in your imagination where you want your fingers to go; performance is then simply connecting the dots – putting your fingers where you already see them. And it's not merely performance accuracy that is affected by visualization: The beauty and color of guitar tone production depends on the precise location of fingers against strings, and the ability to master precise location depends on effective visualization. Furthermore, effective visualization reduces muscle tension and therefore reduces fatigue and injury.

I'm a serious amateur guitarist, and I've been studying with Cobo for five years. He tells me to form images, so I assiduously try to form images. He's frustrated with me because I say I can't do it. "Right now," he says, as he sits across from me playing his guitar, "I'm seeing an image of my left hand: 3 (third finger) on C (fifth string), 1 on A. Now I see 3 guide (slide along the string) to D and 2 set at F# at the fourth fret." He *looks* like someone seeing an image: eyes closed, brow furrowed, fingers moving exactly as he describes in the image. I want to acquire that skill, so I want to know just what kind of images he wants me to create. Therefore I ask him exactly what he sees in that image: Is it from his own perspective – looking down obliquely at the fingerboard? Or is it from perpendicular to the fingerboard? Does he see his actual fingers or some kind of schematic? Is it in color or black-and-white? These are serious guitar-skill-acquisition questions for me; I don't want to create just any old image – I want to create images like those that work for Cobo.

Yet he can't answer my questions about the details of his image, or if he does answer them, the answers are not consistent from one occasion to the next. "Do you see your fingers?" I ask. "Yes! Of course!" he says, but if I ask, "Do you see just your fingertips or your whole fingers?" he can't answer and appears somewhat puzzled. "Do you see the fingerboard?" "Of course I see the fingerboard!" But when I ask, "Do you see, then, steel frets on ebony?" he loses his confidence. "Well, it's like a schematic – I know where the strings are, and I see the fingers as spots – I know this spot is 3 and that spot is 1," he says. "What do you mean, spots? Are these spots in color? Like 1 is green, 3 is yellow?" "Of course I'm seeing an image of my fingers on the fingerboard," he says, but he cannot in good conscience provide any details of what those imaged fingers or the fingerboard look like. My questions frustrate him: It seems to him that he should be able to answer such straightforward questions about the details of his own images, but he can't. They frustrate the guitar student in me, too: *How am I supposed to build this imagine-my-fingers-on-the-fingerboard skill if you can't tell me what I am supposed to imagine?*

As an inner experience investigator I suspect that Cobo's frustrated inability to answer questions about experience may come from his having a *theory* about images (which he has learned from a highly effective and loved teacher, and which he made the center of his view of guitar performance, and about which he has made many public statements, and which has been corroborated in conversation with many other performers) that doesn't square with his actual at-the-moment experience. I've seen that kind of frustration in lots of DES subjects, but I don't really know whether that's true for Cobo. Maybe his frustration arises from my overly aggressive questioning or from some other source.

I suggest to him that we should fit him up with a beeper and see what his images really look like. I'm candidly straightforward with him: I tell him that maybe we will find images, but maybe not – either way is OK with me. I'm doubly motivated to know about his experience when he plays the guitar: (a) As a student of the guitar I might learn something that leads to my improved performance ability; and (b) as a student of experience I might learn something about the experience of a human being who has achieved a level of mastery near the limits of skilled human endeavor. What could be more interesting than that? He agrees to wear the beeper and discuss his beeped experiences with me.

Constraint: Learn how to observe in neutral territory. I tell Cobo something like this:

> At first, please *do not* wear the beeper when you're playing the guitar. Let's master the technique of describing experience in neutral territory. Let's get good at communicating with each other about the details of your experience in situations where you are *less* likely to have strongly held, highly invested preconceptions about how experience is or ought to be. I don't know whether you do or do not have preconceptions about guitar-playing experience, but it seems likely that you have fewer presuppositions about your walking-the-dog experience, your cooking-dinner experience, your paying-the-bills experience; and so on. Let's learn how to observe experience in *those* probably easier situations. If it turns out that you do not have strong guitar-playing presuppositions, that strategy will simply have wasted a few sampling days. But if you do have strong guitar-playing presuppositions, then that strategy may make the exploration of your guitar-playing experience *possible*.

Cobo can see the wisdom in that, agrees, and wears the beeper. But here's the fourth experience on his first sampling day, as best he and I could expose it during the interview:

> Sample 1.4. Cobo has just picked up the guitar and is poised to play. He has looked at the score and is about to play the opening C major chord of the piece. His attention is on the pads (tips) of his fingers, in particular the left hand but also to a lesser degree the right hand. The pads seem to be big, bulging, and tingling. The experience is tactile: His fingertip pads feel big and tingly.

Cobo originally described his experience in this sample using metaphorically visual language: "It's like electricity has run down my arm into the fingertip pads; someone has turned the lights on in my fingertips." However, when we tried as carefully as possible to get to the experience at the moment of the beep, the visual metaphors fell away; what remained was that he *proprioceptively felt* his fingertips to be big and tingling.

This experience was a surprise to Cobo – he didn't know that his fingertip pads might be experienced to swell and tingle in anticipation of playing. On reflection, it makes good sense: All guitar artistry, all sound production and coloration, comes from micro-adjustments in the way fingers touch the strings – move a thousandth of an inch toward the fret and the sound gets brighter; put a thousandth of a pound less pressure on the pad and the sound gets softer; change by a degree the angle the right-hand fingers make with the string and the release gets quicker; and so on. A lot is going on in the pads of a virtuoso guitarist, so from the standpoint of plausibility, it makes perfect sense that Cobo should have heightened tactile awareness of those pads: He has spent maybe 30,000 hours refining the sensations that arise from those couple of square millimeter areas where his fingertips encounter the string. What is remarkable is that despite those 30,000 hours of guitar playing, thousands of which were spent paying particular attention to the way his left hand fingers encounter the string, he is surprised at how his fingers actually feel.

And, also to Cobo's surprise, there was *no* visualization of the fingerboard or his fingers at this beep. He had been of the opinion that he *always* visualized the fingerboard; and if not always, then this would be just the kind of situation that the visualization would be *most likely* to occur – his theory says the player should imagine what he is *about* to do, and he was just *about* to set his fingers on the strings. Yet no visualization was present.

I told Cobo that this was the first sampling day and first-sampling-day apprehensions and descriptions are not to be trusted, and even if they could be trusted, this is still only one sample. I reminded him that I had asked him to use the beeper *away from* the guitar so that we could get some practice at inner-experience conversations in neutral territory. I accepted that it was tempting to beep while playing the guitar, to explore and/or validate prior views, but we should resist that temptation.

This is an example of the necessity of iterative training (Chapter 10): *Now* Cobo has his own *of-himself/for-himself* glimpse of the *real possibility* that he might be mistaken about his view of his own experience and therefore of the necessity of sampling away from the guitar. *Until now* he could (incorrectly) assume that *of course* he understood his own experience, that I was being merely pedantically cautious in my request that he sample away from the guitar.

EVERYDAY SAMPLES

With most DES subjects, I feel as if I have a pretty clear idea of what is experienced and how to communicate about it within about three or four sampling days. It was about nine sampling days before I had gained a sense of Cobo's experience, and even then I wasn't as confident that I had as high fidelity view of his experience as I am accustomed to obtaining in my sampling work. Nine is a lot of (quite frustrating) sampling days. There is no question that he was motivated to perform the sampling task as well as he could; it was simply difficult for us to become confident that I understood what Cobo was apprehending at the moment of the beep. Eventually, after nine days of very careful interviews about his (mostly) non-guitar-playing samples, I came tentatively to understand two salient characteristics of Cobo's experience: sensory awareness and autonomous multiplicity.

Sensory Awareness

Cobo had frequent sensory awarenesses of the kind we will describe in Chapter 16. DES has a specific, narrow definition of sensory awareness: It is the specific attending to the sensory aspects of something, not merely to the something itself. So, for example, if you are seeing the Coke can as you reach for it to take a drink, that is *not* sensory awareness – it is a perception of the can undertaken for its utility in grasping and lifting. However, if as you reach for the can you are drawn to the misty rivulets of condensation on it, then that *is* a sensory awareness – the mistiness is noticed not for its perceptual or instrumental utility but for its purely sensory aspects.

Here are a few typical examples of Cobo's sensory awareness:

> Sample 2.2. Cobo is in the kitchen doing cleanup tasks. At the moment of the beep he is looking at the brown of the floor tile. There are a few drops of water on the tile, but he isn't really paying attention to that; he is attracted for whatever reason to the particular brownness of the tile. He was engaged in some tasks at the time, but those tasks were not in his awareness.

> Sample 6.1. Cobo is sitting on his patio listening on headphones to a Keith Jarrett vinyl jazz improvisation, looking at the frosty edge of the mountains in the distance. As if driven, potentiated, or focused by the music, he is tuning into the frostiness, to the pinks and blues of the mountain edge. The mountain edge is cold; his body is somewhat cold sitting on the patio; he is in some way transported up to the mountain as if he is there feeling even colder/crisper than he currently is on the patio. This is a complex sensory experience: pink/blue, cold in mountain, cold in body, cold as if transported.

> Sample 9.3. Cobo is rinsing the omelet fry pan and particularly interested in/drawn to the sensory details of the flow of the water and the chunks of food being washed away. That is, he is not merely washing the pan; he is noticing the particular way the water flows over the pan and the way the chunks turn and move as they break free of the pan. Simultaneously

he is thinking about how far it is for Russ to drive here – thinking it's a pretty long drive. This thought is not in words or images, but there is no doubt that he's thinking about it at the same time as he is interested in the water/chunks.

Autonomous Multiplicity

The first of those examples is a simple sensory awareness – Cobo is into the brownness of the tile and that's all. But that simplicity is exceptional for Cobo. Most of his experiences have multiple simultaneous strands of experience: there are four separable sensory awarenesses in the Keith Jarrett sample, and two sensory awarenesses and a thought process in the dishwashing sample. Here is a typical sample:

> Sample 7.1. (a) Cobo is sitting at his computer working on a bio for his MySpace site. His wife Julie is leaning her hip against his side, and he's feeling the weight/pressure of it against his body.
>
> (b) He's also in the middle of a thought, shaping what he wants to enter into the MySpace cells, as if he's looking for words and where to put them. But there are no words in this process; he's somehow in the middle of an unarticulated thought. He's letting it flow, not trying to shape it, just understanding what he's doing.
>
> (c) Cobo is also frustrated/puzzled/confused about what he's supposed to do on the MySpace site – the site is not laid out logically. This is a mental process, metaphorically as if he has to wade through the unclarity of the site instructions. But he's not sure this is actually at the moment of the beep – could be in response to the beep.
>
> (d) Cobo also suspects that he's talking to Julie, telling her what he's thinking about the site, but he's not sure about that. He might be talking – babbling on, or she might be talking, or there might have been a pause in the conversation at the moment of the beep. Whichever way, the conversation was just happening and he's not paying much or any attention to it.

Let's discuss that sample one part at a time:

(a) Feeling Julie lean against his side is a typical sensory awareness as described earlier and elaborated in Chapter 16.

(b) Most people, when they are thinking, experience themselves to be the "driver" of their thought process – that they are in some way controlling or initiating the thinking. By contrast, Cobo understands himself to be the observer or receiver of his own thought process. The thought process is happening as if of its own; when it, of its own accord, is finished, he will enter the words into the MySpace cells.

(c) Mental confusion of the kind Cobo describes is not uncommon. It *is* unusual that Cobo is not able to be clear about whether this is at the moment of the beep. This is his seventh sampling day; most subjects have worked out how to pay attention to what is and what is not directly at the moment of the beep by about the third day. This is not for want of trying – we have spent literally hours trying to nail down what is and what is not at the moments of the beeps; it is not for lack of skill in the interview; it is not merely an imprecision of language – we have ironed out that long ago.

(d) Most people, when they are engaged in a conversation, can easily say who is talking at the moment of the beep because there is a distinct phenomenological difference between the experience of talking (I'm in control, the words are coming *from me*) and the experience of listening (I'm dependent on the other, the words are coming *to me*). Cobo apparently does not have that experiential distinction. Whether the words come from Julie or from himself, they are experienced as ongoing words. His own words seem just to happen (as opposed to seeming to be self-created), just like Julie's words seem to happen. (This phenomenon is unusual, but I have written about it before, calling it the "happening of speaking" in Hurlburt, 1993a.)

Cobo and I struggled sample after sample, detail by detail, for nine sampling days to clarify exactly what he meant by such descriptions, to make as sure as we could that we each understood how the other used words, that we were not talking past each other, but usually I did not feel the confidence in the fidelity of my apprehension that I customarily feel after three or four sampling days. I came to understand that our struggle was not merely that Cobo used language in idiosyncratic ways; his experience itself, I came to believe, was different from most of my other subjects in a way I will call "autonomous multiplicity."

Constraint: Idiosyncratic ways of speaking about experience often (but not always) reflect idiosyncratic experience.

Everyone exists in an environment where there is lots of stimulation: external things that could be seen, heard, smelled, touched, and internal events that could be thought, felt, imaged, sensed, proprioceptied, and so on. I referred to this cacophony of possibilities as "the welter" in Chapter 11 (and in Hurlburt & Schwitzgebel, 2011a) – things that are available to be directly experienced. The welter is complex – at any moment there may be hundreds or thousands of simultaneous patterns that *could be* created into pristine experience.

Usually at any moment people directly experience only one or a very few things out of this welter. (The bulimic women in Chapter 2 were exceptional in this regard.) Recall from Chapter 4, for example, that Luke Jones was innerly seeing the equation $g = v^2/R$, as if handwritten in pencil, and simultaneously, but with less intensity, was experiencing something about the textbook he was holding. Figure 14.1 schematizes Luke's experience – the vertical in this

FIGURE 14.1. Schematic of Luke Jones's experience: One main aspect (innerly seeing the equation) and one smaller aspect (seeing the actual textbook).

schematic represents the clarity or salience of experience; the horizontal dimensions represent the various thoughts/feelings/sensations/whatever that might occur in pristine experience. In our schematic of Luke's $g = v^2/R$ sample, there is one main experience, that is, one main, clearly demarcated peak (the innerly seen equation), and one smaller, more diffuse, peak (the seeing of the actual book). There are other non-zero elevations in this schematic to illustrate that there may be other but very minor parts of Luke's experience at that moment. We might quibble about the relative height of the two major mountains – we shouldn't ask too much of this schematic.

By contrast, Figure 14.2 schematizes what I came to understand about Cobo's typical experience. Somewhere, somehow, distributed more or less simultaneously before the footlights of Cobo's consciousness are usually not one or two but quite a few experiences, some more salient than others, but the less salient ones by no means close to nonexistent. Unlike Luke, Cobo does *not* have one central "mountain" of experience; there are several or many mountains, some higher, some lower.

Furthermore, the schematic "mountains" of Cobo's experience are not fixed entities; instead, each individual peak autonomously rises and falls in importance. Imagine the peaks in Figure 14.2 independently rising and falling like a three-dimensional audio equalizer display.

Furthermore, Cobo seems to have multiple perspectives, each from its own mountain peak. That is, there is *not* one particular privileged perspective from

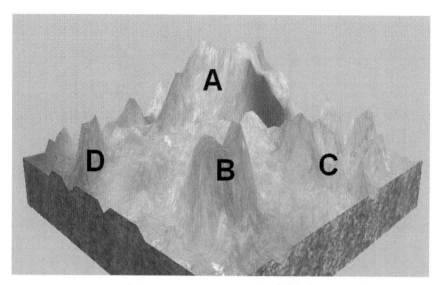

FIGURE 14.2. Schematic of Cobo's autonomously multiple experiences.

which to view all the experiences; *each individual way of experiencing seems to have its own perspective.* This seems to distinguish Cobo's experience from the multiplicity of the bulimic women in Chapter 2; the bulimic women seemed to have one point of view on multiple simultaneous things; Cobo seems to have multiple simultaneous points of view on multiple simultaneous things.

Figure 14.2 schematizes my understanding of Cobo's experience in sample 7.1. Peak *A* schematizes Cobo's feeling of Julie leaning against his hip. There is little doubt about that; it is the highest, strongest mountain peak, and is not rapidly changing at this moment. There is also a thought process ongoing, schematized by peak *B*, which is rising in intensity. The part of Cobo that experiences thought process *B* is inchoately contained in this region; when the peak "rises far enough" the thought will spill out into the action of typing. Thought process *B* isn't aware of the hip pressure *A*, and vice versa: The felt hip pressure is autonomous from and blind to the thought process. The mental confusion, schematized by the bunch of peaks at *C*, has been rising, also autonomously. How high these peaks are at the beep onset is hard to say, because some of them are rising and some falling; it is hard to say whether the rising outweighs the falling, or if enough rise, how they will become organized out of this confusion. Mountain *D* schematizes Cobo's talking, or maybe listening, to Julie. This is a smaller mountain, not as "weighty" to Cobo. Like the other mountains, this talking is autonomous from the rest of Cobo's experience.

Recall that it was quite straightforward for Luke to describe his experience – he was very confident about the innerly seen equation but somewhat less confident about the actually seen textbook. Luke's descriptive straight-forwardness comes, I think, from the straightforwardness of his experience: He has fewer peaks and they rise quickly and unambiguously and disappear equally quickly and unambiguously.

Cobo's experiences wax and wane more or less independently, asynchro-nously, and gradually, so that at any moment some aspects of experience are becoming more salient while others become less salient. Sometimes these aspects are consistent, sometimes contradictory. The aspects are forced into some kind of behavioral unity because they are all contained within the same skin and operate the same neuro-musculo-skeletal structure, but experien-tially they are independent. There is no central "viewer" that apprehends all the experiences. It is this multiple independent asynchrony of experience that makes it difficult for Cobo to apprehend and describe his experience and for me to grasp it. Luke and I had it easy.

The temporality of the "rising of Cobo's mountains" is striking. For example:

> Sample 8.1. It's morning. Cobo has put on the beeper and has been look-ing for the notebook to put into his pocket. He has found it, and has picked it up and has opened it to find a blank page to be ready for the next beep. He's looking at the notebook, which is being held at an angle, waiting for the lines come into focus so he can discover whether he needs to turn to a new page. He sees the pad but it's sort of blurry or out of focus. He has set himself the task of seeing whether it's a blank page, but he is not yet able to see the page clearly enough to know whether it is blank.

In our Figure 14.2 schematic, he is waiting for the seeing-the-page peak to rise high enough to reveal the lines; and connected to this peak is another process that will culminate in either turning or not turning the page. It is very unusual for people to experience their perceptions as gradually coa-lescing; Luke, for example, either innerly sees $g = v^2/R$ or he doesn't see it – he does *not* experience $g = v^2/R$ gradually coming into view. Here's another Cobo example:

> Sample 8.3. Cobo has been in the living room watching TV with Julie, and has gotten up to pick up the dishes to take to the kitchen. As he picks up, Julie tells him what's happening on the TV so he doesn't miss any-thing: "He's sleeping in the same room that Oscar Wilde died in." Cobo is standing in the doorway to the kitchen, looking at an angle toward the TV, trying to discern what's being displayed. At the moment of the beep, his eyes are aimed at the TV screen but he has not yet actually perceived the TV itself or the picture on it; he sees grayness (which as a fact of the uni-verse is reflected from the TV case, but Cobo has not yet seen the TV as an object) and brownness (which as a fact of the universe is emanating from the picture on the TV screen, but he has not yet made out the picture).

Thus it is *not* that he is seeing the room represented on the TV and trying to discern whether, for example, it is in Paris or Madrid; instead, he is not yet seeing whether it is indeed a room at all that is represented on the TV, which itself is not yet made into an experienced object.

In our Figure 14.2 schematic, the peak that will eventually become the television and its picture has not yet coalesced. He's seeing visual phenomena (grays, browns), as separate but adjacent peaks, not yet organized into a television display. Had the beep occurred a bit later, these adjacent sensory awareness peaks may have been transcended into one TV-peak. Such gradual coalescing is common for Cobo, unusual for other DES subjects.

> **Q:** I don't believe you. I think Cobo's experience is just like everyone else's; his language just leads you down an attractive (autonomous multiplicity, slow coalescing) but blind alley.
> **A:** You express what I take to be the prevailing view of most psychologists and philosophers. I think there is good reason for that view: Most opinions that people express about their own and others' experience *are* highly suspect for the variety of reasons (including lack of precision in language) that this book tries to make plain: They don't pay attention to moments, don't carefully attend to experience, don't submit to the constraints that the endeavor imposes.
>
> Against the notion that Cobo simply has a complex way of speaking about things, I note that at the very least that wasn't *always* true for Cobo. For example, here is a quite simple sample:
>
> Sample 9.2. Cobo is wondering if he could die of a heart attack from eating eggs, and whether they would show up in his autopsy. This thought is occurring without words or images – he's just wondering it (an example of unsymbolized thinking; see Chapter 15). In the background of his awareness he's visually seeing the e-mail window on his computer screen. He's seeing it, seeing the lettering and the squareness of the window – taking in the visual aspect of it.
>
> Cobo's experience here is quite similar to the Luke example of Figure 14.1: a main thought and a background seeing. So it seems to me that Cobo is capable of describing a simple experience if simple experience happens, but most of the time it doesn't.

Whereas most people experience the beep as suddenly (most experience it as "instantaneously") "catching" their experience like the flash of a camera, I think it makes sense to think of Cobo's apprehension of the beep as being itself as an experience (peak) that rises and more or less gradually spreads through his ever-shifting landscape of ongoing autonomous experiences, eventually causing Cobo to "catch" the currently high mountains and describe them. The result is Cobo's relative difficulty of determining what he was experiencing precisely at the moment of the beep.

PRACTICING THE GUITAR

We collected twenty-eight beeps while Cobo was practicing the guitar, mostly on the tenth through thirteenth days of sampling. His experience while practicing had the same two characteristics as his non-guitar-playing samples: sensory awareness and autonomous multiplicity.

Sensory Awareness

We described sensory awareness as DES defines it previously and will return to a fuller discussion in Chapter 16. With respect to guitar playing, if Cobo was paying attention to a particular note he was playing simply as part of playing the phrase, that would *not* count as sensory awareness – that would be simply a perceptual awareness experienced for is instrumental utility. To count as sensory awareness, Cobo had to be paying particular attention to some sensory aspect of his inner or external environment.

Sensory awareness was a major focus in most (twenty-two of twenty-eight or 79 percent) of his guitar-practicing samples. Nearly all were directly related to the guitar-playing task. Many of those sensory awarenesses were about the sounds he was producing:

- noting the undesirable "hollow" sound of the cedar-topped guitar he's playing;
- focusing on the smoothness of the passage he's playing;
- absorbed in the blend and color of the sound he's producing;
- focused on the way the first string D is ringing with the fifth string A (the way that interaction affects the color of each);
- hearing a familiar spookiness of the phrase he is playing.

Several of those produced a strong affective reaction:

- He's focused on the way the chord rolls out as he releases each string, and he's enjoying the powerful "juicy" beauty of the chord as it rolls out (it's at a particularly sonorous place in the guitar, and he's drinking in the richness of it "the way a connoisseur would savor a fine wine. I love it.").
- He is hearing the "luminosity" or the "glow" of the high E at the twelfth fret (he's not playing just the E alone – he's playing a series of descending sixteenth note passages all of which begin with that E – but he's focused on the E, and loving this sound – the quality of the sound).

Many of the sensory awarenesses were of the physical mechanics of his guitar technique:

- feeling the muscular resistances in his fingers as he works to "choreograph" their motion to minimize those resistances (and thus to even out the quick passage);

- feeling the sensation of movement in his right arm as his hand sweeps across the strings.

Some of the physical mechanics, like the sound, produce strong affective reaction:

- He's practicing measure twenty-four of the Gnatali *Concert Etude*. As he plays, he says out loud to himself, "From the A! From the E! From the B!" as he plays a sequence of repeated patterns that descend from A, then from E, then from B. He's verbally articulating what he is doing. He's "having a great time"; he's completely warmed up, and this playing and the verbal articulating of it is fully enjoyable. That is, he is verbally articulating not merely as a way to improve some future performance; he's enjoying the verbal articulating and the playing as they occur.

Some of the sensory awarenesses were of issues related to but not intrinsically part of the musical production task:

- feeling his eyeballs physically swing right to left as his eyes pan from the end of one music line to the beginning of the next;
- noticing the particular black and grey shading of the notes on the music he's reading (the imperfections in the printing process);

By contrast, there were *no* sensory awarenesses of things entirely unrelated to the practicing. His non-practice samples had included a wide range of sensory awareness (the brownness of the floor, the shape of the water stream); the practicing seemed to corral or focus his sensory awareness tightly on the practice intention.

The moment-by-moment power of his emotional reaction to his sensory awarenesses was striking. His samples reveal that Cobo *loves* the practicing. He is not merely practicing with the aim of improving skills or preparing for some upcoming concert – he loves the practicing itself, loves the sounds his guitar produces, loves the microscopic sensations of his physical body as he choreographs its motion, loves the ingredients (self-exhortations, etc.) of the practicing itself.

Autonomous Multiplicity

At the same time he was intensely focused on these sensory awarenesses, however, he was also frequently autonomously focused on several or many related or unrelated aspects. Here are examples:

- At the same time as he was hearing the hollowness of the cedar guitar, he was "in a quandary" about whether to play the spruce guitar. This quandary is an evolving process, a simultaneous inchoate considering of lots of factors simultaneously: the current sound of the cedar guitar; his understanding/recollection of the sound of the spruce guitar; the fact that he has just sold the spruce guitar for a lot of money and playing it risks putting a mark on it and screwing up the sale; wanting to play the spruce guitar; knowing he shouldn't really use it because he has sold it; and so on. It's as if each of these considerations are mountains rising and falling as at C of Figure 14.2; sooner or later enough of these mountains will rise and there will be a "majority decision" about whether to play the spruce. Cobo is not guiding this process; experientially it is happening on its own.

- At the same time as he's feeling the muscular resistances in his fingers, Cobo is thinking that Manuel Barrueco (a guitarist with whom Cobo has studied) wouldn't like the way Cobo is playing this passage. Cobo is playing it for its driving emotionality – he's going for the pace, the feel, the sense of urgency, the riding the wave of the speed – not its technical accuracy. He thinks Barrueco wouldn't like the potential inaccuracies.

- At the same time as he's noticing the black and gray shading of the notes of the music, there are three simultaneous thoughts ongoing: (a) thinking about playing A with the left-hand third finger and C with the first finger; (b) ruminating about Los Angeles guitarist Scott Tennant's travel plans. This thought process is definitely experienced as being ongoing, but it is not explicitized. Cobo has arranged for Tennant to play a Las Vegas concert, and Cobo is in some way thinking about Tennant's travel plans coming to Las Vegas and proceeding on thereafter; and (c) thinking about guitarist Bill Snyder's relationship to the Metropolitan Guitar Quartet – Snyder's history with the quartet, how he fits in, and so on. Cobo is not thinking any specific thing about that relationship – he's ruminating about all of it, apparently in one undifferentiated consideration.

- At the same time as he's focused on the powerful "juicy" beauty of the chord he is producing, there is also a background simultaneity of thoughts ongoing that are not related to the guitar. Cobo can't remember what they were, but the gists of them were conspiracy theories about 9/11, the unsatisfactoriness of the presidential candidates, and so on. Maybe 80 percent of his attention was on the enjoyment of the sound; 20 percent on this background thinking.

On the Experience While Practicing

Overall, Cobo's experience while practicing was structurally similar to his experience away from the guitar: dominated by sensory awareness and autonomous multiplicity.

This glimpse into the private experience of a virtuoso is, in my view, worth any effort required by this book. We get to see with as much fidelity as is currently possible directly *how* the beauty of the sound impacts Cobo: It's not just that he thinks the piece is good (which would be an analytical, academic exercise), but that he *loves* the particular sounds that come out of the guitar while he's executing the piece. And he loves the work/effort/practice/repetition/drill *as an end in itself.* Yes, that work has ramifications for the quality of some future performance, but for Cobo, practice is not merely a means to that end – it is a fully enjoyable activity in and of itself. That puts Cobo's artistry in a substantially rich light, opens new insights into his virtuosity, shows that his virtuosity is the real deal: He is organically in touch with the music he is making in his practice room and organically in touch with the physicality of the making of it. He is not practicing so that he can align his performance with some external standard of perfection; he's practicing so that it sounds lovely to him, physically feels right to him.

> **Q:** What difference does it make *to me* whether the playing sounds good to him or is precise according to an external standard? The notes are the notes, if he plays them right.
> **A:** I think you get a glimpse of how music "from the heart" is honed and refined. If instead of loving the sound, Cobo had been, for example, analyzing whether he was playing with perfect precision, then he would have been producing music "from the head." The notes are the same, but the feeling that is transmitted would likely be quite different.
>
> **Q:** So do all virtuosos love their sounds as does Cobo?
> **A:** I don't know. If you think that is an important question (which I do), then you should encourage science to investigate a variety of virtuosos. Such investigation would require paying careful attention to specific moments of experience with a method that genuinely submits to the constraints imposed – remember, it took me nine sampling days mostly away from the guitar before I thought we were ready to *begin* to focus on Cobo's guitar-practicing experience.
>
> It seems pretty clear that retrospective questioning of virtuosos (whether by interview or questionnaire) would *not* be adequate. Because of ego, economics, and presuppositions, it is highly unlikely that a musician would say that he plays from the head, not the heart, regardless of the characteristics of his experience.

THE CONCERT

There are lots of accounts of the experience of music performance, but those accounts are all retrospective and therefore (as we have seen) of questionable validity. So Cobo and I decided, after sampling for the thirteen days described previously, to attempt sampling in a concert situation. Here's what we did.

I arranged to have Cobo give a concert. I invited the audience members, which included professional guitarist peers, guitar society members, university officials, people who knew of my work, friends, graduate students, and so on. The audience was therefore eclectic but knowledgeable and discriminating – the kind of audience that would put realistic musical pressure on Cobo. When I invited the audience, I informed them that there would be an hour-or-so concert, during which Cobo's performance would be interrupted by a half-dozen random beeps. Cobo would immediately suspend playing, jot down notes in a notebook, and then resume from the vicinity of where he had been interrupted. The audience's task while Cobo jotted down his notes was merely to wait quietly. After the hour's performance there would be an intermission. After the intermission, there would be a discussion of what had transpired – perhaps a lecture by me about inner experience, questions from the audience, and so on. The entire event, including audience participation, would be videotaped.

Constraint: Protect privacy. I purposefully left it ambiguous whether Cobo would discuss his during-the-concert samples after the intermission. Cobo and I would make that decision during the intermission, *after* Cobo knew the content of the samples that had been collected.

I delivered the beeps with a computerized random interval generator, rather than the usual beeper, so I would have somewhat more control. The computer-generated beep was a recording of the usual DES beeper's beep, with which Cobo was familiar. The beeps were delivered both through the usual earphone in Cobo's ear and an external speaker so that the audience and videotape would know precisely when the beeps occurred. The beeps were all random with one exception (unbeknownst to Cobo at the time): I specifically arranged to have one beep occur during applause.

As agreed, at intermission Cobo and I discussed whether he should describe to the audience the beeped experiences that had occurred during the concert; he was happy to do so. After intermission, therefore, I interviewed Cobo about his samples, with the audience members looking on and free to ask Cobo (or me) questions. This is, of course, a very non-standard interview procedure, a compromise between faithful apprehension of the beeped experiences and the interpersonal pressures of performing the interview before the live audience.

The Concert Samples

Table 14.1 shows Cobo's concert and the times the beeps occurred:

As far as I know, this is the only time that a virtuoso musician has actually interrupted a real concert to try to capture the ongoing experience. Therefore these are precious bits of experience, and I'll describe all seven.

TABLE 14.1. *Cobo's concert and beep timings*

Composer	Composition	Beep number and timing (min:sec)
Leo Brouwer	*Un Dia de Noviembre*	1 (3:10)
Napoleon Coste	*Deuxieme Polonaise* (Op. 14)	2 (1:25 into 2nd movement)
		3 (0:03 into applause after)
Dilermando Reis	*Se Ela Perguntar*	[no beep]
Maximo Diego Pujol	*Elegy for the Death of a Tanguero*	4 (1:20)
Maximo Diego Pujol	*Stella Australis*	5 (0:00 [first note])
		6 (1:24 into 2nd movement)
Eduardo Martín	*Acrílicos en el Asfalto*	[no beep]
Horacio Salgan	*Don Agustín Bardi*	7 (1:07)

Sample 14.1 ["Un Dia de Noviembre"]. Cobo is focused on the phrasing and joining lines and arches together while the harmony blends in washes and swaths. It is difficult to determine how the lines and arches present themselves to Cobo. There is a peripheral awareness of the DES earpiece.

Sample 14.2 ["Deuxieme Polonaise," second movement]. Cobo is attending to the cadence slur figure, which has three arches and three sets of slurs, as he finishes the A section of the movement. How these arches present themselves to Cobo is difficult to ascertain – perhaps there is a hint of visualization (see later). Also, the earpiece is a distraction – he wonders whether it will fall out.

Sample 14.3 [during the applause after "Deuxieme Polonaise"]. Cobo was focused on the specific space where there is clapping and acknowledgment. He was hearing a white noise that seemed to be filling a hall that was much bigger than the room where the actual concert took place. The noise that he heard was not yet focused upon – not yet really heard to be the actual applause that was actually taking place. Instead, he was attending to the space – an auditorium-sized space that was somehow open and yet also somehow filled with the noise and some visual characteristics as well – the colored air of a large concert hall.

Sample 14.4 ["Elegy for the Death of a Tanguero"]. Background: This beep occurred during one of the climaxes of the piece. A frenetic section climbs to an exposed soprano high F# (one of the highest notes on the guitar) played repetitively against the sustained dissonant G and B: F# – F# – F# – F# – F# – G. The final G resolves the tension by becoming an E-minor chord; the tension relief is completed by playing the E (lowest note on the guitar) that serves as the root of the E-minor. The beep occurs just as that lowest E is being played.

At the beep, Cobo's experience is divided among three aspects: (a) the physicality of his left hand, the way that it sets to play the E-minor structure high on the guitar; (b) the hearing of the soprano line; and (c) wondering about the effectiveness of his phrasing and focus of his concentration. Cobo was unable to provide details of how this wondering took place – couldn't say whether it was in words or not, for example. The wondering was experienced to be just beginning, to be very "backgroundy," a self-analytical wondering whether he was getting the music across: Is he making himself clear to the audience?

Sample 14.5 ["Stella Australis"]. Background: The piece begins with an E-minor melody line E – B – G – F# – B starting on the E that is the lowest note of the guitar, providing the opportunity to display the fullest sound the guitar can produce.

The beep occurs on the first note (the low E). Cobo is "looking inside for how to say" this opening E-minor phrase – how to blend and push energy deep into the phrase. This is a bodily focus, a paying attention to the interior of his chest/thorax, a region bigger than his heart. He is focused on the G as the E-minor phrase would open itself, even though the beep came before he would play this G. He is hearing his playing of the first two notes of this phrase slower than he actually plays them, as if the notes were big and he could work his way in between and around the notes, feeling the weight of the individual notes.

Sample 14.6 ["Stella Australis," second movement]. Cobo "sees" the minor second interval A#/B that he is in the process of playing. That dissonance is powerful and he is taking it in, sensorially focused on it. Additionally, Cobo was just "coming out" of a thinking about triplets and quads and how to nail them. His understanding was that this thinking had been ongoing prior to the current passage, but that his increasing sensory interest in the dissonance of the A#B reduced his interest in the triplets and quads. However, the thinking was not entirely absent, either.

As is usual with Cobo's use of the word "see," we could not determine to what extent this was a sensory awareness, to what extent it was visual, to what extent felt. It was certainly not seen visually clearly (that is, it was *not* seen like Luke saw $g = v^2/R$).

Sample 14.7 ["Don Agustín Bardi"]. Background: The opening theme ends with a series of dissonances followed by a very simple, classical A-major resolution cadence that gives the false impression of being the end of the piece, which, however, actually continues on to a new high-energy second theme. The beep occurred during that A-major resolution chord.

Cobo had a juicy, good feeling from the A-major chord, an emotional hearing of what he was playing. Cobo had in fact played that chord very sweetly, by distinct contrast to the harshness of the dissonances that had preceded it, and now was enjoying the feeling that that beautiful resolution was providing. He was also in some way anticipating the upcoming A-minor theme, which begins with a resolute open-string A.

Discussion

Cobo's concert samples provide a rare look at virtuoso performance from the inside. We have only seven in-concert samples, so it would be a mistake to make too much of them.

Cobo was very experienced with the usual DES procedure, having sampled for thirteen prior sampling days. But now that process, which had been private, was to be performed under public scrutiny. It is reasonable to understand that the first couple of samples were strongly influenced by the novelty of the situation. Cobo the performer, who is accustomed to creating situations for audiences, now had to figure out how to integrate this new performance task of interrupting and note taking, had to evaluate the impact of this interruption on the audience, and so on. It is also reasonable to presume that the shock of this task lessened across samples as it became clear that the audience would patiently wait while he jotted down notes, that the performance was "working" as planned.

Sensory awareness. All seven of Cobo's concert samples included sensory awarenesses. Similar to his non-guitar and his practicing samples, those sensory awarenesses were of sounds (harmony blending in washes and swaths, the powerful dissonance of A#/B) and of the physicality of his body (the sensations of his hand as it sets to play; feeling the interior of his chest/thorax, a region bigger than his heart.)

Two of the concert sensory awarenesses included a kind of distortion of reality: He heard the sound of applause in a large auditorium rather than the relatively small room where the concert was held; hearing the beginning E – B – G – F# – B phrase slower than he is actually playing it so he could work his way in between and around the notes.

Autonomous multiplicity. Five of the seven concert samples included some kind of multiplicity, again somewhat similar to his non-guitar and his practicing samples. However, he was more focused during performance than he was when practicing the guitar or when engaged in non-guitar activities, evidenced in two ways. First, his concert samples were somewhat less complex than were his non-concert samples. In the metaphor of Figure 14.2, Cobo's concert samples had mostly one or two mountains (three in Sample 14.4).

Second, *all* the mountains of *all* of Cobo's concert samples were directly related to the performance. There was *no* thinking about such things as travel plans or conspiracy theories about 9/11 as had populated his while-practicing samples. I'm confident Cobo would have reported them if they had occurred during the concert. There were some thoughts ongoing during the concert, but they were *all* related to the *present* performance: the earphone (14.1 and 14.2), whether he is making himself clear to the audience (14.4), how to nail the triplets and quads (14.6).

Yani Dickens and I (Dickens, 2005) have sampled the experience of golfers as they participated in a golf tournament; one of our findings was that the best golfers were strongly focused on golf throughout the tournament, whereas the not-so-highly skilled players also thought about extraneous issues: the architecture of the houses lining the course, the weather, a business meeting the previous day, and so on. Cobo's experience was 100 percent focused on the performance.

The thought process "mountains" had the same autonomously gradual rising and falling as in the non-concert samples: The applause was not yet fully processed (14.3); the wondering about the effectiveness of his phrasing seemed to be just beginning (14.4); he was "just coming out" of a thinking about triplets and quads (14.6).

VISUALIZATION

At the outset of this chapter, we discussed Cobo's firmly held and often publicly stated belief in the ubiquity and importance of inner visualization while playing the guitar. We trained Cobo, over nine days of mostly non-guitar-playing practice, to observe his experience carefully, as free of presuppositions as possible. When we aimed that new observation skill at his guitar practicing, *we discovered only one instance of visualization* (one of twenty-eight, or 4 percent) *while practicing*. Certainly our sample of Cobo's experience while practicing is small, but the conclusion seems inescapable: Visualization is *not* the ubiquitous feature of Cobo's experience while playing the guitar as he had thought prior to sampling.

Constraint: Be skeptical of general accounts of experience, no matter how fervently held, no matter how competent the holder, no matter how plausible.

Despite the fact that Cobo has spent on the order of 30,000 hours playing the guitar, he was substantially mistaken about at least some of the main characteristics of his experience while doing so. This is *not* a criticism of Cobo. Most people's general characterizations of their experience are mistaken, often substantially so (recall, among others, the bulimia example in Chapter 2 and the Tourette's Syndrome example in Chapter 6). This chapter emphasizes that even the most highly skilled practitioners among us can be substantially mistaken about their experience. The fact that he agreed with other master teachers does not alter the fact that he was mistaken (as are, quite probably, the others as well).

There were two samples from the concert where visualization may have been present (samples 14.2 and 14.6). Yet despite the fourteen days of sampling practice, and despite our joint effort at clarifying the descriptions of his experience, his descriptions remained self-contradictory. For example, about sample 14.2 he said he was seeing arches, and we had this exchange during the after-intermission interview:

> RTH: So are you seeing three arches? Is that what you're saying? [Cobo nods affirmatively] And do these arches, these three arches, have any characteristics to them? Color, shape …?

COBO: No. It's more abstract. In other words, I know there's three arches, and I'm playing with them. I'm making them happen.

RTH: And by "see" do you mean "visually see" or do you mean "understand," as somebody would say, "Oh! I see!"

COBO: It's conceptual.

RTH: OK.

COBO: There is ... In other words, if I were to describe to you what I see, I don't see three arches. I know the shape is there, and I almost see what you would see in a score but without the actual note values, the pitch values. I saw the three phrase marks, but they're not seen – they're felt, they're understood.

This remark is exquisitely self-contradictory: I see but I don't see; I know but I almost see; I saw but they're not seen – they're felt.

RTH: So at this particular beep, there's something that's *three* about it [gestures three arches] ...

COBO: Yep.

RTH: ... and there's something that's visual about that...

COBO: Um hm [nods affirmatively].

RTH: ... but it's not something that you're actually *seeing*...

COBO: Right.

RTH: ...and yet it's also not fair to say, "I'm not seeing it" either. So it's ...

COBO: I'm definitely seeing *something*. I don't know what it is.

Constraint: Embrace the frustration. From the standpoint of trying to apprehend Cobo's experience, his contradictions make for tough going. The temptation may be to discard what he says altogether – if he can't clarify something as straightforward as what "see" means, he simply cannot be trusted. But if the object is to apprehend experience, that temptation has to be overcome. I assure the reader that Cobo was highly motivated to be forthcoming and straightforwardly descriptive about his experience, and I was highly motivated to get it right.

However, I don't have a full understanding of what Cobo is saying about "seeing," and I don't think Cobo does, either. Yes, that is frustrating, in the sense that it would be easier if I understood it. The good news is that we have made a pretty-darn-careful deposit into the bank account of understanding experience: Cobo and I have attempted to apprehend his experience in full submission to the constraints that that endeavor imposes. How that deposit will be redeemed remains to be seen. Perhaps, in the fullness of time, I or the reader will sample with a few or many more virtuoso musicians, and eventually will be able to say, "*That's* what Cobo meant by 'seeing'!" Maybe the sampling will have to be with young musicians, only some of whom actually *become* virtuosos. Maybe the phenomena of Cobo's experience have nothing to do with his musicianship.

That we don't understand all of the details of Cobo's experience does not imply that we know nothing about Cobo's experience. I think it is secure to say that Cobo's seeing of the arches is *not* the same phenomenon as Luke's seeing the equation $g = v^2/R$. That is a fundamentally important step, even if we don't yet fully understand its significance.

> **Q:** You and Cobo are wrestling with language, and that is problematic in conveying the experience. Cobo is having to try to find the words to translate his experience to communicate to you. That's tricky! Maybe he's saying a word and using it in a different way than you would use it.
>
> **A:** I think we are *not* primarily wrestling with language; we are wrestling with the phenomenon. Those are two very different things. To wrestle with language would be, for example, for Luke to call his $g = v^2/R$ experience an *image*, and for me to prefer the term *inner seeing*, and then because of our terminological differences for me to fail to recognize Luke's image is an instance of what I call inner seeing. In that case, there is no question about the phenomenon (Luke is seeing an imaginary $g = v^2/R$ equation), but our linguistic wrestling obscures that phenomenon.
>
> Here, by distinct contrast, we are wrestling about the phenomenon itself. When Cobo says "I see arches," we are *not* primarily wrestling with what he means by "see" or whether there would be some better word for it; we are wrestling about how those arches present themselves to him.
>
> You are correctly squeamish about words: People *do* often use words in a different way from how their listener intends them. But this is the fourteenth interview; for thirteen prior days Cobo and I have been explicitly, relentlessly, repeatedly, skillfully hammering away at clarifying what the words he uses mean, at how I understand what he means, exposing successive approximations of both for each other's view, commentary, clarification, evolution. He has learned to say things differently so that I can understand with higher fidelity. I have learned to ask things differently so that he can respond in ways that I can understand. I have learned to understand what he means when he says *X*. And we have learned to accept the limitations of our endeavor. In particular, we have learned that he uses "see" in a way that is different from Luke, that is somehow visual but does not include seen details, and that neither of us fully understands.
>
> **Q:** This communication might be particularly difficult with music. It reminds me of a quote often attributed to Elvis Costello: "Writing about music is like dancing about architecture." It's very difficult to go from whatever music is to whatever language is.
>
> **A:** I agree that asking Cobo about *music*, or even asking him about his *experience of music*, would be like dancing about architecture – that's why I *don't* ask about either of those. I ask him only about *his pristine experience*, whatever that happens to be, and that is a very different thing, because his pristine experience *already includes* his particular way of focusing on some particular aspect(s) – he has already completed (in whatever way, for

whatever reason) his own task of simplifying the welter of his surroundings (that includes the music, the audience, his proprioceptions, his memories, etc.) and creating his experience, which may (or may not) have involved reacting in some way to the music. Here, for example, his experience is (somehow) of arches, *not* of music *in general* or of "Deuxieme Polonaise" or even of the second movement of "Deuxieme Polonaise." I am asking him only about his particular experience *at the moment of this particular beep.* Writing about music (or dancing about architecture) *is* difficult, if not impossible, at least in part because music (and architecture) is a complexly variable and rapid unfolding of disparate themes, resolutions, and harmonies – music at one moment is quite different from music at another moment, and talk about it cannot possibly keep up with that complexity. Our interview with Cobo reduces this difficulty by focusing on his experience that already has (or at least may have) selected one or a few aspects of that complexity to become the pristine experience at that one moment.

SPECULATION ABOUT VISUALIZATION

Until now we have provided a characterization of Cobo's experience, as faithfully as we can muster, intending to cleave as close as possible to the facts of his experience. Now I relax that cleaving to experience and provide two speculations about Cobo's experience, one about visualization and one about virtuosity. I indulge these speculations *not* because I am committed to their truth, but because the speculations may expose what needs to be done if a science of experience is to mature.

As I have said, in his role as my guitar teacher, Cobo had been exhorting me for years to form a visual image of the fingerboard. When I do so, he has said repeatedly, my accuracy will improve, my security will increase, my tension will reduce, and my tone will improve. "Visualize! See your fingers next to the frets and then put them there!" I have tried hard to visualize as instructed, but I just can't do it. I don't know how to proceed, what to see, or how to see it.

After working unsuccessfully for years at visualizing, it occurred to me that instead of trying to *imagine* my fingers in relation to the frets (as Cobo had exhorted but that I couldn't do), I should simply concentratedly *look at* the exact *real* position on the fingerboard that I wanted my left-hand finger to be in before I set it there. I found that I *could do* this *real* anticipatory seeing, and my performance skill took a substantial step forward in the way Cobo had predicted: My accuracy improved, security increased, tension reduced, and tone improved. There are other potential explanations, but I came to believe that seeing the fingerboard locations in anticipation of placing the fingers does indeed have the virtues Cobo described.

Here's my speculation about Cobo's visualizing. If not before, at age sixteen, when he began studying with Aaron Shearer, Cobo began the systematic real anticipatory seeing of where his fingers should go on the fingerboard, much as I described in the previous paragraph. Over the next several thousand hours of practice, that real seeing became an imaginary seeing, because if the virtues (security, tone) inhere equally in imaginary as in real seeing, imaginary seeing is a substantial improvement: One can imaginarily (but not really) see both left-hand and right-hand position at the same time; and imaginary seeing leaves the real eyes free for other important tasks such as reading the music. Once the transformation from real to imaginary seeing took place, Cobo doubtless completely forgot that the real-seeing phase ever existed.

Over the next thousands of hours of practice, Cobo's imaginarily seeing skill improved – he no longer needed to imagine the actual fingers but instead needed to imagine just a schematic of them. In the service of virtuosity, it is not necessary to waste cognitive resources on the visual details of the left-hand (e.g., fingernails, skin) or the details of the fingerboard (e.g., grain of the ebony, shine of the frets): A schematic that omits such detail is much more efficient.

Over the next thousands of hours of practice, that imaginary schematic-seeing became ever more schematized, ever more implicit rather than actually seeing the schematic in detail. Thus it remains an anticipatory seeing of the fingerboard, but all the extraneous details have been entirely eliminated. Perhaps we could call that "seeingless seeing." If that seems impossible, remember we're considering someone who has honed his skills finer than 99.999 percent of the population, and remember the constraint *Don't judge others by yourself.* That transformation from real seeing to imaginary seeing to schematized imaginary seeing to visual-detail-absent seeing was organically gradual, something that Cobo himself would not notice.

Everything in this sequence involves seeing, so Cobo is entirely correct to say, today, that he always innerly sees the fretboard. However, because this inner seeing is so refined, it is also entirely correct to say that he does *not* innerly see the fretboard – he does not see the pedestrian visual characteristics of everyday $g = v^2/R$–type imagery. And therefore it is entirely appropriate for Cobo to be entirely contradictory when he talks about his seeing experience (as about the arches), depending on the manner of speaking of the word "see."

> **Q:** I was right – he has difficulty with the word "see"!
> **A:** I agree that the words fail him, but the primary difficulty is not verbal. Grant him the ability to inject his experience directly into us, bypassing words altogether, and it will still be difficult (maybe impossible) for those of us who do not have his refined "seeingless" seeing skill to grasp it.

> **Q:** I still don't get it. Cobo didn't spend 30,000 hours refining his inner experience – he spent 30,000 hours refining his finger dexterity.
> **A:** Implied by that question, I think, is the notion that Cobo's experience is pretty much like your own; that you and Cobo differ only in the arena of finger dexterity. I again remind you of the constraint from Chapter 9: *Don't*

judge others by yourself. I happily accept that I don't know what Cobo was refining in those 30,000 hours, but I'd bet a large share of the ranch that it is not only finger dexterity.

And recall the finger-OK story I told at the end of Chapter 13 (Hurlburt, 1976): practicing a finger position for ten days resulted in quite disparate, distal, and major postural and action readjustments. If you believe (as I do) that inner experience is a skill, it's not too large a step to believe that inner experience would be substantially readjusted by 30,000 hours of practice of anything.

SPECULATIONS ABOUT VIRTUOSITY

As we have seen, Cobo's experience had two major characteristics: sensory awareness and autonomous multiplicity. I now speculate that those characteristics of his experience are not accidental; rather, they support his virtuosity, perhaps are essential to virtuosity.

Sensory Awareness

It is probably not surprising that someone who has risen to the top of a profession whose livelihood depends entirely on what you hear coming from his guitar should spend considerable time and attention focusing on sounds coming from the guitar. Therefore it should not be surprising that Cobo had a substantial amount of sensory awareness of sound. What is *not* well known (but see Chapter 16) is that for many people, sensory awareness occurs across modalities – that is, people who experience frequent auditory sensory awareness also experience frequent visual sensory awareness, bodily sensory awareness, and so on. Therefore, I speculate that virtuosos have frequent sensory awarenesses in many modalities (recall Cobo's seeing brownness of the floor, sensing coldness, feeling pressure of Julie's hip against his side, etc.).

Autonomous Multiplicity

Perhaps more surprisingly, I suspect also that Cobo's autonomous multiplicity of experience is fundamentally important to his virtuosity; that characteristic has not been noticed in the literature, as far as I know.

Guitar performance, as we have seen, requires the autonomous but simultaneous operation of left and right hands at opposite ends of the guitar strings. The motions that the right-hand performs are entirely different from and independent of (but coordinated with) the motions of the left hand: The right hand plucks while the left hand stays still; sometimes the right hand moves while the left hand sets and vice versa; sometimes they move in tandem. It is not just the whole hands – each individual finger of each hand must move independently of every other finger, this finger pressing the string against the fret while the others move, for example. This is well known, typically called finger independence.

Furthermore, simultaneous to both hands (or to all the fingers), the performer has to attend to the heard sounds. This hearing is itself a skill, coordinated with but independent of the left-hand and right-hand skills. Simultaneous to all of that are the extraneous events of the concert hall (the sneezes, the doors squeaking) and his ongoing life (family matters, travel arrangements) that may all be ongoing simultaneously.

The music itself is simultaneously multiple, perhaps most obviously in polyphonic music. A fugue, for example, has several (typically three, but as many as six in Bach's *Musical Offering*) "voices" or musical lines that independently weave back and forth among each other. A virtuoso who is playing such music has to hear each line simultaneously and separately, so that each line can be inflected, accented, sped up, slowed down, and so on, in ways that make sense for that particular line, independent of (but harmonized with) the other lines (which are also being separately inflected, etc.).

I speculate that Cobo's autonomously multiple experience capability (as illustrated in Figure 14.2) can deal with musical performance's simultaneity in a highly refined manner. He can have one "mountain" dedicated to the sound of his guitar, another mountain aimed at the right hand, another mountain aimed at the left hand, another mountain aimed at this polyphonic theme, another aimed at the left-hand first finger, and so on, each mountain independently rising and falling as needed as the environment changes. Some new mountain (concern about the heat of the floodlights, the critic in the front row) can rise and fall *without disturbing the "hand" mountains and the "sound" mountain*.

Many, if not most, psychologists and philosophers believe that multiplicity of the kind I'm describing here is impossible – they believe that there is always only one experience at a time. I think they are seriously mistaken. If experience is important (which they think it is), virtuosity may well be *impossible* under science's one-experience-at-a-time model. Suppose I'm a one-experience at a time performer, and I'm absorbed in the sound of my playing. Something happens in the hall – a sneeze, perhaps – and my attention goes to that. No problem, the psychologist says; the playing goes on automatically until the attention returns to the sound. But virtuoso performance isn't just about automatically getting the notes right; it's about a whole series of subtle nuances that require attention to keep consistent. Under the one-thing-at-a-time model, the quality of performance simply *must* degrade when someone in the audience sneezes. By contrast, under my Figure 14.2 model of Cobo's experience, the sneeze causes a new attuned-to-the-sneeze mountain to arise, but the attention-to-the-sound mountain can remain undisturbed.

Doing versus Happening

One more speculation. We have noticed that Cobo seems more a receiver of his experience than a creator of it – for example, the "quandary" about whether to play the spruce guitar was experienced to be many simultaneous thoughts working themselves out on their own, eventually ganging up to present a decision to him – he will play the spruce or not. That is, Cobo does *not* experience himself as *doing* the thinking; the thinking is *happening*, and when enough happens, he will act. This apparently applies not only to inner experience but in his action as well: In the conversation with Julie he didn't know whether she was talking or he was, apparently because both talkings are experienced as happening to him.

All that is quite unusual compared to other DES subjects – most people feel themselves to be the driver of their thoughts, speakings, and actions. I speculate that Cobo's happening of experience is not coincidental – that it serves his virtuosity. I'll give two arguments.

First, let's assume that experiencing takes some time, say δ seconds. For the sake of argument, let's say δ, the time required to form an experience and then initiate action, is on the order of a fourteenth of a second (Libet, 2004, thought it was longer than that, but the actual duration is not essential to my argument). If such a delay exists, I think it is a bad idea for a musician to have his experience *do* (that is, drive) his performance, because his driven-by-experience doings *must* be delayed, out of sync, by δ.

I provide a simple example to demonstrate why this is problematic. Suppose that the performer *does* the maintaining of pitch, as illustrated in Figure 14.3. At some point he recognizes that pitch is "a centimeter" too high, so he initiates an action to lower the pitch by a centimeter. That lowering doesn't begin to take effect until δ later, at which time the pitch lowers by a centimeter and then returns to neutral. (How big is a "centimeter of pitch" is not important.)

Further suppose that the virtuoso uses vibrato, a sinusoidal wavering in pitch with frequency of about 6–8 Hz; for convenience, let's call the vibrato frequency about 7 Hz. That makes the wavelength about on seventh of a second (2δ), as illustrated in the top of Figure 14.4. Most performers and listeners hold vibrato to be beautiful, making the tone "warmer" than a uniform pitch. Now suppose that the performer tries to *do* to his vibrato the same kind of pitch maintenance that was illustrated in Figure 14.3. When the pitch becomes a centimeter too high, he notices it and initiates a centimeter lowering of the pitch. As before, that lowering doesn't begin to take effect until δ later, but by then, the natural sine wave vibrato will *already* have lowered the pitch, so the intentional lowering (initiated when the pitch was too high) will have the effect of *exaggerating* the already occurring natural lowering. Now the performer recognizes that the pitch is two centimeters too low, and initiates a corrective *doing* of raising the pitch, but that raising will not take effect for δ seconds, by which time the sinusoidal wavering will already have raised the pitch. The intentional raising of the pitch will act on top of that, exaggerating the pitch raising. The result of this feedback is that the pitch wavering *amplifies*, rather than lessens, at each oscillation, resulting in an out-of-control

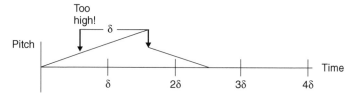

FIGURE 14.3. The doing of pitch correction.

widening wavering of pitch. I wildly speculate that that is the genesis of the tremor due to anxiety: beautiful vibrato distorted by the intentional doing of trying to control it. The speculation that anxiety is related to doing is slightly grounded: Hurlburt (1993a) used DES to investigate anxious individuals and reported a disturbance in their doing of actions. Not coincidentally, the tremor of anxiety (even among non-musicians) has approximately the same frequency as vibrato, for, I think, the same reason: The anxious person is trying to do things (to stay calm, for example) in a frequency realm where this trying leads to the out-of-control amplification illustrated in Figure 14.4.

What makes *doing* problematic is that it is one main driver (one big, coordinated, organismic-wide action), and therefore one main driving frequency. If there is no *doing*, there is instead a bunch of more or less separate processes that independently but coordinately achieve the effect. The pitch starts to rise; the performer's left-arm controller reacts to that rise by relaxing the forearm; the performer's left-third-finger controller reacts by moving slightly toward the fret; the performer's midsection controller reacts by bending forward slightly, and so on. All those reactions coordinately working together successfully lower the pitch. Those reactions don't occur instantaneously, but they occur with differing fundamental frequencies (the finger controller operates faster than the midsection controller, etc.). Because the driving frequencies differ, the out-of-control exaggeration does not occur (which is why soldiers when approaching a bridge stop marching and walk across).

> **Q:** Your example is too contrived. You said that the duration of δ is not essential/meaningful/important for your argument, but then you related it to vibrato's known frequency of about 7 Hz. Your example depends on vibrato's frequency and the time of consciousness being tightly related.
>
> **A:** Perhaps. I accept that I may be wrong about vibrato, but there are lots of natural frequencies occurring in music other than vibrato: the rate of sixteenth notes, for example. And even single occurrences can be Fourier-transformed into the sum of periodic actions of varying frequencies. So the *doing* argument might apply to one of those other frequencies, if not to vibrato.

> **Q:** I still don't know what you mean by *doing*. Everybody is always doing everything. And I don't understand why you're interested in vibrato. What's the big deal?

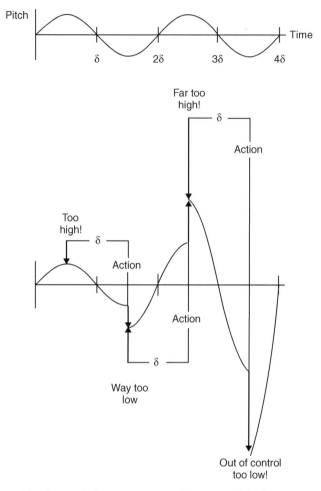

FIGURE 14.4. The doing of vibrato correction. Top: Beautiful vibrato. Bottom: Doing of pitch correction amplifies pitch deviations.

A: There is a huge, but not widely understood, difference between the experience of *doing* something and not doing it. Try this thought experiment. First, I want you to accept that you understand what *doing* is, so I issue this simple instruction: *With your forefinger, tap as fast as you can on the tabletop.* Really, *do it.* That's what it means to *do* something – I can tell you to do something, and you can do it. How fast did you tap? Probably about 7 Hz.

Second, imagine yourself in a cathedral with a large pipe organ. The organist steps on the left-most pedal and the organ blows air through the thirty-two-foot pipe; you hear C four octaves below middle C. Is the hearing of this low C the same as the experience of tapping your finger? Most people say decidedly not – I'm *receiving* or *hearing* or *am impacted by* the organ sound, but I'm *doing* the tapping. Can you *do* the hearing of the organ sound?

That is, can you raise the pitch (speed up the frequency) or lower it? No. Hearing the organ tone is an example of not doing.

The frequency of a thirty-two-foot organ pipe is 16.4 Hz. There are a few organs (not many) that have sixty-four-foot pipes, where the frequency is 8.2 Hz. Whether you draw the line at 8 or 16 Hz isn't too important, so let's call the lower limit of an oscillation's sounding like music "about 10 Hz." Any frequency below about 10 Hz *does not sound*; it is understood as a motion, not a musical tone. Any frequency above about 10 Hz *does not move*; it is understood as a musical tone, not a motion.

So I think that this frequency range from about 7 to about 10 Hz is experientially a very special place in human experience, a transition from frequencies where things can be *done* to frequencies where things *cannot be done*. This "edge of doing" is a very small range, about 3 Hz wide along a spectrum that's about 20,000 Hz wide. Vibrato exists in that range, and is experienced to be a "warming" of an existing tone rather than a tone of its own and rather than an action of its own. You can easily demonstrate how sensitive is the experience in this edge-of-doing region: Take a recording of a performer with a beautiful vibrato and lower the frequencies ("slow it down") by 10 or 20 percent or so (easy to do with modern audio-editing software like Audacity or WavePad). The pitch will go down by a little, of course, but the most salient change will likely be your experience of the vibrato – it no longer warms the tone but instead produces a very unpleasant *wa-wa-wa-wa-wa*. And if you speed it up by 10 or 20 percent, the tone sounds edgy, not warm. There is something experientially special about 7 Hz but no other frequency.

So below about 7 Hz, you can do things. Above about 10 Hz, you cannot do things. True virtuoso musicians know that they shouldn't meddle at the intersection between doing and not doing. That is, they know that vibrato should not be *done*. The musician may have colorful ways of saying this, for example, that vibrato has to "come from the heart."

Second, any intentional *doing* has to involve one thing or one perspective. In virtuoso performance there are always many things happening simultaneously (multiple lines in a polyphonic piece, audience sneezes, etc.), and it is always infelicitous to attend to only one aspect at the expense of the others. In polyphonic performance, it is often desirable to *bring out* one line (call it the "melody"), but to a virtuoso that is not *at the expense* of the others (the "accompaniment" lines); the accompaniment lines as played by a virtuoso are just as important as the melody lines, each serving its own important role.

Perhaps this will make the point: Watch people walking down the street – their action is a quite beautiful coordination of walking, talking with their friends, viewing the sights, and so on. Now aim a TV camera at them in such a way that they notice it. Now they begin to *do* their actions – perhaps *trying* to look cool, perhaps aping for the camera, perhaps intentionally ignoring the camera (walking a straight line looking neither right nor left). The beauty of their coordinated walking has been destroyed by the doing of one aspect of it.

The virtuoso cannot afford to *do* any one line; cannot afford to *do* anything musical. Virtuoso performance is a corralling of happenings: In the Figure 14.2 schematic the audience hushes, the performer's mountains (left hand, right hand, breathing, posture, auditory acuity, visualization of the opening phrase, mood of the whole piece, expectation of the climax, etc.) start to rise, more or less independently, eventually coalescing into coherence, and he begins to play. Thus the playing *happens to him*, more than he *does* the playing.

It seems reasonable to think that this don't-let-experience-meddle-with-performance happening would spill over into a virtuoso's non-performance experiential life: Don't let experience meddle with anything. Or maybe it's the other way around: The person who by nature doesn't *do* experience may have a head start in attaining virtuosity. Or maybe Cobo is atypical. Or maybe I've got it wrong. My aim with this speculation is to be provocative, to open the window a crack into the potential experience of rare individuals, not to provide a definitive view of virtuoso experience.

> **Q:** This is a theory of virtuosity: You considered the demands of virtuosity (lots going on independently and simultaneously) and then theorized about what must be happening in experience. Don't you criticize such theorizing elsewhere in this book?
> **A:** I am here speculating about what goes on behind the scenes (I tried to warn you of that by including "speculation" in the titles of these sections). However, I think your characterization of my procedure is quite backward. I did not *begin* with a theoretical analysis of virtuosity and then try to derive the characteristics of experience. I *began* by recruiting a virtuoso and investigating random samples of his experience, *whatever that experience might be and* not *necessarily connected to his virtuosity* (recall that we sampled for nine days away from the guitar). Cobo's autonomous multiplicity was the *emergent result* of that open-beginninged phenomenological procedure, *not* a hypothesis generated by theory. Then we noted that the simultaneity that we discovered in his experience away from the guitar also occurs when practicing and concertizing. *Only then* did we speculate about the potentially important link between autonomous multiplicity and the requirements of classical guitar playing. That was a remarkable and entirely unexpected speculation.
>
> I happily grant the wildness of the speculations. I advance them in the service of the *Don't judge others by yourself* constraint: There is little reason to suppose that a virtuoso performer (who, by definition, is demonstrably different from 99.999 percent of others) has experience that is just like the other 99.999 percent. I may have the details of the differences partially or entirely wrong; the big picture is the likelihood that there *are* differences, which a science of experience would have to explore. Those differences are not discoverable by any orthodox psychological technique that I know of – they require an exploration of experience in genuine submission to the constraints that such an enterprise imposes.

Q: I could probably accept your sensory awareness and autonomous multiplicity speculations, but your *doing* stuff is over the top.
A: Perhaps. I think, however, there may be millennia of documentation. A favorite exercise of the Buddhists is to watch the breathing but not to interfere with it. Without wishing to stretch the point, I note that in the current vocabulary, the non-interfering with breathing is to let the breathing happen, not to *do* the breathing. Most novice meditators find the not-doing of breathing quite difficult at the start, and its mastery quite beneficial.

Ricardo Cobo responds: First, let me assure the reader of this book that I was fully engaged, as honest and careful about the process of collecting data for the beeps as I knew how to be. I embraced the idea and the process of this task "in full submission to the constraints that that endeavor imposes." Furthermore, when I began discussing my beeped experiences with Russ, I was unaware of the many levels of perception and experience that are taking place seemingly simultaneously.

Furthermore, what had been "routine" or "habitual" details in my playing emerged as surprising details of awareness of things not necessarily related to playing. I have learned that my experiential and sensorial details during my practicing are actually more dominant than the actual notes, notation, or evidence of a systematic approach to playing. That is bewildering to me and suggests, perhaps, that I have automated so much of the mechanics of guitar playing that I operate on a more personal and artistic level while practicing. I've learned that I don't actually see notes but rather experience or feel them and how they strike me.

About the concert, let me corroborate and fully agree with Russ's statement that I was 100 percent focused on the concert. The process of collecting samples "under public scrutiny" was enlightening and reaffirming for me. I believe the pressure of a "live" environment does indeed sharpen my focus and enable me to narrow my experience on the playing rather than a multiplicity of other concerns. That is, live performances raises the bar and elevates the desire for those times in music performance where I seem to be redefined by the music and the performance of it. These times are rare in a practice room, but they make every hour I spend practicing seem worthwhile. Despite the enjoyment of the practicing that my samples revealed, I am always practicing ultimately for a concert or recording.

About some specific details that have been discussed in this chapter, I make four observations. First, I believe the "music from the head" versus the "music from the heart" discussion is invaluable in describing artistry. Speaking for myself, the notes I play aren't just notes, they are pure emotional energy and sound. Anyone can play notes – after all, we play on tempered instruments with frets and concert pitch references. Conveying convincing and beautiful emotion, however, is not merely producing the notes, but more like writing a beautiful poem with sound that goes beyond the actual words, the lines, and grammar (the notes, rhythm, and phrases), produced in a fully realized, choreographed emotion. It is a powerful self-realizing process that pushes the music forward and to higher levels.

Second, Russ's speculations about "anticipatory seeing" and actually "looking" at the exact place your fingers will go to before they move there is revealing to me as a teacher in several ways. As a result of my participation here, I've come to accept that the differing ways that musicians talk about visualizing is probably not a difference in terminology or jargon but rather a difference in their experience. I see that I now have to revise and clarify my way of describing a technique or process to a student: I cannot assume that a student will "see" what I "see," even if we both agree we are seeing the same thing. I can confirm specifically that when I am learning very tricky ornamental figures (as in Baroque and contemporary music) I first, before I play anything, hear them internally. Then, when I start to play, I begin by looking in reality at my fingers on the fingerboard, as if I am videotaping where they go; during that playing I listen for the desired connection and result. Eventually I can execute almost any passage with my eyes closed and my focus guided by an internal experience. Shearer accepted the necessity of "occasionally glancing" at the fingerboard to confirm our "visualization," but Shearer stressed to his students the importance of playing internally, with utter clarity in our own minds, without the need to rely on looking at the fingerboard. I still think Shearer is correct about that, but I have revised my thinking on how I describe visualization and what I actually ask my students to do. I now accept that students initially may have actually to look at their left hand while they play, and that as more highly automated and skilled playing develops, they will rely less and less on actually looking at their hands.

Third, I endorse the importance of the distinction between the doing of playing versus the letting it happen. It is hard to describe this difference, but performing musicians can tell the difference in a few seconds. Many musicians, including me, believe that performance anxiety is the result of "doing too much stuff" rather than "letting it happen." I have learned through many experiments and hundreds of concerts to focus willfully on things that will yield the most "letting it happen," for example, hearing the music in my head the way I would like to play it, grouping lines and shapes clearly and fluently, "grooving" – setting a rhythmic continuity that puts me in the "sweet spot" – and so on.

Fourth, I had never thought before about the possibility, as Russ suggests, that my thousands of hours of guitar practice might impact my inner experience *away* from the guitar – that the multiple, seemingly autonomous happenings in my experience while I clean up dishes or walk the dog might be the result of willful multiple focusing while playing the guitar (or vice versa). It seems reasonable, if a little weird.

15

Unsymbolized Thinking

WITH SARAH A. AKHTER

We have seen in previous chapters (bulimia in Chapter 2, Tourette's Syndrome in Chapter 6, a virtuoso in Chapter 14) that people, including scientists, are often dramatically unaware of salient (hay in the haystack) features of their experience. Against the argument that this blindness is characteristic only of special populations, in the present chapter and the next I present features of inner experience that are extremely common across ordinary people and yet are often unknown to the people themselves and to science. The present chapter discusses unsymbolized thinking; Chapter 16 discusses sensory awareness.

I believe that anyone who attends with adequate care to everyday experience as it is actually lived moment by moment will frequently come across experiences such as these:

> Abigail is wondering whether Julio (her friend who will be giving her a ride that afternoon) will be driving his car or his pickup truck. This wondering is an explicit, unambiguous, "thoughty" phenomenon: It is a thought, not a feeling or an intimation; it is about Julio, and not any other person; and it intends the distinction between Julio's car and truck, not his van or motorcycle, and not any other distinction. But there are no words that carry any of these features – no word "Julio," no "car," no "truck," no "driving." Further, there are no images (visual or otherwise) experienced along with this thought – no image of Julio, or of his car, or of his truck. In fact, there are no experienced symbols whatsoever – Abigail simply apprehends herself to be wondering this and can provide no further description of how this wondering takes place.

> Benito is watching two men carry a load of bricks on a construction site. He is wondering whether the men will drop the bricks. This wondering

Revised with permission from Hurlburt, R. T., & Akhter, S. A. (2008). Unsymbolized thinking. *Consciousness and Cognition*, 17, 1364–1374.

does not involve any symbols, but it is understood to be an explicit cognitive process (Heavey & Hurlburt, 2008).

Charlene is planning her introductory statistics lecture, deciding whether to use the U.S. Census Bureau data or the made-up data that she had used in class last semester. She is deciding between precisely those two data sets and is actively trading off the real-world significance of the Census Bureau data (a desirable feature) against the fact that it might take too long to describe in class. Despite the specificity and detail of this experience, there are no words, images, or other symbols involved in this experience.

Dorothy is tiredly walking down the hall dragging her feet noisily on the carpet. She is thinking, if put into words, something quite like, "Pick up your feet – it sounds like an old lady." However, there are no words, images, or other symbols experienced in that thinking. Despite the lack of words, the sense of the thought is very explicit: "Pick up your feet" is a more accurate rendition of the experienced thought than would be "I should pick up my feet"; and "it sounds like an old lady" is more accurate than "I sound like an old lady" (Seibert, 2009).

Those four examples have some features in common, with each other and with thousands of other examples of inner experience from hundreds of people that my colleagues and I have examined over the past thirty years: Each is the experience of an explicit, differentiated thought that does not include the experience of words, images, or any other symbols. I have called such phenomena unsymbolized thinking (Hurlburt, 1990, 1993a, 1997; Hurlburt & Heavey, 2001, 2002, 2006); this chapter seeks to describe those phenomena: how they present themselves, their manner of appearing, and so on.

Heavey and Hurlburt (2008; Hurlburt & Heavey, 2002) showed that unsymbolized thinking is a feature of roughly one quarter of all moments of waking experience, and is thus one of the five most common features of everyday inner experience (the other four: inner speech, inner seeing, feelings, and sensory awareness). Despite its high frequency of occurrence across many individuals, and despite (or perhaps because of) its potentially substantial theoretical importance, many people, including many professional students of consciousness, believe that a thinking experience that does not involve symbols is impossible; in fact, such phenomena are rarely discussed.

THE APPEARANCE OF UNSYMBOLIZED THINKING

The Abigail, Benito, Charlene, and Dorothy examples are typical products of investigations using the DES procedure. Here is a typical example of the manner in which unsymbolized thinking appears in a DES interview. This verbatim transcript is from a second-sampling-day interview conducted with "Evelyn" by Sharon Jones-Forrester:

EVELYN: I was sitting on the couch watching TV. On the TV there was a commercial for NetZero. And I was listening to the commercial for NetZero, and thinking about, I wonder how much cheaper that is than Cox Cable? [1] And the pager went off. So it ... So as far as I can determine, in my awareness I was holding my coffee mug and y'know kinda wondering to myself, I wonder if Cox ... how much cheaper this NetZero *could be* than Cox Cable. [2] And the pager went off.

SHARON: And is that, "I wonder how much cheaper this NetZero is than cable," is that in your awareness just right at that moment?

E: Um hmm.

S: And is that in words? Or not in words? Or are you saying that? Or thinking that?

E: I was just thinking to myself, I wonder, y'know, if this is actually cheaper [3].

S: And does that "I wonder if that is actually cheaper" ... So it's possible to be thinking that in words or not in words, or in pictures, or in ... How is that thinking coming to you right at that moment?

E: [Looking powerless: palms turning slightly up, eyebrows raised, voice uncertain] I think just ... just *thinking* about it. Not thinking in pictures or ... Just thinking to myself, I wonder if it's really that much cheaper? [4] Because I keep getting bombarded with commercials for it.

S: And, uh, you're holding the mug.

E: Um hmm.

S: Is that in your awareness or is that just kind of a fact of the universe: You're holding it but you're not paying any attention to holding it?

E: I always pay attention to that mug, because it's crystal, and I usually use it only on the weekends, and I like the way it feels – it's real heavy.[1]

S: And so right at this split second, are you noticing the heaviness or the feel or the ...?

E: [returns to the powerless tone of expression] It seems like just the thinking of the Cox Cable versus NetZero [5?] is what's ... what I was actually aware of.

This is a typical early encounter with unsymbolized thinking by a DES subject. First, note that she gives four (five if one counts the final summary) different accounts of her experience, indicated by bracketed numbers in the transcript and restated here for comparison:

1. I wonder how much cheaper that is than Cox Cable?
2. I wonder if Cox ... how much cheaper this NetZero *could be* than Cox Cable.
3. I wonder, y'know, if this is actually cheaper.

---

[1] This comment by Evelyn ("I always pay attention ...") is a "faux generalization" (Chapter 3). Evelyn's statement is not likely to be true, and is largely ignored by the DES process (Chapter 12).

4. I wonder if it's really that much cheaper?
5. Thinking of . . . Cox Cable versus NetZero.

The meaning stays the same across all those statements, but the words used to describe that meaning change somewhat in each expression. By contrast, DES subjects who are describing experiences that are in words (inner speech, for example) quickly learn to be quite confident about the exact words, and their reports of those exact words typically stay much more consistent.

Second, note that Evelyn appears helpless, powerless in the face of her own observation of her experience. Her expression conveys something like the following: I know this sounds weird, and I don't think it's really possible, but you asked me to tell you exactly what is in my experience and this is it. Sorry it doesn't conform to your expectations, but this is what I was thinking.

Third, note that although Sharon gives Evelyn ample opportunity to provide less controversial descriptions of her experience – that it was in words, or in pictures, or that she was experiencing the weight of the mug rather than this weird thought – Evelyn sticks to her description.

Fourth, note that Evelyn uses the phrase "I wonder" to introduce her unsymbolized thought. That is a frequently used term to describe unsymbolized thinking (compare the Abigail and Benito examples earlier). However, many experiences called "wonderings" are not unsymbolized, instead being experienced as involving inner speech or images. Furthermore, many experiences called by terms other than "wondering" (such as "thinking" and "knowing") are unsymbolized experiences (compare the Charlene and Dorothy examples earlier). Thus, Evelyn's use of the term "wonder" is an important clue in discovering that her experience is unsymbolized thinking, but it is only a clue, not a rule.

Sometimes, as here, unsymbolized thinking is the only or main feature of inner experience. At other times, however, unsymbolized thinking is a part of a more complex inner experience that may include other simultaneous instances of unsymbolized thinking, inner speech, inner seeing, feelings, or other kinds of experience. For instance, recall the example in which Dorothy was thinking in an unsymbolized way that her foot dragging sounds like an old lady. At the same moment, she was also thinking in an unsymbolized way that she should throw her dirty clothes in the pile. Those two quite disparate thoughts were experienced to be ongoing simultaneously.

UNSYMBOLIZED THINKING: THE PHENOMENON

As we saw in the examples, unsymbolized thinking is the experience of an explicit, differentiated thought that does not include the experience of words, images, or any other symbols. We turn now to discuss each of the parts of that description.

First, unsymbolized thinking is its own distinct phenomenon – it is not a precursor to some other phenomenon; it is not a part of some other phenomenon; it is not incomplete, unfinished, vague, deficient, implied, or in any other phenomenal way subsidiary to any other phenomenon. Unsymbolized thinking exists in and of itself as a phenomenon, just as inner speaking exists in and of itself as a phenomenon.

Second, unsymbolized thinking is way of *experiencing*, an aspect of a person's phenomenology. It is directly observable, appears directly before the footlights of consciousness, is directly apprehended. It does not need to be inferred or deduced. Evelyn is directly experiencing wondering about Cox Cable versus NetZero, and she clearly distinguishes between that in-awareness experience and processes that are ongoing outside of awareness (holding the mug; the mug's characteristics or significance). Abigail's unsymbolized wondering whether Julio would drive the truck was just as phenomenally present to Abigail as a visual image of Julio's truck would have been had Abigail been seeing such an image (which she wasn't). Benito's unsymbolized wondering whether the workers will drop the bricks was just as phenomenally present to Benito as the words "I wonder whether those guys will drop the bricks?" would have been had Benito been saying those words to himself in inner speech (which he wasn't). Thus, unsymbolized thinking is simply a way of experiencing. There may or may not be some cognitive or organizational process that lies behind the experience, or that causes the experience, or that is caused by the experience; I take no position on that. The term "unsymbolized thinking" refers to the way of experiencing itself and not to any entity or process that may be part of some theoretical explanation.

Third, unsymbolized thinking is experienced to be a *thinking*, not a feeling, not an intention, not an intimation, not a kinesthetic event, not a bodily event. Dorothy is *thinking* about not dragging her feet, and differentiates that thinking confidently from the emotional feeling of tired and old and from the hearing of her feet *scruff-scruff-scruffing* against the carpet. Most people, like Dorothy, confidently discriminate between experiences that are thoughts (using terms such as "mental" or "cognitive") and experiences that are feelings (using terms such as "emotional" or "affective") or sensory awarenesses. The distinction between thoughts and feelings or sensory awarenesses is typically unshakeable in people who are paying careful attention to moments of their experience, and unsymbolized thinking is unwaveringly apprehended as a thought.

Fourth, the content of unsymbolized thinking is *explicit*: The "about what" of the thought is plainly apprehended. Charlene is thinking about a particular census data set and no other; Evelyn is comparing NetZero and Cox Cable and is not thinking about DSL, Earthlink, or any other Internet service provider. That it is about NetZero is doubtless driven by the ongoing

TV commercial, but the commercial is *not* about Cox Cable – that is Evelyn's invention. Furthermore, Evelyn is wondering which is *cheaper*, not which is faster, better, easier to install, more reliable, or any other alternative. That is, this experience is an explicit and differentiated thought.

Fifth, unsymbolized thinking is *differentiated*: The "what about it" is not general or vague. Abigail's thought is concretely and specifically about whether Julio will be driving his car or his truck this afternoon. It is not about whether she likes Julio or about Julio's driving habits; it is about this particular car and that particular truck from the standpoint of whether Julio will be driving them today, not about cars in general or trucks in general, not even about that partic-ular car from some other perspective (not about whether she likes Chevrolets, not about the dent in the door of Julio's Chevrolet), not about yesterday or tomorrow. Taken together, the explicit and differentiated characteristics imply that the thought's sense is quite clearly articulated – there is nothing "hunchy," "hinty," "implied," or "merely suggested" about it.

Sixth, the content of an unsymbolized thought is directly in experience. It is *not* the case that merely the "title" of the thought is experienced and the rest of the thought is subconscious; the unsymbolized thought presents itself directly. The unsymbolized thought is *not* merely a precursor of some sym-bolic (worded or imaged) thinking that is not yet sufficiently conscious for the subject. The unsymbolized thought is itself directly experienced.

Seventh, an unsymbolized thought typically presents itself all at once; there is no rhythm or cadence; no unfolding or sequentiality. The unsymbol-ized thought presents itself as a unit. Further, there is no temporal, spatial, grammatical, or otherwise formal separation between what we called earlier the *explicit* and the *differentiated* characteristics of unsymbolized thinking. The distinction between *explicit* and the *differentiated* is roughly the same as the distinction between the subject and the predicate of a sentence. Just as a com-plete sentence contains a subject (the about what) and a predicate (the what about it), the typical unsymbolized thought can be said to have those charac-teristics. However, those characteristics are not separated from each other as they are in a sentence, not separated temporally (as they would be in a spoken sentence) or spatially (as they would be in a printed sentence). For example, had Benito said to himself in inner speech, "I wonder whether those guys will drop the bricks?" he would have understood himself to be mentioning the guys (the subject) *before* he mentioned the dropping (the predicate). By con-trast, Benito's unsymbolized thought is not first about the guys and then about their dropping; it is inseparably a wondering about the guys/bricks/dropping.

Eighth, unsymbolized thinking *does not include the experience of words, images, or any other symbols*. Charlene does not experience the word "Census Bureau," "data," or "too long." That is, she does not experience herself to be (innerly or outerly) *saying* any of those words, (innerly or outerly) *hearing* any of those words, (innerly or outerly) *seeing* any of those words, or (innerly or outerly) experiencing those words in any other modality. Inner speaking, inner hearing, and inner seeing of words are more or less common ways of experiencing words, and Charlene herself might have such worded experiences at other moments; but at this particular moment, none of those experiences is present to her. Similarly, at that moment Charlene is not experiencing any (inner or outer) seeing of the Census Bureau's data or her own. Instead, Charlene knows, as facts of the universe, that the Census Bureau data set has four columns and her own has two, but no representation of that knowledge is directly apprehended by Charlene at that particular moment.

DISCOVERING THE PHENOMENA OF LIVED EXPERIENCE

Most phenomenological studies start with a targeted concept and seek exemplary lived experiences that can then be examined to discover the phenomenological details of the target. Giorgi (1975), for example, started with the concept of learning as his target; he then asked a series of subjects to describe lived experiences that involved learning with the aim of filling in the phenomenological details of learning. Petitmengin (1999) started with the concept of intuition; she then asked a series of subjects to describe lived experiences that involved intuition. Waddell (2007) started with the concept of the inner voice experience; she then asked a series of subjects to describe lived experiences that involved the hearing of inner voices.

By contrast, the phenomenon of unsymbolized thinking is one of the main features that *emerge* when one starts with *no targeted concept* and carefully asks subjects to describe randomly selected everyday lived experiences, whatever those experiences happen to be. Unsymbolized thinking is thus the end result of an open-beginninged (Chapter 10) phenomenological investigation of pristine or "free-range" lived experience, not the starting point. "Unsymbolized thinking" is the name we apply to a set of frequently occurring phenomena. Our interest in unsymbolized thinking is the result of the frequently occurring nature of the phenomena, not the result of any a priori (theoretical or otherwise) interest.

WHAT UNSYMBOLIZED THINKING IS NOT

When I describe unsymbolized thinking to colleagues unfamiliar with the topic, they frequently jump to incorrect conclusions about the nature of the phenomenon. To forestall that in the reader, here are a few remarks about what unsymbolized thinking is not.

To say that unsymbolized thinking exists as a form of experience is not to make a claim about the nature of thinking. The existence of unsymbolized thinking implies no position whatever about whether words such as

"Julio," "car," or "truck" or images thereof do or do not somehow exist outside Abigail's experience ("too faintly to be apprehended," "unconsciously," "structurally," or the like). That Abigail is experiencing unsymbolized thinking implies no position whatever about Abigail's basic, underlying cognition or about the structure of her consciousness. Unsymbolized thinking is a feature or a phenomenon, something that can be directly observable in consciousness. Interpreting that phenomenon, speculating about its causes or effects, or integrating it into some theory of consciousness are entirely different matters from our aim of simply describing the phenomenon and its manner of appearing.

Unsymbolized thinking is not merely a fleeting thought (Robinson, 2005). Unsymbolized thinkings *can be* fleeting, but typically they are experienced as lasting about as long as other kinds of thinking experiences. Sometimes, in distinct contradistinction to fleetingness, unsymbolized thinkings are experienced as lasting for minutes or hours non-stop (in some very depressed individuals; Hurlburt, 1993a).

An unsymbolized thought is not a hunch, a presentiment, or any other merely not-well-formed thought; it is typically a complete, explicit thought. It is not merely an emotion; it is understood as a thought, not a feeling. It is not a bodily inclination – a "leaning toward," a "physical readiness," or the like; it is a thinking, typically experienced as being in the head, not in the body.

Unsymbolized thinking is not merely a tip of the tongue phenomenon or other accompaniment to occurrent beliefs and desires (Robinson, 2005). Unsymbolized thinking is its own phenomenon, not dependent on any other phenomenon.

Unsymbolized thinking is not merely a feeling of familiarity or rightness – that is, it is more than the non-sensory experiences described by Mangan (2001).

An unsymbolized thought is not merely an aspect of a more complete phenomenon, in, for example, the same way redness is an aspect of an apple whose other aspects include weight, motion, and so on (Horgan & Tienson, 2002). An unsymbolized thought is the entire phenomenon.

Unsymbolized thinking is not merely the "understanding experience" (Strawson, 1994; Pitt, 2004) that lies behind some verbalization; it is the experienced thinking itself. For example, Strawson correctly observed that the understanding experience of the English sentence "Empedocles leaped" is quite different from the understanding experience of the German sentence "Empedocles liebt" ("Empedocles loves"), even though the two sentences are phonologically identical. Some might be led to think that what makes those two phonologically identical utterances distinctly different from each other is the presence of two different unsymbolized thinkings. That is not correct.

I have no position on what distinguishes one understanding experience from another, but it is not unsymbolized thinking: An unsymbolized thought is its own complete experience; it is not a process adjunctive to or interpretive of a verbalization.

Unsymbolized thinking is not the pure thought, pure intention, pure intuitive insight, or a state cultivated by serious practitioners of some contemplative traditions. I have no reason to believe that our subjects who experience unsymbolized thinking frequently are any more or less enlightened than our other subjects.

INDIVIDUAL DIFFERENCES IN THE FREQUENCY OF UNSYMBOLIZED THINKING

We have observed that unsymbolized thinking is frequent, occurring in roughly a quarter of all everyday lived experiences. However, there are large individual differences in the frequency of unsymbolized thinking. Heavey and Hurlburt (2008) stratified large introductory psychology classes on a measure of psychological distress (the SCL-90-R; Derogatis, 1994) and randomly selected thirty individuals. This sample therefore was quite representative of the entering students in a large U.S. state university. They then applied the DES technique to each. Unsymbolized thinking occurred in 22 percent of all sampled experiences. However, within subjects the frequency of unsymbolized thinking ranged from 0 percent to 80 percent; eight of the thirty subjects had no unsymbolized thinking in any of their samples. The median frequency of unsymbolized thinking across subjects was 25 percent, but more than 25 percent of subjects (eight of thirty) had no unsymbolized thinking at all. So although unsymbolized thinking is very common, it is not omnipresent.

IMPEDIMENTS TO THE RECOGNITION OF UNSYMBOLIZED THINKING

I claim that unsymbolized thinking is a robust phenomenon, identifiable by anyone who might genuinely submit to the constraints imposed by the investigation of inner experience. One particularly important constraint, which perhaps has prevented most investigators from discovering the phenomenon, is the failure to bracket the presupposition that all thinking is in words, as I will discuss in detail. But before I turn to that discussion, I describe a second constraint that makes the recognition of unsymbolized thinking somewhat delicate.

Constraint: Carefully disambiguate the usage of "feeling" (a corollary of Chapter 2's constraint, *Remove ambiguities*). Despite the fact that subjects apprehend unsymbolized thinking to be a thought, not a feeling, early in sampling subjects typically waver between using the terms "thought" and "feeling" to describe this phenomenon. That can lead to the mistaken impression that unsymbolized thinking is "on the border" between cognition and affect, but that is simply not the case. Instead, the difficulty comes from the fact that the word "feeling" is often used in two completely different ways, and that can confuse both the subject and the investigator.

"Feeling" sometimes (usually, in fact) refers to an affective or emotional experience, which unsymbolized thinking clearly is *not*. However, the word "feeling" also is used in a non-emotional way, to refer to a consciousness of an inward impression or state of mind, which unsymbolized thinking clearly *is*. DES subjects in their first few sampling days often struggle in the reporting of wordless experiences that they themselves believe to be impossible; those subjects are reluctant to use the word "thinking" and use instead the word "feeling" in the second sense. The practiced DES investigator can easily spot the distress that those subjects face as they struggle to find words to express this phenomenon. Subjects have to be helped to understand the words that they themselves use. Once they learn to make the distinctions necessary, reporting generally becomes easier.

Such an interchange may provide fertile breeding ground for leading the witness, for influencing the subject in the direction of unsymbolized thinking. The skilled DES practitioner must be aware of that possibility and bracket it away.

It should also be noted that some DES subjects are quite comfortable in reporting unsymbolized phenomena – they apparently don't share the thought-must-be-in-words presupposition. For those subjects, there is therefore no particular opportunity for leading the witness.

HISTORICAL COMMENT: THE PHENOMENON BEHIND IMAGELESS THOUGHT

The unsymbolized thinking phenomenon appears to be the same phenomenon that led to the imageless-thought controversy in classical introspection a century ago. Because that imageless-thought controversy was a major contributor to the demise of introspection, we need to understand what is the same and what is different about unsymbolized thinking and imageless thought.

First, the term unsymbolized thinking refers to a phenomenon, something that can be directly apprehended by the person, something that can appear directly before the footlights of consciousness. By contrast, imageless thought was purported by the classical introspectionists (primarily at Würzburg) to be an element of the thinking process. However, the introspectionists at Cornell, led by Titchener, disagreed and believed that the imageless-thought element did not exist – that well-trained introspectionist subjects could always find at

least a faint imaginal element if they looked hard enough. The classical introspectionists spent several decades trying unsuccessfully to resolve that disagreement; their failure to agree about imageless thought is often cited as one
of the major factors in the demise of introspection (there were other factors as
well, see Danziger, 1980).

It is important to note that the disagreement about imageless thought
was about the existence of an *element* of thought, not about the existence of a
phenomenon of thought. That distinction is important. Monson and Hurlburt
(1993) reviewed the introspections that had been performed at Würzburg and
at Cornell and concluded that "*for the most part, introspecting subjects did in
fact agree with each other's reports of the phenomenon which was called imageless thought.* It was only the *interpretation* of these observations, rather than
the observations themselves, which differed from one laboratory to the next"
(Monson & Hurlburt, 1993, p. 20).

Thus Monson and Hurlburt believe that both the Cornell and the
Würzburg investigators observed the same phenomenon that we call unsymbolized thinking (but the Cornell and Würzburg investigators disagreed
strenuously about the interpretation of that phenomenon). Thus the classical
introspections should be seen as *support* for the existence of unsymbolized
thinking *as a phenomenon*. Titchener, to be sure, would deny the existence
of genuine unsymbolized thinking – would probably say that had we pressed
Abigail, Benito, Charlene, Dorothy, and Evelyn harder, they would have found
exquisitely faint but nonetheless existing images. As the history of classical
introspection shows, however, distinguishing the exquisitely faint from the
nonexistent is difficult if not impossible to do (Hurlburt & Schwitzgebel, 2007,
chapter 11; 2011a), so DES declines to try to do it.

MODERN THEORISTS' DESCRIPTIONS
OF UNSYMBOLIZED THINKING

A few, but not many, modern theorists have described phenomena quite similar to unsymbolized thinking. Siewert (1998), for example, describes "noniconic thinking: ... instances in which a thought occurs to you, when not only
do you not image what you think or are thinking of, but you also do not ver-
balize your thought, either silently or aloud, nor are you then understanding
someone else's words" (p. 276). Most of Siewert's examples of noniconic thinking are fairly simple, sudden events. However, he does allow that they can be
complex:

> Walking from my table in a restaurant to pay the bill, I was struck briefly
> by a thought, gone by the time I reached the cashier, about my preoccu-
> pations with this book's topic, the effects of this, and its similarity to other
> preoccupations and their effects. Asked to state more precisely what this

was, I would have to say something like: "My preoccupation with the topic of my book has made the world seem especially alive with examples of it, references to it, so that it can't help but seem to me that the world is more populated with things relevant to it than previously. And it struck me that this is similar to the way in which new parenthood made the world seem to me burgeoning with babies, parents, the paraphernalia of infancy, and talk and pictures of these." Somehow this thought of my philosophical preoccupations and parenthood, and an analogy between their effects, rather complex to articulate, occurred in a couple of moments while I approached the cashier, in the absence of any utterance. (Siewert, 1998, p. 277)

This description of Siewert's noniconic thought is a good description of what we are calling unsymbolized thinking. Such examples are rare in the consciousness science literature, and they are often dismissed. Here, for example, is Robinson's (2005) view of Siewert's restaurant-bill example:

My own introspection leads me to believe that I have had experiences of the kind that Siewert means to be *indicating*; I am denying only that the proffered phenomenological account matches anything in my experience. What then is my positive account of what happens on such occasions? What I believe occurs is a few words in subvocal speech (we might call them "key words"), perhaps a rather vague sense of a diagrammatic sketch, and perhaps some pictorial or kinesthetic imagery. There is also usually a feeling of satisfaction, something I might express by saying I'd thought of something particularly interesting. (Robinson, 2005, 553–554)

Robinson's dismissal of the unsymbolized significance of Siewert's noniconic thinking follows a pattern similar to that used by Titchener against the Würzburgers: The implication is that had Siewert looked harder, he would have found "a few words in subvocal speech … and perhaps some pictorial … imagery." Robinson might be right; however, I think it more likely that Robinson is captured by the all-thinking-is-in-words presupposition, to which we will return.

Horgan and Tienson (2002) and Pitt (2004) are often lumped with Siewert (1998) as supporting the existence of non-symbolic thinking. That is correct, but it is worth emphasizing that whereas Siewert's noniconic thinking does, as we have seen, include the phenomenon that we have called unsymbolized thinking, the topics addressed by Horgan and Tienson and by Pitt do not. For example, Pitt (2004) addresses the distinct change in phenomenology between "buffalo buffalo buffalo buffalo buffalo buffalo buffalo" before it is understood and after its meaning has been comprehended: "the change consists in the presence of cognitive phenomenology: it is the difference made by *thinking*" (Pitt, 2004, p. 28). Pitt's point is that that cognitive phenomenology is not symbolic, and I agree with that. However, that cognitive phenomenology is not unsymbolized thinking, either. Pitt's cognitive phenomenology is a companion to, a feature of, or a conditioning of a verbal process, whereas unsymbolized thinking is its own separate phenomenon, not linked to or subjugated to or ancillary to some other phenomenon. Thus Siewert is perhaps the only modern theorist not associated with DES to describe the phenomenon of unsymbolized thinking.

ON THE PRESUPPOSITION THAT ALL THINKING IS IN WORDS

We have seen that DES studies show unsymbolized thinking to be a robust, frequently occurring phenomenon; and we have observed that despite its ubiquity, unsymbolized thinking is largely overlooked by consciousness studies. It is beyond the scope of this chapter to discuss thoroughly the historical and social-psychological reasons for this overlooking, but we have discussed two of those reasons in previous sections: the impediments to the observation of unsymbolized thinking and the classical introspection–imageless thought debacle. We turn now to a third important reason that unsymbolized thinking is overlooked: the widely held presupposition that all thinking is in words. For example:

> When we introspect our own conscious propositional thoughts, we have access to thoughts expressed in natural language sentences; in other words, we find ourselves engaged in inner speech. This introspective fact is treated as evidence that we do think consciously in a natural language. (Machery, 2005, p. 470)

> Human beings talk to themselves every moment of the waking day. (Baars 2003, p. 106)

> The behaviorist makes no mystery of thinking. He holds that thinking is behavior, is motor organization, just like tennis playing or golf or any other form of muscular activity. But what kind of muscular activity? The muscular activity that he uses in talking. Thinking is merely talking, but talking with concealed musculature.[2] (Watson, in Watson & MacDougall, 1929, p. 33)

---

[2] This quotation is something of an oversimplification of Watson's position; I include it because it is commonly held to be Watson's view. However, a few pages after this widely influential "thinking is merely talking" conclusion, Watson softened this conclusion substantially: "Now a further question comes up for serious consideration: Do we think only in terms of words? I take the position to-day that whenever the individual is thinking, the whole of his bodily organization is at work (implicitly) – even though the final solution shall be a spoken, written or subvocally expressed verbal formulation. In other words, from the moment the thinking problem is set for the individual (by the situation he is in) activity is aroused that may lead finally to adjustment. Sometimes the activity goes on (1) in terms of implicit manual organization; (2) more frequently in terms of implicit verbal organization; (3) sometimes in terms of implicit (or even overt) visceral organization. If (1) or (3) dominates, thinking takes place without words." (Watson, in Watson & McDougall, 1929, p. 34–35.)

> I have accepted Fodor's view that propositional attitudes (beliefs, desires, and so on) are best understood as relations to sentences. The question then is: which sentences? ... I shall present an intuitive, introspection-based, argument for the view that human conscious thinking involves sentences of natural language. (Carruthers, 1996, p. 40)

There are many others that could be cited just as well; the presupposition is extremely widespread.

ON CARRUTHERS'S DISMISSAL OF UNSYMBOLIZED THINKING

In supporting his view that all thinking is in words, Carruthers (1996) considers Hurlburt's reports (1990, 1993a) of unsymbolized thinking and specifically denies the existence of the unsymbolized-thinking phenomenon. Carruthers's argument proceeds as follows. He grants that people often have thoughts that do not involve images or words, but he denies that those thoughts are conscious. When DES subjects report the existence of a conscious non-image, non-worded (that is, unsymbolized) thought, Carruthers believes those subjects are making (probably unknowingly) a swift self-interpretation about their thinking and then are confusing that self-interpretation for a direct observation of phenomena.

To support that notion, Carruthers observes that the subjects in the experiments reviewed by Nisbett and Wilson (1977) make similar mistaken swift inferences. For example:

> When asked to select from a range of identical items, people show a marked preference for items on the right-hand side of the array; but the explanations of their own choices never advert to position, but rather mention superior quality, appearance, and so on. ... The best explanation ... (and the explanation offered by Nisbett and Wilson) is that subjects in such cases lack any form of conscious access to their true thought-processes. Rather, lacking immediate access to their reasons, they engage in a swift bit of retrospective self-interpretation, attributing to themselves the thoughts and feelings which they think they *should* have in the circumstances, or in such a way as to make sense of their own behaviour. (Carruthers, 1996, p. 240)

Carruthers maintains that DES subjects who report unsymbolized thinking make the same kind of mistaken self-interpretation. He examines an example of unsymbolized thinking from Hurlburt (1993a), where at the moment of the beep "Diane" was in the supermarket looking at a box of breakfast cereal.

> She reported that she was wondering – wordlessly – whether to buy the box; and that she was thinking – again wordlessly – that she did not normally eat breakfast, and that the cereal might therefore

be wasted; and that she was also considering the expense involved. (Carruthers, 1996, p. 242)

Carruthers's interpretation is that Diane was *not* observing her thought (unsymbolized or otherwise); instead, she apparently did not have access to any conscious content and therefore was (in a Nisbett-and-Wilson sort of way) attributing to herself thoughts that might naturally be assumed to be ongoing:

> For these are just the thoughts which an observer might naturally attribute to her, who knew what she knew: namely, that she was attending to the price-label on a cereal packet; that she did not normally eat breakfast; and that she was generally careful in matters of expense. (Carruthers, 1996, p. 242)

To the fact that subjects *feel as if* they are reporting an observed thought, Carruthers explains that "when people engage in self-interpretation, this will often take place extremely swiftly, and without self-awareness of what they are doing" (Carruthers, 1996, p. 242).

I acknowledge that it is possible that Carruthers is correct. However, if so, his same arguments might be leveled against *all* introspective reports: of inner speech, of images, and so on. People do not really experience speaking to themselves, he might say; they merely think that it would be *natural* to be speaking to themselves and swiftly mistake that self-interpretation for an introspective observation.

Indeed, that argument seems much *more* compelling as a skeptical view of inner speech and images than of unsymbolized thinking because of the distress some subjects initially experience when reporting unsymbolized thinking (discussed in the section called Impediments to the Recognition of Unsymbolized Thinking; compare the Evelyn example earlier). Carruthers's argument is that subjects give plausible self-interpretations instead of accurate self-observations. Why would subjects, when searching swiftly for a plausible self-interpretation, hit upon unsymbolized thinking, a phenomenon that they themselves (presuppositionally) may believe to be not merely implausible but unquestionably impossible?

DES investigators observe time and time again that DES subjects early in their training give "introspective reports" of inner speech. Subsequent iterations of the method lead to the conclusion that those early reports were erroneous for just the kinds of plausible self-interpretation reasons Carruthers suggests (Hurlburt & Schwitzgebel, 2007): The experience those subjects were trying to describe was not inner speech, but in a self-interpretative way those subjects invoked inner speech as a plausible explanation of the phenomenon (which is likely unsymbolized thinking, sensory awareness, or some other somewhat complex experience). That is quite natural. Inner speech is a well-accepted (in fact, I think overly emphasized), uncontroversial form of inner experience, and it is not surprising that inner speech is mistakenly invoked by unskilled subjects as an explanation of a difficult or controversial phenomenon.

It is thus easy to imagine a person giving an inner-speech explanation for an unsymbolized experience, but it is not at all easy to imagine a person giving an unsymbolized-thinking explanation for a verbal (or absent) experience. If there were in fact no unsymbolized phenomenon, it would have been easy for Diane, for example, to provide some not-held-to-be-impossible self-interpretation; for example, she could have emphasized her feelings of unease about spending that much money for cereal. That appeal to feelings would have been an equally plausible self-interpretation and would not have caused the all-thinking-is-in-words presupposition distress. Why would Diane advance an obviously (to her) impossible explanation if easier explanations are available? The same applies to Evelyn. If there were no direct but unsymbolized phenomenal presentation of NetZero and Cox Cable, why would she consistently aver that there was, even in the face of some distress? I think she sticks to her story because easier explanations are *not* available: She is forced to give an obviously impossible unsymbolized-thinking explanation because the phenomenon drives her to it.

Unsymbolized thinking is *not*, as Carruthers seems to believe, the absence of a phenomenon. Subjects (as for example Evelyn, Diane, Abigail, Benito, Charlene, and Dorothy) directly experience themselves to be thinking. They do not merely infer themselves to be thinking. There is an absence of words, and there is an absence of images, but there is *not* an absence of thinking phenomena. There is a phenomenal presence of thinking, difficult as that might be for many subjects themselves (as well as many consciousness scientists) to believe. When there is a phenomenal *absence* of thinking, subjects do not call that unsymbolized thinking; they merely say they weren't thinking anything.

I have argued against armchair introspection in general in Hurlburt and Schwitzgebel (2007; 2011b). Now I wish to critique the particular armchair introspection used by Carruthers. Here is his description of the armchair introspection task that leads him to the conclusion that thinking involves sentences:

> So what one needs to do, firstly, is to introspect while (or shortly after) *using* some sentence of the natural language in the course of one's daily life; and secondly, while (or shortly after) one has been entertaining privately some complete thought, or sequence of such thoughts. In the first sort of case what one discovers ... is that there is often *no* separable mental process accompanying the utterance of the sentence itself; or, at least, not one that is available to consciousness. In the second sort of case what one discovers, I believe, is that our private thoughts consist chiefly of deployments of natural language sentences in imagination – inner thinking is mostly done in inner speech. (Carruthers, 1995, p. 50, italics in original)

Carruthers's first introspection task (introspecting while using some sentence of the natural language) will of course reveal a sentence of the natural language.

(That introspection while speaking typically yields nothing else is partially but not entirely corroborated by DES, but that is not the point here.) I suspect that Carruthers's second task (introspect while entertaining a complete thought) also tilts the introspection decidedly toward the verbal. Here's why: Carruthers's second task involves a (largely unexamined) pre-introspection task: to determine whether a thought is "complete." That doubtless requires observing the stream of thoughts and making a series of decisions: *No – that's not complete … No – that's not complete … No – that's not complete … Aha! That's a complete thought – Introspect now!* That task may well have substantial impact on the subsequent introspections. I am not in a position to know for certain, but it seems likely that the pre-instrospection decision-making task is performed largely in words, and because the subjects thereby prime themselves with words, they are likely then to observe words when they introspect.

DES avoids, as much as possible, any pre-introspection task. The *Introspect now!* command is given by the external beeper, not the introspector himself or herself.

> **Q:** Even in the beep-triggered case, the introspector still has to initiate the introspection task, has to interpret that the beep means *Introspect now!*
> **A:** That is true, but such beep interpretation, by a subject who has worn the beeper for some number of sampling days and is thus quite experienced at responding to the beep, seems an order of magnitude less word-based and less intrusive/disruptive than the typical (and Carruthers's in particular) self-generated decision about when and when not to introspect.
>
> As a result, I believe that randomly cued introspection is a substantially different procedure from Carruthers's armchair introspection, and as a result, DES finds unsymbolized thinking when that phenomenon is not observed by Carruthers. Additional comments on Carruthers's critique of unsymbolized thinking can be found in Hurlburt and Schwitzgebel, 2007, chapter 11; 2011b).

DISCUSSION

The phenomenon of unsymbolized thinking seems to be robust: It has been found in every DES study since Hurlburt (1990); similar phenomena were found by the classical introspectionists a century ago (Monson & Hurlburt, 1993) and by Siewert (1998). The most consistent modern reports come from DES, but it must be acknowledged that most DES studies have been performed by Hurlburt and his colleagues, so as yet there may be some limitations on the generalizability of their conclusions. In this chapter, I have tried to describe the phenomenon of unsymbolized thinking and to maintain that unsymbolized thinking is as directly observable as is inner speech or visual imagery if an adequate method is used.

At the same time, I have tried *not* to say anything one way or the other about the existence or characteristics of any underlying or fundamental thinking process. I freely accept the possibility that at some substrate level, all thinking (including that for which unsymbolized thinking may be an accompanying phenomenon) is in words; but I just as freely accept the contrary possibility. Part of the phenomenological task is to bracket presuppositions about the nature of underlying processes, real or supposed, so that phenomena can present themselves as they are; as a result, I have not theorized about the nature of consciousness or the characteristics of underlying mental processes.

In fact, I believe that it may well be in the best interests of consciousness science for there to be a distinct division of labor: those who describe phenomena firewalled away from those who theorize about the significance of those phenomena. I have argued (Monson & Hurlburt, 1993; Hurlburt, Heavey, & Seibert, 2006) that part of the reason for the demise of introspection a century ago may have been the failure of the classical introspectors to maintain sufficient distance between the description of phenomena and the attempts at explaining phenomena. I have therefore limited myself to describing the phenomenon, and I am specifically not taking a position on whether there is or is not some kind of symbolic (worded, imaged) thinking that lies behind the unsymbolized phenomenon. Although I have not made such attempts myself, I believe that any theory of consciousness that relies at all on introspection must take the phenomenon of unsymbolized thinking seriously, must allow that thinking can be experienced without the experience of words or images.

We observed that unsymbolized thinking is not discovered by most other investigators. In my opinion, any investigation of free-range lived experience that discovers any characteristic of the form of inner experience (inner speech, inner seeing, etc.) but does not discover unsymbolized thinking must be using a method that is seriously flawed. I happily accept that I may be hugely mistaken; that my opinion is based on the work of a small number of people, mostly my close colleagues. If consciousness science is to advance, it must determine whether I'm right or mistaken. It must bring itself to examine its methods, to recognize that methods are not all equal, to sort out which methods are better than others, for what, and in what situations. The case of unsymbolized thinking should make that clear: It's an elephant in the living room. The question is whether the elephant is merely in my misguided imagination or near the center of conscious phenomena.

16

Sensory Awareness

WITH CHRIS HEAVEY AND ARVA BENSAHEB

Careful examination of pristine experience will reveal moments such as the following:

> Example 1: Andrew is dialing his cell phone. At the moment, he has just "zeroed in" on the shiny blueness of the brushed aluminum phone case. He is not, at that moment, paying attention to the number he is dialing; his experience has momentarily left that task (which continues as if on autopilot) to be absorbed in the shiny blueness.

> Example 2: Betty is in conversation with her friend Wendy, and as Wendy speaks, Betty takes a sip of Dr. Pepper. At that moment, Betty is drawn to the coldness of the liquid as it moves through her throat. Wendy continues to talk, but Wendy's voice is not part of Betty's experience; Betty is focused on the coldness in her throat.

> Example 3: Carol's friend Candy is telling Carol how to log on to a computer Web site. Carol is paying attention to the sweetly longish *a* sound in Candy's slight drawl; at that moment, Carol is not paying attention to what Candy is saying about the log-on procedure.

> Example 4: Damian is checking out at the grocery store, and at the moment is noticing a twinge in the back of his neck – a slight stabbing sensation. He is in the act of putting three candy bars on the conveyer, but at that moment he is not at all noticing candy bars, the checker's activity, or anything else in his environment – his attention is occupied by the neck sensation.

These examples represent a common phenomenon that we have found frequently in the inner experience of the hundreds of people whom we have examined over the last several decades (including Michael Kane of Chapter 6 and Ricardo Cobo of Chapter 14). Each example involves the individual's being immersed in the experience of a particular sensory aspect of his

---

Revised with permission from Hurlburt, R. T., Heavey, C. L., & Bensaheb, A. (2009). Sensory awareness. *Journal of Consciousness Studies, 16*, 231–251.

or her external or internal environment without particular regard for the instrumental aim or perceptually complete objectness. We have called such phenomena "sensory awareness" (Hurlburt, 1990, 1993a, 1997; Hurlburt & Heavey, 2001, 2002, 2006). In example 1, Andrew's momentary interest is not instrumental: He's dialing but he's attending to the shiny-blueness, not the dialing. And his momentary interest is not in the complete object: He is drawn not to the *phone*, which happens to be shiny-blue, but to the *shiny-blueness*, which happens to be of the phone.

Heavey and Hurlburt (2008; Hurlburt & Heavey, 2002) showed that sensory awareness is a feature of roughly one quarter of all apprehended moments of waking experience, and thus appears to be one of the five most common features of everyday inner experience (the other four: inner speech, inner seeing, feelings, and unsymbolized thinking). Despite the prevalence of sensory awareness, it remains little discussed within the consciousness literature.

Sensory awareness is certainly nothing new or unusual: almost everyone can notice a shiny blueness, feel the coldness of an iced drink, hear a feature of a friend's voice, or feel a muscle twitch. What is extraordinary, and what needs to be taken seriously by consciousness science, is that some people may experience such sensory awareness at nearly all their waking moments (Heavey & Hurlburt, 2008), others may experience it at almost none, and others may experience it frequently but not always.

This chapter describes not only the sensory awareness phenomenon but also its manner of appearing, a necessity because of the nature of the phenomenon. Sensory awareness becomes an interesting phenomenon only when it is explored as it naturally occurs in natural environments, as part of pristine experience. In the laboratory, it is easy to contrive situations in which subjects *always* report sensory phenomena and other situations in which subjects *never* report sensory phenomena. If individual differences are important, we will have to use a method that allows those differences to emerge and to be observant about how they emerge.

THE APPEARING OF SENSORY AWARENESS

The previous examples are typical products of DES investigations. Here is a typical example of the manner in which sensory awareness appears in a DES interview. This verbatim (but slightly edited to remove redundancies and irrelevancies) transcript is from a second-sampling-day interview conducted with "Ephraim" by Arva Bensaheb, who begins by asking Ephraim to describe his experience at the fifth beep:

EXAMPLE 5:
EPHRAIM: [laughs nervously] At the moment of the beep I'm eating clam chowder with a relatively large spoon. And at the moment of the beep

I'm pushing ... I had ... I had put the spoon [laughs sheepishly] laying on the top surface of the soup, and I was pushing down slightly, feeling the resistance of it, and then watching the soup spill over the edges really slowly, and watching [laughs sheepishly] the way that it cascaded over the edges of the spoon and filled it up. [Scratches head in apparent resignation] I'd done this quite a few times already, but it was still very fun [smiles sheepishly] – I ate the whole bowl of soup that way. But I was definitely ... the things that stuck out in my mind were the resistance of having to push the spoon down, and the way that – particularly because it's clam chowder – it's [laughs sheepishly] going over the edge: It was like you could see it, the path that it took over the edge, and how it didn't fill, like, symmetrically. Like one part would go over faster, rather than just like going in, in a slowly collapsing circle. It was more of like an amoeba shape [sighs resignedly] getting smaller. [Smiles nervously] At this point there ... I know as a fact of the universe there was music in the background, but I wasn't ... it wasn't there ... anymore.

ARVA BENSAHEB: So right at the moment of the beep you are aware of this resistance of the spoon against the soup ...

EPHRAIM: Um hm.

AB: ... and watching the soup spill into the spoon asymmetrically.

EPHRAIM: [nods affirmatively, nervously]

AB: Anything else [laughs] in your experience at the moment of the beep?

EPHRAIM: [shakes head negatively, resignedly]

AB: The music, you said, was there.

EPHRAIM: Yeah ... I know it was on, but it wasn't ... I wasn't listening to it. I was just really intent on the shape and watching the way that it moved over the spoon. [Pauses, shakes head in resigned sheepishness] That's about it.

AB: And this resistance ... Does it make sense to ask you, like, where you were feeling this resistance? Like, I don't know, if you were holding the spoon, was it in your arm, or in your hand, or ....

EPHRAIM: I felt the resistance in the end of the spoon, like the spoon part of the spoon. Like I don't even know if that makes sense, but ...

AB: The spoon meaning not the handle ...

EPHRAIM: Not in the handle, yeah ...

AB: ... the scoopy part. [laughs]

EPHRAIM: [laughs] Yes, in the scoopy part of the spoon. That's where I perceived the resistance, not in my fingers or in my hand. [Shakes head in resignation] Just kind of weird.

AB: And what is this feeling/sensation? Can you describe it any further?

EPHRAIM: Resistance. Like soft, like, I don't know, it's hard to explain, because it's like [laughs sheepishly] you have to be kind of gentle with how hard you push on the spoon, but the more ... like it builds up [laughs sheepishly]. You have to push the spoon [laughs embarrassedly] rather gently, but in order to do it gently enough the resistance actually feels pretty great, to the point where once the end of the spoon finally gets

right below the surface of the soup, you can feel it just go away, like there
was a *ton* of resistance, but [smiles sheepishly] it's probably not that much
resistance. But just the carefulness of it made it seem that way.

AB: So was there like a different degree of resistance, by any chance? I don't
know if this makes sense, but, like, at the moment of the beep, and I don't
know how much the beep caught, but it seems like there's more resistance
and then the spoon goes in and resistance is less, and … Is there a change,
or anything like that, in your experience, or is it just the initial …

EPHRAIM: Hm. [nods quizzically] I would say that what I was experiencing
was the initial resistance against it. I did just say … I guess I mentioned
… that it changes. But that isn't really at the moment of the beep. That
was just more from doing it a couple … twenty times. I learned! [Laughs
embarrassedly]

AB: And then the soup pouring into the spoon. Is that part of your
experience at the moment of the beep? Or …

EPHRAIM: Yeah.

AB: … the shape of it, or whatever?

EPHRAIM: Yeah. The shape, the way that it looked.

AB: And how is that in …?

EPHRAIM: That was more, I mean, we've focused on the resistance thing,
but the purpose of it [smiles abashedly] was so that I could see what it
would look like. Um, watching like the surface tension build up in the
edge. At the moment of the beep it was … the spoon wasn't completely
through [smiles sheepishly] the soup yet, but there was still a little bit
spilling over from the back end, and there was the residual from the last
[laughs embarrassedly] … from the last attempt that was still there. Just
watching the way that the liquid moved. [laughs resignedly]

This is in some ways a typical relatively early (second sampling day)
encounter with sensory awareness by a DES subject. Here are nine characteristics of the way this experience presents itself to Ephraim:

First, note that the sensory features are a primary focus of Ephraim's
experience: He is aimed at, drawn to, interested in the resistance of the spoon
against the soup and the shape of the pool of soup in the spoon.

Second, Ephraim's interest is in the sensory experience itself, not in the
instrumental aim that employs the sensation. That is, Ephraim is interested in
the resistance of the spoon against the soup for its own sake; he is not merely
eating soup and making the sensory observations that that task requires. The
eating-soup task is secondary or nonexistent in his experience at the moment
of this beep.

Third, note the power of the sensory interest. Ephraim is not merely *idly*
feeling the resistance and seeing the soup patterns – he is drawn directly to
the sensory interests; they grab him to the exclusion of other aspects of his
environment. There is music playing, but he doesn't hear it; there are doubtless

other people and objects in his environment, but they don't exist in his experience at the moment of the beep.

Fourth, note the precision and confidence with which Ephraim describes his experience: He perceives the resistance in the scoopy part of the spoon, not in his hand; he's interested in the shape the soup makes and the paths it takes, not (for example) its color. This is not merely a dim sensation at the edges of his experience; the sensation is not a building block for some subsequent perception; the sensation is at the center of his experience. Ephraim has no doubt about his being focused on this sensory experience at the moment of the beep, no question about whether there is a fully differentiated sensation at the center of his experience.

Fifth, note that Ephraim is quite embarrassed or sheepish about reporting sensory awareness. This embarrassment/sheepishness is quite typical of subjects who frequently report sensory awareness, especially early in their sampling. Our aim is to describe the manner of appearing of sensory awareness; here we observe that descriptions of sensory awareness are frequently accompanied (at least at the outset) by embarrassment or sheepishness. It is not our aim to explain this embarrassment, although we will permit ourselves this speculation: Sensory awareness is a direct access to what looks good, what feels good, what attracts Ephraim, and what repels him in a very elemental, basic, sensual way. Sensual interests are intensely personal, by their very nature exceedingly private. To reveal one's basic sensuality is to stand naked before the observer, and sheepishness is a natural response. Some would say that Ephraim's sheepishness may come from having been "caught" in a childish act (playing with his food), but we think the sheepishness is more elemental, arising from the experience, not the act: The sheepishness (in Ephraim and others) comes from the recognition and admission that the sensations themselves are *fun/attractive/alluring*. I emphasize that this is speculation; it is in accord with our frequent casual observations but requires further study.

Sixth, all five of the samples on this sampling day contained sensory awarenesses. However, none of the samples from the first sampling day contained sensory awareness. It is not uncommon for sensory awareness to be overlooked or avoided on the first sampling day. Whether this is the result of a presupposition that attending to some sensory detail is too trivial to count as a feature of experience, or is a corollary to the embarrassment described previously, or is the result of the punishment of talk about sensory awareness (see the Weihnachten Carousel later), or stems from some other factor remains to be explored. It does illustrate why an iterative approach to studying experience is necessary (see Chapter 10).

Seventh, we note that the embarrassment/sheepishness is a sign that Ephraim is trying to report faithfully his actual experience. It is evidence that he is not making up his experience – why would he make up something that causes distress?

Eighth, there is one aspect that makes this cited example somewhat unusual: Ephraim here is *actively creating* the situation that makes his particular sensory awareness possible. He is actively, repeatedly pressing his spoon slowly into the soup just so he can see the flow and the shape of the soup into the spoon. Most sensory awarenesses, including all the sensory awarenesses in Ephraim's other samples, are not the result of direct creation of the situation, but rather merely involve the specific noticing of the already existing (inner or outer) environment. Ephraim's other samples on this sampling day have this incidental, not actively sought, observational quality: At sample 1, Ephraim was drawn to a shininess on a particular part of a traffic policeman's vest. He had stepped outside to have a cigarette, and the shininess simply attracted him. At sample 2: Ephraim was reading the booklet from a new CD, and while he was reading he happened to be attracted to the shadow that fell diagonally across the page. At sample 3, Ephraim was waiting for a computer game to load; at the moment of the beep he was particularly observing the "8" in "68% Done," noting that the progress bar split the "8" perfectly in half. At sample 4, Ephraim was feeling the sharp edge of the Excedrin package as he opened it. In none of those examples was he manipulating the environment to observe some sensory aspect; on the contrary, it is as if the sensory aspect draws his attention unbidden.

Ninth, had this sensory observational experience not been interrupted by the beep, leading the subject to focus on it, it would likely have been forgotten, like a dream (or like a short-term memory not consolidated into long-term memory), almost immediately. If a friend were to ask him in a few minutes, "How was the soup?" Ephraim will almost certainly not recall the resistance or the flow patterns – even though that was actually what occupied most of his experience while eating the soup – and will instead respond that it tasted good.

SENSORY AWARENESS: THE PHENOMENON

As we have seen in the examples, sensory awareness is the focused, thematic experience of a particular sensory aspect of the external or internal environment without particular regard for the instrumental aim or perceptually complete objectness of that environment. To discriminate sensory awareness from non-sensory-awareness experience, here are some additional examples with brief commentary:

> Example 6: Fatima was playing a computer game. At the beep she was focused on an orange gear that was rotating on the screen, meshing with another gear that lifted the elevator up to the next level. She was paying more attention to the color and shape of the gear than to its function as the mover of the elevator.

Fatima is paying attention to a sensory, non-goal-oriented, non-instrumental aspect of the environment. The color and shape of the gear occupy Fatima's attention, not the instrumental aspect (that it moves the elevator) of the gear. Therefore this is a straightforward sensory awareness.

> Example 7: Georg was looking at the microwave clock to see what time it was. The clock read 4:28, but at the moment of the beep he was focused on the pointy shapes of the line segments that made up the numbers. The pointy appearance of these line segments, rather than the actual time, occupied his awareness.

Georg is not, at the moment of the beep, occupied with the clock as a time-telling instrument; he is occupied with the sensory aspects of the digits. Because he is focused on the sensory, not the instrumental value of his perception, this is a straightforward sensory awareness.

> Example 8: Harold wondered what time it was and looked at the digital clock, which read 8:42. Harold was interested in the time of day represented by the 8:42 display, not its color or shape.

Harold looks at the clock for its instrumental value – to determine the time of day. This is *not* a sensory awareness. Examples 7 and 8 illustrate that sensory awareness is a feature of *experience, not* a characteristic of a sensory process. Georg's and Harold's sensory processes are doubtless quite similar: The pointy line segments impact both Georg's and Harold's retinas the same way, and so on. Yet experientially (for reasons that we do not seek to explain), Georg apprehends the pointiness of the line segments whereas Harold apprehends the time represented by the line segments.

> Example 9: Irma is waiting to cross the street. She is looking at the Walk/ Don't Walk sign, which is displaying a red hand, so she doesn't cross.

There is not enough information here to know whether the red of the hand is apprehended only as a stop signal (in which case the red has instrumental, not sensory-awareness significance), or whether Irma is also interested in the red for its sensory qualities – that it is the same red as her lipstick, for example. Further questioning would be necessary.

The next examples illustrate that sensory awareness can be an aspect of inner seeing (aka seeing an image). The rules for determining whether to call an experience a sensory awareness apply equally to inner as to external seeing.

> Example 10: Juan was talking with his wife, Jill, about Jill's mother, who is ill. At the moment of the beep Juan was innerly seeing Jill's mother in the hospital bed. Juan was particularly aware of the shininess of the oxygen tube in the mother's nose – the shininess seemed to stand out against the otherwise muted inner seeing.

This illustrates that sensory awareness can occur in an inner seeing. Had Juan been attending to the life-support-ness (the instrumentality) of the imaginary oxygen tubes, this would be considered an inner seeing only; but because he is primarily drawn to the shininess, to a sensory aspect, DES would call it a sensory awareness as well as an inner seeing.

> Example 11: Kevin was talking with his wife Kelly about Kelly's mother, who is ill. At the moment of the beep Kevin was innerly seeing Kelly's mother, seeing her as he had seen her the day before in the hospital. Kevin could describe the visual details of this seeing: She was wearing a blue hospital gown; there were oxygen tubes in her nose; he clearly saw the red sore on her cheek. Kevin understands this seeing to be something like an illustration of the conversation he and Kelly were having.

This inner seeing has many sensory qualities (blue of the gown, red of the sore, etc.), but these qualities are not seen for the blueness or the redness themselves. The blueness and the redness are facts of the inner seeing, characteristics of the object being innerly seen, but they are not centrally or particularly in attention. This is *not* a sensory awareness.

> Example 12: Linda was discussing the power steering of her car with her friend Lily. At the moment of the beep Linda was innerly seeing a schematic representation of a power steering system. She saw fluid-filled tubes and pistons; the different parts were in different pastel colors, as though represented in a textbook. Although she doesn't actually know how power steering works, she was imagining how it might work.

The question here is whether the pastel-color quality of the inner seeing counts as sensory awareness, and the answer is that we don't know without further questioning. If these colors were merely incidental facts of the inner seeing, then they would not count as sensory awareness. For example, in Hurlburt and Schwitzgebel (2007), Melanie describes an inner seeing that accompanied a book she was reading. She saw a Greek woman on a road talking with a soldier. She reported that the image was quite detailed: The road went diagonally from close left to far right; there were green shrubs and lighter gray-green olive trees, and so on. In that image, the green and the gray-green were understood to be characteristics of the shrubs/trees, not particularly of interest in and of themselves, and therefore they are *not* sensory awareness. The same logic would apply to the pastel tubes and pistons. If Linda was imagining a schematic drawing of power steering, wherein the pressurized fluid happened to be pink and the low-pressure fluid happened to be green, then, like Melanie's shrubs/trees, this would not be sensory awareness. But if Linda was interested in the pinkness or the greenness; if she created these colors not because they represented a typical schematic drawing but because she was drawn to the pinkness and/or the greenness, then this would have been sensory awareness.

It is therefore not always entirely unambiguous whether a particular sample should be considered an instance of sensory awareness. Let's say schematic drawings are usually in primary colors, and Linda, who happens to be an engineer, knows that. Despite that, she creates an inner seeing of a schematic in pastels. Yet at the moment of the beep, she is interested in the pressures and is not paying attention to the "pastelness" of the pressure representations. Determining whether this experience deserves to be called a sensory awareness would be a tough call.

The good news is that whereas some judgments are tough calls about individual samples, the characteristics of individual *people* are not usually that problematic. For example, Ephraim, in our examples, has a high frequency of sensory awareness *no matter how you make the tough calls*. Whether that high frequency is 75 or 85 percent might depend on the details of the tough calls, but it's a high frequency either way.

> Example 13: Miguel is angry; that anger manifests itself in part by Miguel's sensing the hair on the back of his neck bristle.

DES considers the bodily aspect of a feeling *not* to be sensory awareness. This experience would be called the feeling of anger, not the sensory awareness of hair standing on end. This may seem an arbitrary distinction; should we call this both a feeling and a sensory awareness? DES seeks to apprehend experience. If the organizing principle of the experience seems to be the emotion, and the hair bristling is understood to be an aspect of the emotional experience, then the hair bristling is not considered to be a sensory awareness – there is not a focus on the bristling for its own sake. The bodily aspect of an emotion is not called a sensory awareness by DES unless that bodily aspect is a focus of awareness apart from the emotional experience or any other perceptual/meaning aspect of awareness.[1]

> Example 14: Steven was pacing around his condo engaged in a mental argument. At the beep he was innerly saying the word "whatever" to himself in his own voice, as if directed at the person he was mentally arguing with. He was also aware of a sense of frustration and an accompanying sensation of heat and outward-radiating pressure behind his ears and eyes. Simultaneously, he was also aware of a "frenetic" restless energy in his arms and legs that made him feel like he had to be moving.

---

[1] Science is an evolving process, and I acknowledge that it may, at some future point, be desirable to reverse course on this decision. DES reveals that some people experience emotion with clearly available bodily aspects, whereas others experience emotion without any bodily aspects. Those experiences are phenomenologically quite different, but DES and the emotion literature refers to both as "feelings." I think that an adequate discussion of the phenomenology of feelings is yet to be performed, and when that happens, it may be clearer what to do about the common ground between sensory awareness and feelings.

318 Investigating Pristine Inner Experience

It is possible to have a sensory awareness at the same time as a feeling. Here, the frenetic energy is itself a focus of experience along with (but not part of) the frustration. DES would consider this simultaneously a feeling (frustration) and a sensory awareness (frenetic energy).

INDIVIDUAL DIFFERENCES IN THE FREQUENCY
OF SENSORY AWARENESS

Sensory awareness is a frequently observed phenomenon, occurring in roughly a quarter of all everyday experience samples. However, there are large individual differences in the observed frequency of sensory awareness. Recall that Heavey and Hurlburt (2008) stratified large introductory psychology classes on a measure of psychological distress (the SCL-90-R; Derogatis, 1994) and randomly selected thirty individuals. This stratified sample therefore was quite representative of the entering students in a large U.S. state university. They then applied the DES technique to each. Sensory awareness occurred in 22 percent of all sampled experiences. However, within subjects the observed frequency of sensory awareness ranged from 0 to 100 percent. The median frequency of sensory awareness across subjects was 16 percent, but 30 percent of subjects (nine of thirty) had no sensory awareness at all. So although sensory awareness may be very common, it is by no means omnipresent.

Heavey and Hurlburt (2008) reported that the correlation between the subjects' frequency of sensory awareness and their psychological distress (SCL-90-R) scores was .04. This is only one study with only one measure of distress, but there is no reason to conclude that sensory awareness is unequivocally a beneficial or a detrimental characteristic of experience.

In Chapter 2, we discussed the inner experience of women with bulimia nervosa. We didn't explicitly note it there, but Jones-Forrester and I found that our bulimic women had frequent sensory awareness, averaging about 40 percent across eighteen subjects. For some of these women, the predominance of sensory awareness was striking. For example, Stella (Jones-Forrester, 2006) had sensory awareness in thirty-five of her forty samples (88 percent). Here are some typical samples from Stella:

Sample 3.4. Stella was at work pulling a box off the shelf. She was focused on the dry, dustiness of the box surface and waviness of the surface caused by the corrugations beneath it.

Sample 6.3. Stella was playing with the tips of her hair and was aware of the grainy texture of the tips against her fingers.

Sample 7.4: Stella was changing clothes in the bathroom and was aware of the aqua color of the floor tiles and also was aware of the sensation of cold pressure from the floor on the balls of her feet. (These are two simultaneous sensory awarenesses.)

In seven of her thirty-five sensory-awareness samples (20 percent) Stella seemed to be using sensory awareness actively to avoid potentially distressing stimuli. For example:

> Sample 7.5. Stella was at work eating her lunch. She was focused on the heaviness in her eyebrows as she intentionally furrowed them in an explicit, currently successful attempt to avoid the worry and upset that was currently just outside her awareness.

> Sample 3.6. Stella was on the phone with her father, who was screaming at her. Instead of hearing what her father was screaming, she was noticing the distortion of the sound as the phone loudspeaker was being overdriven by the screams. She was also noticing the vibrating sensation in her skin next to her ear caused by the phone.

> Sample 5.6. Stella was stuck in traffic. She was actively trying to channel her frustration into a sense of calm by looking at the fuzzy blue outline of the sky framed by the spokes of her steering wheel.

> Sample 7.1. Stella was at work in conversation with her new boss. He had physically moved too close to her in a way that Stella found threatening. In response, Stella had leaned back. At the moment of the beep, Stella was feeling the stretching sensations in her back as she arched away from him. Thus, at the moment of the beep Stella was *not* aware of feeling threatened by her boss's advance; in fact, she was not aware of her boss at all. She was focused on the relatively inconsequential arching sensations of her back.

DISCRIMINATING SENSORY AWARENESS

When we describe sensory awareness to colleagues unfamiliar with the topic, they frequently jump to incorrect conclusions about the nature of the phenomenon. Here is what sensory awareness is *not*.

Sensory awareness is not merely some sensory aspect of a perception. If you are driving and you stop for a stop sign, the redness of the sign was doubtless an aspect of the perception that led you to stop. Yet that is *not* a sensory awareness as DES defines it *unless, as a central feature of your experience, you were drawn to, absorbed in, or otherwise particularly noticing the redness.*

Sensory awareness is not part of the subject matter generally called "sensation and perception." Sensory awareness has little or nothing to do with the topics generally called "sensation," topics such as sensory threshold, receptor cells, adaptation, brain projection areas, and so on. Doubtless, sensory awareness depends on processes such as those, but sensory awareness is *the result of* those processes, not merely one more process among many others.

Sensory awareness is not a process, perceptual or otherwise, that occurs or is presumed to occur. Sensory awareness is a phenomenon in its own right – the figure of experience, something directly observed.

Q: I make a distinction between (a) first-order conscious perception (e.g., Andrew's seeing the shiny-blue patch) and (b) second-order conscious reflection or introspection (Andrew's reflecting upon the fact that he is looking at something blue). In which is sensory awareness?
A: The concept of sensory awareness is orthogonal to that distinction. Sensory awareness is a directly apprehended phenomenon. Whether sensory awareness (or any other introspectable event) requires both a first-order perception and a second-order reflection is not known to me; I do not seek to explain how sensory awareness works, only that it exists as a phenomenon. I can say with confidence that we have inquired with substantial care on hundreds of occasions and only very rarely will a subject acknowledge that there is any hint of an awareness of a second-order process. I do not intend this to rule out the existence or necessity of a second-order process; I do intend to say that if there is a second-order process, it escapes the notice of subjects at the moment of the beep, including those subjects who are relatively skilled at knowing the difference between a first-order and a second-order process.

Q: Some would say that mindfulness meditation is designed to increase sensory awareness. For example, Segal, Williams, and Teasdale (2002) describe one of the techniques they use to teach people to be more mindful:

> If there is a window in the room, we ask people to look outside, pay-
> ing attention to the sights as best they can, letting go of the categories
> they normally use to make sense of what they are looking at; rather
> than viewing elements of the scene as trees or cars, or whatever, we
> ask them simply to see them as patterns of color and shapes and move-
> ment. (p. 160)

Is that what you mean by sensory awareness, and are they training that?
A: I agree that his type of mindfulness training attempts to enhance the ability of individuals to focus on sensations without regard to their meaning, symbolism, or other informational significance and thereby to increase the relative frequency of the phenomenon of sensory awareness in the individual's ongoing experience. Furthermore, I have sampled with a few adept meditators, and each had a high frequency of sensory awareness. I don't know whether a natural propensity toward sensory awareness *led to* those meditators becoming adept or their sensory awareness was *the result of* thousands of hours of meditation. I further don't know how much meditation is required to alter in any substantial way the amount of sensory awareness.

IMPEDIMENTS TO THE RECOGNITION OF SENSORY AWARENESS

We claim that sensory awareness is a robust phenomenon, identifiable by anyone who might look carefully at experience moment by moment, occurring in roughly a quarter of sampled moments. However, there is little or no discussion of the phenomenon in the literature. It is our aim to describe the phenomenon, not to explain the social psychology of its absence, but the following ten observations may be useful.

First, it may seem that there is nothing to understand, nothing unknown, about the phenomenon of sensory awareness. A common presupposition is that everybody has sensory awareness most of the time; *of course* we pay attention to sensory details – how else could we navigate our way through the world. That presupposition reflects a serious misunderstanding of sensory awareness as we define it. It is *not* true that everybody has sensory awareness most of the time: As best we can ascertain, roughly one-third of people experience sensory awareness only rarely if at all. Navigating through the world around us does *not* require this thematic sensory awareness: I can easily stop at a stop sign without paying particular attention to the shade of its redness, listen to a lecture without paying particular attention to the timbre of the speaker's voice, and so on. A sensory awareness is *not* merely a building block out of which a perception is constructed. Sensory awareness is a center of interest, not a sub-structure, sub-part, or ingredient of some other perceptual center of interest.

Second, as we observed earlier, sensory awareness is sometimes not reported by DES subjects on their first sampling day, even by those subjects who experience sensory awareness frequently. The iterative nature of DES (Chapter 10) can solve this potential under-reporting. But the non-reporting of sensory awareness on the first sampling day can be a problem for methods that rely on one-shot data gathering and for multiple-occasion methods that train subjects only on one occasion.

Third, and related to the second point, some people who have frequent sensory awareness do not know that they have sensory awareness at all. (Recall Jessica's paradox from Chapter 2.) It was not until Mike Kane (Chapter 6) examined the details of his experiences moment by moment with an external observer that he recognized visual sensory awareness as a frequent characteristic of his experience.

Fourth, many people (including many students of consciousness) assume that everyone's experience is just like their own (this phenomenon led to the constraint in Chapter 9, *Don't judge others by yourself*). This prejudice may lead people who do not have frequent sensory awareness (including many students of consciousness) to fail to recognize the occurrence of sensory awareness in others.

Fifth, it is difficult, if not impossible, to explore sensory awareness using armchair introspection. I have argued (Hurlburt and Heavey, 2004; Hurlburt & Schwitzgebel, 2007, 2011b) against the use of armchair introspection in general. Armchair introspection is particularly problematic in apprehending sensory awareness because the hallmark of sensory awareness is that the sensory aspect grabs you, draws you, attracts you, as if unbidden. This unbidden quality is difficult for armchair introspection to simulate because armchair introspectors have already made themselves purposefully ready to observe.

Sixth, as we saw previously, reporting a sensory awareness, at least at first, is often accompanied by a sense of embarrassment. That embarrassment is likely to cause a substantial (perhaps complete) under-reporting of sensory awareness except in those situations in which subjects trust that the truth and the whole truth about experience is sincerely desired.

Seventh, as we saw earlier, sensory awarenesses, despite their at-the-moment vividness, are, like dreams, almost immediately forgotten. This forgetting would likely lead to a substantial (perhaps complete) under-reporting of sensory awareness by all retrospective methods including questionnaires and interviews.

Eighth, the vocabulary that untrained people use to describe sensory awareness is substantially imprecise. In particular, people (including students of consciousness) frequently use the word "feeling" in three quite distinct ways. We mentioned the first two in Chapter 15: (a) to describe an affective or emotional experience (e.g., "I was feeling anxious"); and (b) to describe an inward impression or state of mind (e.g., "I was feeling that I should take Elm Street instead of Pine Street because there would be less traffic"). "Feeling" is also used (c) to describe bodily sensory awarenesses (e.g., "I was feeling a tickle in my throat"). Those three uses are experientially dramatically different, but the imprecision in the language may make it difficult at the outset to get a clear view of sensory awareness. It is difficult to reduce such imprecision unless an iterative method is employed (Chapter 10).

Ninth, as in the recognition of any phenomenon of inner experience, observers must bracket their presuppositions about what is observed; bracketing presuppositions is not easy (Hurlburt & Akhter, 2006; Hurlburt & Heavey, 2006; Hurlburt & Schwitzgebel, 2007, 2011c).

Tenth, sensory awareness may be systematically punished. We give one example. The family is playing an informal game at the dinner table. It's the Christmas season, and the centerpiece is a candle-lit Weihnachten Carousel (aka windmill carousel or pyramid carousel): The updraft from the candles turns a balsa-wood windmill that rotates carousels on the three levels of the pyramid. On these carousels is a Nativity scene: Mary, Joseph, the crèche, the wise men, the angels, the animals, and so on, all brightly painted and gaily rotating within the wooden framework. The game is a version of *I Spy*. Eight-year-old Peter is "it"; he has "spied" an item on the carousel, and the rest of the family takes turns asking yes/no questions to try to guess which item Peter has selected: Is it moving? No. Is it made of wood? Yes. Is it white or partly white? Yes. The children love this game, which they have made up and elaborated over the years. Eventually the family gives up and requires Peter to tell what he has spied; he says it is the balls that sit on the fence posts around the base of carousel. "Peter! There isn't any white on those balls! They're totally red!" And they are: The balls are, objectively, uniformly painted red, not a speck of white paint on them. The family light-heartedly teases Peter about how much easier it would have been had he given the *correct* answer to his brother's "Is it white or partly white?" question. Peter doesn't enter into this conversation.

However, a more careful look at the red balls reveals that each has the reflection of the two adjacent candle flames on it, two tiny spots of experienced white on the objectively uniformly red-painted balls. The spots are tiny, and they don't count as "white" for anyone except Peter, who may be more sensorially aware than anyone else in the family. Looked at closely, they are indeed experientially white. Peter has been rebuked for his sensory sensitivity, and he doesn't have the confidence to defend himself against attacks on what may actually be his sensorial superiority.

We speculate that inner experiences (sensory awareness, inner speech, inner seeing, etc.) are skills that may be acquired across development. Peter has learned a small lesson: that sensory awareness doesn't count; that talking about your sensory awarenesses will confuse people and get you little reinforcement. We speculate that a long series of that kind of event – in the family, in the classroom, eventually in the workplace – may cause Peter's sensory-awareness skill either to atrophy or to go underground: He will not talk about it, even to himself; he will be embarrassed if he is somehow cornered into talking about it (as was Ephraim); he will deny that he has it; he will not really identify the fact that he has it in his self-narratives.

We do not wish to claim that we know how sensory awareness does or does not develop. However, we think that this example may help the reader overcome the presuppositional stance against accepting the importance of sensory awareness and the individual differences of its occurrence.

SPECULATIONS ABOUT SENSORY AWARENESS

Our experience of observing sensory awareness across many subjects leads us to believe its desirability can be thought of as something of a "razor's edge." On the one hand, sensory awareness seems a highly desirable characteristic of experience: It is a direct apprehension of the sensory features of the world around and within. As we discussed earlier, sensory awareness is the target of many forms of mindfulness training, which train individuals to focus on raw sensations. Mindfulness training has been shown to improve mental health (Segal et al., 2002). This view has been confirmed by my unpublished sampling of the experience of adept meditators, whose inner experience was in fact dominated by sensory awareness.

On the other hand, we have sampled with a number of subjects whose inner experience was dominated by sensory awareness who did not enjoy good mental health. Stella, discussed earlier, is one example of a person for whom sensory awareness often appeared to serve as an escape or distraction from the meaningful demands/requirements of her situation. In Stella and others like her, the immersion in the sensory aspects of experience seemed to lessen the ability to cope effectively with the real-world demands they faced.

Thus we are not in a position to say when sensory awareness is useful or a sign of health and when it is destructive or a symptom of pathology. Neither are we in a position to comment on the directionality of any relationship between sensory awareness and health (as we saw, its correlation with psychological distress was approximately zero in Heavey & Hurlburt, 2008). Our goal here has been to describe a frequent phenomenon of inner experience that deserves more attention so that questions such as whether or when sensory awareness is desirable can someday be answered.

> **Q:** I find it frustrating that you describe sensory awareness but see few connections between it and anything else.
> **A:** I think that is the way of basic science. In 1957, Arthur Schawlow explored the coherent light rays that could be produced by stimulating rubies (a process later called a laser). He didn't immediately say, "Aha! Grocery store checkout tool!" or "Aha! Two hours of video in the palm of your hand!" Those came only at the end of a long series of observations, constructions, false starts, and refinements. For sensory awareness in Western science, it's 1957.

17

The Radical Non-subjectivity of
Pristine Experience

"Karen" sample 3.1. Karen was studying for her psychology test. At the moment of the beep she was seeing the words "abuse treatment," which were experienced to be inside her head, toward the front, as if the point of view was in the back of her head and the words were projected in front of her. The words were seen in bubble letter font, all lower case, and had thin black edges as sketched in Figure 17.1. There was no color in this seeing. The letters of "abuse treatment" floated like balloons, each individual letter independently in motion, moving slightly up and down vertically (and not side to side). She also heard herself innerly saying the word "abuse" (*not* "abuse *treatment*") in her own voice, in a normal volume, but in a flat tone. This voice experience was decidedly a hearing experience rather than a speaking experience, as if she were hearing her own voice as played back by a tape recorder. Although she described her voice as being spoken at a normal volume, she said she experienced it as being loud because she was in a quiet computer lab.

Karen's sample 3.1 is a more or less typical datum from a more or less typical DES subject, a twenty-four-year-old college student. This chapter asks whether we should conceptualize such data as bits of Karen's subjective experience or as bits of Karen's objective experience. Clarifying the terms *subjective* and *objective* as applied to such data is important because it will expose powerful presuppositions regarding the study of inner experience.

There are two separate realms to be explored here: the subjectivity/objectivity of the experience itself and the subjectivity/objectivity of the method used to apprehend that experience.

FIGURE 17.1. "Abuse treatment" as seen by Karen.

IS PRISTINE EXPERIENCE SUBJECTIVE?

Inner experience is often called subjective, and there is certainly an important sense in which that is a fair portrayal. If "subjective" is taken to mean "perception of one's own states and processes" (Merriam-Webster's definition 4c), Karen's innerly seeing "abuse treatment," for example, certainly counts as subjective.

But is that what psychologists generally mean when they call something "subjective"? To answer that, I searched PsycINFO for the keyword "subjective" and looked at the first 10 (of 36,179) articles that search uncovered. Table 17.1 shows excerpts from the abstracts of those studies; I have italicized the authors' use of the term "subjective" in each. Those ten examples are thus more or less randomly selected recent articles, so understanding how "subjective" is used there will open the window on how "subjective" is currently used in psychology.

"Subjective" as "Impressionistic"

In at least nine of the ten examples in Table 17.1 (example 4 is the potential exception), "subjective" means something like "impressionistic." For example, Yacht, Suglia, and Orlander (2007; example 1 in Table 17.1) asked medical residents to fill out a "subjective attitude" questionnaire before and after they participated in a week-long "end-of-life training" rotation that included hospice care and home hospice visits. The subjective attitude questionnaire was composed of twenty-four Likert-scale items, of which these are typical:

- I will be well prepared to deal with terminally ill patients by the time I finish my residency.
- I am comfortable not using IVs for most terminally ill patients in their final days.
- I am comfortable using high-dose narcotics for pain relief, if necessary, for terminally ill patients. (Yacht et al., 2007, p. 443)

"Subjective" could be used interchangeably with "impression" in this example. For example, "*subjective change in knowledge* … [was] assessed … [by] questionnaire" could easily, without substantially altering the meaning, be changed to "*impression of change in knowledge* … [was] assessed … [by] questionnaire." (Note that I am taking no position here on the adequacy of this study for the purpose that it was designed; my interest is in understanding how "subjective" is used in modern science, and Yacht and colleagues' (2007) usage seems quite typical in this regard.)

TABLE 17.1. *Ten "subjective" studies with reference to subjectivity italicized*

1. "Attitudes toward issues relating to end-of-life care and *subjective change in knowledge* were assessed comparing subjects' retrospective preintervention and postintervention responses included in the postintervention questionnaire." (Yacht, Suglia, & Orlander, 2007, p. 439)

2. "Based on previous research and theories on technology acceptance, the questionnaire measured perceived usefulness of e-services, risk perception, worry, perceived behavioural control, *subjective norm*, trust and experience with e-services." (Horst, Kuttschreuter, & Gutteling, 2007, p. 1838)

3. "We explore three analytic methods that can be used to quantify and qualify changes in attitude and similar outcomes that may be encountered in the educational context.... The methods are straightforward and are appropriate when measurements are imperfect, ratings are *subjective* and differences are not necessarily absolute." (Tractenberg, Chaterji, & Haramati, 2007, p. 107)

4. "The effect of opioid blockade on nociceptive flexion reflex (NFR) activity and *subjective pain ratings* was examined in 151 healthy young men and women." (France et al., 2007, p. 95)

5. "We assessed 14 variables reflecting different outcome criteria including *subjective quality of life* (SQOL), self-rated and observer-rated psychopathology, and functioning and disability." (Brieger, Röttig, Röttig, Marneros, & Priebe, 2007, p. 1).

6. "16 euthymic bipolar individuals breathed air and air combined with 5% CO_2 for 15 min each. Respiratory and *subjective anxiety* measures were collected." (MacKinnon, Craighead, & Hoehn-Saric, 2007, p. 45)

7. "This article examines the 50 qualitative studies published in the *Journal of Counseling Psychology* (*JCP*) over a 15-year period in light of methodological principles advocated by qualitative theorists.... Researchers endorsed the need to bracket their own *subjective experiences* and used auditors to enhance reproducibility of findings." (Hoyt & Bhati, 2007, p. 201)

8. "Nature ... has provided evidence that the complexity (*subjective difficulty*) of a Boolean concept is related to the length of its minimum algebraic description." (Lafond, Lacouture, & Mineau, 2007, p. 57)

9. "A questionnaire assessed adolescents' beliefs, *subjective norm*, perceived behavioral control, and self-reported parent-adolescent communication *about sexuality*." (Schouten, van den Putte, Pasmans, & Meeuwesen, 2007, p. 75)

10. "This study was conducted to determine the prevalence and reliability of risk factors collected on uninjured cyclists-pedestrians...Observers recorded cyclist-pedestrian characteristics such as age, sex, clothing color, use of reflectors, flags, helmets, and a *subjective impression of visibility*." (Hagel, Lamy, Rizkallah, Belton, Jhangri, Cherry, & Rowe, 2007, p. 284)

You can check for yourself whether "subjective" means something like "impressionistic" by seeing whether it makes sense to substitute some form of the term "impressionistic" for "subjective" in the nine remaining examples in Table 17.1. In example 2, "the questionnaire measured ... *subjective norm*" becomes "the questionnaire measured ... *the impression of norm*"; in example 3, "The methods are straightforward ... when measurements ... are *subjective*" becomes "The methods are straightforward ... when measurements ... are *impressionistic*"; and so on. I think you will find that "impressionistic" replaces "subjective" without difficulty in at least nine of the ten examples (example 4 excepted).

"Subjective" as "Not Directly Experienced"

In nine of the ten examples (all except example 4), the target of the "subjective" study is a construct that does not refer to any specific directly observed event or phenomenon (including inner experience). For example, the target of the Yacht and colleagues study (example 1 in Table 17.1) is subjective "attitude toward issues relating to end-of-life care," including, apparently, subjective change in knowledge or subjective sense of preparation, or subjective comfort. An attitude is a construct, not a directly encountered thing, not a directly experienced phenomenon, not a directly observable anything. "Attitude toward issues relating to end-of-life care" is *never* directly experienced by anyone at any time. Adam might experience anxiety at 3:47 A.M. when Mrs. Smith, who is dying, asks him for a narcotic and he doesn't know whether to give it to her; Betty might experience arrogance at 3:50 A.M. when stupid (as Betty sees it) Adam asks her whether to give Mrs. Smith the narcotic when Betty knows that *of course* you give Mrs. Smith a narcotic in this situation; Charlie might experience helplessness at 3:51 A.M. because she thinks there isn't really a good choice in Mrs. Smith's situation. Anxiety, arrogance, and helplessness are directly experienced by specific people at specific moments in specific situations. All of those could be said, in some abstract, theoretical, or generalized way, to have something to do with attitude toward issues relating to end-of-life-care. However Adam, Betty, and Charlie did not *experience* an attitude toward end-of-life care; there was no phenomenon experienced by Adam, Betty, or Charlie that was an attitude. "Attitude" is a construct, not a thing, not a phenomenon, not anything experienced.

"Subjective" is used in all these examples except example 4 to signal that the target of the investigation is *not* anything directly experienced. Example 2 is about the subjective norm about e-services; norms are never experienced. Debbie has experiences with e-services, Elisandra has experiences with e-services, Franco has experiences with e-services. Out of reports about all those services, an abstract construct of the way e-services are accepted, the subjective norm, is built. Yet the construct itself, the norm, was *never* experienced by anyone. Example 3 aims at attitudes about education; attitudes are never (or at least not usually) directly experienced. Example 5 concerns quality of life. George can taste a fine wine at 5:53 P.M.; Harriet can experience the joy of seeing her granddaughter for the first time at 8:11 P.M. Such things can be said to be related to the abstract concept of quality of life. However, quality of life, the construct itself, is never (or at least not usually) directly experienced. I leave the analysis of the remaining examples as an exercise for the reader.

Example 4 is the exception. The target of the France et al. (2007) investigation is a directly apprehendable phenomenon. The investigators administered a series of electric shocks to subjects who had taken a narcotic or a placebo. They obtained "subjective pain ratings" following each trial. In this study, *unlike* the other examples, the target of the study is indeed directly experienced: pain, administered at a specific time, to a specific part of the body. Thus, whereas it makes sense to talk about your *impression* of, say, whether you are prepared to deal with terminally ill patients, it does *not* make equally good sense to talk about your *impression* of pain – the *experience* of pain is more to the point.

Pristine Experience Is Radically Non-subjective

The term "subjective" as used in at least nine of the ten studies in Table 17.1 is *not* applicable to pristine experience. For example, it is strongly misleading to say that Karen *subjectively saw* – had an *impression of* innerly seeing – "abuse treatment"; instead, she was *directly seeing* "abuse treatment." Karen's innerly seeing "abuse treatment" is not a reference to a hypothetical construct; instead, it is a directly apprehended phenomenon, specifically present to her (albeit innerly and privately) at a specific moment in time.

> **Q:** I disagree. It is entirely appropriate to say that Karen "had the impression" of seeing "abuse treatment." It is quite possible that Karen had no pristine experience, and that the seeing of "abuse treatment" is an artifact of the procedure you use for trying to apprehend pristine experience.
> **A:** I accept that such a highly skeptical position is irrefutable and perhaps correct. Even so, I urge you to consider carefully your use of the term "impression." It is one thing to say: "Karen, a practiced and reasonably skilled reporter, when interrupted by a carefully delivered beep and interviewed by a highly skilled and quite dispassionate interviewer, *had the impression* that she had been, a fraction of a second earlier, innerly, ongoingly seeing the balloon letters 'abuse treatment'; and further had the impression that this inner seeing continued on, directly experienced, as she paused to report." It is quite another thing to say: "Jason, an entirely unskilled reporter, interviewed by someone who doubtless has an investment in a particular kind of answer, *had the impression*, when asked at the end of a week-long rotation in a hospice, that he had learned quite a lot about end of life care." One of those impressions has (or at least may have) a specific, carefully defined referent; the other does not.
>
> I therefore accept that it might be appropriate to use the term "impression" for Karen's experience as you suggest, so long as you clearly specify that your use of "impression" is far different from its more usual use in psychology.

The "impressionistic" and the "not directly experienced" aspects of "subjective" are opposite sides of the same coin. It is difficult, if not impossible, to describe something more than impressionistically if that something is not directly available to experience at some specified moment in time. That follows directly from the arguments that have been advanced throughout this book.

Karen's pristine experience in sample 3.1 thus has almost nothing in common with any of the subjective examples, except that what is being investigated is not in the plain sight of other people. (Example 4 is a potential exception.) It therefore seems severely misleading to refer to pristine experience as subjective – it simply does not fit with the way "subjective" is typically used in psychology. In fact, pristine experience is radically non-subjective in the etymologically basic sense of the term "radical," which derives from *radix* or root. (Radical surgery is designed to remove the root of a disease or all diseased and potentially diseased tissue.) Pristine experience refers only to actual phenomena that are directly experienced at some moment; all subjective opinions, impressions, and characterizations are radically avoided (pristine experience does not, for example, include Karen's subjective impression of whether she frequently sees images or her subjective impression of the quality of abuse treatment).

IS THE APPREHENSION OF PRISTINE EXPERIENCE SUBJECTIVE?

We have been discussing the *target* of the investigation, discriminating between pristine experience – directly observed at some particular moment – and all other not directly observed constructs. Now we focus on what is meant by "subjective" when applied to the *method* of an investigation.

"Subjective" as "Not Unambiguously Measured"

Let's examine the methods used in our Table 17.1 examples of subjective studies.

Example 1: Yacht and colleagues' (2007) study of end-of-life care asked subjects to rate fifteen "attitude" items such as "I will be well prepared to deal with terminally ill patients by the time I finish my residency" on five-point Likert-type scales, where 1 equals *strongly disagree* and 5 equals *strongly agree*. In this method there is no specification of what "well prepared" means, no consideration of how the subject is to determine whether he or she is well prepared, no specification of what "terminally ill" means, and no specification of any single experience on which the impression of preparation should be based. When the subject responds with, say, 3 to the "I will be well prepared" item, there is no unambiguous understanding of what 3 means.

Example 2: Horst, Kuttschreuter, and Gutteling (2007) asked subjects to use five-point Likert-type scales to rate four "perceived usefulness of e-government services" items. For example, subjects were to rate "the use of personal information by governmental organisations," where 1 equals *pointless* and 5 equals *very useful*. In such items, "use" is not well defined; "personal information" is not well defined; which government organizations are not specified; and no attempt is made unambiguously to ground *pointless* or *very useful*, if that were possible.

Example 3: Tractenberg, Chaterji, and Haramati (2007) asked subjects to rate twenty-one items such as "I believe that such mind-body practices as bio-feedback, guided imagery and meditation can bring about profound physical changes" on five-point Likert-type scales, where 1 equals *strongly disagree* and 5 equals *strongly agree*. As in the previous examples, terms and anchors are not unambiguously specified.

Example 4 is of particular interest to us because, as we saw previously, this was the only case where specific experiences were targeted. France and colleagues (2007) presented electric shock and asked subjects to rate the stimulation intensity on a one-hundred-point scale, where 1 equals *sensory threshold*, 25 equals *uncomfortable*, 50 equals *painful*, 75 equals *very painful*, and 100 equals *maximum tolerable*. However, there is no careful consideration of what *uncomfortable, painful,* or the other terms mean, no careful examination of whether those ratings are used similarly by different subjects. Thus, whereas France and colleagues adequately specified the target experience, their method was not unambiguous.

The remaining examples are similar; I leave their consideration to the reader. I conclude that "subjective" as it applies to the method of data collection means something like "impressionistic," "casual," or "loosely specified." Terms are not unambiguously defined. There is no assurance that rating scales are used in the same way from one subject to the next. These studies rest on the faith that subjects use ratings the same way from one occasion to another (even though how they are used cannot be specified), or that the differing ways that subjects use ratings will average out across large groups of subjects. Whether those assumptions are justified in the individual studies is not our concern here; our focus is on whether the investigator understands what an individual subject means when he or she provides a rating, and the answer is, I think, *no*.

The Apprehension of Pristine Experience Can be Radically Non-subjective

We now contrast the methods used in those studies with the method used to produce Karen's "abuse treatment" sample. That method was DES; there may well be other methods that proceed with equal or better concern for clarity of understanding what is communicated.

The term "subjective" as applied to the methods used in these ten studies is decidedly *not* applicable to the DES method of exploring pristine experience. Unlike all the "subjective" examples, we know with substantial precision what is meant by every word in the description of Karen's "abuse treatment" experience.

DES systematically explored what she intended by every utterance and systematically sought to minimize any ambiguity of expression. We know, for example, that the letters of "abuse treatment" are balloon letters (not, say, Times Roman), that they are empty with thin edges (not, say, boldly filled), that they are moving up and down (and not sideways). Unlike all the subjective examples, DES avoids asking Karen to use rating scales with ill-defined anchors such as *uncomfortable, painful, strongly disagree,* or *strongly agree.* Unlike all the subjective examples except 4, DES did not ask Karen to characterize herself in general terms; DES systematically avoids rating scales that give the illusion of precision. It therefore seems severely misleading to refer to a careful exploration of pristine experience such as DES as a subjective endeavor – it simply does not fit with the way "subjective" is typically used in psychology.

In fact, DES, as a method aimed at pristine experience, systematically tries to *eliminate* all subjectivity from its observations and descriptions, limiting itself to the directly observed facts of experience. If, during the course of her interview about sample 3.4, Karen had referred to something like a subjective change in knowledge (perhaps by saying, "Seeing 'abuse treatment' will cue me to recall the material I'm reading"),or to a subjective quality of life (perhaps by saying, "Seeing images of words is an effective strategy for me"), or to a subjective norm about gender (perhaps by saying, "The balloon font is probably more typical of women than men"), the DES investigator would have conveyed to her that although such things may be important in other contexts, we wish specifically to exclude such subjective impressions from the DES investigation. This is an application of Chapter 11's constraint, *Eliminate mentalisms.*

In its radically non-subjective data gathering, DES *rules out* of consideration subjective constructs such as the self (including self-concept, self-esteem, self-actualization, etc.), meaning, intention, essence, narrative, ego, conscience, attitude, drive, type, momentum, tendency, stage, personality, schema, mental map, need, motive, model, intelligence, interference, explanation, encoding, and the like, unless such a construct appears directly as an observed phenomenon. DES works assiduously in its iterative way to eliminate such reports.

That DES radically and explicitly rules out all subjective topics from its consideration does not imply that such topics are unimportant or that methods might be useful for their investigation; I am not taking a position on that here. DES itself, however, cleaves to directly observed phenomena. It relentlessly seeks to *eradicate from its consideration* exactly the topics that subjective studies seek to make central.

PRETTY DARN CORRECT ANSWERS; HIGH FIDELITY ACCOUNTS

Thus it makes sense to understand that both pristine experience itself and the DES method of its apprehension are radically non-subjective. By this, I have absolutely no wish to pretend that pristine experience or DES somehow over-comes the "perception of one's own states and processes" definition of sub-jective. It does not and cannot. However, Karen's "abuse treatment" sample 3.1 is thoroughly distinguishable from all ten of the subjective examples that we discussed earlier and from the data of nearly all subjective studies in that there are pretty darn correct answers to questions about Karen's experience at the moment of sample 3.1. There are *not*, however, pretty darn correct answers to questions in the subjective studies. Is Karen seeing the words "abuse treat-ment"? There is a pretty darn correct answer to that question: Yes. Are the letters moving? Pretty darn correctly yes. Up and down or side to side? Pretty darn correctly up and down, not side to side. Are the letters in a balloon font, rather than, say, Times Roman? Pretty darn correctly a balloon font, not Times Roman.

By contrast, there is no pretty darn correct way for Adam to determine whether he should, at the end of the hospice rotation, strongly disagree, dis-agree, agree, or strongly agree with the statement "I will be well prepared to deal with terminally ill patients by the time I finish my residency." The correctness of the answer depends on what is meant by "prepared," "well prepared," "strongly agree," and so on, and such terms are never defined. Was the pain uncomfortable? There is no pretty darn correct answer to that question because that depends on what is meant by "uncomfortable," and that is never defined.

By calling the answers about Karen's experience "pretty darn correct," I acknowledge that there may be some mistakes about some details, and that some subjects are doubtless motivated to lie about everything. For the most part, however, if you are interested in reducing the mistakes about details, you can ask ever more careful questions, and you can continue iteratively to build your subject's skill. This is the essence of what I have been calling a "high fidel-ity" apprehension. I think the description of Karen's "abuse treatment" expe-rience is a high fidelity account. It is not a perfectly accurate account; Figure 17.1 shows the *a* slightly higher than the *b* in "abuse," and in Karen's actual experience at the moment of the beep the *b* may well have been higher than the *a*. By contrast, a high fidelity account is simply not possible in any of the ten examples of subjectivity. A subject's endorsing 3 on the Likert question "I will be well prepared to deal with terminally ill patients by the time I finish my residency" is necessarily a low fidelity response.

Pristine experience allows pretty darn right or wrong answers because pristine experience is a directly observed phenomenon that occurs at a specific moment and that can be apprehended with a procedure that genuinely sub-mits to the constraints that the endeavor imposes. As we have seen throughout this book, those three features are essential to a high fidelity apprehension of experience. Perhaps example 4 adequately defines a moment and experience, but it does not use a method that, from the point of view of high fidelity, genuinely submits to the constraints imposed ("uncomfortable," etc., is not adequately defined). None of the remaining nine subjective examples is interested in experience, none defines moments, and none genuinely submits to the constraints that the exploration of experience imposes.

The aim of DES is to cleave relentlessly to questions that have pretty darn correct answers and, as a result, to produce high fidelity descriptions. DES doubtless falls short of perfection in that regard, but most studies of subjectivity do not even begin the attempt. That, in my view, is a very big difference.

IS PRISTINE EXPERIENCE OBJECTIVE?

If both pristine experience and its apprehension can be considered radically non-subjective, then should they be called objective? Merriam-Webster provides two relevant definitions of the adjective "objective." The core of the first definition is "of, relating to, or being an object, phenomenon, or condition in the realm of sensible experience independent of individual thought and perceptible by all observers: having reality independent of the mind." By that definition, which stresses "perceptible by all observers," pristine experience and its apprehension are certainly not objective. However, part *d* of Merriam-Webster's first definition is: "involving or deriving from sense perception or experience with actual objects, conditions, or phenomena <*objective* awareness> <*objective* data>." By that broadened definition, pristine experience *is* objective: Karen's inner seeing of "abuse treatment" seems right in the center of "experience with actual … phenomena." In fact, Merriam-Webster's citing of "*objective* awareness" as a primary exemplar seems clearly to indicate that this definition applies to private, non-corporeal phenomena. It is hard to imagine what kind of awareness would be more objective than Karen's "abuse treatment" pristine experience.

Furthermore, Merriam-Webster's second relevant definition of objective (there is a third, which refers to grammar, as in the object of a preposition, which we ignore here) is "expressing or dealing with facts or conditions as perceived without distortion by personal feelings, prejudices, or interpretations <*objective* art> <an *objective* history of the war>." The DES investigation of pristine experience seems squarely in the center of that definition of objective: The entire aim of DES is to describe experience with as little distortion by personal feelings, prejudices, or interpretations as possible.

> **Q:** Just because DES *aims* to be objective doesn't mean it *is* objective.
> **A:** I agree, but reaching perfection is not, apparently, necessary for Merriam-Webster's definition to apply. Certainly there is no history of any war that perfectly avoids "distortion by personal feelings, prejudices, or interpretations," and yet "an *objective* history of war" is one of

Merriam-Webster's primary exemplars of "objective" by this definition. The balloon-font and moving-up-and-down-letters characteristics of Karen's "abuse treatment" experience seems substantially more likely to be free of personal distortions than are most aspects of any history of war.

More Objective than Objective Tests?

Perhaps the most widespread use of the concept of "objective" in psychology is in objective testing. Here is the definition in Corsini's *The Dictionary of Psychology* (Corsini, 2002):

> *Objective test*: Any examination which leads to identical results regardless of who administers it if the administration is correct. The main issue is to eliminate any subjective aspects of the examiner; for example, a multiple-choice test with a time-limit has printed directions to subjects with an answer key and norms available. Any administrator who follows the simple rules should come up with identical scores for any particular person. (Corsini, 2002, p. 656)

I use the MMPI-2 as a well-known exemplar of an objective test, but the following discussion applies to any good objective test. The MMPI-2 consists of 567 true-false items such as "My father is a good man" and "At times I feel like swearing." The MMPI-2 clearly meets Corsini's definition of an objective test: To obtain a score, an administrator of the MMPI-2 need only count up the number of "true" answers to the specified sets of items. Competent scorers will come up with identical scores.

Such tests are called "objective tests," but it would be more accurate to call them "objectively *scored* tests." This is made explicit in Corsini's definition, which is typical in psychology; Corsini's definition refers only to the objectivity of *administrator*, not to the objectivity of the person taking the test. In fact, the person taking the test is far from objective, left adrift in a sea of subjective ambiguity. Consider the MMPI-2 item "My father is a good man": What does "good" mean? According to whom? All the time or just when the subject was young? Or just when the father wasn't drinking? Or just excepting the year that the father had the affair with the subject's aunt? And good compared to whom? Consider "At times I feel like swearing": What does "at times" mean – twice in my life or twice a day? What does "feel" mean – how strong does that have to be to count? And does "feel like swearing" include actually swearing or just feeling like it but not doing it? There is no attempt made in the MMPI-2 administration to clarify any of those questions, no attempt to refine for the subject what is being asked. In fact, any attempt by the administrator to clarify those issues *invalidates* the test. As a result, there is no way of knowing what the subject means by endorsing "true" for such items. These are typical

MMPI-2 items – most MMPI-2 items are at least as subjectively ambiguous as these – and the MMPI-2 is typical of nearly all "objective" personality tests.

Thus the basic data of the MMPI-2 – the test taker's 567 true or false answers to questions such as "My father is a good man" and "At times I feel like swearing" – are collected with little or no concern for the truth value of the answers. Answering "false" to the item "My father is a good man" elevates your score on the *Sc* scale of the MMPI-2 regardless of how you define "good" and regardless of whether your father is indeed a good man. The validity of the MMPI-2 has nothing to do with the truth of the answers; it depends only on the pattern of answers given between groups, without concern for whether that pattern is the result of the group members responding accurately or group members responding with characteristically widespread misrepresentations.

Thus the data that objective tests collect are, as Frankfurt would say, "description(s) of a certain state of affairs without genuinely submitting to the constraints which the endeavor to provide an accurate representation of reality imposes." Those data are subjected to sophisticated and entirely objective techniques that seek to counter-balance the lack of carefulness in the data themselves. That strategy has had a well-replicated but arguably modest level of success, but that is not my major interest here, which is rather to contrast the methods.

DES is *unlike* an "objective test" both from the perspective of the investigator ("administrator") and the subject. From the perspective of the administrator, DES is *not* an "examination which leads to identical results regardless of who administers it if the administration is correct": DES results *do* depend to some degree on the experience and skill of the investigator; there are no "simple rules" and no guarantee that all competent DES investigators will "come up with identical scores for any particular person." Hurlburt and Heavey (2002) have shown that the inter-observer reliability of DES is very high when making judgments such as "Karen was innerly seeing 'abuse treatment,'" but that high reliability falls short of the "identical results" required by Corsini's definition. (In the real world, even the MMPI-2 administration is not actually identical from one administrator to the next: How to deal with missing values, ambiguous markings on the answer sheet, language issues, and so on varies at least a little across administrators.)

From the perspective of the subject, however, DES is far more objective than the MMPI-2 or any other "objective" test. DES is at every word vitally concerned with the truth of the subject's representations. It works relentlessly to clarify as precisely as possible what subjects intend to convey about their experience. Doubtless it falls short of perfection from this perspective as well, but it certainly seems to do much better than objective tests in this regard.

So is DES an objective method when viewed from the perspective of the MMPI-2? DES strives to be *radically more* objective than the MMPI-2. So-called objective tests strive only to be half objective – objective only on the side of the administrator. DES strives to be objective on both the side of the administrator and the side of the subject. I fully accept that it falls short of perfection on both sides; I fully accept that the falling short of perfection presents problems for science. But science doesn't solve its problems by ignoring them, as it currently does on the subject's side of objective tests. It remains to be seen whether science can work through how to integrate the careful apprehension of experience into its arsenal.

> **Q:** OK. Suppose I accept that you have provided an objective characterization of Karen's "abuse treatment" experience. Big deal! It's one moment, one insignificance, one objectively apprehended but objectively trivial inconsequentiality.
> **A:** Careful! If you accept that, you will have accepted everything I have to say in this book! I fully agree that Karen's "abuse treatment" experience is entirely trivial. Yet if you allow that objective-but-trivial bit, then you allow another objective-but-trivial bit, then another, and then another, eventually you may have a massive structure, just as a sand bar is built out of grains of sand. Sand bars can be huge (Fraser Island is seventy-five miles long, with cities and highways), all made possible by the accumulation of trivial inconsequentialities.
>
> Once you accept that a trivial, inconsequential observation might be objective, then it is possible to accumulate as many objective observations as you like, as for example in the bulimia studies of Chapter 2.

OBJECTIVITY AS VIRTUOUS COORDINATION

I am not claiming that we should call DES results "objective." My point is that there should be no glib confidence in the subjective/objective terminology as applied to inner experience. Pristine experience *is* subjective in a manner of speaking: It presents itself only to one subject, in private. It *is not* subjective (that is, it is radically non-subjective) in a manner of speaking: It radically excludes everything (or nearly everything) that is the target of subjective methods in psychology; it is highly misleading, in a manner of speaking, to lump pristine experience in, intentionally or otherwise, with the targets of typical subjective investigations. Pristine experience is *not* objective in a manner of speaking: It does not concern itself with publicly observable data and does inherently depend on the apprehension by a subject. It *is* objective in a manner of speaking: It is a directly apprehended phenomenon that can be perceived with little distortion by personal feelings, prejudices, or interpretations. It is highly misleading, in a manner of speaking, to imply, intentionally or otherwise, that pristine experience is less objective than the topics investigated by objective tests; in fact, DES can be argued to be *more* objective than objective psychological tests.

It is not within my competence or interest to dive too deeply into the waters that surround the metaphysics of objectivity. However, for the purpose of counter-balancing the prevailing view of objectivity, it may be worth the effort to put a toe into those waters, inspired by Brian Cantwell Smith (1996) and Ron Chrisley (2001). Smith was interested in how objects came to be identified – why, for example, we would see a newspaper as a single object rather than as a stack of separate objects (the pages). If I understand him right, his conclusion is that objectivity is not a characteristic of the object (the newspaper), but is the result of a participation by the subject who creates objects by coordinations of activity.

Smith's idea is that the fundamental nature of objectivity is the creation, stabilization, and maintenance of objects in the face of the underlying flux of perspectival views on the world. Objectivity requires a coordinated participation in this dazzling series that builds and maintains a stable pattern, an object, out of a necessarily subjective welter of experience. Smith uses this metaphor:

> Imagine an acrobat leaping and jumping about on a somewhat darkened stage, putting their body through all kinds of fantastic gyrations, and yet throughout this crazed dance keeping a flashlight pointing absolutely reliably towards some fixed point – a point about four feet off the ground, say, towards the left front center of the stage. What the acrobat would need to do, through a complex series of hand and arm motions – handing the light back and forth from hand to hand, reaching it around behind themselves, and so forth as appropriate – would be to do the opposite with one part of their body (arm and hand, plus flashlight) of what the rest of their body was doing (leaping and dancing), in such a way that the two, when added up together, nullified each other, leaving the focal point of illumination unchanged.
>
> Except of course the word "opposite" is not right. If the acrobat were to leap up four feet, it would not be necessary for them to do the exact opposite – i.e., to drop their arm down four feet, if that were even possible – in order to hold constant the full six-coordinate position and orientation of the flashlight. In fact not a single one of the flashlight's six coordinates needs to remain fixed. It is not the *flashlight* that needs to be stabilized, after all. To freeze the position of the flashlight outright might seem to be overkill, and would anyway be impossible, for example if the acrobat were to rush to the other side of the stage. Ironically, moreover, there is a sense in which keeping the light itself locked into position, as if it were epoxied to a particular point in space, would be underkill, *since there would then be no way to be sure where it was pointing*. For a fixed unmoving flashlight, that is, no single point along its path of illumination is uniquely singled out; all you have is a long gradually dissipating path of light.
>
> Fortunately for the acrobat, there is a better way: it is only necessary to rotate the wrist in just the appropriate manner. The normative requirement is that there be a fixed point at the "end" of (i.e., at some point along)

the line along which the flashlight is pointing – a point that remains stably located in exocentric 3-space. So the dance does not merely compensate for the acrobat's movements; as a method for stabilizing the object, it is superior.... All told, the focal point is much more stably and redundantly identifiable through the acrobat's motion than it would have been had the acrobat stayed put. (Smith, 1996: 237–239)

This notion is that an object is an invariant created in the face of changing conditions by a participatory "virtuous coordination" (Chrisley, 2001) of disparate actions (eyes looking this way, torso rotating that way, arms moving this way, wrist rotating that way) produced by a bag of bones, tendons, receptor cells, and so on.

I like Smith's acrobat metaphor except that it is perhaps too visual: We create objects as the result of sensory interactions that are visual but also of a variety of other modalities. So I would extend the metaphor by saying the acrobat has a flashlight in his left hand, a long stick in his right hand, a ball-on-a-string that he kicks and retrieves with his left foot, a heat and a pain sensor on his right foot, an olfactory sensor in the center of his face, a pressure wave detector on each side of his head, and so on. All of these are coordinated by the acrobat. Some involve a transmission and reception (like the flashlight); some involve reception only (like olfaction); each is useful only in some portion of the stage (the entire stage for the flashlight, within eight feet for the stick, within two feet for the pain); each carries a varying degree of precision (high for the flashlight, lower for the pressure waves, lowest for the olfactory sensor) in its aim at the same point in exocentric three-space; each provides feedback with its appropriate delay (nearly instantaneously for the flashlight, longer for the carom of the kicked ball); and so on. The coordination process includes the recognition of which modality is appropriately useful in which situation.

In most normal adults, this participatory coordination is so well established, so automatic, that it is entirely taken for granted even given its extreme complexity. However, there may be times that one can quite literally watch that frail coordination struggle to exist. For example, Uta Frith, Francesca Happé, and I sampled with Peter, an Asperger Syndrome patient (Hurlburt, Happé, & Frith, 1994). Near the end of the five days of sampling, Peter proudly showed us a photo album of snapshots that he had taken. There were, as I recall, perhaps fifty snapshots (the whole book was full of them); all were nearly identical. Peter responded with apparent glee when we couldn't figure out what they were, nor how one was different from the next. Eventually he told us that they were close-up photos of light fixtures in the ceiling of London railroad cars. The fixtures looked identical to me, but he could tell us with evident satisfaction which car on which train they came from. Here's what we wrote:

He explained that the light fixtures had particular significance for him because he used to see them when he was a young boy riding on the

train. His description of that youthful seeing-of-light-fixtures was as if
he had, there on the train, seen objects for the first time, as if the light-
fixtures had somehow come into existence, had become real visual presences for him, in a way that no other object had ever visually crystallized
for him before, as if out of the dazzle of unconnected visual sensations of
flashes and colours an object had presented itself to him. (Hurlburt et al.,
1994, p. 393)

I think that account is entirely consistent with Smith's view, that the fundamental nature of objectivity is the creation, stabilization, and maintenance of
objects in the face of an ever-changing multi-dazzle of stimulation. I think it
likely that, prior to that London train ride, Peter had never seen any object –
that is, had never been able to create, stabilize, and maintain *anything*. That
afternoon, after years (he had commuted to school daily) of being drawn to
patches and patterns of lights and sounds, of turning his face this way with
a resulting brightness dazzle, of turning his body that way with a resulting
diminishing of brightness, of keeping his body steady but turning his face
back with a resulting increase in brightness; of arching his body upward with
a resulting increase in brightness; of extending his arm, followed by his body
upward with a large increase in brightness and then a painful hotness; and
then a recoil of body with an attendant decrease in hotness and subsidence of
pain; that afternoon, after years of resplendent evanescence, *an object emerged!*
What a remarkable discovery that must have been: There is a *thing* external
from me associated with the flashes and blitzes and dimnesses and bright-
nesses and hardnesses and sharpnesses and clinks and coolnesses and hot-
nesses and pains and proprioceptive patterns! The shock and enlightenment
of such a realization is almost impossible to imagine from the perspective of
someone (like me and doubtless the reader) whose nearly entire life has taken
for granted the existence of things.

My speculation is that for a while after that (days? months?), Peter could
see an object, but *only one kind of object* – light fixtures in the train cars. He
had developed the skill of coordinating the dazzles that are associated with
light fixtures, but could not yet coordinate the dazzles that come from stop
signs and coffee cups. He honed his object-making skills on light fixtures, this
one, that one, today, the next today; eventually, that object-making skill generalized and Peter became able to see objects of many different kinds. But his
first objects were the light fixtures, and he maintained a fascination with them
throughout his life, so much so that he would photograph all of them and display the photo album as a prized possession.

I accept that this is a pretty wild speculation on pretty flimsy evidence.
Yet even if it is not true, entertaining it as a possibility is a worthwhile exercise in bracketing presuppositions. Most people undergo their object-
recognition epiphany when they are infants and so have no recollection of

it, so their presuppositions regarding the nature of objects run deep. But if we accept that Peter's autism-spectrum disability may have made his object-making coordination ability difficult, it can make other characteristics of the autism-spectrum disorders seem reasonable. For example, autistic individuals often scream uncontrollably when a slight change occurs in their environment. If we accept that such individuals have a very tenuous object-making coordination, then a slight change of the multi-dazzle environmental pattern may cause all objects to *evaporate*. If all *your* objects suddenly evaporated, you'd probably scream uncontrollably, too.

One of the other subjects in our Asperger study we called "Nelson." Nearly every time we asked about his inner experience, he began by saying, "The shape of my thoughts is ..." (Hurlburt et al., 1994, p. 390). We came to understand that (a) Nelson's experience was entirely visual and (b) that there was *nothing in experience* outside the registered object. Thus, for example, when I held a pen up in front of Nelson, he said, "The shape of my thoughts is the pen," by which he meant (as we understood it) that he saw the pen, *but he saw nothing else*. He did not see an array of other objects off to the side, indistinct, or dimly presented. He did not have a field of view *in which* was the pen. His entire field of view was *pen shaped* – nothing else. That is, he did not have the kind of figure/ground phenomenon that most people have, where objects in the ground are seen indistinctly and without detail. The ground *was entirely absent from Nelson's experience*. My take on this is that it was very difficult for Nelson to coordinate his seeing of an object; when he was indeed able to see an object, that was *all* he could see, as if he didn't have any resources left over to construct ("ground") objects that might have been slightly off the center of his perception.

Another example: Asperger individual Temple Grandin describes the calming effect of the "squeeze machine," which

> consists of two padded side boards which are hinged at the bottom to form a V shape. The user steps into the machine and lies down on the inside in the V-shaped crevice-like space. The inside surfaces of the device are completely lined with thick foam rubber.... The V-shaped space supports the body fully from head to toe, so that the users can completely relax. The contoured padding provides an even pressure across the entire lateral aspects of the body without generating specific pressure points. (Grandin, 1992, p. 63)

Grandin refers to the "deep touch pressure" of this device that leads to the calming effect, which, of course, may be true. Another explanation, however, is that being pressed into the unmoving position stabilizes both the body and the environment, and therefore dramatically simplifies the virtuous coordination required to create objects. There may well be far fewer objects to create (one can't turn one's head or body to encounter new objects), but the dazzle associated with those that are there to be participated with presents a far easier coordination task.

Ron Chrisley extended Smith's view to the study of consciousness, arguing that "we can have an objective understanding of consciousness through the skilled adoption of the appropriate subjective viewpoint on the experience … just as [Smith's] acrobat keeps their perspectively-oriented torch focused on the same location" (Chrisley, 2001, p. 9). Whereas the participation described by Smith involves the virtuous coordination of stimulation coming from the outside as well as the inside, Chrisley's extension argues that the stimulation may be entirely inner. On this view, inner experience is an acquired skill or set of skills. Chrisley (2008) offered a slight extension of this view, observing that because inner experience is evanescent and ever-changing, it might be useful to extend Smith's metaphor by having the acrobat aim the flashlight not at a fixed point but at a moving butterfly.

Recall that Smith's acrobat must move even if the object remains at a fixed point: If the acrobat is stable and the phenomenon is stable, then the flashlight beam defines a line, whereas an object is just one point on that line. It is only when the acrobat moves but keeps the flashlight trained on the phenomenon that a particular point on the line becomes defined by the convergence of the moving flashlight beams. Chrisley's (2008) addition is that the movement of the butterfly is a *second* reason that the acrobat must move. The butterfly's movement requires that the acrobat's virtuous skill must include the capability of progressive adjustment driven by continuing observation and feedback: Now the butterfly begins to move toward the top of the light beam, now to the left, and so on.

My DES experience accords with Chrisley's view: People participate in the creation of inner phenomena by a virtuous coordination of inner-experience skills. For most adults, this coordination was, at least to some extent, mastered so long ago that the lack of mastery is long forgotten. However, we have seen some examples already in this book where the mastery of this coordination seems to be still in progress; I draw them together here. In Chapter 9, we concluded that inner seeing ("image making") is a skill that, like the experience of feelings, may need to be acquired gradually over a long period of time. We discussed the example of nine-year-old Jimmy who was seeing an image of a hole he had dug in his back yard; apparently this image took some number of *minutes* to construct. Adults presume that inner seeings, when they occur, do so nearly instantaneously, but that, I think, is an adult-centric view that forgets their own skill development. I think it much more reasonable to believe that infants have no ability to create visual images; (some) adults have the ability to create visual images nearly instantaneously; somewhere between infancy and adulthood the skill of creating visual images was acquired; and, like other skills, that acquisition was gradual, at first halting, inefficient, and slow. Most adults uncritically assume that their inner-seeing ability was simply acquired as an intact ability, as if one night I went to sleep unable to create inner seeings and the next day I awoke with the ability to create inner seeings in colorful, immediate detail. That seems highly unlikely. Much more likely is that one day I had a glimpse of a crude inner seeing, and then nothing like that for a few weeks, and then another glimpse, and nothing again for a few days, and then another glimpse, somewhat more detailed, and then nothing again for a day, and then another glimpse, even more detailed and after a shorter delay, until eventually, as the joint result of physiological development and experiential practice, I gradually build the skill of essentially immediately seeing detailed imagery at will.

Monson (1989) described "Wendy's" inner hearing of her junior high school orchestra as apparently a repeated "playing" as a way of acquiring the skill of inner hearing. Wendy reported that for a few months she had been "playing around" with an inner hearing of her school orchestra's performance of a piece from a recent festival. Each time she innerly heard this performance, she "corrected" a bit of it: Now she removed a squeak from the clarinet; now she improved the intonation of a violin note; and so on. As a result, at the moment of Monson's beep she was hearing her orchestra perform, but they sounded better than they ever had in reality. I see this kind of "playing" as an inner-experience equivalent to playing with blocks: Kids play with blocks to build fine-motor coordination; kids play with inner experience to build inner-experience coordination.

Chapter 9 also speculated that in some of our adolescents, emotional processes were occurring as physical events in the body, but with no concomitant emotional experience. For example, at about two-thirds of thirteen-year-old RD's samples he was innerly speaking to himself, and at one-third of those RD recognized his voice as showing emotion such as anger, excitement, sadness, or happiness. Strikingly, he was experiencing a feeling in only one of those samples. I understand that as a lack of coordination/skill of inner processing. The "raw ingredients" of emotion were doubtless present (heart rate elevating, fists clenching, adrenals pumping, etc.), but those disparate events were not (yet) able to be coordinated into an organized experience of feeling.

I take those examples as evidence from the acquisition side that a virtuous coordination is required for the existence of (and for the apprehension of) inner experience – until the coordination is acquired, the experience does not exist. There is also evidence from the deterioration side. The same coordination that I gradually acquired, I can gradually lose. For example, in Chapter 9 we discussed the case of Doris, an eighty-one-year-old woman who saw images in black-and-white, not in color. It seems reasonable to interpret this as a loss of the ability to coordinate experiential details: that as a younger woman, Doris's imagery had been in color, but as she lost the ability to coordinate her physical activities, she similarly lost the ability to coordinate her experiential activities.

In Chapter 9, we discussed the case of Fay, who could not adequately perform the DES task. Todd Seibert and I interpreted that as evidence that Fay had no inner experience, that for some people, somewhere between adulthood (where the coordination of skills that comprise inner experience is easy) and old age, there is a decline in this coordination. For some people, the decline may well be sudden (as in a stroke). But for other people, the decline is gradual, over many years, and is hidden from the view of others and oneself by a variety of coping strategies and habituation.

In 1990 I reported the case of a schizophrenic man whose medication was being unsuccessfully adjusted (Hurlburt, 1990). As his condition worsened, the extent of his ability to form visual images declined. At one point, for example, he was innerly seeing the board of the game Risk, but instead of seeing the whole board, he was seeing only Australia. Earlier, he would have seen the entire board with Australia in the figure and the rest of the board in the ground. Later, he lost his ability to form images or any other kind of experience altogether.

All these examples are consistent with the notion that inner experience is a virtuous coordination of inner skills, and that these skills and the coordination of them may build gradually (across childhood) and decline gradually (across old age). The examples I have cited so far are from unusual (young, old, schizophrenic) individuals, but it is also possible to see the signs of this coordination (or lack thereof) in everyday adults. For example, Chris Heavey and I have shown that inner speech sometimes has "holes" in it – missing words in an otherwise complete inner speaking. The innerly spoken rhythm goes on, leaving a space for the missing word; and continuing on is a coordinated process where the words themselves seem to be produced by a process that is separate from the rhythm of the words. We called this phenomenon "partially unworded speech." For example, "That is a very strong _____ – maybe it is a gas leak!" (Hurlburt & Heavey, 2006, p. 211); the blank had "space" for two syllables, and apparently was created to allow for the word "odor," but that word had not yet appeared. So inner speaking, which might seem to be a unitary process, seems rather to be a coordination of at least two inner processes, one which produces the rhythm and one which produces the words. Sometimes those two processes are happily coordinated, and the words arrive at the same time as the rhythm. But not always.

Hurlburt and Heavey (2006, p. 215) observed a similar phenomenon for inner seeing in normal adults. Some subjects occasionally have the experience of seeing without the experience of anything being seen, a phenomenon Hurlburt and Heavey called "imageless seeing." I see this as another coordination process that can sometimes go awry.

As a result of these considerations, it seems that the virtuous coordination required to participate in the production of inner phenomena is similar to that required to participate in the production of real objects.

THE VIRTUOUS COORDINATION MAY NOT EXIST

Our DES studies show that most normal adults have some sort of this virtuous coordination most of the time – most DES beeps discover some pretty unequivocal form (or forms) of inner experience. Yet as we have just seen, there may be many people (young children, the elderly, some with psychological disorders) who have no inner experience. Thus I conclude that the virtuous coordination that participates in the creation of the "objects" of inner experience need not exist. Hurlburt & Heavey (2006 chapter 2) provided the example of Amy, who, they argued, did not have inner experience at the outset of sampling.

These individuals may navigate through the world satisfactorily, so the external observer might not suspect the absence of inner experience. Therefore I conclude that the virtuous coordination that Chrisley and I are describing is not necessary for human existence.

Many readers, most of whom have inner experience, may find it hard to accept that other seemingly normal people have no inner experience. Hurlburt (in Hurlburt & Schwitzgebel, 2007, chapter 11) discussed the presuppositions behind that view.

DES AS INTERPERSONAL VIRTUOUS COORDINATION

As we saw earlier, Brian Cantwell Smith showed that people create, stabilize, and maintain objects by a virtuous coordination in the face of the underlying flux of perspectival views on the world – the acrobat aiming his flashlight at a fixed point on the stage. Chrisley extended Smith's logic to the creation of the objects of inner experience – the acrobat aiming his flashlight at a butterfly. I elaborated Chrisley's logic by providing some DES examples.

Both Smith's and Chrisley's were *intra*personal accounts: how I create objects for myself (Smith) and how I create inner experience for myself (Chrisley). Now I extend Chrisley's logic by applying it to the *inter*personal problem of apprehending the inner experience of *another person*. What do *I* have to do to apprehend Mike Kane's inner experience (Chapter 6), or to apprehend RD's inner experience (Chapter 9), or to apprehend Ricardo Cobo's experience (Chapter 14)?

The first step is to extend Chrisley's butterfly metaphor by recognizing that not everyone's virtuous coordination is aimed at a butterfly – people's experiences have different characteristics. So Chrisley aims at a butterfly, Jane aims at a gazelle, George aims at the sounds of music (so the flashlight isn't his preferred tool), and so on. The DES skill is to be facile, supple, strong, quick, steady, focused, attentive, patient, responsive, and so on, so that the interviewer's coordinations can become aligned with the subject's coordinations. The required coordinations may differ from one subject to the next, or from one moment to the next within a single subject.

Once the interviewer masters the coordinations necessary for apprehending (for dancing in concert with) any particular subject's coordinations, the interviewer's task is to describe those coordinations to a third party. I think all that is possible but requires substantial delicacy.

Q: So, after all this, should we call pristine experience and DES subjective or objective?

A: In one manner of speaking, pristine experience and DES are entirely subjective (they deal with perception of one's own states and processes), but in another manner of speaking they are not at all subjective (they are not impressionistic). In one manner of speaking they are objective (there are mostly right and wrong answers about what is pristinely experienced at any given moment), but in another manner they are not at all objective (they are not publicly observable). The aim of this chapter is not to resolve that terminological dilemma but to help us see that branding pristine experience as either subjective or objective is a mistake – the connotations of those terms are too polarized. Our aim is to be thoughtful about pristine experience and DES, to see pristine experience and DES for what they are, not blinkered by terminological habits that have been acquired in quite different contexts. I think it makes sense to consider pristine experience "radically non-subjective." That is a mouthful, but it may have the virtue of encouraging you to think about what you're saying.

18

Diamonds versus Glass

Chapter 17 (really the entire book) made the point that bits of pristine experience are radically non-subjective – they have particular, pretty darn directly apprehendable characteristics – and that distinguishes them from other presumed mental structures or processes that are matters of inference, opinion, or impression. Let's call the radically non-subjective bits "diamonds" (following Hurlburt & Heavey, 2006, p. 255) and the other presumed structures/ processes "glass"; I invoke that metaphor to highlight the relatively unyielding phenomenal nature of bits of pristine experience. Karen's innerly seeing bubble-letter "abuse treatment" (Chapter 17), Ephraim's attending to the amoeba shape of the soup in his spoon (Chapter 16), Abigail's wondering whether Julio would be driving his pickup truck (Chapter 15), Ricardo Cobo's not-yet-formed seeing of the TV (Chapter 14), and the other examples in this book – are all diamonds, bits of experience that were the way they were and no other way, impervious to the opinion of others or influence by outside forces. Karen directly (but innerly) saw bubble letters that had thin black borders (not thick, not red, not solid). Ephraim's experience at the moment of the beep was dominated by the soup shape on his spoon (not its taste, the music in the room, or anything else). Abigail directly experienced a wondering, which had no experienced words or images. Cobo saw brown and gray but not the TV from which it emanated. All those experiences are substantially independent of their report: Karen saw bubble letters regardless of whether she was wearing a beeper, regardless of whether the interviewer was or was not skilled. Those experiences could be overlooked or quickly forgotten, in the same way that you could set a diamond ring on the sink and walk away, but the diamond itself would remain as it was regardless of whether it was forgotten. Find the diamond in the trash a week later and it will still be the same diamond, unaltered.

By contrast, the ten examples in Chapter 17's Table 17.1 do not have this diamond-like existence, this direct apprehendability, this existence largely

347

independent of the method of inquiry and largely impervious to outside influence. The state of readiness to deal with terminally ill patients (Table 17.1, example 1) likely does not have an existence independent of the method of inquiring about it; a "state of readiness" is a mentalism like hunger. Recall the discussion of Skinner's view in Chapter 11: Hunger when measured by electric shock is different from hunger as measured by quinine; is different from hunger as measured by weight reduction; is different from hunger as measured by time since eating; is different from hunger as measured by blood sugar. There is, probably, no independent existence of "readiness." Even if there is, that state of readiness is not directly apprehendable, and the readiness itself is probably greatly influenced by outside factors such as who is asking. The same can be said about opinions about the perceived usefulness of e-services (Table 17.1, example 2) and the other examples in Table 17.1. We call those "glass" to reflect the relative ease of breaking or otherwise altering the presumed state or process.

Constraint: Relentlessly distinguish between diamonds and glass – that is, between specific moments of pristine experience and all else. Glass has its place: It is doubtless useful to inquire about medical students' preparation to work with terminally ill patients and about the utility of e-services. But a science of experience has to know the difference between diamonds and glass. This book has tried to show that it may be possible to apprehend diamonds in high fidelity, and that it may be possible to build a useful science of experience on those diamond descriptions – that cleaving to the diamonds might reveal important characteristics of bulimia, adolescence, age-related cognitive decline, Tourette's Syndrome, schizophrenia, virtuosity, and so on. Diamonds *are* precious.

The problem is that the glass is shiny, too, and far easier to accumulate than diamonds. In fact, glass chips at first seem *even shinier* than diamonds because your own glass chips are your own creation, created in perfect alignment with your own favorite presuppositions. Cobo's (prior to sampling) faux-generalizations about his visual experiences were always exactly what he expected, exactly how he expected them, and they behaved exactly how he expected them to. They reflected exactly the light of his own presuppositions. They were perfectly aligned with his presuppositions, but they were *not* aligned at all with his actual experience. It required some substantial work to excavate, cut, and polish Cobo's diamonds until they reflected his real experience with a brilliance that exceeded the presuppositional glassy flash. Once that is accomplished, however, the brilliance may be richer and longer lasting.

SHARON'S CHARACTERIZATION OF HANNAH'S EXPERIENCE

As a way of exploring the distinction between diamonds and glass, we will discuss a characterization of "Hannah's" experience written by Sharon

Jones-Forrester. Hannah is one of the bulimic subjects described in Jones-Forrester (2009; see Chapter 2); the interviews of Hannah were conducted jointly by Sharon and me. Here is Sharon's description of Hannah's experience as revealed by our sampling:

> It is important to convey an as-accurate-as-possible sense of our impressions of Hannah as a whole. Although we can never entirely be "in her skin," the eight days that we spent with her allowed us a brief and captivating glimpse into her inner world. Hannah's inner world is a rich, complex, and profoundly fragmented place. She lives much of her life in a "man's world": she is a semi-truck driver and has been so for many years. Although she has returned to school, she plans to remain in this job for the income and job security it provides her, and in fact, being a truck driver seems to be a core aspect of her self-concept and a source of great pride for her.
>
> At the beginning of sampling, she expressed to us that no one close to her knows the extent of her daily struggles. Although she is physically very strong, her inner world is fragile and fragmented. It is perhaps this contrast that made sampling with Hannah so compelling, and which fostered within us such profound respect for her. It is both her strength *and* her vulnerability that together provide insight into what her daily struggle must be like. This struggle is most apparent in those samples where Hannah was interacting with her boyfriend or engaged in the complex tasks involved in her job. In both of these instances, Hannah's inner world deeply contrasted with her external presentation. In both of these contexts, with her boyfriend and at work, Hannah is likely seen as strong, competent, and fiercely independent, and yet her inner world clearly shows her daily struggles with conflicting pressures. Her undifferentiated emotions and occasional complete withdrawal from conflict by focusing entirely on relatively insignificant sensory details make it very difficult for her to directly experience and resolve conflicts that arise, both within herself and with others in the external world. This is a "snapshot" portrait of Hannah, designed to bring her samples to life.

DISCUSSION OF SHARON'S CHARACTERIZATION

Sharon's characterization of Hannah's experience shows competent psychological thinking; this type/style of description is similar to an initial case conceptualization of a psychotherapy client. It is well written; it is sensitive to Hannah's circumstances; it conveys Hannah and her situation in a convincing way; it appears to give substantial insight into Hannah and some of the current issues in her life. Most psychologists would, I believe, be delighted with this kind of summary.

However, despite its psychological competence, I think this kind of characterization is a great *threat* to the science of experience because it unthinkingly mixes together diamonds and glass, two fundamentally different kinds of material, as if there were no important difference.

Sharon was a student acquiring the DES skills when she wrote this characterization of Hannah, and I thank her for permission to quote and criticize it. I trust that Sharon and the reader understand that my critique is not about Sharon as an individual but about the failure to discriminate diamonds from glass, a failure that she shared with much of psychology, the discipline that taught her to write like that. In her characterization, she was doing what psychologists do – and doing it very well. However, from my point of view, that is *not* good enough to serve as a foundation for a science of experience.

Before I criticize Sharon's characterization, let's be as clear as possible about what a diamond is in this context. Sharon and I had collected forty-four samples of Hannah's experience, each explored in careful expositional interviews. Each sample description is therefore intended to be a high fidelity description of a diamond. Here is an example of a diamond description from Jones-Forrester (2009):

> Sample 3.2. Hannah was in her pickup truck with her boyfriend and had a bodily sensory awareness of the cold air conditioning on her face and neck, and a separate, simultaneous external sensory awareness of the sound of her boyfriend's voice. She was not listening to what he was saying at all, but instead was only aware of the sound of his voice droning on, which she likened to the "wa wa wa wa" of the teacher in the Charlie Brown cartoon movies. (Jones-Forrester, 2009, p. 229)

That is a diamond because at that moment, Hannah was feeling the coldness on her neck and hearing the *wa wa wa* of her boyfriend's voice, regardless of whether she was wearing a beeper, regardless of whether the subsequent DES interview would be skillful or not, regardless of whether, had she not been beeped, she would remember the coldness and *wa wa wa* five minutes or five hours later. The coldness and the *wa wa wa* presented themselves to Hannah directly.

If Sharon's characterization of Hannah is to cleave to the diamonds, it must be a faithful portrayal of that and the forty-three other diamonds. Here is a complete listing of the diamond descriptions in Sharon's characterization of Hannah's experience:

- Diamond: *Hannah's inner world is a rich, complex, and profoundly fragmented place.* Discussion: Hannah's experience at sample 3.2 was, as best we could determine by our careful interview procedure (as free of presuppositions as possible), complex and fragmented: There were two separate, independent, unrelated, but simultaneous sensory awarenesses (the coldness and the *wa wa wa* sound). Likewise, Hannah's experience at sample

2.5 was, as best we could determine, complex and fragmented; Hannah's experience at sample 3.1 was, as best we could determine, complex and fragmented; and so on for twenty-six of her forty-four sampled experiences. A summary of those diamonds – to say, for example, that 59 percent of Hannah's diamonds were complex and fragmented – is again a diamond: It is an actual (*not* a faux) generality, a direct summary of the diamonds, tightly constrained by what we have directly observed through the careful examination of experience at each individual sample. Sharon's statement "Hannah's inner world is a rich, complex, and profoundly fragmented place" is a translation of that diamond-description into everyday English.

- Diamond: *Her inner world is ... fragmented.* A shorter version of the same.
- Diamond: *[She has] undifferentiated emotions.* Again, this is an actual generality about diamonds: Hannah's emotions, as best we could determine by careful interview, were undifferentiated at sample 2.2; her emotions were undifferentiated at sample 2.5, and at a total of seven instances out of the forty-four samples. She never had a clearly experienced emotion. To say that Hannah has undifferentiated emotions is thus an actual generality, a direct summary of the basic diamonds, tightly constrained by what we have directly observed by an adequately careful procedure.
- Diamond: *[She] focuses entirely on relatively insignificant sensory details.* This again is an actual generalization of carefully explored experiences: At twenty-six of her forty-four samples (59 percent) she was, as best we could determine by this careful interview procedure, focused on insignificant sensory details such as the cold of the air conditioner or the *wa wa wa* of the voice.

Thus Sharon's characterization gives some high fidelity descriptions of Hannah's diamonds. However, those diamond descriptions make up only roughly 30 words of the 335 total words of Sharon's characterization. The rest of Sharon's characterization of Hannah is "glass": opinions, casual theorizings, plausible narratives, "clinical impressions," or other unsubstantiated, subjective, and ungrounded notions about Hannah. Anything that appears to be a description of Hannah's experience but is not actually in directly nonsubjective contact with some moment of her experience is glass. Here is some of Sharon's Hannah-glass, chip by chip, with commentary:

- Glass: *It is important to convey an as-accurate-as-possible sense of our impressions of Hannah.* Critique: Carefully considered, we have very little idea what "our impressions of Hannah" means. We don't know whether "our" means Sharon, Sharon and me individually, or Sharon and me jointly. Carefully considered, Sharon's impression of Hannah is a characteristic of *Sharon*, not of Hannah; it is *not* directly tied to Hannah's experience. Sharon's impression arises from an impure, unspecified, and probably unspecifiable mix of the characteristics of Hannah and the characteristics of Sharon. No one including Sharon has examined with any care or clarity what evidence is used in creating this impression, what methodological considerations are employed to specify how one creates an impression, or in what realm, if any, impressions exist. Sharon's impression of Hannah doubtless rests primarily on casual observation, plausibility, presuppositions, and prejudice.

Furthermore, all that presumes that Sharon's impression of Hannah exists, which it probably doesn't. Sharon's impression of Hannah is a mentalism, existing, like the hunger that we described previously, only in a manner of speaking, and differently in each manner of speaking.

Furthermore, and perhaps more importantly, Sharon implies that she will provide an *as-accurate-as-possible* characterization of our impressions of Hannah. Trying to be as accurate as possible about an impression is like trying to be as accurate as possible about the amount of water in a mirage: The closer you look, the harder "our impression" is to define.

Furthermore, and perhaps worst, if Sharon maintains that she can be as accurate as possible about glass, she suggests that she can be no more accurate about diamonds than she can be about glass. In fact, even if she had not used the "as accurate as possible" phrase, her moving back and forth indiscriminately between diamonds and glass, using the same kinds of phrases for both, indicates that she understands no essential distinction between diamonds and glass. That is, her failure relentlessly to distinguish between diamonds and glass diminishes the importance of the diamonds.

Q: You're pretty hard on Sharon. She spent six hours with Hannah, and, presuming Sharon is a sensitive human, did indeed develop an impression of Hannah. Such impressions are not worthless – for example, they often form the basis for psychotherapy.
A: I stipulate that Sharon is sensitive, that she has in some manner of speaking formed an impression, and that that impression may be useful in activities such as psychotherapy. I don't at all want Sharon to be or to pretend to be impressionless, nor do I wish to convey that glass is worthless. However, I do want Sharon (and, vicariously, you) to be perfectly clear about the epistemological distinction between Sharon's through-and-through subjective impression of Hannah (glass) and Hannah's carefully exposed radically non-subjective moments of pristine experience (diamonds). I don't want Sharon to imply, much less explicitly state, that the two are equal. I don't think the science of experience can advance if the distinction between the two is blurred.

- Glass: *…of Hannah as a whole*. Critique: We did not study Hannah as a whole; we examined forty-four moments of Hannah's pristine experience.

Hannah's experience is, as this book argues, important; the careful exploration of forty-four moments of experience gives us important insight into Hannah. But it does not reveal Hannah as a whole; or if it does, that would need to be shown. It is unconstrained speculation (read, "glass") to opine about Hannah as a whole.

- Glass: *Although we can never entirely be "in her skin," the eight days that we spent with her allowed us a brief and captivating glimpse into her inner world.* Critique: That the glimpse was *captivating* is a statement purely *about Sharon* – that she was captivated. It says *nothing whatsoever* about Hannah. Was Hannah captivating because Hannah told Sharon of her hatchet murders? Was Hannah captivating because she told of her great philanthropic contributions? Was she captivating because her choice of words was so beautiful? Was she captivating because she promised forbidden sexual pleasure? I use such extreme and disparate examples to illustrate the non-specific meaninglessness of terms like "captivating" as they are generally used. There is no hard connection between being captivated and *anything else*. We do not know what does and does not captivate Sharon; we do not know the method that is used to determine whether she was captivated. By using such a sentence, Sharon invites the reader into a numbing compact: I'll say nothing about Hannah (actually, nothing specific about anything) if you promise not to notice that I'm saying nothing at all about Hannah and actually nothing specific about anything. This statement does not genuinely submit to the constraints that the endeavor to describe experience imposes.

- Glass: *She lives much of her life in a "man's world": she is a semi-truck driver and has been so for many years.* Critique: The notion of the "man's world" is *not* the result of Sharon's direct observation of Hannah's experience; it is a figment of Sharon's imagination. It is true that Hannah drives a heavy truck and has done so for years. It is true that most of the other drivers for her company are men. It's also true that Hannah *told us* that she works and lives in the "man's world" of semi-truck driving. But Hannah's telling us that she lives in a man's world is *not* a description of her direct, objectively examined experience – it is an impure mixture of opinion/narrative/spin/fact, implied to be important by its position in Sharon's characterization.

It is not my intention here to enter into a discussion of gender discrimination, which I stipulate is an undesirable political and economic reality. My intention is to examine the science of experience and to consider the data on which such a science must rest. Sharon undertook no careful discussion/elaboration/exposition of what Hannah meant by "living in a man's world." There is no consideration of whether Sharon understands "living in a man's world" in the same way as does Hannah. There is absolutely no guarantee that the reader understands what either Sharon or Hannah means by it. Even if living in a man's world is indeed an important factor in Hannah's existence, there is no guarantee that that factor would show up in her pristine experience; and even if it does show up occasionally, there is no guarantee that it would show up in the forty-four samples we collected. Indeed, Sharon had every opportunity to show how living in a man's world manifests itself in Hannah's experience, but did not.

By saying "she lives much of her life in a man's world," Sharon invites the reader into a numbing compact: I won't write in a way that clearly states what I mean if you promise to pretend that you know exactly what I mean.

- Glass: *Although she has returned to school, she plans to remain in this job for the income and job security it provides her.* People often don't know the reasons they do things. Maybe it is indeed the income/job security that motivates her plans. But maybe, instead, she's afraid of applying the education she is obtaining. Maybe she equates education with management, and she's afraid of being part of management – she doesn't like telling other people what to do or firing other people. Hannah indeed told us that she planned to remain for the income and job security, but we did not carefully examine that casual comment and quite possibly neither has Hannah. I don't purport to know what is true about the motivation behind Hannah's vocational plans, but I don't think Sharon knows either, and quite probably neither does Hannah, in some important way.

  Furthermore, and perhaps worst, if Sharon maintains Hannah's casual statements about her motives are important, she implies that they are just as important as the diamonds. That is, her failure relentlessly to distinguish between carefully-investigated-moment diamonds and casual-comment glass diminishes the importance of the diamonds.

- Glass: *Being a truck driver seems to be a core aspect of her self-concept and a source of great pride for her.* The notion of self-concept is not defined. If there is such a thing, how, exactly, did Sharon ascertain it? How many core aspects of self-concept are there (one? two? twenty? two hundred?)? The more one tries to measure/define core aspect or self-concept (or any other mentalism) objectively, the slipperier those concepts become.

  Even if we accept the existence of "core aspects" and "self-concepts," Sharon did not observe them directly in Hannah's experience (or any other direct observation, for that matter), and she didn't *carefully* examine them at all. At the very best, Sharon inferred Hannah's self-concept from some ill-defined set of things Hannah said and didn't say (as interpreted by Sharon), some ways Hannah looked and didn't look (as interpreted by Sharon), some actions she took and didn't take, and so on. But Sharon didn't specify what those observations were; instead, Sharon invites the reader into a numbing compact: I'll say nothing about what self-concept really is, and nothing about the extent to which Hannah does or does not have one, and nothing about how I deduced any of that, if you promise to think that we both know what self-concept is, what I mean when I talk about it, and how I arrived at that meaning.

Inviting the reader into numbing compacts is like crying wolf – when Sharon actually describes a diamond, it will likely be interpreted as the opening move in another numbing compact. That is, her failure relentlessly to distinguish between diamonds and glass diminishes the importance of the diamonds.

I have described the glass in only the first paragraph of Sharon's characterization; I leave as an exercise for the reader the task of identifying the glass in the second paragraph.

A DIAMOND DESCRIPTION OF HANNAH'S EXPERIENCE

The DES task, as I see it, is relentlessly to inquire about and to describe diamonds – to apprehend in high fidelity the actual pristine experiences that occurred at the moments of beeps and carefully to draw actual generalizations about them – and resolutely and unflinchingly to eliminate glass: no opinionating, no psychologizing, no unsubstantiated claims about cause or essence, no collusive appearance of understanding, no theorizing, no narrative making, no economic or political influence, and so on.

Sharon and I had a discussion, more or less like the foregoing, of her characterization of Hannah's experience. Fortified by that discussion, Sharon and I prepared a new characterization of Hannah that is mostly (if not all) diamonds:

> Hannah generally had multiple (two to four or more) simultaneous experiences ongoing at any given time. For example, at one moment she was aware of the salty taste of the sunflower seeds she was eating; separately but simultaneously aware of the vibration of the legal pad that was sitting on her steering wheel; separately but simultaneously thinking/aware that the trailer parked in front of her was in bad repair; separately but simultaneously thinking about parental investment theory from her psychology notes – and this last thinking was itself multiple, including that she didn't like the theory, that it was going to be on the test, that it sounded made up, that it wasn't in her book. All that was experienced to be simultaneously ongoing.
>
> She frequently paid direct attention to sensory aspects, for example, to the saltiness of the sunflower seeds, to the vibration of the legal pad, to the greenness of the picture on the TV, to the scratchiness of her

boyfriend's hand on her back. Occasionally she paid attention to some sensory aspect as a way (apparently) of avoiding something else, as when she was focused in on the crackliness of her ex-husband's voice instead of hearing the criticisms he was shouting at her.

Hannah had frequent emotional reactions, but these were generally not directly experienced. For example, she innerly spoke to herself using an angry tone of voice but was not experiencing anger. She had difficulty differentiating thinking from feeling; for example, she was thinking/feeling of ways she could get her boyfriend to go to the movies with her; this process was inextricably a thinking of anxiety and an anxious feeling about the strategies she could use.

She was frequently occupied with food and weight issues, for example, thinking/sensing the bloatedness of her stomach and its ramifications for which jeans she should wear.

That characterization of Hannah's experience is mostly or all diamonds: It cleaves entirely, it seems to me, to what was directly observed by Hannah at the moments of beeps and relentlessly examined in the interviews within a few hours of the beeps. It includes actual generalizations of those moments – it categorizes experiences, and it uses terms like "frequently" that could be quantified, if desired. I think the reader knows pretty precisely what we are talking about at every step of the characterization. That is, there is no collusive numbing compact between the writer and the reader.

This all-diamond characterization directly describes actually observed characteristics of Hannah's experience. There is little or no ungrounded inference or speculation; there is little or no explicit or implicit theory or favoritism. There is little or no bending or stretching of the facts to make a narrative more plausible or more appealing. This characterization is pretty much pure Hannah with little or no Sharon or Russ or feminism or extrapolation or psychologizing mixed in.

DISCUSSION

The distinction between diamonds and glass is of fundamental importance to a science of inner experience. The diamonds are, or at least should be, the basic data of a science of inner experience – diamonds are the real phenomena of experience. It is through an accumulation of diamonds that generalizations and discriminations about experience can be made, and the relationship between those generalizations/discriminations and other physical and/or psychological constructs can be subsequently evaluated and validated.

The problem with the glass chips is that they are seductively attractive – they *appear to be* direct observations when in fact they are nothing of the sort.

There are four resultant problems: (a) Glass is not strong: A science built on attractive but not real phenomena is of limited utility. (b) Glass mixed with diamonds demeans the diamonds: Glass descriptions give the false impression that a careful description of actually occurring inner experience is no different from and no better than, say, a clinical interpretation about self-concept or gender role. More importantly, (c) glass diminishes the demand for diamonds: A glass description *impedes* real scientific inquiry by giving the false impression that adequate scientific inquiry is *already being done*, that there is no need to look further or to do better. (d) Glass lowers the standards: If it is acceptable to provide an opinion or a clinical impression, then it doesn't seem necessary to maintain a strict discipline about the encounter with pristine experience. (By the way, all this is very similar to what Skinner had to say about mentalisms; e.g., Skinner, 1977.)

> **Q:** I accept that Sharon's original characterization is not a pure description of Hannah's experience. But neither is your "mostly diamond" characterization. If neither is pure, I see no reason to go to the substantial trouble to use the sampling procedure.
> **A:** I agree with your premise but disagree with your conclusion. The scientific value of inner experience does not depend on perfection, but it does depend on the quality of the data. Sharon's glass-heavy narrative about Hannah is a highly impure, inextricably intertwined amalgam of the Hannah's real pristine experience, the mask that Hannah (for whatever reason) presents to the world, the real Sharon, the mask that Sharon presents to the world, and so on. It is low-grade ore, that is, the glass-to-diamonds ratio is high. By contrast, the mostly diamond characterization is high-grade ore. Whether a mine is worth operating depends *not* on the mere *presence* of the mineral, but on the grade of the ore, the cost of separating the mineral from the tailings, and the market value of the mineral.
> In case that metaphor doesn't hit the mark, here's another: The water from your tap is not pure. The water from the sewer is not pure. Therefore, you might as well drink from the sewer.
> **Q:** I accept that Sharon's original characterization is not a pure description of Hannah's experience. However, the all-diamond description of Hannah is totally forgettable – I haven't a clue about what she or her life might be like, generally speaking. Sharon's original description painted a picture of a person, not just of moments. A person is more than moments! Sharon undoubtedly engaged in an emotively impressionistic, self-referential portrayal that may have had a lot of inaccuracies, but the new characterization, accurate though it may be, slices Hannah so thin that I have no sense of a person. I do not see how there could be literature or film or any art form that values narrative for what it tells us about people. I just cannot follow you all the way there. I think that at times your quest for pristineness loses the whole.

A: I don't think it is true that Sharon's original characterization painted a picture of a person. Sharon thought she was painting a picture of a person; you believed her; but in fact she was, as you say, painting a mixture of Hannah, Sharon's own sentiments, and Sharon's take on public myths. You and Sharon jointly suspended disbelief, as Coleridge would say, and entered into a collusion to *accept* Sharon's narrative *as if* it were about Hannah.

I can't say with authority whether literature or film or any other art form can profit from the faithful apprehension of actual experience. But I can say this: There are books and films that purport to convey inner experience, and none does a very good job, as it seems to me. However, I think it is possible to make a film that would convey inner experience as it actually is, and the audience would be genuinely spellbound.

Until the importance of the distinction between diamonds and glass is thoroughly accepted, a science of inner experience will be severely limited, because it will mix a few diamonds in with a heap of glass chips, and then, eventually and quite appropriately, sweep up the whole mess and throw it in the trash. Diamonds and all. Such was the history of introspection a century ago, so this is not an idle speculation.

There is nothing hidden or subtle about the distinction between diamonds and glass. It does not require any supernatural power to write a mostly diamond description of Hannah rather than a glass-heavy description. Sharon wrote a glass-heavy description not because she was dull or dense, but because psychology had trained her to accept glass, had not trained her to discriminate between diamonds and glass. It requires no more time or effort to write the mostly diamond description; it does require knowing the difference between diamonds and glass and the discipline of sticking to the diamonds.

Once again I thank Sharon for allowing herself to be exposed in this way. I re-emphasize that I am not in any way criticizing Sharon in this chapter. My critique is aimed at her psychological training, which had led her, in her original characterization, to accept a mixture of observation, impression, politics, and whatever else as adequate science. That acceptance, which I think is widespread, works against the apprehension of pristine experience. If a science of experience (by which I mean most science, especially psychology and philosophy) is to advance, it will have to distinguish relentlessly between diamonds and glass.

Q: You distinguish between diamonds and glass as if they were fundamentally different entities. But they're not so different. Throughout this book you have described the difficulties that present themselves in apprehending pristine experience. In particular, you have emphasized the operation of presuppositions that prevent people from getting their own experience right and investigators from apprehending them in high fidelity.

Therefore the description of diamonds and glass are both problematic, and therefore diamonds and glass are not essentially different.

A: Your question is at the heart of the matter of a science of experience in that it blurs the important distinction between diamonds and glass as entities and the apprehension thereof. If science can get this distinction straight, I think science can advance. So let's be as clear as we can be about four things:

(a) Diamonds, as entities, are bits of pristine experience, bits of directly observed phenomena directly present before the footlights of consciousness. (b) Glass chips, as entities, have no phenomenal presentings – they are inferred structures or processes, or faux generalizations, taken for granted as existing but not directly observed. (c) The phenomenal characteristics of diamonds can be difficult to apprehend because of diamonds' phenomenal evanescence, because the subject's interest is in what the diamonds present rather than how they present it, and because of the operation of presuppositions. (d) The phenomenal characteristics of glass are impossible to apprehend because glass has no directly apprehendable phenomenal characteristics.

Your question observes that (c) and (d) both present difficulties, and therefore (a) and (b) are the same, but that's similar to saying that getting the view from the top of Mt. Everest is difficult and getting a close-up view of a mirage is difficult, and therefore Mt. Everest and a mirage are the same.

This book tries to show that (a) pristine experience does indeed present itself before the footlights of consciousness, and that presenting is pretty darn impervious to how or whether it is recalled (that is, is radically non-subjective). I have spent a career trying to determine whether that is true, and have answered yes. I accept that I may be mistaken, that science needs to investigate and determine whether or the extent to which I am deluded and have infected my colleagues, to investigate and determine whether there are limitations to the radical non-subjectivity of pristine experience that have escaped my attention, and so on.

But to perform that investigation, science will have to accept at least the possibility that (a) pristine experience exists in an essentially different realm from (b) theoretical constructs, inferred processes, and hypothetical structures; that (a) is directly observed whereas (b) is not. Maybe it will conclude that pristine experience is not directly observable (that I am deluded) and therefore that (a) and (b) are not essentially different. But to reach that conclusion, science will have at least to recognize that there *might be* an essential difference.

You're right, (c) apprehending pristine experience is methodologically difficult. I have emphasized that difficulty throughout this book (and will do so again in Chapters 19 and 20) because that's the way it is and I think science historically either overestimates or underestimates the difficulty (Hurlburt & Heavey, 2001). If science is to advance, it cannot afford either overestimation or underestimation; that is, it will have genuinely to submit to the constraints that the investigation of pristine experience imposes. Whether science can do this effectively remains to be seen – there are all sorts of political, economic, social, and presuppositional impediments. This book has tried to show the *desirability* of overcoming those impediments, but has not opined about the *feasibility* of so doing by the scientific community.

But there is a big difference between (c) difficulty of apprehension and (d) impossibility of apprehension, and science will have to keep that straight. We'll return to that in Chapter 21.

Into the Floor: A Right-or-Wrong-Answer Natural Experiment

WITH CHRIS HEAVEY

Chapters 17 and 18 (really, the entire book) made the case that diamonds of pristine experience exist pretty much independently of the ability to recall or adequately characterize them, that there are "pretty darn right" apprehensions of inner experience. We have also made the case throughout this book that the apprehension of pristine experience is made difficult by the evanescence of the phenomenon, because the subject's interest is in what the diamonds present rather than how they present it, and because of the operation of presuppositions.

However, here is an alternative explanation of the difficulty of apprehension: There is no pristine experience – that pristine experience exists only in a manner of speaking, and if the manner of speaking changes, what is called pristine experience changes. If that is true, then there could be no right or wrong answers about pristine experience – there are only differing manners of speaking about it.

There is no simple or single way to determine which of those explanations to adopt. One approach might be called validational, for example, to see whether we can find ways to verify that bulimic women have distinctive characteristics of experience. Another way, which the present chapter explores, is to try to discover whether there are indeed right or wrong answers about particular experiences. If there are, then there must exist particular pristine experiences about which to have right or wrong answers.

"Naomi" was a nineteen-year-old student in an introductory psychology class who had volunteered to serve as a subject – other than that, we knew nothing about her at the outset of the interviews. Chris Heavey (an experienced DES investigator) conducted the first interview; Chris and Russ conducted the second and third interviews jointly. Russ was unable to attend the fourth interview, so Chris conducted it and wrote descriptions of the sampled experiences.

Here is Chris's description of Naomi's experience at sample 4.1:

> Sample 4.1 [Chris's view] Naomi was in the library sitting on the floor resting with her head on her left arm, which was on a low table. She felt her right wrist moving in a medium size loop. She also felt her muscles relax in a way that felt like they were oozing toward the floor. She also felt sleepy.

The next day, Russ watched the videotape of that interview and concluded that Chris's description missed central features of Naomi's experience. Here is Russ's description of the same sample; we italicize where Russ's description differs substantially from Chris's:

> Sample 4.1 [Russ's view] Naomi was in the library sitting on the floor resting with her head on her left arm, which was on a low table. Her right wrist was moving, *as if of its own accord*, in a medium size loop. She felt her muscles relaxing, and as they did so she felt her body sinking downward *and merging into the floor, her legs having become one with the floor*. She also was sleepy.

In this chapter we will focus on the *merging into the floor* difference between Chris's and Russ's descriptions. On Russ's view, Naomi directly experienced herself *becoming one with* the floor. On Chris's view, by contrast, Naomi was relaxing, feeling her muscles sinking *toward* the floor.

Chris and Russ agreed that Naomi mentioned in the interview "sinking into the floor." Chris's view was that Naomi intended "sinking into the floor" to be taken metaphorically – that it was a colorful description of relaxation. Russ's view was that Naomi intended "sinking into the floor" to be taken literally as a description of direct experience.

Naomi was not, of course, *actually in reality* becoming one with the floor. In Russ's view, Naomi's direct experience of becoming one with the floor is a distortion of reality, which we might call, for lack of a better term, a micro-psychoticism. In Chris's view, Naomi is merely becoming profoundly relaxed.

EXPLORATION

There is a lot at stake for the science of experience in trying to understand Naomi's experience and the two different descriptions of it. If it is impossible to distinguish between literal description and metaphor, impossible to distinguish between everyday relaxation and micro-psychoticism, then that would impose a strong constraint on the exploration of pristine experience – perhaps pristine experience does not exist independently of the ability to recall or adequately characterize it, or perhaps high fidelity apprehensions of pristine experience are impossible (at least in some cases). On the other hand, if it *is* possible to distinguish between literal description and metaphor and *is* possible to distinguish between everyday relaxation and micro-psychoticism, then that would impose a very different constraint on the exploration of pristine experience – high fidelity apprehensions are possible but investigators can get it wrong.

There are also substantial personal stakes involved: This is not merely a matter of one dispassionate theory competing with another theory; it may well be a matter of one of us being right and the other wrong in an observation. Any conversation that we might have about this discrepancy would have to navigate through the thickets of presuppositions, blindnesses, egos, sensitivities, and so on. There are no rules about how or whether to proceed in such situations. The stakes for science seemed to outweigh the personal stakes, so we pressed on.

We decided to ask Naomi to clarify what she meant. We agreed to interview Naomi twice more (her fifth and sixth sampling interviews), a week later and a week after that, about new beeped experiences. We agreed that at the end of the upcoming (fifth) interview, we would ask her again about her experience at the library-relaxing sample 4.1. We would try to ask those questions in ways that were neutral regarding the literality/metaphoricality of her expressions.

A Week Later – The End of the Fifth Interview

Naomi was a subject in a study that dealt with the adequacy of written descriptions of experience, so at the beginning of each sampling interview, she was asked to read the written descriptions of the previous week's samples and rate them on a ten-point scale, where 1 equals *not at all accurate* and 10 equals *completely accurate*. As part of that procedure, at the beginning of the fifth interview, she was given Chris's description of sample 4.1. She rated it a 9.9, explaining that the word "oozing" should have been "sinking," but other than that it looked good.

We then interviewed her about that (fifth) day's samples, and when that interview was completed, we turned out attention back to sample 4.1. Here is a transcript of the relevant segment at the end of the fifth interview:

> RTH:[501] In one of the beeps from last time you were sitting on the floor and relaxing and feeling your legs sinking into the floor or something like that.
> NAOMI:[502] Oh, yeah.
> RTH:[503] And I didn't understand . . . I wasn't sure that I understood what that phenomenon was like. Can you recall that at this moment? I was . . .

RTH[501-503] is Russ's attempt at returning Naomi in a level-playing-field way to sample 4.1. That is, Russ tried to tell Naomi that he was interested in her experience in sample 4.1 without imposing either his viewpoint or Chris's. In RTH[501] he honored both the relaxing and the sinking parts of her earlier description, and in RTH[501] and RTH[503] he repeatedly undermined any implied preference or even understanding of the one or the other ("or something like that," "I didn't understand," "I wasn't sure I understood," and "Can you recall?"). His aim was to get her into the ballpark and then give her a chance to start from the beginning of her own experience, as uncluttered by his own or Chris's expectations/presuppositions as possible. RTH[501–503] is doubtless not a *perfectly* even-handed question, but we think it is pretty darn even-handed, good enough to allow Naomi the opportunity to provide a view of her experience pretty independent of Russ's and Chris's presuppositions.

> NAOMI:[504] I can show you, more [gets off her chair and sits on the floor of the interview room to demonstrate]. You know the tables upstairs at the library?
> RTH:[505] Yeah.
> NAOMI:[506] How they're low?
> RTH:[507] Yeah.
> NAOMI:[508] Well, I was sitting like this with my arm up there, and you just sink down [inaudible while she resumes sitting in her chair].

It seems that Naomi (mis)understood Russ's RTH[501–503] interest to be about her physicality at beep 4.1, which is good news from the desire-to-be-even-handed perspective: It indicates that she knows what sample Russ is interested in and that she recalls this sample in some detail (she duplicates the same posture she had described the previous week); and it indicates that she is not (at least not immediately) too influenced by Russ's particular interests in asking this question (in fact, she misinterprets his interest as being about her physicality).

> RTH:[509] And ...
> NAOMI:[510] [brightens, as if in discovery] Oh, yeah! *That's* what I changed! Instead of *oozing* it was *sitting* ... er, [correcting her misspeaking] *sinking*.

Naomi is recalling here that she rated the written description of her experience as 9.9 instead of 10 because she wanted to change the word *oozing* to *sinking*. This again is evidence that she recalls the beep that Russ is inquiring about without being unduly captured by his view of the interpretation of that experience.

> RTH:[511] OK. And some of the ... in that ... in your descriptions as I recall them, you said that you were ... sort of felt like you were merging into the floor, like your legs were merging into the floor? What ...

This is another example of a skillful level-playing-field question: "sort of felt like you were merging into the floor" is neutrally interpretable as either literal or metaphorical. Russ is still giving Naomi space to maneuver in any way she finds appropriate about this sample.

> NAOMI:[512] Yeah, like I start becoming the floor. Except I wasn't flattening out [laughs].

"Flattening out" appeared to be a reference to a comment from the fourth interview, again indicating that she has good recollection of that interview.

RTH:[513] And what exactly do you mean by "becoming the floor"? What …

Naomi[512] says "like I start becoming the floor," which is consistent with Russ's literal-description interpretation of her experience. Note that Russ does not seize on this interpretation, but instead gives her (by asking "what exactly do you mean?") another opportunity to back away or clarify. This is an example of how bracketing of presuppositions must be done. Her response is consistent with Russ view; therefore Russ *resists* the temptation to accept that he understands her.

NAOMI:[514] I [pause] I became attached to the floor, like if I wanted to get up I couldn't because my legs were in the floor, and I was part of it.

Chris: As Naomi said this, I thought she was embellishing her story; that she was adding "oddness" that was not there initially. I was also mildly annoyed or irritated. I understood that her responses were invalidating my view and supporting Russ's; it was unpleasant. [Note: As here, we are occasionally inserting our best recollections about our own experience during this interview as reconstructed while watching the video. However, we urge the reader to be somewhat skeptical about our ability to reconstruct our experiences even with the aid of videotape (recall the section "A Plausibility Natural Experiment" near the end of Chapter 7).]

Russ: I thought Naomi[514] stated pretty unequivocally that she intended the experience of sinking "into the floor" to be understood literally – "I became attached to the floor" is a straightforward, declarative, mostly unsubjunctified expression. But in a continuing effort to bracket my presuppositions, I resolve to continue to inquire in a neutral manner.

RTH:[515] So there was something about becoming actually a part of the floor in your experience?
NAOMI:[516] Yeah.
RTH:[517] And … and … is that … is that like [pause] *stuck to* the floor, or is that a different kind of a thing?

Part of the art of even-handed, non-leading questioning is to ask questions that lead *away* from what you expect, and to undermine them as equally as you would questions that lead *toward* what you expect. Here "stuck to" implies attached to the surface, rather than merging into it, so with this question Russ leads Naomi slightly *away* from his understanding of what she has said (but to maintain neutrality undermines himself by saying, "or is that a different kind of a thing?").

NAOMI:[518] Kind of like you root … I rooted myself into it.

Naomi[518] indicates that she is not merely being led by whatever Russ asks: she returns to the notion of merging with the floor despite Russ's (RTH[517]) push in an opposite direction.

> RTH:[519] OK. And I gather ... well, I guess I want to ask: Do you mean that metaphorically? Or does it actually feel like you have somehow rooted yourself into the floor at that particular moment?

Again Russ gives her a level-playing-field opportunity to back away from the literal sense of her description.

> NAOMI:[520] Yeah, I think that it was probably around the ... somehow I *did it* to myself, but I don't know how. [laughs nervously]
>
> RTH:[521] So somehow you end up merging somehow physically into the floor?
>
> NAOMI:[522] Yes.
>
> RTH:[523] And is that the ... your entire legs or just ... How does ... What part of you gets ...
>
> NAOMI:[524] The lower half. To where then my upper half is stuck.
>
> RTH:[525] And by your "lower half" you mean the lower half of your body or the lower half of your legs?
>
> NAOMI:[526] Like from here down [gestures to her waist] [laughs nervously]. Like from the middle of my stomach. [laughs nervously]
>
> RTH:[527] OK. So your body has somehow become merged into the floor and your upper half might want to get up but it can't because it's ...
>
> NAOMI:[528] Yes.
>
> RTH:[529] ... the bottom half is stuck to the floor. Is that right?
>
> NAOMI:[530] Yes.

Russ: I concluded that Naomi intended her description of merging into the floor to be straightforwardly literally descriptive, not metaphorical. I thought I asked suitably even-handed questions, and Naomi's responses were consistent (Naomi:[512] "I start becoming the floor"; Naomi:[514] "I became attached to the floor"; Naomi:[518] "I rooted myself into it") and declarative with little subjunctification. What subjunctification she uses seems related to her nervousness, of which there is quite a lot, which I understood reflects that she is worried that this merging with the floor will cause us to think she is crazy.

Chris: I was sure Naomi was changing her story. I accepted that she was confirming Russ's original understanding of the experience, but I was confident that this "new" description of this moment did not align with what she had said in the initial (day 4) interview.

A Week after That

In the interview the following week (her sixth sampling day, interview conducted jointly by Chris and Russ) Naomi happened to use the word *sinking* in the course of describing sample 6.2, and that presented an opportunity to double back and clarify what she meant by "sinking" at both sample 6.2 and at sample 4.1. It turned out that Naomi intended to use the word *sinking* in two different ways: In sample 6.2, *sinking* meant a strong, crushing pressure of her elbows against the table. But she said again that in sample 4.1, she meant *sinking* as a merging into the floor.

Now what? The current status of our exploration was this: (a) Chris and Russ agreed about what Naomi was saying in the fifth and sixth interviews – that she had intended "sinking into" in sample 4.1 to be taken literally; (b) Russ was confident that Naomi had been consistent across all three interviews: "sinking into" was meant to be taken literally from the outset; (c) Chris was confident that he had inquired directly about literalness/metaphoricity in the original (day 4) interview and had determined that she meant "sinking" metaphorically then. That is, Chris thought that in the fifth and sixth interviews, for whatever reason, she was changing her story.

We (Russ and Chris) hadn't resolved anything, hadn't advanced our understanding of the constraints that surround this endeavor. We still had one option open to us: the videotape of the original (day 4) interview. We prepared a transcript of that interview and used it to aid our viewing of the original video, which we watched together, frequently stopping the video when we desired to talk about it. Here is the day 4 transcript with our reactions to it. These reactions were drafted essentially immediately after watching the video, so any references to our experience during the day 4 interview were reconstructed after a month's delay. As noted earlier (after Naomi[514]), the reader and we have reason to be skeptical of our ability to retrospect accurately. We aver that we have retrospected as best we can, and in this situation that is the best we can do.

THE ORIGINAL (DAY 4) INTERVIEW

Chris: Before we display the transcript, let me say that there had been something about Naomi prior to day 4 that challenged my equanimity, as far as I can tell, in two ways. First, Naomi seemed to delight in telling us about her odd inner experience in a way that left me wondering whether oddness was her way of seeking attention. I should say up front that I could be entirely mistaken about this impression, but she struck me as being motivated in the direction of the-weirder-the-better. Although it is hard to say precisely what gave me that impression, it was something like the combination of the smile on her face as she described her unusual experiences and her searching for our reactions of shock or interest or something. She seemed delighted by her oddness and eager to show it to us. She also seemed to be a motivated non-conformist. For example, she did not write down her beeps in order. So when she came to the interview for day 3 and we asked her to describe what was in her experience at the first beep, she laughed while explaining, "I wrote them all out of order, so we're just going to call this beep number 1." This is a small thing, to be sure, but it is the laughing while saying it that catches me.

The second facet of my discomfort with Naomi was on the other side of the equation – my concern that her oddness might be entirely genuine. Years earlier Russ and I had sampled with "Jake," whose unusual experiences were somewhat similar to Naomi's. Jake had worn the beeper for sixteen days, and Russ and I had conducted sixteen sampling interviews trying to figure out what to make of his reports. His experiences were sometimes strange – for example, at one beep he was innerly seeing himself saying goodbye to the residents of a halfway house where he worked. He saw himself traverse through a solid wall in the house and disappear. Furthermore, during the course of the interviews Jake casually reported difficulties navigating real life; bad things just happened to him. For example, he said one day that he had lost his car, and by "lost" he meant that he had simply left it in another state and taken the bus home without it.

Sampling with Jake had been distressing to me. Russ and I discussed a number of times how his unusual inner experience and his difficulty navigating life might be signs of incipient schizophrenia. We were never able to come to a confident understanding of whether or not that was the case. I grew increasingly concerned about the possibility that something bad might happen to Jake "on our watch," so to speak. I was worried for Jake but also worried that if some bad event befell Jake, someone might suggest that our sampling had been the cause. I could imagine some smart lawyer saying, "You saw he was having difficulty hanging on to reality and yet you continued probing his inner experience!?" I believed then and still believe now that our sampling with Jake was probably helping him keep his grasp on reality, but I wouldn't have wanted to defend that position in a courtroom.

Naomi's unusual experiences reminded me of Jake's, though as far as I could tell Naomi was doing OK in life. So I also wondered whether Naomi's unusual inner experience might be a sign of something problematic. As far as I can tell, both of these facets of my reaction to Naomi undermined my equanimity toward Naomi before our discussion of the following beep began.

Russ: I never had the impression that Naomi was seeking our attention. I understood her smile to be a combination of embarrassment and resolve – a sort of pride in her willingness to tell us about something that she suspected we would find odd, perhaps crazy. My view stems, I think, from my pretty darn pure allegiance to the diamonds/glass distinction of Chapter 18. I find diamonds thoroughly attractive; I find glass, no matter how cleverly or adroitly presented, thoroughly boring. I think that interest is revealed by my every interaction, so that if Naomi (or anyone else) seeks my attention, she will figure out pretty quickly that telling me about her real pristine experience is the best way to get it.

Sample 4.1

NAOMI:[401] Just to give back story on the first beep, I was in the library sitting on the floor and my head was resting on my left arm. And at the moment of the beep I felt my wrist [pause] I want to say "flick" but it slowly moved in a circular fashion, to make a loop.

CHRIS (hereafter called CLH):[402] OK.

NAOMI:[403] It was doodling. [pause] And I felt myself sink into the floor, like become grounded. And I was very, very, very sleepy.

Russ: There are two potential oddnesses in the Naomi[401–403] report: First, Naomi refers (twice) to her wrist in the third person: "I felt my wrist flick … *it* slowly moved" at Naomi[401] and "*it* was doodling" at Naomi[403]. It seems much more natural to use the first person: "I flicked my wrist" and "I was doodling." That jangles my *Hm! That's a bit odd!* antenna. Does Naomi's use of "it" reflect something about her experience, or is it just a somewhat unusual verbal style? I don't know; I would be happy with either outcome; I will "keep that ball in the air" awaiting further developments (see Chapter 20). The second oddness is: "I felt myself sink into the floor." A second *Hm!* antenna jangle.

But at the same time I am struck by the carefulness of Naomi's description. First, she distinguishes clearly between context and moment ("Just to give back story …"). Second, this is a very carefully unsubjunctified (Chapter 8) report. There are only two subjunctifiers, and they are used in the service of clarification, not obfuscation. "I want to say 'flick'" is used to signal that she is being very careful in her locution, that "flick" is not exactly right but she doesn't have a better word. "Like become grounded" is an additional detail added onto an absolutely unsubjunctified declarative sentence: "I felt myself sink into the floor."

So to my ear, Naomi has given a very careful description of some things that are a bit odd. What to make of that remains to be seen.

Chris: I do not have a clear recollection of what was going through my mind during this interview. My oddness antennae generally are not as sensitive as are Russ's, and my notes simply say, "Felt wrist move in loop fashion" and "Felt wrist make looping motion." In retrospect her expression is odd, but there was so much odd about her experience that I may have been in "discounting" mode.

CLH:[404] Alright, um. So. You're in the library sitting on the floor, and your head was resting on your arm …

NAOMI:[405] On the table, I'm sorry.

CLH:[406] On your arm on the table or just on the table?

NAOMI:[407] Arm on the table. One of the lower tables. I was just sitting on the floor right in front of the table…

CLH:[408] OK.

NAOMI:[409] … with my arm on it and my head resting on my arm.

CLH:[410] OK. Left arm on the table?

NAOMI:[411] Yes. Left arm on the table.

CLH:[412] OK. And you said that in your awareness at the moment of the
beep…

NAOMI:[413] I felt my arm … my wrist begin to doodle a loop.

Russ: Naomi again refers to her wrist as if it had agency of its own: *I felt…
my wrist begin to doodle*, not *I* began to doodle. Whatever the implication, it
is consistent with the way she spoke at Naomi[401–403]. That raises my oddness
antenna a notch higher. This consistency doesn't satisfy me, doesn't explain
why she would speak like that. It does raise the stakes if our task is to apprehend her experience with fidelity.

CLH:[414] OK.

NAOMI:[415] And I felt myself sinking into the floor. And being very grounded
and being very, very sleepy.

Russ: Another unsubjunctified reference to "Sinking into the floor." That's
an interesting expression; how should we understand it? Colorful metaphor?
Straightforward description? Could be either, so a faithful apprehension will
eventually have to sort this out. The reference to "into the floor" comes as part
of unsubjunctified descriptions of concrete realities (arm on table, head on
arm), so it can't be merely dismissed as metaphor. I'll have to keep both antennae alive – that is, I'll have to bracket both sides of each potential oddness.

CLH:[416] OK.

[For purposes of economy in this chapter, we will focus on the "sinking into
the floor" aspect and excise any further references to the wrist motion.
Here we skip two minutes of conversation about wrist motion.]

CLH:[417] OK. And so the experience of sinking into the floor. That was in
your awareness at the beep?

Russ: Chris has noted the "sinking into the floor" expression and asks
a good, level-playing-field question about it: He returns her attention to this
detail without pre-judging its significance.

NAOMI:[418] Yeah.

CLH:[419] And what was that like?

NAOMI:[420] Well, um, I felt my muscles from my ankles all the way up until
my shoulders relax very, very slowly and kind of drifting on to sleep before
I mentally fall asleep. And I don't mean like a numbing sensation of sleep,
but like right when your muscles relax as you're just about to fall asleep.

Russ: Chris asked about "sinking into the floor" and Naomi responded
with muscle relaxation. Score one for sinking into the floor as merely a colorful

metaphor. Yet at the same time my antennae jangle anew at this reference to her muscles going to sleep before she mentally goes to sleep. What does she mean by that? This utterance is subjunctified ("*Well, um*" and "*kind of* drifting on"), so nothing is resolved for me one way or the other.

Furthermore, the CLH[419] question is slightly ambiguous, and Naomi's subjunctification might have been triggered by that. "What was that *like*?" is *not* necessarily a question about experience. "What was that like?" may invite a metaphor or a comparison: "It was *like* the moon over still water"; "It was *like* the last time I had the flu." Neither of those is a description of direct experience. It is reasonable to understand Naomi's answer as reflecting some confusion: Her initial reticence ("Well, um") signals (perhaps) that she doesn't know what Chris wants from her. On this understanding, she has already told Chris that she was sinking into the floor, and he seems to have understood that, so now he must not be asking about the experience, he must be asking about what the experience *is like*. Naomi doesn't know what to make of that.

Or maybe she does understand Chris's "What was that like?" to be asking directly about her experience, and she is telling him about her experience: Her muscles are relaxing. I don't know. I'll have to keep both options alive.

> CLH:[421] OK. So in your awareness your muscles were relaxing. You were aware of your muscles relaxing.
> NAOMI:[422] Yeah.
> CLH:[423] And it was just … that was the feeling of the muscles relaxing, again, more than a thought about it.
> NAOMI:[424] Yeah.
> CLH:[425] You're not thinking, *Oh! My muscles are relaxing!* You're just feeling in your body relaxed.
> NAOMI:[426] And slowly beginning to drift off, but it didn't work out so well.
> CLH:[427] The beep woke you up! [laughs]
> NAOMI:[428] The beep … I hate that.
> CLH:[429] Yeah. Sorry about that! Um, and the sinking into the floor part. Is that just the muscles … your body relaxing? Or is there an actual sinking-into-the-floorness to it?

Russ: Chris at CLH[427] interprets Naomi's [426] "it didn't work out so well" is referring to Naomi's relaxation's being interrupted by the beep. That might be true, but "it didn't work out so well" might also refer her becoming merged with the floor. I don't know which interpretation is correct, so I think CLH[427] is something of a mistake. However, Chris[429] returns to Naomi's experience of sinking with a good, even handed question. She is left free to say that she is just relaxing, in which case the sinking into the floor is intended to be merely metaphorical (a colorful way of saying that she is becoming ever more relaxed) or literally descriptive (she actually experiences herself as sinking into the floor).

NAOMI:[430] I kind of sunk into it, but I kind of felt like … unknown, like
my body was becoming a part of the floor at the same time, because my
muscles were so relaxed.

Russ: CLH[429] had given her the choice between the merely metaphorical
and the literally descriptive, and I understand Naomi[430] as choosing the literally
descriptive option ("my body was becoming a part of the floor"). However, she
undermines my conviction somewhat by subjunctifying (*kind of, kind of,* and
because) her expression. So what she means remains somewhat ambiguous.

CLH:[431] Um hm.
NAOMI:[432] Kind of like oozing.
CLH:[433] OK. Um, I just want to make sure I get all of this. So the muscle
relaxation feeling is just the muscles relaxing. "Oozing" is just another way
of saying the same thing? Or is …
NAOMI:[434] Yes. Same thing as …
CLH:[435] …there more?

Russ: I worry that Chris here is somewhat estranged from Naomi's con-
veyances. If he is trying here to focus on the muscle-relaxation part, and will
later focus on the "into the floor" part, then there is no problem. But the two
uses of "just" in CLH[433] ("*just* the muscles relaxing; "*just* another way of saying") seem to indicate that he understands her "into the floor" words as being
merely metaphorical, where I think that Naomi[431] has seemed to say that she
means sinking into the floor to be literally descriptive. The "Or is there more"
of CLH[433-435] does leave room for the meant-literally description, but that
seems quite a bit weaker than the "just relaxing" and "just another way" that
emphasizes the merely metaphorical.

NAOMI:[436] … more detailed. Because it's a continuous thing. It's just going
and going and sinking and sinking and sinking. I can't physically sink all
the way into the floor, but it feels like it's still going and I'm getting lower,
although I'm not really moving any further down than I can.

Russ: Naomi brings the discussion back to the literal "sinking into" aspect
of her statement, which I understand as meaning that there is something alive
about her "sinking into" expression that had not been adequately accounted for
by the CLH[433] "just the muscles relaxing." However, what she means here is still
ambiguous. "I can't physically sink *all the way* into the floor" could be understood to mean, "I don't go into the floor at all (that is, I'm going down toward
it but not into it)," but it can also mean, "I sink part way into the floor but not
all the way." For me that raises more questions about Naomi's experience than
it resolves. See Chapter 20.

CLH:[437] And so it seems like there's a part … there's something about your
experience that's going down?

NAOMI:[438] Yeah.

CLH:[439] Like physically going downward? And downward *toward* the floor? Or …

NAOMI:[440] Yeah. Towards the floor.

CLH:[441] … or downwards *into* the floor?

Russ: Chris recognizes that Naomi has refocused the discussion on the "into the floor" aspect, continues to ask skillful, even-handed questions, allowing her to clarify the ambiguity.

NAOMI:[442] Toward and into the floor. 'Cause I was sitting on my knees, and then I moved my legs apart so that I was sitting in between my legs. And then I kind of kept sinking into it.

Russ: By saying "and into," I understand Naomi to be saying that she knows the difference between *toward* and *into*, and that both are correct.

Chris: I remembered her saying the "toward" part, but I somehow missed or blocked out the "into the floor" part of her answer. Now, when I read the transcript and watch the video, I'm surprised to see the "into the floor" part, almost as if it has appeared out of thin air.

CLH:[443] OK. So your body … Your muscles are relaxing so much that there's like a physical sense of actual sinkingness of your body …

NAOMI:[444] Yeah.

CLH:[445] … to become like flat on the floor, or actually to become part of the floor, or …

Russ: CLH[443–445] continues the series of skillful, even-handed question allowing her to clarify her intent.

NAOMI:[446] Part of the floor. Not so much like spreading out so much because I moved into a position that it wouldn't move outward, but just going, sinking further and further down.

Russ: Naomi chooses, now in a quite unsubjunctified way, the "part of the floor" option that CLH[445] had advanced.

Chris: When Russ first told me (the day after the fourth interview) he thought Naomi meant that she directly experienced herself as sinking into the floor, I told him that I agreed that she had said things that might have implied that she experienced herself as sinking into the floor, but that I had asked her specifically about that, which I indeed had (in CLH[439] and CLH[441] and again in CLH[443] and CLH[445]). But for some reason I only took in part of her answer, the part that said *toward*; I ignored or discounted or forgot the part where she added "and into" and "part of."

CLH:[447] OK. And there's no sense of the floor like denting or anything like that? It's just you moving …

NAOMI:[448] Yeah.

CLH:[449] … toward the floor. OK. So kind of like the Wicked Witch of the West, or whatever, it was melting in the *Wizard of Oz*?

Russ: The "toward the floor" and the *Wizard of Oz* reference responds to the "toward" part but does not honor the "into" part of Naomi's description.

NAOMI:[450] Yeah. But she was going outward. I … All my energy was still in this same … Like my self and my body movement was all going into one part of the floor. It wasn't going outward anywhere.

Russ: Here Naomi corrects him. Naomi is "all going into" the floor.

CLH:[451] OK.

[pause]

NAOMI:[452] And the further I sunk into the floor, the more a part of the floor I felt like my legs gradually just became the floor.

Russ: Then she underscores in a mostly unsubjunctified, declarative way that she was speaking literally: "sunk into the floor"; "part of the floor"; "became the floor." Three times she says that she went *into* the floor, not just *toward* the floor. So my understanding is becoming more and more stable; I'm becoming increasingly satisfied that Naomi intends to be saying, in a literally descriptive, non-metaphorical sense, that she experiences herself as sinking into the floor.

Chris: It still did not register or stick with me, and, again, I am surprised to see it here in the transcript. It has the feel as if this "part of the floor" portion of the interview happened when I was in the other room or something.

CLH:[453] OK. And the sleepiness, is that separate?

[We omit seventy-five seconds of conversation about sleepiness, which is not relevant to our present concern.]

CLH:[454] Let me give you a summary of what I've got here, and see if you want to add anything or correct me. Um, you were resting, essentially, and you were aware of your wrist moving in a medium sized circle. Is it your right wrist?

NAOMI:[455] Yes. My right hand.

CLH:[456] Um. And you were feeling your muscles relax in a way that felt like really oozing toward the floor …

NAOMI:[457] Yeah.

CLH:[458] … and feeling sleepy.

NAOMI:[459] Um hm.

CLH:[460] Anything else at that moment?

[Nothing further is said about this beep in the remainder of the interview.]

Russ: The CLH[455–459] summary does not, in my view, honor the "into" portion of Naomi's description. To my ear, in answer to Chris's skillful questions, Naomi has said pretty unequivocally that there is an into-the-floor quality in her experience. Yet in his summary, Chris left that out altogether.

Chris: I must say that the reading of this transcript and the watching of the video is shocking. As I said, when Russ initially mentioned that he thought that Naomi had been saying the she experienced sinking into the floor, I recalled that she had said things that might have implied that. Further, I recalled that I had asked her specifically about that to determine whether her experience was *toward* the floor or *into* the floor. I recalled that she had answered that question by saying that she was simply sinking toward the floor, not into it. I was confident that I had considered the possibilities and correctly resolved the issue.

The transcript and the video shows that I had asked those questions, but her answers had been in the reverse direction of what I recalled. At this point I can only speculate about why I misunderstood or distorted what she had said. I believe that there was something operating in me that interfered with my effectiveness in this instance – a presupposition of some sort. Something blocked or warped my apprehension of what she was saying.

As I mentioned earlier, Naomi's unusual inner experience and manner had made me somewhat uneasy from the outset. Said bluntly, micro-psychoses or whatever we might want to call such experiences make me uncomfortable. So maybe I systematically suppressed the violating-the-rules-of-reality part of her experience to avoid that discomfort. I probably also generally tilt some-what in the direction of seeing what we share in common as opposed to what is unique, in the direction of normalcy rather than distinctiveness. This instance may also reflect that I have not developed my skills to as consistently high a level as I had believed. In reading the transcript I have the feeling of having dropped an easy pass in a game of football – the feeling of "I should have caught (apprehended) that."

The other experience I have reading the transcript is that it is like a slow-motion version of the real thing. The real-time, live interviews are much more challenging than it is made to seem when one reads a transcript of it. The interviewer is trying to pay attention to the content and style of expression as it comes pouring out, to make notes about important facets of the experi-ence that need to be explored, and to construct it into a faithful and complete description of the moment of inner experience. Consistent with this, the cri-tique that evolves out of the review of the videotape and transcript is like the critique of a golf swing in slow motion. Each flaw or imperfection can be dis-covered and highlighted. I cannot say I enjoy the process, but I do accept that looking for and confronting failures and imperfections is part of honing this skill and probably any skill. It is in this spirit that I acknowledge my failure to faithfully apprehend Naomi's experience.

IMPLICATIONS FOR GENUINELY SUBMITTING
TO THE CONSTRAINTS

On the basis of our examination and re-examination of the original interview and two subsequent interviews, we have come to conclude that Naomi meant "sinking into the floor" as a straightforward description of her experience, not a colorful metaphor for relaxation. We have concluded that she was consistent across three interviews three weeks apart, across three perspectives (first a straight-ahead description of the sampled moment, then a revisiting of the sampled moment, then a chance comparison of the sampled moment with another moment), when subjected to multiple questions from two interviewers.

DES is often criticized for its potential for leading the witness: The subject makes things up to tell the interviewer what he wants to hear. This example argues against that position. Why would Naomi describe her experience in a way that clearly made her nervous, that risked her being thought crazy, that clearly was *not* what the interviewer wanted to hear? Chris was clearly *not* leading her in the direction of bodily sinking into the floor – in fact, he may have had presuppositions *directly against* that possibility. So this example provides a situation in which both the subject and the interviewer were motivated, apparently, to *avoid* talking about something, and yet they talked about it, forced against their wills by the intention to describe Naomi's experience in high fidelity.

Furthermore, if Naomi were just trying to be linguistically consistent (another frequent criticism against DES), why would she use the word *sinking* with two different meanings, "penetrating" on the fourth day and "pressing" on the sixth? Naomi's use of language is more reflective of someone trying with some difficulty to describe a clearly apprehended experience than it is of an attempt at linguistic consistency.

CONSTRAINTS

In Chapters 17 and 18 we concluded that there is usually a pretty darn right apprehension of experience. The present example called that conclusion into question, so we explored the example as carefully as we could.

Constraint: It is possible to apprehend inner experience in high fidelity. At the end of our three-week exploration of Naomi's experience at sample 4.1, we found that in this situation, as best we could determine, there indeed *was* a pretty darn right apprehension of experience: Naomi meant to be taken literally when she said she felt herself sinking into the floor, even though it apparently caused her some discomfort to describe it.

Constraint: There is no guarantee that an interviewer will apprehend in high fidelity, even when the interviewing is skillful. This book has observed that an apprehension of experience must be tied to a particular moment, that it must cleave to experience, and that it must avoid other talk that might be mistaken for experience. Chris's sample 4.1 interview was skillful and followed those guidelines, and yet his original apprehension of Naomi's experience was not of high fidelity.

Constraint: The subject cannot be counted upon to judge whether an interviewer's account is of high fidelity. Let's call this Naomi's paradox: The subject (repeatedly) gives high fidelity descriptions of experience but may not point out places where a written characterization of those descriptions departs from high fidelity. Recall that Naomi rated the accuracy of Chris's original description 9.9 on a 10-point scale, the .1 deduction reflecting that the description used "oozing" when it should have used "sinking"; change that word and she doubtless would have rated the description a 10. Yet Chris's description, even with that word change, was not faithful to her experience in at least one important way.

Judging whether a characterization is high fidelity presumes four things: (a) that Naomi herself has a high fidelity apprehension of her own experience; (b) that Naomi understands what Chris means in the description; (c) that Naomi knows what a high fidelity description looks like; and (d) that Naomi is motivated to give an even-handed judgment. The use of the rating scale in judging fidelity presumes all four, as well as (e) that Naomi and Chris have a shared conception of what the points on the rating scale signify.

Much of this book is aimed at (a). That Chris and Russ eventually came to agreement that Naomi had been consistent across three interviews is evidence that she had a high fidelity apprehension of her own experience.

Regarding (b), it is quite likely that Naomi understood Chris's written description to say that she was *merging into* the floor, even though that is *not* what Chris intended and not what the written description said. After all, she had said that she was merging into the floor on several occasions during the interview, and Chris had asked questions repeatedly about the details of that experience. So when Chris's description said, "She also felt her muscles relax in a way that felt like they were oozing toward the floor," Naomi changed the word "oozing" to "sinking" and then may very well have presumed (mistakenly) that that sentence conveyed the merging-into that she knew herself to have described, and that she thought Chris had understood in the interview. That is, Naomi should not be expected fully to grasp that Chris's "sinking toward" specifically excluded her experience of "sinking into."

Regarding (c) and (e), Naomi is simply not at all in a position to know what is or is not a high fidelity description from the standpoint of DES. From Naomi's everyday perspective, Chris's description is doubtless by far the most accurate rendering of a detail of her experience that she has ever seen, so she should give it a 10 on her own reading of the 10-point scale. However, to be able to judge the fidelity of a characterization as DES understands it would require an across-subject knowledge of fidelity, require an appreciation for what is at stake in all aspects of description, and that is more than should be expected from Naomi or any other subject.

Regarding (d), perhaps Naomi recognized that even the corrected "sinking toward" missed the important merging-into aspect of her experience. However, *to point that out to Chris* had two risks: It meant criticizing Chris; and it meant one more time entering into a conversation about her merging with the floor, a conversation that had aroused anxiety the first time, even when Chris seemed to understand, and now might arouse even more anxiety given some evidence that Chris didn't understand or accept her experience.

The 10-point rating scale gives some relatively crude assurance that a description is in the ballpark. If, for example, the description had read, "Naomi was seeing a visual image of a Cadillac Escalade parked next to a Hummer H2," Naomi doubtless would have given it deservedly low marks. But the use of such scales in an exploration aimed at high fidelity is risky: Rating scales give no assurance at all that a description is of high fidelity, they may give the investigator a false sense of security, they give the subject a sense of crudeness of the endeavor, and, perhaps worst, they give the false impression of scientific adequacy at precisely the same time as they undermine scientific value.

Constraint: There is no certain, formulaic way of determining that a description is faithful. In the example at hand, Chris asked very skillful questions and still misapprehended the experience. Corollary: There is no way of certifying that a person will apprehend faithfully. There doubtless could be some minimal level of certification, but whether that would be desirable is dubious. We don't have some minimal level of certification for classical guitarists – the marketplace handles that quite effectively.

Constraint: The required level of fidelity depends on the aim of the investigation. We have been focusing on the *differences* between Chris's and Russ's apprehensions, but we should also note that there are substantial *agreements* between them: They agree that Naomi is sitting on the floor in the library with her head on her arm; that she is not forming an image of a Cadillac Escalade next to a Hummer H2 (or engaged in any other inner seeing); that she is not thinking about the economic crisis (or engaging in any other thought process); that she is not speaking the words "I am sinking" either innerly or aloud (or speaking any other words); that she is not recalling the taste of the pizza she had for lunch (or any other taste); and so on. Chris, Naomi, and Russ all agree that the central aspects of Naomi's experience at the moment of the beep are bodily relaxation and hand moving. That is quite a lot of agreement. Either Chris's or Russ's descriptions would be perfectly adequate for many investigational purposes. For example, if the investigation were a validation of the concept of inner speaking (investigating, say, the conditions under which inner speaking occurs or does not occur), then either of our two descriptions is entirely adequate – Chris's and Russ's descriptions agree that Naomi was *not* innerly speaking at the beeped moment.

However, for other investigations the required level of fidelity might be quite high. For example, if the investigation were an exploration of experience that is or is not a precursor of schizophrenia, then one of our two apprehensions (or both) is *not* of adequate fidelity. The only way to determine whether such micro-psychoticism is or is not a precursor of schizophrenia is to apprehend such micro-psychoticisms in high fidelity every time they occur.

We conclude that the aim of an investigation determines the required level of fidelity. A validation study aimed at a well-known and clearly defined phenomenon such as inner speech is a fundamentally different enterprise from an exploratory study aimed at discovering heretofore unrecognized phenomena. A validation study can operate at a relatively cruder level than can an exploratory study. See Chapter 21.

Constraint: The high fidelity apprehension of inner experience may require long and arduous practice. The high fidelity apprehension of pristine experience is a high-level performance art much as guitar playing is a high-level performance art. Everyone accepts that *many* people try to learn to play the guitar, that *most* drop off along the way, that *some* become quite good at it by neighborhood standards, that *a few* become very good at it by professional standards, and that *very few* become extremely good at it by world-class virtuoso standards. Everyone accepts that there are many different ways to be very good at guitar performance, from bluegrass to rock to jazz to classical; we don't say that the choice of genre makes the guitar playing good or bad; it is just the way it is. Everyone accepts that it takes a long time (measured, perhaps, in decades) to become a skilled guitar player. Everyone accepts that those learning to play the guitar make many mistakes before building the technique that significantly reduces the mistakes. Everyone accepts that learning to play the guitar requires work and practice, discipline, sacrifice, and investment. Everyone accepts that innate talent is a big part of mastery but by no means the total part. Everyone accepts that there are satisfactions and frustrations along the way. Everyone accepts that "He's really good!" has a different meaning when applied to an eight-year-old, to a twenty-eight-year-old, or to a virtuoso.

By contrast, psychological science has almost none of those acceptances when it comes to the apprehension of inner experience. Most of those who think it is possible to apprehend experience think it is easy (Hurlburt & Heavey, 2001), that everyone can do it, that everyone is already doing it. If they think there is a skill to be mastered, it should be masterable in a few weeks. "I read one of your articles. Give me a beeper and I'll do DES!" Psychologists don't raise an eyebrow when they hear that. They'd laugh out loud if they heard someone say, "I heard a recording of Segovia. Give me a guitar and a week of lessons and I'll play Bach's 'Chaconne!'"

In the guitar metaphor, the high fidelity apprehension of pristine experience is more like classical guitar than other genres: In the classical guitar there are right and wrong notes that are created by someone else, and it requires substantial skill, sensitivity, and technique to be able to render those notes faithfully.

Russ: In this and in previous chapters I have pointed out places where my colleagues have failed to cleave to pristine experience. I would have preferred to point out my own presuppositional shortcomings (in fact, I give an example in Chapter 21), rather than those of my colleagues. However, writing plainly about my own presuppositions is impossible for two reasons: (a) it is impossible for me to write about my *current* presuppositions because they are impossible for me to spot (I am blind to my own presuppositions just as Chris is blind to his and you are to yours); (b) it is impossible for me to write plainly about my *former* presuppositions both because retrospection (as we have seen) is fraught with perils, and because thirty years ago when I was struggling with my own most obvious presuppositions regarding inner experience, I didn't have anywhere near as clear a sense as I do today about how presuppositions operate and what the bracketing of presuppositions entails.

I do *not* claim that I have no presuppositions. I do *not* regard myself as the standard against which others should be measured – there is no standard other than the pristine experience itself. I write this book with the intention of contributing to the reawakening of an interest in pristine experience. If the reawakening is successful, I presume that others will become more skillful than I at the apprehension of experience. In the middle of the twentieth century, Andres Segovia contributed to the reawakening of the interest in the classical guitar; now there are many guitarists whose technical ability exceed that of Segovia.

I do think the high fidelity apprehension of pristine experience is a matter of high skill, and the acquiring of that skill takes substantial time. Tom Wolfe reportedly said it takes ten years to learn how to write; the Japanese proverb says, "Even a thief takes ten years to learn his trade." The skills required to apprehend inner experience – to set aside one's own presuppositions and help others set aside theirs, to understand how to discern how others use language – are at least as complex as the skills Wolfe and the Japanese are considering. So it seems to me that it is likely that it would require about ten years of relentless commitment to become moderately skillful at apprehending experience. Maybe it's only five years for some people; maybe fifteen for others; in no way am I making a fine point here.

There are many powerful personal and professional distractions to the consistent attempt to apprehend experience in high fidelity. The science of psychology is structured *in direct opposition* to the apprehension of phenomena: Psychology's taken-for-granted emphasis on validation, its headlong focus on biological aspects, its time pressures, its belief in the adequacy of questionnaires (or at least its rewards for questionnaire studies), its presumption that inner experience is trivially easy (or impossible) to apprehend – all work against the development of the skills necessary for the faithful apprehension of pristine experience.

Constraint: The fact that the high fidelity apprehension of inner experience is possible does not imply that everyone can do it. The virtuoso guitarist can faithfully render Bach's "Chaconne"; that does not imply that you or I can do so, nor that Segovia could have done so without thousands of hours in the practice room.

The apprehension of inner experience with high fidelity is a skill that can be attained (like guitar artistry) by earthly beings. Individuals doubtless differ in their natural ability to faithfully apprehend experience, just as individuals differ in their natural musical ability. Faithful apprehension of inner experience can be cultivated, taught, nurtured, rewarded; in such an environment, a person's ability to faithfully apprehend experience may improve. And that, as this book is trying to show, can be a valuable thing, even if virtuosity is not achieved by everyone. We teach orchestra in middle schools not because we expect all sixth graders to grow up to play the "Chaconne," but because a few will, and the rest will have been enriched by the path and the attempt.

Constraint: Presuppositions are always personal. There is no such thing as a general presupposition. Your presuppositions are always *your* particular blind spots, *your* particular hypersensitivities, *your* desires, *your* exaggerations, *your* avoidances, *your* motivations, *your* history. Therefore, there are only personal ways of illustrating presuppositions. Similarly, there are no general ways of bracketing presuppositions. You have to do what it takes to ferret out your own presuppositions, to do what it takes to steel yourself to the ramifications of that bracketing, to do it as often and often again as you require.

Furthermore, there is no test that unerringly identifies anyone's presuppositions. You can never have any assurance (except, perhaps, in nirvana, about which I have no personal experience) that you have correctly identified your presuppositions, because your own presuppositions operate in you in a prior-to-conceptualization way. Furthermore, what you take to be someone else's presuppositions may be merely a projection of your own presuppositions.

Constraint: Presuppositions are never noticed. Presuppositions always operate contemporaneously, but that operation is always invisible, insidious, or worse than insidious. Presuppositions operate *prior* to your conceptualizations, *prior* to your observations, *prior* to your self-concept. If someone points out your presupposition and you immediately assent ("Yes! You're right! I do have that presupposition!"), then we can be sure that we are *not* talking about your presupposition. A genuine reaction to a true statement about an actual presupposition must be something like: "No way!" "You're mistaken!" "Go to hell!" "I don't understand a thing about what you are saying!" "I have good reasons for that!" "Good science dictates my position!" "There's no other choice!" "You're full of baloney!"

> **Q:** That's reminiscent of the psychoanalytic concept of resistance: If you think your analyst is full of baloney then you are resisting. Yet analysts often *are* full of baloney.
>
> **A:** I agree that that is a danger, but DES has one substantial advantage over the analysts: DES is attempting to apprehend things that are directly observable, whereas the analysts are attempting to infer things that are unconscious. Our Naomi example is typical: The question before us was whether one particular moment of Naomi's directly apprehended, before-the-footlights-of-her-consciousness experience included the sensation of sinking into the floor. We were *not* investigating some psychoanalytic unconscious construct such as whether Naomi's Electra complex led to permeable physical boundaries. There is a directly observable (at least to Naomi) right answer to our Naomi question; there is only a theoretically inferable answer to the psychoanalytic question.

The current example is instructive. For whatever (probably presuppositional) reason, Chris destroyed the *facts* of his own observation. Naomi said "sinking into" and Chris never heard it, as if he were in another room when that was said. It was not that he misinterpreted what was said; he either didn't hear what was said or entirely forgot it within seconds.

Constraint: Acquiring the skill of bracketing of presuppositions is necessarily a far from straightforward endeavor. You have to be willing to go in a direction that you are *sure* (that is, *unquestioningly positive*) is exactly the *wrong* way. Chris was sure that he had ascertained whether Naomi was to be understood metaphorically or literally. Progress is likely to be felt as retrogression. There are plenty of opportunities for confrontation and resentment.

That's just the way it is. Genuinely submitting to the constraints that the exploration of inner experience imposes requires accepting the burdens of the bracketing of presuppositions and doing it anyway, and then doing it some more, and then some more, for a very long time.

Constraint: Presuppositions can be explored. The case transcribed here illustrates the possibility of constructively encountering/discovering presuppositions. If you can find someone you trust who has different sensitivities from yours, and you both are willing to make your differences as bluntly explicit as possible, and you have a stream of new opportunities (an advantage of random sampling) to examine those differences from novel perspectives, and you have a bit of luck, then presuppositions can be exposed and the groundwork laid for bracketing them. Unfortunately, in the current scientific environment there seems to be precious few such opportunities and even less support therefor. That could be because such confrontations are almost always private, and outsiders don't get to see them. Perhaps it will be possible to create an environment that provides some indirect support, that accepts the difficulty and the value of, and even rewards the bracketing of presuppositions – this book is intended in that direction. However, that is not the current environment, and it remains to be seen whether such an environment can be created.

RADICALLY NON-SUBJECTIVE

Russ: We opened this chapter by wondering whether the difficulty of apprehending pristine experience comes from the fact that pristine experience doesn't really exist, that is, that it exists only in a manner of speaking. That is, we wondered whether the difficulty in apprehending diamonds arises from the fact that there are no diamonds. Our consideration of Naomi 4.1 led us to the conclusion that the difficulty in this case arose from the interviewer's presuppositions, not from any vagueness or indeterminacy of Naomi's pristine phenomena. That is, we concluded that there *are* pretty darn right or wrong characterizations of Naomi's experience at sample 4.1; therefore, we conclude that Naomi *did have* pristine experience at sample 4.1.

At the moment of sample 4.1 and elsewhere, we are not operating in the realm of opinions about Naomi, or impressions about Naomi, or about theoretical constructs applied to Naomi, or the interpretation of some test about Naomi; that is, Naomi's "into the floor" experience is not glass. We are operating in the realm of directly (albeit privately) apprehended phenomena that presented themselves to Naomi pretty darn independently of any attempt to apprehend them; that is, Naomi's "into the floor" experience is a radically non-subjective diamond.

Of course, this is just one sample from one subject and one interviewer. I present this example because it is more or less typical: I think that pristine experience *does* exist pretty independently of any attempt to apprehend it. Science's verification of that must be performed by people unrelated to me.

May I re-emphasize: Our goal is not to criticize Chris – on the contrary, he is to be thanked for helping us wade into these important waters.

EXPERIENCE AND *AS IF*

Q: Let me see if I have this straight. Russ, from your perspective Naomi *experienced herself* as if she were sinking into the floor. From Chris's initial perspective Naomi experienced herself as being tired, and she expressed that tiredness metaphorically – she *said* it was as if she were sinking into the floor. So there is a metaphor from each perspective: Both of you say "as if she were sinking into the floor." The difference is that in your view, Russ, the *as if* is in the experience, whereas in Chris's initial perspective the *as if* is in the speaking about it. Is that right?

A: No. There was, as you say, an *as if* metaphor in Chris's original perspective, but there is *no* metaphor from my perspective: Naomi did *not* experience herself *as if sinking* into the floor; she experienced herself *sinking* into the floor, with no *as if* about it. She was mistaken – she was not *really* sinking into the floor, but that is a fact of the physical universe, *not* part of her experience at the moment of the beep.

Q: This doesn't seem like a big deal. She was not sinking into the floor, so it makes sense to say that it was as if she were sinking into the floor.
A: From the standpoint of Naomi's experience, the distinction is a *very* big deal. We have called Naomi's erroneous experience a micro-psychoticism – she experienced something that was not happening in the world of physics. If at the moment of the beep she had experienced herself *as if she were* sinking into the floor – that is, if her experience had included the *as if* – then this would *not* have been a micro-psychoticism: Her experience would have acknowledged reality and simultaneously recognized that her experience, although similar to reality, was not real. That would not have been a micro-psychoticism; it would have been, say, a creative experience. The absence or presence of the *as if* experience distinguishes between the psychotic and the non-psychotic (micro or otherwise). That is a very big deal.

Q: I think you are being overly picky in your language. Whether one says *as if* can't be that important.
A: As usual, it is not the language that I am concerned with, but rather what is meant by the language. It is the *experience* that is important, not what you call it. The question is whether what you say faithfully reflects experience. You wouldn't say, "I experience myself as if I were seeing a red stop sign"; you would say, "I see the red stop sign." Similarly, you shouldn't say, "Naomi experiences herself as if she were sinking into the floor"; you should say, "Naomi feels herself sinking into the floor."

I learned to appreciate the lack of *as if* in psychosis from a catatonic schizophrenia patient called "Harry G." Harry was a twenty-seven-year-old who, at various times during his schizophrenic episode, thought people were trying to poison him; he thought that there were connections to his brain that would cause his own or others' brains to explode if he did not exactly repeat every word that he heard (a behavior called echolalia, e.g., Nurse: "How are you today, Harry?" Harry: "How are you today, Harry?"); he had spent months in a motionless stupor. Psychologist George W. Kisker interviewed Harry when Harry was in remission and asked him about his motionless episodes. Harry told Kisker that during those times he saw huge – "oversized" – animals and was compelled to stay completely still so they wouldn't attack.

> KISKER: Well where were these animals …? Would they be … Did you think they were in the room with you?
> HARRY: (with mild impatience) They *would be* in the room!

KISKER: They would be in the room with you.

HARRY: I mean, it actually seemed like it was real! (Kisker, 1972)

In Harry's experience, there was no *as if*: it was *not* that he *thought* the animals were in the room, the animals *were there*, as far as his experience was concerned. There was no experience of *as if*. In the world of physics there were no animals; thus Harry was psychotic.

LEARNING FROM NAOMI

Q: Was Naomi's micro-psychotic merging into the floor unusual for her?
A: No. We examined eighteen samples from Naomi's third through sixth sampling days (considering the first two days as iterative training). Somewhere between seven and eleven (depending on the definition) could be called micro-psychotic – direct experiences that did not conform with reality, that were not merely a colorful way of describing experience. Some of these were physical phenomena; for example, a monster was chomping down on a corner of her brain (her experience was of a literal monster; in the real world this would be called a headache). Some were visual phenomena; for example, the walls of the bathroom in which she was standing seemed to crumple in on her as if they were made of paper (in the real world the walls remained stationary). Some were multi-sensory phenomena; for example, she was reading on her cell phone a text message from a boy who had texted that he liked her. That surprised her, and she dropped the phone: She felt it slide out of her right hand, saw it fall in slow motion to the floor, heard it crash as it hit, felt the emptiness in her hand (in the real world she had continued to hold the real phone and had not actually dropped it).

Thus it appeared that micro-psychotic moments occurred in roughly half of Naomi's sampled experiences, leading to the speculation that Naomi likely has hundreds or thousands of micro-psychotic experiences each day.

Q: Why do you call these "micro-psychoticisms"? Shouldn't anyone who has hundreds or thousands of "micro-psychotic" experiences each day be called simply "psychotic"?
A: No. We did no formal psychological evaluation of Naomi, but both Chris and I are experienced clinical psychologists and are familiar with schizophrenia and other psychoses, and those diagnoses did not seem to apply to Naomi. The difference between Naomi's micro-psychoticisms and, for example, Harry's frank psychoticism and is that as a result of his misperceived animals, Harry stayed motionless for months and had to be fed through a tube. By micro contrast, a few seconds after Naomi's misperceived "into the floor" experience, Naomi got up off the floor and continued her homework.

Q: Then are Naomi's micro-psychoticms early signs of schizophrenia or other psychosis?

A: I don't know, and neither, I think, does schizophrenia science. That is a crucially important question, but as far as I know, no one (including me) has investigated the pristine experience of people at risk for schizophrenia while submitting to the constraints that that investigation imposes. Therefore we can't answer that question for Naomi.

Q: That seems evasive. I think you owe it to us to state your opinion about the relationship between micro-psychoticisms and psychosis. After all, you've examined each with uncommon care.

A: I can state my opinions about why this is important. It seems to me that there are four possibilities here:

(1) Naomi's experience did *not* involve micro-psychoticisms – that is, I am mistaken in my understanding of Naomi's talk about her experience. For the reasons discussed in this chapter, I doubt that that is true.

(2) Naomi's experience *did* involve micro-psychoticisms, but micro-psychoticisms have no relationship to psychosis. I doubt that that is true. Such experiences are rare in our DES work, and they do involve a perceptual/conceptual distortion of reality, so it seems reasonable that there is some kind of connection between micro- and frank psychosis. However, I accept the possibility that micro-psychoticisms are important for Naomi but not for others.

(3) Naomi's experience *did* involve micro-psychoticisms, and micro-psychoticisms are prodromal to psychosis. The term "prodrome" means an early precursor with an implied inevitability: If micro-psychoticisms are prodromal of schizophrenia, and micro-psychoticisms occur, then inevitably schizophrenia will soon occur (Yung & McGorry, 1996). I don't know whether micro-psychoticisms are prodromal to psychosis, but if they are, discovering that connection would be an important advance in schizophrenia science. There is a strong and growing interest in the early identification of schizophrenia, following the view of Harry Stack Sullivan (among others), who stated in 1927 that schizophrenia might be arrested if incipient cases could be discovered early in their course (see Chapter 13). However, the early identification of schizophrenia has turned out to be difficult; if micro-psychoticisms contribute to early identification, that would be an advance.

(4) Naomi's experience *did* involve micro-psychoticisms, and micro-psychoticisms have some relationship to psychosis other than prodromal. Recall than in Chapter 13 I speculated that some people fall into patterns of inner experience that lead to schizophrenia, whereas others fall into patterns that do not lead to schizophrenia. I further speculated that those patterns are skills that can be unlearned if identified early enough. The micro-psychoticisms are the skills I had in mind: For example, it requires substantial skill to create and coordinate the imaginary hand/tactile experiences, imaginary-seeing experiences, and imaginary-hearing experiences involved in Naomi's imaginary phone dropping. It requires work and practice to become better and better at creating more and more compelling/alluring micro-psychotic experiences.

Naomi is not now psychotic: She has many instances of micro-psychoticisms, but they are followed by instances of recognition of their unreality. Now suppose that, for whatever genetic or environmental/historical reason, Naomi becomes more and more skilled at creating micro-psychoticisms, so that those micro-psychoticisms become ever more compelling/alluring (after all, the micro-psychotic experiences are more fascinating, more creative, more special than mundane reality: I am much more fascinating if I drop the phone upon hearing that the boy likes me than if I merely hold on to it and think, *That's surprising!*). According to this admittedly wild speculation, it is plausible that eventually Naomi will spend more and more time dwelling on the micro-psychotic experience and less and less time in recognizing the real world, and thereby may well lose contact with the real world and become frankly psychotic.

However, if, for whatever reason, Naomi comes to recognize the real as more important than the micro-psychotic, comes to see the admittedly alluring micro-psychotic as an expression of her creativity rather than as a real event, then the micro-psychotic skill may *not* lead to the frankly psychotic. In this sense, Sullivan may have been right: If we knew how to help Naomi to appreciate her creativity without hyper-dwelling on the apparent reality of it, help her to recognize the real importance of the real world, Naomi might be able to avoid frank psychosis.

In this sense, the micro-psychoticism skills might be prerequisites of the frankly psychotic, necessary skills with no inevitability (that is, not prodromal), just as algebra is a prerequisite skill of calculus but does not inevitably lead to calculus.

If (4) is true, there would be huge value to understanding it, because it has implications for the successful avoidance of schizophrenia.

At the current state of the science, there is no way to know which if any of these four possibilities is correct. What does seem to be knowable is that the investigation of pristine experience in those at risk for schizophrenia might be of substantial value.

Q: At-risk-for-schizophrenia researchers have written for a long time that those at risk for schizophrenia show attenuated psychotic features. Is that the same thing that you call micro-psychoticisms?
A: Yes and no. Yes: I think the phenomena are in some ways similar. No: Science's way of exploring attenuated psychotic phenomena have typically led in a very different direction from that described here.

There have been creative attempts to ascertain the phenomena of pre-psychotic experience. For example, Chapman (1966) asked individuals during their first schizophrenic episode what their experience had been like prior to the onset of the episode. Upon noting that patients were reluctant to describe their pre-psychotic characteristics, Chapman adopted a projective approach: Patients were instructed to describe the characteristics *of the interviewer* as if the interviewer were about to become psychotic. Chapman believed that patients would be less reticent when projecting their own experiences in this way. I agree, but I don't think the improvement is enough to outweigh Jessica's paradox (recall Chapter 2). As you will recall, Jessica overlooked important features of her experiences even though they were frequently occurring in her current state; it seems substantially more likely that a schizophrenic individual will overlook important features of the experience that occurred before he became psychotic – not only is the experience to be described distantly retrospective, but the state to be described is presumed to be substantially different from the patient's current state. Such retrospective studies do describe experiences that are in some ways similar to what I would call micro-psychotic, but in general those experiences are (perhaps not surprisingly given the current frankly psychotic state of the interviewee) closer to the frankly psychotic than to the normal. Then the current state of the art reifies such experiences into questionnaires or structured interviews aimed at experience, and such reifications are quite different from the micro-psychoticisms described here. For example, the Structured Interview for Psychosis-Risk Syndromes (SIPS; McGlashan, Walsh, & Woods, 2010) is explicitly based at least in part on the literature regarding attenuated psychotic symptoms; the SIPS has eighty-nine Yes/No questions designed to cover the waterfront of experience of those at risk for schizophrenia.

It is reasonable to inquire whether Naomi's micro-psychoticisms would be discovered by the questionnaires developed for this purpose. Toward that end, I examined the eighty-nine SIPS questions to discern those where Naomi could answer "Yes" when referring to her sinking-into-the-floor, walls-crumpling, or dropping-the-phone experiences. There were only two more or less relevant items:

> Have you ever been confused at times whether something you have experienced is real or imaginary? (McGlashan et al., 2010, p. 190)

> Have you noticed any unusual bodily sensations such as tingling, pulling, pressure, aches, burning, cold, numbness, vibrations, electricity, or pain? (McGlashan et al., 2010, p. 203)

However, I think it likely that Naomi, assuming she is trying to be honest, would answer "No" to both of those items (and to all the other items in the SIPS). She was not *confused* about her sinking into the floor or dropping the phone: It was real, and then it was not real – no confusion in either state. The bodily sensations that corresponded to sinking into the floor and dropping the phone were not *unusual* – they were ordinary sensations of merging with the floor, of dropping a phone.

Q: Are you saying that it is likely that Naomi has micro-psychotic phenomena hundreds or thousands of times a day, and yet a structured interview designed to discover attenuated psychotic symptoms is likely not to discover them? How can that be?

A: Yes, I am saying that, and the explanation follows from all the moments ↔ experience ↔ genuinely-submitting-to-the-constraints reasons discussed throughout this book. First, the SIPS questions do *not* ask about some particular moment. "Have you ever been" at best elicits a (probably faux) generalization about moments and more likely a heuristically guided self-characterization. Second, these questions are ambiguous about pristine experience; the first question asks about *confusion* when the target experience inherently has no confusion. Third, these questions do not submit to the constraints that are discussed in this book. For example, the questions are highly retrospective – "Have you ever been" could refer to last month or last year or years ago – and we have seen again and again that retrospections about experience are not to be trusted.

I emphasize that I am not singling out the SIPS. The same critique applies, I think, to all the instruments used to study experience of those at risk for schizophrenia.

I don't know whether the speculations I've presented here are true, partially true, or entirely false. The take-home message is not about the truth of the speculation, but rather about the manner of exploration: The investigation of pristine experience may make a substantial contribution to science's understanding of the development of schizophrenia, but for that contribution to be realized, pristine experience must be investigated in genuine submission to the constraints that that investigation imposes.

20

The Emergence of Salient Characteristics

In Chapter 9, we met thirteen-year-old RD, a subject in Sarah Akhter's and my exploration of the experience of early adolescents. The aim of that exploration, as you may recall, was to apprehend the phenomena of experience, whatever those phenomena happened to be. For example, at one beep RD was saying in his inner voice, "Why did he kick me in my sore knee?" His voice sounded angry, but RD didn't *feel* angry; he realized that he was angry only by observing the tone of his own inner voice, which he recognized to have an angry sound. That is, he *inferred* that he was angry, rather than *felt* angry. It turned out that other subjects in our small sample were similar, so we speculated that whereas young adolescents may have emotion processes and respond with emotional actions, they may *not* simultaneously *experience* that emotion. We speculated that experiencing feeling emotion is a skill that is acquired across many years.

Somehow in Chapter 9 we got from one adolescent's report about one moment ("I was saying to myself 'Why did he kick me in my sore knee?'") to a speculation about adolescents' experience in general (young adolescents may not experience feelings). That's quite a leap, and it involved noticing both that RD had similar lack of emotional experience on other occasions and also that other children had similar lack of emotional experience. That is, the no-emotional-experience phenomenon *emerged as salient* across several or many samples both within and across subjects.

So far, we have not discussed directly this process of emerging into salience. In Chapter 9, for example, we *began* our account of lack of feelings at the *end* of the story: That section was titled "Feeling is an Acquired Skill," so the reader knew at the outset where we were headed. That is rather like telling the punch line at the beginning of a joke, which makes for efficient scientific writing but is *not* the way a DES investigation actually proceeds. In the present

---

Portions of this chapter are revised with permission from Akhter, S. A. (2008). *Exploring adolescent inner experience.* Unpublished Master's Thesis, University of Nevada, Las Vegas.

chapter, I will present the unfolding of a phenomenon so that the reader may observe how a process that begins with nothing can produce a speculation about something.

So let's go back to the beginning with RD. Let's leave the no-emotional-experience phenomenon aside and observe from scratch the (potential) emergence of a distinctly different phenomenon.

I choose this particular example because it (a) is quite typical of how my DES explorations work and (b) is quite unfinished. I'd like the reader to appreciate the messy way that good observation proceeds, and that requires participating in the mess.

Constraint: Start nowhere. If the aim of observation is to observe faithfully what presents itself, then any presupposition about what will present itself must interfere, at least to some degree, with the faithful apprehension of experience. So Sarah Akhter and I did *not* consult the adolescent literature to learn what is known about adolescent experience and then seek out RD to confirm or disconfirm those views; we simply sought out RD to discover something about RD's experience, whatever that might be. This *Start nowhere* constraint is therefore a corollary to Chapter 9's constraint, *Bracket presuppositions.* Sarah and I were interested in adolescent experience; we invited a few adolescents to wear the beeper and describe their experience. That's all.

RD'S FIRST SAMPLING DAY

We discussed five samples on RD's first sampling day; in all five he said he was "thinking about" one thing or another – thinking about not hitting a rock on his skateboard, thinking about not changing the TV channel, and so on.

Constraint: Understand how people typically describe inner experience. DES is a tool, like a drill or a saw. Part of the woodworking skill is to understand how wood typically reacts to drilling and sawing – to understand the characteristics of the tools and the medium. In particular:

Constraint: Carefully disambiguate the usage of "thinking." As we have seen, one of the characteristics of DES is that subjects often use the word "thinking" in a way that does not at all match the dictionary definition.

> With striking regularity, subjects early in their sampling refer to their own most-frequent kind of inner experience as "thinking," saying things like, "At the moment of the beep I was thinking that I don't want to take that exam." Carefully examining the details of those experiences reveals that people differ substantially in what they mean by "thinking." When Alice says "I was thinking ...," she means that she was saying something to herself in her own naturally inflected inner voice. When Betty says "I was thinking ...," she means that she was seeing a visual image of something. When Carol says "I was thinking ...," she means that she was feeling some

sensation in her heart or stomach and that she had no awareness of cognition whatsoever.

> "Thinking" refers to cognition in its dictionary definition, but it is decidedly *not* necessarily used that way in DES self-descriptions, even by sophisticated subjects. My sense is that this is an unsurprising result of the way children learn language. Children observe adults say "I'm thinking …" and gradually realize that this utterance "thinking" must refer to whatever is going on in the adult out of direct sight of the child. Children then, on this understanding, use the utterance "thinking" to refer to whatever is most frequently going on inside them, out of sight of others. Those whose principal inner experience is inner speech will come to use "thinking" to refer to inner speech; those whose principal inner experience is emotion will come to use "thinking" to refer to emotion. (Hurlburt, in Hurlburt & Schwitzgebel, 2007, p. 61)

So just because RD has said that he was thinking in all five of his first-day samples, I set aside (bracket) any understanding that he is describing a cognitive experience. That is, I bracket my understanding of just about everything that RD said in the first-day sampling interview. This is typical – first-day samples are merely a way of getting the process going, a place to start the iterative process that we described in Chapter 10. Recall the *Maintain a level playing field* constraint from Chapter 5; the interviewer's task here is to maintain a level playing field regarding the term "thinking," so that if by thinking RD means something cognitive, it can emerge with assurance on the second day, but if by thinking RD means something other than cognitive, whatever that other meaning is can emerge with equal assurance.

We had a conversation to that effect with RD and asked him to sample again.

RD'S SECOND SAMPLING DAY

On the second day, apparently as the result of the conversations in the first expositional interview, RD seemed to have a clearer notion of how to describe his experience, which is what we would expect given our discussion of iteration in Chapter 10.

It turned out that all RD's samples from his second day also involved thinking, and now we understood that he indeed meant that he was having a cognitive experience when he said he was thinking. This is a good example of what we mean by maintaining a level playing field. We were not, on the first day, trying to argue RD *out of* his view of the thinking experience; instead, we expressed skepticism in the true sense of that term: We did not merely blindly accept his first offering. On the other hand, we did not discourage RD from describing subsequent samples as thinking. We *leveled* the playing field; we did not tip it either toward or away from a cognitive understanding of thinking.

Q: Isn't bracketing presuppositions often a waste of time? On the first day he said he was thinking; you bracketed presuppositions; and on the second day he still said he was thinking. Nothing happened except you wasted a day!
A: I couldn't disagree more. On the first day he said he was thinking; the skilled observer should understand that we don't really know what RD means, and that even RD may not know what he means. On the second day RD said he was thinking and, informed by the conversation about thinking in the first interview, he could be much more discriminating in his description and we could be much more confident in our understanding. As a result, the skilled observer can now be much less skeptical. The reduction in skepticism comes from the effective bracketing of presuppositions. The alternative is to maintain gullibility throughout.

Your logic, it seems to me, is something like claiming that having a chest X-ray is such a waste of time because yours has never found anything. It is indeed a waste of time until it is not a waste of time.

Here is our description of RD's first sample from the second day:

Sample 2.1. RD was in the act of bowling, in the windup (arm swinging backward) before the release of the ball. At the moment of the beep he was deeply focused on one solid thought: *I have to get a strike.* Though the content of his thought was unambiguously clear to him, the thought was not composed of specific words; its content could have been rendered by *I gotta get a strike*, or *I need a strike*, or *Please let me get a strike*; thus this seemed to be an unsymbolized thought (see Chapter 15). Except for the solid thought, the rest of his thoughts were quiet.

That seems like a pretty straightforward description of unsymbolized thinking, but we know from long sampling experience that before we can be confident that this really is unsymbolized thinking, we will have to maintain a level playing field for a while and see if similar phenomena occur in other samples (an application of the *Understand how people typically describe inner experience* constraint). Also, we didn't hear too much detail about any physical or perceptual phenomenon that might have been ongoing at this beep; certainly physical or perceptual *processes* were ongoing. Does that mean that he really wasn't paying explicit, directly-in-awareness attention to the physical or perceptual processes? We'll have to be alert for that going forward.

Furthermore, there were two somewhat unusual locutions in his talk about this experience: He referred to a "solid thought" and to "quiet thoughts." When we inquired what RD meant by a "solid thought," he said he was locked in to this thinking to the exclusion of all other possible experiences; he was completely absorbed in this thought, and it occupied his entire awareness in a thorough, steady, extended-in-time way. Nothing else, including the act of bowling, could penetrate his awareness at that moment. My reaction was something like: *Hmm. "Solid thought"?! That's interesting. I wonder what that's about. Maybe something, maybe nothing. I know that DES subjects say lots of things that are never mentioned again. Maybe "solid" is a characteristic peculiar to this one thought and I'll never hear about it again. Maybe "solid" is not even a characteristic of this thought, but is a locution that is applied mistakenly (the result of a presupposition, or some perceived pressure from me, or an association to a TV show he watched last night).* So I attend to the use of "solid," file it away in my mind (so to speak) for potential future reference, and move on.

When we inquired what RD meant by "quiet thoughts," he said that except for the solid thought, the rest of his thoughts were quiet, by which he apparently meant that there were other soft, or incompletely articulated, or "hinty" thoughts ongoing at a very low level. The solid thought occupied 90 percent of his experience, he said; the quiet part was 10 percent. We of course don't know what RD's understanding of 90 percent and 10 percent is, but it did seem that he was not confusing 10 percent with zero. That is, he was *not* saying that there were *no other* thoughts; instead, he was saying that there were other thoughts that were quiet. *Hmm. That's interesting, too.* So I file that away as well.

Constraint: Be open to all phenomena. Sample 2.1 puts at least four balls in the air: whether RD is experiencing unsymbolized thinking, how or whether the physical/perceptual processes are represented in direct experience, whether the use of "solid thought" is important, and whether the use of "quiet thoughts" is important. We have answered nothing; instead, we have raised at least four questions – we have rendered ourselves open to the emergence of phenomena. Going forward, we will be sensitive to anything that might elaborate any of these four potentialities.

However, we won't invest ourselves in any of these potentialities. There may be other phenomena that will emerge as far more salient, which for whatever reason weren't part of the sample 2.1 discussion, and which are more important than any of the four potentialities we have observed thus far. We are gradually softening ourselves to RD's experience, and we are only in the beginning of that process.

In Chapter 3 we discussed the constraint that *The exploration of pristine experience is fundamentally idiographic,* and this provides an example. We are interested, or at least potentially interested, in unsymbolized thinking, perceptual awareness, "solid," and "quiet" as part of our attempt to apprehend RD's experience faithfully. In our attempt to apprehend RD's experience, it matters not a whit whether unsymbolized thinking, perceptual awareness, "solid," or "quiet" are terms that apply only to RD, only to pre-adolescents, only to boys, or to all people on the planet. We've seen unsymbolized thinking and perceptual awareness in other subjects, so our task here will be to see if those phenomena occur for RD and, if so, to discover whether there are twists or details that make RD's unsymbolized thinking and perceptual awareness different from that of other people. But we haven't seen other subjects use "solid" or "quiet," so our task will be to grasp what (if anything) RD's use of "solid" and "quiet" reveals about his experience. In all those cases, we will proceed (at least at first) as if RD's experience alone were the only thing of interest. Once we grasp that, then it may be interesting to see whether and how these phenomena apply to other subjects, but that will be later. Now our emphasis is squarely on RD as a solitary individual.

> **Q:** So by "idiographic" do you mean unique to RD?
> **A:** No. Idiographic means pertaining to RD as an individual, regardless of uniqueness or commonness. Here, for example, we are interested in RD's potential unsymbolized thinking (common) and his use of "solid" and "quiet" (potentially unique). An idiographic description of RD will convey both, should they emerge as salient.

Constraint: Avoid leading the witness. The iterative aspect of DES is often criticized for its potential to lead the witness – DES does spend multiple hours with subjects so the opportunity to lead certainly does exist. However, I have argued (e.g., Hurlburt & Schwitzgebel, 2007, pp. 31, 87, 281–284) that that risk is perhaps not as great as some would think. Sample 2.1 provides an example. As we have seen, there are at least four aspects of RD's talk that attracts our (tentative) interest. From the standpoint of leading the witness, that is a good thing: We are not *in fact* particularly interested in any one particular thing (so far, we are interested in four), which makes it easy to *convey* that we are not interested in any one particular thing, which makes it easier not to lead the witness. We will try to get details about all four things to the extent to which those details are available, as well as details about those other things that have yet to emerge as potentially interesting. When we ask about unsymbolized thinking, we will be conveying that we are not particularly interested in "solid"; and when we ask about "solid," we will be conveying that we are not particularly interested in unsymbolized thinking; and so on. In *non*-DES studies there is often substantial risk of leading the witness because there is typically one most important thing of interest (often called the hypothesis). We, by contrast, have no hypothesis. We are open to all potential aspects relatively equally, and will therefore find it relatively easy not to lead in any one particular direction.

Constraint: Be open to the unknown. It bears discussing that Sarah and I *noticed* that RD used the terms "solid" and "quiet." We did not know what, if anything, those terms meant; we did have the impression that other subjects do not use those terms (but we knew we may not be right about that – maybe now that we had noticed RD use those terms we would hear them everywhere). Noticing potentially unusual details of communication is not the natural attitude, which more often simply glosses over (or actively avoids) unknown or unfamiliar details. An aim of DES is not to fall into that natural attitude; instead, the aim is to attend sensitively to everything about the subjects' descriptions of their experiences, regardless of whether the details of that description make sense to our current understandings. Observation of phenomena is something like being a sponge: Sop up whatever comes your way. *Later* we can wring it out and see what's there. Because we noticed "solid" and "quiet" even though they had absolutely no significance *to us*, this constraint is to some degree a corollary to one of the most fundamental constraints discussed in this book (Chapter 9): *Don't judge others by yourself.*

Here is RD's next sample:

> Sample 2.2. RD was doing a trick on his skateboard. The skateboard meets the ground on its thin lateral edge, and RD is momentarily balanced on the opposing lateral edge, mid-trick. At the moment of the beep his mind was open and a light thought was floating through: *I gotta land this trick; please, let me land this trick.* The thought was not in specific words, but it was a clear thought. Roughly half of his awareness was devoted to this light thought floating through, and about a quarter of his awareness was devoted to checking the position of the skateboard and visually confirming that his stance was OK to successfully execute the trick. The remaining quarter of his awareness was just open.

Another unsymbolized thought, probably, so the salience of unsymbolized thinking starts to emerge, but we will maintain skepticism about that because this is only his second sampling day and he is still acquiring the DES skill. This sample does have some specific physical/perceptual awareness, which sheds some light on that aspect. However, there are three new terms that jangle our antennae: a "light thought," an "open mind," and "floating through."

A "light thought," RD said, means that he is not deeply focused on the thought or working on the thought. By a light thought he apparently meant the opposite of a solid thought. A solid thought is heavily concentrated, deeply focused (as in beep 2.1), but here in beep 2.2 RD says he is quite permeable to external stimuli. *Hmm. That makes the concept of "solid" more salient. But light is the opposite of solid? That's a bit strange. Why not "soft" or "weak"? Or why not "heavy" as the opposite of light? What (if anything) is he trying to describe by using these terms?*

It is remarkable how matter-of-factly he uses these terms "solid" and "light" – those seem to be totally concrete descriptors to him, like "sharp" when applied to knives or "salty" when applied to pretzels. He doesn't seem to be searching for some way of describing a phenomenon; he doesn't seem to be invoking a metaphor (that is, he doesn't say, "as if the thought were light," just as he wouldn't say, "as if the knife were sharp"), and he doesn't seem to be making something up on the fly. The thought is simply, declaratively, a light thought. RD said that if we could see into his head, we'd see that light thought easily, whereas we'd have to look deep to find a solid thought.

By "open" he seemed to mean that there is nothing occupying his mind, that it's free from encumbrances, there's no residue of past thoughts, worries about the future, or even "stuckness" on the present thought.

When we asked what he intended when he said the thought was "floating through," he uses his hands to show his thought passing through his head from left to right at about forehead level, but when we ask him if he has a sense of the thought traveling through his head, he says no. *Hmm. It's hard to know what to make of that.*

So now, after just two semi-skilled (second-day as opposed to first-day) samples, we already have seen that RD has quite a complexly particular way of expressing himself about his thinking: solid, light, solid as the opposite of light, quiet thought, open mind, floating through. Our task will be to discover whether he continues to use those terms; if so, what he is trying to describe when he uses those terms; and what that says about his experience. At this point our procedure is to be open for anything in a level-playing-field way: not to make too much of something, not to make too little of something. We now have lots of balls in the air.

Constraint: Let phenomena emerge gradually, organically. As it happened, RD didn't use any of that terminology for the remaining four samples on this (second) sampling day, even though he described thoughts in all those samples. We didn't encourage him to use those terms – for example at the third sample we did *not* ask, "Was that thought solid?" or "Was that thought floating through?" The logic here is that we want phenomena to *emerge*; we want to *discover* what is salient about RD's experience *as phenomena that present themselves to RD*; we don't want to trap RD into continuing to use a term merely because he happened to mention it on his first semi-skilled sample; we don't want to intrude ourselves any more than is necessary into that emergence. If a phenomenon is salient, it will emerge without our encouragement.

Perhaps that constraint might be written as: *Constraint: Drag your feet – mildly resist the emergence of a phenomenon.* This is near the heart of good observation: to be clearly awake to the potential emergence of a phenomenon and yet slightly to discourage its emergence. It might seem that it would be better to be absolutely neutral, neither to encourage nor discourage the arising of a phenomenon, and perhaps that is true at a very high level of purity. Ordinarily, however, I think it better to be somewhat "viscous" – gooily resistive – to new phenomena, for two reasons. First, if you yourself have noticed something that you take to be potentially interesting (as revealed by the *Hmm!*), then unless you are perfectly balanced, there may be a tendency to let that interest amplify things, emphasize things, organize things, overlook other things, and so on. Therefore it is worth cultivating a mild counter-pressure against anything that is interesting – that's what I mean by dragging your feet. Second, RD himself might have found a particular term interesting in itself, or he may have sensitively recognized our interest. It's worth cultivating a counter-pressure against that as well. If a phenomenon or a way of describing a phenomenon is genuinely important, it will continue to express itself against the dragging of your feet, against your mild counter-pressure. So I recommend dragging your feet as long as you can, until it becomes absurd to drag your feet.

Perhaps that constraint might be written as: *Constraint: Resist anything that is interesting.* That is not, of course, the natural attitude, which is to *pursue* that which is interesting. But because of the repetitive nature of DES, if something is genuinely interesting, it will assert itself upon you regardless of your resistance. If it is not genuinely interesting, then your initial interest was probably the result of your own presuppositions, not the phenomenon itself, so your resistance to the interesting is a productive instantiation of the bracketing of presuppositions.

RD'S THIRD SAMPLING DAY

The first sample on the next (third) sampling day is the kick-in-the-knee sample described in Chapter 9:

> Sample 3.1. RD was saying to himself in his head, in an angry voice, "Why did he kick me in my sore knee?" All of his awareness was focused on this thought. RD's inner speech was angry and rapid, yet he was not feeling angry. Immediately after the beep, RD recognized that his voice was angry, and he acknowledged that his angry tone of voice reflected that somehow he was angry. However, at the moment of the beep RD was not experiencing being angry: not experiencing tenseness in his body or any other aspect of experience that might be indicative of anger.

RD, on his own initiative, described this sore-knee thought as solid, and we asked him to clarify what he meant by "solid" here. Note that this is a *triple* application of the *Let phenomena emerge gradually, organically* constraint: (a) We did not originate the discussion of whether the thought was solid; (b) we did not presume that he used the word solid in sample 3.1 *in the same way* as he used it in sample 2.1 (that is, we asked for clarification); and (c) we did not suggest to him that his usages were consistent (that is, we did *not* ask, "Do you mean by 'solid' the same thing as you meant in sample 2.1?"). We dragged our feet; we required him to give a new account of what solid meant.

> **Q:** I think you give yourself too much credit for purity. *Of course* you suggested the conversation about solid! When he said "solid" in sample 2.1 you expressed interest; you reinforced his talk about solid. Maybe you didn't suggest it overtly here, but you did so covertly.

A: I'm far from claiming perfection, but I'm not as worried about such suggestions as you seem to be. He didn't talk about solid during samples 2.3, 2.4, 2.5, and 2.6, and if our reinforcement was an issue in sample 3.1, it should have been even more of an issue then. And we didn't ask about solid in any of those samples, so any pressure was pretty subtle. We were interested in other things as well ("passing through," "open") and he's not talking about them here. (I have discussed why subtle pressures do not have large effects on DES in Hurlburt & Schwitzgebel, 2007, especially pp. 285–289.)

When we inquired, he said that in the sore-knee sample, "solid" meant that all of his awareness is devoted to the thought, he is completely concentrated on the thought, the thought is perfectly clear to him, and due to being so deeply concentrated and focused on the thought, he is deep inside himself, insulated from the outside world, that it seems that someone would have to shake him by the shoulders to rouse him out of that thought. That definition was pretty darn close to what he had said about sample 2.1, but it was not *identical*, as if he had memorized what he had said at 2.1 and was trying to repeat it by rote. Thus his description had all the characteristics of someone describing the same phenomenon in different words on different occasions in different contexts. As a result, against our slight counter-pressure, "solid" gains a bit of salience for us.

Here's the next sample:

> Sample 3.2. RD is saying to himself in his head in a frustrated and irritated tone of voice, "Stupid cat, get away!" RD says this is a "medium" thought. He does not feel any frustration or irritation; after the beep he discovers that he is frustrated and irritated by recognizing those qualities in his inner voice (see Chapter 9).

RD explained that by a "medium" thought he means that the thought is less than solid – it's not a focused, concentrated thought – but it is more than light and fleeting. It is medium because he is partially absorbed in it but it would not be very difficult to get his attention at that moment. These are, again, unsolicited references to solid and light, and are consistent with previous references. The salience of solid and light continues to build.

> Sample 3.4. RD was looking out the car window. At the moment of the beep he was saying to himself in his head, "Oh snap! She's hot!" The words were clear and specific, and it was a light thought in that it seemed to be on the surface of his mind rather than deep within. Most of his awareness was on the thought (85 percent) but a small amount of his awareness was on the girl to whom his thought refers. He was looking at all of her, not a specific part or aspect of her.

Our exploration of this sample caused us to revise somewhat our understanding of the solid-light continuum (an instance of the *Let phenomena emerge gradually, organically* constraint). We had, until this sample, believed that solid-light referred in some important way to the clarity of a thought: Our impression was that solid thoughts were clear and light thoughts were hazy. However, this sample made it evident that a light thought could be clear. So our refined view of solid-light has to do with the depth of the concentration, not the clarity of the thought.

Salient phenomena will emerge, and they will clarify themselves as they do so.

LATER SAMPLES

It would perhaps be overkill to list every sample and our reaction to it; see Akhter, 2008, pp. 186–194 for a complete list). Eventually RD came to characterize seventeen of his twenty-nine day 2 through day 6 samples as being either solid, medium, or light. Over the course of these references, it became less and less tenable to drag our feet, more and more arbitrarily repetitive to ask him to tell us, as if afresh, what he meant by solid or light. We were forced by the phenomenon to accept that RD meant something consistently by these terms, which Sarah and I came to call the "density" of his thinking experience. By solid, RD meant that a thought captured 100 percent of his attention and concentration and seemed to be located deep within his physical head. When having a solid thought, RD was so deeply focused within himself that, he said, a person would have to physically grab and shake him to get his attention. At the other end of the spectrum, RD meant that a light thought involved little if any of his attention, focus, and concentration. A light thought could be absolutely apparent to RD, but it did not require him to be deeply focused or to become impenetrable to external stimuli. RD experienced light thoughts on the outer surface of his head as opposed to deep within. A medium thought was experienced as being somewhere between solid and light.

RD was confident and reliable in these characterizations. By confident, we mean that he deemed these to be important characteristics of his thoughts – he matter-of-factly referred to this thought as solid and that thought as light, as if speaking of a natural, unavoidably obvious characteristic. If you were speaking about two cars, you might say that the red car is in the garage whereas the green car is on the street; you would use "red" and "green" without need of elaboration as being intrinsic features of the cars – those terms would aim your attention at the "garageness" or the "streetness" of the cars, *not* to their redness or the greenness. RD used his thought density terms in a similar, intrinsic-characteristic way. If he wanted to discuss two thoughts, he would say things like, "The solid thought was about my cat, while the light thought was about my friend," apparently because solid and light were palpably evident characteristics that differentiated one thought from the other for him.

Three of RD's samples were solid; the bowling sample (2.1) is an example. Eight of RD's samples were light; the skateboard sample (2.2) is an example. Five of RD's samples were medium (e.g., stupid cat, sample 3.2), and one RD judged (after what seemed to be considerable soul-searching) to be "light-medium."

PASSING THROUGH AND COMING UP

Recall that in sample 2.2, RD had referred to a thought as "floating through" his head. In later samples he referred to thoughts as "passing through," which we took to be a refinement of what he had initially called floating through. This is another instance of the *Let phenomena emerge gradually, organically* constraint; it would have been counter-productive for us to have insisted on continuing to use his first "floating through" term.

As we have seen, there were seventeen samples in which it made sense to describe the density (solid, medium, light) of RD's thought. In eight of these seventeen samples, RD said the thoughts were either passing through (including floating through, five of seventeen) or "coming up" (three of seventeen). Thoughts that passed through started somewhere outside his head, floated through his head (often from left to right), and then passed out of his head. For example:

> Sample 4.4. Just before the beep, RD had heard his friend Steve fart, and RD had said aloud, "Oh! Snap! That smells!" But he had said that based on the *sound* of the fart, *before* he actually smelled it. Now, at the moment of the beep, RD has just caught wind of Steve's fart; he's now actually smelling the fart and quietly exclaiming to himself in his inner voice, "Oh! Crap! That *really does* smell!" About half of his awareness is on the smell of the fart and the other half is on his inner speaking. This is a light thought, not requiring a lot of concentration, and is "just passing through" from left to right. This thought is not deeply focused, and it "did not lodge in my head to be focused on or attended to" for any longer than the one to two seconds it took to pass through.

On the other hand, RD described a thought as coming up when it originated deep within his head and moved forward toward the surface of his head. For example:

> Sample 6.5. RD was thinking to himself an unsymbolized thought that if expressed in words would be "21 to 20," the score of the football game he was watching. This unsymbolized thought came up from the depths of his mind toward the surface. It had started out as a solid thought, but at the moment of the beep, the thought was closer to the surface (but still coming up from the inside toward the outside) and was now becoming a light thought.

RD believed (as a self-characterization that was corroborated by samples) that coming-up thoughts originated deep within his head and were originally experienced to be solid. (Recall that when RD was engaged in a solid thought he was deeply focused, almost entranced, and it would be hard to get through to him.) As that solid thought came up, it became increasingly lighter. The coming-up process seemed to take a second or two. Furthermore, RD believed he could "grab" the thought anywhere along this coming-up process so that it did not become lighter; the longer he waited to grab it, the lighter it would have become. Here's an example of this grabbing of a coming-up thought:

> Sample 5.3. RD was saying to himself in his inner voice, in a quiet yet surprised voice, "Wow! Those *are* nice shoes!" It was a light thought, but it had started off as a solid thought deep inside his head, and then came up through his head getting progressively lighter the closer it got to the surface. As this thought made it's way up from the depths of his mind to the surface it transformed into a medium thought, and then into a light thought – at which point he grabbed it. Thus this thought originated from within the depths of his mind and floated forward, apparently reducing in density along the way.

RD believed (although this was neither corroborated nor disconfirmed by samples) that the density of passing-through thoughts changed in the opposite direction: Thoughts that originated outside his head were originally light, and as they passed through they became more and more solid. However, none of the five passing-through thoughts that actually appeared in his sample showed this solidifying tendency: All the sampled thoughts that passed through were characterized as being light throughout.

QUIET THOUGHTS AND OPEN MIND

You may recall that early in sampling RD used the expressions "quiet thoughts" and "open mind." These references did not continue. We would have been equally ready to encounter quiet thoughts and open mind, to try to discern what RD meant by these terms, but they did not continue to appear. We have no way of knowing whether the lack of subsequent appearance of those characteristics reflects the rarity of the phenomena, the mistaken use of the expressions in the first place, the vagaries of sampling, or the failure of the subsequent interviews to follow through adequately. We could have, had we been so motivated, conducted additional sampling days with RD and perhaps clarified some of those issues.

This illustrates that not everything that a subject mentions continues on the trajectory toward salience. Salient phenomena emerge; not everything that is mentioned emerges.

Constraint: Don't get captured. I notice that students who are learning DES have a tendency to try to follow through on anything a subject says early in sampling. That is, I think, bad strategy. Investigators should *notice* what a subject says early in sampling, so that they are prepared for subsequent mentions *should they occur*, but should not encourage subsequent mentionings.

UNDERSTANDING RD

We have seen that across RD's expositional interviews there came to be a consistent use of the terms solid, medium, and light thoughts, and thoughts that come up or pass through. That is, those terms emerged as salient, refining themselves in the process.

So now we have terms that are salient for RD. What should we make of that? Our aim here is to take a snapshot of that "making-of" process.

First, we have to consider whether RD was using these terms to describe phenomena of his experience. It is of course possible that those terms do not describe RD's experience – perhaps he was merely using words that he thinks will please us regardless of their meaning or connection to his phenomena. That seems pretty unlikely: He was consistent across six weeks; the apparent meanings seemed to change a bit but not much as the weeks progressed – all that is concordant with what you would expect from someone trying to describe a phenomenon, not from one trying merely to be consistent to some definition.

Maybe RD was lying, but that doesn't seem likely as evidenced by the occasions in which he risked his own embarrassment to reveal the details of his inner experience. For example, at sample 3.3 RD was on his bed, with his arms folded behind his head. His arms, head, and upper body were pulsing to music, singing/chanting along in his head to the song on the radio, "I-like-big-butts …" Most of his awareness (75 percent) was on his singing in his head while the rest (25 percent) was on listening to the song. It was quite embarrassing for RD to tell us that he was singing about big butts; by his blushing and stammering it was quite evident that he had to fight down the urge to avoid telling us about this. Yet he told us about his inner experience anyway, despite his embarrassment. It is hard to square that with the notion that he was trying to deceive us about his phenomena.

So it seems likely that RD was telling us about his phenomena. Our task, however, is not merely to catalog what RD *says* about his experience – it is to apprehend faithfully RD's experience itself. RD's (with our help) descriptions are simply (unavoidable) means to an end.

Constraint: Understand the usage. So let's accept for the sake of argument that RD's solid, medium, light, coming up, and passing through are RD's attempts, with our help, of describing his experience of thinking. What does that say about RD's experience itself? First, we have noticed that others do not use that terminology. Does that imply that his phenomena are different from what we have come to expect from others? Maybe he is indeed describing his phenomena using unusual terms, but his phenomena are just like everyone else's – he is merely using those words in an idiosyncratic way. That seems unlikely. We were competent and careful in trying to grasp exactly what RD was trying to convey with all the terms he used. We have seen examples of that carefulness – we didn't blindly accept that "thinking" was a cognitive event; we required new clarification of terms for new samples; we evolved the definition of the solid-light continuum from its original "clarity" to its later "depth"; and so on. We were very careful to ascertain that when he said "passing through" he did indeed intend to be saying that he originally experienced his thought as being outside his head and that he experienced the thought as following a trajectory through his head – that is, passing through was indeed intended in its center-of-the-target literal meaning. The same was true for his other terms. Therefore it seems reasonable to conclude that the most likely understanding is that RD was describing thinking phenomena that are unusual from the standpoint of our sampling experience, which thus far has been mostly with adults.

That may be the most likely understanding, but it is by no means a necessary understanding. Some kind of confirmation would be highly desirable and probably necessary to science – similar phenomena in different children; objective validation; and so on. At present, this is just one child with no objective validation, so we have absolutely no right to be too confident about anything.

> **Q:** Let me see if I understand. Your aim is to examine all the verbal and non-verbal evidence available at the first beep, weigh each bit of evidence appropriately, and thereby ascertain or otherwise figure out what RD's experience was like at the first sample. Then you repeat the same process to ascertain/figure out what RD's experience was like at the second sample, and so on until you have collected all his samples. Then you sift through all those samples looking for commonalities, which you call salient characteristics.
> **A:** Actually, that is a substantial *mischaracterization* of my procedure. I *never* try to *figure out* what RD's experience was like. Instead, at the first sample I try to sensitize myself to *all the possible ways* that RD's experience *might be* that are consonant with what he said, how he said it, and what he didn't say.
> That is, instead of trying to figure out what RD's experience was like, I try to sensitize myself to the possibilities of RD's experience and his way of talking about it, to make myself permeable to his experience, to keep possibilities alive, and to await clarification from subsequent samples. I accept that RD may or may not be skilled at his description, that his description is more or less loosely connected to his experience at the moment of the beep; and I further presume that I may or may not be skilled at understanding RD's particular way of describing. There are thus a lot of unknowns in the

equation, and I try to keep as many of them alive as I can. Then, for the second sample, I continue to try to *expand* my uncertainty, perhaps adding new possibilities to the collection of ways that are broadly consonant with RD's descriptions. And so on, always trying to discern ways to be or to become *more uncertain* about his experience. Usually, I have found, this process eventually adds weight to some possible understandings of RD's experience and subtracts weight from others, until eventually the salient characteristics are left standing and the other characteristics have been washed away. That is, I have faith in the iterative process to clarify what the subject means about his experience.

This process is thus the inverse of the step-by-interpretive-step procedure that you describe. You describe a process that brings closure to the understanding of each beeped experience, whereas my aim is to *resist* such closure for as long as potential ambiguities present themselves. My aim is *not* to select the best interpretation, but rather to keep all possible interpretations alive across multiple samples, perhaps across multiple subjects, until, as the result of multiple perspectives each investigated anew, either (a) only one interpretation is left standing; or (b) the original interpretation no longer seems interesting (because we never revisited it across subsequent samples).

The problem with allowing myself the series of closures that you describe is that each such closure is a micro-capitulation to some presupposition. The weights that you describe are provided by my own presuppositions. The fact is that early in sampling with any subject, I don't know what is important, don't know how to weight things, and therefore don't know how to interpret. If I'm fortunate, over the iterative course of sampling the weights and interpretations will become clear, but that process cannot be rushed.

I might say that for me personally this foot dragging against closure is a quite unpleasant process, a destabilization that feels literally like nausea, as if the body tries to turn away from the "I don't knows" that this process values. I have learned over the years to turn *toward* the nausea as a compass turns toward north, because I have learned to recognize that feeling as a sign that I'm genuinely working at bracketing presuppositions, apparently the price to be paid for the potential to discover something that I didn't anticipate. I don't know whether other investigators must experience the same kind of nausea, but I suspect that others have to figure out for themselves what their own battle for and against presuppositions feels like, have to figure out what caving in to presuppositions feels like, what holding presuppositions at bay feels like, and then have to learn to use those feelings as their own pole stars.

NOMOTHETIC AND PROCESS SPECULATIONS

That's where it stands today: We've done, I think, a good job of exploring RD's experience. It is possible that we have gotten it wrong – that Sarah and I have delusions of one kind or another that block, distort, or otherwise corrupt our apprehensions of his experience. I'd say those probabilities are modest.

I think we did a pretty good job of *arriving* at our interest in solid, medium, light, coming up, and passing through – of being forced into that interest by the data.

What we have said about RD so far is fundamentally idiographic; we have tried to describe RD's experience regardless of whether that experience is or is not similar to anyone else's experience. And what we have said about RD so far is fundamentally phenomenological; we have tried to describe the phenomena of RD's experience regardless of what that said or didn't say about RD's cognitive or other processes. DES is fundamentally an idiographic exploration of phenomena.

However, the aim of science is not primarily to apprehend the single individual RD's phenomena – it aims at discerning from RD those phenomena that might be characteristic of other similarly situated individuals, to piece together idiographic accounts and create a bit of knowledge that transcends individuality. Furthermore, the aim of science is not merely to apprehend phenomena and not merely to discover whether particular phenomena are common – it aims at understanding the processes that underlie the phenomena. Let's see how we might get from an idiographic account of phenomena to a nomothetic speculation about process.

First, we would have to sample with more people, being open to the possibility that they might have phenomena that would make sense to describe as solid, medium, light, coming up, and passing through. It would make sense to sample with more young adolescents, because (a) RD was a young adolescent, (b) we have not sampled with many young adolescents, and (c) we have sampled with many adults and those terms have not been salient. When we perform that sampling, we will be presented with more opportunities for salient phenomena to emerge, now across subjects. There are a whole range of possibilities, including these three: (a) These phenomena will emerge exactly as RD described them for some adolescents (that is, RD was typical of a class of individuals); (b) phenomena that are anywhere close to those described by RD will not emerge across subjects (that is, either RD was an anomaly or misreported); and (c) phenomena will emerge that are similar but not identical to solid, medium, light, coming up, and passing through (that is, the phenomena will be refined as they emerge). The object of the future sampling will be to maintain a level playing field with respect to all these possibilities and any others that may emerge.

So that we can get a glimpse of how this might translate into our understanding, let's assume the simplest case (a): These phenomena will emerge exactly as RD described them for some adolescents. Recall that Chapter 9 speculated that nascent emotion experience may be substantially different from adult emotion experience: AV was (perhaps) just learning how to feel, not yet very good at it, when she said, "I'm sad, I'm sad, I'm sad." A parallel speculation is that nascent thinking may be substantially different from adult thinking: RD may be just learning how to think, and he's not very good at it. His thoughts come and go more or less like wild horses, and he's just learning how to control them, to domesticate them to his own ends. He's semi-good at it – he can grab a thought at a specified density, but sometimes (as in a solid thought) the act of thinking so occupies his attention that nothing short of physically shaking him can dislodge it. By the time RD reaches adulthood, he will have mastered these thought-control skills, and they will have become entirely second nature, taken for granted, and he will have processing capability left over to monitor simultaneously other events in the environment.

This seems an entirely logical process. Think back to what it was like to learn to drive a car: You had to focus all your attention on it, aspect by aspect: As you struggled to remember which way to move the turn-signal lever to indicate the left turn, you forgot to watch the road and veered into the curb. I think it likely that thinking is, similarly, a set of skills. When RD was born, he probably had no ability whatsoever to create inner speakings that could or could not move through his head. When RD is twenty-five, his inner speakings will be stable and controlled. Sometime between zero and twenty-five he has to acquire this thinking skill; at these beeps we see RD in the skill-acquisition phase.

If that is true, it has substantial consequences for our understanding of our own kids and of developmental psychology. If you are a parent of a teenager, you doubtless have the experience of having him ignore you altogether when you speak to him. That ignoring appears to be willful disrespect and elicits parental anger. RD's samples give a quite different explanation: Your teenager may merely be thinking, and he's not very good at it because he is only a teen-ager just in the process of learning how to think. If you happen to talk to him when he is thinking a solid thought, *he in fact doesn't hear you at all*. It *appears that he is willfully ignoring you, but his not-yet-very-skillful thought process simply doesn't allow the multitasking necessary to hear you while he thinks.*

The plausibility of this understanding is increased by the following observations made by Todd Seibert and me of older individuals (Chapter 9). Some of our older subjects failed to respond to the beeper, which emits a quite loud beep through an earphone. Most subjects experience the beep as being "injected" into their consciousness – an impossible to ignore signal that something is to be done. However, when the beep occurs for some of our elderly subjects some of the time, they show no signs of hearing it despite their having normal hearing. Todd and I have altered the situation so we sit with the subject so we can hear the beep "through the back of the earphone," so there is no question whatever about whether the beep is being delivered properly. Our beepers deliver the beep for about eighty seconds before discontinuing beep-ing (to conserve battery). Some of our older subjects can continue whatever they were doing throughout those eighty seconds *and never show the slightest sign that the beep occurred*. How can that be explained?

One plausible speculation is that as the "mental computational power" diminishes with age, the thinking process becomes fragile, and people learn to accommodate to that fragility by systematically ignoring competing events. That is, the multitasking that typical adults take for granted requires too much computation and so gets eliminated from the cognitive repertoire. As a result, thoughts in the elderly at least sometimes become similar to what RD would call solid – recall RD said you have almost to shake him by the shoulders to dislodge an ongoing solid thought.

I am not in any way saying that the thinking produced by a teenager's nascent ability is *the same as* that produced by an older individual's reduced computational power. I am saying that the multitasking that most normal adults take for granted, that allows most normal adults easily to reorient themselves to the beep or to other environmental events, *should not be taken for granted* when trying to apprehend the experience of either younger or older individuals.

Maybe solid, medium, light, coming up, or passing through apply not to adolescents in general, but only some particular adolescent sub-groups. Maybe it doesn't have to do with adolescence at all – maybe it is a fairly rare experience that applies to some adolescents and adults, but not with high frequency, so I haven't seen the phenomenon previously with adults. Maybe those terms applied in some way to RD but to no one else. Maybe those terms didn't apply to RD's experience at all. A large enough sample of adolescents and adults ought to be able to tease those important questions apart, but all would have to be investigated with substantial skill and effective bracketing of presuppositions.

> **Q:** I have a hard time believing that most kids' thoughts go passing through and are solid or light or whatever. That's just not the way thinking is.
>
> **A:** First, this chapter is speculative, so you may be entirely correct. However, it is also likely that you are failing adequately to submit to the *Don't judge others by yourself* constraint, which is a particularly stubborn constraint. *Your* thoughts are stable now, and, because they have been stable for as long as you can remember, you might think they have always been stable, rather than coming up or passing through. *You* have the skill of always monitoring the environment for events that might be dangerous or interesting, but it is entirely possible that you had to acquire that skill. The question you should practice asking, in an entirely level-playing-field kind of way, is, "What was thinking like before you were any good at it?" The problem is that if you're smart enough to ask that question, you're *too* smart to *remember* what it is like. The good news is that you may be smart enough to *observe what is it like for others* if you bracket the presuppositions that prevent your observing it in yourself.

> **Q:** You have written that one of the characteristics of adult schizophrenics is that their thoughts move through their heads (Hurlburt, 1990; see Chapter 13). Could it be that RD is on the path to schizophrenia?

A: This is very crude logic (RD's thoughts move; some schizophrenics' thoughts move; therefore RD is likely to be schizophrenic) and I doubt that it is correct because in our clinical opinion RD is not incipiently schizophrenic. But the fact is that present day science knows very little about the inner experience of thirteen-year-olds, knows very little about the inner experience of schizophrenics, and knows correspondingly much less about the inner experience of thirteen-year-olds who will become schizophrenic as an adult. If your logic *is* correct, its consequences could be enormous: The early identification of schizophrenia, as discussed in Chapter 19, might have substantial personal, social, and scientific consequences.

Q: You seek to understand RD's meanings of terms like solid, light, coming up, and passing through. Is your intention to understand the meaning of adolescence?
A: No. I think you confuse two very different meanings of the term "meaning." When I try to figure out what RD *means* when he says, "I had a solid thought," my aim is simply to discover what RD intends to convey by voicing the phonemes that we recognize as the word "solid." But when you refer to the "meaning of adolescence," your use of *meaning* refers to something's significance to the human condition, particularly to some hidden or special significance. DES does not try to explore significances, whether overt or hidden or special.

Being straight about this distinction is crucial to understanding what is being conveyed in this book. Meaning as you use the term is *not* directly observed or observable – it *lies behind* the observed, it has to be inferred from the observed. (That is, meaning is a mentalism as Skinner used the term; see Chapter 11.) Pristine experience, by distinct contrast, is directly observed, but only by one person. Unless or until a better method exists, that person will have to describe pristine experience, and one main tool (by no means the only tool) in that description will be words. As with most tools, we need to calibrate our usage; with words, that implies that we will need to ensure that we understand what RD's words mean: what he intends to convey by using some particular word.

Q: Yes, but isn't that the crux of the whole exploration-of-pristine-experience enterprise? Given that we can't apprehend the pristine experience directly, we can never be sure that we know how a particular word is intended. You can never know what RD meant by solid, never know whether his experience is just like that of all those others who do *not* use the word solid to describe their experience.
A: I accept that we can never be totally sure, but I do not accept that we cannot be confident, that we cannot apprehend with fidelity. When Ephraim in Chapter 16 uses words like "I had put the spoon [laughs sheepishly] laying on the top surface of the soup, and I was pushing down slightly, feeling the resistance of it, and then watching the soup spill over the edges really slowly, and watching [laughs sheepishly] the way that it cascaded over the

edges of the spoon and filled it up," I think we can be confident (not, of course, absolutely certain) that Ephraim is *not* merely eating soup with the resistance and shape being merely the sensory ingredients of the soup-eating process. We gain that confidence by asking a series of questions that come at resistance from several different directions, observing what he says about it and how he says it.

I happily accept that we are not as confident about what RD meant by solid as about what Ephraim meant by "watching the soup spill over the edges really slowly." It was the point of this chapter to expose you to the potential emergence of a phenomenon, to provide a description about which we are *not* confident, so as to make transparent the emergence into salience.

This book makes the case that if we continue to explore RD's experience genuinely submitting to the constraints that that exploration imposes; if we continue to explore others like RD (whether that means other adolescents, other adolescent boys, others with the same genetic makeup as RD, or whatever); if we allow our understanding of RD's and others' experience iteratively to emerge (always with genuine submission to the constraints); then our confidence in our understanding of what (if anything) RD means by "solid" can increase. That is a process that may be of fundamental importance to our understanding of people, and to which we return in the next chapter.

21

Investigating Pristine Inner Experience

I have tried, over the course of this book, to demonstrate ever more comprehensively that:

- *Pristine experience is personally important.* You live your life entirely immersed in your pristine experiences, a stream of your own creations, tailored by you just for you, perhaps derivative of the surrounding environment, perhaps not. The stream of pristine experience is unfettered by time, place, or reality. At one moment you may be seeing in reality the book you are holding, at the next moment hearing and smelling in imagination the ocean that you visited last year, at the next moment experiencing yourself innerly saying "it's all politics" as part of imagining a conversation that will likely take place this coming evening.

    Your pristine experience is your own ultimate intimacy: You create it; you shape it; you live in it; you're immersed in it every waking minute; no one else can access it.

    You do not occupy the same experiential world as does anyone else. You live in your own individually created stream of pristine experiences and I live in mine, each stream independent of the other, each created more by our own individuality than anchored directly to events in the shared world.

- *Despite its ubiquity, people are often mistaken, sometimes hugely mistaken, about the features of their own pristine experience.*

- *Pristine experience is scientifically important.* Without a careful survey of pristine experience we are unlikely to be able to understand bulimia, adolescence, old age, schizophrenia, emotion, and perhaps most other topics in psychology.

- *Despite its importance, psychological and consciousness science (and, I think, the philosophy of perception, epistemology, and the philosophy of action, among others) has little appreciation for pristine experience.* Science does not make with adequate care the fundamental distinction between pristine experience and all else.

- *Pristine experience inheres in moments and only in moments.* There is nothing "in general" or "usually" about pristine experience.
- *Pristine experience is radically non-subjective* in the sense that there are pretty darn right and pretty darn wrong characterizations of it. Pristine experience is not a matter of opinion, not a matter of impression, not a matter of theory.
- *Pristine experience can be apprehended with fidelity.* Pristine experience is there for the taking. It presents itself directly to you, albeit privately – it is not a mentalism, not an inference. There may well be an upper limit on the fidelity of its apprehension, but that limit is pretty darn high, much higher than is usually supposed in scientific circles.
- *However, the high fidelity apprehension of pristine experience requires genuinely submitting to the constraints that that attempt imposes.* Those constraints involve, at the barest of essentials, the necessity of concretely specifying moments, of forthrightly dealing with the problems of retrospection, of differentiating between experience and not-experience, and of developing the skill of bracketing presuppositions both in the investigator and the subject.
- *Apprehending pristine experience is a skilled performance art.* Those constraints are typically applied in the context of an interview that unfolds in real time, and their execution requires substantial skill.

All this may have raised questions, which I seek to answer as we approach the end of this book.

APPREHENDING PRISTINE EXPERIENCE

Q: There are other ways of apprehending pristine experience – poetry or novels, for example. In particular, "stream-of-consciousness" writers such as Faulkner, James Joyce, and Tolstoy present pristine experience.
A: I agree that there are other ways of exploring and transmitting important views about the human condition, but stream of consciousness is a *literary device*, not a faithful representation of pristine experience.

Q: You say we often don't know what we think or feel or experience. Do you think we are just a bunch of fools, and that we stumble into other similarly afflicted fools, all engaging in meaningless interactions based on false information and faulty presuppositions?
A: That's a complicated question, so let me break it apart.

We often don't know what we think or feel or experience. We know to some extent but are deluded to some extent about our own experience. For generations, the historically dominant branches of psychological science have encouraged us to ignore our experience (behaviorism), or to think that we are blind to or "unconscious of" our most important experiences (psychoanalysis), or to believe that attending to feelings and thoughts is easier than it actually is (humanism). Our modern materialist culture draws our attention away from our experience to all manner of attractive gadgets. The ever-increasing power and immersion in the media encourages us to fulfill roles for each other that are dictated by the media, not by our experience. As a result of these and other pressures, we as individuals often (probably usually) don't take the trouble to distinguish between what we actually think, feel, experience and what we are told we should think, feel, and experience.

Are we a bunch of fools? I'd prefer to say we are a bunch of human beings, which, in my view, means that we are a bunch of complex beings that are partly logical, partly delusional. Some of us are doubtless more delusional than others; I know of no one who is free of delusion (although I accept that freedom from delusion may be possible). Many of us pretend, including to ourselves, that we are free of delusion, and that is foolish, because to the extent that we believe our own pretendings we dig ourselves deeper into whatever delusions we may have – confidence in your own non-delusion is probably evidence of delusion. Delusions are tenacious because they seem so unquestionably true, so incontrovertible, so completely acceptable, so downright virtuous.

We stumble into other similarly afflicted fools ... (recall that I prefer "partly deluded humans"). Sometimes we stumble into, but probably more often we *actively seek out* similarly deluded humans. Such seeking is facilitated by the ever increasing mobility of society, the proliferation of special-interest television, and, of course, the Internet.

...all engaging in meaningless interactions based on false information and faulty presuppositions. Our interactions are by no means meaningless – they are meaningfully constructed, at least to some degree, specifically to support our delusions. But yes, they are based at least to some degree on false information and faulty presuppositions.

So I would say this: *We are mostly a bunch of partially deluded human beings who have only an incomplete sense of our pristine experience. We interact, sometimes purposefully, sometimes accidentally, with other partially deluded human beings in ways that sometimes are in accord with our experience but at other times are perpetuations of our shared delusions.*

Q: Wait a minute! Are you telling me I'm partly deluded?
A: Yes, probably you are. There are two possibilities. You can have attained perfection; or you can be partly delusional. I think most people who claim perfection are partly delusional.

APPREHENDING ANOTHER'S PRISTINE EXPERIENCE

Q: You have said throughout this book that you think the apprehension of one's own or another's pristine experience is difficult (but possible). Could you summarize in a big-picture way why it is difficult? It still seems like it's easy for me to describe my experience.

A: There are four main reasons, all interrelated. First, your take on your experience is (probably) not differentiated. You have direct access to only one kind of experience (your own) and therefore no direct comparisons with the experiences of others, so whatever ways of experiencing you developed as a child or adolescent may continue on into adulthood, entirely taken for granted. For example, if you grow up engaged predominantly in sensory awareness (as described in Chapter 16), you would naturally (but mistakenly) assume that everyone is immersed in sensory awareness, assume that experience couldn't possibly be any other way. Therefore it would never occur to you to notice the existence of sensory awareness even though it is the dominant feature of your experience.

Second, your talk about your inner experience is (probably) not differentiated. As we discussed in Chapter 11, Skinner was right: Your talk about your inner experience has probably never been adequately differentially reinforced by the verbal community. The community carefully refined your talk about external objects: When as a youngster you said, "That stop sign is blue," the community said, "No, that sign is red!" or "I see why you would call it 'bluish,' but I think 'purplish' is better." By contrast, if you said, "I'm feeling blue," there is no way for the verbal community to have access to what you're feeling, whether you mean the same thing when you say "blue" as does someone else. Thus talk about inner experience is only relatively loosely, if at all, related to actual pristine experience.

Third, you (probably) have delusions (which DES generally calls presuppositions) about your experience. Because your and others' talk about experience is not differentiated, what you say about your own inner experience is rarely challenged, leading you to the widely shared delusion that you have infallible access to your own experience (and that others have infallible access to theirs), as well as to the delusion that everyone else's experience is pretty much like your own.

Fourth, you (probably) have little support from the scientific community. Because the delusions of "infallible access to experience" and "everyone is like me" are widely shared including by scientists, science has a difficult time with experience. Either it recognizes the delusion and therefore excludes experience from consideration (as did behaviorism) or it doesn't recognize the delusion and proceeds as if apprehending experience is easy, trying to access it with rating scales and the like. Either way, there is little felt need to improve the apprehension of experience.

Q: What makes you think DES can rise above all that?

A: It remains to be seen whether DES can indeed be productive in science. There are two main aspects that distinguish DES and may make it possible to investigate pristine experience successfully. First, it accepts that presuppositions/delusions about experience abound but then does not avoid experience or pretend the delusions away. Instead, it tries to create and incorporate procedures that bracket those presuppositions.

Second, DES seeks to investigate only those aspects of experience that can be directly apprehended (that is, pristine experience), avoiding all else. For example, DES *avoids* talk about association, the mind, ideas, consciousness, concepts, will, self, causation, inclination, intention, cognitive processes, knowledge, memory, intuition, representations, encoding, storage, retrieval, mental rules, self-concept, decision making, judgment, reasoning, and so on because all are mentalisms (see Chapter 11); none is directly observable and is therefore not part of pristine experience.

SKILL

Q: Suppose (based on your inter-observer reliability studies, your discoveries of novel forms of inner experience, and my own careful observations of your technique) that I accept that *you*, Russ, are a substantially high fidelity observer of inner experience. Suppose that Jane Doe claims to use DES to explore inner experience and finds X. Am I supposed to accept Jane's characterizations of X just because she is using DES? I don't think so. That *you* have demonstrated inter-observer reliability and so on does not imply that *Jane* would be able to do the same if she tried. Even if I were to trust you, how would I determine whether Jane is to be trusted? Certainly there are some Janes who would represent themselves as expert DES practitioners but whom I and probably you would find hopelessly inadequate if we observed them at work.

A: That is indeed the heart of the scientific matter, and I offer three views.

(1) I *don't* think you should blindly trust my (or anyone else's) characterizations of inner experience. I think you should credit my interviewing skill, the care with which I have established my inter-observer reliability, the concern that I have demonstrated about the bracketing of presuppositions, and so on. As a result, I think you should take what I say about experience seriously, perhaps more seriously than you would take someone else's more casual observations. However, that does *not* imply that you (and science) should simply *accept* any particular one of my conclusions – I may be able to bracket my presuppositions in many situations but not in the situation of your interest.

I have made many observations of or speculations about inner experience in this book: that some people's experiences are more complex than others; that some people don't seem to experience emotion; that some people seem to be relatively devoid of inner experience; that there are great individual differences in inner experience; that even scientists seem to assume that all experiences are like theirs; that some people think without words or images; that there are strong regularities in experiences within subjects and even across subjects; that inner voices or mental pictures may seem to be at various places in or around the subject's head; that inner speaking differs from the hearing of oneself speaking; that one might experience viewing oneself from impossible perspectives; that "I was thinking" might variously be used to describe inner speech, inner hearing, mental seeing, feelings, or sensory awareness; that "subjunctifiers" signal when one is not reporting experience; that the happening of experience differs from the doing of experience; that feeling and inner seeing seem to be acquired (through maturation and practice) – and losable – skills; that color in mental imagery might develop after black-and-white imagery and disappear before it; that the *feeling* of emotion is distinct from the *state* of emotion; that a pre-teen's saying of "I'm sad, I'm sad, I'm sad" might reflect a *lack* of feeling; and so on). I expect that some of those observations/ speculations will be proven to be basically correct; others will be mistaken, distorted, or otherwise in need of refinement. How many and which ones are correct or distorted is not known to me. So it seems prudent *not* blindly to accept apprehensions of experience by me, by Jane, or by anyone else.

(2) I think there are at least two ways to make judgments about Jane's (or my) skill:

(a) You can compare Jane's DES results to the DES results of someone whose skills you recognize. If Jane and some skilled DES practitioner independently arrive at similar characterizations of a series of people's experiences, then it is reasonable to judge that Jane is skilled.

(b) You can tell by looking, to a substantial degree, whether someone is skilled at apprehending another's inner experience, even if that other's experience is private. When my granddaughter Hannah was seven or eight, I took her to her first classical orchestra concert. We sat in about the fourth row, a bit to the right of center; the cellos were dead ahead, close enough to see clearly but far enough so that it was impossible to hear each cellist individually. Between pieces I leaned over to Hannah and said, "Let's number the cello players one, two, three …" and I pointed to each one in turn. "During the next piece, you tell me which one has the most beautiful sound." She looked at me quizzically, as if I had set an impossible task: "But I can't hear them!" I said, "Watch them as they play, and just tell me what you think." Half way through the next piece she poked my arm and wrote with her finger on her outstretched palm the number we had assigned to the principal cellist. She was, of course, right – he was the best player and doubtless had the most beautiful sound. Even not knowing anything about cello technique, an eight-year-old was able to discern the best player from a group of excellent players, based on the readily apparent beauty of the vibrato motion, the security of left-hand motion, the consistency of bowing, and so on. Similarly, you can examine Jane's DES interviewing "performance" and determine reliably (not perfectly) whether Jane is skillful at apprehending someone's inner experience with fidelity. If Jane's questioning has very few extraneous, random motions, very few false starts and corrections, moves unerringly toward the moment of the beep, attends to experience and does not attend to theory or generality, understands subjunctification, appropriately distinguishes among known features of pristine experience when they occur, does not impose her own concepts, skillfully levels the playing field where it needs to be leveled, and in short genuinely submits to the constraints described in this book, it is likely (but not certain) that she will apprehend her subject's experience with fidelity.

(3) I don't think it is necessary or perhaps even desirable that there be many highly skilled Janes, just as it is not necessary that there be many violin virtuosos. A hundred or a thousand worldwide may be perfectly adequate to meet the demand for violin virtuosos.

Q: So even if I decide that you or Jane is skilled, science still shouldn't trust your findings?
A: It should not. The apprehension of experience is the beginning of science, not the end. Validation is still the center of science.

Q: I think I could spend 10,000 hours training to do DES and still not be very good at it. I just don't think I have the character for it.
A: I do think there are some character traits that are required for the high fidelity apprehension of pristine experience: tolerance for ambiguity, patience, steadfastness, a willingness to walk very close to one's own and another's sensitivities, and at the same time the ability to be very directive about some things (like cleaving to the moment of the beep), and so on. Certainly those characteristics don't come easily for some people, but whether *you* have or could acquire those traits is not given to me to judge. The good news is that, as we saw in Chapter 3, the randomness of the DES beep can help you acquire those characteristics, if you let it. The bad news is that presuppositions don't give up without a fight.

The situation is similar to violin virtuosity. Not everyone who practices for 10,000 hours becomes a virtuoso.

Q: This has been a pretty negative book. You've given examples of bad DES interviews, examples of the failure to bracket presuppositions even by experienced DES investigators. If you want to convince me that DES is a solid interview method, you should have given me more *good* examples of DES interviewing!
A: I don't believe that my account has been negative. I have tried to describe the situation as it is, and realistic is not negative. Actually, I think I have been quite positive: I have tried to show that pristine experience has a pretty darn radically non-subjective existence, that pristine experience can be faithfully apprehended, that pristine experience is there for the taking, and that it might be useful (recall the list a few questions ago).

However, I have indeed tried to stop far short of saying that DES is a solid interview method. DES is a tool, like a violin is a tool, but it is the skilled application of DES (or of something that resembles it), not DES itself, that allows the faithful apprehending of pristine experience. The story is frequently told about famed violinist Fritz Kreisler who became irritated that the newspaper publicity prior to his concert focused more on his Stradivarius violin than on the performer himself – you should attend this concert, the newspapers said, to hear the famous million dollar violin. Kreisler gave the concert to thunderous applause and then threw the violin to the stage and crushed it with his heel. To make the point that performance is primarily skill, not instrument, he had performed the concert on a cheap violin. That is not to imply that the instrument is not important – there is indeed a substantial difference between a Stradivarius and a violin you might buy at Wal-Mart.[1] And it goes the other way around: You could give me a Stradivarius and I still could not play a note.

Q: How do you expect to "sell" DES if you don't claim it is a solid method?
A: I don't want to sell DES, if by "sell" you mean to convince others to buy it whether they need it or not. I wish to promote the need for something like DES, not DES itself.

There are two kinds of risks in "promoting" the exploration of pristine experience:

Risk I: Fail to convince psychological science that the exploration of pristine experience might be of value. That would be unfortunate because I think it is of value. However, this failure is inconsequential; if pristine experience is indeed important, someone else, sooner or later, will be more convincing.

Risk II: Convince ("sell") psychological science to use DES without imparting the notion that high skill is required. That would be both unfortunate and consequential. Many would-be scientists would read about DES, say, "I can do that!" and get a beeper and charge ahead. However, the results produced by such attempts are not likely, in the long run, to be replicable or productive because of the skills required (particularly the bracketing of presuppositions). The consequence of such attempts, it seems to me, would likely be a discrediting of introspection, which is likely to be even more devastating (because it is the second one) than was the first discrediting of introspection a century ago, and from the shadow of which we are just now barely emerging.

Therefore I think Risk II is worse than Risk I. As a result, I am *not* trying to sell DES. I'm trying to sell the notion that the exploration of pristine experience can be productive if it is performed genuinely submitting to the constraints that that exploration imposes. One of those constraints, a major one, is that it requires substantial skill.

DELUSION

Q: You said that presuppositions are delusions. Do you really mean such a strong word?

---

[1] But most blind comparisons fail to distinguish a Stradivarius from well-made modern violins (Beamont, 2000).

A: Yes. We have discussed in this book about 110 constraints to which one must genuinely submit if one is faithfully to apprehend pristine experience. Most of those constraints have directly or indirectly to do with the bracketing of presuppositions. In an important sense, this entire book is about the bracketing of presuppositions.

Presuppositions are distractions, distortions, blind spots, hypersensitivities, insensitivities that impede the faithful apprehension of pristine experience. And yes, I think presuppositions are mini- or maxi-delusions, insidious, recalcitrant foes that operate in everyone's (and that includes my and probably your, dear reader) own personal blind spots (Hurlburt & Schwitzgebel, 2011c).

A presupposition is a delusion, not merely an ignorance. Ignorance is simply lacking knowledge; delusion is believing that it is not necessary to know. Ignorance is lacking skill; delusion is believing that one's current skill is good enough. Ignorance is a vacuum whose natural tendency is to be filled up by new content; delusion is hyperbaric pressure whose natural tendency is to resist any new content. Ignorance is created by the universe – we are born ignorant. Delusion is self-created – it arises from some prior (but inadequate) skill acquisition. Ignorance is relatively easily recognized; delusion is stubbornly invisible. Ignorance is easily remedied – practice and training easily align with the forces pressing inward. Delusion is hard and perhaps impossible to remedy – practice and training are actively opposed by the hyperbaric pressure forcing outward.

Delusion makes it seem like you already know what you don't actually know; makes it seem like you don't *need* to know what you actually need; makes it seem like you are more skillful than you are; makes the important seem trivial; makes the trivial seem important. Delusion always seems reasonable, seems intelligent, seems necessary, seems Right with a capital *R*, seems Good with a capital *G*, seems True, seems Virtuous.

Delusion always operates behind the scenes and is thus impervious to logic, to argument, to persuasion. It might therefore seem impossible to eliminate a delusion, and in fact many delusions are never eliminated. However, I think it may be within the human condition to eliminate delusions entirely, although that is exceedingly rare (that's what I take true enlightenment to be, about which I have no personal experience). More within our everyday reach is to eliminate some delusions and reduce the effect of others, a process that I generally call bracketing presuppositions (Hurlburt & Schwitzgebel, 2011c; Hurlburt & Raymond, 2011).

Q: You have no right to expose someone else's delusions. You have delusions too!

A: I agree. I consider myself an expert in delusion largely because of substantial personal experience. Like most jokes, that statement has a serious side: I do *not* wish to convey that you're delusional and I'm not. Instead, I wish to convey that you're delusional and so am I. The question is not *whether* you are or I am delusional; I accept that we are *all* (perhaps excepting those who have reached nirvana) delusional. What I would like us to consider is whether we can deal with our delusions in the apprehension of pristine experience, and if so, how. I re-emphasize that I am *not* free of delusion. I *have*, for many years, devoted considerable attention and effort to eliminating the delusions (that is, to bracketing the presuppositions) that stand in the way of apprehending pristine experience. I think I have learned something about that, which I am trying to transmit in this book. But I should not be taken to be the Authority; I am a fellow traveler, perhaps many years ahead of some travelers, perhaps lifetimes behind others.

Let's consider an example of my own delusion. Here is an e-mail (lightly edited for readability here) that I sent to my inner-experience-sampling colleagues and students a few years ago:

Here is a true story.

A few years ago, as some of you know, I started taking guitar lessons from world-class guitarist Ricardo Cobo. I was a pretty good self-taught amateur classical guitarist, nowhere near the league of the teacher. As study progressed, he would occasionally say to me that I needed to be more clear and consistent about the sequencing of my right-hand fingerings, that the order in which my fingers plucked varied from one performance to the next. I smiled to myself in the knowledge that my right-hand sequencing was actually quite advanced, and that it was quite skillful of me to be able to alter fingerings "on the fly" as the situations demanded it.

One day he said, "Here's a movement of Bach's *Cello Suite Number 1* arranged for guitar. Buy a bottle of White-Out and remove all the editor's suggested fingerings from the page. Then pencil in a complete fingering for both left and right hands, indicating for absolutely every note which left- and right-hand fingers are to be used in its execution." On the possibility that he knew what he was talking about, I did so. It was a very arduous task, not merely time consuming but demanding. Most passages could be fingered in any of several ways, and writing them out demanded that I examine all those possibilities and select one. It took most of a week.

At my next lesson we went through my fingerings, and he explained why many of my choices were bad: This fingering would make a rough transition to what comes next – here's an alternative that eases that; that fingering makes it impossible to sustain the F# for its full value – here's an alternative that sustains it; this fingering makes the sound of that note too bright by comparison to this note – play the note on that string instead. He was right in each case. By the time we were done, much of my work had been crossed out and replaced with better fingerings.

Then my task was actually to learn to play the piece with the fingerings that we had indicated. That also was not easy, because I had been in the habit of ignoring whatever right-hand fingering suggestions that music editors had made in the belief that my own choices were good enough. Now I had to develop the skill of paying attention to right-hand fingering notations.

The fact is that once I had, however reluctantly, decided to entertain the possibility that my right-hand fingerings might be problematic (I had to be forced to see for myself that my fingerings were *not* always good, even when I thought hard about them), and then set about the hard, painful, frustrating work of clarifying them, my playing moved to a higher level.

This is, of course, a story about bracketing presuppositions, about the amazing-in-retrospect false pride that led me to believe that my right-hand fingering ability was somehow better than my teacher's, about the fact that this delusion about my fingering ability was an impediment to my own improvement, about the fact that removing the delusion doesn't solve anything but only enables subsequent hard work to be more effective.

In my current view, the final paragraph of that fragment is still somewhat self-protective. It is not a delusion about my *fingering ability*; it is a delusion that *I* am fundamentally superior to my guitar teacher (world-class virtuoso though he may be!). That is a delusion of grandeur, not a delusion about my fingering ability.

Actually, even that minimizes my delusion; makes it seem merely comparative between me and one particular person (Cobo, the guitar virtuoso). Actually, I think my delusion is not in the slightest comparative. The actual delusion of grandeur is something like, *I* am fundamentally superior to Cobo or Segovia or Romero or any other guitarist on the planet, present, past, or future. There is plenty of evidence to the contrary, but that doesn't penetrate the delusion in the slightest.

Q: Why tell us about your guitar playing delusions. That has nothing to do with apprehending pristine experience.
A: I agree, but as I said near the end of Chapter 19, my guitar-playing delusions are easier for me to access than my apprehending-pristine-experience delusions. For thirty years I have been systematically working to abrade away my apprehending-pristine-experience delusions, including many hundreds of hours of co-interviewing (including with noted skeptics), jointly examining videotapes, and so on. I've pretty much worked through the easy-to-access delusions about sampling. The guitar delusions are easier for me to spot.

Anyway, the guitar story illustrates the heart of the kind of delusion that I think typically does characterizes the exploration of inner experience: The topic is something I care about; I have a modicum of skill; I think I have more skill than I actually have; the teacher has a more accurate view of my skill than I do; the teacher tells me repeatedly what I have to do, but I still don't do it; maybe I don't do it because I *can't* do it, but it seems like I don't do it because *I don't have* to do it – that I am *above* doing it; I don't have any experience in doing what I have to do, and therefore I believe that what I don't do doesn't exist or isn't important; I believe that what I can't do is impossible or unnecessary; there's evidence to the contrary that I conveniently ignore or rationalize.

Furthermore, the story illustrates the result of being constructively confronted with my delusion: Nothing changes automatically. Recognizing the existence of a delusion does *not* solve *anything*; it merely opens the door for the substantial, painful, and difficult work whose necessity had been hidden by the delusion, exposes other just as stubborn, just as grandiose delusions about other aspects of playing.

But the point is not about my delusions, guitar or otherwise. I provide my guitar-playing example because it illustrates on my own turf the kind of delusion that I encounter in nearly everyone (perhaps everyone) with whom I interact about pristine experience in lectures and trainings about DES.

"Delusion" has a very negative connotation, some (but not all) of which is justified. To have a delusion means persistently to believe something that is actually false or unreal. It seems to me that that is not inherently negative: Delusion is the human condition. Unless you think of yourself as having attained perfection, you must, it seems to me, accept yourself as delusional. Most people who rankle at thinking of themselves as delusional, it seems to me, rankle because they *do* think of themselves as having attained perfection. I remind the reader that I know firsthand of which I speak.

A main task of advancing a science of experience, or of advancing one's personal understanding of experience, is coming to grips with delusion: accepting its existence, eliminating it where possible, reducing it where possible, bracketing it where possible. The good news is that there is plenty of room for progress, and that progress is attainable.

It is possible, within the human condition, for some everyday mortals to attain virtuosity in guitar or violin; similarly, it is possible for some everyday mortals to master the ability to apprehend pristine experience in high fidelity.

SCIENCE

Q: You have said that psychological science doesn't value experience. I think you are mistaken. If you go to any recent volume of any high quality psychology journal (*Psychological Bulletin*, for example), you'll find empirical studies or reviews of studies in which experience is taken seriously.

A: I don't think experience is taken seriously enough, but I've taken your challenge seriously as follows: I obtained the *Psychological Bulletin* article with the most recent acceptance date and examined it to see how experience is investigated. That haphazardly chosen article happens to be Olatunji and Wolitzky-Taylor (2009; accepted August 17, 2009), which reviews studies of Anxiety Sensitivity (AS). Let's see what role experience has in that article and the studies it reviews.

AS is the fear of anxiety-related bodily sensations, for example the fear that a tremor might be a sign of loss of control. That is, AS is not merely anxiety; it is *anxiety about* anxiety. Because anxiety is both a physiological state and a painful or uneasy experience, it does seem reasonable, as you say, that studies of anxiety about anxiety would take the experience of anxiety about anxiety seriously. At issue is whether those AS studies take that experience seriously *enough*.

Olatunji and Wolitzky-Taylor's first paragraph shows an interest in experience:

> Those high in AS may misinterpret physical sensations as danger signals and, as a result, experience elevated levels of anxiety. An individual with elevated AS might, for example, fear palpitations because of concerns about a heart attack or fear sweating in public based on concerns about negative social evaluation. *Individuals with elevated AS also experience amplified fear in response to stimuli that elicit anxiety and find their own anxiety symptoms to be aversive* (Olatunji & Wolitzky-Taylor, 2009, p. 974, emphasis added)

The sentence I italicized seems to imply that the authors understand that fear and anxiety symptoms are directly experienced phenomena. Yet that is the *only* reference to experience in this twenty-five-page paper. The second paragraph retreats from experience in the direction of theoretical issues (genetics, etc.); the third paragraph continues the retreat from experience by beginning the discussion of how the AS construct is measured.

Q: OK, but this is a review paper. The original articles on which this review is based are interested in experience.

A: I'm afraid that is not true, either. Here's the history of AS: Fear of fear is a very old concept. Freud (1895) discussed it; anxiety about anxiety and its paradoxical-intention treatment was a centerpiece of Frankl's (1975) existentialism, and others discussed it as well (Reiss, 1987).

Reiss and his colleagues brought the concept into its modern manifestation when they created the questionnaire called the Anxiety Sensitivity Index or ASI (Reiss & McNally, 1985; it was originally called there the Reiss-Epstein-Gursky Anxiety Sensitivity Scale; the name was later changed from "Scale" to "Index").

The introduction of the ASI marked a turning point in the investigation of AS. Thereafter, *nearly all* studies of AS operationalize AS by using the ASI (Olatunji & Wolitzky-Taylor, 2009). As a result, the modern literature on AS has, broadly speaking, two threads. One thread might be called "theoretical": examination of the theory behind and improvement of the psychometric characteristics of the ASI. For example, the original theory (Reiss & McNally, 1985) held AS to be a unitary construct; AS was measured by the ASI, which was therefore designed to be uni-dimensional. However, early factor analysis of the ASI revealed three factors, which suggested a refinement to the AS theory: that it was multi-dimensional. That called for refinements of the sixteen-item ASI to improve its ability to measure the three factors of

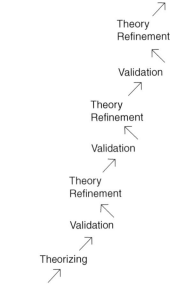

FIGURE 21.1. The scientific development of theory.

AS. For example, Taylor and Cox (1998) created the thirty-six-item ASI-R, which included ten items from the ASI and twenty-six additional items. Taylor and Cox cited an unpublished source for those items and otherwise did not describe how those items were obtained, but the implication was that the items were created on a theoretical or rational basis, something like: There are only two items that load strongly on Factor 3, so we should create additional similar items to make future measurements of that factor more robust.

The second thread might be called "validational": studies attempting to confirm the AS theory. For example, Zinbarg, Brown, Barlow, and Rapee (2001) administered the ASI and then had subjects breathe carbon-dioxide-laden air and rate their subjective anxiety on a nine-point scale (0 = no anxiety, 8 = extreme anxiety) every minute; subjects also rated whether they felt fear or panic and how intense it was on a nine-point scale (0 = not at all, 8 = very strongly felt). The question was whether those who scored high on the ASI would provide high ratings of anxiety and fear.

This example illustrates what I take to be the general procedure of experimental psychology, which I schematize in Figure 21.1. Science begins with a (formal or informal, careful or casual) apprehension of pristine phenomena (by Freud, Frankl, and presumably Reiss, Epstein, and so on). Then a theory is advanced (by Reiss and colleagues: AS is a unitary personality variable as measured by the ASI). Validation studies ensue, correlating ASI scores with a variety of measures and behaviors such as the reaction to breathing carbon dioxide. Those studies reveal potential shortcomings of the original theory, and the theory is refined (AS has three dimensions, leading to the creation of the ASI-R). New validation studies ensue (correlating all three AS factors with other measures), leading to further theory refinement, and so on.

Now I'm (finally) ready to answer your question directly. After the early apprehension of pristine phenomena, *none of the theory-refinement studies or the validation studies carefully examined the phenomena involved in the experience of AS.* In our theory-refinement example, the new items created for the ASI-R were *not*, apparently, the result of carefully re-examining AS phenomena and creating items to match the newly observed phenomena. Instead, they were apparently the result of a rational/analytical (presuppositional?) process that determines that the ASI doesn't have enough items in particular categories and thence creates new items to fit these categories. In our validation example, Zinbarg and colleagues did *not* inquire about potential experiential phenomena of AS while their subjects breathed carbon monoxide. They did inquire about the experience of anxiety and fear (to the extent that that is possible using Likert scales without much training), but the point of AS is that AS is *separate from* anxiety and fear.

As far as I can ascertain, *the AS literature has no careful examination of the phenomena of AS since the ASI was created.* So the answer to your question is no; the original articles on which the (Olatunji & Wolitzky-Taylor, 2009) review is based are *not* interested in experience; they are interested in validating or refining theories about experience.

The scientific strategy schematized in Figure 21.1 rests, as I see it, on the faith that theory validation, refinement, and re-validation will lead to the advancement of science without the need for additional careful observation of phenomena. Figure 21.2, by contrast, shows how science might proceed if it took the apprehension of pristine phenomena seriously.

As in Figure 21.1, the science schematized in Figure 21.2 begins with some (formal or informal, careful or casual) apprehension of pristine phenomena, for example, that some people are anxious about being anxious. And as in Figure 21.1, theorizing and validation may follow that apprehension. However, if a validation study does not perfectly validate the theory (a highly likely outcome), then whereas Figure 21.1 would revise the theory and revalidate, Figure 21.2 goes back to the apprehension of new pristine phenomena. Informed by the failures and successes of the first validation studies, these new apprehensions are likely to be performed in different locations, or with a different kind of apprehensional method, or with different kinds of subjects, and so on, and are therefore likely to penetrate more deeply into the phenomena of interest. In our example, if the first validation studies suggest three factors of AS, then new apprehensions might be sensitive to the existence of more than one AS factor.

These new observations may be quite different from the original observations and may lead to a new theory that is quite orthogonal to the original theory. That new theory could then be validated; but Figure 21.2 also illustrates that the new theory may suggest additional ways of observing pristine phenomena

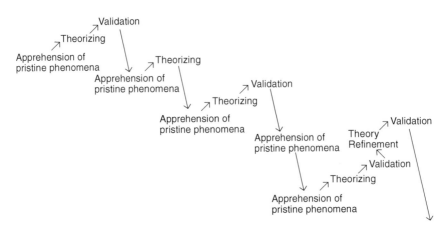

FIGURE 21.2. A science that values the apprehension of pristine phenomena.

(i.e., a ramification of the new theory is that if you look *here*, you should see *this*), which in turn may lead to yet newer theories that may be validated. Figure 21.2 suggests that each apprehension of pristine phenomena is somewhat deeper, more penetrating than the previous one because each new apprehension can be informed by previous apprehensions, theory, and validation. (The alert reader will note advantages similar to the iterative procedure described in Chapter 10, for similar reasons.)

The science of Figure 21.2 does everything that the science of Figure 21.1 does (apprehend pristine phenomena, theorize, validate, refine), except that the Figure 21.2 science recognizes that it is the apprehension of pristine phenomena that nourishes science, recognizes the value of tying theory tightly to pristine phenomena. I am not claiming that the model of Figure 21.2 is always better than that of Figure 21.1. I wish to point out the (largely unexamined) dominance of the Figure 21.1 model, and suggest that the Figure 21.2 model may in some (perhaps many, perhaps most) situations be desirable.

Q: I think Figure 21.1 is a burlesque of science. Scientists are making observations all the time; every validation study involves some observation.
A: I accept that Figure 21.1 is perhaps oversimplified, but I don't think it is too extreme. First, I don't think that many validation studies involve *much* observation. Validation studies are generally designed to be run by relatively unskilled lab assistants operating video or otherwise standardized instructions and collecting data that are as close to keystrokes on a computer keyboard as possible. Second, I have often given formal and informal talks to psychologists about the phenomena DES has discovered – sensory awareness, for example (Chapter 16). Here's the modal reaction: When I'm a quarter or halfway into my description of sensory awareness, some psychologist suggests a validation study. Now I know for a fact that the psychologist doesn't yet understand the phenomenon of sensory awareness (I haven't yet finished my description of it), and yet he is proposing a way to validate it. Third, I urge you to recall the

discussions of orthodox research into emotion in schizophrenia (Chapter 13), which is good orthodox research. Kring cited no careful observations of phenomena since Bleuler's and Sullivan's nearly a century ago, and Bleuler and Sullivan themselves thought of their observations as tentative. Fourth, we have commented throughout this book that questionnaire studies should not be thought of as explorations of phenomena. Fifth, the observations that do underlie most psychological theory are quite casual, clinical, or armchair. As we have seen, casual, clinical, and armchair observations do not typically have sufficient checks and balances to neutralize or otherwise suppress the idiosyncrasies (read presuppositions) of the observing scientist (Hurlburt & Schwitzgebel, 2011b). The scientist assumes that the validation process will correct that, but I think that is overly optimistic. Sixth, graduate programs in experimental (or clinical, for that matter) psychology do not typically teach how to observe phenomena, apparently on the notion that everyone already knows how to do it, or that it is not important anyway. Ask the recent graduates of highly regarded Ph.D. programs how much time was spent in the discussion (or in the supervision of skill acquisition) of such aspects of high-quality investigation as bracketing presuppositions, open-beginninged interviews, level-playing-field questions, and so on. I think the modal answer will be either "none" or "what are you talking about?"

Science needs good apprehensions of pristine phenomena, repeated apprehensions of pristine phenomena, refreshed apprehensions of pristine phenomena, presupposition-bracketed apprehensions of pristine phenomena, apprehensions of pristine phenomena that genuinely submit to the constraints that the faithful apprehension of pristine phenomena imposes. I think psychological science can do a much better job of that than it currently does.

Q: I still think you are being too hard on theoretical/validational science. Such studies *do* advance the understanding of experience. For example, as you said, Taylor and Cox (1998) showed that there are four factors of the ASI: fear of respiratory symptoms, fear of publicly observable anxiety reactions, fear of cardiovascular symptoms, and fear of cognitive dyscontrol. That implies four different kinds of experience, and that difference was discovered by orthodox validation-type studies.

A: That is the heart of the matter: I think the existence of four factors does *not* imply the existence of four kinds or characteristics of experience. None of the ASI's 16 items inquire about experience, and neither do any of the ASI-R's 36 items. The existence of four factors *may* be related to experience, but that is a long extrapolation from items that are not about experience.

Q: How can you say the ASI/ASI-R items are not about experience? They ask about such experiences as "It scares me when I become short of breath" and "When my stomach is upset, I worry that I might become seriously ill" (Reiss, Peterson, Gursky, & McNally, 1986, p. 3).

A: Again, that is at the heart of the matter. Those items are *not* about experience. Experience, as we have stressed, inheres in moments, and *none* of the ASI (or ASI-R) items are about moments of experience. The ASI/ASI-R items invite *faux* generalities, not descriptions of experience. They do *not*, for example, specify any particular moment of shortness of breath; they do *not*, for example, specify whether "worry" is an experience or a state; they are not concerned about retrospection or heuristic problems.

Let me be perfectly clear. I am *not* opposed to validation studies, *not* opposed to so-called objective measures. I enthusiastically support both (evidence: I have written a highly regarded university statistics textbook; Hurlburt, 2006). My objection is to the *over-reliance on* these tools to the exclusion of careful observation. For example, I think it probable that the AS construct is in the vicinity of something genuinely important about anxiety. The question is how to get closer to the AS target. One strategy, which has not been employed, is to follow the example of Figure 21.2: identify, using validated procedures, a sample of individuals that is presumed to be high on AS (that is, who score high on the ASI). Then, in an open-beginninged way, explore their inner experiences, *whatever those experiences might be.* (That is, do *not* inquire about their experience of anxiety; if they have important experiences related to anxiety, that will emerge.) I don't know (nor do AS scientists) what might materialize as salient. Perhaps we would discover that high-ASI subjects engage in frequent bodily sensory awareness; if so, that might suggest that AS is better conceptualized as bodily preoccupation. Perhaps high-ASI subjects engage in bodily sensory awareness at a normal frequency but, when bodily sensory awareness occurs, the experience is profoundly powerful; if so, that might suggest that AS is better conceptualized as bodily hyper-sensitivity. Perhaps high-ASI subjects engage in frequent visual imagery about the body; if so, that might suggest that AS is better conceptualized as visual preoccupation with the body. Perhaps high-ASI subjects engage in frequent multiply simultaneous inner speakings; if so, that might suggest…you get the idea. More likely: We would discover something about the experience of high-ASI subjects that we are not keen enough to predict. If so, such a Figure-21.2 hybrid of selection-by-validity-based-science with careful-observation-of-experiential-phenomena might advance AS science in a way unattainable by validity-based science alone.

Q: Suppose I accept that science needs good observations of phenomena. How should science go about that?

A: I think science needs to consider a division of labor, rather like an army, which has two (I'm oversimplifying a bit) branches: The warriors (tanks, bombers, bazookas, and armored personnel carriers) and the scouts. Warriors should be and want to be equipped with boots, guns, and armor – the more armor, the more bang, the better. The scouts shouldn't want guns and armor; they want listening devices, subterfuge, and delicacy.

Imagine an army with only warriors:

GENERAL: I heard that bin Laden is either in village X or village Y.

TANK COMMANDER: I'll check it out. Captain Smith! Take the Bravo tank division and go see if he's in X. Captain Jones! Take the Charlie tank division and go see if he's in Y.

Modern psychology is like an army without scouts, and I think justifiably deserves criticism for that. It has not developed the scouting specialty, not adequately embraced the need for both scouts and warriors. It believes that the warriors themselves can do adequate intelligence operations (can advance productive hypotheses) and that the warriors' methods (a series of validity studies) can lead to substantial advances. I don't think that's true, and I think the history of psychology shows that it is not true. Psychology needs careful, light-footed, lightly or not at all armed, and nearly invisible infiltrating scouts, who can observe phenomena where and as they lie – trackers who can get the scent of phenomena when there's only a molecule or two in the air, only a broken twig or two on the ground, or only an unguarded word or two in a saloon.

In short, psychology needs to train, support, respect, understand, and value scouts. It's not that the psychology warrior class is bad, but that it is incomplete. We need scouts to determine where bin Laden is; then bring on the tanks and the bunker busters.

Imagine an army with scouts *and* warriors:

GENERAL: I heard that bin Laden is either in village *X* or village *Y*.

TANK COMMANDER: I'll check it out. Captain Smith! Take the Bravo tank division and go see if he's in *X*. Captain Jones! Take Charlie division and go see if he's in *Y*.

GENERAL: No, TC! Your tanks might disturb bin Laden. I'll send a scout instead.

SCOUT COMMANDER: I'll send Aizaz. He speaks fluent Urdu and Pashti.

TANK COMMANDER: But this is a dangerous mission. He should have some protection. Get him to wear a bulletproof vest under his kameez.

SCOUT COMMANDER: Righto.

TANK COMMANDER: I'm still worried about him. I'll send a Predator to fly overhead, and I'll station the Bravo Division just over the hill from *X* and the Charlie Division over the hill from *Y*. People in *X* and *Y* will never notice. And we'll give him the new folding rifle. It's cool – only weighs twelve pounds and will fit easily under his kameez, too. And ...

TC of course thinks like the tank commander that he is, and his justifiable concerns get translated into tank-like maneuvers. The problem, of course, is that his good intentions will likely get Aizaz killed. The good General will have to throttle TC's impulses in this kind of situation.

It's a mistake, of course, to make too much of any metaphor. Yet it seems that psychology under-appreciates the appropriate role of the scout. As both cause and result, psychology does not do a good job of training scouts. And as both cause and result, psychology is likely to resist the creation/exploration/implementation of the scouting role. All that comes from good intentions.

The ramification is that we should try to raise the awareness of the desirability of the scout as an independently valued contributor to the scientific enterprise. It is *not* that the scout should be blindly believed; when Aizaz comes back and reports that bin Laden is in the cellar of a house in the center of *Y*, the general should corroborate that by whatever scout or warrior means are available. Scouts are by no means perfectly reliable – there's politics involved, and double agents, and so forth – so scouts are doubtless far less reliable than the laser-guided aim of the bunker buster that the warriors, with their far superior resources, have developed. The good general accepts this unreliability but values it anyway – values it to the extent that it deserves, no more, no less – and develops ways of using it productively to serve the overall effort.

So what should we do? I think we need to try to convince psychology to value careful observation, not as a replacement for validity-based science but as an interactive guide for it. We should accept that every observation DES makes needs to be corroborated by something outside of DES. That corroboration, to be believable, probably has to be by objective validity-based science. However, we need to convince psychology that the very nature of corroboration is temporal: Observe *first*, corroborate later. Psychology simply does not have that right.

Q: You say that warrior/scout requires a division of labor. I'm a psychological scientist (a "warrior" by your metaphor); I can do my own scouting/observing of phenomena, thank you very much.

A: Perhaps so. But there are at least three overlapping reasons that you may not be very good at it: (a) You probably have little or no formal training in observing phenomena; (b) the training you have in validation is antagonistic to the requirement of bracketing presuppositions; and (c) validation is a fundamentally different skill from observation:

- Observation seeks to discover whatever phenomena exist. Validation focuses on one (or a small number of) pre-determined hypotheses.
- Observation values the bracketing of presuppositions. Validation reifies presuppositions in the form of hypotheses, and once a hypothesis is stated, it is difficult if not impossible to suspend investment in it.
- Observation holds that presuppositions can be (at least partially) bracketed. Validation abandons that attempt, favoring double-blind experiments and the like.
- Observation values qualitative description. Validation values quantitative measurement.
- Observation is a forward looking procedure, designed to discover things that have not been seen before. Validation is a backward looking procedure, designed to confirm previous hypotheses.
- Observation values small revelatory samples (just a few who have the characteristic clearly is better than a lot of low-grade ore). Validation values large representative samples.
- Observation is flexible, following the phenomenon wherever it goes. Validation is rigid, valuing set procedures followed to the letter.
- Observation requires high skill. Validation values low-skill requirements so that narrowly trained research assistants can do the work.
- Observation requires substantial time per subject. Validation values efficiency.

- Observation values the careful observation of all the details of the subject. Validation inspects only those details that correspond (or don't correspond) with the hypotheses.

Both observational and validational skills are essential to good science.
Certainly some scientists, perhaps including you, skillfully incorporate both,
but incorporating both is difficult, perhaps about as difficult as a musician
excelling both at jazz and classical performance. There are a few who do
(Wynton Marsalis, for example) but it is very rare. Whether it is desirable
for science to train both sets of skills in the same individuals remains to be
discovered.

Q: I agree that experimental psychology does not adequately value experience,
but that is not true of the clinical side of psychology. The experience of its
clients is absolutely central to clinical psychology.
A: I wish I could agree with you, but I don't. I think it is fairer to say that
clinical psychology acts *as if* experience were its central value. If experience
really were of central value, then clinical psychology would have worked out
careful methods for observing experience, would have realized the constraints
we have discussed, and this book would be moot. Clinical psychologists don't
get much or any more training than do experimental psychologists in the
bracketing of presuppositions, open-beginninged interviews, level-playing-
field questions, and so on. We have seen, for example, that in bulimia (Chapter 2)
and schizophrenia (Chapter 13), experience was not adequately carefully
explored, and those examples are typical.

Even when experience is thought to be central, it is still not explored
carefully. Hurlburt and Heavey (2006) considered, for example, Obsessive-
Compulsive Disorder (OCD). The defining component of this disorder – the
central feature of its diagnosis – is a characteristic of experience: "recurrent
and persistent thoughts, impulses, or images that are experienced, at some
time during the disturbance, as intrusive and inappropriate and that cause
marked anxiety or distress" (American Psychiatric Association, 2000, p. 462).
That would lead the casual observer to conclude that clinical psychology
does indeed value experience. However, there is *no* careful exploration of
the phenomena of recurrent and persistent thoughts, impulses, or images.
The gold standard of psychological assessment of OCD is the Yale-Brown
Obsessive-Compulsive Scale (Y-BOCS; Goodman et al., 1989), which uses
questions such as:

"How much of your time is occupied by obsessive thoughts?" The interviewer must then score the answer based on the following scale:
   0 = None
   1 = Less than 1hr/day or occasional occurrence
   2 = 1 to 3 hrs/day or frequent
   3 = Greater than 3 and up to 8 hrs/day or very frequent occurrence
   4 = Greater than 8 hrs/day or nearly constant occurrence.

Hurlburt and Heavey observed:

> To give a truly veridical answer to this question, the patient would have had to have kept track of all his minutes during the day, logged those that were occupied by obsessive thoughts, and counted up those minutes. Clearly that is not what people do. Instead, they try to figure out the answer using some unspecifiable process. Such a process is doubtless substantially influenced by a variety of cognitive distortions and heuristics, so the answer to the question may have very little to do with the actual number of hours involved. (Hurlburt & Heavey, 2006, p. 10–11)

The Y-BOCS does not differentiate, for example, between people who actually are occupied more than eight hours a day with obsessive thoughts and people who *think* they are but aren't. Thus in OCD, experience is the center of the disorder but it is not valued enough to examine it carefully.

Heavey and I have sampled with a half dozen OCD individuals. It's premature to draw any specific conclusions, but a preliminary observation is that there are many more samples where there is *nothing* being experienced (a pretty unusual occurrence in most subjects) than when there is an obsession being experienced. That observation must be accepted as tentative, but it illustrates the surprises that clinical psychology might find if it carefully examined experience in OCD. There is no theory within OCD that I know of that suggests that a main feature of OCD is the *lack of any kind of experience.*

The critique that experience is never carefully examined can be applied to nearly all aspects of clinical psychology. Therapists, for example, certainly do inquire about their clients' experiences, but for the most part there is no adequate technique that can be applied to separate the true parts of the client's reports from the parts distorted in the telling by the client and the part distorted in the hearing by the therapist.

CONSTRAINTS

Q: You have provided a lot of constraints throughout this book. It's overwhelming.
A: I don't regard myself as having *provided* constraints. Instead, the constraints have been *imposed on me* by the intention to apprehend pristine experience. I have merely noted those constraints as they appeared. In that regard, I've been simply a reporter, writing down what seems relevant.

Q: How do you expect me to be able to remember all of them?
A: My aim is not to get you to remember *any* of them, much less *all* of them. My aim is to sensitize you to (what I believe is) the fact that, if you genuinely intend to apprehend pristine experience, that intention will impose constraints on you. I have noticed the constraints that arose, not because I wished to provide a constraint catalog, but because I wished to illustrate *that* constraints impose themselves and *how* they impose themselves.

Your task (should you choose to apprehend pristine experience) is not to memorize constraints but to become receptive to the constraints that are imposed by the specific situation in which you find yourself. The constraints imposed on you may be different from those imposed on me both because of the situation and because of our differences in personality, sensitivity, and so forth.

For your easy reference, I list in the Appendix all the constraints imposed on me in the process of apprehending experience in the contexts elaborated in this book. One could attempt to organize these by categories and you, reader, might it find it helpful to organize them for yourself. I did not do it for you, as I do not want to impose my constraints or some interpretation of them on you. The big picture is that the attempt to apprehend pristine experience does impose constraints, and lots of them. If you wish to apprehend pristine experience, you have to submit to all the constraints that impose themselves on you, not the constraints that impose themselves on me. There is likely to be a large but not perfect overlap.

Q: Can you at least tell me which constraints are the most important?
A: That would be like asking a virtuoso violinist to say whether the right hand is more important than the left. All the constraints are important.

Q: Some of those constraints seem pretty similar to each other.
A: I agree. The constraints are not meant to be independent. As I have mentioned, the point here is *not* to provide a catalog of constraints. There is *not* one best way of dividing up the constraints. The constraints are *not* non-overlapping.

A FINAL EXAMPLE

Q: You've covered a lot of ground, and I don't know whether to be excited, depressed, optimistic, or pessimistic.
A: Let me provide one last example that illustrates why I am excited and optimistic. Aadee Mizrachi and I have been investigating the pristine experience of left-handed people. It's well known that there are anatomical asymmetries of the brain associated with right-hand or left-hand preference; in addition, left-handedness has been related to a wide range of psychological and physical problems. So we wondered whether there are experiential differences between left- and right-handed people. There have been no careful explorations of the pristine experience of left-handers – actually, little recognition of the *possibility* that experiential differences might exist.

This is an ongoing study, so what I say here should be viewed as tentative, based on the investigation of about ten left-handers. I'll discuss just one aspect of our findings.

It turns out that left-handers experience words whose meaning is not simultaneously experienced, a phenomenon that we almost never encounter in our studies of the right-handed population. For example, "Serena" was reading a posting on Facebook. At the moment of the beep she experienced herself as inputting a sequence of words ($word_1$ – $word_2$ – $word_3$ – $word_4$, etc.) without any comprehension of their meaning. Her understanding was that at the moment of the beep she is merely taking in a series of words, somehow storing them temporarily. When she finishes a few seconds later, taking in the batch of words, she will extract the meaning from those stored words, and then start the process over again. That is highly unusual for right-handed people, where meaning is experienced as being inextricably, immediately connected to the words that are being read. It is almost inconceivable for a right-hander to think of a word without its associated meaning, to think of a word's being experienced substantially before its meaning.

As a second example, left-handed "Willem" was studying astronomy, and he had placed an asterisk in the margin of his notes to indicate an important concept "*He* flare" (helium flare, a feature of the spectrum of dwarf stars). At the moment of the beep he was saying repeatedly the words "*H–e–*flare, *H–e–*flare, *H–e–*flare," but those words were not experienced as carriers of meaning. His experience at this moment was merely the rote repetition of the words, without any consciousness of what those words meant. His understanding was that such rote repetition was effective studying. I fully accept that there may well have been some sort of processing of meaning ongoing outside of experience. I'm not claiming that the *processing* is different (I don't know anything about that one way or the other); my claim is that the *experience* of words is different for left-handers as for right-handers.

As a third example, "Alan's" mother was talking, and Alan was hearing her words, but the words were experienced as sound patterns, not meaning patterns, more like the output of a musical instrument than a vehicle to transmit semantic meaning.

There is no mention of the phenomena of words separate from their meaning in the literature on left-handedness. There are at least three possibilities: (a) Mizrachi and I are delusional – words without meaning is a figment of our imaginations; (b) our observations are correct but are not about left-handedness. Words without meaning is simply a rare phenomenon, and it is an accident of randomness that the few individuals who show this phenomenon to us happen to be left-handed; (c) our observations are correct, and this words-without-meaning phenomenon does apply to left-handers (or to some large subset thereof). If (c) is correct, that might have substantial impact on our understanding of left-handedness in particular, of cognition in general, and probably of neuroscience.

Here's a thought experiment: What do you think is the probability that (c) is at least approximately correct? I'd say 50 percent is in the ballpark – I happily accept that Mizrachi and I may be mistaken. Now: What do you think is the probability that orthodox science would discover the words-without-meaning phenomenon? I'd say pretty close to zero – there are thousands of psychologists, and as far as I know no remotely similar discoveries have been made.

In hindsight, it seems quite plausible that words are experienced differently by left-handers and right-handers: Science well knows that language is not equally distributed in the two cerebral hemispheres; science well knows that there are anatomical asymmetries in the cerebral hemispheres of left-handed individuals. It therefore seems reasonable that language might be processed differently in left- and right-handed individuals, and therefore experienced differently. Yet as far as I know, this speculation has never before been made. Why not? I think two main reasons: Psychologists (mistakenly) believe that everyone's experience is the same (left-handers included); and psychology has not developed methods of observation sufficiently acute to initiate such speculations.

I think such phenomena are genuinely exciting to discover: At the outset of our investigation of left-handers, I had no notion whatsoever of what we would find.

Q: Yes, but the DES interview is fertile ground for the interviewer to influence the subject!

A: Absolutely. And that makes it doubly exciting, because the bracketing of presuppositions is a personal battle. The object is to be a sensitive interviewer (to *notice*, for example, that left-handers speak of words in slightly unusual ways) and at the same time not to be a *hyper*sensitive interviewer, planting the seeds of phenomena that don't really exist. That is as personally exciting a challenge as I know of. But as I have said before, you shouldn't blindly trust our observations of left-handed experience; they are the starting point for validation and other kinds of exploration.

But here's one additional piece of evidence. We saw in Chapter 6 an example of this words-without-meaning phenomenon. I wrote there about Mike Kane:

> For example, at one sample [Mike] is focused on the redness of the "marks" on the whiteboard. The "marks" are words, but Mike's interest is so focused on the redness that the "wordness" doesn't even register.

Mike, it turns out, is left-handed, a fact that I didn't know when I wrote Chapter 6, and my sampling of Mike was conducted before Mizrachi and I conducted our first study of left-handers. The notion that left-handers experience words without meaning could not possibly have influenced my interview of Mike, and yet I wrote an unambiguous description of the words-without-meaning phenomenon about a person who I did not know was left-handed.

By the way, none of our left-handed subjects suspected, prior to sampling, that they apprehended words in a manner that might be different from right-handed people. How could they? Absolutely every single experience they had ever encountered in their entire lives used words the same way they use words, because they of course have only ever encountered their own experiences. Therefore it would have been absolutely impossible for any of them to report, on their own, their unusual use of words. Recall Jessica's paradox from Chapter 2.

In sum: I think it's possible to apprehend pristine experience in high fidelity; sometimes you get to discover something about experience that is hay-in-the-haystack obvious but heretofore overlooked; such observations are probably useful to the individuals themselves and to science, and that can be genuinely exciting. That's the whole book in fifty words.

APPENDIX

List of Constraints

CONSTRAINTS FROM CHAPTER 1

CONSTRAINTS FROM CHAPTER 2

CONSTRAINTS FROM CHAPTER 3

CONSTRAINTS FROM CHAPTER 5

CONSTRAINTS FROM CHAPTER 6

CONSTRAINTS FROM CHAPTER 7

CONSTRAINTS FROM CHAPTER 8

CONSTRAINTS FROM CHAPTER 9

REFERENCES

Akhter, S. A. (2008). *Exploring adolescent inner experience*. Unpublished Master's thesis, University of Nevada, Las Vegas.

American Psychiatric Association. (2000). *Diagnostic and statistical manual of mental disorders DSM-IV-TR (Text Revision)*. Washington, DC: Author.

Anderson, N, (1980). Aim-directed movement. *Guitarra Magazine, 37*, 10–12.

Baars, B. J. (2003). How brain reveals mind: Neural studies support the fundamental role of conscious experience. *Journal of Consciousness Studies, 10*, 100–114.

Bacon, F. (1620/2000). *The new organon*. Ed. L. Jardine and M. Silverthorne. Cambridge: Cambridge University Press.

Banks, M. S. & Shannon, E. S. (1993). Spatial and chromatic visual efficiency in human neonates. In C. Granrud (ed.), *Visual perception and cognition in infancy*. Hillsdale, N.J.: Erlbaum, pp. 1–46.

Barrett, L. F. (2004). Feelings or words? Understanding the content in self-report ratings of emotional experience. *Journal of Personality and Social Psychology, 87*, 266–281.

(2006). Valence is a basic building block of emotional life. *Journal of Research in Personality, 40*, 35–55.

Barrett, L. F., Mesquita, B., Ochsner, K. N., & Gross, J. J. (2007). The experience of emotion. *Annual Review of Psychology, 58*, 373–403.

Barrett, L. F., Quigley, K.S., Bliss-Moreau, E., & Aronson, K. R. (2004). Interoceptive sensitivity and self-reports of emotional experience. *Journal of Personality and Social Psychology, 87*, 684–697.

Beament, J. (2000). *The violin explained: components, mechanism, and sound*. Oxford: Oxford University Press.

Bensaheb, A. (2009). *Descriptive Experience Sampling interactive multimedia training tool*. Unpublished dissertation, University of Nevada, Las Vegas.

Block, N. (2007). Consciousness, accessibility, and the mesh between psychology and neuroscience. *Behavioral and Brain Sciences, 30*, 481–499.

Bouricius, J. (1989). Negative symptoms and emotions in schizophrenia. *Schizophrenia Bulletin, 15*, 201–208.

Brieger, P., Röttig, S., Röttig, D., Marneros, A., & Priebe, S. (2007). Dimensions underlying outcome criteria in bipolar I disorder. *Journal of Affective Disorders, 99*(1–3), 1–7.

Campos, A., Pérez-Fabello, M., & Gómez-Juncal, R. (2006). Time requirement for formation of mental images. *North American Journal of Psychology, 8*(2), 277–288.

Carruthers, P. (1996). *Language, thought and consciousness*. Cambridge: Cambridge University Press.

Chapman, J. (1966). The early symptoms of schizophrenia. *British Journal of Psychiatry, 112*, 225–251.

Chapman, L. J., Chapman, J. P., & Raulin, M. L. (1976). Scales for physical and social anhedonia. *Journal of Abnormal Psychology, 85*, 374–382.

Chrisley, R. L. (2001). A view from anywhere: Prospects for an objective understanding of consciousness. In P. Pylkkanen & T. Vadén (eds.) *Dimensions of conscious experience*. Amsterdam/Philadelphia: John Benjamins, pp. 3–13.

(2008). *Exploiting the subjective: Science and experience*. Paper presented at the Third Ratna Ling Conference on First-Person Methodologies in the Study of Consciousness. Cazadero, CA: April.

Clark, A.J. (2004). On the meaning of color in early recollections. *Journal of Individual Psychology, 60*(2), 141–154.

Corsini, R. (2002). *The dictionary of psychology*. New York: Brunner-Routledge.

Csikszentmihalyi, M. & Larson, R. (1987). Validity and reliability of the experience-sampling method. *Journal of Nervous and Mental Disease, 175*, 526–536.

Danziger, K. (1980). The history of introspection reconsidered. *Journal of the History of the Behavioral Sciences, 16*, 240–262.

Derogatis, L. R. (1994). *The SCL-90-R: Scoring, administration, and procedures* (3rd ed.). Minneapolis: National Computer Systems.

Descartes, R. (1641/1984). *Meditations on first philosophy*. In J. Cottingham, R. Stoothoff, and D. Murdoch (eds.), *The philosophical writings of Descartes*. Cambridge: Cambridge University Press.

Dickens, Y. L. (2005). *Inner experience and golf performance*. Unpublished dissertation, University of Nevada, Las Vegas.

Doucette, S. (1992). *Sampling the inner experience of bulimic and other individuals*. Unpublished Master's thesis, University of Nevada, Las Vegas.

Doucette, S. & Hurlburt, R. T. (1993a). A bulimic junior high school teacher. In R. T. Hurlburt, *Sampling inner experience in disturbed affect*. New York: Plenum, pp. 139–152.

(1993b). Inner experience in bulimia. In R. T. Hurlburt. *Sampling inner experience in disturbed affect*. New York: Plenum, pp. 153–163.

Dror, I.E. & Kosslyn, S.M. (1994). Mental imagery and aging. *Psychology and Aging, 9*, 90–102.

Fairburn, C. G. & Cooper, Z. (1993). The eating disorder examination (12th edition). In C. G. Fairburn & G. T. Wilson (eds.) *Binge eating: Nature, assessment and treatment*. New York: Guilford, pp. 333–356.

Fairburn, C. G., Cooper, Z., & Shafran, R. (2003). Cognitive behaviour therapy for eating disorders: A "transdiagnostic" theory and treatment. *Behaviour Research and Therapy, 41*, 509–528.

Faw, B. (2008). Review of Hurlburt & Schwitzgebel's *Describing Inner Experience*. *Journal of Consciousness Studies, 15*(8), 119–121.

Flavell, J. H., Green, F. L., & Flavell, E. R. (1995). Young children's knowledge about thinking. *Monographs of the Society for Research in Child Development, 60*(1), Serial No. 243.

(2000). Development of children's awareness of their own thoughts. *Journal of Cognition & Development, 1,* 97–112.

Fodor, J. (1983). *The modularity of mind: An essay on faculty psychology.* Cambridge MA: MIT Press.

Folstein, M.F., Folstein, S.E., & McHugh, P.R. (1975). Mini-mental-state: A practical method for grading the cognitive state of patients for the clinician. *Journal of Psychiatric Research, 12,* 189–198.

France, C. R., al'Absi, M., Ring, C., France, J. L., Harju, A., & Wittmers, L. E. (2007). Nociceptive flexion reflex and pain rating responses during endogenous opiate blockade with naltrexone in healthy young adults. *Biological Psychology, 75*(1), 95–100.

Frankfurt, H. (2005). *On bullshit.* Princeton: Princeton University Press.

Frankl, V. E. (1975). Paradoxical intention and dereflection. *Psychotherapy: Theory, Research and Practice, 12,* 226–237.

Freud, S. (1895). Obsessions and phobias: Their psychical mechanisms and their etiology. In S. Freud (1924), *Collected papers* (Vol. 1). London: Hogarth Press.

Garner, D. M. (2004). *Eating Disorder Inventory-3 Professional Manual.* Lutz, FL: Psychological Assessment Resources, Inc.

Giorgi, A. (1975). An application of phenomenological method in psychology. In A. Giorgi, C. Fischer, & E. Murray (eds.): *Duquesne studies in phenomenological psychology, II* (pp. 82–103). Pittsburgh: Duquesne University Press.

Goodman, W. K, Price, L. H., Rasmussen, S. A., Mazure, C., Fleischmann, R. L., Hill, C. L., Heninger, G. R., & Charney, D. S. (1989). The Yale-Brown Obsessive Compulsive Scale: I. Development, use, and reliability. *Archives of General Psychiatry, 46,* 1006–1011.

Grandin, T. (1992). Calming effects of deep touch pressure in patients with autistic disorder, college students, and animals. *Journal of Child and Adolescent Psychopharmacology, 2.* Downloaded 11/22/10 from http://www.grandin.com/inc/squeeze.html.

Hagel, B. E., Lamy, A., Rizkallah, J. W., Belton, K. L., Jhangri, G. S., Cherry, N., & Rowe, B. H. (2007). The prevalence and reliability of visibility aid and other risk factor data for uninjured cyclists and pedestrians in Edmonton, Alberta, Canada. *Accident Analysis & Prevention, 39*(2), 284–289.

Heavey, C. L. & Hurlburt, R. T. (2008). The phenomena of inner experience. *Consciousness and Cognition, 17,* 798–810.

Heavey, C. L., Hurlburt, R. T., & Lefforge, N. (2010). Descriptive Experience Sampling: A method for exploring momentary inner experience. *Qualitative Research in Psychology, 7,* 345–368.

(in preparation). Toward a phenomenology of feelings.

Horgan, T. & Tienson, J. (2002). The intentionality of phenomenology and the phenomenology of intentionality. In D.J. Chalmers (ed.), *Philosophy of mind.* New York: Oxford University Press.

Horst, M., Kuttschreuter, M. & Gutteling, J. M. (2007). Perceived usefulness, personal experiences, risk perception and trust as determinants of adoption of e-government services in The Netherlands. *Computers in Human Behavior, 23*(4), 1838–1852.

Howes, M. Siegel, M. & Brown, F. (1993). Early childhood memories: Accuracy and effect. *Cognition, 47,* 95–119.

Hoyt, W. T. & Bhati, K. S. (2007). Principles and practices: An empirical examination of qualitative research in the *Journal of Counseling Psychology, 54*(2), 201–210.

Hurlburt, R. T. (1976). Random interval generators and method of behavior modification using same. US Patent #3,986,136.

(1980). Validation and correlation of thought sampling with retrospective measures. *Cognitive Therapy and Research, 4,* 235–238.

(1990). *Sampling normal and schizophrenic inner experience.* New York: Plenum Press.

(1993a). *Sampling inner experience in disturbed affect.* New York: Plenum Press.

(1993b). A bulimic operating-room nurse. In R. T. Hurlburt, *Sampling inner experience in disturbed affect.* New York: Plenum, pp. 123–138.

(1997). Randomly sampling thinking in the natural environment. *Journal of Consulting and Clinical Psychology, 65,* 941–949.

(2006). *Comprehending behavioral statistics* (4th ed.). Belmont, CA: Wadsworth.

(2009). Iteratively apprehending pristine experience. *Journal of Consciousness Studies, 16*(10–12), 156–188.

(2011). Nine clarifications of Descriptive Experience Sampling. *Journal of Consciousness Studies, 18*(1), 274–287.

Hurlburt, R. T. & Akhter, S. A. (2006). The Descriptive Experience Sampling method. *Phenomenology and the Cognitive Sciences, 5,* 271–301.

(2008). Unsymbolized thinking. *Consciousness and Cognition, 17,* 1364–1374.

Hurlburt, R. T., Happé, F., & Frith, U. (1994). Sampling the form of inner experience in three adults with Asperger syndrome. *Psychological Medicine, 24,* 385–395.

Hurlburt, R. T. & Heavey, C. L. (2001). Telling what we know: describing inner experience. *Trends in Cognitive Sciences, 5,* 400–403.

(2002). Interobserver reliability of Descriptive Experience Sampling. *Cognitive Therapy and Research, 26,* 135–142.

(2004). To beep or not to beep: Obtaining accurate reports about awareness. *Journal of Consciousness Studies, 11* (7–8), 113–128.

(2006). *Exploring inner experience: The Descriptive Experience Sampling method.* Amsterdam/Philadelphia: John Benjamins.

Hurlburt, R. T., Heavey, C. L., & Bensaheb, A. (2009). Sensory awareness. *Journal of Consciousness Studies, 16* (10–12), 231–251.

Hurlburt, R. T., Heavey, C.L., & Seibert, T. (2006). Psychological science's prescription for accurate reports about inner experience. In R. T. Hurlburt & C. L. Heavey, *Exploring inner experience: The Descriptive Experience Sampling method.* Amsterdam/Philadelphia: John Benjamins, pp. 41–60.

Hurlburt, R. T., Koch, M., & Heavey, C. L. (2002). Descriptive Experience Sampling demonstrates the connection of thinking to externally observable behavior. *Cognitive Therapy and Research, 26,* 117–134.

Hurlburt, R. T. & Melancon, S. M. (1987a). How are questionnaire data similar to, and different from, thought sampling data? Five studies manipulating retrospectiveness, single-moment focus, and indeterminacy. *Cognitive Therapy and Research, 11,* 681–704.

(1987b). P-technique factor analysis of individuals' thought and mood sampling data. *Cognitive Therapy and Research, 11,* 487–500.

Hurlburt, R. T. & Raymond, N. (2011). Agency: A case study in bracketing presuppositions. *Journal of Consciousness Studies, 18*(1), 295–305.

Hurlburt, R. T. & Schwitzgebel, E. (2007). *Describing inner experience?* Cambridge, MA: MIT Press.

(2011a). Little or no experience outside of attention? *Journal of Consciousness Studies, 18*(1), 234–252.

(2011b). Methodological pluralism, armchair introspection, and DES as the epistemic tribunal. *Journal of Consciousness Studies, 18*(1), 253–273.

(2011c). Presuppositions and background assumptions. *Journal of Consciousness Studies, 18*(1), 206–233.

Husserl, E. (1913/1982) *Ideen zu einer reinen Phänomenologie und phänomenologischen Philosophie. Erstes Buch: Allgemeine Einführung in die reine Phänomenologie.* English translation: *Ideas Pertaining to a Pure Phenomenology and to a Phenomenological Philosophy. First Book: General Introduction to a Pure Phenomenology.* Translated by F. Kersten. The Hague: Nijhoff.

James, W. (1890). *Principles of psychology Vol I.* New York: Holt.

Jones-Forrester, S. (2006). *Inner experience in bulimia.* Unpublished Master's thesis, University of Nevada, Las Vegas.

(2009). *Descriptive Experience Sampling of individuals with bulimia nervosa.* Unpublished dissertation, University of Nevada, Las Vegas.

Kagan, J. (2007). *What is emotion? History, measures, and meaning.* New Haven, CT: Yale University Press.

Kane, M. J. (1994). Premonitory urges as "attentional tics" in Tourette Syndrome. *Journal of the American Academy of Child and Adolescent Psychiatry, 33,* 805–808.

(2011) Describing, debating, and discovering inner experience. *Journal of Consciousness Studies, 18*(1), 150–164.

Kelly, G. A. (1955). *The psychology of personal constructs.* New York: Norton.

Kisker, G. W. (1972). Psychotic Disorders: Schizophrenia II; Catatonia. Recorded case interviews, second series; recorded and with commentary by George W. Kisker. Audiotape accompanying *The disorganized personality* (2nd ed.). New York: McGraw-Hill.

Kosslyn, S. M., Pinker, S., Smith, G., & Schwartz, S. (1981). On the demystification of mental imagery. In N. Block (ed.)., *Imagery* (pp. 131–150). Cambridge, MA: MIT Press.

Kring, A. M. & Germans, M. K (2004). Subjective experience of emotion in schizophrenia. In J. H. Jenkins & R. J. Barrett (eds.). *The Edge of experience: Schizophrenia, culture, and subjectivity.* New York: Cambridge University Press, pp. 329–348.

Kring, A. M. & Neale, J. M. (1996). Do schizophrenic patients show a disjunctive relationship among expressive, experiential, and psychophysiological components of emotion? *Journal of Abnormal Psychology, 105,* 249–257.

Kuhn, T. S. (1962/1970). *The structure of scientific revolutions* (2nd ed.). Chicago: University of Chicago Press.

Lafond, D., Lacouture, Y., & Mineau, G. (2007). Complexity minimization in rule-based category learning: Revising the catalog of Boolean concepts and evidence for non-minimal rules. *Journal of Mathematical Psychology, 51*(2), 57–74.

Lamb, M. E., Bornstein, M. H., & Teti, D. M (2002). *Development in infancy.* Hillsdale, NJ: Erlbaum.

Landman, R., Spekreijse, H., & Lamme, V. A. F. (2003). Large capacity storage of integrated objects before change blindness. *Vision Research, 43,* 149–164.

Larsen, J. T., McGraw, A, P., Cacioppo, J. T. (2001). Can people feel happy and sad at the same time? *Journal of Personality and Social Psychology, 81,* 684–696.

LeDoux, J.E. (2000). Emotion circuits in the brain. *Annual Review of Neuroscience, 23,* 155–184.

Lewis, M. (2008). The emergence of human emotions. In M. Lewis & J. M. Haviland-Jones (eds.) *Handbook of the emotions* (3rd ed.). New York: Guilford, pp. 304–319.

Libet, B. (2004). *Mind time*. Cambridge, MA: Harvard University Press.

Machery, E. (2005). You don't know how you think: Introspection and the language of thought. *British Journal of the Philosophy of Science*, *56*, 469–485.

MacKinnon, D. F., Craighead, B., & Hoehn-Saric, R. (2007). Carbon dioxide provocation of anxiety and respiratory response in bipolar disorder. *Journal of Affective Disorders*, *99*(1–3), 45–49.

Mangan, B. (2001). Sensation's ghost: The non-sensory 'fringe' of consciousness. *Psyche: An Interdisciplinary Journal of Research on Consciousness*, *7*, no. 18.

McGlashan, T. H., Walsh, B. C., & Woods, S. W. (2010). *The Psychosis-Risk Syndrome: Handbook for diagnosis and follow-up*. New York: Oxford University Press.

Merriam-Webster (2009). Merriam-Webster's Word of the Year 2006. (Downloaded October 25, 2009 from http://www.merriam-webster.com/info/06words.htm).

Miller, G.A. (1956). The magical number seven, plus or minus two: Some limits on our capacity for processing information. *The Psychological Review*, *63*, 81–97.

Monson, L. C. (1989). *Sampling inner experience in adolescents*. Unpublished Master's thesis, University of Nevada, Las Vegas.

Monson, C. K. & Hurlburt, R. T. (1993). A comment to suspend the introspection controversy: Introspecting subjects did agree about imageless thought. In R. T. Hurlburt, *Sampling inner experience in disturbed affect*. New York: Plenum.

Myin-Germeys, I., Delespaul, P. A. G., & deVries, M. W. (2000). Schizophrenia patients are more emotionally active than is assumed based on their behavior. *Schizophrenia Bulletin*, *26*, 847–854.

Nisbett, R. E., & Wilson, T. D. (1977). Telling more than we can know: Verbal reports on mental processes. *Psychological Review*, *84*, 231–259.

Olatunji, B. O. & Wolitzky-Taylor, K. B. (2009). Anxiety Sensitivity and the anxiety disorders: A meta-analytic review and synthesis. *Psychological Bulletin*, *135*, 974–999.

Palladino, P. & De Beni, R. (2003). When mental images are very detailed: Image generation and memory performance as a function of age. *Acta Psychologica*, *113*(3), 297–314.

Petitmengin, C. (1999). The intuitive experience. *Journal of Consciousness Studies*, *6*, 43–77.

  (2006). Describing one's subjective experience in the second person: An interview method for the science of consciousness. *Phenomenology and the Cognitive Sciences*, *5*, 229–269.

Pitt, D. (2004). The phenomenology of cognition, or what is it like to think that P? *Philosophy and Phenomenological Research*, *69*, 1–36.

Popper, K. (1935/1959). *The logic of scientific discovery*. London: Routledge.

Reiss, S. (1987). Theoretical perspectives on the fear of anxiety. *Clinical Psychology Review*, *7*, 585–596.

Reiss, S., Peterson, R. A., Gursky, D. M., & McNally, R. J. (1986). Anxiety sensitivity, anxiety frequency, and the prediction of fearfulness. *Behavior Research and Therapy*, *24*, 1–8.

Reiss, S. & McNally, R. J. (1985). Expectancy model of fear. In S. Reiss (ed.), *Theoretical issues in behavior therapy*. New York: Academic Press, pp. 107–121.

Robinson, W.S. (2005). Thoughts without distinctive non-imagistic phenomenology. *Philosophy and Phenomenological Research*, *70*, 534–561.

Rogers, C. R. (1959). A theory of therapy, personality, and interpersonal relationships, as developed in the client-centered framework. In S. Koch (ed.), *Psychology: A study of science*, vol. 3. New York: McGraw-Hill, pp. 184–256.

Saarni, C., Campos, J. J., Camras, L.A., & Witherington, D. (2006). Emotional development: Action, communication, and understanding. In N. Eisenberg (Series ed.), W. Damon & R. M. Lerner (Vol. eds.), *Handbook of child psychology: Vol. 3. Social, emotional, personality development* (6th ed.). Hoboken, NJ: Wiley, pp. 226–299.

Schouten, B. C., van den Putte, B., Pasmans, M., & Meeuwesen, L. (2007). Parent-adolescent communication about sexuality: The role of adolescents' beliefs, subjective norm and perceived behavioral control. *Patient Education and Counseling, 66*(1), 75–83.

Schwitzgebel, E. (2002). Why did we think we dreamed in black and white? *Studies in History and Philosophy of Science, 33*, 649–660.

Segal, Z. V., Williams, J. M. G., & Teasdale, J. D. (2002). *Mindfulness-based cognitive therapy for depression.* New York: Guilford.

Seibert, T. M (2009). *The inner experience of older individuals.* Unpublished dissertation, University of Nevada, Las Vegas.

Siewert, C. P. (1998). *The significance of consciousness.* Princeton: Princeton University Press.

Skinner, B. F. (1953). *Science and human behavior.* New York: Macmillan.

(1974). *About behaviorism.* New York: Vintage.

(1977). Why I am not a cognitive psychologist. *Behaviorism, 5*, 1–10.

Smith, B. C. (1996). *On the origin of objects.* Cambridge, MA: MIT Press.

Sperling, G. (1960). The information available in brief visual presentations. *Psychological Monographs, 74*, 1–29.

Stern, D. N. (2004). *The present moment in psychotherapy and everyday life.* New York: W. W. Norton.

Strawson, G. (1994). *Mental reality.* Cambridge, MA: MIT Press.

Sullivan, H. S. (1927/1994). The onset of schizophrenia. *American Journal of Psychiatry, 151*(6), 135–139.

Taylor, S. & Cox, B. J. (1998). An expanded Anxiety Sensitivity Index: Evidence for a hierarchic structure in a clinical sample. *Journal of Anxiety Disorders, 12*, 463–483.

Tractenberg, R. E., Chaterji, R., Haramati, A. (2007). Assessing and analyzing change in attitudes in the classroom. *Assessment & Evaluation in Higher Education, 32*(2), 107–120.

Vermersch, P. (1997). La référence à l'expérience subjective. *Revue phénoménologique Alter, 5*, 121–136.

Waddell, V. L. (2007). A phenomenological description of the inner voice experience of ordinary people. *Journal of Consciousness Studies, 14*, 35–57.

Watson, D. (2000). *Mood and temperament.* New York: Guilford.

Watson, D., Clark, L. A., & Tellegen, A. (1988). Development and validation of brief measures of positive and negative affect: The PANAS scales. *Journal of Personality and Social Psychology, 54*, 1063–1070.

Watson, J. B. & MacDougall, W. (1929). *The battle of behaviorism: An exposition and an exposure.* New York: Norton.

Whitehead, W. E. & Drescher, V. M. (1980). Perception of gastric contractions and self-control of gastric motility. *Psychophysiology, 17*, 552–558.

Yacht, A. C., Suglia, S. F., & Orlander, J. D. (2007). Evaluating an end-of-life curriculum in a medical residency program. *American Journal of Hospice & Palliative Medicine, 23*(6), 439–446.

Yung, A. R., Killackey, E., Hetrick, S. E., Parker, A. G., Schultze-Lutter F., Klosterkoetter, J., Purcell, R., & McGorry, P. D. (2007). The prevention of schizophrenia. *International Review of Psychiatry, 19*(6), 633–646.

Yung, A. R. & McGorry, P. D. (1996). The prodromal phase of first-episode psychosis: Past and current conceptualizations. *Schizophrenia Bulletin, 22,* 353–370.

Zinbarg, R., Brown, T., Barlow, D., & Rapee, R. (2001). Anxiety sensitivity, panic, and depressed mood: A reanalysis teasing apart the contributions of the two levels in the hierarchical structure of the Anxiety Sensitivity Index. *Journal of Abnormal Psychology, 110*(3), 372–377.

INDEX